Peugeot 206
Owners Workshop Manual

Peter T Gill

Models covered

(4613 - 416 - 7AS1)

Hatchback, Estate (SW) & Coupe Cabriolet, including special/limited editions

Petrol: 1.1 litre (1124cc), 1.4 litre (1360cc 8- & 16-valve), 1.6 litre (1587cc 8-valve) & 2.0 litre (1997cc)
Turbo-Diesel: 1.4 litre (1398cc) & 2.0 litre (1997cc) HDi

Covers major mechanical features of Van
Does NOT cover 1.6 litre HDi or 1.9 litre Diesel engines, 1.6 litre 16-valve petrol engine or GTi 180 models

© Haynes Publishing 2013

ABCDE
FGHI

A book in the **Haynes Owners Workshop Manual Series**

All rights reserved. No part of this book may be reproduced or transmitted in any form or by any means, electronic or mechanical, including photocopying, recording or by any information storage or retrieval system, without permission in writing from the copyright holder.

ISBN **978 0 85733 908 9**

British Library Cataloguing in Publication Data
A catalogue record for this book is available from the British Library.

Printed in the USA

Haynes Publishing
Sparkford, Yeovil, Somerset BA22 7JJ, England

Haynes North America, Inc
861 Lawrence Drive, Newbury Park, California 91320, USA

Haynes Publishing Nordiska AB
Box 1504, 751 45 UPPSALA, Sverige

Printed using 33-lb Resolute Book 65 4.0 from Resolute Forest Products Calhoun, TN mill. Resolute is a member of World Wildlife Fund's Climate Savers programme committed to significantly reducing GHG emissions. This paper uses 50% less wood fibre than traditional offset. The Calhoun Mill is certified to the following sustainable forest management and chain of custody standards: SFI, PEFC and FSC Controlled Wood.

Contents

LIVING WITH YOUR PEUGEOT 206

Roadside Repairs

Weekly checks

Lubricants and fluids

Tyre pressures

MAINTENANCE

Routine Maintenance and Servicing

Petrol models

Diesel models

Illegal Copying

It is the policy of Haynes Publishing to actively protect its Copyrights and Trade Marks. Legal action will be taken against anyone who unlawfully copies the cover or contents of this Manual. This includes all forms of unauthorised copying including digital, mechanical, and electronic in any form. Authorisation from Haynes Publishing will only be provided expressly and in writing. Illegal copying will also be reported to the appropriate statutory authorities.

Contents

The Peugeot 206 range was introduced in the UK in the autumn of 1998. Originally, the 206 was available with a choice of 1.1 litre (1124 cc), 1.4 litre (1360 cc), and 1.6 litre (1587 cc) petrol engines and a 1.9 litre (1868 cc) diesel engine. All models were available in both three- and five-door Hatchback form.

All petrol engines are derived from the well-proven TU series engines, which have appeared in many Peugeot and Citroën vehicles. The engine is of four-cylinder overhead camshaft design, mounted transversely, with the transmission mounted on the left-hand side. In 2003 the 1.4 litre 16-valve petrol engine was introduced, this being a newly developed engine.

The 2.0 litre diesel engine is from the new DW series of diesel engines. The engine has been derived from the original XUD diesel engines, which were also well-proven units, having been fitted to many Peugeot and Citroën vehicles. The engine is of four-cylinder overhead camshaft design, mounted transversely, with the five-speed manual transmission mounted on the left-hand side. In the autumn of 1999, Peugeot introduced the 2.0 litre (1997 cc) turbocharged diesel engine into the 206 range. This engine is also from the new DW series of diesel engines and is fitted with a high-pressure direct injection (HDi) system, which represents the latest in diesel technology. In 2001 the 1.4 litre HDi diesel engine was introduced, this was a newly developed engine.

Other additions to the 206 range include the SW (Sports Wagon) and the CC (Cabriolet Coupe) models.

All models have a five-speed manual transmission, with some models also being offered with the option of a four-speed automatic transmission.

All models have fully independent front suspension, incorporating shock-absorbers, coil springs and an anti-roll bar. The rear suspension is semi-independent, with torsion bars and trailing arms.

A wide range of standard and optional equipment is available within the 206 range to suit most tastes, including central locking, electric windows and front, side and curtain airbags. An air conditioning system is available on all models.

Provided that regular servicing is carried out in accordance with the manufacturer's recommendations, the Peugeot 206 should prove reliable and very economical. The engine compartment is well-designed, and most of the items requiring frequent attention are easily accessible.

Your Peugeot 206 Manual

The aim of this manual is to help you get the best value from your vehicle. It can do so in several ways. It can help you decide what work must be done (even should you choose to get it done by a garage), provide information on routine maintenance and servicing, and give a logical course of action and diagnosis when random faults occur. However, it is hoped that you will use the manual by tackling the work yourself. On simpler jobs it may even be quicker than booking the car into a garage and going there twice, to leave and collect it. Perhaps most important, a lot of money can be saved by avoiding the costs a garage must charge to cover its labour and overheads.

The manual has drawings and descriptions to show the function of the various components so that their layout can be understood. Tasks are described and photographed in a clear step-by-step sequence.

References to the left-hand and right-hand sides of the vehicle are always in the sense of when viewed by a person sat in the driver's seat, facing forwards.

Acknowledgements

Thanks are due to Draper Tools Limited, who provided some of the workshop tools, and to all those people at Sparkford who helped in the production of this manual.

We take great pride in the accuracy of information given in this manual, but vehicle manufacturers make alterations and design changes during the production run of a particular vehicle of which they do not inform us. No liability can be accepted by the authors or publishers for loss, damage or injury caused by errors in, or omissions from, the information given.

Working on your car can be dangerous. This page shows just some of the potential risks and hazards, with the aim of creating a safety-conscious attitude.

General hazards

Scalding

• Don't remove the radiator or expansion tank cap while the engine is hot.
• Engine oil, transmission fluid or power steering fluid may also be dangerously hot if the engine has recently been running.

Burning

• Beware of burns from the exhaust system and from any part of the engine. Brake discs and drums can also be extremely hot immediately after use.

Crushing

• When working under or near a raised vehicle, always supplement the jack with axle stands, or use drive-on ramps.
Never venture under a car which is only supported by a jack.
• Take care if loosening or tightening high-torque nuts when the vehicle is on stands. Initial loosening and final tightening should be done with the wheels on the ground.

Fire

• Fuel is highly flammable; fuel vapour is explosive.
• Don't let fuel spill onto a hot engine.
• Do not smoke or allow naked lights (including pilot lights) anywhere near a vehicle being worked on. Also beware of creating sparks (electrically or by use of tools).
• Fuel vapour is heavier than air, so don't work on the fuel system with the vehicle over an inspection pit.
• Another cause of fire is an electrical overload or short-circuit. Take care when repairing or modifying the vehicle wiring.
• Keep a fire extinguisher handy, of a type suitable for use on fuel and electrical fires.

Electric shock

• Ignition HT and Xenon headlight voltages can be dangerous, especially to people with heart problems or a pacemaker. Don't work on or near these systems with the engine running or the ignition switched on.

• Mains voltage is also dangerous. Make sure that any mains-operated equipment is correctly earthed. Mains power points should be protected by a residual current device (RCD) circuit breaker.

Fume or gas intoxication

• Exhaust fumes are poisonous; they can contain carbon monoxide, which is rapidly fatal if inhaled. Never run the engine in a confined space such as a garage with the doors shut.
• Fuel vapour is also poisonous, as are the vapours from some cleaning solvents and paint thinners.

Poisonous or irritant substances

• Avoid skin contact with battery acid and with any fuel, fluid or lubricant, especially antifreeze, brake hydraulic fluid and Diesel fuel. Don't syphon them by mouth. If such a substance is swallowed or gets into the eyes, seek medical advice.
• Prolonged contact with used engine oil can cause skin cancer. Wear gloves or use a barrier cream if necessary. Change out of oil-soaked clothes and do not keep oily rags in your pocket.
• Air conditioning refrigerant forms a poisonous gas if exposed to a naked flame (including a cigarette). It can also cause skin burns on contact.

Asbestos

• Asbestos dust can cause cancer if inhaled or swallowed. Asbestos may be found in gaskets and in brake and clutch linings. When dealing with such components it is safest to assume that they contain asbestos.

Special hazards

Hydrofluoric acid

• This extremely corrosive acid is formed when certain types of synthetic rubber, found in some O-rings, oil seals, fuel hoses etc, are exposed to temperatures above 4000C. The rubber changes into a charred or sticky substance containing the acid. *Once formed, the acid remains dangerous for years. If it gets onto the skin, it may be necessary to amputate the limb concerned.*
• When dealing with a vehicle which has suffered a fire, or with components salvaged from such a vehicle, wear protective gloves and discard them after use.

The battery

• Batteries contain sulphuric acid, which attacks clothing, eyes and skin. Take care when topping-up or carrying the battery.
• The hydrogen gas given off by the battery is highly explosive. Never cause a spark or allow a naked light nearby. Be careful when connecting and disconnecting battery chargers or jump leads.

Air bags

• Air bags can cause injury if they go off accidentally. Take care when removing the steering wheel and trim panels. Special storage instructions may apply.

Diesel injection equipment

• Diesel injection pumps supply fuel at very high pressure. Take care when working on the fuel injectors and fuel pipes.

⚠️ *Warning: Never expose the hands, face or any other part of the body to injector spray; the fuel can penetrate the skin with potentially fatal results.*

Remember...

DO

• Do use eye protection when using power tools, and when working under the vehicle.

• Do wear gloves or use barrier cream to protect your hands when necessary.

• Do get someone to check periodically that all is well when working alone on the vehicle.

• Do keep loose clothing and long hair well out of the way of moving mechanical parts.

• Do remove rings, wristwatch etc, before working on the vehicle – especially the electrical system.

• Do ensure that any lifting or jacking equipment has a safe working load rating adequate for the job.

DON'T

• Don't attempt to lift a heavy component which may be beyond your capability – get assistance.

• Don't rush to finish a job, or take unverified short cuts.

• Don't use ill-fitting tools which may slip and cause injury.

• Don't leave tools or parts lying around where someone can trip over them. Mop up oil and fuel spills at once.

• Don't allow children or pets to play in or near a vehicle being worked on.

The following pages are intended to help in dealing with common roadside emergencies and breakdowns. You will find more detailed fault finding information at the back of the manual, and repair information in the main chapters.

If your car won't start and the starter motor doesn't turn

- ☐ If it's a model with automatic transmission, make sure the selector is in P or N.
- ☐ Open the bonnet and make sure that the battery terminals are clean and tight.
- ☐ Switch on the headlights and try to start the engine. If the headlights go very dim when you're trying to start, the battery is probably flat. Get out of trouble by jump starting (see next page) using a friend's car.

If your car won't start even though the starter motor turns as normal

- ☐ Is there fuel in the tank?
- ☐ Is there moisture on electrical components under the bonnet? Switch off the ignition, and then wipe off any obvious dampness with a dry cloth. Spray a water-repellent aerosol product (WD-40 or equivalent) on ignition and fuel system electrical connectors like those shown in the photos. Pay special attention to the ignition coil wiring connector and HT leads. (Note that Diesel engines don't normally suffer from damp.)

A Check the security and condition of the battery connections.

B Check the fuel cut-off inertia switch (where fitted) has not tripped. Reset the switch by depressing its button.

C Check that the ignition HT coil (where applicable) is securely connected by pushing it home.

Check that electrical connections are secure (with the ignition switched off) and spray them with a water dispersant spray like WD-40 if you suspect a problem due to damp

D On petrol engines, with the ignition switched off, check the various engine management sensor wiring connectors are all securely connected (crankshaft sensor shown).

E On diesel engines, check the injection pump wiring connectors are securely connected (remove the engine cover for access).

Jump starting

When jump-starting a car using a booster battery, observe the following precautions:

✔ Before connecting the booster battery, make sure that the ignition is switched off.

✔ Ensure that all electrical equipment (lights, heater, wipers, etc) is switched off.

✔ Take note of any special precautions printed on the battery case.

✔ Make sure that the booster battery is the same voltage as the discharged one in the vehicle.

✔ If the battery is being jump-started from the battery in another vehicle, the two vehicles MUST NOT TOUCH each other.

✔ Make sure that the transmission is in neutral (or PARK, in the case of automatic transmission).

> **HAYNES HINT**
>
> *Jump starting will get you out of trouble, but you must correct whatever made the battery go flat in the first place. There are three possibilities:*
>
> **1** *The battery has been drained by repeated attempts to start, or by leaving the lights on.*
>
> **2** *The charging system is not working properly (alternator drivebelt slack or broken, alternator wiring fault or alternator itself faulty).*
>
> **3** *The battery itself is at fault (electrolyte low, or battery worn out).*

1 Connect one end of the red jump lead to the positive (+) terminal of the flat battery

2 Connect the other end of the red lead to the positive (+) terminal of the booster battery.

3 Connect one end of the black jump lead to the negative (-) terminal of the booster battery

4 Connect the other end of the black jump lead to a suitable metal part of the engine on the car to be started

5 Make sure that the jump leads will not come into contact with the fan, drive-belts or other moving parts of the engine.

6 Start the engine using the booster battery and run it at idle speed. Switch on the lights, rear window demister and heater blower motor, then disconnect the jump leads in the reverse order of connection. Turn off the lights etc.

Wheel changing

Some of the details shown here will vary according to model. However, the basic principles apply to all vehicles.

⚠️ *Warning: Do not change a wheel in a situation where you risk being hit by other traffic. On busy roads, try to stop in a lay-by or a gateway. Be wary of passing traffic while changing the wheel – it is easy to become distracted by the job in hand.*

Preparation

☐ When a puncture occurs, stop as soon as it is safe to do so.
☐ Park on firm level ground, if possible, and well out of the way of other traffic.
☐ Use hazard warning lights if necessary.
☐ If you have one, use a warning triangle to alert other drivers of your presence.
☐ Apply the handbrake and engage first or reverse gear.
☐ Chock the wheel diagonally opposite the one being removed – use the jack holder (as described below) or couple of large stones will do for this.
☐ If the ground is soft, use a flat piece of wood to spread the load under the jack.

3 Use the jack holder to chock the wheel diagonally opposite the one being removed. Remove the wheel trim on the wheel to be changed and loosen each wheel bolt by half-a-turn.

6 Remove the punctured wheel from under the sill then lower the vehicle to the ground. Tighten the wheel bolts in a diagonal sequence then refit the wheel trim. Note that the wheel bolts should be slackened and retightened to the specified torque at the earliest possible opportunity.

Changing the wheel

1 Unclip the wheelbrace from its holder at the rear of the luggage compartment. Lift the luggage compartment carpet to gain access to the spare wheel cradle bolt. Use the end of the wheelbrace to slacken the bolt enough to be able to unhook the cradle from its retainer on the bolt.

4 Engage the jack head with the reinforced jacking point nearest the wheel to be changed; the jacking point is the area in between the cut-outs (arrowed) on the sill. Ensure the head of the jack is positioned centrally between the cut-outs then raise the jack until its base is in contact with the ground. Ensure the jack base is located directly below the sill then raise the vehicle until the wheel is clear of the ground. If the tyre is flat, remember to raise the vehicle sufficiently to allow the spare wheel to be fitted.

7 Remove the jack holder from under the wheel. Store the jack and space saver wheel spacer (where fitted – it is not needed when a normal wheel is fitted to the cradle) in the boot then fit the punctured wheel in the cradle. Hook the cradle onto its retainer then raise the cradle fully and secure it in position by tightening the wheel cradle bolt.

2 Unhook and lower the cradle then remove the spare wheel from underneath the vehicle. Where a space saver spare wheel is fitted, unclip the spacer (A) from the top of the wheel. Remove the jack holder (B) then place the wheel under the sill as a precaution against the jack failing.

5 Remove the bolts and lift off the wheel. Place the wheel beneath the sill as a precaution against the jack failing then fit the spare wheel. Fit the wheel bolts and moderately tighten them with the wheelbrace.

Finally . . .

☐ Remove any remaining wheel chocks.
☐ Don't leave the spare wheel cradle empty and unsecured – it could drop onto the ground while the car is moving.
☐ Have the damaged tyre or wheel repaired as soon as possible.
☐ Check the tyre pressure on the wheel just fitted. If it is low, or if you don't have a pressure gauge with you, drive slowly to the nearest garage and inflate the tyre to the right pressure.
☐ The space saver wheel is only designed for emergency use; never exceed 50 mph whilst the wheel is fitted to the vehicle. Never carry the space saver wheel in the cradle without the spacer being fitted.

Identifying leaks

Puddles on the garage floor or drive, or obvious wetness under the bonnet or underneath the car, suggest a leak that needs investigating. It can sometimes be difficult to decide where the leak is coming from, especially if the engine bay is very dirty already. Leaking oil or fluid can also be blown rearwards by the passage of air under the car, giving a false impression of where the problem lies.

 Warning: Most automotive oils and fluids are poisonous. Wash them off skin, and change out of contaminated clothing, without delay.

 The smell of a fluid leaking from the car may provide a clue to what's leaking. Some fluids are distinctively coloured. It may help to clean the car carefully and to park it over some clean paper overnight as an aid to locating the source of the leak.
Remember that some leaks may only occur while the engine is running.

Sump oil

Engine oil may leak from the drain plug...

Oil from filter

...or from the base of the oil filter.

Gearbox oil

Gearbox oil can leak from the seals at the inboard ends of the driveshafts.

Antifreeze

Leaking antifreeze often leaves a crystalline deposit like this.

Brake fluid

A leak occurring at a wheel is almost certainly brake fluid.

Power steering fluid

Power steering fluid may leak from the pipe connectors on the steering rack.

Towing

When all else fails, you may find yourself having to get a tow home – or of course you may be helping somebody else. Long-distance recovery should only be done by a garage or breakdown service. For shorter distances, DIY towing using another car is easy enough, but observe the following points:

☐ Use a proper tow-rope – they are not expensive. The vehicle being towed must display an ON TOW sign in its rear window.
☐ Always turn the ignition key to the 'on' position when the vehicle is being towed, so that the steering lock is released, and that the direction indicator and brake lights will work.

☐ Only attach the tow-rope to the towing eyes provided.
☐ Before being towed, release the handbrake and select neutral on the transmission.
☐ On models with an automatic transmission unit, the vehicle must only be towed forwards with the selector lever in the N position. Never tow the vehicle at speeds in excess of 30 mph or over a distance in excess of 30 miles. Failure to observe these warning will lead to serious transmission damage.
☐ Note that greater-than-usual pedal pressure will be required to operate the brakes, since

the vacuum servo unit is only operational with the engine running.
☐ On models with power steering, greater-than-usual steering effort will also be required.
☐ The driver of the car being towed must keep the tow-rope taut at all times to avoid snatching.
☐ Make sure that both drivers know the route before setting off.
☐ Only drive at moderate speeds and keep the distance towed to a minimum. Drive smoothly and allow plenty of time for slowing down at junctions.

Introduction

There are some very simple checks which need only take a few minutes to carry out, but which could save you a lot of inconvenience and expense.

These *Weekly checks* require no great skill or special tools, and the small amount of time they take to perform could prove to be very well spent, for example;

☐ Keeping an eye on tyre condition and pressures, will not only help to stop them wearing out prematurely, but could also save your life.

☐ Many breakdowns are caused by electrical problems. Battery-related faults are particularly common, and a quick check on a regular basis will often prevent the majority of these.

☐ If your car develops a brake fluid leak, the first time you might know about it is when your brakes don't work properly. Checking the level regularly will give advance warning of this kind of problem.

☐ If the oil or coolant levels run low, the cost of repairing any engine damage will be far greater than fixing the leak, for example.

Underbonnet check points

◀1.4 litre petrol (others similar)

A *Engine oil level dipstick*

B *Engine oil filler cap*

C *Coolant expansion tank*

D *Brake fluid reservoir*

E *Screen washer fluid reservoir*

F *Battery*

G *Power steering fluid reservoir*

◀2.0 litre diesel (1.4 similar)

A *Engine oil level dipstick*

B *Engine oil filler cap*

C *Coolant expansion tank*

D *Brake (and clutch) fluid reservoir*

E *Screen washer fluid reservoir*

F *Battery*

G *Power steering fluid reservoir*

Engine oil level

Before you start
✔ Make sure that your car is on level ground.
✔ Check the oil level before the car is driven, or at least 5 minutes after the engine has been switched off.

The correct oil
Modern engines place great demands on their oil. It is very important that the correct oil for your car is used (see *Lubricants and fluids*).

 HAYNES HINT *If the oil is checked immediately after driving the vehicle, some of the oil will remain in the upper engine components, resulting in an inaccurate reading on the dipstick.*

Car care
● If you have to add oil frequently, you should check whether you have any oil leaks. Place some clean paper under the car overnight, and check for stains in the morning. If there are no leaks, the engine may be burning oil.
● Always maintain the level between the upper and lower dipstick marks (see photo 3).
● If the level is too low severe engine damage may occur. Oil seal failure may result if adding too much oil overfills the engine.
● On models equipped with an oil level gauge, don't be tempted to rely on the gauge alone – verify the level using the dipstick on a regular basis. Equally, don't ignore the gauge if it warns of low oil level.

1 The engine oil level is checked with a dipstick that extends through the dipstick tube and into the sump at the bottom of the engine (1.1 petrol engine shown). The dipstick is located at the front of the engine (see *Underbonnet check points* for exact location). Withdraw the dipstick.

2 Wipe all the oil from the end with a clean rag or paper towel. Insert the clean dipstick back into the tube as far as it will go (2.0 litre diesel engine shown), then withdraw it once more.

3 Note the oil level on the end of the dipstick. Add oil as necessary until the level is between the upper (MAX) mark and lower (MIN) mark on the dipstick. Note that approximately 1.0 litre of oil will be required to raise the level from the lower mark to the upper mark.

4 Oil is added to the engine via the filler cap on the cylinder head cover. Unscrew the cap and top-up the level. A funnel may help to reduce spillage. Add the oil slowly, checking the level on the dipstick frequently. Do not overfill.

Coolant level

Warning: DO NOT attempt to remove the expansion tank pressure cap when the engine is hot, as there is a very great risk of scalding. Do not leave open containers of coolant about, as it is poisonous.

Car care

● With a sealed-type cooling system, adding coolant should not be necessary on a regular basis. If frequent topping-up is required, it is likely there is a leak. Check the radiator, all hoses and joint faces for signs of staining or wetness, and rectify as necessary.

● It is important that antifreeze is used in the cooling system all year round, not just during the winter months. Don't top-up with water alone, as the antifreeze will become too diluted.

1 The coolant level varies with the temperature of the engine. The level is checked in the expansion tank located in the right-hand, rear corner of the engine compartment. When the engine is cold, the coolant level should be between the MAX and MIN level marks on the tank.

2 If topping-up is necessary, **wait until the engine is cold**. Slowly unscrew the expansion tank cap, to release any pressure present in the cooling system, and remove it.

3 Add the specified coolant to the expansion tank until the coolant level is correct. Refit the cap and tighten it securely.

Brake (and clutch) fluid level*

On some models, the fluid reservoir also supplies the clutch master cylinder with fluid

Warning:
● *Brake fluid can harm your eyes and damage painted surfaces, so use extreme caution when handling and pouring it.*
● *Do not use fluid that has been standing open for some time, as it absorbs moisture from the air, which can cause a dangerous loss of braking effectiveness.*

Safety first!

● If the reservoir requires repeated topping-up this is an indication of a fluid leak somewhere in the system, which should be investigated immediately.

● If a leak is suspected, the car should not be driven until the braking system has been checked. Never take any risks where brakes are concerned.

HAYNES HiNT
● *Make sure that your car is on level ground.*
● *The fluid level in the reservoir will drop slightly as the brake pads wear down, but the fluid level must never be allowed to drop below the DANGER mark.*

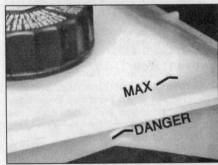

1 The brake fluid reservoir is located on the left-hand side of the engine compartment. The MAX and DANGER marks are indicated on the side of the reservoir. The fluid level must be kept between the marks at all times.

2 If topping-up is necessary, first wipe clean the area around the filler cap to prevent dirt entering the hydraulic system.

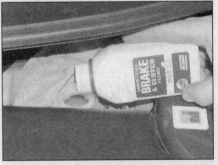

3 Carefully add fluid, taking care not to spill it onto the surrounding components. Use only the specified fluid; mixing different types can cause damage to the system. After topping-up to the correct level, securely refit the cap and wipe off any spilt fluid.

Tyre condition and pressure

It is very important that tyres are in good condition, and at the correct pressure - having a tyre failure at any speed is highly dangerous. Tyre wear is influenced by driving style - harsh braking and acceleration, or fast cornering, will all produce more rapid tyre wear. As a general rule, the front tyres wear out faster than the rears. Interchanging the tyres from front to rear ("rotating" the tyres) may result in more even wear. However, if this is completely effective, you may have the expense of replacing all four tyres at once! Remove any nails or stones embedded in the tread before they penetrate the tyre to cause deflation. If removal of a nail does reveal that

the tyre has been punctured, refit the nail so that its point of penetration is marked. Then immediately change the wheel, and have the tyre repaired by a tyre dealer.

Regularly check the tyres for damage in the form of cuts or bulges, especially in the sidewalls. Periodically remove the wheels, and clean any dirt or mud from the inside and outside surfaces. Examine the wheel rims for signs of rusting, corrosion or other damage. Light alloy wheels are easily damaged by "kerbing" whilst parking; steel wheels may also become dented or buckled. A new wheel is very often the only way to overcome severe damage.

New tyres should be balanced when they are fitted, but it may become necessary to re-balance them as they wear, or if the balance weights fitted to the wheel rim should fall off. Unbalanced tyres will wear more quickly, as will the steering and suspension components. Wheel imbalance is normally signified by vibration, particularly at a certain speed (typically around 50 mph). If this vibration is felt only through the steering, then it is likely that just the front wheels need balancing. If, however, the vibration is felt through the whole car, the rear wheels could be out of balance. Wheel balancing should be carried out by a tyre dealer or garage.

1 *Tread Depth - visual check*
The original tyres have tread wear safety bands (B), which will appear when the tread depth reaches approximately 1.6 mm. The band positions are indicated by a triangular mark on the tyre sidewall (A).

2 *Tread Depth - manual check*
Alternatively, tread wear can be monitored with a simple, inexpensive device known as a tread depth indicator gauge.

3 *Tyre Pressure Check*
Check the tyre pressures regularly with the tyres cold. Do not adjust the tyre pressures immediately after the vehicle has been used, or an inaccurate setting will result.

Tyre tread wear patterns

Shoulder Wear

Underinflation (wear on both sides)
Under-inflation will cause overheating of the tyre, because the tyre will flex too much, and the tread will not sit correctly on the road surface. This will cause a loss of grip and excessive wear, not to mention the danger of sudden tyre failure due to heat build-up.
Check and adjust pressures
Incorrect wheel camber (wear on one side)
Repair or renew suspension parts
Hard cornering
Reduce speed!

Centre Wear

Overinflation
Over-inflation will cause rapid wear of the centre part of the tyre tread, coupled with reduced grip, harsher ride, and the danger of shock damage occurring in the tyre casing.
Check and adjust pressures

If you sometimes have to inflate your car's tyres to the higher pressures specified for maximum load or sustained high speed, don't forget to reduce the pressures to normal afterwards.

Uneven Wear

Front tyres may wear unevenly as a result of wheel misalignment. Most tyre dealers and garages can check and adjust the wheel alignment (or "tracking") for a modest charge.
Incorrect camber or castor
Repair or renew suspension parts
Malfunctioning suspension
Repair or renew suspension parts
Unbalanced wheel
Balance tyres
Incorrect toe setting
Adjust front wheel alignment
Note: *The feathered edge of the tread which typifies toe wear is best checked by feel.*

Power steering fluid level

Before you start
✔ Park the vehicle on level ground.
✔ With the engine idling, turn the steering wheel slowly from lock-to-lock 2 or 3 times. Set the steering wheel straight-ahead position then switch off the engine.

 For the check to be accurate, the steering must not be turned once the engine has been stopped.

Safety first!
● The need for frequent topping-up indicates a leak, which should be investigated immediately.

1 The reservoir is located at the front of the engine on the right-hand side. Wipe clean the area around the reservoir cap, to prevent dirt entering the hydraulic system, and then remove the cap from the reservoir.

2 Wipe all fluid from the cap dipstick with a clean rag. Refit the filler cap fully, then remove it again and note the fluid level on the dipstick. When the engine is cold, the level should be between the lower (ADD) mark and the middle (C) mark on the dipstick. If the engine is warm, the fluid level maybe up to the upper (H) mark.

3 If the fluid level is on or below the lower (ADD) mark, top-up the fluid level to the middle (C) mark using the specified type of fluid (do not overfill). Once the level is correct, securely refit the filler cap to the reservoir.

Washer fluid level

● Screenwash additives not only keep the windscreen clean during foul weather, they also prevent the washer system freezing in cold weather – which is when you are likely to need it most. Don't top-up using plain water as the screenwash will become too diluted, and will freeze during cold weather.

Caution: On no account use coolant antifreeze in the washer system – this could discolour or damage paintwork.

1 The screenwasher fluid reservoir filler neck is located in the right-hand side of the engine compartment, behind the headlight. The screenwasher level cannot easily be seen. Remove the filler cap, and look down the filler neck – if fluid is not visible, topping-up may be required.

2 When topping-up the reservoir, add a screenwash additive in the quantities recommended on the additive bottle. The exact level is not critical – add fluid slowly until the level reaches the base of the filler neck

Electrical systems

✔ Check the operation of all the electrical equipment, ie, lights, direction indicators, horn, etc. Refer to the appropriate Sections of Chapter 12 for details if any of the circuits are found to be inoperative.

✔ Visually check all accessible wiring connectors, harnesses and retaining clips for security, and for signs of chafing or damage

HAYNES HiNT *If you need to check your brake lights and indicators unaided, back up to a wall or garage door and operate the lights. The reflected light should show if they are working properly.*

1 If a single indicator light, stop-light or headlight bulb has failed, it is likely that a bulb has blown and will need renewing. Refer to Chapter 12 for details. If both stop-lights have failed, it is possible that the stop-light switch has failed (see Chapter 9).

2 If more than one indicator light or headlight has failed, it is likely that either a fuse has blown or there is a fault in the circuit (see Chapter 12). The main fuses are located beneath the lower cover on the driver's side of the facia. Rotate the cover fastener 90° and remove the cover to gain access. Additional fuses and relays are located in the fuse/relay box located on the left-hand side of the engine compartment.

3 To renew a blown fuse, remove it using the plastic tool supplied (where applicable). Fit a new fuse of the correct rating, available from car accessory shops. If the new fuse blows immediately, there is a fault, which must be traced and rectified (see *Electrical fault finding* in Chapter 12)

Battery

Caution: Before carrying out any work on the vehicle battery, read the precautions given in 'Safety first!' at the start of this manual.

✔ Make sure that the battery tray is in good condition, and that the clamp is tight. Corrosion on the tray, retaining clamp and the battery itself can be removed with a solution of water and baking soda. Thoroughly rinse all cleaned areas with water. Any metal parts damaged by corrosion should be covered with a zinc-based primer, and then painted.

✔ Periodically (approximately every three months), check the charge condition of the battery as described in Chapter 5A.

✔ If the battery is flat, and you need to jump start your vehicle, see *Roadside Repairs*.

1 The battery is located on the left-hand side of the engine compartment. Unclip the cover from the battery tray to gain access. The exterior of the battery should be inspected periodically for damage such as a cracked case or cover.

2 Check the tightness of the battery cable clamps to ensure good electrical connections, and check the entire length of each cable for cracks and frayed conductors.

HAYNES HiNT

Battery corrosion can be kept to a minimum by applying a layer of petroleum jelly to the clamps and terminals after they are reconnected.

3 If corrosion (visible as white, fluffy deposits) is evident, remove the cables from the battery terminals, clean them with a small wire brush, then refit them. Automotive stores sell tools for cleaning the battery terminals . . .

4 . . . and the battery lead clamps

Wiper blades

1 Check the condition of the wiper blades; if they are cracked or show any signs of deterioration, or if the glass swept area is smeared, renew them. For maximum clarity of vision, wiper blades should be renewed annually, as a matter of course.

2 To remove a windscreen wiper blade, pull the arm fully away from the glass until it locks. Swivel the blade through 90°, then squeeze the locking clip and slide the blade out of the arm's hooked end. On refitting, ensure that the blade locks securely into the arm.

3 Don't forget to check the tailgate wiper blade as well. To remove the blade, pull the arm away from the glass then unclip the blade.

Lubricants and fluids

Engine

Petrol . . . . SAE 10W40, 5W40 or 0W40 Multigrade engine oil to ACEA A3 and API SJ/SL specification*

Diesel . . . . SAE 10W40, 5W40 or 0W40 Multigrade engine oil to ACEA B3 and API CD/CF specification*

Cooling system . . . . BASF Glysantin G33-23F or Gurit Essex Revkogel 2000

Manual transmission . . . . Esso Gear Oil BV 75W80 or Total Transmission BV 75W80

Automatic transmission . . . . Esso 4HP20- AL4 Automatic Transmission Fluid

Brake (and clutch) hydraulic system . . . . Hydraulic fluid to DOT 4 (BP BF PSA DOT4, Shell BF 40 or Gurit Essex Betabrake 303 DOT4)

Power steering . . . . Total Fluide LDS

Due to the extended service intervals Peugeot specify, it is essential that semi-synthetic or fully synthetic engine oil be used.

Tyre pressures

Note: *Always refer to the tyre pressure data sticker on the lower part of the centre door pillar (visible when the door is open) for the correct tyre pressures for your particular vehicle. Pressures apply only to original-equipment tyres, and may vary if any other make or type is fitted; check with the tyre manufacturer or supplier for correct pressures if necessary.*

Chapter 1 Part A:
Routine maintenance and servicing – petrol models

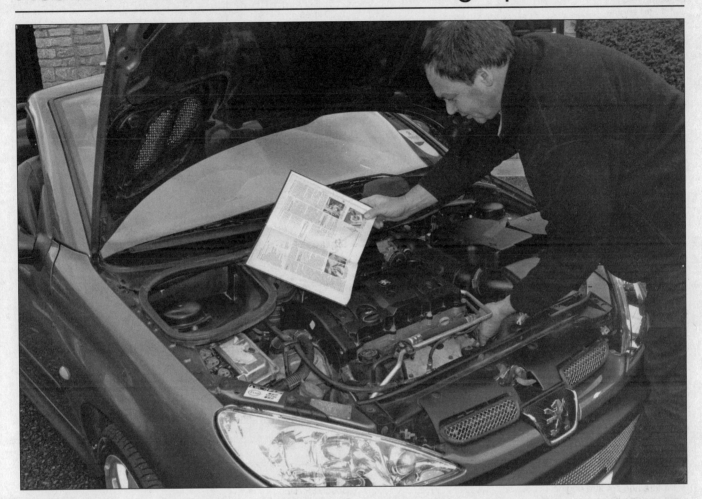

Contents

Degrees of difficulty

Easy, suitable for novice with little experience

Fairly easy, suitable for beginner with some experience

Fairly difficult, suitable for competent DIY mechanic

Difficult, suitable for experienced DIY mechanic

Very difficult, suitable for expert DIY or professional

Lubricants and fluids. . . . . Refer to end of *Weekly checks*

Capacities

Engine oil
Including filter:
   1.1 litre engine . . . . 3.20 litres
   1.4 litre engine:
      SOHC . . . . 3.00 litres
      DOHC . . . . 3.20 litres
   1.6 litre engine . . . . 3.20 litres
   2.0 litre engine . . . . 4.25 litres
Difference between MAX and MIN dipstick marks. . . . . 1.5 litres

Cooling system
1.1, 1.4 and 1.6 litre engines – SOHC . . . . 7.00 litres
1.4 litre engine – DOHC . . . . 5.60 litres
2.0 litre engine . . . . 5.30 litres

Transmission
Manual:
   1.1, 1.4 and 1.6 litre engine . . . . 2.0 litres
   2.0 litre engine . . . . 1.9 litres
Automatic:
   Refilling after draining. . . . . 4.5 litres
   From dry . . . . 6.0 litres

Power-assisted steering (approximate) . . . . 1.0 litres

Fuel tank . . . . 50 litres

Engine

Auxiliary drivebelt tensions (for use with Peugeot tool):
   New belt . . . . 138 SEEM units
   Used belt . . . . 103 SEEM units

Cooling system

Antifreeze mixture:
   50% antifreeze . . . . Protection down to –35°C
Note: *Refer to antifreeze manufacturer for latest recommendations.*

Ignition system

Spark plugs:
   1.1 litre and 1.4 litre engine . . . . Bosch FR7DE
   1.4 litre DOHC engine . . . . Bosch VR8SE
   1.6 litre engine . . . . Bosch FR7ME
   2.0 litre engines . . . . Bosch FR8ME
Electrode gap. . . . . 0.9 mm

Brakes

Brake pad friction material minimum thickness. . . . . 2.0 mm

Tyre pressures . . . . Refer to end of *Weekly checks*

Torque wrench settings

	Nm	lbf ft
Alternator mounting bolts.	37	27
Automatic transmission:		
Filler plug .	24	18
Level plug.	24	18
Auxiliary drivebelt tensioner pulley nut.	45	33
Manual transmission filler/level plug:		
All models except 2.0 litre models.	25	18
2.0 litre models.	20	15
Oil filter cover/cap (element type).	25	18
Roadwheel bolts.	90	66
Spark plugs .	25	18
Sump drain plug.	30	22

Note: *This maintenance schedule is a guide recommended by Haynes, for servicing your own vehicle. For the manufacturer's maintenance schedule, check with your local dealer.*

1 The maintenance intervals in this manual are provided with the assumption that you, not the dealer, will be carrying out the work. These are the minimum maintenance intervals recommended by us for vehicles driven daily. If you wish to keep your vehicle in peak condition at all times, you may wish to perform some of these procedures more often. We encourage frequent maintenance, because it enhances the efficiency, performance and resale value of your vehicle.

2 If the vehicle is driven in dusty areas, used to tow a trailer, or driven frequently at slow speeds (idling in traffic) or on short journeys, more frequent maintenance intervals are recommended.

3 When the vehicle is new, it should be serviced by a dealer service department (or other workshop recognised by the vehicle manufacturer as providing the same standard of service) in order to preserve the warranty. The vehicle manufacturer may reject warranty claims if you are unable to prove that servicing has been carried out as and when specified, using only original equipment parts or parts certified to be of equivalent quality.

4 Valve clearance checking on SOHC engines (Chapter 2A, Section 9) is no longer specified as part of the routine maintenance schedule (other engines have hydraulic adjusters). Check the valve clearances if there is any tapping or rattling from the top of the engine, or in the event of an unexplained lack of performance. The prudent owner may wish to check the clearances, perhaps at 40 000 mile or four-yearly intervals.

Every 250 miles or weekly

☐ Refer to *Weekly checks*

Every 10 000 miles or 12 months – whichever comes sooner

☐ Renew the engine oil and filter* (Section 3).
☐ Check all underbonnet components or fluid leaks (Section 4).
☐ Check the condition of the driveshaft rubber gaiters and CV joints (Section 5).
☐ Lubricate all hinges and locks (Section 6).
☐ Carry out a road test (Section 7).

* Note: *Peugeot recommend the engine oil and filter are changed every 20 000 miles or two years. However, oil and filter changes are good for the engine and we recommend changing the oil at least once a year, especially if the vehicle is used on a lot of short journeys.*

Every 20 000 miles or two years – whichever comes sooner

☐ Reset the service interval indicator (Section 8).
☐ Check the pollen filter (Section 9).
☐ Check the condition of the auxiliary drivebelt (Section 10).
☐ Check the condition of the brake pads (Section 11).
☐ Check the operation of the handbrake (Section 12).
☐ Check the steering and suspension components (Section 13).

Every 40 000 miles

☐ Renew the timing belt (Section 14).
Note: *Although the normal interval for timing belt renewal is 80 000 miles, it is strongly recommended that the interval is reduced to 40 000 miles, especially on vehicles which are subjected to intensive use, ie, mainly short journeys or a lot of stop-start driving. The actual belt renewal interval is therefore very much up to the individual owner, but bear in mind that severe engine damage will result if the belt breaks.*

Every 40 000 miles or two years – whichever comes sooner

☐ Renew the brake fluid (Section 15).
Note: *A hydraulic clutch shares its fluid reservoir with the braking system, and may also need to be bled.*

Every 40 000 miles or four years – whichever comes sooner

☐ Renew the spark plugs (Section 16).
☐ Renew the fuel filter (Section 17).
☐ Renew the air cleaner filter element (Section 18).
☐ Check the manual transmission oil level (Section 19).
☐ Check the automatic transmission fluid level (Section 20).
☐ Check the exhaust emissions (Section 21).
☐ Renew the coolant (Section 22).
☐ Check the brake shoes (Section 23).

Every ten years

☐ Renew the airbags and seat belt pretensioners (Section 24).

Underbonnet view of a 1.4 litre model

1 Engine oil filler cap
2 Engine oil level dipstick
3 Battery
4 Brake/clutch fluid reservoir
5 Fuse/electrical box
6 Air filter housing
7 Radiator
8 Power steering pump/fluid reservoir
9 Washer fluid reservoir
10 Engine management ECU
11 Coolant expansion tank
12 Pollen filter
13 Ignition HT coil
14 Throttle housing
15 Cooling system bleed screws
16 Fuel cut-off inertia switch (where
    fitted)

Front underbody view (manual transmission model)

1 Engine oil drain plug
2 Air conditioning compressor
3 Oil filter
4 Coolant drain plug (where fitted)
5 Air cleaner intake duct
6 Manual transmission filler/level plug
7 Manual transmission drain plug
8 Brake caliper
9 Suspension lower arm
10 Track rod balljoint
11 Anti-roll bar
12 Driveshaft inner CV joint
13 Exhaust system
14 Auxiliary belt

Rear underbody view

1 Spare wheel
2 Exhaust system tailpipe
3 Fuel tank
4 Fuel filter (where fitted)
5 Handbrake cables
6 Rear axle front mounting
7 Rear axle rear mounting
8 Brake pipes
9 Rear shock absorber
10 Rear brake pressure regulating valve
(non ABS models)

1 General information

1 This Chapter is designed to help the home mechanic maintain his/her vehicle for safety, economy, long life and peak performance.
2 The Chapter contains a master maintenance schedule, followed by Sections dealing specifically with each task in the schedule. Visual checks, adjustments, component renewal and other helpful items are included. Refer to the accompanying illustrations of the engine compartment and the underside of the vehicle for the locations of the various components.
3 Servicing your vehicle in accordance with the mileage/time maintenance schedule and the following Sections will provide a planned maintenance programme, which should result in a long and reliable service life. This is a comprehensive plan, so maintaining some items but not others at the specified service intervals will not produce the same results.
4 As you service your vehicle, you will discover that many of the procedures can – and should – be grouped together, because of the particular procedure being performed, or because of the close proximity of two otherwise-unrelated components to one another. For example, if the vehicle is raised for any reason, the exhaust can be inspected at the same time as the suspension and steering components.

5 The first step in this maintenance programme is to prepare yourself before the actual work begins. Read through all the Sections relevant to the work to be carried out, then make a list and gather together all the parts and tools required. If a problem is encountered, seek advice from a parts specialist, or a dealer service department.

2 Routine maintenance

1 If, from the time the vehicle is new, the routine maintenance schedule is followed closely, and frequent checks are made of fluid levels and high-wear items, as suggested throughout this manual, the engine will be kept in relatively good running condition, and the need for additional work will be minimised.
2 It is possible that there will be times when the engine is running poorly due to the lack of regular maintenance. This is even more likely if a used vehicle, which has not received regular and frequent maintenance checks, is purchased. In such cases, additional work may need to be carried out, outside of the regular maintenance intervals.
3 If engine wear is suspected, a compression test (refer to Chapter 2A, 2B or 2C) will provide valuable information regarding the overall performance of the main internal components. Such a test can be used as a basis to decide

on the extent of the work to be carried out. If, for example, a compression test indicates serious internal engine wear, conventional maintenance as described in this Chapter will not greatly improve the performance of the engine, and may prove a waste of time and money, unless extensive overhaul work (Chapter 2E) is carried out first.
4 The following series of operations are those often required to improve the performance of a generally poor-running engine:

Primary operations

a) Clean, inspect and test the battery (See 'Weekly checks').
b) Check all the engine-related fluids (See 'Weekly checks').
c) Check the condition and tension of the auxiliary drivebelt (Section 10).
d) Renew the spark plugs (Section 16).
e) Check the condition of the air cleaner filter element, and renew if necessary (Section 18).
f) Renew the fuel filter (Section 17).
g) Check the condition of all hoses, and check for fluid leaks (Section 4).
5 If the above operations do not prove fully effective, carry out the following operations:

Secondary operations

All items listed under *Primary operations*, plus the following:
a) Check the charging system (Chapter 5A).
b) Check the ignition system (Chapter 5B).
c) Check the fuel system (Chapter 4A).

3.3a Remove the screws . . .

3.3b . . . securing the engine undershield (right-hand side arrowed)

Every 10 000 miles or 12 months

3 Engine oil and filter renewal

Note: *A suitable square-section wrench may be required to undo the sump drain plug. These wrenches can be obtained from most motor factors or your Peugeot dealer.*

1 Frequent oil and filter changes are the most important preventative maintenance procedures, which can be undertaken by the DIY owner. As engine oil ages, it becomes diluted and contaminated, which leads to premature engine wear.

2 Before starting this procedure, gather together all the necessary tools and materials. Also make sure that you have plenty of clean rags and newspapers handy, to mop-up any spills. Ideally, the engine oil should be warm, as it will drain better, and more built-up sludge will be removed with it. Take care, however, not to touch the exhaust or any other hot parts of the engine when working under the vehicle. To avoid any possibility of scalding, and to protect yourself from possible skin irritants and other harmful contaminants in used engine oils, it is advisable to wear gloves when carrying out this work.

Access to the underside of the vehicle will be greatly improved if it can be raised on a lift, driven onto ramps, or jacked up and supported on axle stands (see *Jacking and vehicle support*). Whichever method is chosen, make sure that the vehicle remains level, or if it is at an angle, that the drain plug is at the lowest point.

3 Undo the screws and remove the engine undershield – where fitted **(see illustrations)**.

4 Slacken the drain plug about half a turn **(see illustration)**. Position the draining container under the drain plug, and then remove the plug completely. If possible, try to keep the plug pressed into the sump while unscrewing it by hand the last couple of turns **(see Haynes Hint)**. Recover the sealing ring from the drain plug.

5 Allow some time for the old oil to drain, noting that it may be necessary to reposition the container as the oil flow slows to a trickle.

6 After all the oil has drained, wipe off the drain plug with a clean rag, and fit a new sealing washer. Clean the area around the drain plug opening, and refit the plug, tightening it to the specified torque.

7 Move the container into position under the oil filter, which is located on the front of the cylinder block.

Element type filter

8 On these engines, the filter element is contained within a filter cover. Using a socket or spanner, slacken and remove the filter cover from above **(see illustrations)**. Be prepared for fluid spillage, and recover the O-ring seal from the cover.

9 Pull the filter element from the filter cover.

HAYNES HINT

As the drain plug releases from the sump threads, move it away sharply, so the stream of oil issuing from the sump runs into the container, not up your sleeve.

3.4 Slacken the sump drain plug

3.8a Slacken the filter cover . . .

3.8b . . . and recover the O-ring seal

3.11a Fit the new element into the cover . . .

3.11b . . . and apply a little clean engine oil to the O-ring seal

3.13 Use an oil filter removal tool to slacken the canister type oil filter

10 Use a clean rag to remove all oil, dirt and sludge from the inside and outside of the filter cover.

11 Insert the new filter element in to the cover, then apply a little clean engine oil to the new O-ring seal, and fit it to the filter cover (**see illustrations**).

12 Refit the filter/cover to the housing and tighten the cover to the specified torque.

Canister type filter

13 Using an oil filter removal tool if necessary, slacken the filter initially, then unscrew it by hand the rest of the way (**see illustration**). Empty the oil in the old filter into the container.

14 Use a clean rag to remove all oil, dirt and sludge from the filter sealing area on the engine. Check the old filter to make sure that the rubber sealing ring hasn't stuck to the engine. If it has, carefully remove it.

15 Apply a light coating of clean engine oil to the sealing ring on the new filter, then screw it into position on the engine (**see illustrations**). Tighten the filter firmly by hand only – **do not use any tools.**

All engines

16 Remove the old oil and all tools from under the car, then lower the car to the ground (if applicable).

17 Remove the dipstick, and then unscrew the oil filler cap from the cylinder head cover. Fill the engine, using the correct grade and type of oil (see *Lubricants and fluids*). An oil can spout or funnel may help to reduce spillage. Pour in half the specified quantity of oil first, and then wait a few minutes for the oil to run to the sump. Continue adding oil a small quantity at a time until the level is up to the lower mark on the dipstick. Refit the filler cap.

18 Start the engine and run it for a few minutes; check for leaks around the oil filter seal and the sump drain plug. Note that there may be a delay of a few seconds before the oil pressure warning light goes out when the engine is first started, as the oil circulates through the engine oil galleries and the new oil filter before the pressure builds-up.

19 Refit the engine undershield (where applicable), and secure it in place with the screw fasteners.

3.15a Lubricate the sealing ring of the new filter with clean engine oil . . .

3.15b . . . then screw the filter onto the engine and tighten firmly by hand

20 Switch off the engine, and wait a few minutes for the oil to settle in the sump once more. With the new oil circulated and the filter completely full, recheck the level on the dipstick, and add more oil as necessary.

21 Dispose of the used engine oil safely, with reference to *General repair procedures*.

4 Hose and fluid leak check

1 Visually inspect the engine joint faces, gaskets and seals for any signs of water or oil leaks. Pay particular attention to the areas around the oil filter, cylinder head cover, cylinder head and sump joint faces. Bear in mind that, over a period of time, some very slight seepage from these areas is to be expected – what you are really looking for is any indication of a serious leak. Should a leak be found, renew the offending gasket or oil seal by referring to the appropriate Chapters in this manual.

2 Also check the security and condition of all the engine-related pipes and hoses. Ensure that all cable ties or securing clips are in place, and in good condition. Clips that are broken or missing can lead to chafing of the hoses, pipes or wiring, which could cause more serious problems in the future.

3 Carefully check the radiator hoses and heater hoses along their entire length. Renew any hose which is cracked, swollen or deteriorated. Cracks will show up better if the hose is squeezed. Pay close attention to

the hose clips that secures the hoses to the cooling system components. Hose clips can pinch and puncture hoses, resulting in cooling system leaks. If crimped-type hose clips are used, it may be a good idea to update them with standard worm-drive clips.

4 Inspect all the cooling system components (hoses, joint faces, etc) for leaks (**see Haynes Hint**).

5 Where any problems are found on system components, renew the component or gasket with reference to Chapter 3.

6 Where applicable, inspect the automatic transmission fluid cooler hoses for leaks or deterioration.

7 With the vehicle raised, inspect the petrol tank and filler neck for punctures, cracks and other damage. The connection between

A leak in the cooling system will usually show up as white- or antifreeze-coloured deposits on the area adjoining the leak.

5.1 Check the driveshaft gaiters for signs of damage or deterioration

the filler neck and tank is especially critical. Sometimes a rubber filler neck or connecting hose will leak due to loose retaining clamps or deteriorated rubber.

8 Carefully check all rubber hoses and fuel pipes leading away from the petrol tank. Check for loose connections, deteriorated hoses, crimped lines, and other damage. Pay particular attention to the vent pipes and hoses, which often loop up around the filler neck and can become blocked or crimped. Follow the pipes to the front of the vehicle, carefully inspecting them all the way. Renew damaged sections as necessary.

9 From within the engine compartment, check the security of all fuel pipe attachments and unions, and inspect the fuel pipes and vacuum hoses for kinks, chafing and deterioration.

10 Where applicable, check the condition of the power steering fluid hoses and pipes.

5 Driveshaft gaiter and CV joints check

1 With the vehicle raised and securely supported on stands (see *Jacking and vehicle support*), turn the steering onto full lock, then slowly rotate the roadwheel. Inspect the condition of the outer constant velocity (CV) joint gaiters, squeezing the gaiters to open out the folds **(see illustration)**. Check for signs of cracking, splits or deterioration of the gaiter, which may allow the grease to escape, and lead to water and grit entry into the joint. Also check the security and condition of the retaining clips. Repeat these checks on the inner CV joints.

If any damage or deterioration is found, the gaiters should be renewed (see Chapter 8).

2 At the same time, check the general condition of the CV joints themselves by first holding the driveshaft and attempting to rotate the wheel. Repeat this check by holding the inner joint and attempting to rotate the driveshaft. Any appreciable movement indicates wear in the joints, wear in the driveshaft splines, or a loose driveshaft retaining nut.

6 Hinge and lock lubrication

1 Work around the vehicle, and lubricate the hinges of the bonnet, doors and tailgate with a small amount of general-purpose oil.

2 Lightly lubricate the bonnet release mechanism and exposed section of inner cable with a smear of grease.

3 Check carefully the security and operation of all hinges, latches and locks, adjusting them where required. Check the operation of the central locking system (if fitted).

4 Check the condition and operation of the tailgate struts, renewing them if either is leaking or no longer able to support the tailgate securely when raised.

7 Road test

Instruments and electrical equipment

1 Check the operation of all instruments and electrical equipment.

2 Make sure that all instruments read correctly, and switch on all electrical equipment in turn to check it functions properly.

Steering and suspension

3 Check for any abnormalities in the steering, suspension, handling or road 'feel'.

4 Drive the vehicle, and check that there are no unusual vibrations or noises.

5 Check that the steering feels positive, with no excessive 'sloppiness', or roughness, and check for any suspension noises when cornering, or when driving over bumps.

Drivetrain

6 Check the performance of the engine, clutch, transmission and driveshafts.

7 Listen for any unusual noises from the engine, clutch and transmission.

8 Make sure the engine idles smoothly, and that there is no hesitation when accelerating.

9 Check that the clutch action is smooth and progressive, that the drive is taken up smoothly, and that the pedal travel is not excessive. Also listen for any noises when the clutch pedal is depressed.

10 Check that all gears can be engaged smoothly, without noise, and that the gear lever action is smooth and not vague or 'notchy'.

11 On automatic transmission models, make sure that all gearchanges occur smoothly, without snatching, and without an increase in engine speed between changes. Check that all the gear positions can be selected with the vehicle at rest. If any problems are found, they should be referred to a Peugeot dealer.

12 Listen for a metallic clicking sound from the front of the vehicle, as the vehicle is driven slowly in a circle with the steering on full lock. Carry out this check in both directions. If a clicking noise is heard, this indicates wear in a driveshaft joint; in which case, the complete driveshaft must be renewed (see Chapter 8).

Braking system

13 Make sure that the vehicle does not pull to one side when braking, and that the wheels do not lock when braking hard.

14 Check that there is no vibration through the steering when braking.

15 Check that the handbrake operates correctly, without excessive movement of the lever, and that it holds the vehicle on a slope.

16 Test the operation of the brake servo unit as follows. With the engine off, depress the footbrake four or five times to exhaust the vacuum. Start the engine, holding the brake pedal depressed. As the engine starts, there should be a noticeable 'give' in the brake pedal as vacuum builds-up. Allow the engine to run for at least two minutes, and then switch it off. If the brake pedal is depressed now, it should be possible to detect a hiss from the servo as the pedal is depressed. After about four or five applications, no further hissing should be heard, and the pedal should feel considerably firmer.

Every 20 000 miles or two years

8 Resetting the service indicator

1 On completion of the service, reset the service interval indicator as follows.

2 With the ignition switched off, press and hold the trip meter button **(see illustration)**.

3 Still holding the button, turn the ignition switch on, and the display begins a 10 second

countdown. When the countdown reaches 0, release the trip meter button, and the spanner service symbol in the display will disappear.

4 Turn off the ignition switch.

5 Turn on the ignition switch and check the correct mileage to the next service interval is displayed on the indicator.

Note: *If you need to disconnect the battery after carrying out this procedure, lock the vehicle and wait at least 5 minutes. Otherwise the display reset may not register.*

8.2 Reset the service indicator as described in the text

9 Pollen filter check

1 Open the bonnet.
2 Reach in behind the right-hand suspension strut upper mounting and remove the pollen filter element from the heating/ventilation housing intake, noting which way around the filter is fitted **(see illustrations)**.
3 Check the condition of the filter, and renew it if dirty.
4 Wipe clean the inside of the housing and fit the new pollen filter element, making sure that it is correctly seated.
5 Close the bonnet.

10 Auxiliary drivebelt check and renewal

Note: *On models without power steering and air conditioning, Peugeot specify the use of a special electronic tool (SEEM C.TRONIC type 105.5 belt tension measuring tool) to correctly set the auxiliary drivebelt tension. If access to this equipment cannot be obtained, an approximate setting can be achieved using the method described below. If this method is used, the tension should be checked using the special electronic tool at the earliest opportunity. Models with automatic tensioner do not require the use of a special tool as they are self-adjusting.*

Check

1 Apply the handbrake, slacken the front right-hand roadwheel bolts, then jack up the front of the car and support it on axle stands (see *Jacking and vehicle support*). Remove the right-hand front roadwheel.
2 Remove the plastic expanding rivets (pull out the centre pin then remove the complete rivet) securing the wheel arch liner to the body then manoeuvre the liner out from underneath the wing.
3 Using a suitable socket and extension bar fitted to the crankshaft sprocket bolt, rotate the crankshaft so that the entire length of the drivebelt can be examined. Examine the drivebelt for cracks, splitting, fraying or damage. Check also for signs of glazing (shiny patches) and for separation of the belt plies. Renew the belt if worn or damaged.
4 If the condition of the belt is satisfactory, check the drivebelt tension as described below. **Note:** *On 1.4 litre DOHC and 2.0 litre models, there is no need to check the drivebelt tension (an automatic tensioner is fitted).*
5 Refit the wheel arch liner, securing it in position with the plastic expanding rivets.
6 Refit the roadwheel then lower the vehicle to the ground and tighten the wheel bolts to the specified torque.

9.2a Remove the pollen filter . . .

9.2b . . . noting its fitted position

Models without air conditioning except 1.4 DOHC and 2.0

Renewal

7 If not already done, proceed as described in paragraphs 1 and 2.
8 On 1.1 and 1.4 litre models, slacken both the alternator upper and lower mounting bolts, whilst on 1.6 litre models it is only necessary to slacken the lower mounting bolt.
9 Back off the adjuster bolt to relieve the tension in the drivebelt, then slip the drivebelt from the pulleys. **Note:** *If the belt is going to be re-used, mark the direction of rotation on the belt prior to removal. This will ensure it is refitted the correct way around.*
10 If the belt is being renewed, ensure that the correct type is used. If the original belt is being refitted, use the mark made on removal to ensure it is fitted the correct way around.
11 Fit the belt around the pulleys, and take up the slack in the belt by tightening the adjuster bolt **(see illustrations)**. Tension the drivebelt as described in the following paragraphs.

Tensioning

12 If not already done, proceed as described in paragraphs 1 and 2.
13 If the special measuring tool is available, fit the measuring equipment to the 'lower run' of the belt, approximately midway between the crankshaft and alternator pulleys. The belt tension should be set to the figure given in the Specifications at the start of this Chapter.
14 If the measuring tool is not available, the belt should be tensioned so that, under firm thumb pressure, there is about 5.0 mm of free movement at the mid-point between the pulleys on the lower belt run.
Caution: Correct tensioning of the drivebelt will ensure it has a long life. A belt which is too slack will slip and squeal. Beware of overtightening, as this can cause wear in the alternator bearings.
15 To adjust the belt tension, with the mounting bolt(s) just slackened, turn the adjuster bolt until the correct tension is achieved.
16 Rotate the crankshaft a couple of times, recheck the tension, and then tighten the alternator mounting bolt(s) to the specified torque.
17 Refit the wheel arch liner, securing it in position with the plastic expanding rivets.
18 Refit the roadwheel then lower the vehicle to the ground and tighten the wheel bolts to the specified torque. Reconnect the battery.

10.11a Auxiliary belt adjustment (1.4 litre models without air conditioning)

1 Alternator pivot bolt
2 Adjuster bolt

10.11b Auxiliary belt adjustment (1.6 litre models without air conditioning)

1 Alternator pivot bolt
2 Adjuster bolt

1 Alternator pulley
2 Idler pulley
3 Compressor pulley
4 Crankshaft pulley
5 Tensioner pulley
6 Tensioner bolts

H44692

10.21 Auxiliary belt routing and adjustment (1.4 and 1.6 litre models with air conditioning)

Models with air conditioning except 1.4 DOHC and 2.0

Renewal

19 If not already done, proceed as described in paragraphs 1 and 2.

20 Slacken the tensioner pulley bracket bolts and rotate the adjuster bolt to release the tension in the belt, then remove the belt from the pulleys. **Note:** *If the belt is to be re-used, mark the direction of rotation on the belt prior to removal. This will ensure it is refitted the correct way around.*

21 If the belt is being renewed, ensure that the correct type is used. If the original belt is being refitted, use the mark made on removal to ensure it is fitted the correct way around. Fit the drivebelt around the pulleys in the following order **(see illustration):**

a) *Air conditioning compressor.*
b) *Crankshaft.*
c) *Alternator.*
d) *Idler roller.*
e) *Tensioner pulley.*

22 Ensure that the ribs on the belt are correctly engaged with the grooves in the pulleys, and that the drivebelt is correctly routed. Tension the belt as follows.

Tensioning

23 If not already done, proceed as described in paragraphs 1 and 2.

24 If the special measuring tool is available, fit the measuring equipment to the belt, approximately midway between the crankshaft and air conditioning compressor pulleys. Check the belt tension is as given in the Specifications at the start of this Chapter.

25 If the measuring tool is not available, the belt should be tensioned so that, under firm thumb pressure, there is about 5.0 mm of free movement at the mid-point between the crankshaft and air conditioning compressor pulleys.

Caution: Correct tensioning of the drivebelt will ensure it has a long life. A belt which is too slack will slip and squeal. Beware of overtightening, as this can cause wear in the alternator bearings.

26 To adjust the tension, rotate the adjuster bolt until the correct tension is achieved. Once the belt is correctly tensioned, tighten the tensioner pulley bracket bolts to the specified torque. Rotate the crankshaft a couple of times and recheck the tension.

27 When the belt is correctly tensioned, refit the wheel arch liner, securing it in position with the plastic expanding rivets.

28 Refit the roadwheel then lower the vehicle to the ground and tighten the wheel bolts to the specified torque. Reconnect the battery.

1.4 DOHC and 2.0

Removal

29 If not already done, proceed as described in paragraphs 1 and 2.

30 Move the tensioner pulley away from the drivebelt, using a spanner on the tensioner pulley retaining nut. Rotate the tensioner pulley anti-clockwise away from the belt. **Note:** *On 1.4 litre models, use a locking pin (drill bit) to hold the pulley in the released position* **(see illustration).**

31 Once the tension is released, disengage the belt from all the pulleys, noting its correct routing **(see illustration)**. Remove the drivebelt from the engine. **Note:** *If the belt is going to be re-used, mark the direction of rotation on the belt prior to removal. This will ensure it is refitted the correct way around.*

Refitting and tensioning

32 If the belt is being renewed, ensure that the correct type is used. If the original belt is being refitted, use the mark made on removal to ensure it is fitted the correct way around. Fit the drivebelt around the pulleys in the following order **(see illustration):**

a) *Alternator.*
b) *Idler pulleys*
c) *Air conditioning compressor (where applicable).*
d) *Crankshaft.*
e) *Automatic tensioner pulley.*

H44691

10.32 Auxiliary belt routing and adjustment (2.0 litre models with air conditioning)

1 Alternator
2 Tensioner pulley bolt
3 Compressor
4 Tensioner pulley

10.30 Using a spanner release the tension on the auxiliary belt . . .

10.31 . . . and slip the belt off the pulleys

For a quick check, the thickness of the friction material on each brake pad can be measured through the aperture in the caliper body.

33 Ensure that the ribs on the belt are correctly engaged with the grooves in the pulleys

Caution: Do not allow the tensioner pulley to spring forcefully onto the belt as this could result in damage.

34 Refit the wheel arch liner, securing it in position with the retaining plastic expanding rivets.

35 Refit the roadwheel then lower the vehicle to the ground and tighten the wheel bolts to the specified torque.

11 Brake pad check

1 Slacken the front roadwheel bolts. Firmly apply the handbrake, and then jack up the front of the car and support it securely on axle stands (see *Jacking and vehicle support*). Remove the front roadwheels.

2 For a quick check, the pad thickness can be carried out via the inspection hole on the front caliper **(see Haynes Hint)**. Using a steel rule, measure the thickness of the pad friction material. This must not be less than the specified minimum given in the Specifications.

3 For a comprehensive check, the brake pads should be removed and cleaned. The operation of the caliper can then be checked, and the brake disc itself can be fully examined on both sides. Refer to Chapter 9 for details.

4 If any pad's friction material is worn to the specified minimum thickness or less; all four pads must be renewed as a set. Refer to Chapter 9 for details.

13.4 Check for wear in the hub bearings by grasping the wheel and trying to rock it

5 On completion, refit the roadwheels then lower the vehicle to the ground and tighten the wheel bolts to the specified torque.

6 Slacken the rear roadwheel bolts. Jack up the rear of the car and support it securely on axle stands. Remove the rear roadwheels. Repeat the procedure described in Paragraphs 2 to 5 on the rear brake pads.

12 Handbrake check and adjustment

1 The handbrake should be fully applied before 8 clicks can be heard from the lever ratchet mechanism. Check and, if necessary, adjust the handbrake as described in Chapter 9.

13 Steering and suspension check

Front suspension and steering

1 Raise the front of the vehicle, and securely support it on axle stands (see *Jacking and vehicle support*).

2 Visually inspect the balljoint dust covers and the steering gear gaiters for splits, chafing or deterioration. Any wear of these components will cause loss of lubricant, together with dirt and water entry, resulting in rapid deterioration of the balljoints or steering gear.

3 Check the power steering fluid pipes/hoses for chafing or deterioration, and the pipe and hose unions for fluid leaks. Also check for signs of fluid leakage under pressure from the steering gear rubber gaiters, which would indicate failed fluid seals within the steering gear.

4 Grasp the roadwheel at the 12 o'clock and

6 o'clock positions, and try to rock it **(see illustration)**. Very slight free play may be felt, but if the movement is appreciable, further investigation is necessary to determine the source. Continue rocking the wheel while an assistant depresses the footbrake. If the movement is now eliminated or significantly reduced, it is likely that the hub bearings are at fault. If the free play is still evident with the footbrake depressed, then there is wear in the suspension joints or mountings.

5 Now grasp the wheel at the 9 o'clock and 3 o'clock positions, and try to rock it as before. Any movement felt now may again be caused by wear in the hub bearings or the steering track rod balljoints. If the inner or outer balljoint is worn, the visual movement will be obvious.

6 Using a large screwdriver or flat bar, check for wear in the suspension mounting bushes by levering between the relevant suspension component and its attachment point. Some movement is to be expected as the mountings are made of rubber, but excessive wear should be obvious. Also check the condition of any visible rubber bushes, looking for splits, cracks or contamination of the rubber.

7 With the car standing on its wheels, have an assistant turn the steering wheel back-and-forth about an eighth of a turn each way. There should be very little, if any, lost movement between the steering wheel and roadwheels. If this is not the case, closely observe the joints and mountings previously described, but in addition, check the steering column universal joints for wear, and the steering gear itself.

Suspension strut/ shock absorber

8 Check for any signs of fluid leakage around the suspension strut/shock absorber body, or from the rubber gaiter around the piston rod. Should any fluid be noticed, the suspension strut/shock absorber is defective internally, and should be renewed. **Note:** *Suspension struts/shock absorbers should always be renewed in pairs on the same axle, or the handling of the vehicle will be adversely affected.*

9 The efficiency of the suspension strut/shock absorber may be checked by bouncing the vehicle at each corner. Generally speaking, the body will return to its normal position and stop after being depressed. If it rises and returns on a rebound, the suspension strut/shock absorber is probably suspect. Examine also the suspension strut/shock absorber upper and lower mountings for any signs of wear.

Every 40 000 miles

14 Timing belt renewal

1 Refer to Chapter 2A, 2B or 2C, as applicable.

Every 40 000 miles or two years

15 Brake fluid renewal

⚠️ **Warning: Brake hydraulic fluid can harm your eyes and damage painted surfaces, so use extreme caution when handling and pouring it. Do not use fluid that has been standing open for some time, as it absorbs moisture from the air. Excess moisture can cause a dangerous loss of braking effectiveness.**

Note: *A hydraulic clutch shares its fluid reservoir with the braking system, and may also need to be bled (see Chapter 6).*

1 The procedure is similar to that for the bleeding of the hydraulic system as described in Chapter 9, except that the brake fluid reservoir should be emptied by syphoning, using a clean ladle or similar before starting, and allowance should be made for the old fluid to be expelled when bleeding a section of the circuit.

2 Working as described in Chapter 9, open the first bleed screw in the sequence, and pump the brake pedal gently until nearly all the old fluid has been emptied from the master cylinder reservoir.

3 Top-up to the MAX level with new fluid,

 HAYNES HiNT *Old hydraulic fluid is invariably much darker in colour than the new, making it easy to distinguish the two.*

and continue pumping until only the new fluid remains in the reservoir, and new fluid can be seen emerging from the bleed screw. Tighten the screw, and top the reservoir level up to the MAX level line.

4 Work through all the remaining bleed screws in the sequence until new fluid can be seen at all of them. Be careful to keep the master cylinder reservoir topped-up to above the DANGER level at all times, or air may enter the system and increase the length of the task.

5 When the operation is complete, check that all bleed screws are securely tightened, and that their dust caps are refitted. Wash off all traces of spilt fluid, and recheck the master cylinder reservoir fluid level.

6 Check the operation of the brakes before taking the car on the road.

Every 40 000 miles or four years

16 Spark plug renewal

1 The correct functioning of the spark plugs is vital for the correct running and efficiency of the engine. It is essential that the plugs fitted are appropriate for the engine (see Specifications). If this type is used and the engine is in good condition, the spark plugs should not need attention between scheduled renewal intervals. Spark plug cleaning is rarely necessary, and should not be attempted unless specialised equipment is available, as damage can easily be caused to the firing ends.

2 To gain access to the spark plugs, remove the ignition HT coil as described in Chapter 5B.

3 Unscrew the plugs using a spark plug spanner, suitable box spanner or a deep socket and extension bar **(see illustration)**. Keep the socket aligned with the spark plug – if it is forcibly moved to one side, the ceramic insulator may be broken off. As each plug is removed, examine it as follows.

4 Examination of the spark plugs will give a good indication of the condition of the engine **(see illustration)**. If the insulator nose of the spark plug is clean and white, with no deposits, this is indicative of a weak mixture or too hot a plug (a hot plug transfers heat away from the electrode slowly, a cold plug transfers heat away quickly).

5 If the tip and insulator nose are covered with hard black-looking deposits, then this is indicative that the mixture is too rich. Should the plug be black and oily, and then it is likely that the engine is fairly worn, as well as the mixture being too rich.

6 If the insulator nose is covered with light tan to greyish-brown deposits, then the mixture is correct and it is likely that the engine is in good condition.

7 The spark plug electrode gap is of considerable importance as, if it is too large or too small, the size of the spark and its efficiency will be seriously impaired. The gap should be set to the value given in the Specifications at the beginning of this Chapter. **Note:** *The electrode gap on multi-electrode spark plugs cannot be adjusted.*

8 To set the gap on single-electrode plugs, measure the gap with a feeler blade, and then bend open, or closed, the outer plug electrode until the correct gap is achieved **(see illustration)**. The centre electrode should never be bent, as this may crack the insulator and cause plug failure, if nothing worse. If using feeler blades, the gap is correct when the appropriate-size blade is a firm sliding fit.

9 Special spark plug electrode gap adjusting tools are available from most motor accessory shops, or from spark plug manufacturers.

10 Before fitting the spark plugs, check that the threaded connector sleeves are tight, and

16.3 Unscrew the spark plugs

16.4 Examine the spark plugs to check the condition of the engine – see text

16.8 Measure the spark plug electrode gap with a feeler gauge

HAYNES
HiNT

It is very often difficult to insert spark plugs into their holes without cross-threading them. To avoid this possibility, fit a short length of 8 mm internal diameter rubber hose over the end of the spark plug. The flexible hose acts as a universal joint to help align the plug with the plug hole. Should the plug begin to cross-thread, the hose will slip on the spark plug, preventing thread damage to the cylinder head.

that the plug exterior and threads are clean **(see Haynes Hint)**.

11 Remove the rubber hose (if used), and tighten the plug to the specified torque using the spark plug socket and a torque wrench. Refit the remaining spark plugs in the same manner.

12 Refit the ignition HT coil as described in Chapter 5B.

17 Fuel filter renewal

Warning: Before carrying out the following operation, refer to the precautions given in 'Safety first!' at the beginning of this manual, and follow them implicitly. Petrol is a highly dangerous and volatile liquid, and the precautions necessary when handling it cannot be overstressed.

Note: *On some models the fuel filter is part of the fuel pump/sender unit in the fuel tank (see Chapter 4A). The fuel filter renewal procedure*

17.3 Depress the retaining clips and detach the fuel pipes from the fuel filter

in this Chapter is for models with a separate fuel filter situated at the side of the fuel tank.

1 The fuel filter is situated underneath the rear of the vehicle, on the right-hand side of the front of the fuel tank. To improve access to the filter, chock the front wheels, and then jack up the rear of the vehicle and support it on axle stands (see *Jacking and vehicle support*).

2 Place a container beneath the fuel filter to catch all spilt fuel.

3 Position a large rag around the fuel pipe union, to catch any fuel spray, which may be expelled as the fuel pressure is released, then depress the retaining clips and slowly disconnect the fuel pipe. Disconnect the other pipe from the opposite end of the filter and allow the filter contents to drain into the container **(see illustration)**.

4 Release the retaining clips and slide the fuel filter out of its holder, noting which way around it is fitted **(see illustrations)**. Dispose safely of the old filter; it will be highly inflammable, and may explode if thrown on a fire.

5 Slide the new filter into position, ensuring it is fitted the correct way around; the filter will either have an arrow on its body (indicating the correct direction of fuel flow) or be stamped OUT on one end (indicating the fuel outlet end of the filter) **(see illustration)**.

6 Ensure the filter is clipped securely in its holder then reconnect both fuel pipes. Ensure the pipes 'click' into position on the filter and are securely retained by their quick-release fittings.

7 Start the engine and check the fuel filter for signs leaks.

17.4a Release the retaining clips (arrowed) . . .

17.4b . . . then slide the filter out from its holder

18 Air cleaner filter element renewal

All models except 1.4 DOHC

1 Undo the retaining screws securing the lid to the air cleaner housing **(see illustration)**.

2 Lift the lid and remove the air filter element from the housing, noting which way up it is fitted **(see illustration)**. If necessary, slacken the retaining clip securing the intake duct to the air cleaner housing lid then remove the lid to improve access.

3 Wipe clean the inside of the housing then fit the new element, ensuring it is correctly located.

4 Locate the lid correctly on the housing and securely tighten the retaining screws. Where

17.5 Ensure the new filter is installed with its arrow (shown) or OUT marking facing the right direction

18.1 Undo the air cleaner housing lid screws (arrowed) . . .

18.2 . . . then lift the lid and remove the filter element from the housing

18.5 Unclip the engine upper style cover

18.6 Release the locking clip and remove the air intake pipe

18.7a Release the locking clip . . .

necessary, reconnect the intake duct and securely tighten the retaining clip.

1.4 DOHC models

5 Remove the oil filler cap and unclip the engine upper plastic cover (see illustration).
6 Release the locking clip and disconnect the air intake hose from the front of the air filter housing (see illustration).
7 Release the locking clip and withdraw the air intake resonator housing from the engine bay (see illustrations).
8 Remove the bolt securing the front of the air filter housing (see illustration).
9 Slacken the air intake hose securing clip on the throttle housing (see illustration).
10 Press the locking clips and disconnect the breather pipe from the top of the air filter housing (see illustration).
11 Withdraw the air filter housing from the

18.7b . . . and withdraw the air intake resonator housing

engine bay, unclipping it from its lower locating clip (see illustrations).
12 Undo the retaining screws securing the lid to the air cleaner housing (see illustration).

18.8 Undo the retaining bolt . . .

13 Lift the lid and remove the air filter element from the housing, noting which way up it is fitted (see illustration).
14 Refitting is a reversal of removal.

18.9 . . . slacken the securing clip . . .

18.10 . . . disconnect the breather pipe . . .

18.11a . . . and withdraw the air intake housing . . .

18.11b . . . releasing it from its locating clip – arrowed

18.12 Undo the four retaining screws (arrowed) . . .

18.13 . . . and remove the air filter from the housing

19.2 Push in the centre pin, then lever out the complete plastic rivet

19.3a Oil level/filler plug (MA5 transmission)

19.3b Oil level/filler plug (BE4 transmission)

19 Manual transmission oil level check

Note 1: *A suitable square-section wrench may be required to undo the transmission filler/ level plug on some models. These wrenches can be obtained from most motor factors or your Peugeot dealer.*

Note 2: *On later models, there is no facility for checking the transmission level. If there are signs of oil leaking from the transmission, the oil will need to be drained and the correct amount of oil put back in after the oil leak has been rectified.*

1 Park the car on a level surface. The oil level must be checked before the car is driven, or at least 5 minutes after the engine has been switched off. If the oil is checked immediately after driving the car, some of the oil will remain distributed around the transmission, resulting in an inaccurate level reading.

2 Push in the centre pins a little, then prise out the complete expanding plastic rivets, and remove the left-hand wheel arch liner **(see illustration)**. **Note:** *On some models, the wheel arch liners may be held in place with different types of fasteners.*

3 Wipe clean the area around the filler/level plug, which is on the left-hand end of the transmission. Unscrew the plug and clean it; discard the sealing washer **(see illustrations)**.

4 The oil level should reach the lower edge of the filler/level hole. A certain amount of oil will have gathered behind the filler/level plug, and will trickle out when it is removed; this does **not** necessarily indicate that the level is correct. To ensure that a true level is established, wait until the initial trickle has stopped, then add oil as necessary until a trickle of new oil can be seen emerging. The level will be correct when the flow ceases; use only good-quality oil of the specified type (see *Lubricants and fluids*).

5 Filling the transmission with oil is an extremely awkward operation; above all, allow plenty of time for the oil level to settle properly before checking it. If a large amount is added to the transmission, and a large amount flows out on checking the level, refit the filler/level plug and take the vehicle on a short journey so that the new oil is distributed fully around the transmission components, then recheck the level when it has settled again.

6 If the transmission has been overfilled so that oil flows out as soon as the filler/level plug is removed, check that the car is completely level (front-to-rear and side-to-side), and allow the surplus to drain off into a container.

7 When the level is correct, fit a new sealing washer to the filler/level plug. Refit the plug, tightening it to the specified torque setting. Wash off any spilt oil then refit the wheel arch liner, securing it in position with the screws and fasteners.

20 Automatic transmission fluid level check

Note: *The transmission unit is equipped with a fluid wear sensor to inform the driver when the fluid needs renewing (the ECU flashes the Sport and Snow mode indicator lights when fluid renewal is necessary). Every time the transmission unit is topped-up, this sensor should be adjusted to compensate for the new fluid being added, however this can only be done using the Peugeot diagnostic test box. Adding fluid without adjusting the sensor will not cause any problems but will mean the sensor is giving an inaccurate reading, resulting in fluid renewal being recommended earlier than is actually necessary.*

1 Take the vehicle on a short journey, to warm the transmission up to normal operating temperature, and then park the vehicle on level ground. Firmly apply the handbrake and place the selector lever in the P position.

2 Wipe clean the area around the filler plug, which is situated on the top of the transmission, directly beneath the battery. Remove the battery and battery tray/box as described in Chapter 5A, then unscrew the filler plug from the transmission and recover the sealing washer **(see illustration)**.

3 Carefully add 0.5 litre of the specified type of fluid to the transmission via the filler plug aperture. Fit a new sealing washer to the filler plug then refit the plug, tightening it to the specified torque.

4 Undo the screws and remove the engine undershield – where fitted.

5 Position a suitable container under the drain/filler plug arrangement, situated on the base of the transmission. The level plug is the smaller plug fitted to the centre of the larger drain plug **(see illustration)**.

Caution: Do not remove the drain plug by mistake.

6 Start the engine and allow it to idle. With the engine running, retain the drain plug then slacken and remove the level plug and sealing washer.

⚠️ **Warning: The fluid will be hot, take precautions against scalding.**

7 If there is sufficient fluid in the transmission unit, fluid should trickle out the centre of the drain plug before slowing to a drip. **Note:** *If no fluid trickles out, or just a few drips appear when the plug is removed, the fluid level is*

20.2 Automatic transmission filler plug (1). DO NOT remove the selector shaft bolt (2)

20.5 Unscrew the automatic transmission level plug (1) from the centre of the larger drain plug (2)

22.4a Squeeze together the tabs to release the hose clamp . . .

22.4b . . . or loosen the drain plug (1) and drain the coolant via the outlet tube (2)

too low. Refit the level plug then switch off the engine. Add a further 0.5 litre of fluid to the transmission then refit the filler plug and repeat the check (see paragraphs 3 to 5).

8 Once the flow of fluid stops, the level is correct. Fit a new sealing washer to the level plug then refit the plug and tighten it to the specified torque. Switch off the engine.

21 Emissions control systems check

1 This check specified by Peugeot involves checking the engine management system by plugging an electronic tester into the system diagnostic socket to check the electronic control unit (ECU) memory for faults (see Chapter 4A).

2 In reality, if the vehicle is running correctly and the engine management warning light on the instrument panel is functioning normally, then this check need not be carried out.

22 Coolant renewal

⚠️ *Warning: Wait until the engine is cold before starting this procedure. Do not allow antifreeze to come in contact with your skin, or with the painted surfaces of the vehicle. Rinse off spills immediately with plenty of water. Never leave antifreeze lying around in an open container, or in a puddle in the driveway or on the garage floor. Children and pets are attracted by its sweet smell, but antifreeze can be fatal if ingested.*

Cooling system draining

1 With the engine completely cold, unscrew the expansion tank filler cap.

2 Remove the engine undershield (where

fitted). **Note:** *The undershield may be secured by several screw type fasteners.*

3 Position a suitable container beneath the coolant drain outlet or the lower radiator hose at the left-hand side of the radiator.

4 Release the securing clip and disconnect the lower hose from the radiator, or loosen the drain plug (there is no need to remove it completely), and then allow the coolant to drain into the container **(see illustrations)**.

5 To assist draining, remove the cooling system bleed cap/screw (as applicable) from the heater matrix outlet hose union on the engine compartment bulkhead and, on some models, the bleed screw and sealing washer from the coolant housing on the left-hand end of the cylinder head **(see illustrations)**.

6 If the coolant has been drained for a reason other than renewal, then provided it is clean and less than four years old, it can be re-used, though this is not recommended.

7 Refit the radiator hose and secure it with the hose clip.

Cooling system flushing

8 If coolant renewal has been neglected, or if the antifreeze mixture has become diluted, then in time, the cooling system may gradually lose efficiency, as the coolant passages

become restricted due to rust, scale deposits, and other sediment. The cooling system efficiency can be restored by flushing the system clean.

9 The radiator should be flushed separately from the engine, to avoid excess contamination.

Radiator flushing

10 Disconnect the top and bottom hoses and any other relevant hoses from the radiator (see Chapter 3).

11 Insert a garden hose into the radiator top inlet. Direct a flow of clean water through the radiator, and continue flushing until clean water emerges from the radiator bottom outlet.

12 If after a reasonable period, the water still does not run clear, the radiator can be flushed with a good proprietary cleaning agent. It is important that their manufacturer's instructions are followed carefully. If the contamination is particularly bad, insert the hose in the radiator bottom outlet, and reverse-flush the radiator.

Engine flushing

13 To flush the engine, remove the thermostat (see Chapter 3).

14 With the bottom hose disconnected from the radiator, insert a garden hose into the

22.5a Undo the bleed screw from the heater outlet hose union . . .

22.5b . . . and the bleed screw from the coolant housing on the end of the cylinder head

22.19 Use a 1.0 litre plastic bottle as a header tank

coolant housing. Direct a clean flow of water through the engine, and continue flushing until clean water emerges from the radiator bottom hose.

15 When flushing is complete, refit the thermostat and reconnect the hoses (see Chapter 3).

Cooling system filling

16 Before attempting to fill the cooling system, make sure that all hoses and clips are in good condition, and that the clips are tight. Note that an antifreeze mixture must be used all year round, to prevent corrosion of the engine components (see following sub-Section).

17 Remove the expansion tank filler cap.

18 Remove the cooling system bleed screws (see paragraph 5).

19 Peugeot recommend the use of a 'header tank' when refilling the cooling system, to reduce the possibility of air being trapped in the system. Although Peugeot dealers use a special header tank which screws onto the expansion tank, the same effect can be achieved by using a suitable 1.0 litre bottle, with a seal between the bottle and the expansion tank **(see illustration)**.

20 Fit the header tank to the expansion tank and slowly fill the system whilst observing the bleed holes. Coolant will emerge from each of the bleed holes in turn, starting with the heater matrix hose. As soon as coolant free from air bubbles emerges from the heater matrix hose outlet, securely refit the cap/screw (as applicable) then watch the bleed hole on the coolant housing. Once coolant free from air bubbles emerges from the housing hole, refit the bleed screw and sealing washer and tighten securely.

21 Continue to fill the cooling system until bubbles stop appearing in the expansion tank. Help to bleed the air from the system by repeatedly squeezing the radiator bottom hose.

22 When no more bubbles appear, ensure the header tank is full (at least 1.0 litre of coolant) then start the engine. Run the engine at a fast idle speed (do not exceed 2000 rpm) until the cooling fan cuts in and out TWICE, then when the fan has stopped for the second time, switch the engine off.

Caution: The coolant will be hot. Take great care not to scald yourself.

23 Allow the engine to cool, and then remove the header tank. Wash off any spilt coolant with cold water.

24 When the engine has cooled, check the coolant level with reference to *Weekly checks*. Top-up the level if necessary, and refit the expansion tank cap.

Antifreeze mixture

25 The antifreeze should always be renewed at the specified intervals. This is necessary not only to maintain the antifreeze properties, but also to prevent corrosion, which would otherwise occur as the corrosion inhibitors become progressively less effective.

26 Always use an ethylene glycol-based antifreeze, which is suitable for use in mixed-metal cooling systems.

27 Before adding antifreeze, the cooling system should be completely drained, preferably flushed, and all hoses checked for condition and security.

28 After filling with antifreeze, a label should be attached to the expansion tank, stating the type and concentration of antifreeze used, and the date installed. Any subsequent topping-up should be made with the same type and concentration of antifreeze.

Caution: Do not use engine antifreeze in the windscreen/tailgate washer system, as it will damage the vehicle paintwork. A screen wash additive should be added to the washer system in the quantities stated on the bottle.

23 Brake shoe check

Refer to Chapter 9.

Every ten years

24 Airbags and seat belt pretensioners renewal

1 Peugeot recommends that the airbags and seat belt pretensioners be renewed regardless of their condition every ten years. Refer to Chapter 12 for airbag renewal, and Chapter 11 for seat belt pretensioner renewal.

Chapter 1 Part B:
Routine maintenance and servicing – diesel models

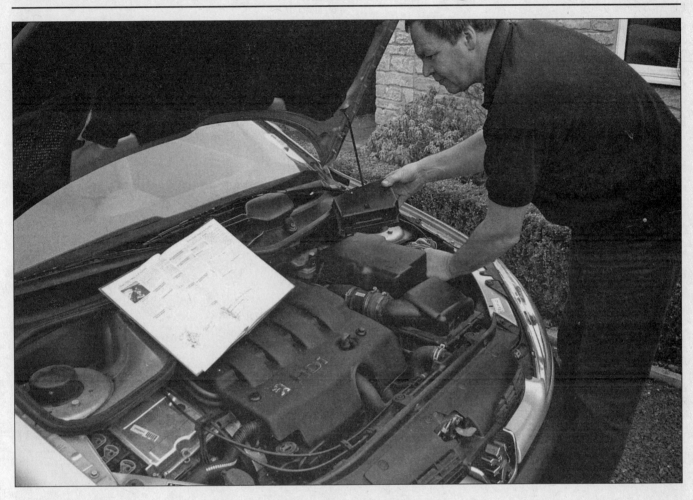

Contents

Degrees of difficulty

Easy, suitable for novice with little experience

Fairly easy, suitable for beginner with some experience

Fairly difficult, suitable for competent DIY mechanic

Difficult, suitable for experienced DIY mechanic

Very difficult, suitable for expert DIY or professional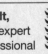

Lubricants and fluids................................ Refer to end of *Weekly checks*

Capacities

Engine oil (including oil filter)

1.4 litre engines	3.75 litres
2.0 litre engines	4.50 litres

Cooling system

1.4 litre engines (approximate)...............................	6.0 litres
2.0 litre engines (approximate)...............................	8.2 litres

Transmission

Manual:

1.4 litre	2.0 litres
2.0 litre	1.9 litres

Automatic:

Drain and refill..	4.5 litres
Total capacity (including torque converter)....................	6.0 litres

Power-assisted steering (approximate)...................... 1.0 litres

Fuel tank .... 50 litres

Cooling system

Antifreeze mixture:

50% antifreeze .... Protection down to −35°C

Note: *Refer to antifreeze manufacturer for latest recommendations.*

Brakes

Brake pad friction material minimum thickness.................... 2.0 mm

Tyre pressures .... Refer to end of *Weekly checks*

Torque wrench settings

	Nm	lbf ft
Automatic transmission:		
Filler plug	24	18
Level plug...	24	18
Engine oil filter cover (1.4 litre engine)	25	18
Engine sump drain plug	16	12
Manual transmission filler/level plug	20	15
Roadwheel bolts..	90	66

The maintenance intervals in this manual are provided with the assumption that you, not the dealer, will be carrying out the work. These are the minimum maintenance intervals recommended by us for vehicles driven daily. If you wish to keep your vehicle in peak condition at all times, you may wish to perform some of these procedures more often. We encourage frequent maintenance, because it enhances the efficiency, performance and resale value of your vehicle.

When the vehicle is new, it should be serviced by a dealer service department (or other workshop recognised by the vehicle manufacturer as providing the same standard of service) in order to preserve the warranty. The vehicle manufacturer may reject warranty claims if you are unable to prove that servicing has been carried out as and when specified, using only original equipment parts or parts certified to be of equivalent quality.

Every 250 miles or weekly

☐ Refer to *Weekly checks*

Every 6000 miles or 12 months – whichever comes sooner

☐ Renew the engine oil and filter* (Section 3)
☐ Drain any water from the fuel filter (Section 4)
☐ Check all underbonnet components and hoses for fluid leaks (Section 5)
☐ Check the steering and suspension (Section 6)
☐ Check driveshaft rubber gaiters and CV joints (Section 7)
☐ Lubricate all hinges and locks (Section 8)

* Note: *Peugeot recommend that the engine oil and filter are changed every 10 000 miles or 2 years. However, oil and filter changes are good for the engine and we recommend that the oil and filter are renewed at least once a year, especially if the vehicle is used on a lot of short journeys.*

Every 12 000 miles

☐ Reset the service interval indicator (Section 9).
☐ Check the pollen filter (Section 10)
☐ Check the condition of the brake pads, and renew if necessary (Section 11)
☐ Check the operation of the handbrake (Section 12)
☐ Carry out a road test (Section 13)
☐ Check the condition of the auxiliary drivebelt, and renew if necessary (Section 14)

Every 24 000 miles

☐ Renew the air filter (Section 15)
☐ Renew the fuel filter (Section 16)
☐ Check the manual transmission oil level, and top-up if necessary (Section 17)
☐ Check the automatic transmission fluid level, and top-up if necessary (Section 18)

Every 36 000 miles

☐ Renew the timing belt (Section 19)

Note: *It is strongly recommended that the timing belt renewal interval is reduced to 36 000 miles on vehicles which are subjected to intensive use, ie, mainly short journeys or a lot of stop-start driving. The actual belt renewal interval is therefore very much up to the individual owner, but bear in mind that severe engine damage will result if the belt breaks.*

Every 36 000 miles or 2 years, whichever comes sooner

☐ Renew the brake fluid (Section 20)*
☐ Check the brake shoes (Section 21)

* Note: *A hydraulic clutch shares its fluid reservoir with the braking system, and may also need to be bled.*

Every 72 000 miles or 5 years, whichever comes sooner

☐ Renew the coolant (Section 22)

Every 10 years

☐ Renew the airbags and seat belt pretensioners (Section 23)

Underbonnet view of a 2.0 litre diesel engine model

1 Engine oil filler cap
2 Engine oil dipstick
3 Battery (under cover)
4 Brake/clutch fluid reservoir
5 Engine compartment fuse/relay box
6 Air cleaner housing
7 Radiator
8 Power steering reservoir filler cap
9 Washer fluid reservoir
10 Electronic Control Unit (ECU)
11 Coolant expansion tank filler cap
12 Pollen filter
13 Preheating control unit
14 Cooling system bleed screws
15 ABS unit

Front underbody view

1 Engine oil drain plug
2 Air conditioning compressor
3 Driveshaft
4 Brake calipers
5 Lower suspension arm
6 Track rod
7 Anti-roll bar
8 Exhaust system
9 Power steering pipes
10 Rear engine mounting

Rear underbody view (Estate model)

1 *Fuel tank*
2 *Axle front mounting*
3 *Handbrake cables*
4 *Shock absorber*
5 *Spare wheel*
6 *Exhaust system rear silencer*
7 *Axle rear mounting*
8 *Axle tie-rods*

1 General information

This Chapter is designed to help the home mechanic maintain his/her vehicle for safety, economy, long life and peak performance.

The Chapter contains a master maintenance schedule, followed by Sections dealing specifically with each task in the schedule. Visual checks, adjustments, component renewal and other helpful items are included. Refer to the accompanying illustrations of the engine compartment and the underside of the vehicle for the locations of the various components.

Servicing your vehicle in accordance with the mileage/time maintenance schedule and the following Sections will provide a planned maintenance programme, which should result in a long and reliable service life. This is a comprehensive plan, so maintaining some items but not others at the specified service intervals, will not produce the same results.

As you service your vehicle, you will discover that many of the procedures can – and should – be grouped together, because of the particular procedure being performed, or because of the proximity of two otherwise-unrelated components to one another. For example, if the vehicle is raised for any reason, the exhaust can be inspected at the same time as the suspension and steering components.

The first step in this maintenance programme is to prepare yourself before the actual work begins. Read through all the Sections relevant to the work to be carried out, then make a list and gather all the parts and tools required. If a problem is encountered, seek advice from a parts specialist, or a dealer service department.

2 Regular maintenance

1 If, from the time the vehicle is new, the routine maintenance schedule is followed closely, and frequent checks are made of fluid levels and high-wear items, as suggested throughout this manual, the engine will be kept in relatively good running condition, and the need for additional work will be minimised.
2 It is possible that there will be times when the engine is running poorly due to the lack of regular maintenance. This is even more likely if a used vehicle, which has not received regular and frequent maintenance checks, is purchased. In such cases, additional work may need to be carried out, outside of the regular maintenance intervals.
3 If engine wear is suspected, a compression test (refer to Chapter 2D) will provide valuable information regarding the overall performance of the main internal components. Such a test can be used as a basis to decide on the extent of the work to be carried out. If, for example,

a compression test indicates serious internal engine wear, conventional maintenance as described in this Chapter will not greatly improve the performance of the engine, and may prove a waste of time and money, unless extensive overhaul work is carried out first.
4 The following series of operations are those most often required to improve the performance of a generally poor-running engine:

Primary operations

a) *Clean, inspect and test the battery (refer to 'Weekly checks').*
b) *Check all the engine-related fluids (refer to 'Weekly checks').*
c) *Check the condition and tension of the auxiliary drivebelt (Section 14).*
d) *Check the condition of the air filter, and renew if necessary (Section 15).*
e) *Check the condition of all hoses, and check for fluid leaks (Section 5).*
f) *Renew the fuel filter (Section 16).*
5 If the above operations do not prove fully effective, carry out the following secondary operations:

Secondary operations

All items listed under *Primary operations*, **plus the following:**
a) *Check the charging system (refer to Chapter 5A).*
b) *Check the preheating system (refer to Chapter 5C).*
c) *Check the fuel system (refer to Chapter 4B).*

Every 6000 miles or 12 months

3 Engine oil and filter renewal

1 Frequent oil and filter changes are the most important preventative maintenance procedures, which can be undertaken by the DIY owner. As engine oil ages, it becomes diluted and contaminated, which leads to premature engine wear.

2 Before starting this procedure, gather together all the necessary tools and materials. Also make sure that you have plenty of clean rags and newspapers handy, to mop-up any spills. Ideally, the engine oil should be warm, as it will drain better, and more built-up sludge will be removed with it. Take care, however, not to touch the exhaust or any other hot parts of the engine when working under the vehicle. To avoid any possibility of scalding, and to protect yourself from possible skin irritants and other harmful contaminants in used engine oils, it is advisable to wear gloves when carrying out this work. Access to the underside of the vehicle will be greatly improved if it can be raised on a lift, driven onto ramps, or jacked up and supported on axle stands. Whichever method is chosen, make sure that the vehicle remains level, or if it is at an angle, that the drain plug is at the lowest point. Release the screws and remove the engine undershield.

3 Slacken the drain plug about half a turn, position the draining container under the drain plug, then remove the plug completely (see illustration). If possible, try to keep the plug pressed into the sump while unscrewing it by hand the last couple of turns (see Haynes Hint). Recover the sealing ring from the drain plug.

4 Allow some time for the old oil to drain, noting that it may be necessary to reposition the container as the oil flow slows to a trickle.

5 After all the oil has drained, wipe off the drain plug with a clean rag, and fit a new sealing washer. Clean the area around the drain plug opening, and refit the plug. Tighten the plug securely.

6 If the filter is also to be renewed, move the container into position under the oil filter, which is located on the front side of the cylinder block.

1.4 litre engines

7 On these engines, the filter element is contained within a filter cover. Using a socket or spanner, slacken and remove the filter cover from above (see illustration). Be prepared for fluid spillage, and recover the O-ring seal from the cover.

8 Pull the filter element from the filter housing.

9 Use a clean rag to remove all oil, dirt and sludge from the inside and outside of the filter cover.

10 Fit the new O-ring to the filter cover, then insert the new filter element into the housing, ensuring that the element locating peg engages correctly with the corresponding hole in the housing (see illustrations).

11 Apply a little clean engine oil to the O-ring seal, then refit the filter/cover to the housing and tighten the cover to the specified torque.

2.0 litre engines

12 Using an oil filter removal tool if necessary, slacken the filter initially, then unscrew it by hand the rest of the way (see illustration). Empty the oil in the old filter into the container.

13 Use a clean rag to remove all oil, dirt and sludge from the filter sealing area on the engine. Check the old filter to make sure that the rubber sealing ring hasn't stuck to the engine. If it has, carefully remove it.

14 Apply a light coating of clean engine oil to the sealing ring on the new filter, then screw it into position on the engine. Tighten the filter firmly by hand only – **do not** use any tools. Where necessary, refit the splash guard under the engine.

All engines

15 Remove the old oil and all tools from under the car, then lower the car to the ground (if applicable).

3.3 Unscrew the sump plug

HAYNES HINT

As the drain plug releases from the threads, move it away sharply so the stream of oil issuing from the sump runs into the container, not up your sleeve.

3.7 Engine oil filter cover (arrowed)

3.10a Fit the new O-ring to the cover

3.10b Ensure the filter locating peg (arrowed) locates into the corresponding hole in the housing (arrowed)

3.12 Use a filter removal tool to slacken the oil filter

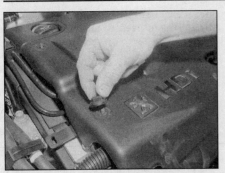

4.1a Remove the fasteners . . .

4.1b . . . then lift off the engine style cover

4.2a Fuel filter water drain plug (arrowed) – 1.4 litre engine . . .

4.2b . . . and 2.0 litre engine drain screw (arrowed)

16 Remove the dipstick, and then unscrew the oil filler cap from the top of the filler tube on the front side of the cylinder block. Fill the engine, using the correct grade and type of oil (*see Lubricants and fluids*). An oil can spout or funnel may help to reduce spillage. Pour in half the specified quantity of oil first, and then wait a few minutes for the oil to fall to the sump. Continue adding oil a small quantity at a time until the level is up to the lower mark on the dipstick. Adding approximately 1.0 litre will bring the level up to the upper mark on the dipstick. Refit the filler cap.

17 Start the engine and run it for a few minutes; check for leaks around the oil filter seal and the sump drain plug. Note that there may be a delay of a few seconds before the oil pressure warning light goes out when the engine is first started, as the oil circulates through the engine oil galleries and the new oil filter (where fitted) before the pressure builds-up.

18 Switch off the engine, and wait a few minutes for the oil to settle in the sump once more. With the new oil circulated and the filter completely full, recheck the level on the dipstick, and add more oil as necessary.

19 Dispose of the used engine oil safely, with reference to *General Repair Procedures*.

4 Fuel filter water draining

1 To gain better access on 1.4 litre models, remove the battery as described in Chapter 5A. On 2.0 litre models, unscrew the four fasteners and remove the plastic cover from the top of the engine **(see illustrations)**.

2 A water drain plug and tube are provided at the base of the fuel filter housing **(see illustrations)**.

3 Place a suitable container beneath the drain tube, and cover the surrounding area with rags.

4 Open the drain plug, and allow fuel and water to drain until fuel which is free from water emerges from the end of the tube. Close the drain plug.

5 Dispose of the drained fuel safely.

6 Start the engine. If difficulty is experienced, bleed the fuel system (Chapter 4B).

5 Hose and fluid leak check

Cooling system

⚠️ **Warning: Refer to the safety information given in 'Safety first!' and Chapter 3 before disturbing any of the cooling system components.**

1 Carefully check the radiator and heater coolant hoses along their entire length. Renew any hose which is cracked, swollen or which shows signs of deterioration. Cracks will show up better if the hose is squeezed. Pay close attention to the clips that secure the hoses to the cooling system components. Hose clips that have been overtightened can pinch and puncture hoses, resulting in cooling system leaks.

2 Inspect all the cooling system components (hoses, joint faces, etc) for leaks. Where any problems of this nature are found on system components, renew the component or gasket with reference to Chapter 3.

3 A leak from the cooling system will usually show up as white or antifreeze-coloured deposits on the area surrounding the leak (see Haynes Hint).

Fuel

⚠️ **Warning: Refer to the safety information given in 'Safety first!' and Chapter 4B before disturbing any of the fuel system components.**

4 Check all fuel lines at their connections to the injection pump, injectors and fuel filter housing.

5 Examine each fuel hose/pipe along its length for splits or cracks. Check for leakage from the union nuts and examine the unions between the metal fuel lines and the fuel filter housing. Also check the area around the fuel injectors for signs of leakage.

6 To identify fuel leaks between the fuel tank and the engine bay, the vehicle should raised and securely supported on axle stands. Inspect the fuel tank and filler neck for punctures, cracks and other damage. The connection between the filler neck and tank is especially critical. Sometimes a rubber filler

neck or connecting hose will leak due to loose retaining clamps or deteriorated rubber.

7 Carefully check all rubber hoses and metal fuel lines leading away from the fuel tank. Check for loose connections, deteriorated hoses, kinked lines, and other damage. Pay particular attention to the vent pipes and hoses, which often loop up around the filler neck and can become blocked or kinked, making tank filling difficult. Follow the fuel supply and return lines to the front of the vehicle, carefully inspecting them all the way for signs of damage or corrosion. Renew damaged sections as necessary.

Engine oil

8 Inspect the area around the oil filter, camshaft cover, cylinder head and sump

A leak in the cooling system will usually show up as white- or antifreeze-coloured deposits on the area adjoining the leak.

joint faces. Bear in mind that, over a period of time, some very slight seepage from these areas is to be expected – what you are really looking for is any indication of a serious leak caused by gasket failure. Engine oil seeping from the base of the timing belt cover or the transmission bellhousing may be an indication of crankshaft or input shaft oil seal failure. Should a leak be found, renew the failed gasket or oil seal by referring to the appropriate Chapters in this manual.

Power steering fluid

9 Examine the hose running between the fluid reservoir and the power steering pump, and the return hose running from the steering rack to the fluid reservoir. Also examine the high-pressure supply hose between the pump and the steering rack.

10 Where applicable, check the hoses leading to the PAS fluid cooler at the front of the engine bay. Look for deterioration caused by corrosion and damage from grounding, or debris thrown up from the road surface.

11 Pay particular attention to crimped unions, and the area surrounding the hoses that are secured with adjustable worm-drive clips.

Air conditioning refrigerant

 Warning: Refer to the safety information given in 'Safety first!' and Chapter 3, regarding the dangers of disturbing any of the air conditioning system components.

12 The air conditioning system is filled with a liquid refrigerant, which is retained under high pressure. If the air conditioning system is opened and depressurised without the aid of specialised equipment, the refrigerant will immediately turn into gas and escape into the atmosphere. If the liquid comes into contact with your skin, it can cause severe frostbite. In addition, the refrigerant contains substances, which are environmentally damaging; for this reason, it should not be allowed to escape into the atmosphere.

13 Any suspected air conditioning system leaks should be immediately referred to a Peugeot dealer or air conditioning specialist. Leakage will be shown up as a steady drop in the level of refrigerant in the system.

14 Note that water may drip from the condenser drain pipe, underneath the car, immediately after the air conditioning system has been in use. This is normal, and should not be cause for concern.

Brake (and clutch) fluid

Warning: Refer to the safety information given in 'Safety first!' and Chapter 9, regarding the dangers of handling brake fluid.

15 With reference to Chapter 9, examine the area surrounding the brake pipe unions at the master cylinder for signs of leakage. Check the area around the base of fluid reservoir, for signs of leakage caused by seal failure. Also examine the brake pipe unions at the ABS hydraulic unit.

16 If fluid loss is evident, but the leak cannot be pinpointed in the engine bay, the brake calipers and underbody brake lines and should be carefully checked with the vehicle raised and supported on axle stands. Leakage of fluid from the braking system is serious fault that must be rectified immediately.

17 Refer to Chapter 6 and check for leakage around the hydraulic fluid line connections to the clutch master cylinder at the bulkhead, and to the clutch slave cylinder, bolted to the side of the transmission bellhousing.

18 Brake/clutch hydraulic fluid is a toxic substance with a watery consistency. New fluid is almost colourless, but it becomes darker with age and use.

Unidentified fluid leaks

19 If there are signs that a fluid of some description is leaking from the vehicle, but you cannot identify the type of fluid or its exact origin, park the vehicle overnight and slide a large piece of card underneath it. Providing that the card is positioned in roughly in the right location, even the smallest leak will show up on the card. Not only will this help you to pinpoint the exact location of the leak, it should be easier to identify the fluid from its colour. Bear in mind, though, that the leak may only be occurring when the engine is running!

Vacuum hoses

20 Although the braking system is hydraulically operated, the brake servo unit amplifies the effort you apply at the brake pedal, by making use of the vacuum created by the pump (see Chapter 9). Vacuum is ported to the servo by means of a large-bore hose. Any leaks that develop in this hose will reduce the effectiveness of the braking system.

21 In addition, many of the underbonnet components, particularly the emission control components, are driven by vacuum supplied from the vacuum pump via narrow-bore hoses. A leak in a vacuum hose means that air is being drawn into the hose (rather than escaping from it) and this makes leakage very difficult to detect. One method is to use an old length of vacuum hose as a kind of stethoscope – hold one end close to (but not in) your ear and use the other end to probe the area around the suspected leak. When the end of the hose is directly over a vacuum leak, a hissing sound will be heard clearly through the hose. Care must be taken to avoid contacting hot or moving components, as the engine must be running, when testing in this manner. Renew any vacuum hoses that are found to be defective.

6 Steering and suspension check

Front suspension and steering

1 Raise the front of the vehicle, and securely support it on axle stands.

2 Visually inspect the balljoint dust covers and the steering rack-and-pinion gaiters for splits, chafing or deterioration (see illustration). Any wear of these components will cause loss of lubricant, together with dirt and water entry, resulting in rapid deterioration of the balljoints or steering gear.

3 Grasp the roadwheel at the 12 o'clock and 6 o'clock positions, and try to rock it (see illustration). Very slight free play may be felt, but if the movement is appreciable, further investigation is necessary to determine the source. Continue rocking the wheel while an assistant depresses the footbrake. If the movement is now eliminated or significantly reduced, it is likely that the hub bearings are at fault. If the free play is still evident with the footbrake depressed, then there is wear in the suspension joints or mountings.

4 Now grasp the wheel at the 9 o'clock and 3 o'clock positions, and try to rock it as before. Any movement felt now may again be caused by wear in the hub bearings or the steering track rod balljoints. If the inner or outer balljoint is worn, the visual movement will be obvious.

5 Using a large screwdriver or flat bar, check for wear in the suspension mounting bushes by levering between the relevant suspension component and its attachment point. Some movement is to be expected as the mountings are made of rubber, but excessive wear should be obvious. Also check the condition

6.2 Check the steering rack gaiters for damage

6.3 Check for wear in the hub bearings by grasping the wheel and trying to rock it

of any visible rubber bushes, looking for splits, cracks or contamination of the rubber.

6 With the car standing on its wheels, have an assistant turn the steering wheel back-and-forth about an eighth of a turn each way. There should be very little, if any, lost movement between the steering wheel and roadwheels. If this is not the case, closely observe the joints and mountings previously described, but in addition, check the steering column universal joints for wear, and the rack-and-pinion steering gear itself.

Suspension strut/shock absorber

7 Check for any signs of fluid leakage around the suspension strut/shock absorber body, or from the rubber gaiter around the piston rod. Should any fluid be noticed, the suspension strut/shock absorber is defective internally, and should be renewed. **Note:** *Suspension struts/shock absorbers should always be renewed in pairs on the same axle.*

8 The efficiency of the suspension strut/shock absorber may be checked by bouncing the vehicle at each corner. Generally speaking, the body will return to its normal position and stop after being depressed. If it rises and returns on a rebound, the suspension strut/shock absorber is probably suspect. Examine also the suspension strut/shock absorber upper and lower mountings for any signs of wear.

7 Driveshaft gaiter and CV joints check

1 With the vehicle raised and securely supported on axle stands, turn the steering to full left or right lock, and then slowly rotate the roadwheel. Inspect the outer constant velocity (CV) joint rubber gaiters, squeezing the gaiters to open out the folds (see illustration). Check for signs of cracking, splits or deterioration of the rubber, which may allow the grease to escape, or water and grit to enter. Also check the security and condition of the retaining clips. Repeat these checks on the inner CV joints. If any damage or deterioration is found, the gaiters should be renewed (see Chapter 8).

2 At the same time, check the general condition of the CV joints themselves by first holding the driveshaft and attempting to rotate the wheel. Repeat this check whilst holding the inner joint and attempting to rotate the driveshaft. Any appreciable movement indicates wear in the CV joints, wear in the driveshaft splines, or a loose driveshaft retaining nut.

7.1 Check the driveshaft gaiter for damage

8 Hinge and lock lubrication

1 Lubricate the hinges of the bonnet, doors and tailgate with light general-purpose oil. Similarly, lubricate all latches, locks and lock strikers – don't overdo it, or it will get on your clothes as you get in! At the same time, check the security and operation of all the locks, adjusting them if necessary (see Chapter 11).

2 Lightly lubricate the bonnet release mechanism and cable with suitable grease.

Every 12 000 miles

9 Resetting the service indicator

1 On completion of the service, reset the service interval indicator as follows.

2 With the ignition switched off, press and hold trip meter button (see illustration).

3 Still holding the button, turn the ignition switch on, and the display begins a 10 second countdown. When the countdown reaches 0, release the trip meter button, and the spanner service symbol in the display will disappear.

4 Turn off the ignition switch.

5 Turn on the ignition switch and check the correct mileage to the next service interval is displayed on the indicator.

Note: *If you need to disconnect the battery after carrying out this procedure, lock the vehicle and wait at least 5 minutes. Otherwise the display reset may not register.*

10 Pollen filter check

1 Open the bonnet.

2 Reach in behind the right-hand suspension strut upper mounting and remove the pollen filter element from the heating/ventilation housing intake, noting which way around the filter is fitted (see illustrations).

3 Check the condition of the filter, and renew it if dirty.

4 Wipe clean the inside of the housing and fit the new pollen filter element, making sure that it is correctly seated.

5 Close the bonnet.

11 Brake pad check

1 Slacken the front roadwheel bolts. Firmly apply the handbrake, and then jack up the front of the car and support it securely on axle stands (see *Jacking and vehicle support*). Remove the front roadwheels.

2 For a quick check, the pad thickness can be carried out via the inspection hole on the

9.2 Reset the service indicator as described in the text

10.2a Remove the pollen filter . . .

10.2b . . . noting its fitted position

front caliper **(see Haynes Hint)**. Using a steel rule, measure the thickness of the pad friction material. This must not be less than the minimum given in the Specifications.

3 For a comprehensive check, the brake pads should be removed and cleaned. The operation of the caliper can then be checked, and the brake disc itself can be fully examined on both sides. Refer to Chapter 9 for details.

4 If any pad's friction material is worn to the specified minimum thickness or less; all four pads must be renewed as a set. Refer to Chapter 9 for details.

5 On completion, refit the roadwheels then lower the vehicle to the ground and tighten the wheel bolts to the specified torque.

6 Slacken the rear roadwheel bolts. Jack up the rear of the car and support it securely on axle stands. Remove the rear roadwheels. Repeat the procedure described in Paragraphs 2 to 5 on the rear brake pads.

12 Handbrake check

1 The handbrake should be fully applied before 8 clicks can be heard from the lever ratchet mechanism. Check and, if necessary, adjust the handbrake as described in Chapter 9.

13 Road test

Instruments and electrical equipment

1 Check the operation of all instruments and electrical equipment.

2 Make sure that all instruments read correctly, and switch on all electrical equipment in turn, to check that it functions properly.

Steering and suspension

3 Check for any abnormalities in the steering, suspension, handling or road 'feel'.

4 Drive the vehicle, and check that there are no unusual vibrations or noises.

5 Check that the steering feels positive, with no excessive 'sloppiness', or roughness, and check for any suspension noises when cornering and driving over bumps.

Drivetrain

6 Check the performance of the engine, clutch, transmission and driveshafts.

7 Listen for any unusual noises from the engine, clutch and transmission.

8 Make sure that the engine runs smoothly when idling, and that there is no hesitation when accelerating.

9 Check that the clutch action is smooth and progressive, that the drive is taken up smoothly, and that the pedal travel is not excessive. Also listen for any noises when the clutch pedal is depressed.

10 Check that all gears can be engaged

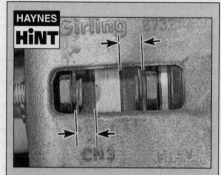

For a quick check, the thickness of the friction material remaining on each brake pad can be measured through the aperture in the caliper body.

smoothly without noise, and that the gear lever action is smooth and not abnormally vague or 'notchy'.

11 On automatic transmission models, make sure that all gearchanges occur smoothly, without snatching, and without an increase in engine speed between changes. Check that all the gear positions can be selected with the vehicle at rest. If any problems are found, they should be referred to a Peugeot dealer.

12 Listen for a metallic clicking sound from the front of the vehicle, as the vehicle is driven slowly in a circle with the steering on full lock. Carry out this check in both directions. If a clicking noise is heard, this indicates wear in a driveshaft joint; in which case, the complete driveshaft must be renewed (see Chapter 8).

Braking system

13 Make sure that the vehicle does not pull to one side when braking, and that the wheels do not lock when braking hard.

14 Check that there is no vibration through the steering when braking.

15 Check that the handbrake operates correctly without excessive movement of the lever, and that it holds the vehicle stationary on a slope.

16 Test the operation of the brake servo unit as follows. With the engine off, depress the footbrake four or five times to exhaust the vacuum. Hold the brake pedal depressed, and then start the engine. As the engine starts, there

14.7 Use an open-ended spanner to rotate the tensioner arm clockwise, then lock it in place by inserting a 4 mm drill into the hole in the tensioner body (arrowed)

J44875

14.5 When the groove (A) lines up with the mark (B) on the mounting bracket, the belt requires renewal (2.0 litre engine)

should be a noticeable 'give' in the brake pedal as vacuum builds-up. Allow the engine to run for at least two minutes, and then switch it off. If the brake pedal is depressed now, it should be possible to detect a hiss from the servo as the pedal is depressed. After about four or five applications, no further hissing should be heard, and the pedal should feel considerably harder.

14 Auxiliary drivebelt check and renewal

1 All models are equipped with a single poly-V type, multi-ribbed auxiliary drivebelt. The belt tension is adjusted automatically by means of a spring-loaded tensioner.

Checking condition

2 Slacken the right-hand front roadwheel bolts. Apply the handbrake, and then jack up the front of the car and support it securely on axle stands (see *Jacking and vehicle support*). Remove the right-hand front roadwheel.

3 Remove the fasteners and withdraw the wheel arch liner from under the right-hand front wing, for access to the crankshaft pulley bolt.

4 Using a suitable socket and bar fitted to the crankshaft pulley bolt, rotate the crankshaft so that the entire length of the drivebelt can be examined. Examine the drivebelt for cracks, splitting, fraying or damage. Check also for signs of glazing (shiny patches) and for separation of the belt plies. Renew the belt if worn or damaged.

5 On 2.0 litre models, the automatic tensioner has markings on the casing to show when the belt is need of renewal **(see illustration)**.

Removal

6 If not already done, proceed as described in paragraphs 2 and 3.

1.4 litre engines

7 Using an open-ended spanner, reach down and rotate the tensioner arm clockwise to release the belt tension. Insert a 4 mm drill bit or rod into the hole in the tensioner body, so that the tensioner arm rests against it and locks it in this position **(see illustration)**. It

14.9 Move the spanner (A) anti-clockwise to release the tension roller (B) from the drivebelt

14.10a Auxiliary drivebelt routing (1.4 litre engine without air conditioning)

A Tensioner   C Idler pulley
B Alternator   D Crankshaft

14.10b Auxiliary drivebelt routing (1.4 litre with air conditioning)

A Tensioner   C Compressor
B Alternator   D Crankshaft

is useful to have a small mirror available to enable the alignment of the locking holes to be more easily seen in the limited space available.

8 Remove the belt from the pulleys. Note that if the belt is to be re-used, mark the direction of rotation. The belt must be refitted the same way around.

2.0 litre engines

9 Using a suitable spanner engaged with the hexagonal stud in the centre of the automatic tensioner pulley, move the pulley towards the rear of the car to release the tension on the drivebelt. Note that considerable effort will be needed to move the pulley against spring tension. Insert a 4 mm drill bit or rod into lock the tensioner in this position **(see illustration)**.

Slip the belt off the pulleys. If the belt is to be re-used, mark the direction of rotation. The belt must be refitted the same way around.

Refitting and tensioning

1.4 litre engines

10 Fit the belt around the pulleys, ensuring that the ribs on the belt are correctly engaged with the grooves in the pulleys, and the drivebelt is correctly routed **(see illustrations)**. If refitting a used belt, use the mark made on removal to ensure it's fitted the correct way around.

11 Using an open-ended spanner, hold the tensioner arm so that the locking drill bit/rod can be removed, then release the pressure on the spanner so that the automatic tensioner

takes up the slack in the drivebelt.

12 Refit the wheel arch liner.

2.0 litre engines

13 Fit the belt around the pulleys, ensuring that the ribs on the belt are correctly engaged with the grooves in the pulleys, and the drivebelt is correctly routed. If refitting a used belt, use the mark made on removal to ensure it's fitted the correct way around.

14 Using a suitable spanner, hold the tensioner pulley so that the locking drill bit/rod can be removed, then release the pressure on the spanner so that the automatic tensioner takes up the slack in the drivebelt.

15 On completion, refit the wheel arch liner. Refit the roadwheel, and lower the vehicle to the ground.

Every 24 000 miles

15 Air filter element renewal

1.4 litre engines

1 Remove the plastic cover from the top of the engine. The cover is retained by rubber grommets, and pulls upwards to release.

2 Undo the three screws at the front of the filter cover, then lift the cover and withdrawn the filter element. Note which way up the element was fitted **(see illustrations)**.

3 Position the new element in the filter housing and refit the filter cover. Note the three lugs at the rear of the cover, which engage with the housing. Tighten the retaining screws securely.

4 Refit the plastic cover to the top of the engine.

2.0 litre engines

5 Undo the screws securing the top to the air filter housing body, lift the top up, disengage the lugs at the rear of the cover, and withdraw the filter element **(see illustrations)**.

6 If required, slacken the clip and disconnect the intake duct from the filter housing top to give better access to the filter housing body.

15.2a Undo the three air filter cover screws (arrowed), lift off the cover . . .

15.2b . . . and remove the filter element

15.5a Undo the air filter cover screws (arrowed), lift off the cover . . .

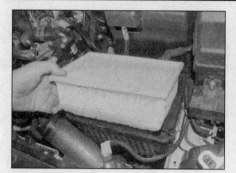

15.5b . . . and remove the filter element

16.2 Undo the vacuum pipe bracket screw (arrowed)

16.5 Depress the button (arrowed) and disconnect the fuel feed and return pipes

7 Where applicable, release any wiring or coolant hoses from their retaining clips on the air filter housing top.

8 Wipe clean the housing body and top.

9 Place the new element in position in the housing body. Refit the filter housing top, securing it in position with its retaining screws.

10 Refit any wiring or coolant hoses (where applicable) to their locating clips in the air filter housing, then reconnect the intake duct and securely tighten its retaining clip.

16 Fuel filter renewal

Note: Check with your dealer for the availability of fuel filter/housing before removal. On some

models the fuel filter/housing may come as a complete assembly.

Removal

1.4 litre engines

1 Remove the battery as described in Chapter 5A.

2 Where applicable, undo the screw, release the retaining bracket, and position the brake servo vacuum pipe to one side (**see illustration**).

3 Place a suitable container beneath the drain screw, and cover the surrounding area with rags. Take care not to allow fuel to enter the transmission bellhousing, which is just below. If available, fit a length of hose over the drain screw (**see illustration 4.2a**).

4 Open the drain plug by turning it anti-clockwise. Allow fuel and water to drain. Close the drain plug.

5 Release the retaining clips and disconnect the fuel feed and return pipes from the filter (**see illustration**). Plug the pipes to prevent dirt ingress and fuel loss.

6 Undo the single filter retaining screw, and manoeuvre the filter from the bracket. Disconnect the fuel heater and water detector wiring plugs (where fitted) as the filter is withdrawn (**see illustrations**).

7 Unscrew the fuel heater and water detector (where fitted) from the filter. Discard the O-ring seals; new ones must be fitted.

2.0 litre engines

8 Undo the four fasteners and remove the plastic cover from the top of the engine.

9 Position a suitable container under the end of the fuel filter drain hose. Open the drain screw on the base of the filter housing and allow the fuel to drain completely (**see illustration 4.2b**).

10 Where applicable, disconnect the wiring connector from the top of the fuel filter (**see illustration**).

11 Disconnect the fuel lines from the top of the fuel filter housing by releasing the quick-release fittings using a small screwdriver. Move to one side, covering the ends of the fuel lines to prevent dirt entry.

12 Unscrew the top of the fuel filter and lift the filter from the housing (**see illustrations**).

Note: Although in theory the collar on top of the filter unscrews, in practice we have found it impossible to unscrew the filter without damaging the housing, necessitating the renewal of the complete filter housing. The housing is secured to the engine by two bolts.

16.6a Undo the filter retaining screw (arrowed) . . .

16.6b . . . then disengage the filter lug from the bracket

16.10 Disconnect the filter wiring plug

16.12a Unscrew the top of the filter

16.12b Depress the clip to disconnect the fuel pipe

17.3 Manual transmission oil filler/level plug

17.4 Add oil until a trickle emerges

Refitting

1.4 litre engines

13 Renew the water detector and fuel heater O-ring seals, and refit them to the new filter, tightening them securely.

14 Manoeuvre the filter into position and secure it in place with the fixing screw.

15 Reconnect the fuel feed/return pipes and the wiring plugs.

16 Refit the retaining bracket – tighten the screw securely.

17 Close the fuel drain plug and prime the fuel system as described in Chapter 4B. The remainder of refitting is a reversal of removal.

2.0 litre engines

18 Refitting is a reversal of removal. Place the new filter in the housing, making sure that a new seal is fitted before refitting the top to the filter housing. If the complete assembly is being renewed, refit the filter to the engine and tighten the bolts securely.

19 Refit the filter housing assembly, close the fuel filter drain screw and prime the fuel system (see Chapter 4B).

17 Manual transmission oil level check

Note 1: *A new sealing washer will be required for the transmission filler/level plug, when refitting.*

Note 2: *On later models, there is no facility for checking the transmission level. If there are signs of oil leaking from the transmission, the oil will need to be drained and the correct amount of oil put back in after the oil leak has been rectified.*

1 Slacken the left-hand front roadwheels bolts. Jack up the front and rear of the car and securely support it on axle stands so that it remains level (see *Jacking and vehicle support*). If the car has been recently driven, wait at least 5 minutes after the engine has been switched off. If the oil level is checked immediately after driving the car, some of the oil will remain distributed around the transmission components, resulting in an inaccurate level reading.

2 Remove the left-hand front roadwheel then

push in the centre pins a little, prise out the complete plastic expanding rivet, and remove the wheel arch liner from under the wing for access to the filler/level plug.

3 Wipe clean the area around the filler/level plug. The filler/level plug is the largest bolt among those securing the end cover to the transmission. Unscrew the plug and clean it; discard the sealing washer **(see illustration)**.

4 The oil level should reach the lower edge of the filler/level hole. A certain amount of oil will have gathered behind the filler/level plug, and will trickle out when it is removed; this does *not* necessarily indicate that the level is correct. To ensure that a true level is established, wait until the initial trickle has stopped, then add oil as necessary until a trickle of new oil can be seen emerging **(see illustration)**. The level will be correct when the flow ceases; use only good-quality oil of the specified type.

5 Refilling the transmission is an awkward operation; above all, allow plenty of time for the oil level to settle properly before checking it. If a large amount had to be added to the transmission, or if a large amount flowed out on checking the level, refit the filler/level plug and take the vehicle on a short journey. With the new oil distributed fully around the transmission components, recheck the level after allowing time for it to settle again.

6 If the transmission has been overfilled so

that oil flows out as soon as the filler/level plug is removed, first check that the car is completely level (front-to-rear and side-to-side). Allow any surplus oil to drain off into a suitable container.

7 When the level is correct, fit a new sealing washer to the filler/level plug. Tighten the plug to the specified torque wrench setting. Wash off any spilt oil. Refit the wheel arch liner, and secure it in position with its plastic rivets. Refit the roadwheel then lower the car to the ground.

8 Frequent need for topping-up indicates a leak, which should be found and corrected before it becomes serious.

18 Automatic transmission fluid level check

Note: *The transmission unit is equipped with a fluid wear sensor to inform the driver when the fluid needs renewing (the ECU flashes the Sport and Snow mode indicator lights when fluid renewal is necessary). Every time the transmission unit is topped-up, this sensor should be adjusted to compensate for the new fluid being added, however this can only be done using the Peugeot diagnostic test box. Adding fluid without adjusting the sensor will not cause any problems but will mean the sensor is giving an inaccurate reading, resulting in fluid renewal being recommended earlier than is actually necessary.*

1 Take the vehicle on a short journey, to warm the transmission up to normal operating temperature, and then park the vehicle on level ground. Firmly apply the handbrake and place the selector lever in the P position. Undo the screws and remove the engine undershield.

2 Wipe clean the area around the filler plug, which is situated on the top of the transmission, directly beneath the battery. Unscrew the filler plug from the transmission and recover the sealing washer **(see illustration)**.

18.2 Transmission oil filler plug (1) as viewed from above

3 Carefully add 0.5 litre of the specified type of fluid to the transmission via the filler plug aperture. Fit a new sealing washer to the filler plug then refit the plug, tightening it to the specified torque.

4 Position a suitable container under the drain/filler plug arrangement, situated on the base of the transmission. The level plug is the smaller plug fitted to the centre of the larger drain plug **(see illustration)**.
Caution: Do not remove the drain plug by mistake.

5 Start the engine and allow it to idle. With the engine running, retain the drain plug then slacken and remove the level plug and sealing washer.
Warning: The fluid will be hot, take precautions against scalding.

6 If there is sufficient fluid in the transmission unit, fluid should trickle out the centre of the drain plug before slowing to a drip. **Note:** *If no fluid trickles out, or just a few drips appear when the plug is removed, the fluid level is too low. Refit the level plug then switch off the engine. Add a further 0.5 litre of fluid to the transmission then refit the filler plug and repeat the check (see paragraphs 3 to 5).*

7 Once the flow of fluid stops, the level is correct. Fit a new sealing washer to the level plug then refit the plug and tighten it to the specified torque. Switch off the engine.

18.4 Transmission oil drain plug (1) and oil level plug (2), inside the drain plug

Every 36 000 miles

19 Timing belt renewal

Refer to Chapter 2D.

Every 36 000 miles or 2 years

20 Brake fluid renewal

Warning: Brake hydraulic fluid can harm your eyes and damage painted surfaces, so use extreme caution when handling and pouring it. Do not use fluid that has been standing open for some time, as it absorbs moisture from the air. Excess moisture can cause a dangerous loss of braking effectiveness.

Note: *A hydraulic clutch shares its fluid reservoir with the braking system, and may also need to be bled (see Chapter 6).*

1 The procedure is similar to that for the bleeding of the hydraulic system as described in Chapter 9, except that the brake fluid reservoir should be emptied by syphoning, using a clean ladle or similar before starting, and allowance should be made for the old fluid to be expelled when bleeding a section of the circuit.

2 Working as described in Chapter 9, open the first bleed screw in the sequence, and pump the brake pedal gently until nearly all the old fluid has been emptied from the master cylinder reservoir.
Haynes hint: *Old hydraulic fluid is invariably much darker in colour than the new, making it easy to distinguish the two.*

3 Top-up to the MAX level with new fluid, and continue pumping until only the new fluid remains in the reservoir, and new fluid can be seen emerging from the bleed screw. Tighten the screw, and top the reservoir level up to the MAX level line.

4 Work through all the remaining bleed screws in the sequence until new fluid can be seen at all of them. Be careful to keep the master cylinder reservoir topped-up to above the DANGER level at all times, or air may enter the system and increase the length of the task.

5 When the operation is complete, check that all bleed screws are securely tightened, and that their dust caps are refitted. Wash off all traces of spilt fluid, and recheck the master cylinder reservoir fluid level.

6 Check the operation of the brakes before taking the car on the road.

21 Brake shoe check

Refer to Chapter 9.

Every 72 000 miles or 5 years

22 Coolant renewal

⚠️ **Warning: Wait until the engine is cold before starting this procedure. Do not allow antifreeze to come in contact with your skin, or with the painted surfaces of the vehicle. Rinse off spills immediately with plenty of water. Never leave antifreeze lying around in an open container, or in a puddle in the driveway or on the garage floor. Children and pets are attracted by its sweet smell, but antifreeze can be fatal if ingested.**

Cooling system draining

1 Remove the battery and battery tray/box as described in Chapter 5A.

1.4 litre engine

2 Undo the screws and remove the engine undershield.

3 Position a suitable container beneath the radiator lower hose outlet at the lower left-hand side of the radiator.

4 Release the retaining clip and disconnect the radiator lower hose **(see illustration)**. Be prepared for coolant spillage.

5 With the engine completely cold, reach under the scuttle and unscrew the bleed screw located in the heater hose at the bulkhead connection **(see illustration)**.

6 To drain the engine, pull out the clip and remove the plug located in the coolant manifold at the rear of the cylinder head **(see illustration)**. The plug must be refitted with a new clip and O-ring.

2.0 litre engines

7 With the engine completely cold, unscrew and remove the expansion tank cap.

8 Position a suitable container beneath the radiator lower hose outlet.

9 Slacken the bleed screw at the heater hose bulkhead connection, and the screw at the coolant outlet housing **(see illustration)**.

10 Release the radiator lower hose retaining clip, and pull the hose from the fitting. Be prepared for coolant spillage.

11 When the flow of coolant stops, reposition the container below the cylinder block drain plug, located at the rear of the cylinder block.

12 Remove the drain plug, and allow the coolant to drain into the container.

All engines

13 If the coolant has been drained for a reason other than renewal, then provided it is clean and less than five years old, it can be re-used, though this is not recommended.

14 Refit the cylinder block drain plug on completion of draining.

Cooling system flushing

15 If coolant renewal has been neglected, or if the antifreeze mixture has become diluted, then in time, the cooling system may gradually lose efficiency, as the coolant passages become restricted due to rust, scale deposits,

and other sediment. The cooling system efficiency can be restored by flushing the system clean.

16 The radiator should be flushed independently of the engine, to avoid unnecessary contamination.

Radiator flushing

17 To flush the radiator first tighten the radiator bleed screw, where applicable.

18 Disconnect the top hose and any other relevant hoses from the radiator, with reference to Chapter 3.

19 Insert a garden hose into the radiator top inlet. Direct a flow of clean water through the radiator, and continue flushing until clean water emerges from the radiator bottom outlet.

20 If after a reasonable period, the water still does not run clear, the radiator can be flushed with a good proprietary cleaning agent. It is important that their manufacturer's instructions are followed carefully. If the contamination is particularly bad, insert the hose in the radiator bottom outlet, and reverse-flush the radiator.

Engine flushing

21 To flush the engine, first refit the cylinder

22.4 Squeeze together the tabs to release the hose retaining clip

22.5 Undo the heater outlet hose union bleed screw cap (arrowed)

22.6 Prise out the retaining clip (arrowed) and pull out the drain plug

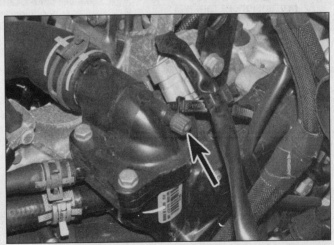

22.9 Coolant outlet housing bleed screw (arrowed)

block drain plug, and tighten the cooling system bleed screws.

22 Remove the thermostat as described in Chapter 3, then temporarily refit the thermostat cover.

23 With the top and bottom hoses disconnected from the radiator, insert a garden hose into the radiator top hose. Direct a clean flow of water through the engine, and continue flushing until clean water emerges from the radiator bottom hose.

24 On completion of flushing, refit the thermostat and reconnect the hoses with reference to Chapter 3.

Cooling system filling

25 Before attempting to fill the cooling system, make sure that all hoses and clips are in good condition, and that the clips are tight. Note that an antifreeze mixture must be used all year round, to prevent corrosion of the engine components (see following sub-Section. Also check that the radiator and cylinder block drain plugs are in place and tight.

26 Remove the expansion tank filler cap.

27 Open all the cooling system bleed screws (see paragraphs 5 and 9).

28 Some of the cooling system hoses are positioned at a higher level than the top of the radiator expansion tank. It is therefore necessary to use a 'header tank' when refilling the cooling system, to reduce the possibility of air being trapped in the system. Although Peugeot dealers use a special header tank, the same effect can be achieved by using a suitable 1.0 litre bottle with the bottom cut off, with a seal between the bottle and the expansion tank **(see illustrations)**.

29 Fit the header tank to the expansion tank

22.28a A plastic bottle and sealing ring (arrowed) can be used as a substitute header tank

22.28b Fit the header tank to the expansion tank and slowly fill the cooling system

and slowly fill the system. Coolant will emerge from the bleed screw. As soon as coolant free from air bubbles emerges from the screw, tighten the screw.

30 Ensure that the header tank is full (at least 1.0 litre of coolant). Refit the battery, start the engine, and run it at a fast idle speed (do not exceed 2000 rpm) until the cooling fan cuts in, and then cuts out. Stop the engine. **Note:** *Take great care not to scald yourself with the hot coolant during this operation.*

31 Allow the engine to cool, and then remove the header tank.

32 When the engine has cooled, check the coolant level as described in *Weekly checks*. Top-up the level if necessary, and refit the expansion tank cap.

Antifreeze mixture

33 The antifreeze should always be renewed at the specified intervals. This is necessary not only to maintain the antifreeze properties, but also to prevent corrosion, which would

otherwise occur as the corrosion inhibitors become progressively less effective.

34 Always use an ethylene glycol-based antifreeze, which is suitable for use in mixed-metal cooling systems. The quantity of antifreeze and levels of protection are indicated in the Specifications.

35 Before adding antifreeze, the cooling system should be completely drained, preferably flushed, and all hoses checked for condition and security.

36 After filling with antifreeze, a label should be attached to the expansion tank, stating the type and concentration of antifreeze used, and the date installed. Any subsequent topping-up should be made with the same type and concentration of antifreeze.

Caution: Do not use engine antifreeze in the washer system, as it will cause damage to the vehicle paintwork. A screenwash additive should be added to the washer system in the quantities stated on the bottle.

Every 10 years

23 Airbags and seat belt pretensioners renewal	

1 Peugeot recommends that the airbags and seat belt pretensioners be renewed regardless of their condition every ten years. Refer to Chapter 12 for airbag renewal, and Chapter 11 for seat belt pretensioner renewal.

Chapter 2 Part A:
SOHC petrol engine in-car repair procedures

Contents

Degrees of difficulty

Easy, suitable for novice with little experience 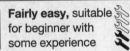	**Fairly easy,** suitable for beginner with some experience	**Fairly difficult,** suitable for competent DIY mechanic	**Difficult,** suitable for experienced DIY mechanic	**Very difficult,** suitable for expert DIY or professional

Specifications

Engine (general)

Capacity:
1.1 litre engine	1124 cc
1.4 litre engine	1360 cc
1.6 litre engine	1587 cc

Designation:
1.1 litre engine	TU1
1.4 litre engine	TU3
1.6 litre engine	TU5

Engine codes*:
1.1 litre engine	HFX, HFY and HFZ (TU1JP)
1.4 litre engine	KFV (TU3A)
1.4 litre engine	KFW and KFX (TU3JP)
1.6 litre engine	NFZ (TU5JP)

Bore:
1.1 litre engine	72.00 mm
1.4 litre engine	75.00 mm
1.6 litre engine	78.50 mm

Stroke:
1.1 litre engine	69.00 mm
1.4 litre engine	77.00 mm
1.6 litre engine	82.00 mm
Direction of crankshaft rotation	Clockwise (viewed from right-hand side of vehicle)
No 1 cylinder location.	At transmission end of engine

Compression ratio (typical):
1.1 litre engine	9.7:1
1.4 and 1.6 litre engine.	10.5:1

* The engine code is situated on front, left-hand end of the cylinder block. On cast-iron block engines, the code is stamped directly onto the cylinder block. On aluminium block engines the code can be stamped directly onto the block and/or stamped on a plate, which is riveted to the block. The code given in brackets is the factory identification number.

Camshaft

Drive	Toothed belt
Number of bearings	5

Camshaft bearing journal diameter (outside diameter):

No 1	36.950 to 36.925 mm
No 2	40.650 to 40.625 mm
No 3	41.250 to 41.225 mm
No 4	41.850 to 41.825 mm
No 5	42.450 to 42.425 mm

Cylinder head bearing journal diameter (inside diameter):

No 1	37.000 to 37.039 mm
No 2	40.700 to 47.739 mm
No 3	41.300 to 41.339 mm
No 4	41.900 to 41.939 mm
No 5	42.500 to 42.539 mm

Valve clearances (engine cold)

Inlet	0.20 mm
Exhaust	0.40 mm

Lubrication system

Oil pump type	Gear-type, chain-driven off the crankshaft
Minimum oil pressure at 80°C	4 bars at 4000 rpm
Oil pressure warning switch operating pressure	0.8 bars

Torque wrench settings

	Nm	lbf ft
Big-end bearing cap nuts	38	28
Camshaft sprocket retaining bolt		
M11	80	59
M10	45	33
Camshaft thrust fork retaining bolt	16	12
Crankshaft oil seal housing bolts – cast-iron block engine	8	6
Crankshaft pulley retaining bolts	25	18
Crankshaft sprocket retaining bolt	100	74
Cylinder head bolts (aluminium block engine):		
Stage 1	20	15
Stage 2	Angle-tighten a further 240°	
Cylinder head bolts (cast-iron block engine):		
Stage 1	20	15
Stage 2	Angle-tighten a further 120°	
Stage 3	Angle-tighten a further 120°	
Cylinder head cover nuts:		
M8 nuts	16	12
M6 nuts	7	5
Driveplate bolts	67	49
Engine-to-transmission bolts:		
Manual transmission models	40	30
Automatic transmission models	35	26
Engine/transmission left-hand mounting:		
Mounting centre nut	65	48
Mounting-to-bracket bolts	30	22
Mounting bracket-to-body bolts	19	14
Mounting bracket-to-manual transmission nuts	25	18
Mounting bracket-to-automatic transmission bolts	45	33
Mounting stud (automatic transmission)	50	37
Engine/transmission rear mounting:		
Mounting-to-cylinder block bolts	40	30
Mounting link-to-mounting bolt	50	37
Mounting link-to-subframe bolt	39	29
Vibration damper-to-mounting bolt	32	24
Engine/transmission right-hand mounting:		
Mounting bracket nuts	45	33
Support bracket:		
Bracket to mounting bracket	45	33
Bracket to engine	26	19
Mounting to body	40	30
Mounting vibration damper	32	24

Torque wrench settings (continued)

	Nm	lbf ft
Flywheel bolts	67	49
Main bearing cap bolts (cast-iron block engine):		
Stage 1	20	15
Stage 2	Angle-tighten a further 49°	
Main bearing ladder casting (aluminium block engine):		
M11 bolts:		
Stage 1	20	15
Stage 2	Angle-tighten a further 44°	
M6 bolts	8	6
Oil pump retaining bolts	9	7
Piston oil jet spray tube bolts (cast-iron block engine)	10	7
Roadwheel bolts	90	66
Sump drain plug	30	22
Sump retaining nuts and bolts	8	6
Timing belt cover bolts	8	6
Timing belt tensioner pulley nut	22	16

1 General information

How to use this Chapter

1 This Part of Chapter 2 describes those repair procedures that can reasonably be carried out on the petrol engine while it remains in the car. If the engine has been removed from the car and is being dismantled, as described in Part E, any preliminary dismantling procedures can be ignored.

2 Note that, while it may be possible physically to overhaul items such as the piston/connecting rod assemblies while the engine is in the car, such tasks are not normally carried out as separate operations. Usually, several additional procedures (not to mention the cleaning of components and of oilways) have to be carried out. For this reason, all such tasks are classed as major overhaul procedures, and are described in Part E of this Chapter.

3 Part E describes the removal of the engine/transmission from the vehicle, and the full overhaul procedures that can then be carried out.

TU series engine

4 All petrol engines in this Chapter are from the TU series of engines and are well-proven engines, which has been fitted to many previous Peugeot and Citroën vehicles. The engine is of the in-line four-cylinder, single overhead camshaft (SOHC) type, mounted transversely at the front of the car with the transmission attached to its left-hand end. The 206 range was offered with a choice of 1.1 litre (1124 cc), 1.4 litre (1360 cc) and 1.6 litre (1587 cc) engines.

5 The crankshaft runs in five main bearings. Thrustwashers are fitted to No 2 main bearing (upper half) to control crankshaft endfloat.

6 The connecting rods rotate on horizontally split bearing shells at their big-ends. The pistons are attached to the connecting rods by gudgeon pins, which are an interference fit in the connecting rod small-end eyes. The aluminium alloy pistons are fitted with three piston rings – two compression rings and an oil control ring.

7 On 1.1 and 1.4 litre engines, the cylinder block is made of aluminium, and renewable wet liners are fitted to the cylinder bores. Sealing O-rings are fitted at the base of each liner, to prevent the escape of coolant into the sump.

8 On 1.6 litre engines, the cylinder block is made from cast-iron, and the cylinder bores are an integral part of the cylinder block. On this type of engine, the cylinder bores are sometimes referred to as having dry liners.

9 The inlet and exhaust valves are each closed by coil springs, and operate in guides pressed into the cylinder head; the valve seat inserts are also pressed into the cylinder head, and can be renewed separately if worn.

10 The camshaft is driven by a toothed timing belt, and operates the eight valves via rocker arms. Valve clearances are adjusted by a screw-and-locknut arrangement. The camshaft rotates directly in the cylinder head. The timing belt also drives the coolant pump.

11 Lubrication is by means of an oil pump, which is driven (via a chain and sprocket) off the right-hand end of the crankshaft. It draws oil through a strainer located in the sump, and then forces it through an externally mounted filter into galleries in the cylinder block/crankcase. From there, the oil is distributed to the crankshaft (main bearings) and camshaft. The big-end bearings are supplied with oil via internal drillings in the crankshaft, while the camshaft bearings also receive a pressurised supply. The camshaft lobes and valves are lubricated by splash, as are all other engine components.

Operations with engine in car

12 The following work can be carried out with the engine in the car:

a) Compression pressure – testing.
b) Cylinder head cover – removal and refitting.
c) Timing belt covers – removal and refitting.
d) Timing belt – removal, refitting and adjustment.
e) Timing belt tensioner and sprockets – removal and refitting.
f) Camshaft oil seal – renewal.
g) Camshaft and rocker arms – removal, inspection and refitting*.
h) Cylinder head – removal and refitting.
i) Cylinder head and pistons – decarbonising.
j) Sump – removal and refitting.
k) Oil pump – removal, overhaul and refitting.
l) Crankshaft oil seals – renewal.
m) Engine/transmission mountings – inspection and renewal.
n) Flywheel/driveplate – removal, inspection and refitting.

* The cylinder head must be removed for the successful completion of this work. Refer to Section 10 for details.

2 Compression test – description and interpretation

1 When engine performance is down, or if misfiring occurs which cannot be attributed to the ignition or fuel systems, a compression test can provide diagnostic clues as to the engine's condition. If the test is performed regularly, it can give warning of trouble before any other symptoms become apparent.

2 The engine must be fully warmed-up to normal operating temperature, the battery must be fully-charged. The aid of an assistant will also be required.

3 Remove the ignition HT coil assembly (see Chapter 5B) then remove the spark plugs (see Chapter 1A).

4 Fit a compression tester to the No 1 cylinder spark plug hole – the type of tester which screws into the plug thread is to be preferred.

5 Have the assistant hold the throttle wide open, and crank the engine on the starter motor; after one or two revolutions, the compression pressure should build-up to a maximum figure, and then stabilise. Record the highest reading obtained.

6 Repeat the test on the remaining cylinders, recording the pressure in each.

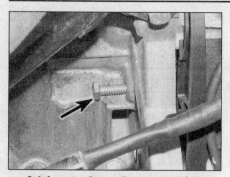

3.4 Insert a 6 mm diameter bolt/pin (arrowed) into the hole in the cylinder block flange and locate it in the flywheel/driveplate hole

3.5 Lock the camshaft sprocket in position with a 10 mm diameter bolt/pin (arrowed)

7 All cylinders should produce very similar pressures; a difference of more than 2 bars between any two cylinders indicates a fault. Note that the compression should build-up quickly in a healthy engine; low compression on the first stroke, followed by gradually increasing pressure on successive strokes, indicates worn piston rings. A low compression reading on the first stroke, which does not build-up during successive strokes, indicates leaking valves or a blown head gasket (a cracked head could also be the cause). Deposits on the undersides of the valve heads can also cause low compression.

8 Although Peugeot do not specify exact compression pressures, as a guide, any cylinder pressure of below 10 bars can be considered as less than healthy. Refer to a Peugeot dealer or other specialist if in doubt as to whether a particular pressure reading is acceptable.

9 If the pressure in any cylinder is low, carry out the following test to isolate the cause. Introduce a teaspoonful of clean oil into that cylinder through its spark plug hole, and repeat the test.

10 If the addition of oil temporarily improves the compression pressure, this indicates that bore or piston wear is responsible for the pressure loss. No improvement suggests that leaking or burnt valves, or a blown head gasket, may be to blame.

11 A low reading from two adjacent cylinders is almost certainly due to the head gasket having blown between them; the presence of coolant in the engine oil will confirm this.

12 If one cylinder is about 20 percent lower than the others and the engine has a slightly rough idle; a worn camshaft lobe could be the cause.

13 If the compression reading is unusually high, the combustion chambers are probably coated with carbon deposits. If this is the case, the cylinder head should be removed and decarbonised.

14 On completion of the test, refit the spark plugs and ignition HT coil (see Chapters 1A and 5B).

3 Engine assembly/valve timing holes – general information and usage

Note: *Do not attempt to rotate the engine whilst the crankshaft/camshaft are locked in position. If the engine is to be left in this state for a long period of time, it is a good idea to place warning notices inside the vehicle, and in the engine compartment. This will reduce the possibility of the engine being accidentally cranked on the starter motor, which is likely to cause damage with the locking pins in place.*

1 On all models, timing holes are drilled in the camshaft sprocket and in the rear of the flywheel/driveplate. The holes are used to ensure that the crankshaft and camshaft are correctly positioned when assembling the engine (to prevent the possibility of the valves contacting the pistons when refitting the cylinder head), or refitting the timing belt.

When the timing holes are aligned with access holes in the cylinder head and the front of the cylinder block, suitable diameter bolts/pins can be inserted to lock both the camshaft and crankshaft in position, preventing them from rotating. Proceed as follows.

2 Remove the timing belt upper cover as described in Section 5.

3 The crankshaft must now be turned until the timing hole in the camshaft sprocket is aligned with the corresponding hole in the cylinder head. The holes are aligned when the camshaft sprocket hole is in the 2 o'clock position, when viewed from the right-hand end of the engine. The crankshaft can be turned by using a spanner on the crankshaft sprocket bolt, noting that it should always be rotated in a clockwise direction (viewed from the right-hand end of the engine).

4 With the camshaft sprocket hole correctly positioned, insert a 6 mm diameter bolt or pin through the hole in the front, left-hand flange of the cylinder block, and locate it in the timing hole in the rear of the flywheel/driveplate **(see illustration)**. Note that it may be necessary to rotate the crankshaft slightly to get the holes to align.

5 With the flywheel correctly positioned, insert a 10 mm diameter bolt or a pin through the timing hole in the camshaft sprocket, and locate it in the hole in the cylinder head **(see illustration)**.

6 The crankshaft and camshaft are now locked in position, preventing unnecessary rotation.

4 Cylinder head cover – removal and refitting

Removal

1 Disconnect the battery negative lead.

2 Release the retaining clip and disconnect the breather hose from the cylinder head cover **(see illustration)**.

3 Remove the ignition HT coil as described in Chapter 5B.

4 Undo the two retaining nuts and sealing washers (where fitted) then lift off the cylinder head cover, complete with its rubber seal **(see illustrations)**. Examine the seal for signs of

4.2 Disconnect the breather hose from the cylinder head cover

4.4a Unscrew the retaining nuts (arrowed) . . .

4.4b . . . then lift off the cylinder cover

4.5a Remove the spacers (arrowed) from the studs . . .

4.5b . . . then lift off the baffle plate

4.7 Ensure the rubber seal is correctly located on the cylinder head cover

damage and deterioration, and if necessary, renew it.

5 Remove the spacer from each cover stud then lift off the oil baffle plate **(see illustrations)**.

Refitting

6 Carefully clean the cylinder head and cover mating surfaces, and remove all traces of oil.

7 Fit the rubber seal over the edge of the cylinder head cover, ensuring that it is correctly located along its entire length **(see illustration)**.

8 Refit the oil baffle plate then fit the spacers to the cover studs.

9 Carefully refit the cylinder head cover to the engine, taking great care not to displace the rubber seal.

10 Fit the sealing washers (where fitted) and cover retaining nuts, tightening them to the specified torque. **Note:** *There are two possible sizes of cylinder head cover nut; some early engines have M8 cap nuts which are fitted with sealing washers whereas later engines have M6 cap nuts which are fitted without sealing washers. The torque wrench settings are different for each type of nut; ensure they are tightened to the correct torque (see Specifications).*

11 Refit the ignition HT coil (see Chapter 5B) then reconnect the breather hose securely to the cylinder head cover. On completion reconnect the battery negative lead.

5 Timing belt covers – removal and refitting

Note: *On some early engines, a three-piece timing belt cover assembly is fitted (consisting of upper, centre and lower covers), on all later engines a two-piece cover is used (the centre and lower covers are integrated into one large lower cover).*

Removal

Upper cover

1 Slacken and remove the two retaining bolts (one at the front and one at the rear),

and remove the upper timing cover from the cylinder head **(see illustrations)**.

Centre cover (of three-piece assembly)

2 Remove the upper cover as described in paragraph 1.

3 Firmly apply the handbrake then jack up the front of the vehicle and support it securely on axle stands (see *Jacking and vehicle support*). Remove the right-hand front roadwheel.

4 Undo the screws securing the front section of the right-hand wheel arch liner to the base of the bumper. Remove the fasteners (pull out the centre pin then remove the complete fastener) securing the liner section to the body then manoeuvre the

5.1a Unscrew the retaining bolts (arrowed) . . .

5.8a Unscrew the retaining bolts (arrowed) . . .

front section of the liner out from underneath the wing.

5 Slacken and remove the retaining bolts and manoeuvre the centre cover out of position.

Lower cover

6 Remove the upper cover as described in paragraph 1.

7 Remove the auxiliary drivebelt as described in Chapter 1A.

8 Undo the three crankshaft pulley retaining bolts and remove the pulley, noting which way round it is fitted **(see illustrations)**.

9 On models with a three-piece timing cover assembly, remove the centre cover as described above.

10 On all models, slacken and remove the

5.1b . . . and remove the timing belt upper cover

5.8b . . . then remove the crankshaft pulley

5.10a Unscrew the bolts (arrowed) . . .

5.10b . . . and remove the timing belt lower cover from the engine

6.6a Unscrew the nut and lift off the bracket . . .

retaining bolts then remove the lower cover from the engine (see illustrations).

Refitting

Upper cover

11 Refitting is the reverse of removal.

Centre cover (of three-piece assembly)

12 Refitting is the reverse of removal, tightening the wheel bolts to the specified torque.

Lower cover

13 Locate the lower cover over the timing belt sprocket, and tighten its retaining bolts.

14 Fit the pulley to the end of the crankshaft, ensuring it is fitted the correct way round, and tighten its bolts to the specified torque.

15 Refit the centre (where fitted) and upper covers as described above.

16 Refit and tension the auxiliary drivebelt as described in Chapter 1A.

6 Timing belt – general information, removal and refitting

Note: *Peugeot specify the use of a special electronic tool (SEEM C.TRONIC type 105.5 belt tensioning measuring tool) and the rocker arm contact plate (0132-AE) to correctly set the timing belt tension. If access to this equipment cannot be obtained, an approximate setting can be achieved using the method described below.*

6.6b . . . then free the ECU mounting plate from the body and position it clear of the engine

If this method is used, the tension must be checked using the special electronic tool at the earliest possible opportunity. Do not drive the vehicle over large distances, or use high engine speeds, until the belt tension is known to be correct. Refer to a Peugeot dealer for advice.

General information

1 The timing belt drives the camshaft and coolant pump from a toothed sprocket on the end of the crankshaft. If the belt breaks or slips in service, the pistons are likely to hit the valve heads, resulting in extensive (and expensive) damage.

2 The timing belt should be renewed at the specified intervals (see Chapter 1A), or earlier if it is contaminated with oil or if it is at all noisy in operation (a 'scraping' noise due to uneven wear).

3 If the timing belt is being removed, it is a wise precaution to check the condition of the coolant pump at the same time (check for signs of coolant leakage). This may avoid the need to remove the timing belt again at a later stage, should the coolant pump fail.

Removal

4 Disconnect the battery negative terminal.

5 Align the engine assembly/valve timing holes as described in Section 3, and lock both the camshaft sprocket and the flywheel/driveplate in position.

Caution: Do not attempt to rotate the engine whilst the locking tools are in position.

6 Unclip the wiring harness from the front of

6.8 Slacken the nut then pivot the tensioner pulley clockwise to relieve the timing belt tension

the engine management ECU to gain access to the mounting plate nut. Slacken and remove the nut using a pair of grips (the plate is secured in position with an anti-tamper nut) then remove the bracket. Free the ECU mounting plate from the body and position it clear of the engine (see illustrations).

7 Remove the timing belt lower cover as described in Section 5.

8 Loosen the timing belt tensioner pulley retaining nut (see illustration). Pivot the pulley in a clockwise direction, using a square-section key (on early models), or a hexagonal key (on later models), fitted to the hole in the pulley hub, then retighten the retaining nut (see Tool Tip).

9 If the timing belt is to be re-used, use white paint or similar to mark the direction of rotation on the belt (if markings do not already exist). Slip the belt off the sprockets.

10 Check the timing belt carefully for any signs of uneven wear, splitting, or oil contamination. Pay particular attention to the roots of the teeth. Renew the belt if there is the slightest doubt about its condition. If the engine is undergoing an overhaul, and has covered more than 40 000 miles with the existing belt fitted, renew the belt as a matter of course, regardless of its apparent condition. The cost of a new belt is nothing when compared to the cost of repairs should the belt break in service.

If you're having difficulty finding a square-section tool that will fit the tensioner pulley, obtain a length of standard 8 mm door handle rod from a DIY shop and cut it to length (A). Insert the rod into the pulley hub and rotate the pulley with an 8 mm spanner (B).

6.14 Pivot the tensioner pulley anti-clockwise to remove all free play from the timing belt then tighten the pulley nut

If signs of oil contamination are found, trace the source of the oil leak, and rectify it. Wash down the engine timing belt area and all related components, to remove all traces of oil.

Refitting

11 Prior to refitting, thoroughly clean the timing belt sprockets. Check that the tensioner pulley rotates freely, without any sign of roughness. If necessary, renew the tensioner pulley as described in Section 7. Make sure that the locking tools are still in place, as described in Section 3.

Early engines up to engine no. 3666765

12 Manoeuvre the timing belt into position, ensuring that the arrows on the belt are pointing in the direction of rotation (clockwise, when viewed from the right-hand end of the engine).
13 Do not twist the timing belt sharply while refitting it. Fit the belt over the crankshaft and camshaft sprockets. Make sure that the 'front run' of the belt is taut – ie, ensure that any slack is on the tensioner pulley side of the belt. Fit the belt over the coolant pump sprocket and tensioner pulley. Ensure that the belt teeth are seated centrally in the sprockets.
14 Loosen the tensioner pulley retaining nut. Pivot the pulley anti-clockwise to remove all free play from the timing belt, and then retighten the nut **(see illustration)**. Tension the timing belt as described under the relevant sub-heading.

Tensioning without the special tool

Note: If this method is used, ensure that the belt tension is checked by a Peugeot dealer at the earliest possible opportunity.
15 If the special tool is not available, an approximate setting may be achieved by pivoting the tensioner pulley anti-clockwise until it is just possible to twist the timing belt through 90° by finger and thumb, midway between the crankshaft and camshaft sprockets. The deflection of the belt at the mid-point between the sprockets should be approximately 6.0 mm.
16 Remove the locking tools from the camshaft sprocket and flywheel/driveplate.
17 Using a suitable socket and extension bar on the crankshaft sprocket bolt, rotate the crankshaft through four complete rotations in

6.26 Fit the rocker arm plate (1) to the cylinder head and use the contact bolts (2) to lift the rocker arms clear of the camshaft (see text). Note the correct location for the measuring tool (3)

a clockwise direction (viewed from the right-hand end of the engine). Refit the flywheel/driveplate locking tool and check that the camshaft timing hole is correctly aligned with the cylinder head hole.
Caution: Do not at any time rotate the crankshaft anti-clockwise.
18 Slacken the tensioner pulley nut, retension the belt as described in paragraph 15, then tighten the tensioner pulley nut to the specified torque.
19 Remove the flywheel/driveplate locking tool then rotate the crankshaft through a further two turns clockwise. Check that both the camshaft sprocket and flywheel timing holes are still correctly aligned.
20 If all is well, refit the timing belt covers as described in Section 5.
21 Locate the engine management ECU bracket assembly on its mounting, refit the bracket and secure it in position with a new anti-tamper nut or standard nut.
22 Clip the wiring harness back into position then reconnect the battery negative terminal.

Tensioning using the special tool

23 Fit the special belt tensioning measuring equipment to the 'front run' of the timing belt, approximately midway between the camshaft and crankshaft sprockets. Position the tensioner pulley so that the belt is tensioned to a setting of 44 SEEM units, then retighten its retaining nut.
24 Remove the locking tools from the camshaft sprocket and flywheel/driveplate, and remove the measuring tool from the belt.
25 Using a suitable socket and extension bar on the crankshaft sprocket bolt, rotate the crankshaft through four complete rotations in a clockwise direction (viewed from the right-hand end of the engine). Refit the flywheel/driveplate locking tool and check that the camshaft timing hole is correctly aligned with the cylinder head hole.

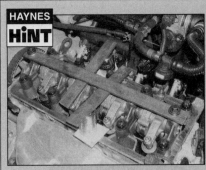

HAYNES HINT

If the rocker arm plate is not available, slacken the locknuts and back off the adjusting screws on all the necessary rocker arms. It will be found that two of the rocker arms remain in contact with the camshaft, even with the adjusting screws backed fully off. To hold these arms clear of the camshaft, fix a stout metal bar to the cylinder head cover studs with the nuts and lift the arms using shorter lengths of metal bar pivoted on large sockets.

Caution: Do not at any time rotate the crankshaft anti-clockwise.
26 To ensure an accurate reading, it is necessary to remove the valve spring load from the camshaft by fitting the rocker arm plate (0132-AE). Remove the cylinder head cover (see Section 4) then back off all the rocker arm contact bolts on the plate (0132-AE). Fit the plate to the cylinder head cover studs, ensuring it is fitted the correct way around then secure it in position with the cylinder head cover nuts **(see illustration)**. Tighten each rocker arm contact bolt until all rockers are lifted clear of the camshaft lobes. If the rocker arm plate is not available, obtain clearance between the rocker arms and camshaft by slackening the locknut and backing off the adjusting screws on all the necessary rocker arms. It will be found that two of the rocker arms remain in contact with the camshaft, even with the adjusting screws backed off fully. To hold these arms clear of the camshaft, use an arrangement similar to that shown **(see Tool Tip)**.
Caution: Do not overtighten the contact bolts any more than is necessary to obtain a small amount of clearance between the rocker arm roller and cam lobe. If the bolts are overtightened, there is a risk of the valves being forced into contact with the pistons, resulting in serious engine damage.
27 Refit the tensioning measuring equipment to the front run of the belt.
28 Slacken the tensioner pulley retaining nut whilst holding the pulley stationary. Gradually release the tensioner pulley until a tension setting of between 29 and 33 SEEM units is indicated on the measuring equipment. With the belt correctly tensioned, hold the pulley

**6.36 Timing belt tensioner
(later 1.4 litre engine)**

1 *Hole for hexagonal key*
2 *Normal tension position*
3 *Maximum tension position*

stationary and tighten its retaining nut to the specified torque.

29 Remove the measuring tool from the belt then unscrew the nuts and remove the rocker arm contact plate (or home-made alternative) from the cylinder head.

30 Remove the flywheel/driveplate locking tool, then rotate the crankshaft through another four complete rotations in a clockwise direction. Refit the flywheel/driveplate locking tool and check that the camshaft timing hole is correctly aligned with the cylinder head hole.

31 If all is well refit the timing belt covers and cylinder head cover as described in Sections 4 and 5. **Note:** *If the rocker arm adjusting screws were moved, adjust the valve clearances before refitting the cylinder head cover.*

32 Locate the engine management ECU bracket assembly on its mounting, refit the bracket and secure it in position with a new anti-tamper nut or standard nut. Clip the wiring harness back into position then reconnect the battery negative terminal.

Later engines from engine no. 3666766

33 These engines are equipped with a spring-loaded tensioner, so access to the belt tensioning gauge is unnecessary.

34 Manoeuvre the timing belt into position, ensuring that the arrows on the belt are pointing in the direction of rotation (clockwise when viewed from the right-hand end of the engine).

35 Do not twist the timing belt sharply while refitting it. Fit the belt over the crankshaft and camshaft sprockets, Make sure that the 'front run' of the belt is taut – ie, ensure that any slack is on the tensioner pulley side of the belt. Fit the belt over the coolant pump sprocket and tensioner pulley. Ensure that the belt teeth are seated centrally in the sprockets.

36 Remove the crankshaft and camshaft locking tools, then slacken the tensioner pulley nut and, using a hexagonal key, rotate the pulley anti-clockwise until the index arm is in the maximum tension position **(see illustration)**. Tighten the pulley retaining nut.

37 Using a socket on the crankshaft pulley bolt, rotate the crankshaft clockwise 10 complete revolutions, and refit the crankshaft locking tool as described in Section 3.

38 Check the timing is correct by inserting the camshaft sprocket locking tool (Section 3). If the tool cannot be inserted, slacken the tensioner, remove the belt, refit the locking tools, and start again from Paragraph 34.

39 Remove the crankshaft and camshaft locking tools.

40 Rotate the crankshaft two complete revolutions, and check that the crankshaft camshaft locking tools can still be inserted.

41 The remainder of refitting is a reversal of removal.'

7 Timing belt tensioner and sprockets – removal, inspection and refitting

Removal

1 Disconnect the battery negative terminal.

2 Position the engine assembly/valve timing holes as described in Section 3, and lock both the camshaft sprocket and flywheel/driveplate in position. *Do not* attempt to rotate the engine whilst the pins are in position.

Camshaft sprocket

3 Remove the timing belt as described in Section 6. **Note:** *On engines with a three-piece timing belt cover assembly, the sprocket can be removed without removing the belt completely. Referring to Sections 5 and 6, remove the centre timing belt cover then*

slacken the tensioner pulley retaining nut. Release the belt tension then disengage the timing belt from the camshaft sprocket, and move the belt clear, taking care not to bend or twist it sharply.

4 Remove the locking pin from the camshaft sprocket.

5 Slacken the camshaft sprocket retaining bolt and remove it, along with its washer. To prevent the camshaft rotating as the bolt is slackened, a sprocket-holding tool will be required. In the absence of the special Peugeot tool, an acceptable substitute can be fabricated as follows. Use two lengths of steel strip (one long, the other short), and three nuts and bolts; one nut and bolt forms the pivot of a forked tool, with the remaining two nuts and bolts at the tips of the 'forks' to engage with the sprocket spokes (see **Tool Tip** in *Refitting*).
Caution: Do not attempt to use the sprocket locking pin to prevent the sprocket from rotating whilst the bolt is slackened.

6 With the retaining bolt removed, slide the sprocket off the end of the camshaft. If the sprocket locating pin is a loose fit, remove it for safe-keeping. Examine the camshaft oil seal for signs of oil leakage and, if necessary, renew it as described in Section 8.

Crankshaft sprocket

7 Remove the timing belt as described in Section 6.

8 Slacken the crankshaft sprocket bolt. To prevent crankshaft rotation on manual transmission models, select top gear, and have an assistant apply the brakes firmly. If the engine has been removed from the vehicle or the vehicle is equipped with an automatic transmission unit, it will be necessary to lock the flywheel/driveplate (see Section 15).
Caution: Do not be tempted to use the flywheel/driveplate locking pin to prevent the crankshaft from rotating; temporarily remove the locking pin prior to slackening the pulley bolt, then refit it once the bolt has been slackened.

9 Unscrew the retaining bolt and washer, then slide the sprocket off the end of the crankshaft **(see illustrations)**.

10 If the Woodruff key is a loose fit in the crankshaft, remove it and store it with the

7.9a Remove the retaining bolt and washer . . .

7.9b . . . then slide off the crankshaft sprocket

7.10 Remove the Woodruff key and flanged spacer (where fitted) from the crankshaft

Using a home-made tool to hold the camshaft sprocket stationary whilst the bolt is tightened (shown with the cylinder head removed).

sprocket for safe-keeping. If necessary, also slide the flanged spacer (where fitted) off the end of the crankshaft **(see illustration)**. Examine the crankshaft oil seal for signs oil leakage and, if necessary, renew as described in Section 14.

Tensioner pulley

11 On models with a three-piece timing belt cover assembly, remove the centre timing belt cover; on models with a two-piece timing belt cover assembly, remove the lower cover (see Section 5).

12 Slacken and remove the timing belt tensioner pulley retaining nut, and slide the pulley off its mounting stud. Examine the mounting stud for signs of damage and, if necessary, renew it.

Inspection

13 Clean the sprockets thoroughly, and renew any that show signs of wear, damage or cracks.

14 Clean the tensioner assembly, but do not use any strong solvent, which may enter the pulley bearing. Check that the pulley rotates freely about its hub, with no sign of stiffness or of free play. Renew the tensioner pulley if there is any doubt about its condition, or if there are any obvious signs of wear or damage.

15 Inspect the timing belt (see Section 6). Renew the belt is there is any doubt about its condition.

Refitting

Camshaft sprocket

16 Refit the locating pin (where removed) then locate the sprocket on the end of the camshaft. Ensure that the locating pin is correctly engaged with the sprocket and the cut-out in the camshaft end.

17 Refit the sprocket retaining bolt and washer. Tighten the bolt to the specified torque, whilst retaining the sprocket with the tool used on removal **(see Tool Tip)**.

18 Realign the timing hole in the camshaft sprocket (see Section 3) with the corresponding hole in the cylinder head, and refit the locking pin.

19 Refit the timing belt as described in Section 6.

Crankshaft sprocket

20 Locate the Woodruff key in the crankshaft end, then slide on the flanged spacer (where fitted) aligning its slot with the Woodruff key.

21 Align the crankshaft sprocket slot with the Woodruff key, and slide it onto the end of the crankshaft.

22 Temporarily remove the locking pin from the rear of the flywheel/driveplate, and then refit the crankshaft sprocket retaining bolt and washer. Tighten the bolt to the specified torque, whilst preventing crankshaft rotation using the method employed on removal. Refit the locking pin to the rear of the flywheel/driveplate.

23 Refit the timing belt as described in Section 6.

Tensioner pulley

24 Refit the tensioner pulley to its mounting stud, and fit the retaining nut.

25 Ensure that the 'front run' of the belt is taut – ie, ensure that any slack is on the pulley side of the belt. Check that the belt is centrally located on all its sprockets. Rotate the pulley anti-clockwise to remove all free play from the timing belt, then tighten the pulley retaining nut securely.

26 Tension the timing belt as described in Section 6.

27 Once the belt is correctly tensioned, refit the timing belt covers as described in Section 5.

8 Camshaft oil seal – renewal

Note: *If the camshaft oil seal has been leaking, check the timing belt for signs of oil contamination; the belt must be renewed if signs of oil contamination are found. Ensure that all traces of oil are removed from the sprockets and surrounding area before the new belt is fitted.*

1 Remove the camshaft sprocket as described in Section 7.

2 Punch or drill two small holes opposite each other in the oil seal. Screw a self-tapping screw into each, and pull on the screws with pliers to extract the seal. Alternatively, carefully prise the seal out using a flat-bladed screwdriver **(see illustration)**.

3 Clean the seal housing, and polish off any burrs or raised edges, which may have caused the seal to fail in the first place.

4 Lubricate the lips of the new seal with clean engine oil, and drive it into position until it seats on its locating shoulder. Use a suitable tubular drift, such as a socket, which bears only on the hard outer edge of the seal. Take care not to damage the seal lips during fitting. Note that the seal lips should face inwards.

5 Refit the camshaft sprocket as described in Section 7.

8.2 Carefully prise the camshaft oil seal out with a flat-bladed screwdriver

9 Valve clearances – checking and adjustment

Note: *The valve clearances must be checked and adjusted only when the engine is cold.*

1 The importance of having the valve clearances correctly adjusted cannot be overstressed, as they vitally affect the performance of the engine. If the clearances are too big, the engine will be noisy (characteristic rattling or tapping noises) and engine efficiency will be reduced, as the valves open too late and close too early. A more serious problem arises if the clearances are too small, however. If this is the case, the valves may not close fully when the engine is hot, resulting in serious damage to the engine (eg, burnt valve seats and/or cylinder head warping/cracking). The clearances are checked and adjusted as follows.

2 Remove the cylinder head cover as described in Section 4.

3 The engine can now be turned using a suitable socket and extension bar fitted to the crankshaft sprocket bolt.

4 It is important that the clearance of each valve is checked and adjusted only when the valve is fully closed, with the rocker arm resting on the heel of the cam (directly opposite the peak). This can be ensured by carrying out the adjustments in the following sequence, noting that No 1 cylinder is at the transmission end of the engine. The correct valve clearances are given in the Specifications at the start of this Chapter. The valve locations can be determined from the position of the manifolds.

Valve fully open	Adjust valves
No 1 exhaust	No 3 inlet and No 4 exhaust
No 3 exhaust	No 4 inlet and No 2 exhaust
No 4 exhaust	No 2 inlet and No 1 exhaust
No 2 exhaust	No 1 inlet and No 3 exhaust

5 With the relevant valve fully open, check the clearances of the two valves specified. The clearances are checked by inserting a feeler blade of the correct thickness between the valve stem and the rocker arm adjusting screw. The feeler blade should be a light, sliding fit. If adjustment is necessary, slacken the adjusting screw locknut, and turn the screw as necessary

9.5 Adjusting a valve clearance

10.4 Remove the circlip and slide the components off the end of the rocker arm

10.5 Lock two nuts together to enable the stud to be unscrewed from the left-hand end pedestal

(see illustration). Once the correct clearance is obtained, hold the adjusting screw and tighten the locknut securely. Once the locknut has been tightened, recheck the valve clearance, and adjust again if necessary.

6 Rotate the crankshaft until the next valve in the sequence is fully open, and check the clearances of the next two specified valves.

7 Repeat the procedure until all eight valve clearances have been checked (and if necessary, adjusted), then refit the cylinder head cover as described in Section 4.

10 Camshaft and rocker arms – removal, inspection and refitting

General information

1 The rocker arm assembly is secured to the top of the cylinder head by the cylinder head bolts. Although in theory it is possible to undo the head bolts and remove the rocker arm assembly without removing the head, in practice, this is not recommended. Once the bolts have been removed, the head gasket will be disturbed, and the gasket will almost certainly leak or blow after refitting. For this reason, removal of the rocker arm assembly cannot be done without removing the cylinder head and renewing the head gasket.

2 The camshaft is slid out of the right-hand end of the cylinder head, and it therefore cannot be removed without first removing the cylinder head, due to a lack of clearance.

Removal

Rocker arm assembly

3 Remove the cylinder head as described in Section 11.

4 To dismantle the rocker arm assembly, carefully prise off the circlip from the right-hand end of the rocker shaft; retain the rocker pedestal, to prevent it being sprung off the end of the shaft. Slide the various components off the end of the shaft, keeping all components in their correct fitted order (see illustration). Make a note of each component's correct fitted position and orientation as it is removed, to ensure it is fitted correctly on reassembly. **Note:** *Avoid touching the rocker arm roller bearing surfaces with your fingers.*

5 To separate the left-hand pedestal and shaft, first unscrew the cylinder head cover retaining stud from the top of the pedestal; this can be achieved using a stud extractor, or two nuts locked together (see illustration). With the stud removed, unscrew the grub screw from the top of the pedestal, and withdraw the rocker shaft.

Camshaft

6 Remove the cylinder head as described in Section 11.

7 With the head on a bench, remove the locking pin, then remove the camshaft sprocket as described in paragraphs 5 and 6 of Section 7.

8 Unbolt the coolant housing from the left-hand end of the cylinder head.

9 Undo the retaining bolt and slide out the camshaft thrust fork (see illustration).

10 Using a large flat-bladed screwdriver,

carefully prise the oil seal out of the right-hand end of the cylinder head, and then slide out the camshaft (see illustrations). **Note:** *On 1.4 litre engines equipped with air injection, take care not to damage the camshaft sensor lug as the camshaft is removed. Discard the seal – a new one must be used on refitting.*

Inspection

Rocker arm assembly

11 Examine the rocker arm roller surfaces which contact the camshaft lobes for wear ridges and scoring. Renew any rocker arms on which the rollers show signs of damage. If a rocker arm roller surface is badly scored, also examine the corresponding lobe on the camshaft for wear, as both will likely be worn. Renew worn components as necessary. The rocker arm assembly can be dismantled as described in paragraphs 4 and 5.

12 If necessary, inspect the ends of the (valve clearance) adjusting screws for signs of wear or damage, and renew as required.

13 If the rocker arm assembly has been dismantled, examine the rocker arm and shaft bearing surfaces for wear ridges and scoring. If there are obvious signs of wear, the relevant rocker arm(s) and/or the shaft must be renewed.

Camshaft

14 Examine the camshaft bearing surfaces and cam lobes for signs of wear ridges and scoring. Renew the camshaft if any of these conditions are apparent. Examine the condition of the bearing surfaces, both on the camshaft journals and in the cylinder head. If the head

10.9 Undo the retaining bolt and slide out the camshaft thrust fork

10.10a Prise out the oil seal . . .

10.10b . . . then slide the camshaft out from the cylinder head

bearing surfaces are worn excessively, the cylinder head will need to be renewed. If the necessary measuring equipment is available, camshaft bearing journal wear can be checked by direct measurement, noting that No 1 journal is at the transmission end of the head.

15 Examine the thrust fork for signs of wear or scoring, and renew as necessary.

Refitting
Rocker arm assembly

16 If the rocker arm assembly was dismantled, refit the rocker shaft to the left-hand pedestal, aligning its locating hole with the pedestal threaded hole. Refit the grub screw, and tighten it securely. With the grub screw in position, refit the cylinder head cover mounting stud to the pedestal, and tighten it securely. Apply a smear of clean engine oil to the shaft, and then slide on all removed components, ensuring each is correctly fitted in its original position. **Note:** *Avoid touching the rocker arm roller bearing surfaces with your fingers.* Once all components are in position on the shaft, compress the right-hand pedestal and refit the circlip. Ensure that the circlip is correctly located in its groove on the shaft.

17 Refit the cylinder head and rocker arm assembly as described in Section 11.

Camshaft

18 Ensure that the cylinder head and camshaft bearing surfaces are clean, and then liberally oil the camshaft bearings and lobes. Slide the camshaft back into position in the cylinder head. **Note:** *On 1.4 litre engines equipped with air injection, take care not to damage the camshaft sensor lug as the camshaft is refitted.*

19 Locate the thrust fork with the left-hand end of the camshaft. Refit the fork retaining bolt, tightening it to the specified torque setting.

20 Ensure that the coolant housing and cylinder head mating surfaces are clean and dry, then apply a smear of sealant to the housing mating surface. Refit the housing to the left-hand end of the head, and securely tighten its retaining bolts.

21 Lubricate the lips of the new seal with clean engine oil, then drive it into position until

it seats on its locating shoulder. Use a suitable tubular drift, such as a socket, which bears only on the hard outer edge of the seal. Take care not to damage the seal lips during fitting. Note that the seal lips should face inwards.

22 Refit the camshaft sprocket as described in paragraphs 16 to 18 of Section 7.

23 Refit the cylinder head as described in Section 11.

---

11 Cylinder head –
removal and refitting

Note: *Ensure the engine is cold before removing the cylinder head.*

Removal

1 Disconnect the battery negative lead.

2 Drain the cooling system as described in Chapter 1A.

3 Remove the ignition HT coil assembly (see Chapter 5B) then remove the spark plugs (see Chapter 1A).

4 Remove the cylinder head cover as described in Section 4.

5 Align the engine assembly/valve timing holes as described in Section 3, and lock both the camshaft sprocket and flywheel/driveplate in position.

Caution: Do not attempt to rotate the engine whilst the tools are in position.

6 Note that the following text assumes that the cylinder head will be removed with both inlet and exhaust manifolds attached; this is easier, but makes it a bulky and heavy assembly to handle. If it is wished to remove the manifolds first, proceed as described in Chapter 4A.

7 Carry out the following operations as described in Chapter 4A:

a) *Disconnect the exhaust system front pipe from the manifold. Disconnect or release the oxygen sensor wiring, so that it is not strained by the weight of the exhaust.*

b) *Remove the air cleaner housing inlet duct assembly.*

c) *Disconnect the fuel feed hose from the fuel rail (plug all openings, to prevent loss of fuel and entry of dirt into the fuel system).*

11.9 Unscrew the bolts (arrowed) and free the wiring/power steering pipe bracket from the left-hand end of the cylinder head

d) *Disconnect the accelerator cable.*

e) *Disconnect the relevant electrical connectors and vacuum/breather hoses from the inlet manifold.*

f) *Where necessary unbolt the support bracket from the inlet manifold.*

g) *On 1.4 litre models with air injection, disconnect the hose from the injection valve which is fitted to the exhaust manifold.*

8 Remove the timing belt as described in Section 6. **Note:** *On engines with a three-piece timing belt cover assembly, the cylinder head can be removed without removing the belt completely. Referring to Sections 5 and 6, remove the centre timing belt cover then slacken the tensioner pulley retaining nut. Release the belt tension then disengage the timing belt from the camshaft sprocket, and move the belt clear, taking care not to bend or twist it sharply*

9 Unscrew the bolts and free the wiring/power steering pipe bracket from the coolant housing **(see illustration)**.

10 Slacken the retaining clips, and disconnect the coolant hoses from the housing on the left-hand end of the cylinder head. Disconnect the wiring connectors from the electrical sensors which are screwed into the coolant housing/cylinder head.

11 On models with power steering, referring to Chapter 10, unbolt the power steering pump from its mounting bracket. Undo the power steering pipe retaining clip screws then position the pump clear of the engine **(see illustrations)**. Support the weight of the pump

11.11a Unscrew the front . . .

11.11b . . . and rear mounting bolts . . .

11.11c . . . then free the power steering pump from its mounting bracket and position it clear of the engine

11.12 Slacken and remove the cylinder head bolts as described in text . . .

11.13 . . . then lift off the rocker arm assembly

by tying it to the vehicle body to prevent any excess strain being placed on the hydraulic pipes/hoses. **Note:** *There is no need to disconnect the pipe/hose from the pump.*

12 Working in the *reverse* of the sequence shown in illustration 11.31a, progressively slacken the ten cylinder head bolts by half a turn at a time, until all bolts can be unscrewed by hand **(see illustration).**

13 With all the cylinder head bolts removed, lift the rocker arm assembly off the cylinder head **(see illustration). Note:** *Avoid touching the rocker arm roller bearing surfaces with your fingers.* Note the locating pins, which are fitted to the base of each rocker arm pedestal. If any pin is a loose fit in the head or pedestal, remove it for safe-keeping.

14 On engines with a cast-iron cylinder block, lift the cylinder head away; seek assistance if possible, as it is a heavy assembly, especially if it is being removed complete with the manifolds.

15 On engines with an aluminium cylinder block, the joint between the cylinder head and gasket and the cylinder block/crankcase must now be broken without disturbing the wet liners. To break the joint, obtain two stout screwdrivers, which fit into the cylinder head bolt holes. Gently 'rock' the cylinder head free towards the front of the car **(see illustration).** Do not try to swivel the head on the cylinder block/crankcase; it is located by dowels, as well as by the tops of the liners. **Note:** *If care is not taken and the liners are moved, there is also a possibility of the bottom seals being*

disturbed, causing leakage after refitting the head. When the joint is broken, lift the cylinder head away; seek assistance if possible, as it is a heavy assembly, especially if it is being removed complete with the manifolds.

16 On all models, remove the gasket from the top of the block, noting the two locating dowels. If the locating dowels are a loose fit, remove them and store them with the head for safe-keeping. Do not discard the gasket – on some models it will be needed for identification purposes (see paragraphs 21 and 22). Operations that require the rotation of the crankshaft (eg, cleaning the piston crowns) should only be carried out on aluminium block engines once the cylinder liners are firmly clamped in position **(see illustration).** In the absence of the special Peugeot liner clamps, the liners can be clamped in position using large flat washers positioned underneath suitable-length bolts. Alternatively, the original head bolts could be temporarily refitted, with suitable spacers fitted to their shanks.

Caution: On aluminium block engines, do not attempt to rotate the crankshaft with the cylinder head removed; otherwise the wet liners may be displaced.

17 If the cylinder head is to be dismantled for overhaul, remove the camshaft as described in Section 10, then refer to Part E of this Chapter.

Preparation for refitting

18 The mating faces of the cylinder head and cylinder block/crankcase must be perfectly

clean before refitting the head. Use a hard plastic or wood scraper to remove all traces of gasket and carbon; also clean the piston crowns. **Note:** *On aluminium block engines, clamp the liners in position before turning the crankshaft (see paragraph 16).* Take particular care during the cleaning operations, as aluminium alloy is easily damaged. Also, make sure that the carbon is not allowed to enter the oil and water passages – this is particularly important for the lubrication system, as carbon could block the oil supply to the engine's components. Using adhesive tape and paper, seal the water, oil and bolt holes in the cylinder block/crankcase. To prevent carbon entering the gap between the pistons and bores, smear a little grease in the gap. After cleaning each piston, use a small brush to remove all traces of grease and carbon from the gap, and then wipe away the remainder with a clean rag. Clean all the pistons in the same way.

19 Check the mating surfaces of the cylinder block/crankcase and the cylinder head for nicks, deep scratches and other damage. If slight, they may be removed carefully with a file, but if excessive, machining may be the only alternative to renewal.

20 If warpage of the cylinder head gasket surface is suspected, use a straight-edge to check it for distortion. Refer to Part E of this Chapter if necessary.

21 When purchasing a new cylinder head gasket, it is essential that a gasket of the correct thickness be obtained. On some models only one thickness of gasket is available, so this is not a problem. On other models, there are two different thicknesses available – the standard gasket, and a slightly thicker 'repair' gasket (+ 0.2 mm). The gaskets can be identified as described in the following paragraph, using the cut-outs on the left-hand end of the gasket.

22 With the gasket fitted the correct way up on the cylinder block, there will be a single or double cut-out at the rear of the left-hand side of the gasket identifying the engine type (eg, TU3JP engine). In the centre of the gasket there will likely be another series of between 0 and 4 cut-outs, identifying the manufacturer of the gasket and whether or not it contains asbestos (these cut-outs are of little importance). The important cut-out location is at the front of the gasket; on the standard gasket there will be no cut-out in this position, whereas on the thicker 'repair' gasket there will be a single cut-out **(see illustration).** Identify the gasket type, and ensure that the new gasket obtained is of the correct thickness. If there is any doubt as to which gasket is fitted, take the old gasket along to your Peugeot dealer, and have him confirm the gasket type.

23 Check the condition of the cylinder head bolts, and particularly their threads, whenever they are removed. Wash the bolts in suitable solvent, and wipe them dry. Check each for any sign of visible wear or damage, renewing any bolt if necessary. Measure the length of each

11.15 On aluminium block engines, use two stout screwdrivers to rock the cylinder head free from the block

11.16 On aluminium block engines clamp the cylinder liners in position before rotating the crankshaft (clamps arrowed)

11.22 Cylinder head gasket identification markings

A Engine type identification cut-out locations
B Gasket manufacturer identification cut-out locations
C Gasket thickness identification cut-out location

11.23 Measure the length of each cylinder head bolt (Y) to check for stretching – see text

bolt, from the underside of its head to the bolt end, to check for stretching **(see illustration)**. The bolts are 175.5 mm in length when new; if any bolt has stretched to more than 176.5 mm; renew all the cylinder head bolts as a set. Although Peugeot do not actually specify that the bolts must be renewed, it is strongly recommended that the bolts should be renewed as a complete set, regardless of their apparent condition, whenever they are disturbed.

24 On aluminium block engines, prior to refitting the cylinder head, check the cylinder liner protrusion as described Chapter 2E, Section 12.

Refitting

25 Wipe clean the mating surfaces of the cylinder head and cylinder block/crankcase. Check that the two locating dowels are in position at each end of the cylinder block/crankcase surface and, if necessary, remove the cylinder liner clamps **(see illustration)**.

26 Position a new gasket on the cylinder block/crankcase surface, ensuring that its identification cut-outs are at the left-hand end of the gasket.

27 Check that the flywheel/driveplate and camshaft sprocket are still correctly locked in position with their respective tools then, with the aid of an assistant, carefully refit the cylinder head assembly to the block, aligning it with the locating dowels.

28 Ensure that the locating pins are in position in the base of each rocker pedestal, and then refit the rocker arm assembly to the cylinder head.

29 Lubricate the threads and underside of the heads of the cylinder head bolts lightly with clean engine oil.

30 Carefully enter each bolt into its relevant hole (do not drop them in) and screw in, by hand only, until finger-tight.

31 Working progressively and in sequence, tighten the cylinder head bolts to their Stage 1 torque setting, using a torque wrench and suitable socket **(see illustrations)**.

32 Once all the bolts have been tightened to their Stage 1 setting, working again in the given sequence, angle-tighten the bolts through the specified Stage 2 angle, using a socket and extension bar. It is recommended that an angle-measuring gauge is used during this stage of the tightening, to ensure accuracy **(see illustration)**. If a gauge is not available, use white paint to make alignment marks between the bolt head and cylinder head prior to tightening; the marks can then be used to check that the bolt has been rotated through the correct angle during tightening.

33 On cast-iron block engines, it will then be necessary to tighten the bolts through the specified Stage 3 angle setting.

34 Refit and tension the timing belt as described in Section 6.

35 Reconnect the wiring connectors to the coolant temperature sensors on the coolant housing/cylinder head.

36 Reconnect the coolant hoses to the cylinder head coolant housing.

37 On models with power steering, ensure the mounting spacer (where fitted) is correctly fitted to the rear mounting then locate the pump on its mounting bracket Apply locking compound (Peugeot recommend the use of Loctite Frenetanch) to the pump lower front mounting bolt then install all the bolts; tighten the pump front (drivebelt pulley end) bolts to the specified torque first then tighten the rear bolts (see Chapter 10).

38 Secure the wiring/power steering pipe bracket to the cylinder head coolant housing, tightening its retaining bolts securely.

39 Working as described in the Chapter 4A, carry out the following tasks:

a) Refit all disturbed wiring, hoses and control cable(s) to the inlet manifold and fuel system components.
b) Reconnect and adjust the accelerator cable.

11.25 Ensure the locating dowels (arrowed) are in position then fit the new head gasket

11.31a Cylinder head bolt tightening sequence

11.31b Working in the specified sequence, tighten the cylinder head bolts to the specified Stage 1 torque setting . . .

11.32 . . . and then through the specified Stage 2 angle

c) *Reconnect the exhaust system front pipe to the manifold and reconnect the oxygen sensor wiring connector.*

d) *Refit the air cleaner and inlet duct.*

40 Check and, if necessary, adjust the valve clearances as described in Section 9.

41 Refit the spark plugs and install the ignition HT coil (see Chapters 1A and 5B).

42 On completion, reconnect the battery, and refill the cooling system as described in Chapter 1A.

12 Sump – removal and refitting

Removal

1 Firmly apply the handbrake, and then jack up the front of the vehicle and support it on axle stands (see *Jacking and vehicle support*). Disconnect the battery negative lead.

2 Drain the engine oil, then clean and refit the engine oil drain plug, tightening it to the specified torque. If the engine is nearing the service interval when the oil and filter are due for renewal, it is recommended that the filter is also removed, and a new one fitted. After reassembly, the engine can then be refilled with fresh oil. Refer to Chapter 1A for further information.

3 Remove the exhaust system front pipe as described in Chapter 4A.

4 Progressively slacken and remove all the sump nuts and bolts and position the wiring harness guide clear of the sump **(see illustration)**. On cast-iron block engines, it may be necessary to unbolt the flywheel cover plate from the transmission to gain access to the left-hand sump fasteners.

5 Break the joint by striking the sump with the palm of your hand, then lower and withdraw the sump from under the car.

6 While the sump is removed, take the opportunity to check the oil pump pick-up/strainer for signs of clogging or splitting. If necessary, remove the pump as described in Section 13, and clean or renew the strainer.

Refitting

7 Clean all traces of sealant from the mating surfaces of the cylinder block/crankcase and

sump, then use a clean rag to wipe out the sump and the engine's interior.

8 Ensure that the sump and cylinder block/crankcase mating surfaces are clean and dry, then apply a coating of suitable sealant to the sump mating surface.

9 Offer up the sump and locate it on its studs. Locate the wiring harness guide back in position then refit the sump retaining nuts and bolts. Tighten the nuts and bolts evenly and progressively to the specified torque.

10 Refit the exhaust front pipe as described in Chapter 4A.

11 Replenish the engine oil (see Chapter 1A).

13 Oil pump – removal, inspection and refitting

Removal

1 Remove the sump (see Section 12).

2 Slacken and remove the three bolts securing the oil pump in position **(see illustration)**. Disengage the pump sprocket from the chain, and remove the oil pump. If the pump locating-dowel is a loose fit, remove and store it with the bolts for safe-keeping.

Inspection

3 Examine the oil pump sprocket for signs of damage and wear, such as chipped or missing teeth. If the sprocket is worn, the pump assembly must be renewed, as the sprocket is not available separately. It is also recommended that the chain and drive sprocket, fitted to the crankshaft, is renewed at the same time. On aluminium block engines, renewal of the chain and drive sprocket is an involved operation requiring the removal of the main bearing ladder, and therefore cannot be carried out with the engine still fitted to the vehicle. On cast-iron block engines, the oil pump drive sprocket and chain can be removed with the engine *in situ*, once the crankshaft sprocket has been removed and the crankshaft oil seal housing has been unbolted.

4 Slacken and remove the bolts securing the strainer cover to the pump body, and then lift off the strainer cover. Remove the relief valve piston and spring (and guide pin – cast-iron

block engines only), noting which way round they are fitted.

5 Examine the pump rotors and body for signs of wear ridges and scoring. If worn, the complete pump assembly must be renewed.

6 Examine the relief valve piston for signs of wear or damage, and renew if necessary. The condition of the relief valve spring can only be measured by comparing it with a new one; if there is any doubt about its condition, it should also be renewed. Both the piston and spring are available individually.

7 Thoroughly clean the oil pump strainer with a suitable solvent, and check it for signs of clogging or splitting. If the strainer is damaged, the strainer and cover assembly must be renewed.

8 Locate the relief valve spring, piston and (where fitted) the guide pin in the strainer cover, then refit the cover to the pump body. Align the relief valve piston with its bore in the pump. Refit the cover retaining bolts, tightening them securely.

Refitting

9 Ensure that the locating dowel is in position, and then engage the pump sprocket with its drive chain. Locate the pump on its dowel, and refit the pump retaining bolts, tightening them to the specified torque setting.

10 Refit the sump as described in Section 12.

14 Crankshaft oil seals – renewal

Right-hand oil seal

1 Remove the crankshaft sprocket and flanged spacer (where fitted) as described in Section 7.

2 Make a note of the correct fitted depth of the seal in its housing then carefully punch or drill two small holes opposite each other in the seal. Screw a self-tapping screw into each, and pull on the screws with pliers to extract the seal. Alternatively, the seal can be levered out of position using a suitable flat-bladed screwdriver, taking great care not to damage the crankshaft/oil pump drive gear shoulder or seal housing **(see illustration)**.

12.4 Unscrew the sump nut (1) and position the wiring harness guide (2) clear of the sump

13.2 Unscrew the three bolts securing the oil pump in position

14.2 Using a screwdriver to lever the crankshaft right-hand oil seal out of position

3 Clean the seal housing, and polish off any burrs or raised edges which may have caused the seal to fail in the first place.

4 Lubricate the lips of the new seal with clean engine oil, and carefully locate the seal on the end of crankshaft. Note that its sealing lip must face inwards. Take care not to damage the seal lips during fitting.

5 Using a suitable tubular drift (such as a socket), which bears only on the hard outer edge of the seal, tap the seal into position, to the same depth in the housing as the original was prior to removal. The inner face of the seal must be flush with the inner wall of the crankcase.

6 Wash off any traces of oil, then refit the crankshaft sprocket as described in Section 7.

Left-hand oil seal

7 Remove the flywheel/driveplate (see Section 15).

8 Make a note of the correct fitted depth of the seal in its housing. Punch or drill two small holes opposite each other in the seal. Screw a self-tapping screw into each, and pull on the screws with pliers to extract the seal.

9 Clean the seal housing, and polish off any burrs or raised edges, which may have caused the seal to fail in the first place.

10 Lubricate the lips of the new seal with clean engine oil, and carefully locate the seal on the end of the crankshaft.

11 Using a suitable tubular drift, which bears only on the hard outer edge of the seal, drive the seal into position, to the same depth in the housing as the original was prior to removal.

12 Wash off any traces of oil, then refit the flywheel/driveplate as described in Section 15.

15 Flywheel/driveplate –
removal, inspection and refitting

Flywheel

Removal

1 Remove the transmission as described in Chapter 7A, then remove the clutch assembly as described in Chapter 6.

2 Prevent the flywheel from turning by locking the ring gear teeth **(see illustration)**.

15.2 Use a tool similar to that shown to lock the flywheel ring gear and prevent rotation

Alternatively, bolt a strap between the flywheel and the cylinder block/crankcase.

Caution: Do not attempt to lock the flywheel in position using the locking pin described in Section 3.

3 Slacken and remove the flywheel retaining bolts.

4 Remove the flywheel. Do not drop it, as it is very heavy. If the locating dowel is a loose fit in the crankshaft end, remove and store it with the flywheel for safe-keeping.

Inspection

5 If the flywheel's clutch mating surface is deeply scored, cracked or otherwise damaged, the flywheel must be renewed. However, it may be possible to have it surface-ground; seek the advice of a Peugeot dealer or engine reconditioning specialist.

6 If the ring gear is badly worn or has missing teeth, it must be renewed. This job is best left to a Peugeot dealer or engine reconditioning specialist. The temperature to which the new ring gear must be heated for installation is critical and, if not done accurately, the hardness of the teeth will be destroyed.

Refitting

7 Clean the mating surfaces of the flywheel and crankshaft.

8 Remove any traces of locking compound from the threads of the flywheel bolts and apply a small amount of fresh locking compound (Peugeot recommend Loctite Frenbloc) to the bolt threads.

9 Ensure that the locating dowel is in position. Offer up the flywheel, locating it on the dowel, and fit the retaining bolts.

10 Lock the flywheel using the method employed on dismantling, and tighten the retaining bolts evenly and progressively to the specified torque.

11 Refit the clutch as described in Chapter 6. Remove the locking tool, and refit the transmission as described in Chapter 7A.

Driveplate

Removal

12 Remove the transmission as described in Chapter 7B.

13 Prevent the driveplate from turning by locking the ring gear teeth with a similar arrangement to that shown in illustration 15.2. Alternatively, bolt a strap between the driveplate and the cylinder block/crankcase.

Caution: Do not attempt to lock the driveplate in position using the locking pin described in Section 3.

14 Slacken and remove the driveplate retaining bolts and remove the outer spacer plate and torque converter mounting plate.

15 Remove the driveplate and inner spacer plate from the end of the crankshaft. If the locating dowel is a loose fit in the crankshaft end, remove and store it with the driveplate for safe-keeping. *Note: The inner and outer spacer plates are different and are not interchangeable.*

Inspection

16 Inspect the driveplate and torque converter mounting plate for signs of wear or damage. If damage is found, the worn component must be renewed (it is not possible to renew the driveplate ring gear separately).

Refitting

17 Ensure all mating surfaces are clean and dry.

18 Remove any traces of locking compound from the threads of the driveplate bolts and apply a small amount of fresh locking compound (Peugeot recommend Loctite Frenbloc) to the bolt threads.

19 Ensure that the locating dowel is in position then refit the inner spacer plate, driveplate, torque converter mounting plate and outer spacer plate. Ensure all components are correctly located on the dowel then fit the retaining bolts.

20 Lock the driveplate using the method employed on dismantling, and tighten the retaining bolts evenly and progressively to the specified torque.

21 Refit the transmission as described in Chapter 7B.

16 Engine/transmission
mountings – inspection and renewal

Inspection

1 If improved access is required, raise the front of the car and support it on axle stands (see *Jacking and vehicle support*).

2 Check the mounting rubber to see if it is cracked, hardened or separated from the metal at any point; renew the mounting if any such damage or deterioration is evident.

3 Check that all the mounting's fasteners are securely tightened; use a torque wrench to check if possible.

4 Using a large screwdriver or a crowbar, check for wear in the mounting by carefully levering against it to check for free play. Where this is not possible, enlist the aid of an assistant to move the engine/transmission back-and-forth, or from side-to-side, while you watch the mounting. While some free play is to be expected even from new components, excessive wear should be obvious. If excessive free play is found, check first that the fasteners are secure, and then renew any worn components as described below.

Renewal

Right-hand mounting

5 Disconnect the battery negative lead.

6 Unclip the wiring harness from the front of the engine management ECU to gain access to the mounting plate nut. Slacken and remove the nut using a pair of grips (the plate is secured in position with an anti-tamper nut) then free the mounting plate from the body and position it clear of the engine mounting **(see illustrations 6.6a and 6.6b)**.

16.8 Unscrew the mounting nut and bolts and remove the support bracket from the front of the right-hand mounting

16.10 Unscrew the nuts (1) and unclip the wiring harness (2) . . .

7 Place a jack beneath the engine, with a block of wood on the jack head. Raise the jack until it is supporting the weight of the engine.
8 Slacken and remove the mounting nut and bolts and remove the support bracket securing the mounting to the front of the engine unit **(see illustration)**.
9 Unscrew the vibration damper (where fitted) from the top of the mounting rubber then slacken and remove the nut and washer securing the mounting bracket to the mounting rubber **(see illustration)**.
10 Slacken and remove the three nuts securing the right-hand engine mounting

bracket to the bracket/housing on the rear of the cylinder block **(see illustration)**.
11 Unclip the wiring harness then lift off the mounting bracket **(see illustration)**.
12 Make identification marks on the movement restrictors (the front and rear restrictors are different and are not interchangeable) then unscrew the nuts and remove both restrictors **(see illustration)**.
13 Using a strap wrench, unscrew the mounting rubber from the body **(see illustration)**.
14 Check for signs of wear or damage on all components, and renew as necessary.

15 On reassembly, screw the mounting rubber into the body, tightening it to the specified torque.
16 Refit the front and rear movement restrictors in their original locations. Ensure the restrictor pegs are correctly located in their holes then securely tighten their retaining nuts **(see illustration)**.
17 Install the mounting bracket and tighten its retaining nuts to the specified torque setting. Clip the wiring harness back into position then, where necessary, refit the vibration damper to the mounting, tightening it to the specified torque.
18 Remove the jack from under the engine. Refit the support bracket, tightening its fixings to the specified torque.
19 Locate the engine management ECU assembly on its mounting and secure it in position with a new anti-tamper nut or standard nut. Clip the wiring harness back into position then reconnect the battery negative terminal.

Left-hand mounting
20 Remove the battery, battery tray and mounting plate as described in Chapter 5A.
21 Place a jack beneath the transmission, with a block of wood on the jack head. Raise the jack until it is supporting the weight of the transmission.
22 Slacken and remove the mounting rubber's

16.11 . . . then lift off the right-hand mounting bracket

16.12 Unscrew the nuts and remove the front and rear movement restrictors

16.9 Unscrew the nut (arrowed) securing the mounting bracket to the mounting

16.13 Use a strap wrench to unscrew the mounting rubber from the body

16.16 Ensure the movement restrictors are fitted in the correct locations with their pegs located in the body holes (arrowed)

16.22a Unscrew the centre nut (1) and the mounting bolts (2) . . .

16.22b . . . then remove the left-hand mounting rubber

16.23 Unscrew the mounting bolts (locations arrowed) and remove the mounting bracket from the body

16.24 On manual transmission models disconnect the clutch cable then unscrew the nuts (arrowed) and remove the bracket from the transmission

16.33 Slacken and remove the mounting nuts and bolts . . .

16.34 . . . then remove the rear mounting link from the vehicle

centre nut and two retaining bolts and remove the mounting from the engine compartment **(see illustrations)**.

23 If necessary, undo the retaining bolts and remove the mounting bracket from the body **(see illustration)**.

24 To remove the transmission bracket on manual transmission models, disconnect the clutch cable from the transmission (see Chapter 6) then unscrew the retaining nuts and remove the bracket from the top of the transmission **(see illustration)**.

25 On automatic transmission models, the mounting stud is a screw-fit into its mounting bracket and the bracket is secured to the transmission by two bolts. If the mounting stud is tight, a universal stud extractor can be used to unscrew it.

26 Check carefully for signs of wear or damage on all components, and renew them where necessary.

27 On manual transmission models, refit the bracket to the transmission, tightening

its mounting nuts to the specified torque. Reconnect the clutch cable as described in Chapter 6.

28 On automatic transmission models, ensure the transmission mounting bracket bolts and the stud are tightened to the specified torque. Slide the spacer onto the stud.

29 On all models, refit the mounting bracket to the vehicle body and tighten its bolts to the specified torque.

30 Fit the mounting rubber to the bracket and tighten its retaining bolts to the specified torque. Refit the mounting centre nut, and tighten it to the specified torque.

31 Remove the jack from underneath the transmission, then refit the battery as described in Chapter 5A.

Rear mounting

32 If not already done, firmly apply the handbrake, then jack up the front of the vehicle and support it securely on axle stands (see *Jacking and vehicle support*).

33 Unscrew and remove the bolt securing the

rear mounting link to the mounting on the rear of the cylinder block **(see illustration)**.

34 Remove the bolt securing the rear mounting link to the subframe and remove the mounting link **(see illustration)**.

35 To remove the mounting assembly it will first be necessary to remove the right-hand driveshaft as described in Chapter 8.

36 With the driveshaft removed, undo the retaining bolts and remove the mounting from the rear of the cylinder block.

37 Check carefully for signs of wear or damage on all components, and renew them where necessary.

38 On reassembly, fit the rear mounting assembly to the rear of the cylinder block, and tighten its retaining bolts to the specified torque. Refit the driveshaft as described in Chapter 8.

39 Refit the rear mounting link, and tighten both its bolts to their specified torque settings.

40 Lower the vehicle to the ground.

Notes

Chapter 2 Part B:
1.4 litre DOHC petrol engine in-car repair procedures

Contents

Degrees of difficulty

Easy, suitable for novice with little experience	**Fairly easy,** suitable for beginner with some experience	**Fairly difficult,** suitable for competent DIY mechanic	**Difficult,** suitable for experienced DIY mechanic	**Very difficult,** suitable for expert DIY or professional

Specifications

Engine (general)

Capacity	1.4 litre (1360cc) DOHC 16V
Designation	ET3J4
Engine codes*	KFU
Bore	75.00 mm
Stroke	77.00 mm
Direction of crankshaft rotation	Clockwise (viewed from right-hand side of vehicle)
No 1 cylinder location..............................	At transmission end of the engine
Compression ratio	11:1
Maximum power output	65 kW @ 5250 rpm
Maximum torque output	135 Nm @ 3250 rpm

* The engine code is situated on the front, left-hand end of the cylinder block.

Camshaft(s)
Drive . . . . Toothed belt
No of bearings 5

Lubrication system
Oil pump type . . . . Gear type, chain-driven off the crankshaft
Minimum oil pressure at 80°C . . . . 4 bars @ 4000 rpm
Oil pressure warning switch operating pressure . . . . 0.8 bars

Torque wrench settings

	Nm	lbf ft
Big-end bearing cap nuts*:		
Stage 1	30	22
Stage 2	Angle-tighten a further 45°	
Camshaft sprocket retaining bolt:		
Exhaust sprocket retaining bolt	45	33
Inlet sprocket retaining bolt cover	40	30
Inlet sprocket retaining bolt:		
Stage 1	20	15
Stage 2	60	44
Camshaft upper bearing cap casing bolts	9	7
Crankshaft pulley retaining bolts	25	18
Crankshaft sprocket retaining bolt*:		
Stage 1	40	30
Stage 2	Angle-tighten a further 45°	
Cylinder head bolts:		
Stage 1	15	11
Stage 2	25	18
Stage 3	Angle-tighten a further 200°	
Cylinder head cover bolts	10	7
Engine-to-transmission bolts:		
Manual transmission models	40	30
Automatic transmission models	35	26
Engine/transmission left-hand mounting:		
Mounting centre nut	65	48
Mounting-to-bracket bolts	30	22
Mounting bracket-to-body bolts	25	18
Mounting bracket-to-manual transmission nuts	25	18
Engine/transmission rear mounting:		
Mounting-to-cylinder block bolts	40	30
Mounting link-to-mounting bolt	50	37
Mounting link-to-subframe bolt	40	30
Lower bracket-to-mounting link bolt	20	15
Lower bracket-to-sump nuts	40	30
Engine/transmission right-hand mounting:		
Upper mounting support to cylinder head bolts	60	44
Upper mounting support to mounting nut	45	33
Support bracket to cylinder block	45	33
Flywheel/driveplate bolts*	67	49
Main bearing ladder casting:		
Stage 1	20	15
Stage 2	Angle-tighten a further 44°	
Main bearing ladder upper casing bolts	8	6
Oil filter cover	25	18
Oil filter housing-to-cylinder block mounting bolts	10	7
Oil level sensor	32	24
Oil pressure switch	20	15
Oil pump retaining bolts	9	7
Roadwheel bolts	90	66
Sump drain plug	30	22
Sump retaining nuts and bolts	8	6
Timing belt cover bolts	8	6
Timing belt idler pulley bolt	20	15
Timing belt tensioner pulley nut	20	15

* Do not re-use

1 General information

How to use this Chapter

1 This Part of Chapter 2 describes those repair procedures that can reasonably be carried out on the petrol engine while it remains in the car. If the engine has been removed from the car and is being dismantled, as described in Part E, any preliminary dismantling procedures can be ignored.

2 Note that, while it may be possible physically to overhaul items such as the piston/connecting rod assemblies while the engine is in the car, such tasks are not normally carried out as separate operations. Usually, several additional procedures (not to mention the cleaning of components and of oilways) have to be carried out. For this reason, all such tasks are classed as major overhaul procedures, and are described in Part E of this Chapter.

3 Part E describes the removal of the engine/transmission from the vehicle, and the full overhaul procedures that can then be carried out.

ET3 series engine

4 The engine is of in-line four-cylinder, double-overhead camshaft, 16-valve type, mounted transversely at the front of the car. The clutch and transmission are attached to its left-hand end.

5 The cylinder block is made of aluminium, and wet liners are fitted to the cylinder bores. Sealing O-rings are fitted at the base of each liner, to prevent the escape of coolant into the sump.

6 The crankshaft runs in five main bearings. Thrustwashers are fitted to No 4 main bearing cap, to control crankshaft endfloat.

7 The connecting rods rotate on horizontally-split bearing shells at their big-ends. The pistons are attached to the connecting rods by gudgeon pins. The gudgeon pins are an interference fit in the connecting rod small-end eyes. The aluminium alloy pistons are fitted with three piston rings – two compression rings and an oil control ring.

8 The camshafts are driven by a toothed timing belt, and operate sixteen valves by followers located beneath each cam lobe. The valve clearances are self-adjusting by means of hydraulic tappets fitted to the cam followers. The camshaft runs in bearing cap housings, which are bolted to the top of the cylinder head. The inlet and exhaust valves are each closed by coil springs, and operate in guides pressed into the cylinder head. Both the valve seats and guides can be renewed separately if worn. The inlet camshaft sprocket is a sealed unit that is fed by oil pressure to give variable valve timing (VVT).

9 The coolant pump is driven by the timing belt and located in the right-hand end of the cylinder block.

10 Lubrication is by means of an oil pump driven off the crankshaft right-hand end. It draws oil through a strainer located in the sump, and then forces it through an externally mounted filter into galleries in the cylinder block/crankcase. From there, the oil is distributed to the crankshaft (main bearings) and camshaft. The big-end bearings are supplied with oil via internal drillings in the crankshaft; the camshaft bearings also receive a pressurised supply. The camshaft lobes and valves are lubricated by splash, as are all other engine components.

11 Throughout the manual, it is often necessary to identify the engines not only by their cubic capacity, but also by their engine code. The engine code consists of three digits (eg, KFU). The code is stamped on the front, left-hand end of the cylinder block, on the machined surface located just above the oil filter **(see illustration)**.

1.11 Engine code (arrowed) stamped on the front of the cylinder block

Operations with engine in car

12 The following work can be carried out with the engine in the car:

a) *Compression pressure – testing.*
b) *Cylinder head cover – removal and refitting.*
c) *Timing belt covers – removal and refitting.*
d) *Timing belt – removal, refitting and adjustment.*
e) *Timing belt tensioner and sprockets – removal and refitting.*
f) *Camshaft oil seal(s) – renewal.*
g) *Camshaft(s) and rocker arms/followers – removal, inspection and refitting.*
h) *Cylinder head – removal and refitting.*
i) *Cylinder head and pistons – decarbonising.*
j) *Sump – removal and refitting.*
k) *Oil pump – removal, overhaul and refitting.*
l) *Crankshaft oil seals – renewal.*
m) *Engine/transmission mountings – inspection and renewal.*
n) *Flywheel/driveplate – removal, inspection and refitting.*

2 Compression test – description and interpretation

1 When engine performance is down, or if misfiring occurs which cannot be attributed to the ignition or fuel systems, a compression test can provide diagnostic clues as to the engine's condition. If the test is performed regularly, it can give warning of trouble before any other symptoms become apparent.

2 The engine must be fully warmed-up to normal operating temperature, the battery must be fully-charged. The aid of an assistant will also be required.

3 Remove the ignition HT coil assembly (see Chapter 5B) then remove the spark plugs (see Chapter 1A).

4 Fit a compression tester to the No 1 cylinder spark plug hole – the type of tester which screws into the plug thread is to be preferred.

5 Have the assistant hold the throttle wide open, and crank the engine on the starter motor; after one or two revolutions, the compression pressure should build-up to a maximum figure, and then stabilise. Record the highest reading obtained.

6 Repeat the test on the remaining cylinders, recording the pressure in each.

7 All cylinders should produce very similar pressures; a difference of more than 2 bars between any two cylinders indicates a fault. Note that the compression should build-up quickly in a healthy engine; low compression on the first stroke, followed by gradually increasing pressure on successive strokes, indicates worn piston rings. A low compression reading on the first stroke, which does not build-up during successive strokes, indicates leaking valves or a blown head gasket (a cracked head could also be the cause). Deposits on the undersides of the valve heads can also cause low compression.

8 Although Peugeot do not specify exact compression pressures, as a guide, any cylinder pressure of below 10 bars can be considered as less than healthy. Refer to a Peugeot dealer or other specialist if in doubt as to whether a particular pressure reading is acceptable.

9 If the pressure in any cylinder is low, carry out the following test to isolate the cause. Introduce a teaspoonful of clean oil into that cylinder through its spark plug hole, and repeat the test.

10 If the addition of oil temporarily improves the compression pressure, this indicates that bore or piston wear is responsible for the pressure loss. No improvement suggests that leaking or burnt valves, or a blown head gasket, may be to blame.

11 A low reading from two adjacent cylinders is almost certainly due to the head gasket having blown between them; the presence of coolant in the engine oil will confirm this.

12 If one cylinder is about 20 percent lower than the others and the engine has a slightly rough idle, a worn camshaft lobe could be the cause.

13 If the compression reading is unusually high, the combustion chambers are probably

3.4 Insert a 6 mm diameter bolt/pin (arrowed) into the hole in the cylinder block flange and into the flywheel hole

3.5 Lock the camshaft sprockets in position using 5 mm and 8 mm diameter drill bits/bolts (arrowed)

coated with carbon deposits. If this is the case, the cylinder head should be removed and decarbonised.

14 On completion of the test, refit the spark plugs and ignition HT coil (see Chapters 1A and 5B).

3 Engine assembly/valve timing holes – general information and usage

Note: *Do not attempt to rotate the engine whilst the crankshaft/camshaft are locked in position. If the engine is to be left in this state for a long period of time, it is a good idea to place warning notices inside the vehicle, and in the engine compartment. This will reduce the possibility of the engine being accidentally*

cranked on the starter motor, which is likely to cause damage with the locking pins in place.

1 The timing holes are drilled in the camshaft sprockets and in the rear of the flywheel/driveplate. The holes are used to ensure that the crankshaft and camshaft(s) are correctly positioned when assembling the engine (to prevent the possibility of the valves contacting the pistons when refitting the cylinder head), or refitting the timing belt. When the timing holes are aligned with access holes in the cylinder head and the front of the cylinder block, suitable diameter bolts/pins can be inserted to lock both the camshaft and crankshaft in position, preventing them from rotating. Proceed as follows.

2 Remove the timing belt upper cover as described in Section 5.

3 The crankshaft must now be turned until

the timing holes in the camshaft sprocket is aligned with the corresponding hole in the cylinder head. The crankshaft can be turned by using a spanner on the crankshaft sprocket bolt, noting that it should always be rotated in a clockwise direction (viewed from the right-hand end of the engine).

4 With the camshaft sprocket holes correctly positioned, insert a 6 mm diameter stud or pin, 90 mm long, welded to a length of weld rod bent to the appropriate shape, through the hole in the front left-hand flange of the cylinder block (behind the oil filter cover), and locate it in the timing hole in the rear of the flywheel **(see illustration).** A purpose-made Peugeot tool No 0132-QY is available from dealers. Note that it may be necessary to rotate the crankshaft slightly to get the holes to align.

5 With the flywheel correctly positioned. Insert a 5 mm diameter bolt or a pin through the timing hole in the inlet camshaft sprocket, and locate it in the hole in the cylinder head. Insert an 8 mm diameter bolt or a pin through the timing hole in the exhaust camshaft sprocket, and locate it in the hole in the cylinder head **(see illustration).**

6 The crankshaft and camshafts are now locked in position, preventing unnecessary rotation.

4 Cylinder head covers – removal and refitting

Note: *Wait 15 minutes after the ignition is switched off, before disconnecting the battery. This is to make sure the ECU stores all the various information in its memory.*

Removal

1 Remove the plastic style covers from the top of the engine and the battery, then disconnect the battery earth lead (see Chapter 5A). Unclip the coil wiring loom retaining clip from the end of the rear cylinder head cover **(see illustration).**

2 Depress the clips and disconnect the breather hose from the rear cylinder head cover **(see illustration).**

3 Working in a spiral pattern, progressively and evenly slacken the cylinder head cover bolts starting from the outside. Remove the covers and recover the gaskets **(see illustrations).** **Note:** *It may be necessary to slacken the inlet manifold retaining bolts, and then move the inlet manifold away from the engine, to allow the removal of the rear camshaft cover.*

Refitting

4 Carefully clean the cylinder head and cover mating surfaces, and remove all traces of oil.

5 Check the condition of the cover's composite gasket, and re-use it if undamaged. If it is damaged, a repair may be effected using silicone sealing compound.

6 On the rear (inlet camshaft) cover, the oil baffle plate is part of the seal; make sure it

4.1 Unclip the wiring loom from the end of the camshaft cover

4.2 Disconnect the breather hoses from the inlet camshaft cover and manifold

4.3a Removing the exhaust camshaft cover . . .

4.3b . . . and the inlet camshaft cover

is located correctly with no damage **(see illustration)**.

7 Carefully refit the cylinder head covers to the engine, taking great care that the pegs on the covers are located correctly **(see illustration)**.

8 With the covers in place, tighten the bolts in a spiral sequence to the specified torque setting; starting from the inner bolts working outwards.

9 Reconnect the breather hose securely to the cylinder head cover and clip into place.

10 Reconnect the battery and refit the plastic engine and battery covers.

4.6 The oil baffle plate forms part of the cover seal

4.7 Make sure the locating pegs (arrowed) are lined up correctly when fitting the camshaft covers

5 Timing belt covers – removal and refitting

Upper (outer) cover removal

1 Remove the plastic cover from the top of the engine.

2 Release the securing clips and withdraw the cover upwards away from the camshaft sprockets **(see illustrations)**.

Upper (inner) cover removal

3 Remove the camshaft sprockets and tensioner pulley as described in Section 7.

4 Undo the bolts and remove the inner cover **(see illustrations)**.

Lower cover removal

5 Remove the auxiliary drivebelt as described in Chapter 1A.

6 Undo the three crankshaft pulley retaining bolts and remove the pulley, noting which way round it is fitted **(see illustration)**.

7 Slacken and remove the retaining bolts then remove the lower cover from the engine **(see illustration)**.

Refitting

8 Refitting is the reverse of removal, noting the following points.

 a) Tighten all retaining bolts to their specified torque setting, where applicable.

 b) Refit the camshaft sprockets as described in Section 7.

 c) Refit and tension the auxiliary drivebelt as described in Chapter 1A.

 d) Refit the plastic cover to the top of the engine

6 Timing belt, tensioner and idler pulleys – general information, removal and refitting

Note: *Wait 15 minutes after the ignition is switched off before disconnecting the battery. This is to make sure the ECU stores all the various information in its memory.*

General information

1 The timing belt drives the camshafts and coolant pump from a toothed sprocket on the end of the crankshaft. If the belt breaks or slips in service, the pistons are likely to hit the valve heads, resulting in extensive (and expensive) damage.

2 The timing belt should be renewed at the specified intervals (see Chapter 1A), or earlier

5.2a Release the locking clip . . .

5.2b . . . and withdraw the upper timing belt cover

5.4a Undo the bolts (arrowed) . . .

5.4b . . . and withdraw the inner cover from the cylinder head

5.6 Remove the crankshaft pulley

5.7 Unscrew the bolts and remove the timing belt lower cover

6.8 Slacken the tension on the timing belt

6.9 Remove the timing belt, noting its fitted position

6.12 Remove the tensioner from the cylinder block

if it is contaminated with oil or if it is at all noisy in operation (a 'scraping' noise due to uneven wear).

3 If the timing belt is being removed, it is a wise precaution to check the condition of the coolant pump at the same time (check for signs of coolant leakage). This may avoid the need to remove the timing belt again at a later stage, should the coolant pump fail.

Caution: It is recommended that the timing belt should always be renewed if it has been removed, along with the tensioner pulley and the idler pulley.

Removal

4 Remove the plastic engine cover and battery cover, and then disconnect the battery earth lead (see Chapter 5A).

5 Align the engine assembly/valve timing holes as described in Section 3, and lock both the camshaft sprockets and the flywheel/driveplate in position.

Caution: Do not attempt to rotate the engine whilst the locking tools are in position.

6 Remove the timing belt lower cover as described in Section 5.

7 Position a trolley jack under the engine, placing a block of wood between the jack head and the sump. Take the weight of the engine, undo the bolts/nuts and remove the

right-hand engine mounting and support bracket (see Section 15).

8 Loosen the timing belt tensioner pulley retaining nut **(see illustration)**. Turn the pulley in a clockwise direction, using an Allen key fitted to the hole in the pulley hub, and then temporarily retighten the retaining nut.

> ⚠️ *Warning: Do not turn the pulley more than three quarters of a turn.*

9 If the timing belt is to be re-used, use white paint or similar to mark the direction of rotation on the belt (if markings do not already exist). Slip the belt off the sprockets **(see illustration)**. **Note:** *Peugeot recommend that the timing belt, tensioner and idler pulley should be renewed as a complete assembly.*

10 Check the timing belt carefully for any signs of uneven wear, splitting, or oil contamination. Pay particular attention to the roots of the teeth. Renew the belt if there is the slightest doubt about its condition. If the engine is undergoing an overhaul, and has covered more than 40 000 miles with the existing belt fitted, renew the belt as a matter of course, regardless of its apparent condition. The cost of a new belt is nothing when compared to the cost of repairs should the belt break in service. If signs of oil contamination are found, trace the source of the oil leak, and rectify it.

Wash down the engine timing belt area and all related components, to remove all traces of oil.

11 Prior to refitting, thoroughly clean the timing belt sprockets. Check that the tensioner pulley rotates freely, without any sign of roughness. If necessary, renew the tensioner pulley as described in Section 7. Make sure that the locking tools are still in place, as described in Section 3.

12 Remove the tensioner pulley retaining nut and withdraw the tensioner from the cylinder block **(see illustration)**. Examine the mounting stud for signs of damage and, if necessary, renew it.

13 Remove the idler pulley retaining bolt and withdraw it from the cylinder block **(see illustration)**.

Refitting

14 Refit the new idler pulley to the cylinder block and tighten the retaining bolt to the specified torque setting.

15 Refit the new tensioner pulley; making sure the fork on the bracket is located correctly on the casting of the cylinder block. Refit the retaining nut to hold the tensioner in position **(see illustration)**.

16 Manoeuvre the timing belt into position, ensuring that the arrows on the belt are

6.13 Undo the retaining bolt and remove the idler pulley

6.15 Make sure the tensioner is located correctly on the cylinder block (arrowed)

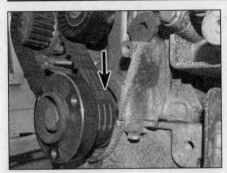

6.16a Make sure the arrows on the timing belt (arrowed) are pointing in the direction of rotation

6.16b Align the white lines on the timing belt with the marks on the camshaft sprockets (arrowed) . . .

6.16c . . . and the line on the crankshaft sprocket centre hub

pointing in the direction of rotation (clockwise, when viewed from the right-hand end of the engine). Note that there are three marks on a new belt, which correspond to marks on the crankshaft and camshaft sprockets **(see illustrations)**.

17 Do not twist the timing belt sharply while refitting it. Fit the belt over the crankshaft and camshaft sprockets aligning the marks on the belt with those on the crankshaft and camshaft sprockets. Make sure that the 'front run' of the belt is taut – ie, ensure that any slack is on the tensioner pulley side of the belt. Fit the belt over the coolant pump sprocket and tensioner pulley **(see illustration)**. Ensure that the belt teeth are seated centrally in the sprockets.

18 Remove the locking pin from the new tensioner pulley bracket **(see illustration)**

19 Insert the hexagonal key on the tensioner pulley, slacken the pulley nut and rotate the key to bring the index arm to the position just above the locking-pin hole in the tensioner bracket **(see illustration)**. When in position, tighten the tensioner retaining nut to 10 Nm (7 lbf ft).

Caution: Do not let the index arm go lower than the locking-pin hole in the tensioner bracket.

20 Remove the camshaft and crankshaft

6.17 Refit the timing belt over the tensioner pulley last

locking tools, and rotate the crankshaft 4 complete revolutions clockwise, and then refit the crankshaft locking tool.

Caution: Do not at any time rotate the crankshaft anti-clockwise.

21 Insert the hexagon key in the tensioner, slacken the nut and rotate the tensioner using the key, until the index arm is in the normal tension position **(see illustration)**. Tighten the tensioner nut to the specified torque.

22 Remove the crankshaft locking tool, and rotate the crankshaft two complete revolutions clockwise. Check the position of the tensioner

6.18 Remove the locking pin from the new tensioner

index arm – it should be no more than 2.0 mm away from the normal tension position. If it is not, repeat the belt tensioning procedure from Paragraph 19.

23 To check the settings, align the engine assembly/valve timing holes as described in Section 3, and lock both the camshaft sprockets and the flywheel/driveplate in position.

24 If everything aligns correctly, remove all locking pins and refit the timing belt covers.

25 The remainder of refitting is a reversal of removal.

6.19 Turn the Allen key until the index arm (arrowed) aligns just above the locking pin hole

6.21 Turn the Allen key until the index arm aligns in the normal position (arrowed)

7.3a Slacken the retaining bolt cover . . .

7.3b . . . and remove it from the inlet sprocket

7.4 Slacken and remove the retaining bolt . . .

7 Camshaft and crankshaft sprockets – removal, inspection and refitting

Removal

1 Remove the timing belt as described in Section 6.

2 Withdraw the crankshaft locking tool and, using a spanner or socket on the crankshaft pulley bolt, rotate the crankshaft backwards (anti-clockwise) 90°. This is to prevent any accidental contact between the pistons and valves.

Caution: Do not attempt to use the sprocket locking pin to prevent the sprocket from rotating whilst the bolt is slackened.

Inlet camshaft sprocket

3 Slacken the camshaft sprocket retaining bolt cover and remove it, along with its seal **(see illustrations)**. To prevent the camshaft rotating as the cover is slackened, a Peugeot sprocket-holding tool or similar will be required. **Note:** *There is oil inside the inlet camshaft sprocket for the VVT (variable valve timing).*

4 Slacken the camshaft sprocket retaining bolt and remove it from the sprocket **(see illustration)**. To prevent the camshaft rotating as the bolt is slackened, a Peugeot sprocket-holding tool or similar will be required.

5 With the retaining bolt removed, slide the sprocket off the end of the camshaft **(see illustration)**. Note that the key is integral with the sprocket. Examine the camshaft oil

7.5 . . . and withdraw the inlet camshaft sprocket

seal for signs of oil leakage and, if necessary, renew it as described in Section 8.

Exhaust camshaft sprocket

6 Slacken the camshaft sprocket retaining bolt and remove it from the sprocket **(see illustration)**. To prevent the camshaft rotating as the bolt is slackened, a Peugeot sprocket-holding tool or similar will be required.

7 With the retaining bolt removed, slide the sprocket off the end of the camshaft **(see illustration)**. Note that the key is integral with the sprocket. Examine the camshaft oil seals for signs of oil leakage and, if necessary, renew it as described in Section 8.

Crankshaft sprocket

8 Remove the timing belt as described in Section 6.

9 Slacken the crankshaft sprocket retaining bolt. To prevent crankshaft rotation on manual

7.6 Slacken and remove the retaining bolt . . .

transmission models, select top gear, and have an assistant apply the brakes firmly. If the engine has been removed from the vehicle or the vehicle is equipped with an automatic transmission unit, it will be necessary to lock the flywheel/driveplate.

Caution: Do not be tempted to use the flywheel/driveplate locking pin to prevent the crankshaft from rotating; temporarily remove the locking pin prior to slackening the pulley bolt, then refit it once the bolt has been slackened.

10 Unscrew the retaining bolt, then slide the sprocket off the end of the crankshaft **(see illustration)**.

11 If the Woodruff key is a loose fit in the crankshaft, remove it and store it with the sprocket for safe-keeping **(see illustration)**. Examine the crankshaft oil seal for signs oil leakage and, if necessary, renew as described in Section 13.

7.7 . . . and withdraw the exhaust camshaft sprocket

7.10 Slacken and remove the retaining bolt and withdraw the crankshaft sprocket

7.11 Make sure the woodruff key (arrowed) is secure in the crankshaft

7.15 Slot in the end of the camshaft to locate sprocket

7.17 Using drill bits (arrowed) to align the sprockets in the correct position

Inspection

12 Clean the sprockets thoroughly, and renew any that show signs of wear, damage or cracks.

13 Clean the tensioner assembly, but do not use any strong solvent, which may enter the pulley bearing. Check that the pulley rotates freely about its hub, with no sign of stiffness or of free play. Renew the tensioner pulley if there is any doubt about its condition, or if there are any obvious signs of wear or damage.

14 Inspect the timing belt (see Section 6). Renew the belt if there is any doubt about its condition.

Refitting

Camshaft sprockets

15 Refit the camshaft sprockets on the end of the camshafts aligning the locating key on the back of the sprockets with the slots in the end of the camshaft **(see illustration)**.

16 Refit the new sprocket retaining bolts. Tighten the bolts to the specified torque, whilst retaining the sprocket/camshaft with the method used on removal.

17 Re-align the timing hole in the camshaft sprockets (see Section 3) with the corresponding hole in the cylinder head, and refit the locking pins **(see illustration)**.

18 Refit the new inlet sprocket retaining bolt cover **(see illustration)**. Tighten the cover to the specified torque, whilst retaining the sprocket/camshaft with the method used on removal.

19 Rotate the crankshaft back 90° in the normal direction of rotation (clockwise), until the crankshaft locking pin can be inserted.

20 Refit the timing belt as described in Section 6.

Crankshaft sprocket

21 Check the Woodruff key is located in the crankshaft end, and then slide the crankshaft sprocket onto the end of the crankshaft.

22 Temporarily remove the locking pin from the rear of the flywheel/driveplate, and then refit the crankshaft sprocket retaining bolt. Tighten the bolt to the specified torque and angle **(see illustration)**, whilst preventing

7.18 Fit new inlet sprocket retaining bolt cover

crankshaft rotation using the method employed on removal. Refit the locking pin to the rear of the flywheel/driveplate.

23 Refit the timing belt as described in Section 6.

8 Camshaft oil seals – renewal

Note: *If a camshaft oil seal has been leaking, check the timing belt for signs of oil contamination; the belt must be renewed if signs of oil contamination are found. Ensure that all traces of oil are removed from the sprockets and surrounding area before the new belt is fitted.*

8.4a Slide the new seal complete with sleeve over the end of the camshaft . . .

7.22 Tightening the crankshaft sprocket to the specified torque and angle

1 Remove the camshaft sprocket as described in Section 7.

2 Punch or drill two small holes opposite each other in the oil seal. Screw a self-tapping screw into each, and pull on the screws with pliers to extract the seal. Alternatively, carefully prise the seal out using a flat-bladed screwdriver, taking care not to damage the seal housing.

3 Clean the seal housing, and polish off any burrs or raised edges, which may have caused the seal to fail in the first place.

4 The seal comes in packaging complete with plastic sleeve to protect the seal. Slide the protective sleeve complete with oil seal over the end of the camshaft and push into position in the housing **(see illustrations)**.

8.4b . . . and press the seal into position

5 Use a suitable tubular drift, such as a socket, which bears only on the hard outer edge of the seal and a threaded bar with nut and washer **(see illustration)**. Take care not to damage the seal lips during fitting. Note that the seal lips should face inwards.

6 With the seal in the fitted position, carefully remove the protective sleeve from the end of the camshaft **(see illustration)**.

7 Refit the camshaft sprocket as described in Section 7.

8.5 Using a socket to press the seal squarely into the end of the cylinder head

8.6 Carefully withdraw the protective sleeve from the seal

9 Camshafts, rocker arms and hydraulic lifters – removal, inspection and refitting

General information

1 The valves are operated via rockers arms between the camshaft and the top of the valves. One end of the rocker arm is clipped to the hydraulic lifter and the other end rests on top of the valve stem. The camshafts and rocker arms/hydraulic lifters can be removed without disturbing the cylinder head.

Removal

2 Remove the cylinder head covers as described in Section 4.

3 Remove the camshaft sprockets as described in Section 7.

4 Undo the bolts and remove the upper inner timing cover to the cylinder head as described in Section 5.

5 It may be necessary to slacken the inlet manifold retaining bolts, and then move the inlet manifold away from the engine to allow the removal of the rear camshaft bearing cap casting.

6 Starting from the outside, working in a spiral pattern, progressively and evenly slacken the camshaft bearing housing retaining bolts, and lift the housing from the cylinder head **(see illustration)**.

Caution: Some of the valves will be in the open position and the spring under tension; make sure the camshaft bearing housing lifts evenly.

7 Identify each camshaft for position – the intake camshaft is at the rear and the exhaust camshaft is at the front of the cylinder head **(see illustration)**. Also note the

TDC position of each camshaft for correct refitting.

8 Remove the oil seal from the timing belt end of the camshaft and lift the camshaft from the cylinder head **(see illustrations)**.

9 Obtain 16 small, clean plastic containers, and number them intake 1 to 8 and exhaust 1 to 8; alternatively, use a larger container which is divided into 16 compartments and number each compartment accordingly. Withdraw each rocker arm complete with hydraulic lifter, and place it in its respective container **(see illustrations)**. Don't interchange the followers; the wear rate will be much increased.

Inspection

Rocker arm assembly

10 Examine the rocker arm roller surfaces

9.6 Remove the camshaft bearing housing

9.7 The inlet camshaft has a rotor fitted (arrowed) for the camshaft position sensor

9.8a Remove the seal (arrowed) . . .

9.8b . . . and lift the camshaft from the cylinder head

9.9a Remove the rocker arms complete with hydraulic lifter . . .

9.9b . . . and keep them in a clean container

9.10 Check the roller surface (arrowed) on the rocker arm

9.15a Refit the rocker arm and hydraulic lifter . . .

9.15b . . . making sure the hydraulic lifter is clipped into the rocker arm securely

(see illustration), which contact the camshaft lobes for wear ridges and scoring. Renew any rocker arms on which the rollers show signs of damage. If a rocker arm roller surface is badly scored, also examine the corresponding lobe on the camshaft for wear, as both will likely be worn. Renew worn components as necessary.
11 Inspect the ends of the rocker arm for signs of wear or damage, and renew as required.

Camshafts

12 Examine the camshaft bearing surfaces and cam lobes for signs of wear ridges and scoring. Renew the camshaft if any of these conditions are apparent. Examine the condition of the bearing surfaces, both on the camshaft journals and in the cylinder head/bearing housing. If the head bearing

surfaces are worn excessively, the cylinder head will need to be renewed. If the necessary measuring equipment is available, camshaft bearing journal wear can be checked by direct measurement.
13 Examine the hydraulic lifter surfaces which contact the rocker arm for wear. Renew any follower where these conditions are apparent.

Refitting

14 Before commencing refitting, remove all traces of oil from the bearing housing retaining bolts holes in the cylinder head, using a clean rag. Also ensure that both the cylinder head and bearing housing mating faces are clean and free from oil.
15 Liberally oil the hydraulic lifters and carefully refit the lifters to the cylinder head,

ensuring that each lifter is refitted to its original bore. Make sure the rocker arms are clipped to the hydraulic lifter securely (see illustrations).
16 Liberally oil the camshaft bearings in the cylinder head and the camshaft lobes, and then refit the camshafts to the cylinder head in the previously-noted positions (see illustrations).
17 Apply a bead of silicone-based jointing compound around the perimeter of the mating faces (see illustration).
18 Refit the bearing housing, and tighten the bolts progressively, in sequence, to the specified torque (see illustrations).
19 Fit new camshaft oil seals with reference to Section 8.
20 Refit the upper inner timing cover as described in Section 5.

9.16a Oil the camshaft bearing in the cylinder head . . .

9.16b . . . and refit the camshaft

9.17 Apply a bead of sealant around the upper camshaft bearing housing

9.18a Lower the upper camshaft bearing housing into position . . .

9.18b . . . and tighten in the sequence shown

21 Refit the camshaft sprockets as described in Section 7.

22 Refit the cylinder head covers as described in Section 4.

23 Where applicable, refit the inlet manifold.

10 Cylinder head – removal and refitting

Note: *Ensure the engine is cold before removing the cylinder head.*

Removal

1 Disconnect the battery (see Chapter 5A).

2 Drain the cooling system as described in Chapter 1A.

3 Remove the ignition HT coil assembly (see Chapter 5B) then remove the spark plugs (see Chapter 1A).

4 Remove the camshafts, rocker arms and hydraulic lifters as described in Section 9.

5 Align the engine assembly/valve timing holes as described in Section 3, and lock both the camshaft sprocket(s) and flywheel/driveplate in position.

Caution: Do not attempt to rotate the engine whilst the tools are in position.

6 Note that the following text assumes that the cylinder head will be removed with both intake and exhaust manifolds attached; this is easier, but makes it a bulky and heavy assembly to handle. If it is wished to remove the manifolds first, proceed as described in Chapter 4A.

7 Carry out the following operations as described in Chapter 4A:

a) *Disconnect the exhaust system front pipe/catalytic converter from the manifold. Disconnect or release the oxygen sensor wiring.*

b) *Remove the air cleaner housing and intake duct assembly.*

c) *Disconnect the fuel feed and return hoses from the fuel rail (plug all openings, to prevent loss of fuel and entry of dirt into the fuel system).*

d) *Note their fitted positions, then disconnect the relevant electrical connectors and vacuum/breather hoses from the intake manifold.*

e) *Where necessary unbolt the support bracket from the intake manifold.*

8 If not already removed, undo the retaining bolts and remove the timing belt upper inner cover (see Section 5).

9 Undo the mounting bolt and remove the upper section of the oil dipstick guide tube.

10 Note their fitted positions, then slacken the retaining clips, and disconnect the coolant hoses from the cylinder head. Likewise, note the routing, and then disconnect all electrical connectors from the cylinder head.

11 Working in the *reverse* of the tightening sequence **(see illustration 11.28)**, progressively slacken the cylinder head bolts by half a turn at a time, until all bolts can be unscrewed by hand.

12 The joint between the cylinder head and gasket, and the cylinder block/crankcase must now be broken without disturbing the wet liners. To break the joint, obtain two stout screwdrivers, which fit into the cylinder head bolt holes. Gently 'rock' the cylinder head free towards the front of the car. Do not try to swivel the head on the cylinder block/crankcase; it is located by dowels, as well as by the tops of the liners. **Note:** *If care is not taken and the liners are moved, there is also a possibility of the bottom seals being disturbed, causing leakage after refitting the head.*

13 When the joint is broken, lift the cylinder head away; seek assistance if possible, as it is a heavy assembly, especially if it is being removed complete with the manifolds.

14 Remove the gasket from the top of the block, noting the two locating dowels. If the locating dowels are a loose fit, remove them and store them with the head for safe-keeping. Do not discard the gasket – it will be needed for identification purposes (see paragraphs 19 and 20). Operations that require the rotation of the crankshaft (eg, cleaning the piston crowns) should only be carried out once the cylinder liners are firmly clamped in position **(see illustration)**. In the absence of the special Peugeot liner clamps, the liners can be clamped in position using large flat washers positioned underneath suitable-length bolts. Alternatively, the original head bolts could be temporarily refitted, with suitable spacers fitted to their shanks.

Caution: Do not attempt to rotate the crankshaft with the cylinder head removed, otherwise the wet liners may be displaced.

15 If the cylinder head is to be dismantled for overhaul, remove the camshaft as described in Section 9, then refer to Part E of this Chapter.

Preparation for refitting

16 The mating faces of the cylinder head and cylinder block/crankcase must be perfectly clean before refitting the head. Use a hard plastic or wood scraper to remove all traces of gasket and carbon; also clean the piston crowns. **Note:** *Clamp the liners in position before turning the crankshaft (see paragraph 14).* Take particular care during the cleaning operations, as aluminium alloy is easily damaged. Also, make sure that the carbon is not allowed to enter the oil and water passages – this is particularly important for the lubrication system, as carbon could block the oil supply to the engine's components. Using adhesive tape and paper, seal the water, oil and bolt holes in the cylinder block/crankcase. To prevent carbon entering the gap between the pistons and bores, smear a little grease in the gap. After cleaning each piston, use a small brush to remove all traces of grease and carbon from the gap, and then wipe away the remainder with a clean rag. Clean all the pistons in the same way.

17 Check the mating surfaces of the cylinder block/crankcase and the cylinder head for nicks, deep scratches and other damage. If slight, they may be removed carefully with a file, but if excessive, machining may be the only alternative to renewal.

18 If warpage of the cylinder head gasket surface is suspected, use a straight-edge to check it for distortion. Refer to Part E of this Chapter if necessary.

19 When purchasing a new cylinder head gasket, it is essential that a gasket of the correct thickness be obtained. On some models only one thickness of gasket is available, so this is not a problem. On other models, there are two different thicknesses available – the standard gasket, and a slightly thicker 'repair' gasket (+ 0.2 mm). The gaskets can be identified as described in the following paragraph, using the cut-outs on the left-hand end of the gasket.

20 With the gasket fitted the correct way up on the cylinder block, there will be a single or double cut-out at the rear of the left-hand side of the gasket identifying the engine type (eg, ET3JP engine). In the centre of the gasket there will likely be another series of between 0 and 4 cut-outs, identifying the manufacturer of the gasket and whether or not it contains asbestos (these cut-outs are of little importance). The important cut-out location is at the front of the gasket; on the standard gasket there will be no cut-out in this position, whereas on the thicker 'repair' gasket there will be a single cut-out **(see illustrations)**. Identify the gasket type,

10.14 Clamp (arrowed) the cylinder liners in position before rotating the crankshaft

H44751

10.20a Cylinder head gasket identification markings

A *Engine type identification cut-out locations*
B *Gasket manufacturer identification cut-out locations*
C *Gasket thickness identification cut-out locations*

10.20b Cylinder head gasket identification markings viewed with gasket still in place

H44749

10.21 Measure the bolt length from the underside of the bolt head to the end of the bolt

and ensure that the new gasket obtained is of the correct thickness. If there is any doubt as to which gasket is fitted, take the old gasket along to your Peugeot dealer, and have him confirm the gasket type.

21 Check the condition of the cylinder head bolts, and particularly their threads, whenever they are removed. Wash the bolts in suitable solvent, and wipe them dry. Check each for any sign of visible wear or damage, renewing any bolt if necessary. Measure the length of each bolt, from the underside of its head to the bolt end, to check for stretching **(see illustration)**. The bolts when measured from under the head of the bolt to the end of the bolt must be less than 119.0 mm; renew all the cylinder head bolts as a set. Peugeot recommend that the bolts should only be re-used twice, regardless of this measurement.

22 Prior to refitting the cylinder head, check the cylinder liner protrusion as described in Chapter 2E.

Refitting

23 Wipe clean the mating surfaces of the cylinder head and cylinder block/crankcase. Check that the two locating dowels are in position at each end of the cylinder block/crankcase surface and, if necessary, remove the cylinder liner clamps **(see illustration)**.

24 Position a new gasket on the cylinder block/crankcase surface, ensuring that its identification cut-outs are at the left-hand end of the gasket, and the side marked TOP is uppermost.

25 Check that the flywheel/driveplate and camshaft sprocket(s) are still correctly locked in position with their respective tools then,

with the aid of an assistant, carefully refit the cylinder head assembly to the block, aligning it with the locating dowels.

26 Lubricate the threads and underside of the heads of the cylinder head bolts lightly with clean engine oil.

27 Carefully enter each bolt into its relevant hole (do not drop them in) and screw in, by hand only, until finger-tight.

28 Working progressively and in sequence, tighten the cylinder head bolts to their Stage 1 torque setting, using a torque wrench and suitable socket **(see illustration)**.

29 Tighten the bolts further to their Stage 2 setting in the same sequence.

30 Once all the bolts have been tightened to their Stage 2 setting, working again in the given sequence, angle-tighten the bolts through the specified Stage 3 angle, using a socket and extension bar. It is recommended that an angle-measuring gauge is used during this stage of the tightening, to ensure accuracy. If a gauge is not available, use white paint to make alignment marks between the bolt head and cylinder head prior to tightening; the marks can then be used to check that the bolt has been rotated through the correct angle during tightening.

31 Refit the timing belt upper inner cover as described in Section 5.

32 Reconnect the all wiring plugs to the cylinder head and manifold.

33 Working as described in the Chapter 4A, carry out the following tasks:

a) Refit all disturbed wiring, hoses and control cable(s) to the intake manifold and fuel system components.

b) Reconnect and adjust the accelerator cable (where fitted).

c) Reconnect the exhaust system front pipe to the manifold and reconnect the oxygen sensor wiring connector.

d) Refit the air cleaner and intake duct.

34 Refit the cylinder head cover(s) as described in Section 4.

35 Refit the spark plugs and install the ignition HT coil (see Chapters 1A and 5B).

36 On completion, reconnect the battery (Chapter 5A), and refill the cooling system as described in Chapter 1A.

11 Sump – removal and refitting

Removal

1 Firmly apply the handbrake, and then jack up the front of the vehicle and support it on axle stands (see Jacking and vehicle support). Remove the right-hand front wheel and inner wheel arch liner, where applicable remove the engine undershield.

2 Drain the engine oil, then clean and refit the engine oil drain plug, tightening it to the specified torque. If the engine is nearing the service interval when the oil and filter are due for renewal, it is recommended that the filter is also removed, and a new one fitted. After reassembly, the engine can then be refilled with fresh oil. Refer to Chapter 1A for further information.

3 Remove the exhaust system front pipe as described in Chapter 4A.

4 Undo the retaining bolts and remove the rear lower mounting link bracket **(see illustration)**, see Section 15 for further information.

10.23 Ensure the locating dowels (arrowed) are in position then fit the new head gasket

H44707

10.28 Cylinder head bolt tightening sequence

11.4 Remove the lower mounting bracket (arrowed)

11.5 Unbolt the wiring loom carrier (arrowed) from the end of the sump

11.9 Apply a bead of sealant around the mating surface of the sump

11.10 Offer the sump into position on the two locating studs (arrowed)

5 Progressively slacken and remove all the sump nuts and bolts/nuts and position the wiring harness guide clear of the sump **(see illustration)**.
6 Break the joint by striking the sump with the palm of your hand, then lower and withdraw the sump from under the car.
7 While the sump is removed, take the opportunity to check the oil pump pick-up/strainer for signs of clogging or splitting. If necessary, remove the pump as described in Section 12, and clean or renew the strainer.

Refitting

8 Clean all traces of sealant from the mating surfaces of the cylinder block/crankcase and sump, and then use a clean rag to wipe out the sump and the engine's interior.
9 Ensure that the sump and cylinder block/crankcase mating surfaces are clean and dry then apply a coating of suitable sealant to the sump mating surface **(see illustration)**.
10 Offer up the sump and locate it on its studs **(see illustration)**. Locate the wiring harness guide back in position then refit the sump retaining nuts and bolts. Tighten the nuts and bolts evenly and progressively to the specified torque.
11 Refit the exhaust front pipe as described in Chapter 4A.
12 Refit the rear lower mounting link bracket with reference to Section 15.
13 Replenish the engine oil and change the oil filter if required (see Chapter 1A).

14 Refit the inner wheel arch liner and front right-hand road wheel.
15 Where applicable refit the engine under shield, then lower the vehicle to the ground and tighten the wheel bolts to their specified torque settings.

12 Oil pump – removal, inspection and refitting

Removal

1 Remove the sump as described in Section 11.
2 Slacken and remove the three bolts securing the oil pump in position **(see illustration)**. Disengage the pump sprocket from the chain, and remove the oil pump. If the oil pump locating dowel is a loose fit, remove and store it with the bolts for safe-keeping.

Inspection

3 Examine the oil pump sprocket for signs of damage and wear, such as chipped or missing teeth. If the sprocket is worn, the pump assembly must be renewed, as the sprocket is not available separately. It is also recommended that the chain and drive sprocket, fitted to the crankshaft, are renewed at the same time. Renewal of the chain and drive sprocket is an involved operation requiring the removal of the main bearing

ladder, and therefore cannot be carried out with the engine still fitted to the vehicle.
4 Slacken and remove the bolts securing the strainer cover to the pump body, and then lift off the strainer cover. Remove the relief valve piston and spring, noting which way round they are fitted **(see illustration)**.
5 Examine the pump rotors and body for signs of wear ridges and scoring. If worn, the complete pump assembly must be renewed.
6 Examine the relief valve piston for signs of wear or damage, and renew if necessary. The condition of the relief valve spring can only be measured by comparing it with a new one; if there is any doubt about its condition, it should also be renewed. Both the piston and spring are available individually.
7 Thoroughly clean the oil pump strainer with a suitable solvent, and check it for signs of clogging or splitting. If the strainer is damaged, the strainer and cover assembly must be renewed.
8 Locate the relief valve spring and piston in the pump body and refit the strainer cover to the pump body. Refit the cover retaining bolts, tightening them securely.

Refitting

9 Ensure that the locating dowel is in position **(see illustration)**, and then engage the pump sprocket with its drive chain. Locate the pump on its dowel, and refit the pump retaining bolts, tightening them to the specified torque setting.
10 Refit the sump as described in Section 11.

12.2 Unscrew the three bolts securing the oil pump in position

12.4 Note the position of the relief valve spring when pump is parted

12.9 Make sure the pump is located correctly on the dowel (arrowed)

13.2 Using a screw and pliers to remove the crankshaft right-hand oil seal

13.4a Slide the new seal complete with sleeve over the end of the crankshaft . . .

13.4b . . . and press the seal into position

13 Crankshaft oil seals – renewal

Right-hand oil seal

1 Remove the crankshaft sprocket as described in Section 7.

2 Make a note of the correct fitted depth of the seal in its housing then carefully punch or drill a hole in the seal. Screw a self-tapping screw into the hole, and pull on the screw with a pair of pliers to extract the seal **(see illustration)**. Alternatively, the seal can be levered out of position using a suitable flat-bladed screwdriver, taking great care not to damage the crankshaft/oil pump drive gear shoulder or seal housing

3 Clean the seal housing, and polish off any burrs or raised edges, which may have caused the seal to fail in the first place.

4 The seal comes in packaging complete with plastic sleeve to protect the seal. Slide the protective sleeve complete with oil seal over the end of the crankshaft and push into position in the housing **(see illustrations)**.

5 Use a suitable tubular drift, such as a socket, which bears only on the hard outer edge of the seal and a threaded bar with nut and washer **(see illustration)**. Take care not to damage the seal lips during fitting. Note that the seal lips should face inwards.

6 With the seal in the fitted position, carefully remove the protective sleeve from the end of the crankshaft.

7 Wash off any traces of oil, then refit the crankshaft sprocket as described in Section 7.

Left-hand oil seal

7 Remove the flywheel/driveplate as described in Section 14.

8 Make a note of the correct fitted depth of the seal in its housing. Punch or drill two small holes opposite each other in the seal. Screw a self-tapping screw into each, and pull on the screws with pliers to extract the seal **(see illustration 13.2)**.

9 Clean the seal housing, and polish off any burrs or raised edges, which may have caused the seal to fail in the first place.

10 Lubricate the lips of the new seal with clean engine oil, and carefully locate the seal on the end of the crankshaft.

11 Using a suitable tubular drift, which bears only on the hard outer edge of the seal, drive the seal into position, to the same depth in the housing as the original was prior to removal.

12 Wash off any traces of oil, then refit the flywheel/driveplate as described in Section 14.

14 Flywheel/driveplate – removal, inspection and refitting

Flywheel

Removal

1 Remove the transmission as described in Chapter 7A, then remove the clutch assembly as described in Chapter 6.

2 Prevent the flywheel from turning by locking the ring gear teeth **(see illustration)**. Alternatively, bolt a strap between the flywheel and the cylinder block/crankcase.

Caution: Do not attempt to lock the flywheel in position using the locking pin described in Section 3.

3 Slacken and remove the flywheel retaining bolts.

4 Remove the flywheel. Do not drop it, as it is very heavy. If the locating dowel is a loose fit

in the crankshaft end, remove and store it with the flywheel for safe-keeping.

Inspection

5 If the flywheel's clutch mating surface is deeply scored, cracked or otherwise damaged, the flywheel must be renewed. However, it may be possible to have it surface-ground; seek the advice of a Peugeot dealer or engine reconditioning specialist.

6 If the ring gear is badly worn or has missing teeth, it must be renewed. This job is best left to a Peugeot dealer or engine reconditioning specialist. The temperature to which the new ring gear must be heated for installation is critical and, if not done accurately, the hardness of the teeth will be destroyed.

Refitting

7 Clean the mating surfaces of the flywheel and crankshaft.

8 If the new flywheel retaining bolts are not supplied with their threads already precoated, apply a suitable thread-locking compound to the threads of each bolt.

9 Ensure that the locating dowel is in position. Offer up the flywheel, locating it on the dowel, and fit the retaining bolts.

10 Lock the flywheel using the method employed on dismantling, and tighten the retaining bolts evenly and progressively to the specified torque.

11 Refit the clutch as described in Chapter 6. Remove the locking tool, and refit the transmission as described in Chapter 7A.

13.5 Using a socket to press the seal squarely into the housing

14.2 Use a tool to lock the flywheel ring gear and prevent rotation

Driveplate

Removal

12 Remove the transmission as described in Chapter 7B.

13 Prevent the driveplate from turning by locking the ring gear teeth with a similar arrangement to that for the flywheel (see illustration 14.2). Alternatively, bolt a strap between the driveplate and the cylinder block/crankcase.

Caution: Do not attempt to lock the driveplate in position using the locking pin described in Section 3.

14 Slacken and remove the driveplate retaining bolts and remove the outer spacer plate and torque converter mounting plate.

15 Remove the driveplate and inner spacer plate from the end of the crankshaft. If the locating dowel is a loose fit in the crankshaft end, remove and store it with the driveplate for safe-keeping. **Note:** *The inner and outer spacer plates are different and are not interchangeable.*

Inspection

16 Inspect the driveplate and torque converter mounting plate for signs of wear or damage. If damage is found, the worn component must be renewed (it is not possible to renew the driveplate ring gear separately).

Refitting

17 Ensure all mating surfaces are clean and dry.

18 Remove any traces of locking compound from the threads of the driveplate bolts and apply a small amount of fresh locking compound (Peugeot recommend Loctite Frenbloc) to the bolt threads.

19 Ensure that the locating dowel is in position then refit the inner spacer plate, driveplate, torque converter mounting plate and outer spacer plate. Ensure all components are correctly located on the dowel then fit the retaining bolts.

20 Lock the driveplate using the method employed on dismantling, and tighten the retaining bolts evenly and progressively to the specified torque.

21 Refit the transmission as described in Chapter 7B.

15 Engine/transmission mountings – inspection and renewal

Inspection

1 If improved access is required, raise the front of the car and support it on axle stands (see *Jacking and vehicle support*).

2 Check the mounting rubber to see if it is cracked, hardened or separated from the metal at any point; renew the mounting if any such damage or deterioration is evident.

3 Check that all the mounting's fasteners are securely tightened; use a torque wrench to check if possible.

4 Using a large screwdriver or a crowbar, check for wear in the mounting by carefully levering against it to check for free play. Where this is not possible, enlist the aid of an assistant to move the engine/transmission back-and-forth, or from side-to-side, while you watch the mounting. While some free play is to be expected even from new components, excessive wear should be obvious. If excessive free play is found, check first that the fasteners are secure, and then renew any worn components as described below.

Renewal

Right-hand mounting

5 Place a jack beneath the engine, with a block of wood on the jack head. Raise the jack until it is supporting the weight of the engine.

6 Unclip the upper timing belt cover with reference to Section 5.

7 Undo the retaining nut and withdraw the ECU from the top of the right-hand inner wing panel and move it to one side (see illustration).

8 Unclip the wiring loom from the top of the engine-mounting bracket (see illustration).

9 Undo the two retaining bolts and remove the bracket from across the top of the engine mounting (see illustration)

10 Slacken and remove the nut securing the mounting bracket to the rubber engine mounting, and the mounting bracket to the bracket bolted to the cylinder block (see illustration).

11 Withdraw the mounting bracket from the engine bay (see illustration)

12 If required, undo the bolts and remove the lower bracket from the cylinder head (see illustration).

15.7 Move the ECU to one side

15.8 Unclip the wiring loom from the top of the mounting bracket

15.9 Slacken and remove the two bracket bolts (arrowed)

15.10 Remove the bolts (arrowed) . . .

15.11 . . . and remove the upper engine mounting bracket

15.12 Removing the lower engine mounting bracket

15.13a Remove the shield from the mounting . . .

15.13b . . . and check the condition of the rubber mountings

15.21 Remove the bolts and nut (arrowed)

15.28 Slacken and remove the mounting centre bolt arrowed) . . .

29.29 . . . and the lower mounting bracket bolt and nuts (arrowed)

15.31 Mounting bracket-to-cylinder block retaining bolts (arrowed)

13 Remove the shield from the mounting and check the condition of the rubber engine mounting (see illustrations)

14 Check for signs of wear or damage on all components, and renew as necessary.

15 On reassembly, refit the lower bracket to the cylinder block, tightening the bolts/nuts to the specified torque.

16 Install the upper mounting bracket and tighten its retaining bolts and nut to the specified torque setting.

17 Refit the ECU to the inner wing panel and refit the upper timing belt cover, making sure all wiring and cables are secured in the securing clips.

18 Remove the jack from under the engine.

Left-hand mounting

19 Remove the battery, and battery tray/box as described in Chapter 5A.

20 Place a jack beneath the transmission, with a block of wood on the jack head. Raise the jack until it is supporting the weight of the transmission.

21 Slacken and remove the mounting rubber's centre nut and two retaining bolts and remove the mounting from the engine compartment (see illustration).

22 If necessary, undo the retaining bolts and remove the mounting bracket from the body.

23 Check carefully for signs of wear or damage on all components, and renew them where necessary.

24 Refit the mounting bracket to the vehicle body and tighten its bolts to the specified torque.

25 Fit the mounting rubber to the bracket and tighten its retaining bolts to the specified torque. Refit the mounting centre nut, and tighten it to the specified torque.

26 Remove the jack from underneath the transmission, then refit the battery as described in Chapter 5A.

Rear mounting

27 If not already done, firmly apply the handbrake, then jack up the front of the vehicle and support it securely on axle stands (see Jacking and vehicle support).

28 Unscrew and remove the bolt securing the rear mounting link to the mounting on the rear of the cylinder block (see illustration).

29 Remove the bolt and nuts securing the bracket from the sump to the mounting bracket (see illustration).

30 To remove the mounting assembly it will first be necessary to remove the right-hand driveshaft as described in Chapter 8.

31 With the driveshaft removed, undo the retaining bolts and remove the mounting from the rear of the cylinder block (see illustration).

32 Check carefully for signs of wear or damage on all components, and renew them where necessary.

33 On reassembly, fit the rear mounting assembly to the rear of the cylinder block, and tighten its retaining bolts to the specified torque. Refit the driveshaft as described in Chapter 8.

34 Refit the bolt securing the rear mounting link to the mounting on the rear of the cylinder block.

35 Refit the rear mounting lower bracket, and tighten both its bolts to their specified torque settings.

36 Lower the vehicle to the ground.

Chapter 2 Part C:
2.0 litre DOHC petrol engine in-car repair procedures

Contents

Degrees of difficulty

Easy, suitable for novice with little experience	**Fairly easy,** suitable for beginner with some experience	**Fairly difficult,** suitable for competent DIY mechanic	**Difficult,** suitable for experienced DIY mechanic	**Very difficult,** suitable for expert DIY or professional

Specifications

Engine (general)

Type	2.0 litre (1997cc) DOHC 16V
Designation	EW10J4
Engine code*	RFN
Bore	85.00 mm
Stroke	88.00 mm
Direction of crankshaft rotation	Clockwise (viewed from the right-hand side of vehicle)
No 1 cylinder location......................	At the transmission end of the engine
Compression ratio	10.8 : 1
Maximum power output......................	100 kW @ 6000 rpm
Maximum torque output.....................	190 Nm @ 4100 rpm

* The engine code is stamped on a plate attached to the front right-hand end of the cylinder block, below the right-hand branch of the exhaust manifold. The code is the first 3-digits on the first line, and this is the code most often used by Peugeot.

Camshafts

Drive......................................	Toothed belt
No of bearings	5

Lubrication system

Oil pump type..............................	Crescent-type driven directly from crankshaft
Minimum oil pressure at 80°C:	
1000 rpm	1.5 bars
3000 rpm	5.0 bars
Oil pressure warning switch operating pressure	0.5 bars

Torque wrench settings

	Nm	lbf ft
Big-end bearing bolts*:		
Stage 1	10	7
Stage 2	Slacken each bolt 180°	
Stage 3	25	18
Stage 4	Angle-tighten a further 46° ± 5°	
Camshaft bearing housings:		
Stage 1	5	4
Stage 2	10	7
Camshaft sprocket/hub-to-camshaft retaining bolts	75	55
Crankshaft pulley retaining bolt	21	15
Crankshaft sprocket centre bolt (with gold washer):		
Stage 1	40	30
Stage 2	Angle-tighten a further 53°	
Crankshaft sprocket centre bolt (with metallic washer):		
Stage 1	40	30
Stage 2	Angle-tighten a further 40°	
Cylinder head bolts:		
Stage 1	15	11
Stage 2	50	37
Stage 3	Slacken fully	
Stage 4	20	15
Stage 5	Angle-tighten a further 285° (maximum of two steps)	
Cylinder head cover bolts	11	8
Engine-to-transmission fixing bolts	45	33
Flywheel/driveplate retaining bolts*:		
Stage 1	25	18
Stage 2	Slacken fully	
Stage 3	20	15
Stage 4	Angle-tighten a further 22°	
Left-hand engine/transmission mounting:		
Mounting bracket-to-body bolts	22	16
Mounting stud to transmission bracket	50	37
Rubber mounting centre nut.	65	48
Rubber mounting-to-bracket nuts	30	22
Main bearing cap housing:		
Stage 1 – 11.0 mm diameter bolts	10	7
Stage 2 – 6.0 mm diameter bolts	5	4
Stage 3 – 11.0 mm diameter bolts	Slacken fully	
Stage 4 – 11.0 mm diameter bolts	20	15
Stage 5 – 11.0 mm diameter bolts	Angle-tighten a further 70° ± 5°	
Stage 6 – 6.0 mm diameter bolts	10	7
Oil pressure switch.	30	22
Oil pump-to-engine bolts	9	7
Rear engine/transmission mounting:		
Connecting link-to-mounting bracket bolt	40	30
Connecting link-to-subframe bolt	55	41
Mounting bracket-to-cylinder block bolts	45	33
Right-hand engine/transmission mounting:		
Mounting bracket to support bracket.	60	44
Rubber mounting to body	60	44
Support bracket to engine	45	33
Roadwheels	90	66
Sump retaining bolts	8	6
Sump baffle plate bolts	20	15
Sump drain plug.	30	22
Timing belt tensioner pulley bolt	21	15
Timing belt idler pulley bolt:		
Stage 1	15	11
Stage 2	37	27

* Do not re-use

1 General information

How to use this Chapter

This Part of Chapter 2 describes those repair procedures that can reasonably be carried out on the engine, while it remains in the car. If the engine has been removed from the car and is being dismantled as described in Part E, any preliminary dismantling procedures can be ignored.

Note that, while it may be possible physically to overhaul items such as the piston/connecting rod assemblies while the engine is in the car, such tasks are not usually carried out as separate operations. Usually, several additional procedures (not to mention the cleaning of components and oilways) have to be carried out. For this reason, all such tasks are classed as major overhaul procedures, and are described in Part E of this Chapter.

Part E describes the removal of the engine/transmission unit from the vehicle, and the full overhaul procedures that can then be carried out.

EW series engine

The engine is of in-line four-cylinder, double-overhead camshaft, 16-valve type, mounted transversely at the front of the car. The clutch and transmission are attached to its left-hand end.

The engine is of conventional 'dry-liner' type, and the cylinder block is cast in aluminium.

The crankshaft runs in five main bearings. Thrustwashers are fitted to No 2 main bearing cap, to control crankshaft endfloat.

The connecting rods rotate on horizontally-split bearing shells at their big-ends. The pistons are attached to the connecting rods by gudgeon pins. The gudgeon pins are an interference fit in the connecting rod small-end eyes. The aluminium alloy pistons are fitted with three piston rings – two compression rings and an oil control ring.

The camshafts are driven by a toothed timing belt, and operate sixteen valves by followers located beneath each cam lobe. The valve clearances are self-adjusting by means of hydraulic tappets fitted to the cam followers. The camshaft runs in bearing cap housings, which are bolted to the top of the cylinder head. The inlet and exhaust valves are each closed by coil springs, and operate in guides pressed into the cylinder head. Both the valve seats and guides can be renewed separately if worn.

The coolant pump is driven by the timing belt and located in the right-hand end of the cylinder block.

Lubrication is by means of an oil pump driven off the crankshaft right-hand end. It draws oil through a strainer located in the sump, and then forces it through an externally-mounted filter into galleries in the cylinder block/crankcase. From there, the oil is distributed to the crankshaft (main bearings) and camshaft. The big-end bearings are supplied with oil via internal drillings in the crankshaft; the camshaft bearings also receive a pressurised supply. The camshaft lobes and valves are lubricated by splash, as are all other engine components.

Throughout the manual, it is often necessary to identify the engines not only by their cubic capacity, but also by their engine code. The engine code consists of three digits (eg, RFN). The code is stamped on a plate attached to the front, left-hand end of the cylinder block, or stamped directly onto the front face of the cylinder block, on the machined surface located just to the left of the oil filter (next to the crankcase vent hose union).

Operations with engine in car

The following work can be carried out with the engine in the car:

a) Compression pressure – testing.
b) Cylinder head covers – removal and refitting.
c) Crankshaft pulley – removal and refitting.
d) Timing belt covers – removal and refitting.
e) Timing belt – removal, refitting and adjustment.
f) Timing belt tensioner and sprockets – removal and refitting.
g) Camshaft oil seals – renewal.
h) Camshafts and followers – removal, inspection and refitting.
i) Cylinder head – removal and refitting.
j) Cylinder head and pistons – decarbonising.
k) Sump – removal and refitting.
l) Oil pump – removal, overhaul and refitting.
m) Crankshaft oil seals – renewal.
n) Engine/transmission mountings – inspection and renewal.
o) Flywheel/driveplate – removal, inspection and refitting.

2 Compression test – description and interpretation

Refer to Chapter 2A, Section 2.

3 Engine assembly/valve timing holes – general information and usage

Note: *Do not attempt to rotate the engine whilst the crankshaft/camshaft are locked in position. If the engine is to be left in this state for a long period of time, it is a good idea to place suitable warning notices inside the vehicle, and in the engine compartment. This will reduce the possibility of the engine being accidentally cranked on the starter motor, which is likely to cause damage with the locking pins in place.*

1 Timing holes are drilled in the crankshaft sprocket endplate and in the two camshaft sprockets. The holes are used to ensure that the crankshaft and camshafts are correctly positioned when assembling the engine (to prevent the possibility of the valves contacting the pistons when refitting the cylinder head), or refitting the timing belt. When the timing holes are aligned with corresponding holes in the cylinder head and oil pump housing, suitable diameter pins or bolts can be inserted to lock both the camshafts and crankshaft in position, preventing them from rotating. To set the engine in the timing position, proceed as follows.

2 Remove the crankshaft pulley as described in Section 5.

3 Remove the timing belt upper (outer) and lower covers as described in Section 6.

4 Using a socket and extension bar fitted to the crankshaft sprocket centre bolt, turn the crankshaft in the normal direction of rotation (clockwise) until the timing holes in both camshaft sprockets are aligned with their corresponding holes in the cylinder head. The holes are aligned when the inlet camshaft sprocket hole is in approximately the 5 o'clock position and the exhaust camshaft sprocket hole is in approximately the 7 o'clock position, when viewed from the right-hand end of the engine. Use a small mirror to accurately observe the position of the holes.

5 With the camshaft sprocket holes correctly positioned, insert an 8.0 mm diameter drill bit or bolt through the timing hole in the crankshaft sprocket endplate, and locate it in the corresponding hole in the oil pump housing (see illustration). **Note:** *It may be found that an 8.0 mm drill is too large, in which case a 5/16 in drill may be required.*

6 The camshaft sprockets can now be locked in position using the Peugeot camshaft setting rods, or suitable homemade alternatives (see **Tool Tip overleaf**). With the crankshaft locked in position, insert the Peugeot special tools, or alternatives, through the timing hole in each camshaft sprocket and locate it in the

3.5 Insert an 8.0 mm drill bit or bolt through the hole in the crankshaft sprocket endplate, and into the corresponding hole in the oil pump housing

Camshaft sprocket locking tools can be made from 10.0 mm diameter steel bar, fabricated to the dimensions shown.

3.6 Camshaft sprocket locking tools (arrowed) inserted through the timing hole in each sprocket

corresponding hole in the cylinder head (see illustration).

7 The crankshaft and camshafts are now locked in position, preventing rotation. In this position the crankshaft is at 90° BTDC and all the pistons are positioned halfway down their cylinder bores.

4 Cylinder head covers – removal and refitting

Removal

1 Undo the six screws and remove the plastic cover from the top of the engine. Remove the crankcase ventilation hose and camshaft position sensor from the rear cylinder head cover (see illustrations).

2 Progressively unscrew the bolts securing the cylinder head covers to the cylinder head. The bolts must be unscrewed in a spiral sequence starting from the outside.

3 Remove the cylinder head covers and gaskets (see illustrations). Unless they are obviously damaged, do not attempt to remove the rubber gaskets from the covers.

Refitting

4 Thoroughly clean the surfaces of the covers and cylinder head.

4.1a Disconnect the crankcase breather hose from the rear cylinder head cover

4.1b Disconnect the camshaft position sensor wiring connector . . .

4.1c . . . then undo the bolt and remove the sensor from the rear cylinder head cover

4.3a Undo the retaining bolts and lift off the front . . .

4.3b . . . and rear cylinder head covers

4.5 Locate the cylinder head cover seal in the groove, ensuring it is fully seated along its entire length

4.6 Cylinder head cover bolt tightening sequence

5.3a Undo the four crankshaft pulley retaining bolts . . .

5.3b . . . and remove the pulley from the crankshaft endplate

5 If necessary, fit new seals and locate the covers on the head (see illustration). Insert the retaining bolts and finger-tighten them.

6 Progressively tighten the bolts in sequence (see illustration).

7 Check the condition of the O-ring seal on the camshaft position sensor and renew the seal if it is in any way suspect.

8 Refit the camshaft position sensor and secure with the retaining bolt. Reconnect the sensor wiring connector.

9 Reconnect the breather hose to the rear cover.

10 The remainder of refitting is a reversal of removal.

5 Crankshaft pulley – removal and refitting

Removal

1 Remove the auxiliary drivebelt (Chapter 1A).

2 To prevent the crankshaft turning whilst the pulley retaining bolt is being slackened on manual transmission models, select 5th gear and have an assistant apply the brakes firmly. On automatic transmission models it will be necessary to remove the starter motor (Chapter 5A) and lock the driveplate with a suitable tool. If the engine has been removed from the vehicle, lock the flywheel ring gear as described in Section 8. *Do not* attempt to lock the pulley by inserting a bolt/drill through the timing hole. If the locking pin is in position, temporarily remove it prior to slackening the pulley bolt, then refit it once the bolt has been slackened.

3 Undo the four crankshaft pulley retaining bolts and remove the pulley from the crankshaft sprocket endplate (see illustrations).

Refitting

4 Locate the pulley on the crankshaft sprocket endplate, refit the four retaining bolts and tighten them to the specified torque.

5 Refit and tension the auxiliary drivebelt as described in Chapter 1A.

6 Timing belt covers – removal and refitting

Removal

Upper (outer) cover

1 Undo the screws and remove the engine undershield (where fitted).

2 Position a trolley jack under the engine, placing a block of wood between the jack head and the sump. Take the weight of the engine, undo the bolts/nuts and remove the right-hand engine mounting and bracket (see Section 16).

3 Undo the bolt securing the power steering pipe bracket adjacent to the coolant pump. Move the pipes to one side to improve access.

4 Remove the plastic cover from over the coolant and washer reservoirs. The cover is secured by plastic expanding rivets. Push in the centre pins a little, then prise out the complete rivets and release the side clip. Release the side retaining clip.

5 Undo the upper and lower retaining bolts securing the outer cover to the inner cover (see illustration). Slide the cover retaining clip upwards to release it from its fasteners.

6 Ease the outer cover upwards and away from the engine, freeing it from its lower locations (see illustration).

6.5 Undo the upper timing belt cover retaining bolts (A) . . .

6 6 . . . and withdraw the cover from the cylinder head

6.9 Undo the lower timing belt cover retaining bolts (B)

6.12 Upper (inner) timing belt cover retaining bolts (C)

Lower cover

7 Remove the crankshaft pulley as described in Section 5.

8 Remove the upper (outer) cover as described above.

9 Slacken and remove the retaining bolts, then remove the lower timing belt cover from the engine **(see illustration)**. Note that on some models it may be necessary to unbolt the auxiliary drivebelt tensioner assembly and remove it from the engine in order to allow the cover to be removed.

Upper (inner) cover

10 Remove the timing belt as described in Section 7.

11 Remove both camshaft sprockets as described in Section 8.

12 Remove the bolts securing the cover to the side of the cylinder head, and remove the cover from the engine **(see illustration)**.

Refitting

13 Refitting is a reversal of the relevant removal procedure, ensuring that each cover section is correctly located, and that the cover retaining nuts and/or bolts are securely tightened. When refitting the upper (inner) cover, apply thread-locking compound to the retaining bolts.

---

7 Timing belt – general information, removal and refitting

General information

1 The timing belt drives the camshafts and coolant pump from a toothed sprocket on the end of the crankshaft. If the belt breaks or slips in service, the pistons are likely to hit the valve heads, resulting in extensive (and expensive) damage.

2 The timing belt should be renewed at the specified intervals (see Chapter 1A), or earlier if it is contaminated with oil, or if it is at all noisy in operation (a 'scraping' noise due to uneven wear).

3 If the timing belt is being removed, it is a wise precaution to check the condition of the coolant pump at the same time (check for signs of coolant leakage). This may avoid the need to remove the timing belt again at a later stage, should the coolant pump fail.

4 The crankshaft sprocket is a two-piece assembly consisting of the toothed sprocket itself and an outer endplate. The endplate is locked to the crankshaft by means of a conventional Woodruff key. When the sprocket retaining bolt is slackened, the sprocket is free to turn on the crankshaft within the limits afforded by an additional keyway within the endplate. When the sprocket retaining bolt is tightened the complete assembly is locked to the crankshaft. This arrangement allows accurate tensioning of the timing belt when refitting, provided that the procedures contained in this Section are strictly adhered to.

7.7 Using an Allen key in the hole (arrowed) on the tensioner pulley, rotate it clockwise to relieve tension from the belt

Removal

5 Remove the upper (outer) and lower timing belt covers as described in Section 6.

6 Align the engine assembly/valve timing holes as described in Section 3, and lock the crankshaft sprocket and camshaft sprockets in position. *Do not* attempt to rotate the engine whilst the locking tools are in position.

7 Loosen the timing belt tensioner pulley retaining bolt. Using an Allen key in the hole provided on the front of the pulley, rotate the pulley in a clockwise direction, to relieve the tension from the timing belt **(see illustration)**. Retighten the tensioner pulley retaining bolt to secure it in the slackened position.

8 If the timing belt is to be re-used, use white paint or chalk to mark the direction of rotation on the belt (if markings do not already exist), then slip the belt off the sprockets and pulleys. Note that the crankshaft must not be rotated whilst the belt is removed.

9 Check the timing belt carefully for any signs of uneven wear, splitting, or oil contamination. Pay particular attention to the roots of the teeth. Renew it if there is the slightest doubt about its condition. If the engine is undergoing an overhaul, it is advisable to renew the belt as a matter of course, regardless of its apparent condition. The cost of a new belt is nothing compared with the cost of repairs should the belt break in service. If signs of oil contamination are found, trace the source of the oil leak and rectify it. Wash down the engine timing belt area and all related components, to remove all traces of oil.

Refitting

10 Before refitting, thoroughly clean the timing belt sprockets. Check that the tensioner and idler pulleys rotate freely, without any sign of roughness. If necessary, renew the relevant pulley as described in Section 8.

7.12 Locate the timing belt on the crankshaft sprocket, with the arrows on the belt pointing in the direction of rotation

7.13a Retain the belt on the crankshaft sprocket and feed it over the idler pulley . . .

7.13b . . . inlet camshaft sprocket . . .

11 Ensure that the crankshaft and camshaft sprocket locking tools are still in position.

12 Locate the timing belt on the crankshaft sprocket, ensuring that any arrows on the belt are pointing in the direction of rotation (clockwise when viewed from the right-hand end of the engine) **(see illustration)**.

13 Retain the timing belt on the crankshaft sprocket then, keeping it taut, feed the belt over the remaining sprockets and pulleys in the following order **(see illustrations)**:

  a) *Idler pulley.*
  b) *Inlet camshaft.*
  c) *Exhaust camshaft.*
  d) *Coolant pump.*
  e) *Tensioner pulley.*

14 Remove the locking tool from the exhaust camshaft sprocket.

15 Slacken the tensioner pulley retaining bolt and turn the tensioner pulley hub anti-clockwise, by means of the Allen key, so that the upper edge of the index pointer is positioned approximately 10° clockwise past the slot in the backing plate **(see illustrations)**. If the index pointer will not attain a position of at least 10° past the backing plate slot, then the tensioner pulley, or both the tensioner pulley and the timing belt, must be renewed.

16 Now rotate the tensioner pulley hub

7.13c . . . exhaust camshaft sprocket . . .

7.13d . . . coolant pump sprocket and tensioner pulley

clockwise until the index pointer is exactly aligned with the slot in the backing plate **(see illustration 7.15b)**. Hold the pulley in this position and tighten the retaining bolt to the specified torque. With the timing belt tensioned and the tensioner pulley retaining bolt tightened, the Allen key slot in the pulley should be below the cylinder head gasket level. If this is not the case, then the tensioner pulley, or both the tensioner pulley and the timing belt, must be renewed.

17 Remove the remaining camshaft and crankshaft locking tools and rotate the crankshaft through ten complete rotations in a clockwise direction (viewed from the right-

hand end of the engine). Realign the engine assembly/valve timing holes and refit the inlet camshaft sprocket locking tool.

18 Check that the tensioner pulley index pointer is still aligned with the slot in the backing plate. If not repeat the tensioning operation.

19 With the inlet camshaft sprocket locking tool in place, it should now also be possible to fit the crankshaft sprocket locking tool. If so, continue with the refitting procedure. If the crankshaft sprocket locking tool will not engage, then the crankshaft sprocket endplate must be repositioned as follows.

20 Slacken the crankshaft sprocket retaining

7.15a Using an Allen key, turn the tensioner pulley anti-clockwise . . .

H34032

7.15b . . . until the upper edge of the index pointer (A) is positioned approximately 10° past the slot (B) in the backing plate

7.22a Hold the crankshaft sprocket endplate with the holding tool and tighten the retaining bolt to the specified torque . . .

7.22b . . . then through the specified angle

bolt while holding the sprocket endplate stationary using Peugeot special tool 6310-T or a suitable home-made alternative **(see Tool Tip in Section 8)**. *Do not* attempt to use only the

To make a sprocket holding tool, obtain two lengths of steel strip about 6 mm thick by about 30 mm wide or similar, one 600 mm long, the other 200 mm long (all dimensions are approximate). Bolt the two strips together to form a forked end, leaving the bolt slack so that the shorter strip can pivot freely. At the other end of each 'prong' of the fork, drill a suitable hole and fit a nut and bolt to engage with the spokes of holes in the sprocket. The same tool can be used to hold both the inlet camshaft sprocket and the crankshaft sprocket.

sprocket locking tools inserted in the engine assembly/valve timing holes to prevent rotation whilst the bolt is slackened.

21 With the sprocket retaining bolt slackened, turn the endplate until the sprocket locking tool can be fully inserted through the endplate and into the hole in the oil pump housing.

22 Hold the endplate with the holding tool and tighten the sprocket retaining bolt to the specified torque, then through the specified angle **(see illustrations)**.

23 Refit the lower and upper (outer) timing belt covers as described in Section 6.

24 Refit the crankshaft pulley as described in Section 5.

25 Refit the auxiliary drivebelt with reference to Chapter 1A.

26 Refit the right-hand front wheel arch liner.

27 Refit the roadwheel and lower the vehicle to the ground.

28 Reconnect the battery.

8 Timing belt tensioners, sprockets and pulleys – removal, inspection and refitting

Removal

1 Remove the timing belt as described in Section 7.

Camshaft sprockets

2 The camshafts must now be prevented from rotating to allow the sprocket retaining bolts to be slackened. If working on the exhaust camshaft sprocket, it will be necessary to remove the rear cylinder head cover (see Section 4) to allow a spanner to be engaged with a square section of the camshaft, provided for this purpose. This is because the sprocket contains a rubber vibration damper incorporated into the sprocket hub. If the sprocket itself is held as the bolt is slackened, the rubber hub will be damaged. The inlet camshaft sprocket is conventional and can be held using Peugeot tool 6016-T, or an acceptable substitute can be fabricated at home **(see Tool Tip)**. Alternatively, remove the front cylinder head cover and hold the camshaft with a spanner as described for the exhaust camshaft. *Do not* attempt to use the engine assembly/valve timing hole locking tools to prevent the sprockets from rotating whilst the bolts are slackened.

3 Remove the engine assembly/valve timing hole locking tool from the relevant sprocket, then slacken the centre retaining bolt. If a spanner is being used to prevent camshaft rotation, the spanner should be engaged with the square section of the camshaft adjacent to No 8 cam lobe **(see illustration)**.

4 Remove the previously-slackened sprocket retaining bolt and washer, and withdraw the relevant sprocket from the end of the camshaft **(see illustrations)**.

Crankshaft sprocket

5 With the crankshaft pulley removed from the flange on the front of the crankshaft, remove the timing locking pin. **Note:** *Do not use the pin to lock the crankshaft when loosening the crankshaft pulley bolt.*

6 The crankshaft must now be locked. To do this, remove the starter motor and have an assistant insert a wide-bladed screwdriver between the teeth of the ring gear and the transmission casing. Unscrew and remove the bolt and washer, and remove

8.3 The camshafts can be held with a spanner engaged with the square section adjacent to the No 8 cam lobe

8.4a Remove the retaining bolt and washer . . .

8.4b . . . and withdraw the sprocket from the end of the camshaft

8.6a Hold the crankshaft sprocket endplate with the home-made tool while the retaining bolt is slackened

8.6b Withdraw the crankshaft sprocket endplate . . .

8.6c . . . and the sprocket itself

8.7 Remove the Woodruff key from the end of the crankshaft

8.9a Remove the timing belt tensioner pulley . . .

8.9b . . . and the idler pulley

the crankshaft sprocket and flange from the end of the crankshaft. Alternatively a home-made tool may be used **(see illustrations)**.

7 Remove the Woodruff key from the crankshaft, and store it with the sprocket for safe-keeping **(see illustration)**. Where necessary, also slide the spacer (where fitted) off the end of the crankshaft.

8 Examine the crankshaft oil seal for signs of oil leakage and, if necessary, renew it as described in Section 14.

Tensioner and idler pulleys

9 Unscrew the retaining bolts from the tensioner and idler pulleys, then remove the pulleys from the engine **(see illustrations)**. Note that the tensioner roller bracket locates over the rib on the cylinder block.

Inspection

10 Clean the camshaft/crankshaft sprockets thoroughly, and renew any that show signs of wear, damage or cracks. Where applicable, check the condition of the rubber vibration damper in the exhaust camshaft sprocket and renew the sprocket if there is any sign of deterioration of the rubber.

11 Clean the tensioner/idler pulleys but do not use any strong solvent, which may enter the pulley bearings. Check that the pulleys rotate freely, with no sign of stiffness or free play. Renew them if there is any doubt about there condition, or if there are any obvious signs of wear or damage.

Refitting

Camshaft sprockets

12 Locate the relevant sprocket on the end of the camshaft, engaging the lug in the sprocket hub with the slot in the end of the camshaft.

13 Refit the sprocket retaining bolt and washer, and tighten it to the specified torque. Prevent the sprocket from turning as the bolt is tightened using the method employed for removal.

14 Realign the hole in the camshaft sprocket with the corresponding hole in the cylinder head, and refit the locking tool. Check that the crankshaft pulley locking tool is still in position.

15 Where removed, refit the cylinder head cover(s) as described in Section 4.

16 Refit and tension the timing belt as described in Section 7.

8.22 Ensure the slot (arrowed) on the tensioner pulley body engages with the web on the cylinder block when refitting

Crankshaft sprocket

17 Where fitted, refit the spacer, and then locate the Woodruff key in the crankshaft groove, making sure that it is parallel with the surface of the crankshaft.

18 Locate the sprocket and flange onto the end of the crankshaft and engage the groove with the Woodruff key.

19 Apply locking fluid to the threads of the crankshaft pulley bolt then insert it, together with the washer, and screw it in finger-tight.

20 Hold the crankshaft stationary with the method used for removal, then tighten the bolt to the specified torque.

21 Refit and tension the timing belt as described in Section 7.

Tensioner and idler pulleys

22 Locate the tensioner pulley on the engine, making sure that the roller bracket engages over the rib on the cylinder block **(see illustration)**. Insert the bolt and finger-tighten it at this stage.

23 Locate the idler pulley on the engine, insert the bolt, and tighten it to the specified torque and angle.

24 Refit and tension the timing belt as described in Section 7.

9 Camshaft oil seals – renewal

1 Remove the camshaft sprockets as described in Section 8.

9.3 Use pliers and a self-tapping screw to extract the camshaft oil seal

9.5 Locate the new seal in position with the seal lips facing inwards

10.7 Progressively slacken and remove the retaining bolts, then lift off the camshaft bearing cap housing(s)

2 Note the fitted depth of the oil seals as a guide to fitting the new ones.

3 Punch or drill two small holes opposite each other in the oil seal. Screw a self-tapping screw into each, and pull on the screws with pliers to extract the seal **(see illustration)**.

4 Clean the seal housing, and polish off any burrs or raised edges, which may have caused the seal to fail in the first place.

5 Lubricate the lips of the new seal with clean engine oil, and drive it into position until it seats on its locating shoulder **(see illustration)**. Use a suitable tubular drift, such as a socket, which bears only on the hard outer edge of the seal. If available, use the Peugeot tool No 0189-D1/D2. Take care not to damage the seal lips during fitting. Note that the seal lips should face inwards.

6 Refit the camshaft sprockets as described in Section 8.

10 Camshafts and followers – removal, inspection and refitting

Removal

1 Remove the timing belt as described in Section 7.

2 Progressively unscrew the bolts securing the cylinder head covers to the cylinder head. The bolts must be unscrewed in a spiral sequence starting from the outside (see Section 4).

3 Remove the cylinder head covers and gaskets.

4 Refer to Section 8 and remove both camshaft sprockets.

5 Unbolt and remove the inner timing cover from the cylinder head. At this stage, note the fitted depth of the oil seals as a guide to fitting new seals during reassembly.

6 Evenly and progressively slacken the camshaft bearing housing retaining bolts by one turn at a time, in a spiral sequence, starting from the outside. This will relieve the valve spring pressure on the bearing housing gradually and evenly. Once the pressure has been relieved, the bolts can be fully unscrewed, together with their washers.

7 Lift the camshaft bearing housings from the cylinder head, noting that the housings are located on dowels **(see illustration)**.

8 Identify each camshaft for position – the exhaust camshaft is at the rear and the inlet camshaft is at the front of the cylinder head. Also note the TDC position of each camshaft for correct refitting.

9 Remove the camshafts by pressing on their transmission ends to release the opposite ends from the bearings. Withdraw the camshafts from the cylinder head and slide the oil seals from the ends **(see illustration)**.

10 Obtain sixteen small, clean plastic containers, and number them inlet 1 to 8 and exhaust 1 to 8; alternatively, divide a larger container into sixteen compartments and number each compartment accordingly. Using a rubber sucker, withdraw each hydraulic tappet in turn, and place it in its respective container **(see illustration)**. Do not interchange the tappets, or the rate of wear will be much increased.

Inspection

11 Examine the camshaft bearing surfaces and cam lobes for signs of wear ridges and scoring. Renew the camshaft if any of these conditions are apparent. Examine the condition of the bearing surfaces, both on the camshaft journals and in the cylinder head and bearing housing. If the head bearing surfaces are worn excessively, the cylinder head will need to be renewed. If suitable measuring equipment is available, camshaft bearing journal wear can be checked by direct measurement, noting that No 1 journal is at the transmission end of the head.

12 Examine the hydraulic tappet bearing surfaces, which contact the camshaft lobes for wear ridges and scoring. Renew any tappet where these conditions are apparent. If a tappet bearing surface is badly scored, also examine the corresponding lobe on the camshaft for wear, as it is likely that both will be worn. Renew worn components as necessary.

Refitting

13 Before commencing refitting, remove all traces of oil from the bearing housing retaining bolt holes in the cylinder head, using a clean rag. Also ensure that both the cylinder head and bearing housing mating faces are clean and free from oil.

14 Liberally oil the cylinder head hydraulic tappet bores and the tappets. Carefully refit the tappets to the cylinder head; ensuring that each tappet is refitted to its original bore **(see illustrations)**. Some care will be required

10.9 Carefully lift out the camshaft(s) up and out of their locations

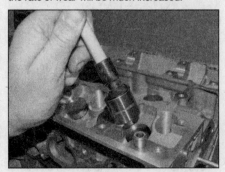

10.10 Use a rubber sucker to withdraw the hydraulic tappets

10.14a Lubricate the hydraulic tappet bores and the tappets . . .

10.14b . . . then refit the tappets ensuring that each is refitted to its original bore

10.15 Liberally oil the camshaft bearings and lobes, then lay the camshaft in the cylinder head

10.17 Apply a bead of sealing compound around the perimeter of the cylinder head mating faces

to enter the tappets squarely into their bores. Check that each tappet rotates freely in its bore.

15 Liberally oil the camshaft bearings in the cylinder head and the camshaft lobes, then refit the camshafts to the cylinder head in their previously-noted positions **(see illustration)**. Note that the exhaust camshaft has a sensor ring on its left-hand end and must be fitted at the rear of the cylinder head.

16 Ensure that the four locating dowels are in position, one at each corner of the cylinder head.

17 Apply a bead of silicone-based jointing compound (Peugeot E10 jointing paste) around the perimeter of the mating faces and around the retaining bolt hole locations **(see illustration)**.

18 Liberally oil the camshaft bearings and carefully locate the bearing housings over the camshafts. Refit the retaining bolts ensuring that each has a washer under its head **(see illustration)**. Note that the bearing housing with the sensor hole is located over the exhaust camshaft. Initially finger-tighten the bolts.

19 Progressively tighten the bearing housing retaining bolts to the specified torque, in the order given in Section 4. It is suggested that the bolts are initially tightened to 5 Nm (4 lbf ft), then tightened to their final torque.

20 Refit the inner timing cover to the cylinder head and tighten the retaining bolts securely.

21 Clean the jointing compound from the oil seal seatings in the cylinder head and camshaft housing.

22 Fit new oil seals with reference to Section 9.
23 Refit the sprockets to the camshafts with reference to Section 8.
24 Refit the cylinder head covers together with new gaskets, with reference to Section 4.
25 Refit the timing belt with reference to Section 7.

11 Cylinder head – removal and refitting

Removal

1 Disconnect the battery (see Chapter 5A).
2 Apply the handbrake, then jack up the front of the vehicle and support it on axle stands (see *Jacking and vehicle support*). Undo the screws and remove the engine undershield. For improved access, remove the bonnet as described in Chapter 11.
3 Drain the cooling system as described in Chapter 1A.
4 Unbolt the exhaust downpipe from the exhaust manifold on the rear of the engine with reference to Chapter 4A.
5 Undo the 6 screw fasteners and remove the plastic cover from the engine.
6 Release the fuel pressure from the fuel system by placing cloth rags around and over the Shrader valve on the fuel rail, and depressing the valve core.
7 Disconnect the fuel supply pipe from the fuel rail.

8 Remove the timing belt as described in Section 7.
9 Remove the timing belt tensioner roller as described in Section 8.
10 Remove the air cleaner and intake pipe with reference to Chapter 4A.
11 Remove the engine oil dipstick from its tube, then remove the tube itself from the block.
12 Disconnect the crankcase breather hose from the camshaft cover.
13 Note their fitted positions and routing, then disconnect all coolant hoses and wiring connectors/looms from the cylinder head.
14 Remove the camshaft position sensor from the left-hand end of the exhaust camshaft cover.
15 Remove the ignition coil module from the top of the cylinder head with reference to Chapter 5B.
16 Unscrew the bolts/nuts securing the inlet manifold to the front of the cylinder head, then support the manifold away from the cylinder head.
17 Remove both cylinder head covers and gaskets with reference to Section 4.
18 Refit the right-hand engine mounting support bracket to the cylinder head.
19 Using a Torx key socket and working in the *reverse* of the tightening sequence (see paragraph 33), progressively slacken the ten cylinder head bolts by half a turn at a time, until all bolts can be unscrewed by hand. Recover the washers where fitted.
20 With all the cylinder head bolts removed, the joint between the cylinder head and gasket, and the cylinder block/crankcase must now be broken. To break the joint, obtain two L-shaped metal bars which fit into the cylinder head bolt holes, and gently 'rock' the cylinder head free towards the front of the car. *Do not* try to swivel the head on the cylinder block/crankcase; it is located by dowels. When the joint is broken, lift the cylinder head away. Use a hoist or seek assistance if possible, as it is a heavy assembly **(see illustration)**. Remove the gasket from the top of the block, noting the two locating dowels. If the locating dowels are a loose fit, remove them and store them with the head for safe-keeping. Do not discard the gasket; it will be needed for identification purposes. During removal, check that the

10.18 Carefully locate the bearing cap housings over the camshafts

11.20 Remove the cylinder head from the engine block

11.25 Measure the length of the cylinder head bolts from the underside of the head to the end of the bolt

11.27a Check the cylinder head locating dowels (arrowed) are in place . . .

11.27b . . . and the camshaft oil supply non-return valve (arrowed) is in place in the cylinder head

camshaft oil supply non-return valve (located in the underside of the cylinder head at the timing belt end) does not drop out; it is easily lost if it does.

21 If the cylinder head is to be dismantled for overhaul, remove the camshafts as described in Section 10, then refer to Part E of this Chapter. Also remove the rigid pipe from the outlet housing.

Preparation for refitting

22 The mating faces of the cylinder head and cylinder block/crankcase must be perfectly clean before refitting the head. Use a hard plastic or wooden scraper to remove all traces of gasket and carbon and also clean the piston crowns. Make sure that the carbon is not allowed to enter the oil and water passages – this is particularly important for the lubrication system, as carbon could block the oil supply to the engine's components. Using adhesive tape and paper, seal the water, oil and bolt holes in the cylinder block/crankcase. To prevent carbon entering the gap between the pistons and bores, smear a little grease in the gap. After cleaning each piston, use a small brush to remove all traces of grease and carbon from the gap, and then wipe away the remainder with a clean rag. Clean all the pistons in the same way.

23 Check the mating surfaces of the cylinder block/crankcase and the cylinder head for nicks, deep scratches and other damage. If slight, they may be removed carefully with a file, but if excessive, machining may be the

only alternative to renewal. If warpage of the cylinder head gasket surface is suspected, use a straight-edge to check it for distortion. Refer to Part E of this Chapter if necessary.

24 Obtain a new cylinder head gasket before starting the refitting procedure. At the time of writing, there are two different thicknesses available – the standard gasket that is fitted at the factory, and a slightly thicker 'repair' gasket (+0.3 mm), for use once the head gasket face has been machined. If the cylinder head has been machined, it should be marked '–0.3' on the upper corner, on the inlet manifold side, at the timing belt end. Note that modifications to the cylinder head gasket material, type, and manufacturer are constantly taking place; seek the advice of a Peugeot dealer as to the latest recommendations.

25 Check the condition of the cylinder head bolts, and particularly their threads, whenever they are removed. Wash the bolts in a suitable solvent, and wipe them dry. Check each bolt for any sign of visible wear or damage, renewing them if necessary. Measure the length of each bolt from the underside of its head to the end of the bolt (see illustration). The bolts may be re-used if their length does not exceed 147.00 mm. If any one bolt is longer than the specified length, *all* of the bolts should be renewed as a complete set. Considering the stress, which the cylinder head bolts are under, it is highly recommended that they be renewed, regardless of their apparent condition. Also check that the thickness of the head bolt washers is 4.00 ± 0.2 mm.

Refitting

26 Where removed, refit the camshafts, and the rigid pipe to the outlet housing on the cylinder head.

27 Wipe clean the mating surfaces of the cylinder head and cylinder block/crankcase. Check that the two locating dowels are in position at each end of the cylinder block/crankcase surface. Peugeot recommend that the camshaft oil supply non-return valve in the oil feed bore at the timing belt end of the cylinder head is renewed (see illustrations).

28 Position a new gasket on the cylinder block/crankcase surface, ensuring that the TOP mark is uppermost and at the front of the block (see illustration).

29 Check that the crankshaft pulley and camshaft sprockets are still at their locked positions (see Section 3).

30 With the aid of an assistant, carefully lower the cylinder head assembly onto the block, aligning it with the locating dowels.

31 Apply a smear of grease to the threads, and to the underside of the heads, of the cylinder head bolts. Peugeot recommend the use of Molykote G Rapid Plus (available from your Peugeot dealer); in the absence of the specified grease, any good-quality high melting-point grease may be used.

32 Carefully enter each bolt and washer into its relevant hole (*do not drop it in*) then screw them in finger-tight.

33 Working progressively and in sequence (see illustration), tighten the cylinder head bolts to their Stage 1 torque setting.

34 Once all the bolts have been tightened to their Stage 1 torque setting, proceed to tighten them through the remaining stages as given in the Specifications. When carrying out Stage 3, slacken each bolt 1 turn working in the *reverse* of the tightening sequence. It is recommended that an angle-measuring gauge be used for the angle-tightening stages, however, if a gauge is not available, use white paint to make alignment marks between the bolt head and cylinder head prior to tightening; the marks can then by used to check that the bolt has rotated sufficiently. Where a maximum of 2 steps is given for angle-tightening, each step must be completed in one movement without stopping.

11.28 Position the cylinder head gasket with the work TOP uppermost and toward the oil filter side of the engine block

11.33 Cylinder head bolt tightening sequence

12.4 Undo the upper and lower retaining bolts and remove the dipstick guide tube

12.7a Oil pump pick-up tube retaining nuts and retaining bolt locations (arrowed)

12.7b Crankcase baffle plate retaining bolts locations (arrowed)

35 The remainder of the refitting procedure is a reversal of removal, referring to the relevant Chapters or Sections as required. On completion, refill the cooling system as described in Chapter 1A. Initialise the engine management ECU as follows. Start the engine and run to normal temperature. Carry out a road test during which the following procedure should be made. Engage third gear and stabilise the engine at 1000 rpm. Now accelerate fully to 3500 rpm.

12 Sump – removal and refitting

Removal

1 Apply the handbrake, then jack up the front of the vehicle and support it on axle stands (see *Jacking and vehicle support*). Undo the screws and remove the engine undershield (where fitted).
2 Drain the engine oil then clean and refit the engine oil drain plug, tightening it securely. If the engine is nearing the service interval when the oil and filter are due for renewal, it is recommended that the filter is also removed, and a new one fitted. After reassembly, the engine can then be refilled with fresh oil. Refer to Chapter 1A for further information.
3 Withdraw the engine oil dipstick from the guide tube.
4 Undo the bolt securing the upper end of the dipstick guide tube to the ancillary

components mounting bracket. Undo the bolt securing the base of the guide tube to the sump and remove the guide tube **(see illustration)**. Collect the two O-rings from the base of the guide tube, noting that new O-rings will be required for refitting.
5 Where applicable, move the power steering pipe supports from the oil pump. Also disconnect the wiring from the oil temperature sender unit.
6 Progressively slacken and remove all the sump retaining bolts. Since there are nineteen 25.0 mm bolts and seven 110.0 mm bolts, remove each bolt in turn, and store it in its correct fitted order by pushing it through a clearly-marked cardboard template. This will avoid the possibility of installing the bolts in the wrong locations on refitting.
7 Break the joint by striking the sump with the palm of your hand. Lower the sump, and withdraw it from underneath the vehicle. While the sump is removed, take the opportunity to check the oil pump pick-up/strainer for signs of clogging or splitting. If necessary, remove the pump as described in Section 13, and clean or renew the strainer. Also unbolt the oil baffle plate from the bottom of the main bearing ladder; noting which way round it is fitted **(see illustrations)**. Note that the sump is located on a dowel.

Refitting

8 Where removed, refit the baffle plate to the main bearing ladder and tighten the bolts securely.
9 Where removed, refit the oil pump and pick-up/strainer with reference to Section 13.

10 Clean all traces of sealant/gasket from the mating surfaces of the main bearing ladder and sump, then use a clean rag to wipe out the sump and the engine's interior.
11 Ensure that the sump mating surfaces are clean and dry, and then apply a thin coating of suitable sealant to the sump mating surface **(see illustration)**.
12 Check that the location dowel is in place, then refit the sump onto the main bearing ladder and insert the bolts and finger-tighten them at this stage, so that it is still possible to move the sump. Make sure the bolts are refitted in their correct locations **(see illustrations)**.
13 Using a straight-edge, align the flywheel end of the sump with the main bearing ladder and cylinder block, then progressively tighten the sump bolts to the specified torque **(see illustration)**.

12.11 Apply a thin bead of RTV sealant to the sump mating surface

12.12a Four of the long sump retaining bolts are fitted at the transmission end . . .

12.12b . . . and three are fitted at the timing belt end on the oil filter side

12.13 Use a straight-edge to ensure the rear faces of the cylinder block and sump are flush

13.3 Oil pump housing retaining bolt locations (arrowed)

13.4a Slide the oil pump drive collar off the crankshaft . . .

14 Check that the oil drain plug is tightened securely, then refit the engine undershield (where applicable) and lower the vehicle to the ground.
15 Refill the engine with oil as described in Chapter 1A.

13 Oil pump – removal, inspection and refitting

Removal

1 Remove the timing belt and crankshaft sprocket as described in Sections 7 and 8.
2 Remove the sump and oil pump pick-up/ strainer as described in Section 12.
3 Unscrew the nine bolts securing the oil pump to the main bearing ladder and cylinder block, then withdraw the oil pump over the nose of the crankshaft **(see illustration)**. Note it is located on dowels, and therefore it may be necessary to carefully prise it away to release it.
4 Slide the oil pump drive collar off the end of the crankshaft and collect the O-ring located behind the collar **(see illustrations)**.
5 With the oil pump removed, note the fitted

depth of the crankshaft oil seal, and then drive it from the oil pump housing. A new oil seal must be obtained for refitting.

Inspection

6 At the time of writing, checking specifications for the oil pump were not available, however, if the oil pump is to be re-used, the internal gears should be cleaned. To do this, unbolt the cover, then mark the gears for location and remove them **(see illustrations)**. Clean the gears and inspect them for damage and excessive wear.
7 Lubricate the gears with oil, then refit them

in their locations noted during removal. Refit the cover and tighten the bolts securely.
8 Thoroughly clean the oil pump strainer with a suitable solvent, and check it for signs of clogging or splitting. If the strainer is damaged, the strainer and cover assembly must be renewed.

Refitting

9 Clean the mating surfaces of the oil pump and main bearing ladder/cylinder block. Check that the locating dowels are in position on the pump flange then locate a new O-ring over the oil pump outlet stub **(see illustration)**.

13.4b . . . and collect the O-ring behind the collar

13.6a Undo the five screws and lift off the oil pump rear cover

13.6b Remove the inner rotor . . .

13.6c . . . and outer rotor from the pump housing

13.9 Locate a new O-ring over the oil pump outlet stub

13.10 Apply a thin bead of RTV sealant to the oil pump mating surface

13.13 Position a new oil pump drive collar O-ring on the end of the crankshaft

13.14a Lubricate the sealing lips of the new crankshaft right-hand oil seal . . .

10 Apply a thin coating of suitable sealant to the mating face of the oil pump housing **(see illustration)**.

11 Prime the oil pump by injecting clean engine oil into the outlet stub, then place the pump in position on the cylinder block, engaging the locating dowels.

12 Apply thread-locking compound to the threads of the nine oil pump retaining bolts, then refit the bolts and tighten them to the specified torque.

13 Position a new oil pump drive collar O-ring on the end of the crankshaft **(see illustration)**.

14 Lubricate the sealing lips of the new crankshaft right-hand oil seal and carefully fit the seal over the oil pump drive collar **(see illustrations)**. Note that the open part of the seal must be towards the shoulder of the drive collar.

15 Slide the drive collar over the end of the crankshaft and engage it with the oil pump inner rotor **(see illustration)**. As the collar engages with the pump inner rotor, push the oil seal initially into place in the oil pump housing. Tap the seal fully into position using a suitable drift.

16 Refit the pick-up/strainer and sump as described in Section 12, and the crankshaft sprocket and timing belt as described in Sections 7 and 8.

17 Before starting the engine, prime the oil pump as follows. Disconnect the fuel injector wiring connectors, then spin the engine on the starter until the oil pressure light goes out. Reconnect the injector wiring on completion.

14 Crankshaft oil seals – renewal

Right-hand oil seal

1 Remove the crankshaft sprocket and (where fitted) spacer, referring to Section 8. Secure the timing belt clear of the working area, so that it cannot be contaminated with oil. Make a note of the correct fitted depth of the seal in its housing.

2 Punch or drill two small holes opposite each other in the seal. Screw a self-tapping screw into each, and pull on the screws with pliers

13.14b . . . and carefully fit the seal over the oil pump drive collar

to extract the seal. Alternatively, the seal can be levered out of position. Use a flat-bladed screwdriver, and take great care not to damage the crankshaft shoulder or seal housing.

3 Clean the seal housing, and polish off any burrs or raised edges, which may have caused the seal to fail in the first place.

4 Lubricate the lips of the new seal with clean engine oil, and carefully locate the seal on the end of the crankshaft. Note that its sealing lip must be facing inwards. Take care not to damage the seal lips during fitting.

5 Fit the new seal using a suitable tubular drift, such as a socket, which bears only on the hard outer edge of the seal. Tap the seal into position, to the same depth in the housing as the original was prior to removal **(see illustration)**.

6 Wash off any traces of oil, then refit the crankshaft sprocket as described in Section 8.

14.5 Tap the crankshaft right-hand oil seal into position using a suitable drift

13.15 Slide the drive collar onto the crankshaft and engage it with the oil pump inner rotor

Left-hand oil seal

7 Remove the flywheel/driveplate as described in Section 15. Make a note of the correct fitted depth of the seal in its housing.

8 Punch or drill two small holes opposite each other in the seal. Screw a self-tapping screw into each, and pull on the screws with pliers to extract the seal.

9 Clean the seal housing, and polish off any burrs or raised edges, which may have caused the seal to fail in the first place.

10 Lubricate the lips of the new seal with clean engine oil, and carefully locate the seal on the end of the crankshaft. The new seal will normally be supplied with a plastic fitting sleeve to protect the seal lips as the seal is fitted. If so, lubricate the fitting sleeve and locate it over the end of the crankshaft **(see illustration)**.

14.10 Lubricate the crankshaft left-hand oil seal fitting sleeve and locate it over the end of the crankshaft

14.11 Locate the oil seal over the fitting sleeve and over the end of the crankshaft

11 Lubricate the lips of the new seal with clean engine oil, and carefully locate the seal over the fitting sleeve and onto the end of the crankshaft **(see illustration)**. Drive the seal into position, to the same depth in the housing as the original was prior to removal.

12 Wash off any traces of oil, then refit the flywheel/driveplate as described in Section 15.

15 Flywheel/driveplate – removal, inspection and refitting

Removal

Flywheel

1 Remove the transmission as described in Chapter 7A, then remove the clutch assembly as described in Chapter 6.

2 Prevent the crankshaft from turning by locking the flywheel with a wide-bladed screwdriver between the ring gear teeth and the transmission casing. Alternatively, bolt a strap between the flywheel and the cylinder block/crankcase. *Do not* attempt to lock the flywheel in position using the crankshaft pulley locking pin described in Section 3.

3 Slacken and remove the flywheel retaining bolts, and remove the flywheel from the end of the crankshaft. Be careful not to drop it; it is heavy. If the flywheel locating dowel is a loose fit in the crankshaft end, remove it and store it with the flywheel for safe-keeping. Discard the flywheel bolts; new ones must be used on refitting.

Driveplate

4 Remove the transmission as described in Chapter 7B. Lock the driveplate as described in paragraph 2. Mark the relationship between the torque converter plate and the driveplate, and slacken all the driveplate retaining bolts.

5 Remove the retaining bolts, along with the torque converter plate and (where fitted) the two shims (one fitted on each side of the torque converter plate). Note that the shims are of different thickness, the thicker one being on the outside of the torque converter plate. Discard the driveplate retaining bolts; new ones must be used on refitting.

6 Remove the driveplate from the end of the crankshaft. If the locating dowel is a loose fit in the crankshaft end, remove it and store it with the driveplate for safe-keeping.

Inspection

7 On models with manual transmission, examine the flywheel for scoring of the clutch face, and for wear or chipping of the ring gear teeth. If the clutch face is scored, the flywheel may be surface-ground, but renewal is preferable. Seek the advice of a Peugeot dealer or engine reconditioning specialist to see if machining is possible. If the ring gear is worn or damaged, the flywheel must be renewed, as it is not possible to renew the ring gear separately.

8 On models with automatic transmission, check the torque converter driveplate carefully for signs of distortion. Look for any hairline cracks around the bolt holes or radiating outwards from the centre, and inspect the ring gear teeth for signs of wear or chipping. If any sign of wear or damage is found, the driveplate must be renewed.

Refitting

Flywheel

9 Clean the mating surfaces of the flywheel and crankshaft. Remove any remaining locking compound from the threads of the crankshaft holes, using the correct-size tap, if available.

> **HAYNES HINT**
> *If a suitable tap is not available, cut two slots into the threads of one of the old flywheel bolts and use the bolt to remove the locking compound from the threads.*

10 If the new flywheel retaining bolts are not supplied with their threads already precoated, apply a suitable thread-locking compound to the threads of each bolt.

11 Ensure the locating dowel is in position. Offer up the flywheel, locating it on the dowel, and fit the new retaining bolts.

12 Lock the flywheel using the method employed on dismantling, and tighten the retaining bolts to the specified torque and angle.

13 Refit the clutch as described in Chapter 6. Remove the flywheel locking tool, and refit the transmission as described in Chapter 7A.

Driveplate

14 Carry out the operations described above in paragraphs 9 and 10, substituting 'driveplate' for all references to the flywheel.

15 Locate the driveplate on its locating dowel.

16 Offer up the torque converter plate, with the thinner shim positioned behind the plate and the thicker shim on the outside, and align the marks made prior to removal.

17 Fit the new retaining bolts, then lock the driveplate using the method employed on dismantling. Tighten the retaining bolts to the specified torque wrench setting and angle.

18 Remove the driveplate locking tool, and refit the transmission as described in Chapter 7B.

16 Engine/transmission mountings – inspection and renewal

Inspection

1 If improved access is required, raise the front of the car and support it securely on axle stands.

2 Check the mounting rubber to see if it is cracked, hardened or separated from the metal at any point; renew the mounting if any such damage or deterioration is evident.

3 Check that all the mounting's fasteners are securely tightened; use a torque wrench to check if possible.

4 Using a large screwdriver or a crowbar, check for wear in the mounting by carefully levering against it to check for free play. Where this is not possible, enlist the aid of an assistant to move the engine/transmission unit back-and-forth, or from side-to-side, while you watch the mounting. While some free play is to be expected even from new components, excessive wear should be obvious. If excessive free play is found, check first that the fasteners are correctly secured, and then renew any worn components as described below.

Renewal

Right-hand mounting

5 Release all the relevant hoses and wiring from their retaining clips. Place the hoses/ wiring clear of the mounting so that the removal procedure is not hindered.

6 Undo the screws and remove the engine undershield (where fitted), then place a jack beneath the engine, with a block of wood on the jack head. Raise the jack until it is supporting the weight of the engine.

7 Undo the bolts securing the engine mounting to the body and the support bracket.

8 If required, undo the bolts/nuts securing the support bracket to the cylinder head/cylinder block.

9 Check all components carefully for signs of wear or damage, and renew as necessary.

10 Where removed, refit the support bracket to the cylinder head, and tighten the bolts securely.

11 Refit the mount to the body and support bracket, and then tighten the bolts to the specified torque.

12 Remove the jack from underneath the engine, and refit the engine undershield (where applicable).

Left-hand mounting

13 Remove the battery and battery tray (see Chapter 5A).

14 Undo the screws and remove the engine

16.15a Slacken the centre nut (arrowed) then undo the mounting retaining nuts (arrowed)

16.15b Undo the nut/bolts (arrowed) and remove the mounting plate

16.16 Unscrew the mounting stud from the mounting

undershield (where fitted), then place a jack beneath the transmission, with a block of wood on the jack head. Raise the jack until it is supporting the weight of the transmission.

15 Slacken and remove the centre nut and washer from the left-hand mounting, then undo the nuts securing the mounting in position and remove it from the engine compartment. If necessary undo the nut/bolts and remove the mounting plate **(see illustrations)**.

16 If necessary, slide the spacer (where fitted) off the mounting stud, then unscrew the stud from the top of the transmission housing, and remove it along with its washer **(see illustration)**. If the mounting stud is tight, a universal stud extractor can be used to unscrew it.

17 Check all components carefully for signs of wear or damage, and renew as necessary.

18 Clean the threads of the mounting stud, and apply a coat of thread-locking compound to its threads. Refit the stud and washer to the top of the transmission, and tighten it securely.

19 Slide the spacer (where fitted) onto the mounting stud, then refit the rubber mounting. Tighten both the mounting-to-body bolts and the mounting centre nut to their specified torque settings, and remove the jack from underneath the transmission. Refit the engine undershield.

20 Refit the battery and tray as described in Chapter 5A.

Lower engine movement limiter

21 If not already done, chock the rear wheels, then jack up the front of the vehicle and support it securely on axle stands (see *Jacking and vehicle support*). Undo the screws and remove the engine undershield (where fitted).

22 Unscrew and remove the bolt securing the movement limiter link to the driveshaft intermediate bearing housing **(see illustration)**.

23 Remove the bolt securing the link to the subframe. Withdraw the link.

24 To remove the intermediate bearing housing assembly it will first be necessary to remove the right-hand driveshaft as described in Chapter 8.

25 With the driveshaft removed, undo the retaining bolts and remove the bearing housing from the rear of the cylinder block.

26 Check carefully for signs of wear or damage on all components, and renew them where necessary. The rubber bush fitted to the bearing housing is available as a separate item

16.22 Undo the link-to-engine block bracket bolt (A) and the link-to-subframe bolt (B)

(at the time of writing), and can be pressed out of, and back into place.

27 On reassembly, fit the bearing housing assembly to the rear of the cylinder block, and tighten its retaining bolts securely. Refit the driveshaft as described in Chapter 8.

28 Refit the movement limiter link, and tighten both its bolts to their specified torque settings. Refit the engine undershield (where applicable).

29 Lower the vehicle to the ground.

Notes

Chapter 2 Part D:
Diesel engine in-car repair procedures

Contents

Degrees of difficulty

Easy, suitable for novice with little experience	Fairly easy, suitable for beginner with some experience	Fairly difficult, suitable for competent DIY mechanic	Difficult, suitable for experienced DIY mechanic	Very difficult, suitable for expert DIY or professional

Specifications

General

Designation:
1.4 litre (1398 cc engine)	DV4TD
2.0 litre (1997 cc engine)	DW10TD

Engine codes*:
1.4 litre engine	8HX and 8HZ
2.0 litre engine	RHY

Bore:
1.4 litre engine	73.70 mm
2.0 litre engine	85.00 mm

Stroke:
1.4 litre engine	82.00 mm
2.0 litre engine	88.00 mm
Direction of crankshaft rotation	Clockwise (viewed from the right-hand side of vehicle)
No 1 cylinder location	At the transmission end of the engine

Maximum power output:
1.4 litre engine	50 kW @ 4000 rpm
2.0 litre engine	66 kW @ 4000 rpm

Maximum torque output:
1.4 litre engine	160 Nm @ 2000 rpm
2.0 litre engine	205 Nm @ 1900 rpm

Compression ratio:
1.4 litre engine	18.0 : 1
2.0 litre engine	17.6 : 1

* The engine code is stamped on a plate attached to the front of the cylinder block, next to the oil filter

Compression pressures (engine hot, at cranking speed)

Normal	25 to 30 bars (363 to 435 psi)
Minimum	18 bars (261 psi)
Maximum difference between any two cylinders	5 bars (73 psi)

Timing belt

Tension setting – 2.0 litre engine only (see Section 7):
Initial setting	98 ± 2 SEEM units
Final setting	54 ± 3 SEEM units

Lubrication system

Oil pump type:	
1.4 litre engine	Gear type, driven directly by the right-hand end of the crankshaft, by two flats machined along the crankshaft journal
2.0 litre engine	Gear-type, chain-driven off the crankshaft right-hand end
Minimum oil pressure:	
1.4 litre engine (@ 110°C)	3.5 bars @ 4000 rpm, 2.3 bars @ 2000 rpm
2.0 litre engine (@ 80°C)	4.0 bars @ 4000 rpm, 2.0 bars @ 2000 rpm
Oil pressure warning switch operating pressure	0.8 bars

Torque wrench settings

1.4 litre engine

	Nm	lbf ft
Auxiliary drivebelt tensioner roller	20	15
Big-end bolts*:		
Stage 1	10	7
Stage 2	Slacken 180°	
Stage 3	10	7
Stage 4	Angle-tighten a further 100°	
Camshaft bearing housing	10	7
Camshaft position sensor bolt	5	4
Camshaft sprocket	45	33
Coolant outlet housing bolts	10	7
Crankshaft position/speed sensor bolt	5	4
Crankshaft pulley/sprocket bolt:		
Stage 1	30	22
Stage 2	Angle-tighten a further 180 °	
Cylinder head bolts:		
Stage 1	20	15
Stage 2	40	30
Stage 3	Angle-tighten a further 230°	
Cylinder head cover bolts	10	7
Engine-to-transmission fixing bolts	45	33
Flywheel bolts*:		
Stage 1	15	11
Stage 2	Angle-tighten a further 75°	
Fuel pump sprocket nut	50	37
Left-hand engine/transmission mounting:		
Mounting bracket-to-body bolts	20	15
Mounting stud-to-transmission bolts	20	15
Mounting to bracket	30	22
Rubber mounting centre nut	60	44
Main bearing ladder seam bolts:		
Stage 1	5	4
Stage 2	10	7
Main bearing ladder to cylinder block*:		
Stage 1	10	7
Stage 2	Slacken 180°	
Stage 3	30	22
Stage 4	Angle-tighten a further 140°	
Piston oil jet spray tube bolt	20	15
Oil pump to cylinder block	10	7
Rear engine/transmission mounting:		
Connecting link to mounting assembly	55	41
Connecting link-to-subframe nut/bolt	40	30
Mounting to engine	45	33
Right-hand engine mounting:		
Mounting to body	60	44
Mounting to support bracket	60	44
Support bracket to engine	55	41
Sump bolts/nuts	10	7
Sump plug	16	12
Timing belt idler pulley	35	26
Timing belt tensioner pulley	25	18

Torque wrench settings (contiued)

	Nm	lbf ft
2.0 litre engine		
Big-end bearing cap nuts*:		
Stage 1	20	15
Stage 2	Angle-tighten a further 70°	
Camshaft bearing housing bolts	10	7
Camshaft sprocket hub-to-camshaft bolt	43	32
Camshaft sprocket-to-hub bolts	20	15
Clutch bellhousing closure plate	18	13
Coolant outlet manifold:		
Stage 1 – studs	25	18
Stage 2 – stud nuts	20	15
Stage 3 – 3 bolts	20	15
Crankshaft pulley bolt:		
Early engines (see Section 7):		
Stage 1	50	37
Stage 2	Angle-tighten a further 62°	
Later engines (see Section 7):		
Stage 1	70	52
Stage 2	Angle-tighten a further 60°	
Crankshaft right-hand oil seal housing bolts	14	10
Cylinder head bolts:		
Stage 1	22	16
Stage 2	60	44
Stage 3	Angle-tighten a further 220° ± 5°	
Cylinder head cover bolts	10	7
Engine-to-transmission fixing bolts	45	33
Flywheel/driveplate bolts*	50	37
Fuel pump sprocket nut	50	37
Left-hand engine/transmission mounting:		
Mounting bracket-to-body bolts	20	15
Mounting stud-to-transmission bolts	20	15
Mounting to bracket	30	22
Rubber mounting centre nut	60	44
Main bearing cap bolts:		
Stage 1	25	18
Stage 2	Angle-tighten a further 60°	
Oil pump mounting bolts	18	13
Piston oil jet spray tube bolt	10	7
Rear engine/transmission mounting:		
Connecting link to mounting assembly	55	41
Connecting link-to-subframe nut/bolt	40	30
Mounting to engine	45	33
Right-hand engine mounting:		
Mounting to body	60	44
Mounting to support bracket	60	44
Support bracket to engine	55	41
Sump bolts	16	12
Sump plug	16	12
Timing belt idler roller bolt	25	18
Timing belt tensioner	23	17

* Do not re-use

1 General information

How to use this Chapter

This Part of Chapter 2 describes the repair procedures that can reasonably be carried out on the engine while it remains in the vehicle. If the engine has been removed from the vehicle and is being dismantled as described in Part E, any preliminary dismantling procedures can be ignored.

Note that, while it may be possible physically to overhaul items such as the piston/connecting rod assemblies while the engine is in the car, such tasks are not usually carried out as separate operations. Usually, several additional procedures are required (not to mention the cleaning of components and oilways); for this reason, all such tasks are classed as major overhaul procedures, and are described in Part E of this Chapter.

Part E describes the removal of the engine/transmission from the car, and the full overhaul procedures that can then be carried out.

DW and DV series engines

The DW series engine is based on the well-proven XUD series engine, which has appeared in many Peugeot and Citroën vehicles. In particular, the cylinder block components are very similar to the XUD; however, the remainder of the engine has been completely redesigned. The 1.4 litre DV series engine is the result of development collaboration between Peugeot/Citroën and Ford.

Both engines are of single overhead camshaft 8-valve design. The turbocharged, four-cylinder engines are mounted transversely, with the transmission mounted on the left-hand side.

A toothed timing belt drives the camshaft, high-pressure fuel pump and coolant pump. The camshaft operates the inlet and exhaust valves via rocker arms, which are supported at their pivot ends by hydraulic self-adjusting tappets. The camshaft is supported by bearings machined directly in the cylinder head and camshaft bearing housing.

The high-pressure fuel pump supplies fuel to the fuel rail, and subsequently to the electronically-controlled injectors, which inject the fuel direct into the combustion chambers. This design differs from the previous type where an injection pump supplies the fuel at high pressure to each injector. The earlier, conventional type injection pump required fine calibration and timing, and these functions are now completed by the high-pressure pump, electronic injectors and engine management ECU.

The crankshaft runs in five main bearings of the usual shell type. Endfloat is controlled by thrustwashers either side of No 2 main bearing.

The pistons are selected to be of matching weight, and incorporate fully-floating gudgeon pins retained by circlips.

On the 2.0 litre engine, the oil pump is chain-driven from the right-hand end of the crankshaft, whilst on the 1.4 litre engine, the gear type pump is fitted over the end of the crankshaft, and is driven by interlocking machined flats on the crankshaft and pump gear.

Throughout the manual, it is often necessary to identify the engines not only by their cubic capacity, but also by their engine code. The engine code, consists of three letters (eg, RHY). The code is stamped on a plate attached to the front of the cylinder block.

Precautions

The engine is a complex unit with numerous accessories and ancillary components. The design of the engine compartment is such that every conceivable space has been utilised, and access to virtually all of the engine components is extremely limited. In many cases, ancillary components will have to be removed, or moved to one side, and wiring, pipes and hoses will have to be disconnected or removed from various cable clips and support brackets.

When working on this engine, read through the entire procedure first, look at the car and engine at the same time, and establish whether you have the necessary tools, equipment, skill and patience to proceed. Allow considerable time for any operation, and be prepared for the unexpected. Any major work on these engines is not for the faint-hearted!

Because of the limited access, many of the engine photographs appearing in this Chapter were, by necessity, taken with the engine removed from the vehicle.

⚠️ **Warning: It is essential to observe strict precautions when working on the fuel system components of the engine, particularly the high-pressure side of the system. Before carrying out any engine operations that entail working on, or near, any part of the fuel system, refer to the special information given in Chapter 4B, Section 2.**

Operations with engine in car

a) Compression pressure – testing.
b) Cylinder head cover(s) – removal and refitting.
c) Crankshaft pulley – removal and refitting.
d) Timing belt covers – removal and refitting.
e) Timing belt – removal, refitting and adjustment.
f) Timing belt tensioner and sprockets – removal and refitting.
g) Camshaft oil seal – renewal.
h) Camshaft, rocker arms and hydraulic tappets – removal, inspection and refitting.
i) Sump – removal and refitting.
j) Oil pump – removal and refitting.
k) Crankshaft oil seals – renewal.
l) Engine/transmission mountings – inspection and renewal.
m) Flywheel/driveplate – removal, inspection and refitting.

2 Compression and leakdown tests – description and interpretation

Compression test

Note: *A compression tester specifically designed for diesel engines must be used for this test.*

1 When engine performance is down, or if misfiring occurs which cannot be attributed to the fuel system, a compression test can provide diagnostic clues as to the engine's condition. If the test is performed regularly, it can give warning of trouble before any other symptoms become apparent.

2 A compression tester specifically intended for diesel engines must be used, because of the higher pressures involved. The tester is connected to an adapter, which screws into the glow plug or injector hole. On these engines, an adapter suitable for use in the glow plug holes will be required, so as not to disturb the fuel system components. It is unlikely to be worthwhile buying such a tester for occasional use, but it may be possible to borrow or hire one – if not, have the test performed by a garage.

3 Unless specific instructions to the contrary are supplied with the tester, observe the following points:

a) The battery must be in a good state of charge, the air filter must be clean, and the engine should be at normal operating temperature.

b) All the glow plugs should be removed as described in Chapter 5C before starting the test.

c) The wiring connector on the engine management system ECU (located in the plastic box behind the battery) must be disconnected.

4 The compression pressures measured are not so important as the balance between cylinders. Values are given in the Specifications.

5 The cause of poor compression is less easy to establish on a diesel engine than on a petrol one. The effect of introducing oil into the cylinders ('wet' testing) is not conclusive, because there is a risk that the oil will sit in the swirl chamber or in the recess on the piston crown instead of passing to the rings. However, the following can be used as a rough guide to diagnosis.

6 All cylinders should produce very similar pressures; any difference greater than that specified indicates the existence of a fault. Note that the compression should build-up quickly in a healthy engine; low compression on the first stroke, followed by gradually increasing pressure on successive strokes, indicates worn piston rings. A low compression reading on the first stroke, which does not build-up during successive strokes, indicates leaking valves or a blown head gasket (a cracked head could also be the cause). Deposits on the undersides of the valve heads can also cause low compression.

7 A low reading from two adjacent cylinders is almost certainly due to the head gasket having blown between them; the presence of coolant in the engine oil will confirm this.

8 If the compression reading is unusually high, the cylinder head surfaces, valves and pistons are probably coated with carbon deposits. If this is the case, the cylinder head should be removed and decarbonised (see Part E).

Leakdown test

9 A leakdown test measures the rate at which compressed air fed into the cylinder is lost. It is an alternative to a compression test, and in many ways it is better, since the escaping air provides easy identification of where pressure loss is occurring (piston rings, valves or head gasket).

10 The equipment needed for leakdown testing is unlikely to be available to the home mechanic. If poor compression is suspected, have the test performed by a suitably-equipped garage.

3 Engine assembly/valve timing holes – general information and usage

Note: *Do not attempt to rotate the engine whilst the crankshaft and camshaft are locked in position. If the engine is to be left in this state for a long period of time, it is a good idea to place suitable warning notices inside*

3.7a Use a mirror to observe the camshaft sprocket hub timing slot (DW10 engine)

3.7b Camshaft sprocket hub timing slot (A) aligned with the cylinder head timing hole (B) (DW10 engine)

3.8 Rod (arrowed) inserted through the cylinder block into the flywheel timing hole (2.0 litre engine)

the vehicle, and in the engine compartment. This will reduce the possibility of the engine being accidentally cranked on the starter motor, which is likely to cause damage with the locking pins in place.

1 Timing holes or slots are located only in the flywheel/driveplate (2.0 litre) or crankshaft pulley flange (1.4 litre) and camshaft sprocket hub. The holes/slots are used to align the crankshaft and camshaft at the TDC position for Nos 1 and 4 on 2.0 litre models, or position the pistons halfway up the cylinder bores on the 1.4 litre models. This will ensure that the valve timing is maintained during operations that require removal and refitting of the timing belt. When the holes/slots are aligned with their corresponding holes in the cylinder block and cylinder head, suitable diameter bolts/pins can be inserted to lock the crankshaft and camshaft in position, preventing rotation. **Note:** *On 2.0 litre models, with the timing holes aligned, No 4 piston is at TDC on its compression stroke.*

2 Note that the HDi type fuel system used on these engines does not have a conventional diesel injection pump, but instead uses a high-pressure fuel pump that does not have to be timed. The alignment of the fuel pump sprocket (and hence the fuel pump itself) with respect to crankshaft and camshaft position, is therefore irrelevant.

3 To align the engine assembly/valve timing holes, proceed as follows.

4 Apply the handbrake, then jack up the front of the vehicle and support it on axle stands (see *Jacking and vehicle support*). Remove the right-hand front roadwheel.

5 To gain access to the crankshaft pulley, to enable the engine to be turned, the wheel arch plastic liner must be removed. The liner is secured by several plastic expanding rivets. To remove the rivets, push in the centre pins a little, and then prise the clips from place. Remove the liner from under the front wing. Where necessary, unclip the coolant hoses from under the wing to improve access further. The crankshaft can then be turned using a suitable socket and extension bar fitted to the pulley bolt.

6 Remove the upper and lower timing belt covers as described in Section 6.

7 Turn the crankshaft until the timing hole in the camshaft sprocket hub is aligned with the corresponding hole in the cylinder head. Note that the crankshaft must always be turned in a clockwise direction (viewed from the right-hand side of vehicle). Use a small mirror so that the position of the sprocket hub timing slot can be observed **(see illustrations)**. When the slot is aligned with the corresponding hole in the cylinder head, the camshaft is positioned correctly. **Note:** *On 2.0 litre engines, make sure that the centre part of the slot is aligned with the hole in the cylinder head, as it is possible to incorrectly align the area to each side of the slot.*

2.0 litre engines

8 Insert an 8 mm diameter bolt, rod or drill through the hole in the left-hand flange of the cylinder block by the starter motor; if necessary, carefully turn the crankshaft either way until the rod enters the timing hole in the flywheel/driveplate **(see illustration)**.

9 Insert an 8 mm bolt, rod or drill through the hole in the camshaft sprocket hub and into engagement with the cylinder head **(see illustration)**.

1.4 litre engines

10 Remove the crankshaft drivebelt pulley as described in Section 5.

11 Insert a 5 mm diameter bolt, rod or drill through the hole in crankshaft sprocket flange and into the corresponding hole in the oil pump **(see illustration)**, if necessary, carefully turn the crankshaft either way until the rod enters the timing hole in the pump.

12 Insert an 8 mm bolt, rod or drill through the hole in the camshaft sprocket hub and into engagement with the cylinder head **(see illustration)**.

All engines

13 The crankshaft and camshaft are now locked in position, preventing unnecessary rotation.

3.9 Insert an 8 mm bolt (arrowed) through the sprocket timing slot and into the cylinder head to lock the camshaft (2.0 litre engine)

3.11 Insert a 5 mm drill through the hole in the crankshaft sprocket flange, and into the corresponding hole in the oil pump

3.12 Insert an 8 mm drill through the hole in the camshaft sprocket, and into the corresponding hole in the cylinder head

4.1 Rotate the four fasteners (arrowed) 90° anti-clockwise and pull up the plastic cover

4.8 Disconnect the mass airflow meter wiring plug

4.9 Slacken the retaining clamps and disconnect the turbo outlet hose

4 Cylinder head cover – removal and refitting

Removal

1 Remove the plastic cover from the top of the engine. On 1.4 litre engines, the cover pulls up from its locating pegs, and on 2.0 litre models, the cover is retained by four fasteners **(see illustration)**

2 Remove the timing belt upper cover, as described in Section 6.

2.0 litre engines

3 As applicable, slacken or release the clips securing the crankcase ventilation hoses to the cylinder cover and disconnect the hoses.

4 Undo the bolts and move the engine cover and cable guide support bracket clear of the right-hand end of the cylinder head cover.

5 Disconnect the camshaft position sensor wiring connector.

6 Release the wiring harness from the clip on the cylinder head cover and move the harness to one side.

7 Progressively unscrew the bolts securing the cylinder head cover to the camshaft carrier or inlet manifold (as applicable) and collect the washers. Carefully lift off the cover, taking care not to damage the camshaft position sensor as the cover is removed. Recover the seal from the cover.

1.4 litre engines

8 The cylinder head cover is integral with the inlet manifold and oil separator. Disconnect the mass airflow meter wiring plug **(see illustration)**.

9 Slacken the retaining clip, and remove the turbocharger outlet elbow **(see illustration)**.

10 Undo the retaining bolts, lift up the right-hand end and remove the resonator **(see illustrations)**. Recover the O-ring seal.

11 Slacken the retaining clips and remove the air intake ducting and turbocharger intake hose. Slide up the plastic trim in the left-hand front corner of the engine compartment, push in the centre pin a little, prise out the rivet and remove the intake ducting from the bonnet slam panel.

12 Unscrew the air filter housing bolts, and the filter cover bolts, then remove the cover and filter element – refer to Chapter 4B **(see illustration)**. Release the diesel priming pump bulb from its retaining brackets at the right-hand end of the cylinder head, and remove the air filter housing. Disconnect any wiring plugs as necessary as the housing is withdrawn, having first noted their fitted positions.

13 Remove the diesel fuel filter as described in Chapter 1B, then undo the bolts securing the diesel filter support bracket.

14 Disconnect the wiring plugs from the top of each injector, then make sure all wiring harnesses are freed from any retaining brackets on the cylinder head cover/intake manifold. Disconnect any vacuum pipes as necessary, having first noted their fitted positions.

15 Prise out the retaining clips and disconnect the fuel return pipes from the injectors. Plug the openings to prevent dirt ingress.

16 Disconnect the fuel feed and return pipes at the right-hand end of the cylinder head cover. Undo the Torx screw securing the fuel pipes bracket **(see illustration)**.

17 Unclip the fuel temperature sensor from the retaining bracket and move the pipe/priming bulb assembly to the rear.

18 Undo the two screws securing the EGR pipe to the cylinder head cover, and the bolt

4.10a Undo the bolts (arrowed) and lift up the right-hand end . . .

4.10b . . . to disengage the resonator box from the turbocharger

4.16 Depress the locking buttons (arrowed) and disconnect the fuel feed and return hoses

4.18 Undo the bolt securing the EGR pipe to the rear of the block (arrowed)

4.12 Undo the two bolts (arrowed) and pull the air filter housing up from its place

4.20a Undo the 8 bolts (arrowed) at the front . . .   **4.20b . . . and the 2 bolts (arrowed) at the rear**

securing the pipe to the rear of the cylinder head **(see illustration)**.

19 Undo the two bolts securing the EGR valve to the left-hand end of the cylinder head, disconnect the vacuum hose, and then remove the valve along with the EGR pipe. Recover the O-ring seal from the pipe.

20 Undo the eight bolts securing the cylinder head cover and intake manifold at the front, and the two retaining bolts along the rear edge of the cover. Lift the assembly away **(see illustrations)**. Recover the manifold rubber seals.

Refitting

21 Refitting is a reversal of removal, bearing in mind the following points:

a) Examine the cover seal(s) for signs of damage and deterioration, and renew if necessary. On 1.4 litre engines, smear a little clean engine oil on the manifold seals.

b) Tighten the cylinder head cover bolts to the specified torque. On 1.4 litre engines, in the order shown **(see illustration)**.

c) On 2.0 litre engines, before refitting the timing belt upper cover, adjust the camshaft position sensor air gap as described in Chapter 4B, Section 13.

5 Crankshaft pulley – removal and refitting

Removal

1 Remove the auxiliary drivebelt as described in Chapter 1B. Turn the tensioner anti-clockwise and insert a pin or drill to hold it **(see illustrations)**.

2.0 litre engines

2 To prevent crankshaft turning whilst the pulley retaining bolt is being slackened, the flywheel/driveplate ring gear can be locked using a suitable tool made from steel angle **(see illustration)**. Remove the cover plate from the base of the transmission bellhousing and bolt the tool to the bellhousing flange so it engages with the ring gear teeth. Do not attempt to *lock* the pulley by inserting a bolt/drill through the timing hole. If the timing hole bolt/drill is in position from a previous operation, temporarily remove it prior to slackening the pulley bolt, then refit it once the bolt has been slackened. **Note:** *On later 2.0 engines (see Section 7), it is essential that the crankshaft and camshaft timing pins*

4.21 Cylinder head cover tightening sequence (1.4 litre engine)

are in place as described in Section 3. This is because, on these engines, the crankshaft sprocket has a wider keyway, to allow it to rotate a little independently of the crankshaft. Failure to lock the crankshaft and camshaft could result in the timing being lost.

1.4 litre engines

3 To lock the crankshaft, working underneath the engine, insert Peugeot tool No 0194-C into the hole in the right-hand face of the engine block casting over the lower section of the flywheel. Rotate the crankshaft until the tool engages in

5.1a Insert a drill or pin to lock the auxiliary drivebelt tensioner in position on 2.0 litre engine . . .

5.1b . . . and 1.4 litre engine

5.2 Use a fabricated tool similar to this to lock the flywheel ring gear and prevent crankshaft rotation

5.3 The locking pin/bolt (arrowed) must locate in the hole in the flywheel (arrowed) to prevent rotation

5.4 Undo the crankshaft pulley retaining bolt

5.6 On 1.4 litre engines, the notch in the pulley (arrowed) must align with the key in the sprocket (arrowed)

the corresponding hole in the flywheel. In the absence of the Peugeot tool, insert a 12 mm rod or drill into the hole **(see illustration)**. Note: *The hole in the casting and the hole in the flywheel are provided purely to lock the crankshaft whilst the pulley bolt is undone, it does **not** position the crankshaft at TDC.*

All engines

4 Using a suitable socket and extension bar, unscrew the retaining bolt, remove the washer, then slide the pulley off the end of the crankshaft **(see illustration)**. If the pulley is tight fit, it can be drawn off the crankshaft using a suitable puller. If a puller is being used, refit the pulley retaining bolt without the washer, to avoid damaging the crankshaft as the puller is tightened.
Caution: On 1.4 litre engines, do not touch the outer magnetic sensor ring of the

sprocket with your fingers, or allow metallic particles to come into contact with it.
5 On 2.0 litre engines, if the pulley locating key is a loose fit, remove it and store it with the pulley for safe-keeping.

Refitting

6 Ensure that the key is correctly located in its crankshaft groove (2.0 litre engines only), and then refit the pulley to the end of the crankshaft **(see illustration)**.
7 Thoroughly clean the threads of the pulley retaining bolt, then apply a coat of locking compound to the bolt threads. Peugeot recommend the use of Loctite (available from your Peugeot dealer); in the absence of this, any good-quality locking compound may be used.
8 Refit the crankshaft pulley retaining bolt and washer. Tighten the bolt to the specified

torque, then through the specified angle, preventing the crankshaft from turning using the method employed on removal.
9 Refit and tension the auxiliary drivebelt as described in Chapter 1B.

6 Timing belt covers – removal and refitting

 Warning: Refer to the precautionary information contained in Section 1 before proceeding.

Upper cover removal

1.4 litre engines

1 Remove the plastic cover from the top of the engine.
2 Release the wiring harness and fuel pipes from the upper cover **(see illustration)**.
3 Undo the five screws and remove the timing belt upper cover **(see illustration)**.

2.0 litre engines

4 Remove the plastic covers from the top of the engine, then undo the screws and remove the engine undershield. The cover over the engine is release by rotating the four fasteners anti-clockwise whilst gently pulling up the cover. Push in the centre pins and prise out the two plastic expanding rivets, release the side clip and remove the cover over the coolant/washer reservoirs.
5 Position a trolley jack under the engine and, using a piece of wood on the jack head, support the weight of the engine.
6 Undo the bolts and remove the right-hand engine mounting and support bracket – see Section 17.
7 At the connections above the fuel pump, disconnect the fuel supply and return hose quick-release fittings using a small screwdriver to press down and release the locking clip **(see illustration)**. Cover the open unions to prevent dirt entry, using small plastic bags, or fingers cut from clean rubber gloves.
8 Release the two hoses from the retaining clips on the upper timing belt cover and move them to one side **(see illustration)**.

6.2 Release the wiring harness from the timing belt upper cover

6.3 Undo the 5 screws (arrowed) and remove the upper timing belt cover

6.7 Disconnect the fuel supply and return hose quick-release fittings

6.8 Release the two fuel hoses from the retaining clips on the upper timing belt cover

6.10 Timing belt cover retaining bolt locations (arrowed)

1 Upper cover
2 Intermediate cover
3 Lower cover

9 Release the EGR solenoid valve vacuum hose from the clip on the upper cover.
10 Undo the bolt securing the upper timing belt cover to the cylinder head cover **(see illustration)**.
11 Undo the upper bolt on the edge of the cover nearest to the engine compartment bulkhead.
12 Undo the lower bolt/nut on the bulkhead side of the cover at the join between the upper and lower covers. Note that this bolt/stud also retains the coolant pump. Where a bolt is fitted, to avoid coolant leakage after the upper cover is removed, refit the bolt fitted with a 17.0 mm spacer, and tighten it securely.
13 Undo the remaining bolt in the centre of the cover.
14 Disengage the upper cover from the intermediate cover and manipulate the upper cover from its location.

Intermediate cover removal

2.0 litre engines

15 Remove the upper cover as described previously.
16 Undo the upper bolt on the top edge of the intermediate cover.
17 Undo the two remaining bolts at the join between the intermediate cover and lower cover, then manipulate the intermediate cover from its location.

Lower cover removal

1.4 litre engines

18 Remove the upper cover as described previously.
19 Remove the crankshaft pulley as described in Section 5.
20 Undo the five bolts and remove the lower cover **(see illustration)**.

6.20 Lower cover retaining bolts (arrowed)

2.0 litre engines

21 Remove the upper and intermediate covers as described previously.
22 Remove the crankshaft pulley as described in Section 5.
23 Undo the two remaining bolts on the edge of the cover, one on either side of the crankshaft pulley location.
24 Lift the cover off the front of the engine.

Refitting

25 Refitting of all the covers is a reversal of the relevant removal procedure, ensuring that each cover section is correctly located, and that the cover retaining bolts are securely tightened. Ensure that all disturbed hoses are reconnected and retained by their relevant clips.

---

7 Timing belt – removal, inspection, refitting and tensioning

Note: *On 2.0 litre engines, Peugeot specify the use of an electronic belt tension checking tool (SEEM CTG 105.M) to correctly set the timing belt tension. The following procedure assumes that this equipment (or suitable alternative equipment calibrated to display belt tension in SEEM units) is available. Accurate tensioning of the timing belt is essential, and if the electronic equipment is not available, it is recommended that the work is entrusted to a Peugeot dealer or suitably-equipped garage.*
Note: *Early 2.0 litre models are identified by three bolts securing the camshaft sprocket to the hub. Later engines are identified by*

the camshaft sprocket being retained by one central bolt.

General

1 The timing belt drives the camshaft(s), high-pressure fuel pump, and coolant pump from a toothed sprocket on the end of the crankshaft. If the belt breaks or slips in service, the pistons are likely to hit the valve heads, resulting in expensive damage.
2 The timing belt should be renewed at the specified intervals, or earlier if it is contaminated with oil, or at all noisy in operation (a 'scraping' noise due to uneven wear).
3 If the timing belt is being removed, it is a wise precaution to check the condition of the coolant pump at the same time (check for signs of coolant leakage). This may avoid the need to remove the timing belt again at a later stage, should the coolant pump fail.

Removal

4 Apply the handbrake, then jack up the front of the vehicle and support it on axle stands (see *Jacking and vehicle support*). Remove the front right-hand roadwheel, wheel arch liner (to expose the crankshaft pulley) and the engine undershield. The wheel arch liner is secured by several plastic expanding rivets. Push the centre pins in a little then prise the rivet from place. The engine undershield is retained by several screw fasteners. Rotate the fasteners 90 degrees anti-clockwise and remove them.
5 Refer to Chapter 4B and remove the complete exhaust system.
Caution: If the exhaust system is not removed, the front pipe flexible section will be damaged when the right-hand engine mounting is detached.
6 Remove the auxiliary drivebelt as described in Chapter 1B.

1.4 litre engines

7 Remove the upper and lower timing belt covers, as described in Section 6.
8 Undo the screw and remove the crankshaft position sensor adjacent to the crankshaft sprocket flange, and move it to one side **(see illustration)**.
9 Undo the retaining screw and remove the timing belt protection bracket, again adjacent to the crankshaft sprocket flange **(see illustration)**.

7.8 Undo the bolt securing the crankshaft position sensor (arrowed)

7.9 Timing belt protection bracket retaining bolt (arrowed)

7.13 Insert an Allen key into the hole (arrowed), slacken the pulley bolt and allow the tensioner to rotate

7.18a Unscrew the crankshaft pulley bolt . . .

7.18b . . . then remove the pulley

10 Lock the crankshaft and camshaft in the correct position as described in Section 3. If necessary, temporarily refit the crankshaft pulley bolt to enable the crankshaft to be rotated.

11 Position a trolley jack under the engine, and using a block of wood on the jack head, take the weight of the engine.

12 Undo the bolts and remove the right-hand engine mounting and support bracket – see Section 17.

13 Insert a hexagon key into belt tensioner pulley centre, slacken the pulley bolt, and allow the tensioner to rotate, relieving the belt tension **(see illustration)**. With belt slack, temporarily tighten the pulley bolt.

14 Note its routing, then remove the timing belt from the sprockets.

2.0 litre engines

15 Remove the turbocharger air inlet pipe.

16 Unbolt the closure plate from the bottom of the clutch housing

17 Using a suitable tool, lock the flywheel/driveplate, and then loosen the crankshaft pulley bolt. Peugeot technicians use a tool which engages the teeth of the starter ring gear and is bolted to the clutch bellhousing. A similar tool may be made out of a length of angle iron, bent to engage the teeth, or alternatively an assistant may restrain the starter ring gear with a wide-bladed screwdriver.

18 Unscrew and remove the crankshaft pulley bolt, then remove the pulley from the crankshaft **(see illustrations)**. If it is tight, refit the bolt without its washer, leaving sufficient room to release the pulley. Using a puller, remove the pulley from the front of the crankshaft.

19 Unbolt the rear engine mounting link piece – see Section 17.

20 An 8.0 mm diameter flywheel/driveplate locking pin is now required, and may be obtained from a Peugeot dealer or car accessory shop.

21 Temporarily refit the crankshaft pulley bolt, and then turn the engine until the TDC hole in the flywheel/driveplate is aligned with the hole in the front engine flange (next to the transmission bellhousing – see Section 3). Insert the locking pin to lock the engine.

22 Remove the upper, intermediate and lower

timing belt covers as described in the previous Section.

23 As a precaution against damage to the radiator, place a card or piece of hardboard over it on the engine side.

24 Insert a suitable drill or metal dowel through the TDC hole in the camshaft sprocket flange, and into the cylinder head (see Section 3).

25 Loosen the bolt on the tensioner roller, and turn the tensioner clockwise to release the tension on the timing belt. If available, use an 8 mm square drive extension in the hole provided to turn the tensioner bracket against the spring tension **(see Tool Tip)**. Retighten the bolt sufficiently to hold the tensioner in its released position; do not fully tighten the bolt in this position.

26 Mark the timing belt with an arrow to indicate its running direction, if it is to be re-used. Remove the belt from the sprockets.

Inspection

27 Renew the belt as a matter of course, regardless of its apparent condition. The cost of a new belt is nothing compared with the cost of repairs should the belt break in service. If signs of oil contamination are found, trace the source of the oil leak and rectify it. Wash down the engine timing belt

A square section tool to fit the timing belt tensioner pulley can be made from a length of standard 8 mm door handle rod (A), obtained from a DIY shop, and then cut to size. Once the rod has been fitted to the tensioner, the timing belt can be tensioned by turning the rod with an 8 mm spanner (B).

area and all related components, to remove all traces of oil. Check that the tensioner and idler pulleys rotate freely without any sign of roughness, and also check that the coolant pump pulley rotates freely. If necessary, renew these items. **Note:** *Peugeot recommend that the tensioner and idler pulleys should not be re-used, regardless of apparent condition.*

Refitting and tensioning

28 Commence refitting by ensuring that the crankshaft and camshaft timing pins are still in position correctly.

1.4 litre engines

29 Locate the timing belt on the crankshaft sprocket then, keeping it taut, locate it around the idler pulley, camshaft sprocket, high-pressure pump sprocket, coolant pump sprocket, and the tensioner roller **(see illustration)**.

7.29 Timing belt routing (1.4 litre engine)

1 *Camshaft sprocket*
2 *Idler pulley*
3 *Crankshaft sprocket*
4 *Coolant pump sprocket*
5 *Tensioner pulley*
6 *High-pressure fuel pump pulley*

30 Refit the timing belt protection bracket and tighten the retaining bolt securely.

31 Slacken the tensioner pulley bolt and, using a hexagonal key, rotate the tensioner anti-clockwise, which moves the index arm clockwise, until the index arm is aligned **(see illustration)**.

32 Remove the camshaft and crankshaft timing pins and, using a socket on the crankshaft pulley bolt, rotate the engine clockwise 10 complete revolutions. Refit the crankshaft and camshaft locking pins.

33 Check that the tensioner index arm is still aligned between the edges of the area **(see illustration 7.31)**. If it is not, remove and belt and begin the refitting process again, starting at Paragraph 29.

34 The remainder of refitting is a reversal of removal. Tighten all fasteners to the specified torque where given.

Early 2.0 litre engines

35 Early models are identified by three bolts securing the camshaft sprocket to the hub. Loosen the three bolts securing the camshaft sprocket to the camshaft, so that the sprocket can be turned on its hub **(see illustration)**. To do this, either use a tool engaged with the holes in the sprocket, or alternatively, hold the sprocket with an old timing belt.

36 Finger-tighten the sprocket bolts, and then slacken each bolt by one sixth of a turn. Turn the sprocket clockwise to the end of the slots.

37 Locate the timing belt on the crankshaft pulley splines then, keeping it taut, locate

7.31 Align the index arm (A) with the locating stud (B)

it around the idler pulley and onto the high-pressure pump pulley **(see illustrations)**. Peugeot technicians use a plastic clip to retain the belt on the crankshaft pulley; if necessary, use a plastic cable tie to hold it.

38 Locate the belt onto the camshaft sprocket teeth. If the teeth do not align correctly, turn the camshaft sprocket slightly anti-clockwise until the belt engages. **Note:** *Do not turn the pulley anti-clockwise more than one tooth space.*

39 Continue to locate the belt onto the tensioner pulley and coolant pump sprocket, then loosen the bolt and turn the tensioner *anti-clockwise* to tension the belt moderately. Pretighten the bolt to 1.0 Nm, and then remove the holding clip or cable tie.

40 A timing belt tension setting tool is now required to apply the correct tension. A tool which checks SEEM units is necessary, and

7.35 Slacken the three camshaft sprocket-to-sprocket hub retaining bolts

should be fitted to the belt run between the camshaft sprocket and high-pressure pump sprocket.

41 Loosen the bolt, then turn the tensioner *anti-clockwise* until 98.0 ± 2.0 SEEM units is read on the tool **(see illustrations)**. At this point, tighten the tensioner bolt to the specified torque.

42 Temporarily remove one of the three bolts securing the sprocket to the camshaft, and check that the bolts are not at the anti-clockwise limit of their slots. If they are, repeat the refitting procedure.

43 Tighten the camshaft sprocket bolts to the specified torque.

44 Remove the crankshaft and camshaft TDC setting pins. Also remove the tensioning tool.

45 Turn the engine clockwise 8 times. Do not turn the engine anti-clockwise during this operation.

7.37a Retain the timing belt on the crankshaft sprocket and feed it around the idler roller . . .

7.37b . . . high-pressure fuel pump sprocket . . .

7.37c . . . camshaft sprocket . . .

7.37d . . . coolant pump and tensioner pulley

7.41a Pivot the tensioner pulley anti-clockwise, then tighten the retaining bolt . . .

7.41b . . . when the specified tension value is shown on the measuring equipment

7.59 Insert a 2 mm rod (A) on the left-hand side of the Woodruff key (B)

46 Refit the crankshaft and camshaft TDC setting pins.

47 Loosen the camshaft sprocket bolts again, then finger-tighten them, and loosen each by one sixth of a turn.

48 Refit the tensioning tool midway between the camshaft and high-pressure pump sprocket.

49 Loosen the tensioner bolt, then turn the tensioner anti-clockwise until the tool reads 54.0 ± 2.0 SEEM units. With the tensioner held in this position, tighten the bolt to the specified torque. It is important to apply the correct tension to the timing belt, otherwise the belt may be noisy in operation, or worse still, may break.

50 Tighten the camshaft sprocket bolts to the specified torque.

51 Remove the tensioning tool to release its internal forces, then refit it and check the tension of the belt is between 51.0 and 57.0 SEEM units. If necessary, repeat the tensioning procedure.

52 Remove the tensioning tool and TDC setting pins.

53 Turn the engine clockwise 2 times. Do not turn the engine anti-clockwise during this operation.

54 Refit the crankshaft and camshaft TDC setting/locking pins.

55 Visually check that the offset between the camshaft hub hole and the corresponding setting hole does not exceed 1.0 mm.

56 Remove the TDC setting/locking pins.

57 The remainder of refitting is a reversal of removal. Tighten all fasteners to the specified torque where given.

Later 2.0 litre engines

58 Later engines are identified by the camshaft sprocket being retained by one central bolt.

59 Set the crankshaft sprocket by inserting a 2 mm diameter rod on the left-hand side of the woodruff key **(see illustration)**. Check the flywheel and camshaft timing pins are still in place.

60 Locate the timing belt on the camshaft sprocket splines then, keeping it taut, locate it around the high-pressure pump pulley, idler pulley, crankshaft sprocket, coolant pump sprocket and tensioner pulley. Peugeot technicians use a plastic clip to retain the belt on the camshaft sprocket; if necessary, use a plastic cable tie to hold it.

61 Loosen the bolt and turn the tensioner *anti-clockwise* to tension the belt moderately. Pretighten the bolt to 1.0 Nm, then remove the holding clip or cable tie. Remove the 2 mm diameter rod from alongside the crankshaft sprocket key.

62 A timing belt tension setting tool is now required to apply the correct tension. A tool which checks SEEM units is necessary, and should be fitted to the belt run between the camshaft sprocket and high-pressure pump sprocket.

63 Loosen the bolt, then turn the tensioner *anti-clockwise* until 98.0 ± 2.0 SEEM units is read on the tool **(see illustrations 7.41a and 7.41b)**. At this point, tighten the tensioner bolt to the specified torque.

64 Immobilise the flywheel as described in Paragraph 17, then refit the crankshaft auxiliary belt pulley, and tighten its retaining bolt to 70 Nm.

65 Remove the crankshaft and camshaft timing pins, and the flywheel locking tool.

66 Turn the engine clockwise 8 times. Do not turn the engine anti-clockwise during this operation.

67 Refit the crankshaft and camshaft TDC setting pins, then lock the flywheel as described in Paragraph 17.

68 Undo the bolt and remove the auxiliary drivebelt pulley.

69 Refit the tensioning tool midway between the camshaft and high-pressure pump sprocket.

70 Loosen the tensioner bolt, then turn the tensioner anti-clockwise until the tool reads 54.0 ± 2.0 SEEM units. With the tensioner held in this position, tighten the bolt to the specified torque. It is important to apply the correct tension to the timing belt, otherwise

Tool Tip 1: A sprocket holding tool can be made from two lengths of steel strip bolted together to form a forked end. Bend the end of the strip through 90° to form the fork 'prongs'.

the belt may be noisy in operation, or worse still, may break.

71 Remove the tensioning tool to release its internal forces, then refit it and check the tension of the belt is between 51.0 and 57.0 SEEM units. If necessary, repeat the tensioning procedure.

72 Remove the crankshaft and camshaft timing pins, and the flywheel locking tool.

73 The remainder of refitting is a reversal of removal, noting the following points.
a) Ensure the timing covers engage correctly with each other.
b) When refitting the crankshaft auxiliary drivebelt pulley, apply a few drops of thread-locking compound to the pulley bolt.
c) Tighten all fasteners to the specified torque where given.

8 Timing belt sprockets and tensioner – removal and refitting

Camshaft sprocket

Removal

1 Remove the timing belt as described in Section 7.

2 Remove the locking tool from the camshaft sprocket/hub. Slacken the sprocket hub retaining bolt, and the three sprocket-to-hub retaining bolts (where applicable). To prevent the camshaft rotating as the bolt(s) are slackened, a sprocket-holding tool will be required. In the absence of the special Peugeot tool, an acceptable substitute can be fabricated at home **(see Tool Tip 1)**. *Do not* attempt to use the engine assembly/valve timing locking tool to prevent the sprocket from rotating whilst the bolt is slackened.

3 Remove the sprocket hub retaining bolt and washer (where fitted), and slide the sprocket and hub off the end of the camshaft **(see illustration)**. If the Woodruff key is a loose fit in the camshaft on 2.0 litre engines, remove it for safe-keeping. Examine the camshaft oil seal for signs of oil leakage and, if necessary, renew it as described in Section 14.

4 If necessary on early 2.0 litre engines, the

8.3 Undo the retaining bolt and remove the camshaft sprocket (1.4 litre engine)

8.7 On 1.4 litre engines, align the sprocket lug with the notch in the end of the camshaft (arrowed)

8.13a Slide the crankshaft sprocket off the end of the crankshaft . . .

8.13b . . . and collect the Woodruff key (2.0 litre engine)

sprocket can be separated from the hub after removing the three retaining bolts.

5 Clean the camshaft sprocket thoroughly, and renew it if there are any signs of wear, damage or cracks.

Refitting

6 If removed on early 2.0 litre engines, refit the sprocket to the hub and secure with the three retaining bolts, tightened finger tight only at this stage.

7 Where applicable, refit the Woodruff key to the end of the camshaft, and then refit the camshaft sprocket and hub **(see illustration)**.

8 Refit the sprocket hub retaining bolt and washer. Tighten the bolt to the specified torque, preventing the camshaft from turning as during removal.

9 Align the engine assembly/valve timing slot in the camshaft sprocket hub with the hole in the cylinder head and refit the timing pin to lock the camshaft in position.

10 Fit the timing belt around the pump sprocket and camshaft sprocket, and tension the timing belt as described in Section 7.

Crankshaft sprocket

Removal

11 Remove the timing belt as described in Section 7.

12 Check that the engine assembly/valve timing holes are still aligned as described in Section 3, and the camshaft sprocket/hub and flywheel/driveplate are locked in position.

13 Slide the sprocket off the end of the

crankshaft and collect the Woodruff key **(see illustrations)**.

14 Examine the crankshaft oil seal for signs of oil leakage and, if necessary, renew it as described in Section 14.

15 Clean the crankshaft sprocket thoroughly, and renew it if there are any signs of wear, damage or cracks. Recover the crankshaft locating key.

Refitting

16 Refit the key to the end of the crankshaft, then refit the crankshaft sprocket (with the flange nearest the cylinder block on the 2.0 litre engine, and facing the crankshaft pulley on the 1.4 litre engine).

17 Fit the timing belt around the crankshaft sprocket, and tension the timing belt as described in Section 7.

Fuel pump sprocket

Removal

18 Remove the timing belt as described in Section 7.

19 Using a suitable socket, undo the pump sprocket retaining nut. The sprocket can be held stationary by inserting a suitably-sized locking pin, drill or rod through the hole in the sprocket, and into the corresponding hole in

the backplate **(see illustration)**, or by using a suitable forked tool engaged with the holes in the sprocket **(see Tool Tip 1 – paragraph 2)**.

20 The pump sprocket is a taper fit on the pump shaft and it will be necessary to make up another tool to release it from the taper **(see Tool Tip 2)**.

21 Partially unscrew the sprocket retaining nut, fit the home-made tool, and secure it to the sprocket with two suitable bolts. Prevent the sprocket from rotating as before, and unscrew the sprocket retaining nut **(see illustration)**. The nut will bear against the tool as it is undone, forcing the sprocket off the shaft taper. Once the taper is released, remove the tool, unscrew the nut fully, and remove the sprocket from the pump shaft.

22 Clean the sprocket thoroughly, and renew it if there are any signs of wear, damage or cracks.

Refitting

23 Refit the pump sprocket and retaining nut, and tighten the nut to the specified torque. Prevent the sprocket rotating as the nut is tightened using the sprocket holding tool.

24 Fit the timing belt around the pump sprocket, and tension the timing belt as described in Section 7.

Coolant pump sprocket

25 The coolant pump sprocket is integral with the pump, and cannot be removed. Coolant pump removal is described in Chapter 3.

8.19 On 1.4 litre engines insert a suitable drill bit through the sprocket into the hole in the backplate

Tool Tip 2: Make a sprocket releasing tool from a short strip of steel. Drill two holes in the strip to correspond with the two holes in the sprocket. Drill a third hole just large enough to accept the flats of the sprocket retaining nut.

8.21 Using the home-made tools to remove the fuel pump sprocket (2.0 litre engine)

Tensioner pulley
Removal

26 Remove the timing belt as described in Section 7.

27 Remove the tensioner pulley retaining bolt, and slide the pulley off its mounting stud.

28 Clean the tensioner pulley, but do not use any strong solvent, which may enter the pulley bearings. Check that the pulley rotates freely, with no sign of stiffness or free play. Renew the pulley if there is any doubt about its condition, or if there are any obvious signs of wear or damage.

29 Examine the pulley mounting stud for signs of damage and if necessary, renew it.

Refitting

30 Refit the tensioner pulley to its mounting stud, and fit the retaining bolt.

31 Refit the timing belt as described in Section 7.

Idler pulley
Removal

32 Remove the timing belt as described in Section 7.

33 Undo the retaining bolt/nut and withdraw the idler pulley from the engine.

34 Clean the idler pulley, but do not use any strong solvent, which may enter the bearings. Check that the pulley rotates freely, with no sign of stiffness or free play. Renew the idler pulley if there is any doubt about its condition, or if there are any obvious signs of wear or damage.

Refitting

35 Locate the idler pulley on the engine, and fit the retaining bolt/nut. Tighten the bolt/nut to the specified torque.

36 Refit the timing belt as described in Section 7.

> **9 Camshaft, rocker arms and hydraulic tappets** – removal, inspection and refitting

Removal

1 Remove the cylinder head cover as described in Section 4.

2 Remove the camshaft sprocket as described in Section 8.

9.10 Remove the rocker arms

9.4 Undo the vacuum pump bolts (arrowed)

1.4 litre engines

3 Refit the right-hand engine mounting, but only tighten the bolts moderately; this will keep the engine supported during the camshaft removal.

4 Undo the bolts and remove the vacuum pump. Recover the pump O-ring seals **(see illustration)**.

5 Disconnect the wiring plug, unscrew the retaining bolt, and remove the camshaft position sensor from the cylinder head.

6 Working in a spiral pattern, progressively and evenly unscrew the camshaft upper bearing housing bolts **(see illustration)**. Carefully lift the housing away.

7 Note the orientation of the camshaft, then lift it upwards from the housing and slide off and discard the oil seal.

8 To remove the rocker arms and hydraulic tappets, undo the 13 bolts and remove the lower half of the camshaft bearing housing.

9 Obtain eight small, clean plastic containers, and number them 1 to 8; alternatively, divide a larger container into eight compartments.

10 Lift out each rocker arm. Place the rocker arms in their respective positions in the box or containers **(see illustration)**.

11 A compartmentalised container filled with engine oil is now required to retain the hydraulic tappets while they are removed from the cylinder head. Withdraw each hydraulic follower and place it in the container, keeping them each identified for correct refitting. The tappets must be totally submerged in the oil to prevent air entering them.

12 Recover the 5 O-ring seals between the housing and the cylinder head.

9.18 Remove the camshaft bearing housing from the cylinder head . . .

9.6 Upper camshaft bearing housing bolts (arrowed)

2.0 litre engines

13 Slacken the retaining clamps and disconnect the air intake hose from the left-hand end of the cylinder head. Remove the intercooler air duct from the left-hand end of the cylinder head.

14 Refit the right-hand engine mounting, but only tighten the bolts moderately; this will keep the engine supported during the camshaft removal.

15 Disconnect the vacuum pipe from the brake vacuum pump on the left-hand end of the cylinder head.

16 Remove the vacuum pump from the cylinder head with reference to Chapter 9.

17 Working in a spiral pattern from the outside-in, progressively loosen the camshaft bearing cap housing bolts until they can be removed.

18 Withdraw the bearing cap housing from the cylinder head. The housing is likely to be initially tight to release as it is located by two dowels on the forward-facing side of the cylinder head. If necessary, very carefully prise up the housing using a screwdriver inserted in the slotted lug adjacent to each dowel location. Once the bearing housing is free, lift it squarely from the cylinder head **(see illustration)**. The camshaft will rise up slightly under the pressure of the valve springs – be careful it doesn't tilt and jam in the cylinder head or bearing housing section.

19 Carefully lift the camshaft from its location and remove the oil seal **(see illustration)**. Discard the seal, a new one should be used on refitting.

9.19 . . . then lift out the camshaft

9.21 Lift out the rocker arms . . .

9.22a . . . followed by the hydraulic tappets . . .

9.22b . . . and place all the components in their respective positions in a box

20 Obtain eight small, clean plastic containers, and number them 1 to 8; alternatively, divide a larger container into eight compartments.

21 Lift out each rocker arm and release it from the spring clip on the tappet. Place the rocker arms in their respective positions in the box or containers **(see illustration)**.

22 A compartmentalised container filled with engine oil is now required to retain the hydraulic tappets while they are removed from the cylinder head. Using a rubber sucker, withdraw each hydraulic follower and place it in the container, keeping them identified for correct refitting **(see illustrations)**. The tappets must be totally submerged in the oil to prevent air entering them.

Inspection

23 Inspect the cam lobes and the camshaft bearing journals for scoring or other visible evidence of wear. Once the surface hardening of the cam lobes has been eroded, wear will occur at an accelerated rate. **Note:** *If these symptoms are visible on the tips of the camshaft lobes, check the corresponding rocker arm, as it will probably be worn as well.*

24 Examine the condition of the bearing surfaces in the cylinder head and camshaft bearing housing. If wear is evident, the cylinder head and bearing housing will both have to be renewed, as they are a matched assembly.

25 Inspect the rocker arms and tappets for scuffing, cracking or other damage and renew any components as necessary. Also check the condition of the tappet bores in the cylinder head. As with the camshafts, any wear in this area will necessitate cylinder head renewal.

Refitting

26 Thoroughly clean the sealant from the mating surfaces of the cylinder head and camshaft bearing housing. Use a suitable liquid gasket dissolving agent (available from Peugeot dealers) together with a soft putty knife; do not use a metal scraper or the faces will be damaged. As there is no conventional gasket used, the cleanliness of the mating faces is of the utmost importance.

27 Clean off any oil, dirt or grease from both components and dry with a clean lint-free cloth. Ensure that all the oilways are completely clean.

28 On 2.0 litre engines, to prevent any possibility of the valves contacting the pistons as the camshaft is refitted, remove the locking pin/drill from the flywheel/driveplate/crankshaft sprocket and turn the crankshaft a quarter turn in the *opposite* direction to normal rotation (ie, anti-clockwise), to position all the pistons at mid-stroke. On 1.4 litre engines, with the timing marks aligned as described in

Section 3, the pistons are already positioned halfway down the cylinder bores.

29 Liberally lubricate the hydraulic tappet bores in the cylinder head with clean engine oil.

30 Insert the hydraulic tappets into their original bores in the cylinder head unless they have been renewed.

31 Lubricate the rocker arms and place them over their respective tappets and valve stems. On 2.0 litre engines, ensure that the ends of the rocker arms engage with the spring clips on the tappets.

32 On 2.0 litre engines, lubricate the camshaft bearing journals in the cylinder head sparingly with oil, taking care not to allow the oil to spill over onto the camshaft bearing housing contact areas.

1.4 litre engines

33 Sparingly apply a bead of silicone sealant to the mating face of the cylinder head-to-camshaft lower bearing housing, and position the 5 new O-ring seals **(see illustration)**.

34 Insert two 12 mm rods or drill bits into the locating holes in the cylinder head to guide the bearing housing into position. Suitable guide rods, No 194-N, are available from Peugeot dealers. Refit the lower bearing housing over the tools, insert the bolts and finger-tighten them in order **(see illustration)**.

35 Remove the guide pins/rods and tighten

9.33 Apply a bead of sealant, and fit the new O-rings (arrowed)

H44706

9.34 Insert guide pins/rods into the guide holes (A), fit the housing and tighten the bolts in sequence

9.37 Lay the camshaft in position, and apply a bead of sealant to the housing mating face

9.39 Upper camshaft housing bolts tightening sequence

the housing bolts in the sequence shown previously to the specified torque.

36 Lubricate the camshaft bearing journals with clean engine oil, and lay the camshaft in position.

37 Sparingly apply a bead of silicone sealant to the mating face of the camshaft lower bearing housing **(see illustration)**.

38 Insert two 12 mm rods or drill bits into the locating holes in the lower camshaft bearing housing to guide the upper housing into position. Suitable guide rods, No 194-N, are available from Peugeot dealers.

39 Lower the upper housing over the guide pins/rods, and finger-tighten the bolts gradually and evenly, in sequence until the housing makes firm contact with the lower housing **(see illustration)**.

40 Remove the guides pins/rods and tighten the housing to the specified torque in the same sequence.

41 Fit a new camshaft oil seal as described in Section 14.

42 Ensure the key is fitted to the camshaft, then refit the camshaft sprocket to the camshaft and tighten the bolt to the specified torque.

43 Refit the camshaft position sensor to the camshaft housing, and position the sensor so that the gap between the sprocket and the sensor end is 1.2 mm for a used sensor. If fitting a new sensor, the small tip of the sensor must be just touching one of the three webs of the signal ring **(see illustration)**. Tighten the bolt to the specified torque.

44 Turn the camshaft sprocket the position where the timing tool can be inserted, then refit the timing belt as described in Section 7.

45 The remainder of refitting is a reversal of removal.

2.0 litre engines

46 Lay the camshaft in the cylinder head. On early engines position the camshaft so that the engine assembly/valve timing slot in the sprocket hub is approximately aligned with the timing hole in the cylinder head.

47 Ensure that the mating faces of the cylinder head and camshaft bearing housing are clean and free of any oil or grease.

48 Sparingly apply a bead of silicone sealant to the mating face of the camshaft bearing housing, taking care not to allow the product to contaminate the camshaft bearing journal areas **(see illustration)**.

49 Locate the bearing housing over the camshaft and into position on the cylinder head.

50 Insert all the bearing housing retaining bolts and *progressively* tighten them to the specified torque, in sequence **(see illustration)**.

51 Fit a new camshaft oil seal as described in Section 14.

52 Refit the camshaft hub and/or sprocket as described in Section 8.

53 Rotate the crankshaft clockwise until the timing rod can be re-inserted through the hole in the block and into the flywheel/driveplate (see Section 3).

54 Refit the timing belt as described in Section 7.

55 The remainder of refitting is a reversal of removal.

10 Cylinder head – removal and refitting

Note: *This is an involved procedure, and it is suggested that the Section is read thoroughly before starting work. To aid refitting, make notes on the locations of all relevant brackets and the routing of hoses and cables before removal.*

Removal

1 Apply the handbrake, then jack up the front of the vehicle and support it on axle stands (see *Jacking and vehicle support*). Remove the front right-hand roadwheel, the engine undershield, and the front wheel arch liner. The undershield is secured by several screws, and the wheel arch liner is secured by several plastic expanding rivets. Push the centre pins in a little, then prise the rivet from place.

2 Remove the battery (see Chapter 5A).

3 Drain the cooling system as described in Chapter 1B. For improved general access, remove the bonnet as described in Chapter 11.

1.4 litre engines

4 Remove the cylinder head cover as described in Section 4.

5 Remove the timing belt as described in Section 7.

6 Disconnect the exhaust front pipe from the manifold, as described in Chapter 4B. **Note:** *Do not allow any strain to be placed on the*

9.43 When fitting a used sensor, the gap between the sensor end and the sensor ring web should be 1.2 mm

9.48 Apply a bead of silicone sealant to the mating face of the camshaft bearing housing

9.50 Camshaft bearing housing bolt tightening sequence

10.8 Auxiliary drivebelt tensioner bolts (arrowed)

10.13a Fuel pump rear support bracket bolts (arrowed) . . .

flexible section of the exhaust pipe, as damage will result.

7 Remove the glow plugs as described in Chapter 5C.

8 Undo the three bolts and remove the auxiliary drivebelt tensioner from the front of the engine **(see illustration)**.

9 Remove the catalytic converter as described in Section 18 of Chapter 4B.

10 Remove the alternator (see Chapter 5A) and mounting bracket.

11 Undo the union bolts and remove the oil feed pipe from the engine block and the turbocharger. Recover the unions sealing washers.

12 Slacken the retaining clamp and disconnect the turbocharger oil return hose from the engine block.

13 Slacken and remove the high-pressure fuel pump rear support bracket bolts and front support bracket upper bolt **(see illustrations)**.

14 Remove the injectors as described in Chapter 4B.

15 Undo the coolant outlet housing (left-hand end of the cylinder head) retaining bolts, slacken the two bolts securing the housing support bracket to the top of the transmission bellhousing, and move the outlet housing away from the cylinder head a little **(see illustration)**. There is no need to disconnect the hoses.

16 Disconnect the wiring plug, then undo the bolt and remove the camshaft position sensor from the cylinder head.

17 Undo the 13 bolts and remove the camshaft bearing housing from the cylinder head, complete with camshaft. Recover the 5 small O-ring seals between the housing and the cylinder head.

18 Obtain eight small, clean plastic containers, and number them 1 to 8; alternatively, divide a larger container into eight compartments.

19 Lift out each rocker arm. Place the rocker arms in their respective positions in the box or containers **(see illustration 9.10)**.

20 A compartmentalised container filled with engine oil is now required to retain the hydraulic tappets while they are removed from the cylinder head. Withdraw each hydraulic follower and place it in the container, keeping

them identified for correct refitting. The tappets must be totally submerged in the oil to prevent air entering them.

21 Working in the *reverse* of the tightening sequence **(see illustration 10.54)** undo the cylinder head bolts.

2.0 litre engines

22 Remove the air cleaner assembly, airflow meter and inlet air ducts, fuel injectors, common fuel rail and turbocharger as described in Chapter 4B.

23 Remove the EGR valve with reference to Chapter 4C.

24 Remove the timing belt as described in Section 7.

10.13b . . . and front support bracket upper bolt

10.28a Unscrew the nuts . . .

25 Temporarily refit the right-hand engine mounting to support the engine whilst the cylinder head is removed.

26 Note their fitted positions and routing, then disconnect all coolant and vacuum hoses from the cylinder head.

27 Unscrew the bolts securing the oil level dipstick tube to the cylinder head.

28 Unscrew the nuts on the two studs securing the coolant outlet manifold to the left-hand end of the cylinder head, then unscrew and remove the studs. Use a stud extractor or alternatively tighten two nuts together on the stud before unscrewing it. Note the location of brackets on the studs for correct refitting **(see illustrations)**.

10.15 Coolant housing bolts (arrowed)

10.28b . . . then remove the studs from the coolant outlet manifold

10.29a Unscrew the bolts . . .

10.29b . . . and move the coolant outlet manifold away from the cylinder head

10.30 Remove the camshaft position sensor

29 Without disconnecting the hoses, unscrew the mounting bolts and move the coolant outlet manifold away from the left-hand end of the cylinder head (see illustrations). If necessary, tie it to one side. Recover the seal. Note: *At the time of writing, the coolant outlet manifold seal was not available separately. If damaged, the complete outlet manifold must be renewed. Check with a Peugeot dealer.*
30 Disconnect the wiring from the camshaft position sensor then undo the screw and remove the sensor (see illustration). Check that all relevant wiring is disconnected from the sensors on the cylinder head, then move the wiring harness to one side.
31 Remove the cylinder head cover as described in Section 4.
32 Progressively slacken the cylinder head bolts, in the *reverse* order to that for tightening (see illustration 10.62). A Torx socket will be required for this.
33 When all the bolts are loose, unscrew them fully and remove them from the cylinder head.

All engines

34 Release the cylinder head from the cylinder block and location dowels by rocking it. The Peugeot tool for doing this consists simply of two metal rods with 90-degree angled ends (see illustration). Do not prise between the

10.34 Free the cylinder head using angled rods

mating faces of the cylinder head and block, as this may damage the gasket faces.
35 Lift the cylinder head from the block, and recover the gasket.
36 If necessary, remove the manifolds (if not already done so) with reference to Chapter 4B.

Preparation for refitting

37 The mating faces of the cylinder head and cylinder block must be perfectly clean before refitting the head. Peugeot recommend the use of a scouring agent for this purpose, but acceptable results can be achieved by using a hard plastic or wood scraper to remove all traces of gasket and carbon. The same method can be used to clean the piston crowns. Take particular care to avoid scoring or gouging the cylinder head/cylinder block mating surfaces during the cleaning operations, as aluminium alloy is easily damaged. Make sure that the carbon is not allowed to enter the oil and water passages – this is particularly important for the lubrication system, as carbon could block the oil supply to the engine's components. Using adhesive tape and paper, seal the water, oil and bolt holes in the cylinder block. To prevent carbon entering the gap between the pistons and bores, smear a little grease in the gap. After cleaning each piston, use a small brush to remove all traces of grease and carbon from the gap, and then wipe away the remainder with a clean rag.
38 Check the mating surfaces of the

10.43 Measure the piston protrusion using a DTI gauge

cylinder block and the cylinder head for nicks, deep scratches and other damage. If slight, they may be removed carefully with a file, but if excessive, machining may be the only alternative to renewal. If warpage of the cylinder head gasket surface is suspected, use a straight-edge to check it for distortion. Refer to Part E of this Chapter if necessary.
39 Thoroughly clean the threads of the cylinder head bolt holes in the cylinder block. Ensure that the bolts run freely in their threads, and that all traces of oil and water are removed from each bolt hole.

Gasket selection

40 Remove the crankshaft timing pin, then turn the crankshaft until pistons 1 and 4 are at TDC (Top Dead Centre). Position a dial test indicator (dial gauge) on the cylinder block adjacent to the rear of No 1 piston, and zero it on the block face. Transfer the probe to the crown of No 1 piston (10.0 mm in from the rear edge), and then slowly turn the crankshaft back-and-forth past TDC, noting the highest reading on the indicator. Record this reading as protrusion A.
41 Repeat the check described in paragraph 40, this time 10.0 mm in from the front edge of the No 1 piston crown. Record this reading as protrusion B.
42 Add protrusion A to protrusion B, then divide the result by 2 to obtain an average reading for piston No 1.
43 Repeat the procedure described in paragraphs 40 to 42 on piston 4, then turn the crankshaft through 180° and carry out the procedure on the piston Nos 2 and 3 (see illustration). Check that there is a maximum difference of 0.07 mm protrusion between any two pistons.
44 If a dial test indicator is not available, piston protrusion may be measured using a straight-edge and feeler blades or Vernier calipers. However, this is much less accurate, and cannot therefore be recommended.
45 Note the greatest piston protrusion measurement, and use this to determine the correct cylinder head gasket from the following table. The series of notches/holes on

10.45a Cylinder head gasket thickness identification notches (arrowed) on 1.4 litre engine . . .

10.45b . . . and 2.0 litre engine (arrowed)

10.46 Measure the length of from under the bolt head to its end (1.4 litre engine)

the side of the gasket are used for thickness identification (**see illustrations**).

1.4 litre engines

Piston protrusion	Gasket identification
0.618 to 0.725 mm	2 notches
0.726 to 0.775 mm	3 notches
0.776 to 0.825 mm	1 notch
0.826 to 0.875 mm	4 notches
0.876 to 0.983 mm	5 notches

2.0 litre engines

Piston protrusion	Gasket identification
0.470 to 0.604 mm	1 notch
0.605 to 0.654 mm	2 notches
0.655 to 0.704 mm	3 notches
0.705 to 0.754 mm	4 notches
0.755 to 0.830 mm	5 notches

Head bolt examination

46 Carefully examine the cylinder head bolts for signs of damage to the threads or head, and for any sign of corrosion. If the bolts are in a satisfactory condition, measure the length of each bolt from the underside of the head, to the end of the shank. The bolts may be re-used providing that the measured length does not exceed 149.0 mm on the 1.4 litre engine, and 133.3 mm on the 2.0 litre engine (**see illustration**). **Note:** *Considering the stress to which the cylinder head bolts are subjected, it is highly recommended that they be all renewed, regardless of their apparent condition.*

Refitting

47 Turn the crankshaft and position Nos 1

and 4 pistons at TDC, then turn the crankshaft a quarter turn (90°) anti-clockwise.
48 Thoroughly clean the surfaces of the cylinder head and block.
49 Make sure that the locating dowels are in place, then fit the correct gasket the right way round on the cylinder block (**see illustration**).

1.4 litre engines

50 If necessary, refit the exhaust manifold to the cylinder head as described in Chapter 4B.
51 Carefully lower the cylinder head onto the gasket and block, making sure that it locates correctly onto the dowels.
52 Apply a smear of grease to the threads, and to the underside of the heads, of the cylinder head bolts. Peugeot recommend the use of Molykote G Rapid Plus (available from your Peugeot dealer); in the absence of the specified grease, any good-quality high melting-point grease may be used.
53 Carefully insert the cylinder head bolts into their holes (*do not drop them in*) and initially finger-tighten them.
54 Working progressively and in sequence, tighten the cylinder head bolts to their Stage 1 torque setting, using a torque wrench and suitable socket (**see illustration**).
55 Once all the bolts have been tightened to their Stage 1 torque setting, working again in the specified sequence, tighten each bolt to the specified Stage 2 setting. Finally, angle-tighten the bolts through the specified Stage 3 angle. It is recommended that an angle-measuring gauge be used during this stage of tightening, to ensure accuracy. **Note:**

Retightening of the cylinder head bolts after running the engine is not required.
56 Refit the hydraulic tappets, rocker arms, and camshaft housing (complete with camshaft) as described in Section 9.
57 Refit the timing belt as described in Section 7.

2.0 litre engines

58 If necessary, refit the inlet and exhaust manifolds with reference to Chapter 4B.
59 Check that the camshaft TDC timing pin is in position, then carefully lower the cylinder head onto the gasket and block, making sure that it locates correctly onto the dowels.
60 Apply a smear of grease to the threads, and to the underside of the heads, of the cylinder head bolts. Peugeot recommend the use of Molykote G Rapid Plus (available from your Peugeot dealer); in the absence of the specified grease, any good-quality high-melting-point grease may be used.
61 Carefully insert the cylinder head bolts into their holes (*do not drop them in*) and initially finger-tighten them.
62 Working progressively and in the sequence shown, tighten the cylinder head bolts to their Stage 1 torque setting, using a torque wrench and suitable socket (**see illustration**).
63 Once all the bolts have been tightened to their Stage 1 torque setting, working again in the specified sequence, tighten each bolt to the specified Stage 2 setting. Finally, angle-tighten the bolts through the specified Stage 3 angle. It is recommended that an angle-measuring gauge be used during this stage of tightening,

10.49 Ensure the gasket fits correctly over the locating dowels

10.54 Cylinder head bolt tightening sequence (1.4 litre engine)

10.62 Cylinder head bolt tightening sequence (2.0 litre engine)

to ensure accuracy. **Note:** *Retightening of the cylinder head bolts after running the engine is not required.*

64 Refit the cylinder head cover with reference to Section 4.

65 Refit the timing belt as described in Section 7.

All models

66

The remainder of refitting is a reversal of removal, noting the following points.

  a) Use a new seal when refitting the coolant outlet housing.
  b) When refitting a cylinder head, it is good practice to renew the thermostat.
  c) Refit the camshaft position sensor and set the air gap with reference to Chapter 4B.
  d) Tighten all fasteners to the specified torque where given.
  e) Refill the cooling system as described in Chapter 1B.
  f) The engine may run erratically for the first few miles, until the engine management ECU relearns its optimum running values.

11 Sump – removal and refitting

Removal

1 Drain the engine oil, then clean and refit the engine oil drain plug, tightening it securely. If the engine is nearing the service interval when the oil and filter are due for renewal, it is recommended that the filter is also removed, and a new one fitted. After reassembly, the engine can then be refilled with fresh oil. Refer to Chapter 1B for further information.

2 Apply the handbrake, then jack up the front of the vehicle and support it on axle stands (see *Jacking and vehicle support*). Undo the screws and remove the engine undershield.

3 On 1.4 litre models, to improve access,

11.7 On later 2.0 litre models the dipstick tube extends to the bottom of the sump

remove the exhaust front pipe as described in Chapter 4B.

4 On 2.0 litre models with air conditioning, where the compressor is mounted onto the side of the sump, remove the drivebelt as described in Chapter 1B. Unbolt the compressor, and position it clear of the sump. Support the weight of the compressor by tying it to the vehicle, to prevent any excess strain being placed on the compressor lines. *Do not* disconnect the refrigerant lines from the compressor (refer to the warnings given in Chapter 3).

5 Where necessary, disconnect the wiring connector from the oil temperature sender unit, which is screwed into the sump.

6 Progressively slacken and remove all of the sump retaining bolts/nuts. Since the sump bolts vary in length, remove each bolt in turn, and store it in its correct fitted order by pushing it through a clearly marked cardboard template. This will avoid the possibility of installing the bolts in the wrong locations on refitting.

7 Try to break the joint by striking the sump with the palm of your hand, then lower and withdraw the sump from under the car. If the sump is stuck (which is quite likely) use a putty knife, or similar, carefully inserted between the sump and block. Ease the knife along the joint until the sump is released. While the sump is

11.9 Apply a bead of sealant to the sump or crankcase-mating surface

removed, take the opportunity to check the oil pump pick-up/strainer for signs of clogging or splitting. If necessary, remove the pump as described in Section 12, and clean or renew the strainer. Note that on later 2.0 litre models, the oil dipstick tube extends to the bottom of the sump in order to allow the oil to be sucked out of the sump using special equipment **(see illustration)**.

Refitting

8 Clean all traces of sealant/gasket from the mating surfaces of the cylinder block/crankcase and sump, and then use a clean rag to wipe out the sump and the engine's interior.

9 On engines where the sump was fitted without a gasket, ensure that the sump mating surfaces are clean and dry, and then apply a thin coating of suitable sealant to the sump or crankcase-mating surface **(see illustration)**.

10 Offer up the sump to the cylinder block/crankcase. Refit its retaining bolts/nuts, ensuring that each bolt is screwed into its original location. Tighten the bolts evenly and progressively to the specified torque setting. On 2.0 litre engines, note the concealed bolts at one end of the sump **(see illustrations)**.

11 Where necessary, align the air conditioning

11.10a Refit the sump and tighten the bolts (1.4 litre engine)

11.10b Concealed bolts (arrowed) at one end of the sump (2.0 litre engine)

12.4 Undo the three Allen bolts (arrowed) and remove the oil pick-up tube

12.5 Undo the 8 bolts (arrowed) and remove the oil pump

12.7 Disengage the chain and remove the oil pump

compressor with its mountings on the sump, and insert the retaining bolts. Securely tighten the compressor retaining bolts, then refit the drivebelt as described in Chapter 1B.

12 Reconnect the wiring connector to the oil temperature sensor (where fitted).

13 Lower the vehicle to the ground, then refill the engine with oil as described in Chapter 1B.

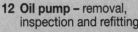

12 Oil pump – removal, inspection and refitting

Removal

1 Remove the sump as described in Section 11.

1.4 litre engines

2 Remove the crankshaft sprocket as described in Section 8. Recover the locating key from the crankshaft.

3 Disconnect the wiring plug, undo the bolts and remove the crankshaft position sensor, located on the right-hand end of the cylinder block.

4 Undo the three Allen bolts and remove the oil pump pick-up tube from the pump/block, complete with the dipstick guide tube **(see illustration)**. Discard the oil seal; a new one must be fitted.

5 Undo the 8 bolts, and remove the oil pump **(see illustration)**.

2.0 litre engines

6 Unscrew and remove the bolts securing the oil pump to the base of the cylinder block/ crankcase.

7 Disengage the pump sprocket from the chain, and remove the oil pump **(see illustration)**. Where necessary, also remove the spacer plate, which is fitted behind the oil pump.

Inspection

1.4 litre engine

8 Undo and remove the Torx screws securing the cover to the oil pump **(see illustration)**. Examine the pump rotors and body for signs of wear and damage. If worn, the complete pump must be renewed.

9 Remove the circlip, and extract the cap, valve piston and spring, noting which way

12.8 Undo the Torx screws and remove the pump cover

around they are fitted **(see illustrations)**. The condition of the relief valve spring can only be measured by comparing it with a new one; if there is any doubt about its condition, it should be renewed.

10 Refit the relief valve piston and spring, and then secure them in place with the circlip.

11 Refit the cover to the oil pump, and tighten the Torx screws securely.

2.0 litre engines

12 Examine the oil pump sprocket for signs of damage and wear, such as chipped or missing teeth. If the sprocket is worn, the pump assembly must be renewed, since the sprocket is not available separately. It is also recommended that the chain and drive sprocket, fitted to the crankshaft, be renewed at the same time. To renew the chain and drive sprocket, first remove

12.9a Remove the circlip . . .

12.9b . . . the cap . . .

12.9c . . . the spring . . .

12.9d . . . and the piston

12.13a Remove the oil pump cover bolts . . .

12.13b . . . then lift off the cover and remove the spring . . .

12.13c . . . and relief valve piston, noting which way round it is fitted

the crankshaft timing belt sprocket, then unbolt the oil oil seal carrier from the cylinder block. The sprocket, spacer (where fitted) and chain can then be slid off the end of the crankshaft.

13 Unscrew and remove the bolts (along with the baffle plate, where fitted) securing the strainer cover to the pump body. Lift off the strainer cover, and take off the relief valve piston and spring, noting which way round they are fitted **(see illustrations)**.

14 Examine the pump rotors and body for signs of wear ridges or scoring. If worn, the complete pump assembly must be renewed.

15 Examine the relief valve piston for signs of wear or damage, and renew if necessary. The condition of the relief valve spring can only be measured by comparing it with a new one; if there is any doubt about its condition,

it should be renewed. Both the piston and spring are available individually.

16 Thoroughly clean the oil pump strainer with a suitable solvent, and check it for signs of clogging or splitting. If the strainer is damaged, the strainer and cover assembly must be renewed.

17 Locate the relief valve spring and piston in the strainer cover. Refit the cover to the pump body, aligning the relief valve piston with its bore in the pump. Refit the baffle plate (where fitted) and the cover retaining bolts, and tighten them securely.

18 Prime the pump by filling it with clean engine oil before refitting.

Refitting
1.4 litre engines

19 Remove all traces of sealant, and

thoroughly clean the mating surfaces of the oil pump and cylinder block.

20 Apply a 4 mm wide bead of silicone sealant to the mating face of the cylinder block **(see illustration)**. Ensure that no sealant enters any of the holes in the block.

21 With a new oil seal fitted, refit the oil pump over the end of the crankshaft, aligning the flats in the pump drive gear with the flats machined in the crankshaft **(see illustrations)**. Note that new oil pumps are supplied with the oil seal already fitted, and a seal protector sleeve. The sleeve fits over the end of the crankshaft to protect the seal as the pump is fitted.

22 Install the oil pump bolts and tighten them to the specified torque.

23 Refit the oil pick-up tube to the pump/cylinder block using a new O-ring seal. Ensure the oil dipstick guide tube is correctly refitted.

24 Refit the Woodruff key to the crankshaft, and slide the crankshaft sprocket into place.

25 The remainder of refitting is a reversal of removal.

2.0 litre engines

26 Offer up the spacer plate (where fitted), then engage the pump sprocket with its drive chain, and seat the pump on the base of the cylinder block/crankcase. Refit the pump retaining bolts, and tighten them to the specified torque setting.

27 Refit the sump as described in Section 11.

12.21a Fit a new oil seal . . .

12.20 Apply a bead of sealant to the cylinder block mating surface

12.21c . . . with those of the crankshaft (arrowed)

13 Oil cooler –
removal and refitting

Removal

1 Apply the handbrake, then jack up the front of the vehicle and support it on axle stands (see *Jacking and vehicle support*). Undo the screws and remove the engine undershield.

1.4 litre engine

2 The oil cooler is fitted to the front of the oil filter housing. Drain the coolant as described in Chapter 1B.

12.21b . . . align the pump gear flats (arrowed) . . .

13.4a Undo the bolts (arrowed), remove the oil cooler . . .

13.4b . . . and recover the O-ring seals

13.8 Oil cooler/oil filter mounting bolt (A) and locating notch (B)

3 Drain the engine oil as described in Chapter 1B, or be prepared for fluid spillage.

4 Undo the bolts and remove the oil cooler. Recover the O-ring seals **(see illustrations)**.

2.0 litre engines

5 Drain the cooling system as described in Chapter 1B. Alternatively, clamp the oil cooler coolant hoses directly above the cooler, and be prepared for some coolant loss as the hoses are disconnected.

6 Position a suitable container beneath the oil filter on the front of the engine. Unscrew the filter using an oil filter removal tool if necessary, and drain the oil into the container. If the oil filter is damaged or distorted during removal, it must be renewed. Given the low cost of a new oil filter relative to the cost of repairing the damage which could result if a re-used filter leaks, it is probably a good idea to renew the filter in any case.

7 Release the hose clips, and disconnect the coolant hoses from the oil cooler.

8 Unscrew the oil cooler/oil filter mounting bolt/stud from the cylinder block, and withdraw the cooler. Note the locating notch in the cooler flange, which fits over the lug on the cylinder block **(see illustration)**. Discard the oil cooler sealing ring; a new one must be used on refitting.

Refitting

1.4 litre engine

9 Fit new O-ring seals into the recesses in the oil filter housing, and refit the cooler. Tighten the bolts securely.

2.0 litre engines

10 Fit a new sealing ring to the recess in the rear of the cooler, then offer the cooler to the cylinder block.

11 Ensure that the locating notch in the cooler flange is correctly engaged with the lug on the cylinder block. Apply locking fluid to the threads of the mounting bolt/stud, then insert it through the oil cooler and tighten securely.

12 Fit the oil filter, then lower the vehicle to the ground.

All engines

13 Refill or top-up the cooling system and engine oil level as described in Chapter 1B

or *Weekly Checks* (as applicable). Start the engine, and check the oil cooler for signs of leakage.

14 Oil seals – renewal

Crankshaft right-hand oil seal

1 Remove the crankshaft sprocket as described in Section 8.

2 Measure and note the fitted depth of the oil seal.

3 Pull the oil seal from the housing using a hooked instrument. Alternatively, drill a small hole in the oil seal, and use a self-tapping screw and a pair of pliers to remove it **(see illustration)**.

4 Clean the oil seal housing and the crankshaft sealing surface.

5 On 2.0 litre engines, dip the new oil seal in clean engine oil, and press it into the housing (open end first) to the previously-noted depth, using a suitable tube or socket.

 HAYNES HINT *A piece of thin plastic or tape wound around the front of the crankshaft is useful to prevent damage to the oil seal as it is fitted.*

6 On 1.4 litre engines, the seal has a Teflon lip and must not be oiled or marked. The new seal

14.3 Drill a hole then use a self-tapping screw and pliers to extract the oil seal

should be supplied with a protector sleeve, which fits over the end of the crankshaft to prevent any damage to the seal lip. With the sleeve in place, press the seal (open end first) into the pump to the previously-noted depth, using a suitable tube or socket.

7 Where applicable, remove the plastic or tape from the end of the crankshaft.

8 Refit the timing belt crankshaft sprocket as described in Section 8.

Crankshaft left-hand oil seal

9 Remove the flywheel/driveplate, as described in Section 16.

10 Measure and note the fitted depth of the oil seal.

11 Pull the oil seal from the housing using a hooked instrument. Alternatively, drill a small hole in the oil seal, and use a self-tapping screw and a pair of pliers to remove it **(see illustration 14.3)**.

12 Clean the oil seal housing and the crankshaft sealing surface.

13 On 2.0 litre engines, dip the new oil seal in clean engine oil, and press it into the housing (open end first) to the previously-noted depth, using a suitable tube or socket. A piece of thin plastic or tape wound around the end of the crankshaft is useful to prevent damage to the oil seal as it is fitted.

14 On 1.4 litre engines, the seal has a Teflon lip and must not be oiled or marked. The new seal should be supplied with a protector sleeve, which fits over the end of the crankshaft to prevent any damage to the seal lip **(see illustration)**. With the sleeve in place,

14.14 The new oil seal comes with a protective sleeve (arrowed) which fits over the end of the crankshaft

14.20 Locate the new seal in the cylinder head

14.21 Use a tube or socket to press the new seal into place

14.22 The new oil seal comes with a protective sleeve (arrowed) which fits over the end of the camshaft

press the seal (open end first) into the housing to the previously-noted depth, using a suitable tube or socket.

15 Where applicable, remove the plastic or tape from the end of the crankshaft.

16 Refit the flywheel/driveplate, as described in Section 16.

Camshaft right-hand oil seal

17 Remove the camshaft sprocket (and hub where applicable) as described in Section 8. In principle there is no need to remove the timing belt completely, but remember that if the belt has been contaminated with oil, it must be renewed.

18 Pull the oil seal from the housing using a hooked instrument. Alternatively, drill a small hole in the oil seal and use a self-tapping screw and a pair of pliers to remove it **(see illustration 14.3)**.

19 Clean the oil seal housing and the camshaft sealing surface.

2.0 litre engines

20 Smear the new oil seal with clean engine oil, then fit it over the end of the camshaft, open first **(see illustration)**. A piece of thin plastic or tape wound around the front of the camshaft is useful to prevent damage to the oil seal as it is fitted.

21 Press the seal into the housing until it is flush with the end face of the cylinder head. Use an M10 bolt (screwed into the end of the camshaft), washers and a suitable tube or socket that bears only on the outer

edge of the seal to press it into position **(see illustration)**.

1.4 litre engines

22 The seal has a Teflon lip and must not be oiled or marked. The new seal should be supplied with a protector sleeve, which fits over the end of the camshaft to prevent any damage to the seal lip **(see illustration)**. With the sleeve in place, press the seal (open end first) into the housing using a suitable tube or socket, which bears only of the outer edge of the seal.

All engines

23 Refit the camshaft sprocket (and hub where applicable) as described in Section 8.

24 Where necessary, fit a new timing belt with reference to Section 7.

Camshaft left-hand oil seal

25 No oil seal is fitted to the left-hand end of the camshaft. The sealing is provided by an O-ring fitted to the endplate flange. The O-ring can be renewed after unbolting the plate from the cylinder head.

---

15 Oil pressure switch and level sensor – removal and refitting

Removal

Oil pressure switch

1 The oil pressure switch is located at the front of the cylinder block, adjacent to the oil

dipstick guide tube (1.4 litre engines) or above the oil filter mounting (2.0 litre engines). Note that on some models, access to the switch may be improved if the vehicle is jacked up and supported on axle stands, then undo the screws and remove the engine undershield so that the switch can be reached from underneath (see *Jacking and vehicle support*).

2 Remove the protective sleeve from the wiring plug (where applicable), and then disconnect the wiring from the switch.

3 Unscrew the switch from the cylinder block, and recover the sealing washer **(see illustrations)**. Be prepared for oil spillage, and if the switch is to be left removed from the engine for any length of time, plug the hole in the cylinder block.

Oil level sensor

4 The oil level sensor is located at the rear of the cylinder block. Jack up the front of the vehicle and support it securely on axle stands (see *Jacking and vehicle support*). Undo the screws and remove the engine undershield.

5 Reach up between the driveshaft and the cylinder block and disconnect the sensor wiring plug **(see illustration)**.

6 Using an open-ended spanner, unscrew the sensor and withdraw it from position. On 2.0 litre engines, discard the sealing washer; a new one must be fitted.

Refitting

Oil pressure switch

7 Examine the sealing washer for any signs

15.3a On 1.4 litre engines, the oil pressure switch is on the front face of the cylinder block

15.3b Oil pressure switch (2.0 litre engine)

15.5 Oil level sensor (arrowed)

of damage or deterioration, and if necessary renew.

8 Refit the switch, complete with washer, and tighten it securely.

9 Refit the engine undershield, and lower the vehicle to the ground.

Oil level sensor

10 Smear a little silicone sealant on the threads and refit the sensor to the cylinder block, tightening it securely. On 2.0 litre models renew the sealing washer prior to refitting the sensor.

11 Reconnect the sensor wiring plug.

12 Refit the engine undershield, and lower the vehicle to the ground.

16 Flywheel/driveplate – removal, inspection and refitting

Flywheel removal

1 Remove the transmission as described in Chapter 7A, then remove the clutch assembly as described in Chapter 6.

2 Prevent the flywheel from turning by locking the ring gear teeth (see illustration 5.2). Alternatively, bolt a strap between the flywheel and the cylinder block/crankcase. *Do not* attempt to lock the flywheel in position using the crankshaft pulley locking tool described in Section 3. On 1.4 litre engines, insert a 12 mm diameter rod or drill bit through the hole in the flywheel cover casting, and into a slot in the flywheel (see illustration 5.3)

3 Make alignment marks between the flywheel and crankshaft to aid refitment. Slacken and remove the flywheel retaining bolts, and remove the flywheel from the end of the crankshaft. Be careful not to drop it; it is heavy. If the flywheel locating dowel (where fitted) is a loose fit in the crankshaft end, remove it and store it with the flywheel for safe-keeping. Discard the flywheel bolts; new ones must be used on refitting.

Driveplate removal

4 Remove the transmission as described in Chapter 7B. Lock the driveplate as described in paragraph 2 of this Section. Mark the

16.10 If the new bolts are not supplied with their threads precoated, apply thread-locking compound to them . . .

relationship between the torque converter plate and the driveplate, and slacken all the driveplate retaining bolts.

5 Remove the retaining bolts, along with the torque converter plate and the two shims (one fitted on each side of the torque converter plate). Note that the shims are of different thickness, the thicker one being on the outside of the torque converter plate. Discard the driveplate retaining bolts; new ones must be used on refitting.

6 Remove the driveplate from the end of the crankshaft. If the locating dowel is a loose fit in the crankshaft end, remove it and store it with the driveplate for safe-keeping.

Inspection

7 On models with manual transmission, examine the flywheel for scoring of the clutch face, and for wear or chipping of the ring gear teeth. If the clutch face is scored, the flywheel may be surface-ground, but renewal is preferable. Seek the advice of a Peugeot dealer or engine-reconditioning specialist to see if machining is possible. If the ring gear is worn or damaged, the flywheel must be renewed, as it is not possible to renew the ring gear separately.

8 On models with automatic transmission, check the torque converter driveplate carefully for signs of distortion. Look for any hairline cracks around the bolt holes or radiating outwards from the centre, and inspect the ring gear teeth for signs of wear or chipping. If any sign of wear or damage is found, the driveplate must be renewed.

Flywheel refitting

9 Clean the mating surfaces of the flywheel and crankshaft. Remove any remaining locking compound from the threads of the crankshaft holes, using the correct size of tap, if available.

> **HAYNES HINT** *If a suitable tap is not available, cut two slots along the threads of one of the old flywheel bolts, and use the bolt to remove the locking compound from the threads.*

10 If the new flywheel retaining bolts are not supplied with their threads already precoated,

16.15 . . . then refit the flywheel and tighten the bolts to the specified torque

apply a suitable thread-locking compound to the threads of each bolt (see illustration).

2.0 litre with dual mass flywheel

11 The dual mass flywheel is designed to reduce harshness and vibration in the action of the engine, clutch and transmission. With this type of flywheel, two flywheel centralising tools are needed (0216-L – available from Peugeot dealers). These are screwed into two opposite flywheel bolt holes in the crankshaft. As the tools are screwed down, their conical shape centralises the flywheel with regard to the crankshaft.

12 With the flywheel centralised, fit the new bolts into the remaining flywheel holes, then lock the flywheel using the same method employed on dismantling, and tighten the bolts to the specified torque.

13 Remove the two centralising tools, fit the new bolts and tighten them to the specified torque.

All other engines

14 Ensure that the locating dowel is in position. Offer up the flywheel, locating it on the dowel (where fitted) and fit the new retaining bolts. Where no locating dowel is fitted, align the previously-made marks to ensure the flywheel is refitted in its original position.

15 Lock the flywheel using the method employed on dismantling, and tighten the retaining bolts to the specified torque (see illustration).

All engines

16 Refit the clutch as described in Chapter 6. Remove the flywheel locking tool, and refit the transmission as described in Chapter 7A.

Driveplate refitting

17 Carry out the operations described above in paragraphs 9 and 10, substituting 'driveplate' for all references to the flywheel.

18 Locate the driveplate on its locating dowel.

19 Offer up the torque converter plate, with the thinner shim positioned behind the plate and the thicker shim on the outside, and align the marks made prior to removal.

20 Fit the new retaining bolts, then lock the driveplate using the method employed on dismantling. Tighten the retaining bolts to the specified torque wrench setting.

21 Remove the driveplate locking tool, and refit the transmission (see Chapter 7B).

17 Engine/transmission mountings – inspection and renewal

Inspection

1 If improved access is required, firmly apply the handbrake, then jack up the front of the car and support it on axle stands (see *Jacking and vehicle support*). Undo the screws and remove the engine undershield.

2 Check the mounting rubbers to see if they are cracked, hardened or separated from the metal at any point; renew the mounting if any such damage or deterioration is evident.

3 Check that all the mountings' fasteners are securely tightened; use a torque wrench to check if possible.

4 Using a large screwdriver or a crowbar, check for wear in each mounting by carefully levering against it to check for free play. Where this is not possible, enlist the aid of an assistant to move the engine/transmission back-and-forth, or from side-to-side, while you watch the mounting. While some free play is to be expected even from new components, excessive wear should be obvious. If excessive free play is found, check first that the fasteners are correctly secured, and then renew any worn components as described below.

Renewal

Right-hand mounting

5 Disconnect the battery negative lead then remove the engine upper cover.

6 Remove the undercover (where fitted) then place a jack beneath the engine, with a block of wood on the jack head. Raise the jack until it is supporting the weight of the engine.

7 Unclip the wiring harness from the front of the injection system ECU. Slacken and remove the ECU mounting plate nut, remove the cable/hose bracket then free the mounting plate from the body and position it clear of the engine.

8 Slacken and remove the mounting bolts and remove the bracket from the top of the mounting.

9 Unscrew the vibration damper (where fitted) from the top of the mounting rubber then slacken and remove the nut securing the mounting bracket to the mounting rubber.

10 Slacken and remove the three bolts securing the right-hand engine mounting bracket to the bracket on the side of the cylinder block then lift off the mounting bracket, taking care not to lose the locating dowels (where fitted).

11 Make identification marks on the movement restrictors (the front and rear restrictors are different and are not interchangeable) then unscrew the nuts and remove both restrictors.

12 Using a strap wrench, unscrew the mounting rubber from the body

13 Check for signs of wear or damage on all components, and renew as necessary.

14 On reassembly, screw the mounting rubber into the body, tightening it to the specified torque.

15 Refit the front and rear movement restrictors in their original locations. Ensure the restrictor pegs are correctly located in their holes then securely tighten their retaining nuts.

16 Ensure the dowels (where fitted) are in position then install the mounting bracket, tightening its retaining bolts and nut to their specified torque settings

17 Refit the vibration damper (where fitted) to the mounting, tightening it to the specified torque.

18 Fit the bracket over the vibration damper, tightening its bolts to the specified torque.

19 Remove the jack from under the engine then refit the undercover (where fitted). Reconnect the battery negative lead then refit the engine cover.

Left-hand mounting

20 Remove the battery, battery tray and mounting plate as described in Chapter 5A.

21 Remove the undercover (where fitted) and place a jack beneath the transmission, with a block of wood on the jack head. Raise the jack until it is supporting the weight of the transmission.

22 Slacken and remove the mounting rubber's centre nut and two retaining bolts and remove the mounting from the engine compartment.

23 If necessary, undo the retaining bolts and remove the mounting bracket from the body.

24 The mounting stud is a screw-fit into its mounting bracket and the bracket is secured to the transmission by two bolts. If the mounting stud is tight, a universal stud extractor can be used to unscrew it.

25 Check carefully for signs of wear or damage on all components, and renew them where necessary.

26 Where necessary, refit the mounting bracket to the top of the transmission unit and tighten its bolts to the specified torque. Apply locking compound (Peugeot recommend the use of Loctite Frenetanch) to the stud threads then refit the stud to the bracket, tightening it to the specified torque. Slide the spacer onto the stud.

27 Refit the mounting bracket to the vehicle body and tighten its bolts to the specified torque.

28 Fit the mounting rubber to the bracket and tighten its retaining bolts to the specified

17.34 Lower engine movement limiter

torque. Refit the mounting centre nut, and tighten it to the specified torque.

29 Remove the jack from underneath the transmission and refit the undercover (where fitted).

30 Refit the battery as described in Chapter 5A.

Rear mounting

31 If not already done, firmly apply the handbrake, then jack up the front of the vehicle and support it securely on axle stands (see *Jacking and vehicle support*).

32 Where necessary, remove the retaining bolts, screws and clips and remove the undershield from beneath the engine/transmission unit.

33 Unscrew and remove the bolt securing the rear mounting link to the mounting on the rear of the cylinder block.

34 Remove the bolt securing the rear mounting link to the subframe **(see illustration)**.

35 To remove the mounting assembly it will first be necessary to remove the right-hand driveshaft as described in Chapter 8.

36 With the driveshaft removed, undo the retaining bolts and remove the mounting from the rear of the cylinder block.

37 Check carefully for signs of wear or damage on all components, and renew them where necessary.

38 On reassembly, fit the rear mounting assembly to the rear of the cylinder block, and tighten its retaining bolts to the specified torque. Refit the driveshaft as described in Chapter 8.

39 Refit the rear mounting link, and tighten both its bolts to their specified torque settings.

40 Refit the undershield (where fitted) then lower the vehicle to the ground.

Chapter 2 Part E:
Engine removal and overhaul procedures

Contents

Degrees of difficulty

Easy, suitable for novice with little experience | **Fairly easy,** suitable for beginner with some experience | **Fairly difficult,** suitable for competent DIY mechanic | **Difficult,** suitable for experienced DIY mechanic | **Very difficult,** suitable for expert DIY or professional

Specifications

Cylinder head

Maximum gasket face distortion	0.05 mm
New cylinder head height:	
Petrol engines:	
1.1, 1.4 and 1.6 litre SOHC	111.20 mm
1.4 litre DOHC....................................	N/A
2.0 litre	138.00 mm
Diesel engines:	
1.4 litre	88.00 mm
2.0 litre	133.00 mm
Minimum cylinder head height after machining:	
Petrol engines:	
1.1, 1.4 and 1.6 litre SOHC...........................	111.00 mm
1.4 litre DOHC....................................	N/A
2.0 litre	137.70 mm
Diesel engines:	
1.4 litre	87.60 mm
2.0 litre	132.80 mm
Valve head-to-cylinder head measurement – diesel engines:	
1.4 litre	1.25 mm maximum
2.0 litre	0.20 mm maximum

Valves

Valve head diameter:	Inlet	Exhaust
Petrol engines:		
1.1 and 1.4 litre SOHC	36.7 mm	29.4 mm
1.4 litre DOHC.	28.25 mm	24.38 mm
1.6 litre	39.35 mm	31.4 mm
2.0 litre	33.3 mm	29.0 mm
Diesel engines:		
1.4 litre	32.8 mm	30.3 mm
2.0 litre	35.6 mm	33.8 mm
Valve stem diameter:		
Petrol engines:		
1.1 and 1.4 litre SOHC	6.965 to 6.980 mm	6.945 to 6.960 mm
1.4 litre DOHC.	5.485 mm	5.475 mm
1.6 litre	6.956 to 6.970 mm	6.955 to 6.970 mm
2.0 litre	5.985 to 5.970 mm	5.975 to 5.960 mm
Diesel engines:		
1.4 litre	N/A	N/A
2.0 litre	5.978 mm (nominal)	5.978 mm (nominal)

Cylinder block

Cylinder bore diameter:	
Petrol engines:	
1.1 litre	72.00 mm (nominal)
1.4 litre	75.00 mm (nominal)
1.6 litre	78.50 mm (nominal)
2.0 litre	85.00 mm (nominal)
Diesel engines:	
1.4 litre	73.70 mm (nominal)
2.0 litre	85.00 mm (nominal)
Liner protrusion – aluminium block petrol engine:	
Standard.	0.03 to 0.10 mm
Maximum difference between any two liners.	0.05 mm

Pistons

Piston diameter:	
Petrol engines:	
1.1 litre	71.950 mm (nominal)
1.4 litre	74.950 mm (nominal)
1.6 litre	78.455 mm (nominal)
2.0 litre	84.948 mm (nominal)
Diesel engines:	
1.4 litre	73.520 mm (nominal)
2.0 litre	84.210 mm (nominal)

Check with your Peugeot dealer or engine specialist regarding piston oversizes

Crankshaft

Endfloat:	
Petrol engines:	
1.1, 1.4 and 1.6 litre	0.07 to 0.27 mm
2.0 litre	0.07 to 0.32 mm
Diesel engines:	
1.4 litre	0.10 to 0.30 mm
2.0 litre	0.07 to 0.32 mm
Main bearing journal diameter:	
Petrol engines:	
1.1, 1.4 and 1.6 litre	49.965 to 49.981 mm
2.0 litre	60.00 mm (nominal)
Diesel engines:	
1.4 litre	49.962 to 49.981 mm
2.0 litre	59.977 to 60.000 mm
Big-end bearing journal diameter:	
Petrol engines:	
1.1, 1.4 and 1.6 litre	44.975 to 44.991 mm
2.0 litre	60.00 mm (nominal)
Diesel engines:	
1.4 litre	44.975 to 44.991 mm
2.0 litre	49.980 to 50.000 mm

Piston rings

End gaps:

Petrol engines:

Top compression ring . . . .   0.20 to 0.45 mm
Second compression ring. . . . .   0.30 to 0.50 mm
Oil control ring . . . .   0.30 to 0.50 mm

Diesel engines:

1.4 litre:

Top compression ring . . . .   0.20 to 0.35 mm
Second compression ring. . . . .   0.20 to 0.40 mm
Oil control ring. . . . .   0.80 to 1.00mm

2.0 litre:

Top compression ring . . . .   0.20 to 0.35 mm
Second compression ring. . . . .   0.80 to 1.00 mm
Oil control ring. . . . .   0.25 to 0.50 mm

Torque wrench settings

1.1, 1.4 (SOHC) and 1.6 litre petrol engines

Refer to Chapter 2A Specifications

1.4 (DOHC) petrol engines

Refer to Chapter 2B Specifications

2.0 litre petrol engines

Refer to Chapter 2C Specifications

Diesel engines

Refer to Chapter 2D Specifications

1 General information

Included in this Part of Chapter 2 are details of removing the engine/transmission from the car and general overhaul procedures for the cylinder head, cylinder block/crankcase and all other engine internal components.

The information given ranges from advice concerning preparation for an overhaul and the purchase of parts, to detailed step-by-step procedures covering removal, inspection, renovation and refitting of engine internal components.

After Section 5, all instructions are based on the assumption that the engine has been removed from the car. For information concerning in-car engine repair, as well as the removal and refitting of those external components necessary for full overhaul, refer to Part A, B, C or D of this Chapter, as applicable and to Section 5. Ignore any preliminary dismantling operations described in Parts A, B, C or D that are no longer relevant once the engine has been removed from the car.

Apart from torque wrench settings, which are given at the beginning of Parts A, B, C and D, all specifications relating to engine overhaul are at the beginning of this Part of Chapter 2.

2 Engine overhaul – general information

1 It is not always easy to determine when, or if, an engine should be completely overhauled, as a number of factors must be considered.

2 High mileage is not necessarily an indication that an overhaul is needed, while low mileage does not preclude the need for an overhaul. Frequency of servicing is probably the most important consideration. An engine which has had regular and frequent oil and filter changes, as well as other required maintenance, should give many thousands of miles of reliable service. Conversely, a neglected engine may require an overhaul very early in its life.

3 Excessive oil consumption is an indication that piston rings, valve seals and/or valve guides are in need of attention. Make sure that oil leaks are not responsible before deciding that the rings and/or guides are worn. Perform a compression test, as described in Part A, B, C or D of this Chapter (as applicable), to determine the likely cause of the problem.

4 Check the oil pressure with a gauge fitted in place of the oil pressure switch, and compare it with that specified. If it is extremely low, the main and big-end bearings, and/or the oil pump, are probably worn out.

5 Loss of power, rough running, knocking or metallic engine noises, excessive valve gear noise, and high fuel consumption may also point to the need for an overhaul, especially if they are all present at the same time. If a complete service does not remedy the situation, major mechanical work is the only solution.

6 A full engine overhaul involves restoring all internal parts to the specification of a new engine. During a complete overhaul, the pistons and the piston rings are renewed, and the cylinder bores are reconditioned. New main and big-end bearings are generally fitted; if necessary, the crankshaft may be reground, to compensate for wear in the journals. The valves are also serviced as well, since they are usually in less-than-perfect condition at this point. Always pay careful attention to the condition of the oil pump when overhauling the engine, and renew it if there is any doubt as to its serviceability. The end result should be an as-new engine that will give many trouble-free miles.

7 Critical cooling system components such as the hoses, thermostat and water pump should be renewed when an engine is overhauled. The radiator should be checked carefully, to ensure that it is not clogged or leaking. Also, it is a good idea to renew the oil pump whenever the engine is overhauled.

8 Before beginning the engine overhaul, read through the entire procedure to familiarise yourself with the scope and requirements of

the job. Overhauling an engine is not difficult if you follow carefully all of the instructions, have the necessary tools and equipment, and pay close attention to all specifications. It can, however, be time-consuming. Plan on the car being off the road for a minimum of two weeks, especially if parts must be taken to an engineering works for repair or reconditioning. Check on the availability of parts and make sure that any necessary special tools and equipment are obtained in advance. Most work can be done with typical hand tools, although a number of precision measuring tools are required for inspecting parts to determine if they must be renewed. Often the engineering works will handle the inspection of parts and offer advice concerning reconditioning and renewal.

9 Always wait until the engine has been completely dismantled, and until all components (especially the cylinder block/crankcase and the crankshaft) have been inspected, before deciding what service and repair operations must be performed by an engineering works. The condition of these components will be the major factor to consider when determining whether to overhaul the original engine, or to buy a reconditioned unit. Do not, therefore, purchase parts or have overhaul work done on other components until they have been thoroughly inspected. As a general rule, time is the primary cost of an overhaul, so it does not pay to fit worn or sub-standard parts.

10 As a final note, to ensure maximum life and minimum trouble from a reconditioned engine, everything must be assembled with care, in a spotlessly-clean environment.

3 Engine removal – methods and precautions

1 If you have decided that the engine must be removed for overhaul or major repair work, several preliminary steps should be taken.

2 Locating a suitable place to work is extremely important. Adequate workspace,

along with storage space for the car, will be needed. If a workshop or garage is not available, at the very least, a flat, level, clean work surface is required.

3 Cleaning the engine compartment and engine/transmission before beginning the removal procedure will help keep tools clean and organised.

4 An engine hoist or A-frame will also be necessary. Make sure the equipment is rated in excess of the weight of the engine. Safety is of primary importance, considering the potential hazards involved in lifting the engine/transmission out of the car.

5 If this is the first time you have removed an engine, an assistant should ideally be available. Advice and aid from someone more experienced would also be helpful. There are many instances when one person cannot simultaneously perform all of the operations required when lifting the engine out of the vehicle.

6 Plan the operation ahead of time. Before starting work, arrange for the hire of or obtain all of the tools and equipment you will need. Some of the equipment necessary to perform engine/transmission removal and installation safely and with relative ease (in addition to an engine hoist) is as follows: a heavy duty trolley jack, complete sets of spanners and sockets (see *Tools and working facilities*), wooden blocks, and plenty of rags and cleaning solvent for mopping-up spilled oil, coolant and fuel. If the hoist must be hired, make sure that you arrange for it in advance, and perform all of the operations possible without it beforehand. This will save you money and time.

7 Plan for the car to be out of use for quite a while. An engineering works will be required to perform some of the work, which the do-it-yourselfer cannot accomplish without special equipment. These places often have a busy schedule, so it would be a good idea to consult them before removing the engine, in order to accurately estimate the amount of time required to rebuild or repair components that may need work.

8 Always be extremely careful when removing and refitting the engine/transmission. Serious injury can result from careless actions. Plan

ahead and take your time, and a job of this nature, although major, can be accomplished successfully.

Note: *Such is the complexity of the power unit arrangement on these vehicles, and the variations that may be encountered according to model and optional equipment fitted, that the following should be regarded as a guide to the work involved, rather than a step-by-step procedure. Where differences are encountered, or additional component disconnection or removal is necessary, make notes of the work involved as an aid to refitting.*

4 Engine – removal and refitting

Note: *This is an involved operation. Read through the procedure thoroughly before starting work, and ensure that adequate lifting tackle and jacking/support equipment is available. Make notes during dismantling to ensure that all wiring/hoses and brackets are correctly repositioned and routed on refitting.*
Note: *The engine can be removed from the car only as a complete unit with the transmission; the two are then separated for overhaul.*

Removal

1 Park the vehicle on firm, level ground. Chock the rear wheels, then firmly apply the handbrake. Jack up the front of the vehicle, and securely support it on axle stands (see *Jacking and vehicle support*). Remove both front roadwheels.

2 Remove the battery, battery tray and mounting plate as described in Chapter 5A.

3 Remove the complete air cleaner housing and duct assembly, as described in Chapter 4A or 4B.

4 If the engine is to be dismantled, working as described in Chapter 1A or 1B, first drain the oil and remove the oil filter. Clean and refit the drain plug, tightening it securely.

5 Remove the auxiliary drivebelt as described in Chapter 1A or 1B.

6 Remove the radiator and coolant expansion tank as described in Chapter 3.

7 On models with power steering, referring to Chapter 10, unbolt the power steering pump from its mounting bracket. Undo the power steering pipe retaining clip screws then position the pump clear of the engine **(see illustrations)**. Support the weight of the pump by tying it to the vehicle body to prevent any excess strain being placed on the hydraulic pipes/hoses. **Note:** *There is no need to disconnect the pipe/hose from the pump.*

8 On models with air conditioning, disconnect the compressor wiring connector then unscrew the compressor mounting bolts and nuts **(see**

4.7a Unscrew the power steering pipe clip screws and the pump mounting bolt . . .

4.7b . . . then free the pump from its mounting bracket and position it clear of the engine

4.8a Disconnect the wiring connector . . .

4.8b . . . unscrew the mounting bolts and nuts (lower fixings arrowed) and free the air conditioning compressor from the engine

illustrations). Free the compressor from the engine and support its weight by tying it to the vehicle, to prevent any excess strain being placed on the compressor lines. Take care not to lose the spacers from the compressor rear mountings (where fitted).

Caution: Do not disconnect the refrigerant lines from the compressor (refer to the warnings given in Chapter 3). Ensure the compressor is securely supported to prevent the refrigerant lines being damaged.

9 Remove the alternator as described in Chapter 5A.

10 Working as described in Chapter 4A or 4B, carry out the following operations.

a) *Depressurise the fuel system and disconnect the fuel hose from the fuel rail.*

b) *Where applicable, disconnect the*

accelerator cable.

c) *Disconnect the purge valve and braking system servo vacuum hoses from the inlet manifold.*

d) *Remove the exhaust system front pipe.*

e) *On diesel models, disconnect the braking system servo vacuum hose from the vacuum pump.*

11 Unclip the wiring harness then slacken and remove the ECU mounting plate nut (the plate is secured in position with an anti-tamper nut, unscrew the nut using a pair of grips). Free the mounting plate from the body then disconnect the wiring connectors from the ECU and relay. Rotate the locking ring anti-clockwise and disconnect the engine harness

connector, then unscrew the locking nut and free the harness from the bracket. Remove the bracket assembly and secure the harness to the engine unit **(see illustrations)**.

12 Release the retaining clips and disconnect the heater matrix hoses from their connection on the engine compartment bulkhead **(see illustrations)**.

13 On manual transmission models, carry out the following operations using the information in Chapters 6 and 7A.

a) *Disconnect the clutch cable from the transmission.*

b) *Drain the transmission oil or be prepared for some spillage as the engine/ transmission unit is removed.*

c) *Disconnect the gearchange mechanism link rods from the transmission.*

d) *Unbolt the body earth lead from the transmission.*

14 On automatic transmission models, carry out the following operations using the information in Chapter 7B.

a) *Disconnect the selector cable from the transmission.*

b) *Drain the transmission fluid or be prepared for some fluid spillage as the engine/transmission unit is removed.*

c) *Disconnect the main transmission wiring connector and unbolt the earth lead(s) from the transmission.*

15 Remove both driveshafts as described in Chapter 8.

4.11a Unscrew the mounting nut and remove the bracket . . .

4.11b . . . then free the ECU mounting plate and disconnect the engine harness connector

4.11c Disconnect the ECU wiring harness . . .

4.11d . . . and the relay wiring connector, and then unscrew the locking nut (arrowed) and free the harness from the mounting plate

4.12a Release the retaining clips . . .

4.12b . . . and disconnect the coolant hoses from the heater matrix unions on the bulkhead

4.16 Rotate the locking ring anti-clockwise and disconnect the wiring harness connector

4.17a Unscrew the nuts (arrowed) . . .

4.17b . . . and disconnect the engine wiring harness from the fuse/relay box

4.19a Unscrew the nuts and bolts . . .

4.19b . . . and remove the rear mounting link

4.20a Unscrew the centre nut (1) and bolts (2) . . .

16 Trace the wiring harness back from the engine to the wiring connector in the front, left-hand corner of the engine compartment. Rotate the locking ring anti-

4.20b . . . and remove the rubber mounting from the left-hand mounting

clockwise and disconnect the connector (see illustration).
17 Remove the fuse/relay box lid then undo the nuts and disconnect the engine wiring harness leads from the terminals (see illustrations). Release the wiring harness from its clips so that it is free to be removed with the engine/transmission.
18 Manoeuvre the engine hoist into position, and attach it to the lifting brackets bolted onto the cylinder head. Raise the hoist until it is supporting the weight of the engine.
19 From underneath the vehicle, slacken and remove the nuts and bolts securing the rear mounting link to the mounting assembly and subframe, and remove the link (see illustrations).
20 Slacken and remove the centre nut and washer from the engine/transmission left-

hand mounting. Undo the two bolts securing the mounting to its bracket, and remove the mounting from the engine compartment. Undo the retaining bolts and remove the mounting bracket from the body (see illustrations).
21 Working on the right-hand engine/transmission mounting, slacken and remove the mounting nut/bolts and remove the support bracket securing the mounting to the front of the engine unit (see illustration).
22 Unscrew the vibration damper (where fitted) from the top of the right-hand mounting rubber. Slacken and remove the nut and washer securing the mounting bracket to the mounting rubber and the three nuts securing the right-hand engine mounting bracket to the bracket/housing on the rear of the cylinder block. Unclip the wiring harness then lift off the bracket (see illustrations).

4.20c Unscrew the mounting bolts (locations arrowed) and remove the left-hand mounting bracket from the body

4.21 Unscrew the nut and bolts and remove the support bracket from the right-hand mounting

4.22a Unscrew the nuts (1) and unclip the wiring harness (2) . . .

4.22b . . . then lift off the right-hand engine bracket

4.24 Lifting the engine/transmission unit out of position

4.28 Unscrew the mounting bolts (arrowed) and remove the starter motor

23 Make a final check that any components which would prevent the removal of the engine/transmission from the car have been removed or disconnected. Ensure that components such as the gearchange selector link rods are secured so that they cannot be damaged on removal.

24 Lift the engine/transmission out of the car, ensuring that nothing is trapped or damaged **(see illustration)**. Enlist the help of an assistant during this procedure, as it will be necessary to tilt the assembly slightly to clear the body panels

Caution: On models equipped with air conditioning, care must be taken to ensure the auxiliary drivebelt pulleys do not damage the air conditioning pipes on the right-hand side of the engine compartment. As a precaution, cover the condenser with a stout piece of cardboard to ensure it is not damaged.

25 Once the engine is high enough, lift it out over the front of the body, and lower the unit to the ground.

Separation

Engine and manual transmission

26 With the engine/transmission assembly removed, support the assembly on suitable blocks of wood, on a workbench (or failing that, on a clean area of the workshop floor).

27 Undo the retaining bolts and remove the lower cover plate (where fitted) from the transmission.

28 Slacken and remove the retaining bolts and remove the starter motor from the transmission, taking care not to lose the locating dowel **(see illustration)**.

29 Ensure that both engine and transmission are adequately supported, then slacken and remove the remaining bolts securing the transmission housing to the engine. Note the correct fitted positions of each bolt (and the relevant brackets) as they are removed, to use as a reference on refitting.

30 Carefully withdraw the transmission from the engine, ensuring that the weight of the transmission is not allowed to hang on the input shaft while it is engaged with the clutch friction disc.

31 If they are loose, remove the locating

dowels from the engine or transmission, and keep them in a safe place.

Engine and automatic transmission

Note: *New torque converter nuts will be required on refitting.*

32 With the engine/transmission assembly removed, support the assembly on suitable blocks of wood, on a workbench (or failing that, on a clean area of the workshop floor).

33 Undo the retaining bolts, and remove the lower cover plate (where fitted) from the transmission.

34 Slacken and remove the retaining bolts and remove the starter motor from the transmission, taking care not to lose the locating dowel **(see illustration 4.28)**.

35 Access to the torque converter retaining nuts is gained via the starter motor aperture. Use a socket and extension bar to rotate the crankshaft pulley to align the first nut with the aperture **(see illustration)**. Unscrew the nut then rotate the crankshaft 120°. Remove the second nut then rotate the crankshaft another 120°. Unscrew the third and final nut and discard all three nuts; new ones must be used on refitting.

36 To ensure that the torque converter does not fall out as the transmission is removed,

secure it in position using a length of metal strip bolted to one of the starter motor bolt holes.

37 Ensure that both engine and transmission are adequately supported, then slacken and remove the remaining bolts securing the transmission housing to the engine. Note the correct fitted positions of each bolt (and the relevant brackets) as they are removed, to use as a reference on refitting.

38 Carefully withdraw the transmission from the engine, ensuring that the weight of the transmission is not allowed to hang on the torque converter while it is engaged with the driveplate.

39 If they are loose, remove the locating dowels from the engine or transmission, and keep them in a safe place.

Refitting

Engine and manual transmission

40 If the engine and transmission have been separated, perform the operations described below in paragraphs 41 to 46. If not, proceed as described from paragraph 47 onwards.

41 Check the clutch release mechanism components are correctly assembled (see Chapter 6)

4.35 Working through the starter motor aperture, unscrew the torque converter nuts (1), rotating the crankshaft as necessary

42 Ensure that the locating dowels are correctly positioned in the engine or transmission.

43 Carefully offer the transmission to the engine, until the locating dowels are engaged. Ensure that the weight of the transmission is not allowed to hang on the input shaft as it is engaged with the clutch friction disc.

44 Refit the transmission housing-to-engine bolts, ensuring that all the necessary brackets are correctly positioned, and tighten them to the specified torque.

45 Ensure the locating dowel is in position then refit the starter motor, tightening its retaining bolts securely.

46 Refit the flywheel cover plate (where fitted) to the transmission, and securely tighten its retaining bolts.

47 Reconnect the hoist and lifting tackle to the engine lifting brackets. With the aid of an assistant, lift the assembly over the engine compartment.

48 The assembly should be tilted as necessary to clear the surrounding components, as during removal; lower the assembly into position in the engine compartment, manipulating the hoist and lifting tackle as necessary.

49 With the engine/transmission in position, refit the right-hand engine/transmission mounting bracket, tightening the nuts by hand only at this stage.

50 Working on the left-hand mounting, refit the mounting bracket to the body and tighten its retaining bolts to the specified torque. Refit the mounting rubber and refit the mounting retaining bolts and washers and the centre nut and washer, tightening them lightly only.

51 From underneath the vehicle, refit the rear mounting link and install both its bolts.

52 Rock the engine to settle it on its mountings. Ensure the left-hand mounting is centralised on its bracket then go around and tighten all the mounting nuts and bolts to their specified torque settings. The hoist can then be detached from the engine and removed.

53 Refit the vibration damper (where fitted) to the right-hand mounting and tighten it to the specified torque.

54 The remainder of the refitting procedure is a direct reversal of the removal sequence, noting the following points:

a) *Ensure that the wiring loom is correctly routed and retained by all the relevant retaining clips; all connectors should be correctly and securely reconnected.*

b) *Ensure all disturbed hoses are correctly and securely reconnected.*

c) *On models with air conditioning, ensure the mounting spacers (where fitted) are correctly fitted to the rear mountings. Tighten the compressor front (drivebelt pulley end) mounting bolts to the specified torque first then tighten the rear bolts (see Chapter 3).*

d) *On models with power steering, ensure the mounting spacer (where fitted) is correctly fitted to the rear mounting. Apply locking compound (Peugeot recommend the use of Loctite Frenetanch) to the pump lower front mounting bolt then install all the bolts; tighten the pump front (drivebelt pulley end) bolts to the specified torque first then tighten the rear bolts (see Chapter 10).*

e) *Tighten all fixings to the specified torque (where given).*

f) *Prior to refitting the driveshafts to the transmission, renew the driveshaft oil seals as described in Chapter 7A.*

g) *Reconnect the clutch cable and gearchange linkage link rods to the transmission and refill/top-up the transmission unit with oil (see Chapters 6 and 7A).*

h) *On diesel models, reconnect the brake servo vacuum hose back to the vacuum pump.*

i) *Where applicable, adjust the accelerator cable as described in Chapter 4A or 4B.*

j) *Refill the cooling system and engine oil as described in Chapter 1A or 1B.*

Engine and automatic transmission

55 If the engine and transmission have been separated, perform the operations described below in paragraphs 56 to 62. If not, proceed as described from paragraph 63 onwards.

56 Ensure that the bush fitted to the centre of the crankshaft is in good condition, and apply a little Molykote BR2 grease to the torque converter centring pin.

Caution: Do not apply too much; otherwise there is a possibility of the grease contaminating the torque converter.

57 Ensure that the engine/transmission locating dowels are correctly positioned.

58 Carefully offer up transmission, aligning the torque converter studs with the driveplate holes, then engage the transmission unit with the engine.

Caution: Do not allow the weight of the transmission unit to hang on the torque converter as the unit is installed.

59 With the transmission and engine correctly joined, refit the transmission-to-engine unit bolts, ensuring that all the necessary brackets are correctly positioned, and tighten them to the specified torque.

60 Screw the new nuts onto the torque converter studs, tightening them lightly only, rotating the crankshaft as necessary. Tighten all three nuts to the specified Stage 1 torque setting. Once all have been tightened to the Stage 1 torque, go around and tighten them to the specified Stage 2 torque setting.

61 Ensure the locating dowel is in position then refit the starter motor, tightening its retaining bolts securely.

62 Refit the cover plate (where fitted) to the transmission, and securely tighten its retaining bolts.

63 Install the engine/transmission unit as described in paragraphs 47 to 53.

64 The remainder of the refitting procedure is a direct reversal of the removal sequence, noting the following points:

a) *Ensure that the wiring loom is correctly routed and retained by all the relevant retaining clips; all connectors should be correctly and securely reconnected.*

b) *Ensure all disturbed hoses are correctly and securely reconnected.*

c) *On models with air conditioning, ensure the mounting spacers (where fitted) are correctly fitted to the rear mountings. Tighten the compressor front (drivebelt pulley end) mounting bolts to the specified torque first then tighten the rear bolts (see Chapter 3).*

d) *On models with power steering, ensure the mounting spacer (where fitted) is correctly fitted to the rear mounting. Apply locking compound (Peugeot recommend the use of Loctite Frenetanch) to the pump lower front mounting bolt then install all the bolts; tighten the pump front (drivebelt pulley end) bolts to the specified torque first then tighten the rear bolts (see Chapter 10).*

e) *Tighten all fixings to the specified torque (where given).*

f) *Prior to refitting the driveshafts to the transmission, renew the driveshaft oil seals as described in Chapter 7B.*

g) *Reconnect and adjust the selector cable refill/top-up the transmission unit with oil as described in Chapter 7B.*

h) *Where applicable, adjust the accelerator cable as described in Chapter 4A or 4B.*

i) *Refill the cooling system and engine oil as described in Chapter 1A or 1B.*

5 Engine overhaul – dismantling sequence

1 It is much easier to dismantle and work on the engine if it is mounted on a portable engine stand. These stands can often be hired from a tool hire shop. Before the engine is mounted on a stand, the flywheel/driveplate should be removed, so that the stand bolts can be tightened into the end of the cylinder block/crankcase.

2 If a stand is not available, it is possible to dismantle the engine with it blocked up on a sturdy workbench, or on the floor. Be extra careful not to tip or drop the engine when working without a stand.

3 If you are going to obtain a reconditioned engine, all the external components must be removed first, to be transferred to the new engine (just as they will if you are doing a complete engine overhaul yourself). These components include the following:

a) *Ancillary unit mounting brackets (oil filter, starter, alternator, power steering pump, etc).*

b) *Thermostat and housing (Chapter 3).*

c) *Dipstick tube/sensor.*

d) *All electrical switches and sensors.*

e) *Inlet and exhaust manifolds – where applicable (Chapter 4A or 4B).*

f) *Ignition coils and spark plugs – as applicable (Chapter 5B and 1A).*

g) *Flywheel/driveplate (Part A, B, C or D of this Chapter).*

Note: *When removing the external components from the engine, pay close attention to details that may be helpful or important during refitting. Note the fitted position of gaskets, seals, spacers, pins, washers, bolts, and other small items.*

4 If you are obtaining a 'short' engine (which consists of the engine cylinder block/crankcase, crankshaft, pistons and connecting rods all assembled), then the cylinder head, sump, oil pump, and timing belt will have to be removed also.

5 If you are planning a complete overhaul, the engine can be dismantled, and the internal components removed, in the order given below, referring to Part A, B, C or D of this Chapter unless otherwise stated.

a) *Inlet and exhaust manifolds – where applicable (Chapter 4A or 4B).*
b) *Timing belts, sprockets and tensioner(s).*
c) *Cylinder head.*
d) *Flywheel/driveplate.*
e) *Sump.*
f) *Oil pump.*
g) *Piston/connecting rod assemblies (Section 9). Note: On 1.4 litre diesel engines, remove the crankshaft before the pistons.*
h) *Crankshaft (Section 10).*

6 Before beginning the dismantling and overhaul procedures, make sure that you have all of the correct tools necessary. Refer to *Tools and working facilities* for further information.

6 Cylinder head – dismantling

Note: *New and reconditioned cylinder heads are available from the manufacturer, and from engine overhaul specialists. Be aware that some specialist tools are required for the dismantling and inspection procedures, and new components may not be readily available. It may therefore be more practical and economical for the home mechanic to purchase a reconditioned head, rather than*

6.6a Compress the valve spring using a spring compressor . . .

6.6b . . . then extract the collets and release the spring compressor

6.6c Remove the spring retainer . . .

6.6d . . . followed by the valve spring . . .

dismantle, inspect and recondition the original head.

1 Remove the cylinder head as described in Part A, B, C or D of this Chapter (as applicable).

2 If not already done, remove the inlet and exhaust manifolds with reference to Chapter 4A or 4B. Remove any remaining brackets or housings as required.

3 Remove the camshaft(s), hydraulic tappets and rockers (as applicable) as described in Part A, B, C or D of this Chapter.

4 If not already done on petrol models, remove the spark plugs as described in Chapter 1A.

5 If not already done on diesel models, remove the glow plugs as described in Chapter 5C.

6 On all models, using a valve spring compressor, compress each valve spring in turn until the split collets can be removed. Release the compressor, and lift off the spring

retainer, spring and, where fitted, the spring seat. Using a pair of pliers, carefully extract the valve stem oil seal from the top of the guide. On some engines, the valve stem oil seal also forms the spring seat **(see illustrations)**.

7 If, when the valve spring compressor is screwed down, the spring retainer refuses to free and expose the split collets, gently tap the top of the tool, directly over the retainer, with a light hammer. This will free the retainer.

8 Withdraw the valve from the combustion chamber. Remove the valve stem oil seal from the top of the guide, then lift out the spring seat where fitted.

9 It is essential that each valve is stored together with its collets, retainer, spring, and spring seat. The valves should also be kept in their correct sequence, unless they are so badly worn that they are to be renewed. If they are going to be kept and used again,

6.6e . . . and the spring seat (not all models)

6.6f Use a pair of pliers to remove the valve stem oil seal. On some models the spring seat is integral with the seal

6.9 Place each valve and its associated components in a labelled bag

place each valve assembly in a labelled polythene bag or similar small container (see illustration). Note that No 1 valve is nearest to the transmission (flywheel/driveplate) end of the engine.

7 Cylinder head and valves – cleaning and inspection

1 Thorough cleaning of the cylinder head and valve components, followed by a detailed inspection, will enable you to decide how much valve service work must be carried out during the engine overhaul. Note: If the engine has been severely overheated, it is best to assume that the cylinder head is warped – check carefully for signs of this.

Cleaning

2 Scrape away all traces of old gasket material from the cylinder head.

3 Scrape away the carbon from the combustion chambers and ports, then wash the cylinder head thoroughly with paraffin or a suitable solvent.

4 Scrape off any heavy carbon deposits that may have formed on the valves, then use a power-operated wire brush to remove deposits from the valve heads and stems.

Inspection

Note: Be sure to perform all the following inspection procedures before concluding that the services of a machine shop or engine overhaul specialist are required. Make a list of all items that require attention.

Cylinder head

5 Inspect the head very carefully for cracks, evidence of coolant leakage, and other damage. If cracks are found, a new cylinder head should be obtained. Use a straight-edge and feeler blade to check that the cylinder head gasket surface is not distorted (see illustration). If it is, it may be possible to have it machined, provided that the cylinder head height is not significantly reduced.

6 Examine the valve seats in each of the combustion chambers. If they are severely

7.5 Check the cylinder head gasket surface for distortion

pitted, cracked, or burned, they will need to be renewed or recut by an engine overhaul specialist. If they are only slightly pitted, this can be removed by grinding-in the valve heads and seats with fine valve-grinding compound, as described below.

7 Check the valve guides for wear by inserting the relevant valve, and checking for side-to-side motion of the valve. A very small amount of movement is acceptable. If the movement seems excessive, remove the valve. Measure the valve stem diameter (see below), and renew the valve if it is worn. If the valve stem is not worn, the wear must be in the valve guide, and the guide must be renewed. The renewal of valve guides is best carried out by a Peugeot dealer or engine overhaul specialist, who will have the necessary tools available. Where no valve stem diameter is specified, seek the advice of a Peugeot dealer on the best course of action.

8 If renewing the valve guides, the valve seats should be recut or reground only after the guides have been fitted.

9 On the 2.0 litre petrol engines, examine the camshaft oil supply non-return valve in the oil feed bore at the timing belt end of the cylinder head. Check that the valve is not loose in the cylinder head and that the ball is free to move within the valve body. If the valve is a loose fit in its bore, or if there is any doubt about its condition, it should be renewed. The non-return valve can be removed (assuming it is not loose), using compressed air, such as

that generated by a tyre foot pump. Place the pump nozzle over the oil feed bore of the inlet camshaft No 4 bearing journal and seal the corresponding oil feed bore in the exhaust camshaft with a rag. Apply the compressed air and the valve will be forced out of its location in the underside of the cylinder head (see illustrations). Fit the new non-return valve to its bore on the underside of the head ensuring it is fitted the correct way. Oil should be able to pass upwards through the valve to the camshafts, but the ball in the valve should prevent the oil from returning back to the cylinder block. Use a thin socket or similar to push the valve fully into position.

Valves

10 Examine the head of each valve for pitting, burning, cracks, and general wear. Check the valve stem for scoring and wear ridges. Rotate the valve, and check for any obvious indication that it is bent. Look for pits or excessive wear on the tip of each valve stem. Renew any valve that shows any such signs of wear or damage.

11 If the valve appears satisfactory at this stage, measure the valve stem diameter at several points using a micrometer (see illustration). Any significant difference in the readings obtained indicates wear of the valve stem. Should any of these conditions be apparent, the valve must be renewed.

12 If the valves are in satisfactory condition, they should be ground (lapped) into their respective seats, to ensure a smooth, gas-tight seal. If the seat is only lightly pitted, or if it has been recut, fine grinding compound only should be used to produce the required finish. Coarse valve-grinding compound should not be used, unless a seat is badly burned or deeply pitted. If this is the case, the cylinder head and valves should be inspected by an expert, to decide whether seat recutting, or even the renewal of the valve or seat insert (where possible) is required.

13 Valve grinding is carried out as follows. Place the cylinder head upside-down on a bench.

14 Smear a trace of (the appropriate grade of) valve-grinding compound on the seat face, and press a suction grinding tool onto

7.9a Apply compressed air to the oil feed bore of the inlet camshaft, seal the bore in the exhaust camshaft bore with a rag . . .

7.9b . . . and the camshaft oil supply non-return valve will be ejected from the underside of the cylinder head

7.11 Measure the valve stem diameter with a micrometer

7.14 Grinding-in a valve

8.1a Locate the valve stem oil seal on the valve guide . . .

8.1b . . . and press the seal firmly onto the guide using a suitable socket

the valve head **(see illustration)**. With a semi-rotary action, grind the valve head to its seat, lifting the valve occasionally to redistribute the grinding compound. A light spring placed under the valve head will greatly ease this operation.

15 If coarse grinding compound is being used, work only until a dull, matt even surface is produced on both the valve seat and the valve, then wipe off the used compound, and repeat the process with fine compound. When a smooth unbroken ring of light grey matt finish is produced on both the valve and seat, the grinding operation is complete. *Do not* grind-in the valves any further than absolutely necessary, or the seat will be prematurely sunk into the cylinder head.

16 When all the valves have been ground-in, carefully wash off *all* traces of grinding compound using paraffin or a suitable solvent, before reassembling the cylinder head.

Valve components

17 Examine the valve springs for signs of damage and discoloration. No minimum free length is specified by Peugeot, so the only way of judging valve spring wear is by comparison with a new component.

18 Stand each spring on a flat surface, and check it for squareness. If any of the springs are damaged, distorted or have lost their tension, obtain a complete new set of springs. It is normal to renew the valve springs as a matter of course if a major overhaul is being carried out.

19 Renew the valve stem oil seals regardless of their apparent condition.

8 Cylinder head – reassembly

1 Working on the first valve assembly, refit the spring seat then dip the new valve stem oil seal in fresh engine oil. Locate the seal on the valve guide and press the seal firmly onto the guide using a suitable socket **(see illustrations)**. Note that on 2.0 litre diesel engines no spring lower seat is fitted, whilst on some of the other engines, the valve stem oil seal is integral with the lower spring seat.

2 Lubricate the stem of the first valve, and insert it in the guide **(see illustration)**.

3 Locate the valve spring on top of its seat, and then refit the spring retainer. Note that on the 2.0 litre petrol engines, the larger diameter of the spring must face the cylinder head.

4 Compress the valve spring, and locate the split collets in the recess in the valve stem. Release the compressor, then repeat the procedure on the remaining valves. Ensure that each valve is inserted into its original location. If new valves are being fitted, insert them into the locations to which they have been ground.

 Use a little dab of grease to hold the collets in position on the valve stem while the spring compressor is released.

5 With all the valves installed, support the cylinder head and, using a hammer and

interposed block of wood, tap the end of each valve stem to settle the components.

6 Refit the camshafts, hydraulic tappets and rocker arms (as applicable) as described in Part A, B, C or D of this Chapter.

7 Refit any remaining components using the reverse of the removal sequence and with new seals or gaskets as necessary.

8 The cylinder head can then be refitted as described in Part A, B, C or D of this Chapter.

9 Piston/connecting rod assembly – removal

Note: On 1.4 litre diesel engines, the main bearing ladder must be removed before the piston/connecting rods.

1 Remove the cylinder head, sump and oil pump as described in Part A, B, C or D of this Chapter.

2 If there is a pronounced wear ridge at the top of any bore, it may be necessary to remove it with a scraper or ridge reamer, to avoid piston damage during removal. Such a ridge indicates excessive wear of the cylinder bore.

3 Using quick-drying paint, mark each connecting rod and big-end bearing cap with its respective cylinder number on the flat machined surface provided; if the engine has been dismantled before, note carefully any identifying marks made previously **(see illustration)**. Note that No 1 cylinder is at the transmission (flywheel) end of the engine.

4 Turn the crankshaft to bring pistons 1 and 4

8.1c On some models, the valve stem oil seal is integral with the spring seat

8.2 Lubricate the stem of the valve and insert it into the guide

9.3 Connecting rod and big-end bearing cap identification marks (No 3 shown)

9.5 Remove the big-end bearing shell and cap

9.6 To protect the crankshaft journals, tape over the connecting rod stud threads

10.21 On 1.4 litre diesel engines, prise up the two caps to expose the main bearing bolts at the flywheel end

to BDC (bottom dead centre). On 1.4 litre diesel engines, remove the main bearing ladder as described in Section 10 of this Chapter.

5 Unscrew the nuts or bolts, as applicable, from No 1 piston big-end bearing cap. Take off the cap, and recover the bottom half bearing shell **(see illustration)**. If the bearing shells are to be re-used, tape the cap and the shell together.

6 To prevent the possibility of damage to the crankshaft bearing journals, tape over the connecting rod stud threads where fitted **(see illustration)**.

7 Using a hammer handle, push the piston up through the bore, and remove it from the top of the cylinder block. Recover the bearing shell, and tape it to the connecting rod for safe-keeping.

8 Loosely refit the big-end cap to the connecting rod, and secure with the nuts/bolts – this will help to keep the components in their correct order.

9 Remove No 4 piston assembly in the same way.

10 Turn the crankshaft through 180° to bring pistons 2 and 3 to BDC (bottom dead centre), and remove them in the same way.

10 Crankshaft – removal

1 Remove the crankshaft sprocket and the oil pump as described in Part A, B, C or D of this Chapter (as applicable).

2 Remove the pistons and connecting rods, as described in Section 9. If no work is to be done on the pistons and connecting rods, there is no need to remove the cylinder head, or to push the pistons out of the cylinder bores. The pistons should just be pushed far enough up the bores so that they are positioned clear of the crankshaft journals. **Note:** On 1.4 litre diesel engines, the main bearing ladder must be removed before the piston/connecting rods.

3 Check the crankshaft endfloat as described in Section 13, then proceed as follows.

1.1 and 1.4 litre petrol engine

4 Work around the outside of the cylinder block, and unscrew all the small (M6) bolts securing the main bearing ladder to the base of the cylinder block. Note the correct fitted depth of both the left- and right-hand crankshaft oil seals in the cylinder block/main bearing ladder.

5 Working in a diagonal sequence, evenly and progressively slacken the ten large (M11) main bearing ladder retaining bolts by a turn at a time. Once all the bolts are loose, remove them from the ladder.

6 With all the retaining bolts removed, carefully lift the main bearing ladder casting away from the base of the cylinder block. Recover the lower main bearing shells, and tape them to their respective locations in the casting. If the two locating dowels are a loose fit, remove them and store them with the casting for safekeeping.

7 Lift out the crankshaft, and discard both the oil seals. Remove the oil pump drive chain from the end of the crankshaft. Where necessary, slide off the drive sprocket, and recover the Woodruff key.

8 Recover the upper main bearing shells, and store them along with the relevant lower bearing shell. Also recover the two thrustwashers from the cylinder block.

1.6 litre petrol engine

9 Unbolt and remove the crankshaft left- and right-hand oil seal housings from each end of the cylinder block, noting the correct fitted locations of the locating dowels. If the locating dowels are a loose fit, remove them and store them with the housings for safe-keeping.

10 Remove the oil pump drive chain, and slide the drive sprocket off the end of the crankshaft. Remove the Woodruff key, and store it with the sprocket for safe-keeping.

11 The main bearing caps should be numbered 1 to 5 from the transmission (flywheel/driveplate) end of the engine. If not, mark them accordingly using a centre-punch or paint.

12 Unscrew and remove the main bearing cap retaining bolts, and withdraw the caps. Recover the lower main bearing shells, and tape them to their respective caps for safe-keeping.

13 Carefully lift out the crankshaft, taking

care not to displace the upper main bearing shell.

14 Recover the upper bearing shells from the cylinder block, and tape them to their respective caps for safe-keeping. Remove the thrustwasher halves from the side of No 2 main bearing, and store them with the bearing cap.

2.0 litre petrol engine

15 Work around the outside of the cylinder block, and unscrew all the small bolts securing the main bearing ladder to the base of the cylinder block. Note the correct fitted depth of the left-hand crankshaft oil seal in the cylinder block/main bearing ladder.

16 Working in a diagonal sequence, evenly and progressively slacken the large main bearing ladder retaining bolts by a turn at a time. Once all the bolts are loose, remove them from the ladder.

17 With all the retaining bolts removed, carefully lift the main bearing ladder casting away from the base of the cylinder block. Recover the lower main bearing shells, and tape them to their respective locations in the casting. If the two locating dowels are a loose fit, remove them and store them with the casting for safe-keeping.

18 Lift out the crankshaft, and discard both the oil seals.

19 Recover the upper main bearing shells, and store them along with the relevant lower bearing shell. Also recover the two thrustwashers (one fitted either side of No 2 main bearing) from the cylinder block.

1.4 litre diesel engine

20 Work around the outside of the cylinder block, and unscrew all the small bolts securing the main bearing ladder to the base of the cylinder block. Note the correct fitted depth of the left-hand crankshaft oil seal in the cylinder block/main bearing ladder.

21 Working in a diagonal sequence, evenly and progressively slacken the large main bearing ladder retaining bolts by a turn at a time. Once all the bolts are loose, remove them from the ladder. **Note:** Prise up the two caps at the flywheel end of the ladder to expose the two end main bearing bolts **(see illustration)**.

10.25 Remove the oil seal housing from the right-hand end of the block

10.28 Note the thrustwashers (arrowed) fitted to the No 2 bearing cap

22 With all the retaining bolts removed, carefully lift the main bearing ladder casting away from the base of the cylinder block. Recover the lower main bearing shells, and tape them to their respective locations in the casting. If the two locating dowels are a loose fit, remove them and store them with the casting for safe-keeping. Undo the big-end bolts and remove the pistons/connecting rods as described in Section 9.

23 Lift out the crankshaft, and discard both the oil seals.

24 Recover the upper main bearing shells, and store them along with the relevant lower main bearing shell. Also recover the two thrustwashers (one fitted either side of No 2 main bearing) from the cylinder block.

2.0 litre diesel engine

25 Slacken and remove the retaining bolts, and remove the oil seal housing from the right-hand (timing belt) end of the cylinder block **(see illustration)**.

26 Remove the oil pump drive chain, and slide the drive sprocket off from the crankshaft. Remove the Woodruff key, and store it with the sprocket for safe-keeping then remove the sealing ring (where fitted) from the crankshaft.

27 The main bearing caps should be numbered 1 to 5, starting from the transmission (flywheel) end of the engine. If not, mark them accordingly using a centre-punch. Also note the correct fitted depth of the crankshaft oil seal in the bearing cap.

28 Slacken and remove the main bearing cap retaining bolts, and lift off each bearing cap.

Recover the lower bearing shells, and tape them to their respective caps for safe-keeping. Also recover the lower thrustwasher halves from the side of No 2 main bearing cap **(see illustration)**. Remove the sealing strips from the sides of No 1 main bearing cap, and discard them.

29 Lift out the crankshaft, and discard the left-hand (flywheel end) oil seal.

30 Recover the upper bearing shells from the cylinder block, and tape them to their respective caps for safe-keeping. Remove the upper thrustwasher halves from the side of No 2 main bearing, and store them with the lower halves.

11 Cylinder block/crankcase – cleaning and inspection

Cleaning

1 Remove all external components and electrical switches/sensors from the block. For complete cleaning, the core plugs should ideally be removed **(see illustration)**. Drill a small hole in the plugs, and then insert a self-tapping screw into the hole. Pull out the plugs by pulling on the screw with a pair of grips, or by using a slide hammer.

2 On aluminium block petrol engines with wet liners (1.4 litre), remove the liners – see paragraph 18.

3 Where applicable, undo the retaining bolts and remove the piston oil jet spray tubes (there is one for each piston) from inside the cylinder block **(see illustration)**.

4 Scrape all traces of gasket from the cylinder block/crankcase, and from the main bearing ladder/caps (as applicable), taking care not to damage the gasket/sealing surfaces.

5 Remove all oil gallery plugs (where fitted). The plugs are usually very tight – they may have to be drilled out, and the holes retapped. Use new plugs when the engine is reassembled.

6 If any of the castings are extremely dirty, all should be steam-cleaned.

7 After the castings are returned, clean all oil holes and oil galleries one more time. Flush all internal passages with warm water until the water runs clear. Dry thoroughly, and apply a light film of oil to all mating surfaces, to prevent rusting. On cast-iron block engines, also oil the cylinder bores. If you have access to compressed air, use it to speed up the drying process, and to blow out all the oil holes and galleries.

⚠️ *Warning: Wear eye protection when using compressed air.*

8 If the castings are not very dirty, you can do an adequate cleaning job with hot (as hot as you can stand), soapy water and a stiff brush. Take plenty of time, and do a thorough job. Regardless of the cleaning method used, be sure to clean all oil holes and galleries very thoroughly, and to dry all components well. On cast-iron block engines, protect the cylinder bores as described above, to prevent rusting.

9 All threaded holes must be clean, to ensure accurate torque readings during reassembly. To clean the threads, run the correct-size tap into each of the holes to remove rust, corrosion, thread sealant or sludge, and to restore damaged threads **(see illustration)**. If possible, use compressed air to clear the holes of debris produced by this operation.

10 Apply suitable sealant to the new oil gallery plugs, and insert them into the holes in the block. Tighten them securely. Also apply suitable sealant to new core plugs, and drive them into the block using a tube or socket.

11 Where applicable, clean the threads of the piston oil jet retaining bolts, and apply a drop of thread-locking compound (Peugeot recommend Loctite Frenetanch) to each bolt threads. Refit the piston oil jet spray tubes to the cylinder block, and tighten the retaining bolts to the specified torque setting.

11.1 Cylinder block core plugs (arrowed)

11.3 Piston oil jet spray tube (arrowed) in the cylinder block

11.9 Use a suitable tap to clean the cylinder block threaded holes

11.18a On aluminium block engines, remove each liner . . .

11.18b . . . and recover the bottom O-ring seal (arrowed)

12.2 Remove the piston rings with the aid of a feeler gauge

12 If the engine is not going to be reassembled right away, cover it with a large plastic bag to keep it clean; protect all mating surfaces and the cylinder bores as described above, to prevent rusting.

Inspection

Cast-iron cylinder block

13 Visually check the castings for cracks and corrosion. Look for stripped threads in the threaded holes. If there has been any history of internal water leakage, it may be worthwhile having an engine overhaul specialist check the cylinder block/crankcase with special equipment. If defects are found, have them repaired if possible, or renew the assembly.

14 Check each cylinder bore for scuffing and scoring. Check for signs of a wear ridge at the top of the cylinder, indicating that the bore is excessively worn.

15 If the necessary measuring equipment is available, measure the bore diameter of each cylinder at the top (just under the wear ridge), centre, and bottom of the cylinder bore, parallel to the crankshaft axis.

16 Next, measure the bore diameter at the same three locations, at right-angles to the crankshaft axis. Compare the results with the figures given in the Specifications. Where no figures are stated by Peugeot, or if there is any doubt about the condition of the cylinder bores, seek the advice of a Peugeot dealer or suitable engine reconditioning specialist.

17 At the time of writing, it was not clear whether oversize pistons were available for all models. Consult your Peugeot dealer or engine specialist for the latest information on piston availability. If oversize pistons are available, then it may be possible to have the cylinder bores rebored and fit the oversize pistons. If oversize pistons are not available, and the bores are worn, renewal of the block seems to be the only option.

Aluminium cylinder block

18 Remove the liner clamps (where used), and then use a hardwood drift to tap out each liner from the inside of the cylinder block. When all the liners are released, tip the cylinder block/crankcase on its side and remove each liner from the top of the block. As each liner is removed, stick masking tape on its left-hand

(transmission side) face, and write the cylinder number on the tape. No 1 cylinder is at the transmission (flywheel/driveplate) end of the engine. Remove the sealing ring from the base of each liner, and discard **(see illustrations)**.

19 Check each cylinder liner for scuffing and scoring. Check for signs of a wear ridge at the top of the liner, indicating that the bore is excessively worn.

20 Take the liners to a Peugeot dealer or engine reconditioning specialist and have their bores measured to determine if renewal is necessary. If it is, the dealer or specialist will be able to advise you regarding piston/liner availability.

21 Prior to installing the liners, check the liner protrusion as follows. Thoroughly clean the mating surfaces of the liner and cylinder block. Insert the liners into the block ensuring each one is correctly seated; if the original liners are being refitted, ensure the liners are fitted in their original locations. With all four liners correctly installed, use a dial gauge (or a straight-edge and feeler blade) to check that the protrusion of each liner above the upper surface of the cylinder block is within the limits given in the Specifications. The maximum difference between any two liners must not be exceeded. **Note:** *If new liners are being fitted, it is permissible to interchange them to bring the difference in protrusion within limits. Remember to keep each piston with its respective liner.* If liner protrusion is not within the specified limits, seek the advice of a Peugeot dealer or engine reconditioning specialist before proceeding with the engine rebuild.

22 Once the protrusions have been checked, remove the liners from the block and fit a new sealing ring carefully to the base of each liner. Lubricate the base of each liner with a smear of oil to aid installation.

23 Insert each liner into the cylinder block, taking care not to damage the O-ring, and press it home as far as possible by hand. Using a hammer and a block of wood, tap each liner lightly but fully onto its locating shoulder. If the original liners are being refitted, use the marks made on removal to ensure that each is refitted the correct way round, and is inserted into its original bore.

24 Wipe clean, then lightly oil all exposed liner

surfaces, to prevent rusting. Where necessary, clamp the liners back in position.

12 Piston/connecting rod assembly – inspection

1 Before the inspection process can begin, the piston/connecting rod assemblies must be cleaned, and the original piston rings removed from the pistons.

2 Carefully expand the old rings over the top of the pistons. The use of two or three old feeler blades will be helpful in preventing the rings dropping into empty grooves **(see illustration)**. Be careful not to scratch the piston with the ends of the ring. The rings are brittle, and will snap if they are spread too far. They are also very sharp – protect your hands and fingers. Note that the third ring incorporates an expander. Always remove the rings from the top of the piston. Keep each set of rings with its piston if the old rings are to be re-used.

3 Scrape away all traces of carbon from the top of the piston. A hand-held wire brush (or a piece of fine emery cloth) can be used, once the majority of the deposits have been scraped away.

4 Remove the carbon from the ring grooves in the piston, using an old ring. Break the ring in half to do this (be careful not to cut your fingers – piston rings are sharp). Be careful to remove only the carbon deposits – do not remove any metal, and do not nick or scratch the sides of the ring grooves.

5 Once the deposits have been removed, clean the piston/connecting rod assembly with paraffin or a suitable solvent, and dry thoroughly. Make sure that the oil return holes in the ring grooves are clear.

6 If the pistons and cylinder bores are not damaged or worn excessively, and if the cylinder block does not need to be rebored (where possible), the original pistons can be refitted. Normal piston wear shows up as even vertical wear on the piston thrust surfaces, and slight looseness of the top ring in its groove. New piston rings should always be used when the engine is reassembled.

7 Carefully inspect each piston for cracks

12.15a Prise out the circlip . . .

12.15b . . . and withdraw the gudgeon pin

12.19 Piston and connecting rod assembly – 1.4 litre diesel engine

1 *Connecting rod*   4 *Piston rings*
2 *Big-end shells*   5 *Gudgeon pin*
3 *Big-end bolt*   6 *Circlips*

around the skirt, around the gudgeon pin holes, and at the piston ring 'lands' (between the ring grooves).

8 Look for scoring and scuffing on the piston skirt, holes in the piston crown, and burned areas at the edge of the crown. If the skirt is scored or scuffed, the engine may have been suffering from overheating, and/or abnormal combustion, which caused excessively high operating temperatures. The cooling and lubrication systems should be checked thoroughly. Scorch marks on the sides of the pistons show that blow-by has occurred. A hole in the piston crown, or burned areas at the edge of the piston crown, indicates that abnormal combustion (pre-ignition, knocking, or detonation) has been occurring. If any of the above problems exist, the causes must be investigated and corrected, or the damage will occur again. The causes may include incorrect ignition/injection pump timing, or a faulty injector (as applicable).

9 Corrosion of the piston, in the form of pitting, indicates that coolant has been leaking into the combustion chamber and/ or the crankcase. Again, the cause must be corrected, or the problem may persist in the rebuilt engine.

10 On aluminium block engines with wet liners, it is not possible to renew the pistons separately; pistons are only supplied with piston rings and a liner, as a part of a matched assembly (see Section 11). On iron-block engines, pistons can be purchased from a Peugeot dealer or engine reconditioning specialist.

11 Examine each connecting rod carefully for signs of damage, such as cracks around the big end and small-end bearings. Check that the rod is not bent or distorted. Damage is highly unlikely, unless the engine has been seized or badly overheated. Detailed checking of the connecting rod assembly can only be carried out by a Peugeot dealer or engine specialist with the necessary equipment.

12 The connecting rod big-end cap nuts must be renewed whenever they are disturbed. Although Peugeot do not specify that the bolts must also be renewed, it is recommended that the nuts and bolts are renewed as a complete set.

13 On petrol engines, the gudgeon pins

are an interference fit in the connecting rod small-end bearing. Therefore, piston and/or connecting rod renewal should be entrusted to a Peugeot dealer or engine repair specialist, who will have the necessary tooling to remove and install the gudgeon pins.

14 On diesel engines, the gudgeon pins are of the floating type, secured in position by two circlips. On these engines, the pistons and connecting rods can be separated as follows.

15 Using a small flat-bladed screwdriver, prise out the circlips, and push out the gudgeon pin **(see illustrations)**. Hand pressure should be sufficient to remove the pin. Identify the piston and rod to ensure correct reassembly. Discard the circlips – new ones *must* be used on refitting.

16 Examine the gudgeon pin and connecting rod small-end bearing for signs of wear or damage. Wear can be cured by renewing both the pin and bush (where possible) or connecting rod. Bush renewal, however, is a specialist job – press facilities are required, and the new bush must be reamed accurately.

17 The connecting rods themselves should not be in need of renewal, unless seizure or some other major mechanical failure has occurred. Check the alignment of the connecting rods visually, and if the rods are not straight, take them to an engine overhaul specialist for a more detailed check.

18 Examine all components, and obtain any new parts from your Peugeot dealer. If new pistons are purchased, they will be supplied complete with gudgeon pins and circlips. Circlips can also be purchased individually.

19 On 1.4 litre diesel engines, position the piston as shown **(see illustration)**.

20 On 2.0 litre diesel engines, position the piston so that the valve recesses on the piston crown are on the opposite side to the connecting rod big-end bearing shell cut-outs.

21 Ensure the piston and connecting rod are correctly positioned then apply a smear of clean engine oil to the gudgeon pin. Slide it into the piston and through the connecting rod small-end. Check that the piston pivots freely on the rod, then secure the gudgeon pin in position with two new circlips. Ensure that each circlip is correctly located in its groove in the piston.

13 Crankshaft – inspection

Checking endfloat

1 If the crankshaft endfloat is to be checked, this must be done when the crankshaft is still installed in the cylinder block/crankcase, but is free to move (see Section 10).

2 Check the endfloat using a dial gauge in contact with the end of the crankshaft. Push the crankshaft fully one way, and then zero the gauge. Push the crankshaft fully the other way, and check the endfloat. The result can be compared with the specified amount, and will give an indication as to whether new thrustwashers are required **(see illustration)**.

3 If a dial gauge is not available, feeler blades can be used. First push the crankshaft fully towards the flywheel end of the engine, and

13.2 The crankshaft endfloat can be checked with a dial gauge . . .

13.3 . . . or with feeler gauges

then use feeler blades to measure the gap between the web of the crankpin and the thrustwasher **(see illustration)**.

Inspection

4 Clean the crankshaft using paraffin or a suitable solvent, and dry it, preferably with compressed air if available. Be sure to clean the oil holes with a pipe cleaner or similar probe, to ensure that they are not obstructed.

 Warning: Wear eye protection when using compressed air.

5 Check the main and big-end bearing journals for uneven wear, scoring, pitting and cracking.

6 Big-end bearing wear is accompanied by distinct metallic knocking when the engine is running (particularly noticeable when the engine is pulling from low speed) and some loss of oil pressure.

7 Main bearing wear is accompanied by severe engine vibration and rumble – getting progressively worse as engine speed increases – and again by loss of oil pressure.

8 Check the bearing journal for roughness by running a finger lightly over the bearing surface. Any roughness (which will be accompanied

14.2 Typical bearing failures

by obvious bearing wear) indicates that the crankshaft requires regrinding (where possible) or renewal.

9 Check the oil seal contact surfaces at each end of the crankshaft for wear and damage. If the seal has worn a deep groove in the surface of the crankshaft, consult an engine overhaul specialist; repair may be possible, but otherwise a new crankshaft will be required.

10 Take the crankshaft to a Peugeot dealer or engine reconditioning specialist to have it measured for journal wear. If excessive wear is evident, they will be able to advise you with regard to regrinding the crankshaft and supplying new bearing shells.

11 If the crankshaft has been reground, check for burrs around the crankshaft oil holes (the holes are usually chamfered, so burrs should not be a problem unless regrinding has been carried out carelessly). Remove any burrs with a fine file or scraper, and thoroughly clean the oil holes as described previously.

12 At the time of writing, it was not clear whether Peugeot produce undersize bearing shells for all of these engines. On some engines, if the crankshaft journals have not already been reground, it may be possible to have the crankshaft reconditioned, and to fit undersize shells. If no undersize shells are available and the crankshaft has worn beyond the specified limits, it will have to be renewed. Consult your Peugeot dealer or engine specialist for further information on parts availability.

14 Main and big-end bearings – inspection

1 Even though the main and big-end bearings should be renewed during the engine overhaul, the old bearings should be retained for close examination, as they may reveal valuable information about the condition of the engine. The bearing shells are graded by thickness, the grade of each shell being indicated by the colour code marked on it.

2 Bearing failure can occur due to lack of lubrication, the presence of dirt or other foreign particles, overloading the engine, or corrosion **(see illustration)**. Regardless of the cause of bearing failure, the cause must be corrected (where applicable) before the engine is reassembled, to prevent it from happening again.

3 When examining the bearing shells, remove them from the cylinder block/crankcase, the connecting rods and the connecting rod big-end bearing caps. Lay them out on a clean surface in the same general position as their location in the engine. This will enable you to match any bearing problems with the corresponding crankshaft journal. *Do not* touch any shell's bearing surface with your fingers while checking it, or the delicate surface may be scratched.

4 Dirt and other foreign matter gets into the

engine in a variety of ways. It may be left in the engine during assembly, or it may pass through filters or the crankcase ventilation system. It may get into the oil, and from there into the bearings. Metal chips from machining operations and normal engine wear are often present. Abrasives are sometimes left in engine components after reconditioning, especially when parts are not thoroughly cleaned using the proper cleaning methods. Whatever the source, these foreign objects often end up embedded in the soft bearing material, and are easily recognised. Large particles will not embed in the bearing, and will score or gouge the bearing and journal. The best prevention for this cause of bearing failure is to clean all parts thoroughly, and keep everything spotlessly clean during engine assembly. Frequent and regular engine oil and filter changes are also recommended.

5 Lack of lubrication (or lubrication breakdown) has a number of interrelated causes. Excessive heat (which thins the oil), overloading (which squeezes the oil from the bearing face) and oil leakage (from excessive bearing clearances, worn oil pump or high engine speeds) all contribute to lubrication breakdown. Blocked oil passages, which usually are the result of misaligned oil holes in a bearing shell, will also oil-starve a bearing, and destroy it. When lack of lubrication is the cause of bearing failure, the bearing material is wiped or extruded from the steel backing of the bearing. Temperatures may increase to the point where the steel backing turns blue from overheating.

6 Driving habits can have a definite effect on bearing life. Full-throttle, low-speed operation (labouring the engine) puts very high loads on bearings, tending to squeeze out the oil film. These loads cause the bearings to flex, which produces fine cracks in the bearing face (fatigue failure). Eventually, the bearing material will loosen in pieces, and tear away from the steel backing.

7 Short-distance driving leads to corrosion of bearings, because insufficient engine heat is produced to drive off the condensed water and corrosive gases. These products collect in the engine oil, forming acid and sludge. As the oil is carried to the engine bearings, the acid attacks and corrodes the bearing material.

8 Incorrect bearing installation during engine assembly will lead to bearing failure as well. Tight-fitting bearings leave insufficient bearing running clearance, and will result in oil starvation. Dirt or foreign particles trapped behind a bearing shell result in high spots on the bearing, which lead to failure.

9 *Do not* touch any shell's bearing surface with your fingers during reassembly; there is a risk of scratching the delicate surface, or of depositing particles of dirt on it.

10 As mentioned at the beginning of this Section, the bearing shells should be renewed as a matter of course during engine overhaul; to do otherwise is false economy.

16.5 Measure the piston rings end gaps with a feeler gauge

J44877

16.9a Piston ring fitting diagram (typical)

1 *Oil control ring*
2 *Second compression ring*
3 *Top compression ring*

H44714

16.9b Piston rings (1.4 litre diesel engine)

1 *Top compression ring*
2 *Second compression ring*
3 *Oil control ring*

15 Engine overhaul – reassembly sequence

1 Before reassembly begins, ensure that all new parts have been obtained, and that all necessary tools are available. Read through the entire procedure to familiarise yourself with the work involved, and to ensure that all items necessary for reassembly of the engine are at hand. In addition to all normal tools and materials, thread-locking compound will be needed. A tube of suitable liquid sealant will also be required for the joint faces that are fitted without gaskets. It is recommended that Peugeot's own product(s) are used, which are specially formulated for this purpose; the relevant product names are quoted in the text of each Section where they are required.

2 In order to save time and avoid problems, engine reassembly can be carried out in the following order, referring to Part A, B, C or D of this Chapter unless otherwise stated:

a) *Crankshaft (See Section 17).* **Note:** *On 1.4 litre diesel engines, the piston/ connecting rods must be fitted before the crankshaft.*
b) *Piston/connecting rod assemblies (See Section 18).*
c) *Oil pump.*
d) *Sump.*
e) *Flywheel/driveplate.*
f) *Cylinder head.*
g) *Injection pump and mounting bracket – diesel engine (Chapter 4B).*
h) *Timing belt tensioner pulley(s) and sprockets, and timing belt.*
i) *Engine external components.*

3 At this stage, all engine components should be absolutely clean and dry, with all faults repaired. The components should be laid out (or in individual containers) on a completely clean work surface.

16 Piston rings – refitting

1 Before fitting new piston rings, the ring end gaps must be checked as follows.

2 Lay out the piston/connecting rod assemblies and the new piston ring sets, so that the ring sets will be matched with the same piston and cylinder during the end gap measurement and subsequent engine reassembly.

3 Insert the top ring into the first cylinder, and push it down the bore using the top of the piston. This will ensure that the ring remains square with the cylinder walls. Position the ring near the bottom of the cylinder bore, at the lower limit of ring travel. Note that the top and second compression rings are different. The second ring can be identified by its taper; on petrol engines it also has a step on its lower surface. On 1.4 litre diesel engines, the top ring has a chamfer on its upper/outer edge.

4 Measure the end gap using feeler blades.

5 Repeat the procedure with the ring at the top of the cylinder bore, at the upper limit of its travel **(see illustration)**, and compare the measurements with the figures given in the Specifications. If the end gaps are incorrect, check that you have the correct rings for your engine and for the cylinder bore size.

6 Repeat the checking procedure for each ring in the first cylinder, and then for the rings in the remaining cylinders. Remember to keep rings, pistons and cylinders matched up.

7 Once the ring end gaps have been checked and if necessary corrected, the rings can be fitted to the pistons.

8 Fit the oil control ring expander (where fitted) then install the ring.

9 The second and top rings are different and can be identified from their cross-sections; the

17.5 Fit the grooved bearing shells to No 2 and 4 main bearings (1.4 litre petrol engine)

top ring is symmetrical whilst the second ring is tapered. Fit the second ring, ensuring its identification (TOP) marking is facing upwards, and then install the top ring **(see illustrations)**. Arrange the oil control, second and top ring end gaps so they are equally spaced 120° apart. **Note:** *Always follow any instructions supplied with the new piston ring sets – different manufacturers may specify different procedures. Do not mix up the top and second compression rings, as they have different cross-sections.*

17 Crankshaft – refitting

Selection of bearing shells

1 Have the crankshaft inspected and measured by a Peugeot dealer or engine reconditioning specialist. They will be able to carry out any regrinding/repairs, and supply suitable main and big-end bearing shells.

Crankshaft refitting

Note: *New main bearing cap/lower crankcase bolts must be used when refitting the crankshaft.*

2 Where applicable, ensure that the oil spray jets are fitted to the bearing locations in the cylinder block.

1.1 and 1.4 litre petrol engine

3 Using a little grease, stick the upper thrustwashers to each side of the relevant main bearing upper location; ensure that the oilway grooves on each thrustwasher face outwards (away from the block).

4 Clean the backs of the bearing shells, and the bearing locations in both the cylinder block/crankcase and the main bearing ladder/ bearing caps.

5 Press the bearing shells into their locations, ensuring that the tab on each shell engages in the notch in the cylinder block/crankcase or main bearing ladder/bearing cap. Take care not to touch any shell's bearing surface with your fingers. Note that the grooved bearing shells, both upper and lower, are fitted to Nos 2 and 4 main bearings **(see illustration)**.

17.7 Fit the oil pump drive chain and sprocket

17.8 Apply a thin film of sealant to the cylinder block mating surface

17.10 Tighten the ten main bearing bolts to the specified torque

6 Liberally lubricate each bearing shell in the cylinder block/crankcase with clean engine oil.

7 Refit the Woodruff key, then slide on the oil pump drive sprocket, and locate the drive chain on the sprocket **(see illustration)**. Lower the crankshaft into position so that Nos 2 and 3 cylinder crankpins are at TDC; Nos 1 and 4 cylinder crankpins will be at BDC, ready for fitting No 1 piston. Check the crankshaft endfloat as described in Section 13.

8 Thoroughly degrease the mating surfaces of the cylinder block/crankcase and the main bearing ladder. Apply a thin bead of suitable sealant to the cylinder block mating surface of the main bearing ladder casting, then spread to an even film **(see illustration)**.

9 Ensure the locating dowels are in position then lubricate the lower bearing shells with clean engine oil. Refit the main bearing ladder to the cylinder block, ensuring that the lower bearings remain correctly fitted.

10 Install the main bearing ladder retaining bolts, and tighten them all by hand only. Working in a spiral pattern from the centre bolts outwards, evenly and progressively tighten the bolts to the specified Stage 1 torque wrench setting. Once all the bolts have been tightened to the Stage 1 setting, working in the same sequence, angle-tighten the bolts through the specified Stage 2 angle using a socket and extension bar. It is recommended that an angle-measuring gauge is used during this stage of the tightening, to ensure accuracy **(see illustration)**. If a gauge is not

available, use a dab of white paint to make alignment marks between the bolt head and casting prior to tightening; the marks can then be used to check that the bolt has been rotated sufficiently during tightening.

11 Refit all the smaller bolts securing the main bearing ladder to the base of the cylinder block, and tighten them to the specified torque. Check that the crankshaft rotates freely.

12 Refit the piston/connecting rod assemblies to the crankshaft as described in Section 18.

13 Ensuring that the drive chain is correctly located on the sprocket, refit the oil pump and sump as described in Part A or B of this Chapter.

14 Fit two new crankshaft oil seals as described in Part A or B.

15 Refit the flywheel/driveplate as described in Part A or B of this Chapter.

16 Refit the cylinder head (where removed) as described in Part A or B. Also refit the crankshaft sprocket and timing belt (see Part A or B).

1.6 litre petrol engine

17 Using a little grease, stick the upper thrustwashers to each side of the No 2 main bearing upper location. Ensure that the oilway grooves on each thrustwasher face outwards (away from the cylinder block) **(see illustration)**.

18 Place the bearing shells in their locations as described in paragraphs 4 and 5 **(see illustration)**. If new shells are being fitted,

ensure that all traces of protective grease are cleaned off using paraffin. Wipe dry the shells and connecting rods with a lint-free cloth. Liberally lubricate each bearing shell in the cylinder block/crankcase and cap with clean engine oil.

19 Lower the crankshaft into position so that Nos 2 and 3 cylinder crankpins are at TDC; Nos 1 and 4 cylinder crankpins will be at BDC, ready for fitting No 1 piston. Check the crankshaft endfloat as described in Section 13.

20 Lubricate the lower bearing shells in the main bearing caps with clean engine oil. Make sure that the locating lugs on the shells engage with the corresponding recesses in the caps.

21 Fit the main bearing caps to their correct locations, ensuring that they are fitted the correct way round (the bearing shell lug recesses in the block and caps must be on the same side).

22 Lightly lubricate the threads and the underside of the heads of the main bearing cap bolts with engine oil then refit the bolts. Working in a spiral sequence from the centre bolts outwards, tighten the main bearing cap bolts evenly and progressively to the specified Stage 1 torque wrench setting. Once all the bolts have been tightened to the Stage 1 setting, working in the same sequence, angle-tighten the bolts through the specified Stage 2 angle, using a socket and extension bar. It is recommended that an angle-measuring gauge is used during this stage of the tightening, to ensure accuracy. If a gauge is not available, use a dab of white paint to make alignment marks between the bolt head and casting prior to tightening; the marks can then be used to check that the bolt has been rotated sufficiently during tightening.

23 Check that the crankshaft rotates freely.

24 Refit the piston/connecting rod assemblies to the crankshaft as described in Section 18.

25 Refit the Woodruff key to the crankshaft groove, and slide on the oil pump drive sprocket. Locate the drive chain on the sprocket.

26 Ensure that the mating surfaces of right-hand (timing belt end) oil seal housing and cylinder block are clean and dry. Note the correct fitted depth of the oil seal then, using

17.17 Fit the thrustwashers to either side of the No 2 main bearing, with the oilway grooves facing outwards

17.18 Ensure the tab (arrowed) is located in the cut-out when fitting the bearing shells

17.36 Insert the thrustwashers to either side of the No 2 main bearing upper location

17.37 Apply a thin bead of RTV sealant to the bearing cap housing mating surface

17.40 Main bearing ladder retaining bolt tightening sequence (2.0 litre petrol engine)

a large flat-bladed screwdriver, lever the seal out of the housing.

27 Apply a smear of suitable sealant to the oil seal housing mating surface, and make sure that the locating dowels are in position. Slide the housing over the end of the crankshaft, and into position on the cylinder block. Tighten the housing retaining bolts securely.

28 Repeat the operations in paragraphs 26 and 27, and fit the left-hand (flywheel/driveplate end) oil seal housing.

29 Fit new crankshaft oil seals as described in Part A of this Chapter.

30 Ensuring that the chain is correctly located on the drive sprocket, refit the oil pump and sump as described in Part A of this Chapter.

31 Refit the flywheel/driveplate as described in Part A of this Chapter.

32 Refit the cylinder head (where removed) and install the crankshaft sprocket and timing belt as described in the relevant Sections of Part A.

2.0 litre petrol engine

33 Clean the backs of the bearing shells in both the cylinder block/crankcase and the main bearing ladder. If new shells are being fitted, ensure that all traces of protective grease are cleaned off using paraffin. Wipe dry the shells with a lint-free cloth.

34 Press the bearing shells into their locations, ensuring that the tab on each shell engages in the notch in the cylinder block/crankcase and bearing ladder. Take care not to touch any shell's bearing surface with your fingers. Note that the upper bearing shells all have a grooved surface, whereas the lower shells have a plain bearing surface.

35 Liberally lubricate each bearing shell in the cylinder block with clean engine oil then lower the crankshaft into position.

36 Insert the thrustwashers to either side of No 2 main bearing upper location and push them around the bearing journal until their edges are horizontal **(see illustration)**. Ensure that the oilway grooves on each thrustwasher face outwards (away from the cylinder block).

37 Thoroughly degrease the mating surfaces of the cylinder block and the crankshaft bearing cap housing/main bearing ladder. Apply a thin bead of RTV sealant to the

bearing cap housing mating surface **(see illustration)**. Peugeot recommend the use of Loctite Autojoint Noir for this purpose.

38 Lubricate the lower bearing shells with clean engine oil, then refit the bearing cap housing, ensuring that the shells are not displaced, and that the locating dowels engage correctly.

39 Install the large and small crankshaft bearing cap housing/ladder retaining bolts, and screw them in until they are just making contact with the housing.

40 Working in sequence, tighten all the M11 bolts to the Stage 1 torque setting given in the Specifications **(see illustration)**. Now tighten all the M6 bolts to the Stage 2 torque setting (finger-tight).

41 Fully slacken all the M11 bolts (Stage 3), and then tighten them to the Stage 4 setting, working in the correct sequence.

42 Finally tighten all the M11 bolts, in the correct sequence, through the specified Stage 5 angle, using an angle-tightening gauge.

43 The M6 bolts can now be tightened to the Stage 6 torque setting.

44 With the bearing cap housing in place, check that the crankshaft rotates freely.

17.50 Main bearing shell refitment (1.4 litre diesel engine)

1 Bearing shell
2 Main bearing ladder
3 Peugeot tool No 0194-Q
4 Aligning pins

45 Refit the piston/connecting rod assemblies to the crankshaft as described in Section 18.

46 Refit the oil pump and sump as described in Part C.

47 Fit a new crankshaft left-hand oil seal, then refit the flywheel as described in Part C.

48 Where removed, refit the cylinder head, crankshaft sprocket and timing belt also as described in Part C.

1.4 litre diesel engine

49 Clean the backs of the bearing shells in both the cylinder block/crankcase and the main bearing ladder. If new shells are being fitted, ensure that all traces of protective grease are cleaned off using paraffin. Wipe dry the shells with a lint-free cloth.

50 Press the bearing shells into their locations, ensuring that the tab on each shell engages in the notch in the cylinder block/crankcase and bearing ladder. Take care not to touch any shell's bearing surface with your fingers. Note that the upper bearing shells all have a grooved surface, whereas the lower shells have a plain bearing surface. It is essential that the lower bearing shell halves are centrally located in the ladder. To ensure this use a Peugeot tool positioned over the ladder, and insert the bearing shells through the slots in the tool **(see illustration)**.

51 Liberally lubricate each bearing shell in the cylinder block with clean engine oil then lower the crankshaft into position.

52 Insert the thrustwashers to either side of No 2 main bearing upper location and push them around the bearing journal until their edges are horizontal. Ensure that the oilway grooves on each thrustwasher face outwards (away from the cylinder block). Now refit the piston and connecting rod assemblies as described in Section 18.

53 Thoroughly degrease the mating surfaces of the cylinder block and the crankshaft bearing cap housing/main bearing ladder. Apply a thin bead of RTV sealant to the bearing cap housing mating surface. Peugeot recommend the use of Loctite Autojoint Noir for this purpose. Use two aligning pins (available from Peugeot) inserted into the main bearing ladder, to ensure the correct positioning of the assembly.

17.56 Main bearing ladder bolts tightening sequence (1.4 litre diesel engine)

17.63 Fit the upper thrustwashers to the No 2 main bearing location with the oilway grooves facing outwards

17.64a Ensure the grooved main bearing shells are fitted to the cylinder block . . .

54 Lubricate the lower bearing shells with clean engine oil, then refit the bearing cap housing, ensuring that the shells are not displaced, and that the locating dowels engage correctly. Remove the aligning pins from the bearing ladder.

55 Install the large and small crankshaft bearing cap housing/ladder retaining bolts, and screw them in until they are just making contact with the housing. Note that new large (M11) bolts must be used.

56 Tighten all the main bearing ladder bolts to their Stage 1 setting in sequence **(see illustration)**.

57 Slacken (Stage 2) the large diameter bearing ladder bolts half a turn (180°), then tighten them in sequence to the Stage 3 torque setting, followed by the Stage 4 angle-

17.64b . . . and plain bearing shells to the bearing caps

tightening setting. Apply sealant to the two new bearing ladder bolt caps, and tap them into place over the two flywheel end bolts.

58 Finally, tighten the small diameter bearing ladder bolts to their Stage 2 setting.

59 With the bearing cap housing in place, check that the crankshaft rotates freely.

60 Refit the oil pump and sump as described in Part D.

61 Fit a new crankshaft left-hand oil seal, then refit the flywheel as described in Part D.

62 Where removed, refit the cylinder head, crankshaft sprocket and timing belt also as described in Part D.

2.0 litre diesel engine

63 Using a little grease, stick the thrustwashers to each side of No 2 main bearing upper location and bearing cap **(see illustration)**. Ensure that the oilway grooves on each thrustwasher face outwards (away from the cylinder block).

64 Place the bearing shells in their locations as described in paragraphs 4 and 5 **(see illustrations)**. If new shells are being fitted, ensure that all traces of protective grease are cleaned off using paraffin. Wipe dry the shells and connecting rods with a lint-free cloth. Liberally lubricate each bearing shell in the cylinder block/crankcase and cap with clean engine oil.

65 Lower the crankshaft into position so that Nos 2 and 3 cylinder crankpins are at TDC;

Nos 1 and 4 cylinder crankpins will be at BDC, ready for fitting No 1 piston.

66 Lubricate the lower bearing shells in the main bearing caps with clean engine oil. Make sure that the locating lugs on the shells engage with the corresponding recesses in the caps.

67 Fit main bearing caps Nos 2 to 5 to their correct locations, ensuring that they are fitted the correct way round (the bearing shell tab recesses in the block and caps must be on the same side) **(see illustration)**. Ensure the thrustwashers remain correctly fitted to No 2 bearing cap then refit the bearing cap bolts, tightening them only lightly at this stage. Check the crankshaft endfloat as described in Section 13.

68 Apply a small amount of sealant to the No 1 main bearing cap mating face on the cylinder block, around the sealing strip holes **(see illustration)**.

69 Locate the tab of each sealing strip over the pins on the base of No 1 bearing cap, and press the strips into the bearing cap grooves. It is now necessary to obtain two thin metal strips, of 0.25 mm thickness or less, in order to prevent the strips moving when the cap is being fitted. Peugeot garages use the tool shown, which acts as a clamp. Metal strips (such as old feeler blades) can be used, provided all burrs, which may damage the sealing strips, are first removed **(see illustrations)**.

70 Where applicable, oil both sides of the

17.67 Fit the No 2 to 5 bearing caps and install the bearing cap bolts

17.68 Apply sealant to the No 1 main bearing cap mating face on the cylinder block, around the sealing strip holes and in the corners

17.69a Fit the sealing strips to each side of No 1 main bearing cap, ensuring they are correctly engaged with the pins

17.69b Using the Peugeot special tool to fit the No 1 main bearing cap

17.70 Fit the No 1 main bearing cap using metal strips to retain the sealing strips

17.71 Main bearing cap bolt tightening sequence (2.0 litre diesel engines)

metal strips, and hold them on the sealing strips. Fit the No 1 main bearing cap, insert the bolts loosely, and then carefully pull out the metal strips in a horizontal direction, using a pair of pliers **(see illustration)**.

71 Working in sequence **(see illustration)**, tighten the main bearing cap bolts evenly and progressively to the specified Stage 1 torque wrench setting. Once all the bolts have been tightened to the Stage 1 setting, working in the specified sequence, angle-tighten the bolts through the specified Stage 2 angle, using a socket and extension bar. It is recommended that an angle-measuring gauge is used during this stage of the tightening, to ensure accuracy. If a gauge is not available, use a dab of white paint to make alignment marks between the bolt head and casting prior to tightening; the marks can then be used to check that the bolt has been rotated sufficiently during tightening.

72 Check that the sealing strips protrude slightly from above the cylinder block/crankcase mating surface by approximately 1 mm. If not, remove the bearing cap again and refit; the seals are supplied the correct length and should not be cut. Also check that the crankshaft rotates freely.

73 Fit a new crankshaft left-hand (flywheel end) oil seal as described in Part D.

74 Refit the piston/connecting rod assemblies to the crankshaft as described in Section 18.

75 Fit a new sealing ring (where fitted) the crankshaft then refit the Woodruff key and slide on the oil pump drive sprocket and spacer. Locate the drive chain on the sprocket.

76 Ensure that the mating surfaces of the right-hand (timing belt end) oil seal housing and cylinder block are clean and dry. Note the correct fitted depth of the oil seal then, using a large flat-bladed screwdriver, lever the old seal out of the housing.

77 Apply a smear of suitable sealant to the oil seal housing mating surface. Ensure that the locating dowels are in position, and then slide the housing over the end of the crankshaft and into position on the cylinder block. Tighten the housing retaining bolts to the specified torque.

78 Fit a new crankshaft right-hand (timing belt end) oil seal as described in Part D.

79 Ensuring that the drive chain is correctly located on the sprocket, refit the oil pump and sump as described in Part D.

80 Refit the flywheel as described in Part C of this Chapter.

81 Refit the cylinder head (where removed) as described in Part D. Also refit the crankshaft sprocket and timing belt (see Part D).

18 Piston/connecting rod assembly – refitting

Note: *New big-end cap nuts/bolts must be used on refitting.*

1 Note that the following procedure assumes that the cylinder liners (aluminium block petrol engines) are in position in the cylinder block/crankcase as described in Section 11, and that the crankshaft and main bearing ladder/

caps are in place – except on the 1.4 litre diesel engine where the crankshaft is fitted after the pistons (see Section 17).

2 Clean the backs of the bearing shells, and the bearing locations in both the connecting rod and bearing cap.

All engines except 1.4 litre diesel

3 Press the bearing shells into their locations, ensuring that the tab on each shell engages in the notch in the connecting rod and cap. Take care not to touch any shell's bearing surface with your fingers **(see illustration)**.

All engines

4 Lubricate the cylinder bores, the pistons, and piston rings, then lay out each piston/connecting rod assembly in its respective position.

5 Start with assembly No 1. Make sure that the piston rings are still spaced as described in Section 16, and then clamp them in position with a piston ring compressor.

6 Insert the piston/connecting rod assembly into the top of cylinder/liner No 1; ensuring the piston is correctly positioned as follows.

a) On petrol engines, ensure that the arrow on the piston crown is pointing towards the timing belt end of the engine.

b) On 1.4 litre diesel engines, ensure that the DIST mark or arrow on the piston crown is towards the timing belt end of the engine.

c) On 2.0 litre diesel engines, ensure that the valve recesses on the piston crown are towards the rear of the cylinder block.

7 Once the piston is correctly positioned, using a block of wood or hammer handle against the piston crown, tap the assembly into the cylinder/liner until the piston crown is flush with the top of the cylinder/liner **(see illustration)**.

All engines except 1.4 litre diesel

8 Ensure that the bearing shell is still correctly installed. Liberally lubricate the crankpin and both bearing shells. Taking care not to mark the cylinder/liner bores; pull the piston/connecting rod assembly down the bore and onto the crankpin. Refit the big-end bearing cap and fit the new nuts, tightening them

18.3 Ensure the bearing shell tab (arrowed) locates correctly in the cut-out

18.7 Tap the piston into the bore using a hammer handle

18.8 Fit the big-end bearing cap, ensuring it is fitted the right way around, and screw on the new nuts

finger-tight at first **(see illustration)**. Note that the faces with the identification marks must match (which means that the bearing shell locating tabs abut each other).

9 On petrol engines, tighten the bearing cap retaining nuts evenly and progressively to the specified torque setting.

10 On 2.0 litre diesel engines, tighten the bearing cap retaining nuts evenly and progressively to the Stage 1 torque setting. Once both nuts have been tightened to the Stage 1 setting, angle-tighten them through the specified Stage 2 angle, using a socket and extension bar. It is recommended that an angle-measuring gauge is used during this stage of the tightening, to ensure accuracy. If a gauge is not available, use a dab of white paint to make alignment marks between the nut and bearing cap prior to tightening; the marks can then be used to check that the nut has been rotated sufficiently during tightening.

1.4 litre diesel engine

11 On these engines, the connecting rod is made in one piece, and the big-end bearing cap is 'cracked' off. This ensures that the cap fits onto the connecting rod only in one position, and with maximum rigidity. Consequently, there are no locating notches for the bearing shells to fit into.

12 To ensure that the big-end bearing shells

H44712

18.12 Big-end bearing shell positioning (1.4 litre diesel engine)

1 *Peugeot tool No 0194-P*
2 *Bearing shell*

are centrally located in the connecting rod and cap, two special tools are available from Peugeot. These half-moon shaped tools are pressed in from either side of the rod/cap and locate the shell exactly in the centre **(see illustration)**. Fit the shells into the connecting rods and big-end caps and lubricate them with plenty of clean engine oil.

13 Pull the connecting rods and pistons down the bores and onto the crankshaft journals. Fit the big-end caps – they will only fit properly one way round (see paragraph 11), and insert the new bolts.

14 Tighten the bolts to the Stage 1 torque setting, then slacken them 180° (Stage 2). Tighten the bolts to the Stage 3 setting, followed by the Stage 4 angle-tightening setting.

15 Continue refitting the main bearing shells and ladder as described in Section 17.

All engines

16 Once the bearing cap retaining nuts have

been correctly tightened, rotate the crankshaft. Check that it turns freely; some stiffness is to be expected if new components have been fitted, but there should be no signs of binding or tight spots.

17 Refit the cylinder head and oil pump as described in Part A, B C or D of this Chapter (as applicable).

19 Engine –
initial start-up after overhaul

1 With the engine refitted in the vehicle, double-check the engine oil and coolant levels. Make a final check that everything has been reconnected, and that there are no tools or rags left in the engine compartment.

2 Switch on the ignition and immediately turn the engine on the starter (do not allow the glow plugs to heat up on diesel engines) until the oil pressure warning light goes out.

3 Pressurise/prime the fuel system as described in Chapter 4A, Section 7, or Chapter 4B, Section 3, then start the engine, noting that this may take a little longer than usual, due to the fuel system components having been disturbed.

4 While the engine is idling, check for fuel, water and oil leaks. Don't be alarmed if there are some odd smells and smoke from parts getting hot and burning off oil deposits.

5 Assuming all is well; keep the engine idling until hot water is felt circulating through the top hose, then switch off the engine.

6 Allow the engine to cool then recheck the oil and coolant levels as described in *Weekly checks*, and top-up as necessary.

7 If new pistons, rings or crankshaft bearings have been fitted, the engine must be treated as new, and run-in for the first 500 miles. *Do not* operate the engine at full-throttle, or allow it to labour at low engine speeds in any gear. It is recommended that the oil and filter be changed at the end of this period.

Chapter 3
Cooling, heating and ventilation systems

Contents

Degrees of difficulty

| **Easy,** suitable for novice with little experience | | **Fairly easy,** suitable for beginner with some experience | | **Fairly difficult,** suitable for competent DIY mechanic | | **Difficult,** suitable for experienced DIY mechanic | | **Very difficult,** suitable for expert DIY or professional | |

Specifications

General
Maximum system pressure .... 1.4 bars

Thermostat
Start of opening temperature:
  Petrol engine models .... 89°C
  1.4 litre diesel engine models........................... 88°C
  2.0 litre diesel engine models........................... 83°C

Air conditioning compressor oil
Quantity .... 135 cc
Type SP10

Refrigerant
Quantity .... 585 ± 25 g
Type R134a

Torque wrench settings	Nm	lbf ft
Air conditioning compressor mounting bolts:		
1.1, 1.4 and 1.6 litre petrol engine	25	18
2.0 litre petrol engine	45	33
1.4 litre diesel engine	25	18
2.0 litre diesel engine	40	30
Coolant outlet elbow	10	7

1 General information and precautions

General information

1 The cooling system is of pressurised type, comprising a coolant pump driven by the timing belt, an aluminium radiator, an expansion tank, an electric cooling fan, a thermostat, a heater matrix, and all associated hoses and switches.

2 The system functions as follows. Cold coolant in the bottom of the radiator passes through the bottom hose to the coolant pump, where it is pumped around the cylinder block and head passages. After cooling the cylinder bores, combustion surfaces and valve seats, the coolant reaches the underside of the thermostat, which is initially closed. The coolant passes through the heater, and is returned via the cylinder block to the coolant pump. On models fitted with an engine oil cooler, the coolant is also passed through the oil cooler.

3 When the engine is cold, the coolant circulates only through the cylinder block, cylinder head, and heater. When the coolant reaches a predetermined temperature, the thermostat opens, and the coolant passes through the top hose to the radiator. As the coolant passes down through the radiator, it is cooled by the inrush of air when the car is in forward motion. The airflow is supplemented by the action of the electric cooling fan when necessary. Upon reaching the bottom of the radiator, the coolant has now cooled, and the cycle is repeated.

4 On models with automatic transmission, a proportion of the coolant is recirculated through the transmission fluid cooler mounted on the transmission.

5 On models without air conditioning a single-speed cooling fan is fitted. This is controlled by a thermostatic sensor on petrol engines, and by the injection system electronic control unit on diesel engines (see Section 7).

6 Models with air conditioning have a two-speed cooling fan, which is controlled by a 'Bitron' control unit on petrol engines. On diesel engines the fan is controlled by the injection system electronic control unit (see Section 7)

Precautions

⚠️ **Warning: Do not attempt to remove the expansion tank filler cap, or to disturb any part of the cooling system, while the engine is hot, as there is a high risk of scalding. If the expansion tank filler cap must be removed before the engine and radiator have fully cooled (even though this is not recommended), the pressure in the cooling system must first be relieved. Cover the cap with a thick layer of cloth to avoid scalding, and slowly unscrew the filler cap until a hissing sound is heard. When the hissing has stopped, indicating that the pressure has reduced, slowly unscrew the filler cap until it can be removed; if more hissing sounds are heard, wait until they have stopped before unscrewing the cap. At all times keep well away from the filler cap opening, and protect your hands.**

⚠️ **Warning: Do not allow antifreeze to come into contact with your skin, or with the painted surfaces of the vehicle. Rinse off spills immediately, with plenty of water. Never leave antifreeze lying around in an open container, or in a puddle in the driveway or on the garage floor. Children and pets are attracted by its sweet smell, but antifreeze can be fatal if ingested.**

⚠️ **Warning: If the engine is hot, the electric cooling fan(s) may start rotating even if the engine is not running. Be careful to keep your hands, hair, and any loose clothing well clear when working in the engine compartment.**

⚠️ **Warning: Refer to Section 11 for precautions to be observed when working on models equipped with air conditioning.**

2 Cooling system hoses – disconnection and renewal

Note: *Refer to the warnings given in Section 1 of this Chapter before proceeding. Hoses should only be disconnected once the engine has cooled sufficiently to avoid scalding.*

1 If the checks described in the *Hose and fluid leak check* Section in Chapter 1A or 1B reveal a faulty hose, it must be renewed as follows.

2 First drain the cooling system (see Chapter 1A or 1B). If the coolant is not due for renewal, it may be re-used, providing it is collected in a clean container.

3 To disconnect a hose, proceed as follows, according to the type of hose connection.

Conventional hose connections

4 On conventional connections, the clips used to secure the hoses in position may be standard worm-drive clips, spring clips or disposable crimped types. The crimped type of clip is not designed to be re-used and should be updated with a worm-drive type on reassembly.

5 To disconnect a hose, release the retaining clips and move them along the hose, clear of the relevant inlet/outlet. Carefully work the hose free. The hoses can be removed with relative ease when new – on an older car; they may have stuck. On later models, press the quick-release retaining clips and pull the hose to disconnect **(see illustrations)**.

6 If a hose proves to be difficult to remove, try to release it by rotating its ends before attempting to free it. Gently prise the end of the hose with a blunt instrument (such as a flat-bladed screwdriver), but do not apply too much force, and take care not to damage the pipe stubs or hoses. Note in particular that the radiator inlet stub is fragile; do not use excessive force when attempting to remove the hose. If all else fails, cut the hose with

2.5a Disconnecting the expansion tank hose from the radiator

2.5b Releasing the expansion tank hose from the radiator on later models

2.12 Where click-fit hose connectors are used, remove the circlip then disconnect the hose

2.13 Ensure the sealing ring and circlip (arrowed) are correctly fitted to the hose union before reconnecting a click-fit connector

a sharp knife, then slit it so that it can be peeled off in two pieces. Although this may prove expensive if the hose is otherwise undamaged, it is preferable to buying a new radiator. Check first, however, that a new hose is readily available.

7 When fitting a hose, first slide the clips onto the hose, and then work the hose into position. If crimped-type clips were originally fitted, use standard worm-drive clips when refitting the hose.

8 Work the hose into position, checking that it is correctly routed, and then slide each clip back along the hose until it passes over the flared end of the relevant inlet/outlet, before tightening the clip securely.

> **HAYNES HiNT**
> *If the hose is stiff, use a little soapy water as a lubricant or soften the hose by soaking it in hot water. Do not use oil or grease as these may attack the rubber.*

9 Refill the cooling system (see Chapter 1A or 1B).

10 Check thoroughly for leaks as soon as possible after disturbing any part of the cooling system.

Click-fit connections

Note: *New sealing ring should be used when reconnecting the hose.*

11 On certain models, some cooling system hoses are secured in position with click-fit connectors where the hose is retained by a large circlip.

12 To disconnect this type of hose fitting, carefully prise the circlip out of position then disconnect the hose connection **(see illustration)**. Once the hose has been disconnected, refit the circlip to the hose union. Inspect the hose unit sealing ring for signs of damage or deterioration and renew if necessary.

13 On refitting, ensure that the sealing ring is in

position and the circlip is correctly located in the groove in the union **(see illustration)**. Lubricate the sealing ring with a smear of soapy water, to ease installation, and then push the hose into its union until it is heard to click into position.

14 Ensure the hose is securely retained by the circlip then refill the cooling system as described in Chapter 1A or 1B.

15 Check thoroughly for leaks as soon as possible after disturbing any part of the cooling system.

3 Coolant expansion tank – removal and refitting

Removal

1 Referring to Chapter 1A or 1B, drain the cooling system sufficiently to empty the contents of the expansion tank. Do not drain any more coolant than is necessary.

2 Release the retaining clip(s) and disconnect the hose(s) from the top of the expansion tank.

3 On petrol engine models, unhook the retaining strap and free the expansion tank from its mounting bracket **(see illustration)**.

4 On diesel engine models, unscrew the mounting bolt from the left-hand side of the

3.3 On petrol engine models, unhook the retaining strap and free the expansion tank from its bracket

tank then free the tank from its mounting bracket. Take care not to lose the mounting rubbers from the tank lower mountings.

5 On all models, prise out the circlip from the coolant hose end fitting then free expansion tank from the lower hose and remove it from the engine compartment. Refit the circlip correctly to the groove in the hose end fitting **(see illustrations 2.12 and 2.13)**. Where fitted, disconnect the level sensor wiring plug as the coolant expansion tank is being removed.

6 If necessary, slacken and remove the mounting nuts/bolts and remove the mounting bracket from the vehicle **(see illustration)**.

Refitting

7 Refitting is the reverse of removal, ensuring the hoses are securely reconnected. On completion, top-up the coolant level as described in *Weekly checks*.

4 Radiator – removal, inspection and refitting

Note: *If leakage is the reason for removing the radiator, bear in mind that minor leaks can often be cured using a radiator sealant with the radiator in situ.*

3.6 Unscrew the nut and bolts and remove the expansion tank mounting bracket (petrol engine model shown)

4.4a Release the retaining clips and disconnect the upper . . .

4.4b . . . and lower hoses from the radiator

4.5a Undo the retaining screws (arrowed) . . .

4.5b . . . and remove the upper mounting brackets from the radiator

4.6a Lift the radiator out of position . . .

4.6b . . . and recover the lower mounting rubbers from the front panel

Removal

1 Disconnect the battery negative lead.
2 Drain the cooling system (see Chapter 1A or 1B).
3 Where necessary, disconnect the wiring connector from the cooling fan switch fitted to the top of the radiator.
4 Release the retaining clips and disconnect the expansion tank hose, and the upper and lower coolant hoses from the radiator **(see illustrations)**.
5 Slacken and remove the retaining screws securing the radiator upper mounting brackets to the front panel. Unclip both brackets from the panel and remove them from the radiator **(see illustrations)**.
6 Carefully lift the radiator out of position, taking care not to damage the radiator fins.

Recover the radiator lower mounting rubbers **(see illustrations)**.

Inspection

7 If the radiator has been removed due to suspected blockage, reverse-flush it as described in Chapter 1A or 1B. Clean dirt and debris from the radiator fins, using an airline (in which case, wear eye protection) or a soft brush. Be careful, as the fins are sharp, and easily damaged.
8 If necessary, a radiator specialist can perform a 'flow test' on the radiator, to establish whether an internal blockage exists.
9 A leaking radiator must be referred to a specialist for permanent repair. Do not attempt to weld or solder a leaking radiator, as damage to the plastic components may result.

10 Inspect the condition of the radiator mounting rubbers, and renew them if necessary.

Refitting

11 Refitting is a reversal of removal, bearing in mind the following points:
a) Ensure that the lower lugs on the radiator are correctly engaged with the mounting rubbers in the body panel.
b) Reconnect the hoses with reference to Section 2, using new sealing rings where applicable.
c) On completion, refill the cooling system as described in Chapter 1A or 1B.

5 Thermostat – removal, testing and refitting

Removal

1 Disconnect the battery negative lead.
2 Drain the cooling system (see Chapter 1A or 1B).

Petrol engine

3 The thermostat is fitted to the coolant housing on the left-hand end of the cylinder head.
4 Unscrew the retaining bolts and free the outlet union from the coolant housing **(see illustration)**.
5 On early models with a separate thermostat, recover the thermostat and sealing ring from the coolant housing, noting which way around it is fitted **(see illustration)**.

5.4 On petrol engines, unscrew the retaining bolts (locations arrowed) and free the outlet union from the coolant housing

5.5 On early models remove the thermostat and sealing ring from the coolant housing

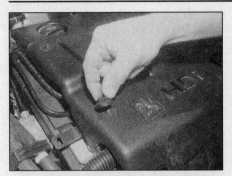

5.7a On 2.0 litre diesel engines, rotate each fastener 90° to release it . . .

5.7b . . . then lift off the engine cover

5.8a Press down the release button and disconnect the hose

5.8b Coolant outlet housing retaining bolts

5.9a Lift the thermostat out from its housing . . .

5.9b . . . and remove the sealing ring (2.0 litre diesel engine shown)

6 On later models where the thermostat is an integral part of the outlet union. Recover the sealing ring then release the retaining clip and remove the union from the coolant hose.

Diesel engine

7 On 1.4 litre engines the plastic engine cover simply pulls up away from its mountings. On 2.0 litre engines remove the fasteners (rotate them 90° to release them) and lift off the plastic engine cover **(see illustrations)**. On 1.4 litre engines, the thermostat is integral with the coolant outlet housing on the left-hand end of the cylinder head. On 2.0 litre engines, the thermostat is fitted to the top of the coolant outlet housing on the left-hand end of the cylinder head.

8 On 1.4 litre engines, disconnect the coolant hoses from the outlet housing, and the wiring plug from the coolant temperature sensor. Note that some of the hoses are disconnected after pressing down on the white-coloured release button. Undo the four screws and remove the housing **(see illustrations)**.

9 On 2.0 litre engines, unscrew the retaining bolts and free the outlet union from the housing to expose the thermostat, taking care not to strain the hose. Remove the thermostat from the housing, noting which way around it is fitted, and recover the sealing ring **(see illustrations)**.

Testing

10 A rough test of the thermostat may be made by suspending it with a piece of string in a container full of water. Heat the water to

bring it to the boil – the thermostat must open by the time the water boils. If not, renew it.

11 If a thermometer is available, the precise opening temperature of the thermostat may be determined; compare with the figures given in the Specifications. The opening temperature is also marked on the thermostat.

12 A thermostat which fails to close as the water cools, must also be renewed.

Refitting

13 Refitting is a reversal of removal, bearing in mind the following points.
  a) *Examine the sealing ring for damage or deterioration, and if necessary, renew. On 1.4 litre diesel engines, the seal is not available separately from the housing.*
  b) *Where a separate thermostat is fitted, ensure that it is fitted the correct way round, with the spring(s) facing into the housing.*

6.3a Unscrew the fan mounting bolts and washers . . .

  c) *On completion, refill the cooling system as described in Chapter 1A or 1B.*

6 Electric cooling fan – removal and refitting

Electric fan removal

1 The cooling fan can be removed on its own or complete with the front panel assembly. Proceed as described under the relevant sub-heading.

Cooling fan

2 Remove the front bumper as described in Chapter 11.

3 Slacken and remove the three bolts and washers securing the cooling fan to the front panel. Recover the collar from the rear of each mounting rubber **(see illustrations)**.

6.3b . . . and recover the collar from the rear of each mounting rubber

6.4a Disconnect the fan wiring connector (arrowed) . . .

6.4b . . . then manoeuvre the fan assembly out of position

6.6 Remove the retaining clips (arrowed) and free the bonnet release cable from the front panel

4 Free the fan assembly from the front panel to gain access to the wiring connector. Lift the retaining clip then disconnect the wiring connector and manoeuvre the fan assembly out of position (see illustrations).

Cooling fan and front panel assembly

5 Remove the radiator as described in Section 4.
6 Remove the bonnet lock as described in Chapter 11. Remove the retaining clips and free the bonnet release cable from the front panel (see illustration).
7 Slacken and remove the retaining screws securing the front trim panel in position. Carefully unclip the trim panel from the inner edge of each headlight then unclip the ends of the panel from each wing and remove the panel from the vehicle (see illustrations).
8 Remove the air filter housing as described in Chapter 4A or 4B (as applicable).
9 Unclip and remove the cooling duct (where fitted) connecting the battery box to the front panel. Rotate the cooling duct elbow to free it from the left-hand end of the front panel and remove it from the vehicle (see illustrations).
10 Unscrew the bolt and detach the cooling fan earth lead, located at the base of the fan/radiator mounting panel, from the body (see illustration).

6.7a Undo the retaining screws (arrowed) . . .

6.7b . . . then unclip the ends of the panel from the wings (clips arrowed) . . .

6.9a Remove the battery box cooling duct . . .

6.7c . . . and remove the front trim panel from the vehicle

6.9b . . . and unclip the elbow from the front panel

6.10 Unscrew the bolt and detach the cooling fan earth lead from the body

6.11a Unscrew the bolts (arrowed) securing the dehydrator . . .

6.11b . . . and the refrigerant pipe to the front panel . . .

6.11c . . . then position the condenser clear, taking care not to lose its mounting rubbers

11 On models with air conditioning, unscrew the bolts securing the dehydrator reservoir to the fan/radiator mounting panel and the bolt securing the refrigerant pipe to the base of the panel. Free the dehydrator and condenser, and position them clear of the front panel, taking care not to strain the refrigerant pipes/hoses. Also take care not to lose the condenser upper and lower mounting rubbers **(see illustrations)**.
Caution: Do not disconnect the refrigerant lines from the dehydrator/condenser (refer to the warnings given in Section 11). Ensure the compressor is securely supported to prevent the refrigerant lines being damaged.
12 On models with air conditioning, remove both headlights as described in Chapter 12, Section 7.
13 On all models, disconnect the cooling fan wiring connector located on the left-hand side of the panel **(see illustration)**.
14 Trace the fan wiring back to the fuse/relay box, releasing its retaining clips from the body. Remove the fuse/relay box cover and pull out the large cooling fan fuse. Carefully prise out the locking clip then unclip the fan wiring connector from the fuse/relay box so it is free to be removed with the front panel assembly **(see illustrations)**. **Note:** *The position of the cooling fan wiring in the fuse/relay box may vary depending on model, see Chapter 12.*
15 Unclip the wiring harness from the right-hand side of the front panel.
16 Unscrew the four bolts securing the top of the front panel to the body then carefully

6.13 Disconnect the cooling fan wiring connector from the left-hand side of the panel

6.14b . . . then prise out the locking clip . . .

6.14a Remove the cooling fan fuse . . .

6.14c . . . and free the fan connector from the fuse/relay box

manoeuvre the assembly upwards and out of position **(see illustrations)**. On models with air conditioning, take great care not to damage the condenser as the panel is removed.
17 With the mounting panel removed,

disconnect the wiring connector then unscrew the mounting bolts and remove the fan assembly **(see illustrations)**. Recover the spacers and washers from the fan mounting rubbers.

6.16a Unscrew the mounting bolts (arrowed) . . .

6.16b . . . then lift the front panel assembly out of position

6.17a Disconnect the wiring connector . . .

6.17b . . . then undo the retaining bolts (arrowed) and remove the fan assembly

6.21a Remove the fasteners (arrowed – pull out the centre pins then remove the complete fastener) . . .

6.21b . . . and free the cover from the front panel to gain access to the cooling fan relays (arrowed)

6.24 Disconnect the cooling fan resistor wiring connector

Electric fan refitting

18 Refitting is a reversal of removal.

Cooling fan relays

19 The relays are fitted to the front panel and are located behind the cover on the right-hand side of the cooling fan.
20 To gain access to the relays, remove the front bumper as described in Chapter 11.

21 Release the fasteners and remove the cover from the front panel. The relays can then be removed (see illustrations).

Cooling fan resistor – models with air conditioning

22 The cooling fan resistor is fitted to the front panel and is also located on the right-hand side of the cooling fan.

23 To gain access to the resistor, remove the front bumper as described in Chapter 11.
24 Disconnect the wiring connector then undo the retaining screws and remove the resistor from the front panel (see illustration).

7 Cooling system electrical sensors – general information, removal and refitting

General information

1 There is only one coolant temperature sensor on most models, which is fitted to the coolant outlet housing on the left-hand end of the cylinder head (see illustrations). The coolant temperature gauge and the cooling fan are all operated by the engine management ECU using the signal supplied by this sensor. However, on some models, two sensors are fitted. The one fitted to the outlet housing is for the temperature gauge, and the one screwed into the left-hand end of the cylinder head is for the engine management ECU.

7.1a Engine management system coolant temperature sensor (1) and air conditioning control system (Bitron) temperature sensor (2) locations – petrol engine

7.1b On petrol engines the coolant temperature gauge temperature sensor (arrowed) is screwed into the left-hand end of the cylinder head

7.4a Prise out the retaining clip (arrowed) to release the coolant temperature sensor . . .

7.4b . . . on 2.0 litre diesel engines

7.4c Prise out the retaining clip (arrowed) on 1.4 litre diesel engine

Removal

Note: *Ensure the engine is cold before removing a temperature sensor.*

2 Partially drain the cooling system to just below the level of the sensor (as described in Chapter 1A or 1B). Alternatively, have ready a suitable bung to plug the sensor aperture whilst the sensor is removed. If this method is used, take great care not to damage the switch aperture or use anything, which will allow foreign matter to enter the cooling system. On diesel models, to improve access, remove the battery as described in Chapter 5A.

3 Disconnect the wiring connector from the sensor.

4 On some engines, the sensor is clipped in place. Prise out the sensor retaining circlip then remove the sensor and sealing ring from the housing **(see illustrations)**. If the system

has not been drained, plug the sensor aperture to prevent further coolant loss.

5 On all other engines, unscrew the sensor and recover the sealing washer (where applicable). If the system has not been drained, plug the sensor aperture to prevent further coolant loss.

Refitting

6 Where the sensor was clipped in place, fit a new sealing ring to the sensor. Push the sensor firmly into the housing and secure it in position with the circlip, ensuring it is correctly located in the housing groove.

7 On all other engines, if the sensor was originally fitted using sealing compound, clean the sensor threads thoroughly, and coat them with fresh sealing compound. If the sensor was originally fitted using a sealing washer, use a new sealing washer. Fit the sensor and tighten securely.

8 Reconnect the wiring connector then refit any components removed from access. If removed, refit the battery.

9 Top-up the cooling system as described in *Weekly checks*.

8 Coolant pump – removal and refitting

Removal

1 Drain the cooling system (see Chapter 1A or 1B).

2 Remove the timing belt as described in Chapter 2A, 2B, 2C or 2D as applicable.

3 On 2.0 litre petrol engines, remove the heat shield from the pump, and then undo the bolts securing the pump to the cylinder block **(see illustration)**. Do not undo the bolts securing the two halves of the pump together. Withdraw the pump.

4 On all other models, remove the retaining bolts and withdraw the pump assembly from the engine. Recover the pump sealing ring/gasket (as applicable) and discard it; a new one must be used on refitting **(see illustrations)**.

8.3 Coolant pump retaining nut (A) and bolts (B)

8.4a Remove the coolant pump . . .

8.4b . . . and recover the sealing ring/ gasket (1.4 litre petrol engine shown)

8.4c Undo the coolant pump bolts (arrowed) – 1.4 litre diesel engine

8.4d Coolant pump bolts (A) – 2.0 litre diesel engine

H44736

Refitting

5 Ensure that the pump and cylinder block/housing mating surfaces are clean and dry.

6 Fit the new sealing ring/gasket (as applicable) to the pump then refit the pump assembly, tightening its retaining bolts securely.

7 Refit the timing belt as described in Chapter 2A, 2B, 2C or 2D (as applicable).

8 Refill the cooling system as described in Chapter 1A or 1B (as applicable).

9 Heating and ventilation system – general information

Note: *Refer to Section 11 for information on the air conditioning side of the system.*

Manual heating/ventilation system

1 The heating/ventilation system consists of a four-speed blower motor (housed behind the facia), face level vents in the centre and at each end of the facia, and air ducts to the front footwells.

2 The control unit is located in the facia, and the controls operate flap valves to deflect and mix the air flowing through the various parts of the heating/ventilation system. The flap valves are contained in the air distribution housing, which acts as a central distribution unit, passing air to the various ducts and vents.

3 Cold air enters the system through the grille on the right-hand side of the bonnet. If required, the airflow is boosted by the blower, and then flows through the various ducts, according to the settings of the controls. Stale air is expelled through ducts at the rear of the vehicle. If warm air is required, the cold air is passed over the heater matrix, which is heated by the engine coolant.

4 A recirculation lever enables the outside air supply to be closed off, while the air inside the vehicle is recirculated. This can be useful to prevent unpleasant odours entering from outside the vehicle, but should only be used briefly, as the recirculated air inside the vehicle will soon become stale.

5 On some diesel engine models an electric coolant heater is fitted to the feed hose to the heater matrix. When the coolant temperature is cold, the heater warms the coolant before it enters the heater matrix. This quickly increases the temperature of the heater matrix on cold starts, resulting in warm air being available to heat the vehicle interior soon after start-up.

Automatic climate control system

6 A fully automatic electronic climate control system was offered as an option on some models. The main components of the system are exactly the same as those described for the manual system, the only major difference being that the temperature and distribution flaps in the heating/ventilation housing are operated by electric motors rather than cables.

7 The operation of the system is controlled by the electronic control module (which is incorporated in the blower motor assembly) along with the following sensors.

a) *The passenger compartment sensor – informs the control module of the temperature of the air inside the passenger compartment.*

b) *Evaporator temperature sensor – informs the control module of the evaporator temperature.*

c) *Heater matrix temperature sensor – informs the control module of the heater matrix temperature.*

8 Using the information from the above sensors, the control module determines the appropriate settings for the heating/ventilation system housing flaps to maintain the passenger compartment at the desired setting on the control panel.

9 If the system develops a fault, the vehicle should be taken to a Peugeot dealer. A complete test of the system can then be carried out, using a special electronic diagnostic test unit, which is simply plugged into the system's diagnostic connector (located next to the fusebox).

10 Heater/ventilation components – removal and refitting

Heating/ventilation control panel

1 Remove the audio unit as described in Chapter 12.

2 Carefully unclip the clock/multifunction unit surround from the top of the facia and remove it, disconnecting the wiring connector from the hazard warning light switch **(see illustration)**.

3 Slacken and remove the retaining screws securing the top of the centre vent panel to the facia. Carefully unclip the panel and remove it from the facia **(see illustrations)**.

4 Slacken and remove the four screws then release the upper retaining clip(s) and free the heating/ventilation control unit from the facia **(see illustrations)**.

5 On models with a manual control panel, disconnect the wiring connector from the rear of the control panel. Note the correct fitted location of each control cables (the end

10.2 Unclip the clock/multifunction unit surround from the facia and disconnect the wiring connector (arrowed)

10.3a Undo the retaining screws (arrowed) . . .

10.3b . . . then unclip the centre vent panel from the facia

10.4a Undo the retaining screws (arrowed) . . .

10.4b . . . then unclip the control panel and manoeuvre it out from the facia

10.5 On models with a manual control panel, disconnect the wiring connector then release the retaining clips and detach the cables

10.7 Ensure the control cables are correctly reconnected and securely held by the retaining clips

10.12 Clamp the heater matrix coolant hoses to minimise coolant loss

fittings are colour-coded) then unhook the cable retaining clips. Detach the cables and remove the control panel from the vehicle (**see illustration**).

6 On models with an automatic climate control system, disconnect the wiring connectors and remove the control panel from the vehicle.

7 Refitting is the reverse of removal. On models with a manual control panel ensure the control cables are correctly reconnected and securely held by the retaining clips; check the operation of the control knobs before securing the control panel to the facia (**see illustration**).

Heater/ventilation control cables

8 Remove the facia as described in Chapter 11.

9 Release the retaining clip and detach the relevant cable from the rear of the control panel and the heating/ventilation housing. Remove the cable, noting its correct routing.

10 Refitting is the reverse of removal, ensuring the cable is securely retained by its clips. Check the operation of the control panel and cables before refitting the facia (see Chapter 11).

10.13a Release the retaining clips . . .

Heater matrix

Note: *New matrix pipe sealing rings must be used on refitting. Suitable screws/bolts will also be required to secure the matrix/pipe unions in position.*

11 To improve access to the matrix unions on the bulkhead, remove the battery and battery tray as described in Chapter 5A. Where necessary also remove the air cleaner housing intake duct (see Chapter 4A or 4B).

12 Drain the cooling system (see Chapter 1A or 1B). Alternatively, clamp the heater matrix

10.13b . . . and disconnect both coolant hoses from the heater matrix pipe unions

coolant hoses to minimise coolant loss (**see illustration**).

13 Release the retaining clips and disconnect the coolant hoses from the heater matrix pipe unions on the engine compartment bulkhead (**see illustrations**).

14 Slacken and remove the screw securing the heater matrix pipes to the bulkhead and remove the retaining plate and seal (**see illustrations**).

15 Remove the facia assembly as described in Chapter 11.

16 Position a container beneath the heater

10.14a Undo the retaining screw (location arrowed) and remove the retaining plate . . .

10.14b . . . and seal from the pipes

10.18a Manoeuvre the heater matrix pipes out of position . . .

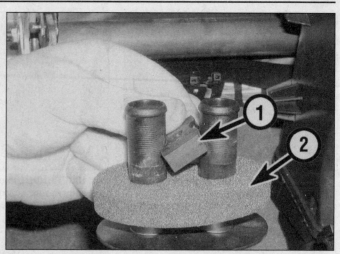

10.18b . . . taking care not to lose the retaining plate (1) or seal (2) from the bulkhead end of the pipes

matrix pipe union on the left-hand side of the heating/ventilation housing to catch any spilt coolant.

17 Slacken and remove the screws securing the matrix pipes to the housing and release the clips securing the pipes to the matrix. **Note:** *The clips are designed to be snapped off and bolts used on refitting.*

18 Free the pipes from the matrix, catching the coolant in the container, then free them from the bulkhead and remove them from the vehicle. Recover the sealing rings fitted to the pipe unions and discard them; new ones

should be used on refitting. Take care not to lose the bulkhead seal or retaining plate from the pipes **(see illustrations)**.

19 Release the retaining clips then slide the matrix out from the housing. **Note:** *The clips are designed to be snapped off and bolts used on refitting.* Keep the matrix unions uppermost as the matrix is removed to prevent coolant spillage **(see illustrations)**.

20 Ease the matrix into the housing and clip it into position. If the retaining clips where broken on removal, secure the matrix in

position using self-tapping screws fitted to the holes provided **(see illustration)**.

21 Ensure the bulkhead seal and retaining plate are correctly fitted to the matrix pipes and fit a new sealing ring to each of the pipe unions. Manoeuvre the pipe assembly into position and secure it to the matrix using screws/nuts and bolts fitted to the three holes provided **(see illustrations)**.

22 Working in the engine compartment, refit the seal and retaining plate to the heater matrix pipes and securely tighten the retaining screw. Remove the clamps (where fitted) then reconnect the coolant hoses, securing them in position with the retaining clips.

23 Refit the facia assembly (see Chapter 11).

24 Refit the battery (see Chapter 5A).

25 Refill the cooling system (see Chapter 1A or 1B).

Heater blower motor

26 The blower motor is fitted to the top of the heating/ventilation housing, on the left-hand side.

27 On right-hand drive models, remove the glovebox as described in Section 27 of Chapter 11. Access to the motor can then be gained through the glovebox aperture.

10.19a Release the retaining clips (arrowed) . . .

10.19b . . . then slide the heater matrix out from the housing

10.20 Secure the heater matrix in position with self-tapping screws (arrowed) if the retaining clips are no longer any use

10.21a Fit new sealing rings to the matrix pipe unions . . .

10.21b . . . and secure the pipes in position using screws and nuts (arrowed) in the holes provided

10.30 Disconnect the wiring connector from the blower motor . . .

10.31 . . . then rotate the motor clockwise to free it from the housing (arrow indicates hole provided for retaining screw – if fitted)

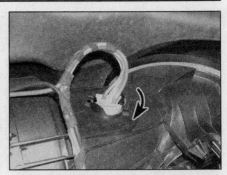

10.35a Rotate the blower motor resistor and pull it into the duct . . .

28 On left-hand drive models, remove the steering column as described in Chapter 10 to gain access to the motor.

29 Where necessary, slacken and remove the retaining screw securing the motor to the housing (this screw may not be fitted).

30 Disconnect the wiring connector(s) from the blower motor **(see illustration)**.

31 Rotate the motor clockwise to free it from the housing then manoeuvre it out of position **(see illustration)**.

32 Refitting is the reverse of removal. If the motor is not a secure fit in the housing, fix it in position by fitting a self-tapping screw to the hole provided.

Heater blower motor resistor

33 On left-hand drive models, remove the glovebox as described in Section 27 of Chapter 11.

34 On all models, set the air recirculation flap lever to the recirculation position. Access to the resistor can then be gained via recirculation intake aperture on the underside of the heating/ventilation housing duct.

35 Rotate the resistor to free it from the duct and pull it into the duct. Disconnect the wiring connector and remove the resistor from the housing **(see illustrations)**. **Note:** *If access proves difficult, remove the blower motor and remove the resistor through the blower motor aperture.*

36 Manoeuvre the resistor into position and securely connect it to the wiring connector.

Once the connector is securely fitted located the resistor in the duct and clip it in position. Refit any components removed for access.

Heating/ventilation housing

Models without air conditioning

37 To improve access to the matrix unions on the bulkhead, remove the battery and battery tray as described in Chapter 5A. Where necessary also remove the air cleaner housing intake duct (see Chapter 4A or 4B).

38 Drain the cooling system (see Chapter 1A or 1B). Alternatively, working in the engine compartment, clamp the heater matrix coolant hoses to minimise coolant loss **(see illustration 10.12)**.

39 Release the retaining clips and disconnect the coolant hoses from the heater matrix pipe unions on the engine compartment bulkhead **(see illustrations 10.13a and 10.13b)**.

40 Slacken and remove the screw securing the heater matrix pipes to the bulkhead and remove the retaining plate and seal **(see illustrations 10.14a and 10.14b)**.

41 Slacken and remove the bolt securing the heating/ventilation housing to the bulkhead **(see illustration)**.

42 Remove the facia assembly as described in Chapter 11.

43 Disconnect the wiring connectors from the heating/ventilation housing components then remove the housing and control panel assembly from the vehicle. Keep the heater

matrix pipe unions uppermost as the assembly is removed to prevent coolant spillage.

44 Recover the seal and retaining plate from the heater matrix pipes **(see illustration 10.18b)** and the seal from the housing mounting. Renew the seals if they show signs of damage or deterioration.

45 Refitting is the reverse of removal, ensuring the seals are in position on the pipes and housing mounting. On completion, refill the cooling system (see Chapter 1A or 1B).

Models with air conditioning

⚠️ *Warning: Refer to Section 11 for precautions to be observed when working on models equipped with air conditioning. Do not attempt the following procedure unless the system has been professionally discharged.*

46 Have the air conditioning system discharged by an air conditioning specialist and obtain some plugs to seal the air conditioning pipe unions whilst the system is disconnected.

47 Carry out the operations described in paragraphs 37 to 41.

48 Unscrew the two nuts securing the air conditioning pipe union to the bulkhead **(see illustration)**. Separate the pipes from the evaporator and quickly seal the pipe and evaporator unions to prevent the entry of moisture into the refrigerant circuit. Discard the sealing rings, new ones must be used on refitting.

10.35b . . . then disconnect it from the wiring connector and manoeuvre it out of position (shown being removed through blower motor aperture – facia removed for clarity)

10.41 Slacken and remove the bolt (arrowed) securing the heating/ventilation housing to the bulkhead

10.48 Air conditioning pipe union retaining nuts (arrowed)

10.57 Remove the rubber insulation covers then unscrew the nuts (arrowed) and disconnect the wiring from the coolant heater terminals (2.0 litre diesel engine shown)

⚠ **Warning: Failure to seal the refrigerant pipe unions will result in the dehydrator reservoir become saturated, necessitating its renewal.**

49 Remove the heating/ventilation housing assembly as described in paragraphs 42 to 44 and recover the seal from the evaporator.
50 Ensure the bulkhead seals are correctly fitted to the evaporator, matrix pipes and housing mounting. Manoeuvre the housing assembly into position, locating the housing drain hose correctly in its hole in the floor.
51 Loosely refit the housing mounting bolt then refit the retaining plate to the heater matrix pipe and loosely install the retaining screw.
52 Lubricate the new evaporator union sealing rings with compressor oil. Remove the plugs and install the sealing rings then quickly fit the refrigerant pipe union to the evaporator. Ensure the refrigerant pipes and evaporator are correctly joined then refit the retaining nuts, tighten them securely.

TOOL TiP

Many car accessory shops sell one-shot air conditioning recharge aerosols. These generally contain refrigerant, compressor oil, leak sealer and system conditioner. Some also have a dye to help pinpoint leaks.

⚠ *Warning: These products must only be used as directed by the manufacturer, and do not remove the need for regular maintenance.*

53 Tighten the matrix pipe retaining screw securely and securely tighten the housing mounting bolt.
54 The remainder of refitting is the reverse of removal. On completion, refill the cooling system (see Chapter 1A or 1B).

Automatic climate control system

55 The automatic climate control system sensors and motors are all fitted to the heating/ventilation housing. At the time of writing it was unclear whether they were available separately or were an integral part of the housing assembly. Refer to your Peugeot dealer for the latest information on parts availability.

Coolant heater

56 Remove the battery and battery tray as described in Chapter 5A to gain access to the heater which is mounted on the top of the transmission unit.
57 Remove the rubber insulation covers then unscrew the nuts and disconnect the wiring connectors from the heater terminals **(see illustration)**.
58 Drain the cooling system (see Chapter 1B). Alternatively, clamp the coolant hoses on each side of the heater to minimise coolant loss.
59 Release the retaining clips and disconnect the coolant hoses from the heater.
60 Unscrew the bolts securing the heater bracket to the transmission unit and remove the heater from the engine compartment.
61 Refitting is the reverse of removal. On completion, refill the cooling system (see Chapter 1B).

---

11 Air conditioning system – general information and precautions

General information

1 An air conditioning system is available on certain models. It enables the temperature of incoming air to be lowered, and also dehumidifies the air, which makes for rapid demisting and increased comfort.
2 The cooling side of the system works in the same way as a domestic refrigerator.

11.6a Air conditioning high pressure pipe connection (arrowed) . . .

Refrigerant gas is drawn into a belt-driven compressor, and passes into a condenser mounted on the front of the radiator, where it loses heat and becomes liquid. The liquid passes through an expansion valve to an evaporator, where it changes from liquid under high pressure to gas under low pressure. This change is accompanied by a drop in temperature, which cools the evaporator. The refrigerant returns to the compressor, and the cycle begins again.
3 Air blown through the evaporator passes to the heating/ventilation housing, where it is mixed with hot air blown through the heater matrix to achieve the desired temperature in the passenger compartment.
4 The heating side of the system works in the same way as on models without air conditioning (see Section 9).
5 The operation of the system is controlled electronically by the 'Bitron' control unit, which controls the electric cooling fan, the compressor and the facia-mounted warning light. Any problems with the system should be referred to a Peugeot dealer **(see Tool Tip)**.

Precautions

6 When an air conditioning system is fitted, it is necessary to observe special precautions whenever dealing with any part of the system, or its associated components. The refrigerant is potentially dangerous, and should only be handled by qualified persons **(see illustrations)**. Uncontrolled discharging of the refrigerant is dangerous and damaging to the environment for the following reasons.
  a) *If it is splashed onto the skin, it can cause frostbite.*
  b) *The refrigerant is heavier then air and so displaces oxygen. In a confined space, which is not adequately ventilated, this could lead to a risk of suffocation. The gas is odourless and colourless so there is no warning of its presence in the atmosphere.*
  c) *Although not poisonous, in the presence of a naked flame (including a cigarette) it forms a noxious gas, which causes headaches, nausea, etc.*

⚠ *Warning: Never attempt to open any air conditioning system refrigerant pipe/hose*

11.6b . . . and low pressure pipe connection (arrowed)

union without first having the system fully discharged by an air conditioning specialist. On completion of work, have the system recharged with the correct type and amount of fresh refrigerant.

⚠ **Warning: Always seal disconnected refrigerant pipe/hose unions as soon as they are disconnected.** Failure to form an air-tight seal on any union will result in the dehydrator reservoir become saturated, necessitating its renewal. Also renew all sealing rings disturbed.

Caution: Do not operate the air conditioning system if it is known to be short of refrigerant as this could damage the compressor.

12 Air conditioning system components – removal and refitting

⚠ **Warning: Refer to the precautions given in Section 11 and have the system discharged by an air conditioning specialist before carrying out any work on the air conditioning system**

Compressor

Removal

1 Have the air conditioning system fully discharged by an air conditioning specialist.

2 Remove the auxiliary drivebelt as described in Chapter 1A or 1B (as applicable).

3 Disconnect the compressor wiring connector from the engine harness **(see illustration)**.

4 Unscrew the bolt securing the refrigerant pipe retaining plate to the compressor **(see illustration)**. Separate the pipes from the compressor and quickly seal the pipe and compressor unions to prevent the entry of moisture into the refrigerant circuit. Discard the sealing rings, new ones must be used on refitting.

⚠ **Warning: Failure to seal the refrigerant pipe unions will result in the dehydrator reservoir become saturated, necessitating its renewal.**

5 Unscrew the compressor mounting bolts and nuts then free the compressor from its mounting bracket and remove it from the engine **(see illustrations)**. Take care not to lose the spacers from the compressor rear mountings (where fitted).

Refitting

6 Ensure the spacers are correctly fitted to the rear mountings then manoeuvre the compressor into position and fit the mounting bolts and nuts. Tighten the compressor front (drivebelt pulley) end mounting bolts to the specified torque first then tighten the rear bolts.

7 Lubricate the new refrigerant pipe sealing rings with compressor oil. Remove the plugs

12.3 Disconnect the wiring connector from the air conditioning compressor

and install the sealing rings then quickly fit the refrigerant pipes to the compressor. Ensure the refrigerant pipes are correctly joined then refit the retaining bolt, tighten it securely.

8 Reconnect the wiring connector then refit the auxiliary drivebelt (see Chapter 1A or 1B).

9 Have the air conditioning system recharged with the correct type and amount of refrigerant by a specialist before using the system.

Condenser

Removal

10 Have the air conditioning system fully discharged by an air conditioning specialist.

11 Remove the radiator as described in Section 4.

12 Unscrew the nut/bolt and disconnect the dehydrator pipe from the right-hand side of the condenser then release the retaining clip and detach the compressor pipe from the condenser. Quickly seal the pipe and condenser unions to prevent the entry of moisture into the refrigerant circuit. Discard the sealing ring(s); new one(s) must be used on refitting.

⚠ **Warning: Failure to seal the refrigerant pipe unions will result in the dehydrator reservoir become saturated, necessitating its renewal.**

13 Free the condenser from the front panel and remove it from the vehicle, taking care not to lose the condenser upper and lower mounting rubbers.

12.5a Compressor front and rear lower mounting bolts (arrowed) – petrol engine

12.4 Refrigerant pipe retaining plate bolt (arrowed)

Refitting

14 Ensure the upper and lower mounting rubbers are correctly fitted then seat the condenser in position in the front panel.

15 Lubricate the sealing rings with compressor oil. Remove the plugs and install the sealing rings then quickly fit the refrigerant pipes to the condenser. Securely tighten the dehydrator pipe union nut/bolt and ensure the compressor pipe is correctly joined.

16 Refit the radiator as described in Section 4.

17 Have the air conditioning system recharged with the correct type and amount of refrigerant by a specialist before using the system.

Dehydrator reservoir

Removal

18 The dehydrator reservoir is located on the right-hand side of the condenser where it is mounted onto the front panel.

19 Have the air conditioning system fully discharged by an air conditioning specialist.

20 Unscrew the nuts and disconnect the pipes from the dehydrator reservoir. Quickly seal the pipe and dehydrator unions to prevent the entry of moisture into the refrigerant circuit. Discard the sealing rings, new ones must be used on refitting.

⚠ **Warning: Failure to seal the refrigerant pipe unions will result in the dehydrator reservoir become saturated, necessitating its renewal.**

12.5b Compressor front and rear lower mounting bolts and nuts (arrowed) – diesel engine

21 Unscrew the mounting bolts and remove the dehydrator reservoir from the vehicle.

Refitting

22 Fit the dehydrator reservoir to the front panel and securely tighten its mounting bolts.
23 Lubricate the new sealing rings with compressor oil. Remove the plugs and install the sealing rings then quickly fit the refrigerant pipes to the dehydrator, tightening their retaining nuts securely.
24 Have the air conditioning system recharged with the correct type and amount of refrigerant by a specialist before using the system.

Evaporator

Removal

25 Have the air conditioning system fully discharged by an air conditioning specialist.
26 Remove the heating/ventilation housing as described in Section 9.
27 Release the retaining clips and slide the evaporator out from the front of the housing.

Refitting

28 Install the evaporator in the housing then refit the housing as described in Section 9.

Chapter 4 Part A:
Fuel/exhaust systems – petrol engine

Contents

Degrees of difficulty

| **Easy,** suitable for novice with little experience | | **Fairly easy,** suitable for beginner with some experience | | **Fairly difficult,** suitable for competent DIY mechanic | | **Difficult,** suitable for experienced DIY mechanic | | **Very difficult,** suitable for expert DIY or professional | |

Specifications

System type
1.1 litre models	Magneti Marelli 1AP or 4.8P2
1.4 litre models	
SOHC	Bosch Motronic MP7.3, Magneti Marelli 1AP or 6LP, Sagem S2000 PM1 or Johnson Controls J34P
DOHC	Sagem S2000
1.6 litre models	Bosch Motronic MP7.2
2.0 litre models	Magneti Marelli 4.8P

Fuel system data
Fuel pump type	Electric, immersed in tank
Fuel pump regulated constant pressure.	3.5 ± 0.2 bars
Specified idle speed.	850 ± 100 rpm (not adjustable – controlled by ECU)
Idle mixture CO content	Less than 1.0 % (not adjustable- controlled by ECU)

Recommended fuel
Minimum octane rating	95 RON unleaded (UK unleaded premium). Leaded/lead replacement fuel (LRP) must **not** be used

Torque wrench settings
	Nm	lbf ft
Exhaust manifold nuts:		
Long nuts	16	12
Short nuts.	25	18
Inlet manifold nuts	8	6
Knock sensor	20	15
Roadwheel bolts.	90	66

2.2 Disconnect the breather hose(s) . . .

1 General information and precautions

1 The fuel supply system consists of a fuel tank (which is mounted under the rear of the car, with an electric fuel pump immersed in it), a fuel filter, fuel feed and return lines. The fuel pump supplies fuel to the fuel rail, which acts as a reservoir for the four fuel injectors which inject fuel into the inlet tracts. The fuel filter incorporated in the feed line from the pump to the fuel rail ensures that the fuel supplied to the injectors is clean.

2 Refer to Section 6 for further information on the operation of the engine management system, and to Section 16 for information on the exhaust system.

2.4a Lift the air cleaner housing to free it from its mounting bracket (arrowed) . . .

2.4b . . . then recover the lower mounting rubber (1) and rubber sealing ring (2)

2.3 . . . then slacken the retaining clips and remove the duct connecting the air cleaner housing to the manifold (1.4 litre engine shown)

 Warning: Many of the procedures in this Chapter require the removal of fuel lines and connections, which may result in some fuel spillage. Before carrying out any operation on the fuel system, refer to the precautions given in 'Safety first!' at the beginning of this manual, and follow them implicitly. Petrol is a highly dangerous and volatile liquid, and the precautions necessary when handling it cannot be overstressed.
Note: *Residual pressure will remain in the fuel lines long after the vehicle was last used. When disconnecting any fuel line, first depressurise the fuel system as described in Section 7.*

2 Air cleaner assembly and intake ducts – removal and refitting

Removal

1 On 1.4 litre DOHC engines, remove the air filter and housing as described in Chapter 1A, Section 18.

2 On all other models, unclip and disconnect the breather hose(s) from the manifold end of the duct connecting the air cleaner housing to the inlet manifold **(see illustration)**.

3 Slacken the retaining clips then free the duct from the manifold and air cleaner housing, and remove it from the engine compartment **(see illustration)**.

4 Lift the air cleaner housing assembly off of

its mounting bracket and remove it from the engine compartment. Recover the mounting rubber fitted to the housing lower locating peg and the sealing ring from the housing intake duct **(see illustrations)**.

5 To remove the intake duct, firmly apply the handbrake then jack up the front of the car and support it on axle stands (see *Jacking and vehicle support*). Undo the screws securing the front section of the left-hand wheel arch liner to the base of the bumper then remove the fasteners securing the liner to the body (pull out the centre pin then remove the complete fastener) and manoeuvre it out from underneath the wing. Remove the retaining bolts and remove the duct assembly from the vehicle (on 1.4 and 1.6 litre SOHC engines a resonator chamber is incorporated into the duct to reduce intake noise).

Refitting

6 Refitting is a reversal of the removal procedure, ensuring that all hoses and ducts are properly reconnected and correctly seated and, where necessary, securely held by their retaining clips. Refer to Chapter 1A, Section 18, for air filter element refitting.

3 Accelerator cable – removal, refitting and adjustment

Note: *Not all models have an accelerator cable.*

Removal

1 Working in the engine compartment, free the accelerator inner cable from the throttle housing cam, then pull the outer cable out from its mounting bracket rubber grommet. Recover the spring clip from the outer cable **(see illustration)**.

2 Working back along the length of the cable, free it from any retaining clips or ties, noting its correct routing.

3 Working inside the vehicle, reach up behind the facia then release the retaining clip and detach the inner cable from the top of the accelerator pedal **(see illustration)**.

3.1 Remove the spring clip from the accelerator outer cable

3.3 Free the inner cable end fitting (1) from the accelerator pedal and remove the retaining clip (2) from the outer cable (shown with facia removed)

4.2 Accelerator pedal retaining clip (arrowed)

4 Remove the retaining clip which secures the outer cable end fitting to the bulkhead, then tie a length of string to the end of the cable.

5 Return to the engine compartment, release the cable grommet from the bulkhead and withdraw the cable. When the end of the cable appears, untie the string and leave it in position – it can then be used to draw the cable back into position on refitting.

Refitting

6 Tie the string to the end of the cable, then use the string to draw the cable into position through the bulkhead. Once the cable end is visible, untie the string, then secure the outer cable in position with the retaining clip and attach the inner cable into the pedal end.

7 From within the engine compartment, ensure the outer cable is correctly seated in the bulkhead grommet, and then work along the cable, securing it in position with the retaining clips and ties, and ensuring that the cable is correctly routed.

8 Pass the outer cable through its mounting bracket grommet, and reconnect the inner cable to the throttle cam. Adjust the cable as described below.

Adjustment

9 Remove the spring clip from the accelerator outer cable **(see illustration 3.1)**. Ensuring that the throttle cam is fully against its stop, gently pull the cable out of its grommet until all free play is removed from the inner cable.

10 With the cable held in this position, refit the spring clip to the last exposed outer cable groove in front of the rubber grommet. When the clip is refitted and the outer cable is released, there should be only a small amount of free play in the inner cable.

11 Have an assistant depress the accelerator pedal, and check that the throttle cam opens fully and returns smoothly to its stop.

Note: *On models with an automatic transmission unit, Peugeot specify that the automatic transmission electronic control unit (ECU) should be reprogrammed every time the accelerator cable is adjusted. If the transmission performance has been adversely affected by accelerator cable adjustment, take the vehicle to a Peugeot dealer to have the transmission ECU reprogrammed with the necessary diagnostic equipment.*

4 Accelerator pedal – removal and refitting

Removal

1 Working inside the vehicle, reach up behind the facia then release the retaining clip and detach the inner cable from the top of the accelerator pedal.

2 On right-hand drive models, remove the retaining clip then slide out the pivot pin and remove the accelerator pedal from the pedal mounting bracket **(see illustration)**.

3 On left-hand drive models, remove the retaining clip then slide the pedal off its pivot shaft. The pivot shaft is a screw fit in the body.

Refitting

4 Refitting is a reversal of the removal procedure, applying a little multi-purpose grease to the pedal pivot point. On completion, adjust the accelerator cable as described in Section 3.

5 Unleaded petrol – general information and usage

Note: *The information given in this Chapter is correct at the time of writing. If updated information is thought to be required, check with a Peugeot dealer. If travelling abroad, consult one of the motoring organisations (or a similar authority) for advice on the fuel available.*

1 The fuel recommended by Peugeot is given in the Specifications Section of this Chapter, followed by the equivalent petrol currently on sale in the UK.

2 All models are designed to run on fuel with a minimum octane rating of 95 (RON). All models have a catalytic converter, and so must be run on unleaded fuel only. Under no circumstances should leaded/lead replacement fuel (UK 4-star/LRP) be used, as this may damage the converter.

3 Super unleaded petrol (98 octane) can also be used in all models if wished, though there is no advantage in doing so.

6 Engine management system – general information

Note: *The fuel injection ECU is of the 'self-learning' type, meaning that, as it operates, it also monitors and stores the settings, which give optimum engine performance under all operating conditions. When the battery is disconnected, these settings are lost and the ECU reverts to the base settings programmed into its memory at the factory. On restarting, this may lead to the engine running/idling roughly for a short while, until the ECU has relearned the optimum settings. This process is best accomplished by taking the vehicle on a road test (for approximately 15 minutes), covering all engine speeds and loads, concentrating mainly in the 2500 to 3500 rpm region.*

On all engines, the fuel injection and ignition functions are combined into a single engine management system. The systems fitted are manufactured by Bosch, Magneti Marelli, Sagem and Johnson Controls, and are very similar to each other in most respects, the only significant differences being in the software contained in the system ECU, and specific component location according to engine type. Each system incorporates a closed-loop catalytic converter and an evaporative emission control system, and complies with the latest emission control standards. Refer to Chapter 5B for information on the ignition side of each system; the fuel side of the system operates as follows.

The fuel pump supplies fuel from the tank to the fuel rail, on some models via a renewable cartridge filter mounted on the side of the fuel tank, on other models the filter is part of the fuel pump/sender unit. The pump itself is mounted inside the tank, with the pump motor permanently immersed in fuel, to keep it cool. The fuel rail is mounted directly above the fuel injectors and acts as a fuel reservoir.

Fuel rail supply pressure is controlled by the pressure regulator, also located in the fuel tank. The regulator contains a spring-loaded valve, which lifts to allow excess fuel to recirculate within the tank when the optimum operating pressure of the fuel system is exceeded (eg, during low speed, light load cruising).

The fuel injectors are electromagnetic pintle valves, which spray atomised fuel into the combustion chambers under the control of the engine management system ECU. There are four injectors, one per cylinder, mounted in the inlet manifold close to the cylinder head. Each injector is mounted at an angle that allows it to spray fuel directly onto the back of the inlet valve(s). The ECU controls the volume of fuel injected by varying the length of time for which each injector is held open. The fuel injection systems are typically of the sequential type, whereby each injector operates individually in cylinder sequence.

The electrical control system consists of the ECU, along with the following sensors:

a) *Throttle potentiometer – informs the ECU of the throttle valve position, and the rate of throttle opening/closing (not all models).*

b) *Coolant temperature sensor – informs the ECU of engine temperature.*

c) *Inlet air temperature sensor – informs the ECU of the temperature of the air passing through the throttle housing.*

d) *Oxygen sensors – inform the ECU of the oxygen content of the exhaust gases (explained in greater detail in Part C of this Chapter).*

e) *Manifold pressure sensor – informs the*

ECU of the load on the engine (expressed in terms of inlet manifold vacuum).

f) *Crankshaft position sensor – informs the ECU of engine speed and crankshaft angular position.*

g) *Vehicle speed sensor – informs the ECU of the vehicle speed (not all models).*

h) *Knock sensor – informs the ECU of pre-ignition (detonation) within the cylinders.*

i) *Camshaft sensor – informs the ECU of which cylinder is on the firing stroke on systems with sequential injection (not all models).*

j) *Accelerator pedal position sensor – informs the ECU of the pedal position and rate of change (not all models)*.*

k) *Throttle valve position motor – allows the ECU to control the throttle valve position (not all models)*.*

* *2.0 litre petrol engines may be fitted with a manual throttle body with an accelerator cable, or a motorised throttle body with no cable.*

Signals from each of the sensors are compared by the ECU and, based on this information; the ECU selects the response appropriate to those values, and controls the fuel injectors (varying the pulse width – the length of time the injectors are held open – to provide a richer or weaker air/fuel mixture, as appropriate). The air/fuel mixture is constantly varied by the ECU, to provide the best settings for cranking, starting (with either a hot or cold engine) and engine warm-up, idle, cruising and acceleration.

The ECU also has full control over the engine idle speed, via a stepper motor fitted to the throttle housing. The stepper motor either controls the amount of air passing through a bypass drilling at the side of the throttle or controls the position of the throttle valve itself, depending on model. On some models, a sensor informs the ECU of the position, and rate of change, of the accelerator pedal. The ECU then controls the throttle valve by means of a throttle positioning motor integral with the throttle body – no accelerator cable is fitted. The ECU also carries out 'fine tuning' of the idle speed by varying the ignition timing to increase or reduce the torque of the engine as it is idling. This helps to stabilise the idle speed when electrical or mechanical loads (such as headlights, air conditioning, etc) are switched on and off.

The throttle housing is also fitted with an electric heating element. The heater is supplied with current by the ECU, warming the throttle housing on cold starts to help prevent icing of the throttle valve.

The exhaust and evaporative loss emission control systems are described in more detail in Chapter 4C.

If there is any abnormality in any of the readings obtained from the coolant temperature sensor, the inlet air temperature sensor or the lambda sensor, the ECU enters its 'back-up' mode. If this happens, the erroneous sensor signal is overridden, and the ECU assumes a preprogrammed 'back-up' value, which will allow the engine to continue running, albeit at reduced efficiency. If the ECU enters this mode, the warning lamp on the instrument panel will be illuminated, and the relevant fault code will be stored in the ECU memory.

If the warning light illuminates, the vehicle should be taken to a Peugeot dealer or specialist at the earliest opportunity. Once there, a complete test of the engine management system can be carried out, using a special electronic diagnostic test unit, which is plugged into the system's diagnostic connector, located behind the trim panel to the right of the steering column.

7 Fuel system – depressurisation and pressurising

Note: *Refer to the warning note in Section 1 before proceeding.*

Depressurisation

⚠️ *Warning: The following procedure will merely relieve the pressure in the fuel system – remember that fuel will still be present in the system components and take precautions accordingly before disconnecting any of them.*

1 The fuel system referred to in this Section is defined as the tank-mounted fuel pump, the fuel filter, the fuel injectors, the fuel rail and the pipes of the fuel lines between these components. All these contain fuel which will be under pressure while the engine is running, and/or while the ignition is switched on. The pressure will remain for some time after the ignition has been switched off, and must be relieved in a controlled fashion when any of these components are disturbed for servicing work.

2 Disconnect the battery negative terminal.

3 Some models are equipped with a pressure relief valve on the fuel rail. On these models, unscrew the cap from the valve and position a container beneath the valve. Hold a wad of rag over the valve and relieve the pressure in the system by depressing the valve core with a suitable screwdriver. Be prepared for the squirt of fuel as the valve core is depressed and catch it with the rag. Hold the valve core down until no more fuel is expelled from the valve. Once the pressure is relieved, securely refit the valve cap.

4 Where no valve is fitted to the fuel rail, it will be necessary to release the pressure as the fuel pipe is disconnected. Place a container beneath the union and position a large rag around the union to catch any fuel spray, which may be expelled. Slowly release and disconnect the fuel pipe and catch any spilt fuel in the container. Plug the pipe/union to minimise fuel loss and prevent the entry of dirt into the fuel system.

Pressurising

5 After any work is carried out on the fuel system, the system should be pressurised as follows.

6 Depress the accelerator pedal fully then switch on the ignition. Hold the pedal depressed for approximately 1 second then release it. The ECU should then operate the fuel pump for between 20 and 30 seconds to refill the fuel system. Once the fuel pump stops the ignition can be switched off.

8 Fuel pump – removal and refitting

Note: *A pop rivet gun and new rivets will be required on refitting.*

Removal

1 Disconnect the battery negative lead.

2 For access to the fuel pump, tilt or remove the right-hand rear seat cushion (see Chapter 11).

3 Carefully drill the heads off the three rivets securing the fuel pump cover plate (where fitted) to the floor, taking care not to damage the plate/vehicle body **(see illustration)**. Remove the plate from the vehicle.

4 Using a screwdriver, carefully prise the plastic access cover from the floor to expose the fuel pump **(see illustration)**.

5 Disconnect the wiring connector from the fuel pump, and tape the connector to the

8.3 Drill the heads off the rivets (arrowed) then remove the cover plate (where fitted) from the floor

8.4 Remove the plastic cover to gain access to the fuel pump

8.5 Disconnect the wiring connector . . .

8.6 . . . then unclip the fuel feed and return pipes from the pump

8.8 Manoeuvre the fuel pump assembly out of position taking care not to bend the float arm (arrowed)

8.10 On refitting fit a new sealing ring to the fuel tank

8.13 Tighten the locking ring until its alignment mark (1) is correctly aligned with the pump cover mark (2) and the fuel tank mark (not shown)

8.17 Secure the cover plate in position with new pop rivets

vehicle body to prevent it from disappearing behind the tank (see illustration).

6 Depress the retaining clips and detach both fuel pipes from the top of the pump, bearing in mind the information given in Section 7 on depressurising the fuel system (the hose end fittings are colour-coded for identification) (see illustration). Plug the pipe ends to minimise fuel loss and prevent the entry of dirt.

7 Noting the alignment marks on the tank, pump cover and the locking ring, unscrew the ring and remove it from the tank. This is best accomplished by using a screwdriver on the raised ribs of the locking ring. Carefully tap the screwdriver to turn the ring anti-clockwise until it can be unscrewed by hand.

8 Carefully lift the fuel pump assembly out of the fuel tank, taking great care not to damage the fuel gauge sender unit float arm, or to spill fuel onto the interior of the vehicle (see illustration). Recover the rubber sealing ring and discard it – a new one must be used on refitting.

9 Note that the fuel pump is only available as a complete assembly – no components are available separately.

Refitting

10 Ensure the fuel pump pick-up filter is clean and free of debris. Fit the new sealing ring to the top of the fuel tank (see illustration).

11 Carefully manoeuvre the pump assembly into the fuel tank, taking care not to damage the float arm.

12 Align the arrow on the fuel pump cover with the arrow on the fuel tank and clip the pump assembly into position.

13 Refit the locking ring and tighten it securely until its alignment mark aligns with the pump cover and tank arrows (see illustration).

14 Securely reconnect the feed and return pipes to the pump cover then reconnect the pump wiring connector.

15 Reconnect the battery negative terminal and pressurise the fuel system (see Section 7). Start the engine and check the fuel pump feed and return hoses unions for signs of leakage.

16 If all is well, refit the plastic access cover ensuring its locating tab is at the front.

17 Where applicable, refit the cover plate and secure it in position with new pop rivets (see illustration). Refit the rear seat cushion (see Chapter 11).

10.3 Removing the right-hand rear wheel arch liner front section

9 Fuel gauge sender unit – removal and refitting

The fuel gauge sender unit is an integral part of the fuel pump assembly and is not available separately. Refer to Section 8 for removal and refitting details.

10 Fuel tank – removal and refitting

Note: Refer to the warning note in Section 1 before proceeding.

Removal

1 Before removing the fuel tank, all fuel must be drained from the tank. Since a fuel tank drain plug is not provided, it is therefore preferable to carry out the removal operation when the tank is nearly empty. Before proceeding, disconnect the battery negative lead and syphon or hand-pump the remaining fuel from the tank.

2 Chock the front wheels then jack up the rear of the vehicle and support it on axle stands (see Jacking and vehicle support). Remove the right-hand rear roadwheel

3 Remove the retaining screws and fasteners (pull out the centre pin then remove the complete fasteners) and remove the front section of the right-hand rear wheel arch liner to gain access to the fuel tank filler neck (see illustration).

10.4 Undo the screws (arrowed) securing the fuel filler neck to the body

10.7 Prise off the retaining clips (arrowed) and free the handbrake cables from the fuel tank

10.8 Disconnect the vent pipe (1) and fuel pipe (2) from their unions near the fuel filter

4 Remove the fuel filler cap then slacken and remove the three screws securing the filler neck to the body **(see illustration)**.

5 Remove the exhaust system and relevant heat shield(s) as described in Section 16.

6 Disconnect the two handbrake cables from the handbrake lever – see Chapter 9.

7 From underneath the vehicle, remove the retaining clips, and release each handbrake cable from its clip on the underside of the fuel tank **(see illustration)**. Position both cables clear of the tank, so that they will not hinder the removal procedure.

8 Depress the retaining clips and detach the fuel pipe and vent pipe from their unions located next to the fuel filter; bear in mind the information given in Section 7 on depressurising the fuel system when disconnecting the fuel pipe **(see illustration)**. Plug the pipe ends to minimise fuel loss and prevent the entry of dirt. **Note:** *On some models, the fuel filter is part of the fuel sender unit, this type do not have a separate filter at the side of the fuel tank.*

9 Place a trolley jack with an interposed block of wood beneath the tank, then raise the jack until it is supporting the weight of the tank.

10 Slacken and remove the four nuts securing the fuel tank to the body and remove the support strap from the right-hand mountings **(see illustration)**.

11 Slowly lower the fuel tank out of position until access can be gained to the top of the tank. Disconnect the wiring connector from the fuel pump then manoeuvre the tank and filler neck assembly out from underneath the vehicle.

12 If the tank is contaminated with sediment or water, remove the fuel pump (Section 8), and swill the tank out with clean fuel. The tank is injection-moulded from a synthetic material – if seriously damaged, it should be renewed. However, in certain cases, it may be possible to have small leaks or minor damage repaired. Seek the advice of a specialist before attempting to repair the fuel tank.

13 To separate the filler neck from the tank, it will be necessary to cut the hard plastic vent/breather pipes. Remove the retaining clips securing the flexible connectors to the tank/filler neck then cut both pipes at the locations shown **(see illustration)**. Mark the pipes to ensure they are correctly reconnected then remove the filler neck. **Note:** *The filler neck*

can be removed without disturbing the fuel tank.

Refitting

14 Refitting is the reverse of the removal procedure, noting the following points:

a) *If necessary, refit the filler neck to the tank. Reconnect the vent/breather pipes with quick-release couplings (available from your Peugeot dealer) and secure the flexible connector to the filler neck/tank with new retaining clips.*

b) *Ensure wiring connector and fuel/vent pipes are securely reconnected and retained by all the relevant clips. When lifting the tank back into position, take care to ensure that the pipes/wiring do not become trapped between the tank and vehicle body.*

c) *Reconnect the handbrake cables and adjust the handbrake as described in Chapter 9.*

d) *Refit the exhaust as described in Section 16.*

e) *On completion, refill the tank with a small amount of fuel and pressurise the fuel system as described in Section 7. Check for signs of leakage prior to taking the vehicle out on the road.*

10.10 Unscrew the mounting nuts (2) and remove the support strap (1) from the fuel tank right-hand mountings

10.13 Cut the vent/breather pipes at the points shown when separating the fuel tank and filler neck

1 Retaining clips
2 Vent/breather pipe – cut at X (55 mm up from bend A)
3 Vent/breather pipe – cut at Y (150 mm down from union B)

12.4 Disconnect the wiring connectors from all the throttle housing components

12.5a Undo the three retaining screws (arrowed) . . .

12.5b . . . then remove the throttle housing from the manifold and recover the sealing ring – 1.4 litre engine shown

11 Engine management system – testing and adjustment

Testing

1 If a fault appears in the engine management system, first ensure that all the system wiring connectors are securely connected and free of corrosion. Ensure that the fault is not due to poor maintenance; ie, check that the air cleaner filter element is clean, the spark plugs are in good condition and correctly gapped, the cylinder compression pressures are correct and that the engine breather hoses are clear and undamaged, referring to Chapters 1A, 2A and 5B for further information.

2 If these checks fail to reveal the cause of the problem, the vehicle should be taken to a suitably-equipped Peugeot dealer for testing using a diagnostic tester, which is connected into the diagnostic socket next to the fusebox. The tester will locate the fault quickly and simply, alleviating the need to test all the system components individually, which is a time-consuming operation that carries a risk of damaging the ECU.

Adjustment

3 Whilst it is possible to check the exhaust CO level and the idle speed, if these are found to be in need of adjustment, the car *must* be taken to a suitably-equipped Peugeot

12.6 On refitting ensure the new sealing ring is correctly fitted to the manifold

dealer for further testing. Neither the mixture adjustment (exhaust gas CO level) nor the idle speed are adjustable, and should either be incorrect, a fault must be present in the engine management system.

12 Throttle housing – removal and refitting

Removal

1 Remove the plastic style covers from the top of the engine, and then disconnect the battery negative terminal.

2 Unclip and disconnect the breather hose(s) from the manifold end of the duct connecting the air cleaner housing to the inlet manifold. Slacken the retaining clips then free the duct from the manifold and air cleaner housing and remove it from the engine compartment.

3 Free the accelerator inner cable from the throttle cam (where applicable).

4 Depress the retaining clip and disconnect the wiring connectors from the throttle potentiometer, intake air temperature sensor and, where necessary, from the idle speed stepper motor and electric heating element (as applicable) **(see illustration)**.

5 Slacken and remove the three retaining screws and remove the throttle housing from the inlet manifold **(see illustrations)**. Recover the sealing ring from manifold and discard it; a new one must be used on refitting.

13.5 Depress the retaining clip (arrowed) and disconnect the fuel hose from the fuel rail

Refitting

6 Refitting is a reversal of the removal procedure, noting the following points:

a) *Fit a new sealing ring to the manifold, then refit the throttle housing and securely tighten its retaining screws (see illustration).*

b) *Ensure all wiring is correctly routed, and that the connectors are securely reconnected.*

c) *On completion, adjust the accelerator cable as described in Section 3 (where applicable).*

13 Engine management system components – removal and refitting

Fuel rail and injectors

Note: *Refer to the warning note in Section 1 before proceeding.*

Note: *If a faulty injector is suspected, before condemning the injector it is worth trying the effect of one of the proprietary injector-cleaning treatments, which are available from car accessory shops.*

1 Slacken the retaining clips then free the duct from the throttle housing and air cleaner housing and remove it from the engine compartment.

1.1 litre and 1.4 litre SOHC models

2 Remove the ignition HT coil as described in Chapter 5B.

3 Free the accelerator inner cable (where fitted) from the throttle housing cam, then pull the outer cable out from its mounting bracket rubber grommet, complete with its spring clip **(see illustration 3.1)**.

4 Unscrew the bolts and remove the accelerator cable bracket (where fitted) from the manifold/cylinder head.

5 Depress the retaining clip and disconnect the fuel pipe from the right-hand end of the fuel rail, bearing in mind the information given in Section 7 on depressurising the fuel system **(see illustration)**.

6 Slacken and remove the two bolts securing the fuel rail to the cylinder head, and the nut securing the rail to the manifold. Loosen the

13.6a Unscrew the fuel rail mounting bolts (1) and the nut (2) . . .

13.6b . . . then loosen the bolt (arrowed) and lift off the centre bracket

13.8 Remove the seal from the end of each injector

bolt securing the fuel rail centre bracket to the inlet manifold, then lift off the bracket (the bracket is slotted to ease removal) **(see illustrations)**.

7 Disconnect the injector wiring harness connector, and then unclip the connector from the rear of the inlet manifold. Also disconnect the wiring connectors from the throttle housing and position the wiring harness clear of the manifold so that it does not hinder fuel rail removal.

8 Carefully ease the fuel rail and injector assembly out from the cylinder head and manoeuvre it out of position. Remove the seals from the end of each injector and discard them; they must be renewed whenever they are disturbed **(see illustration)**.

9 Refitting is a reversal of the removal procedure, noting the following points.

a) *Fit new seals to all disturbed injector unions.*

b) *Apply a smear of engine oil to the seals to aid installation, then ease the injectors and fuel rail into position ensuring that none of the seals are displaced.*

c) *On completion, pressurise the fuel system as described in Section 7. Start the engine and check for fuel leaks.*

1.4 DOHC and 1.6 litre models

10 Remove the inlet manifold as described in Section 14.

11 Undo the two bolts and remove the fuel rail with injectors from the manifold **(see illustration)**.

12 Disconnect the wiring connector(s) then slide out the retaining clip(s) and remove the relevant injector(s) from the fuel rail. Remove the seals from each disturbed injector and discard; all disturbed seals must be renewed **(see illustration)**.

13 Refitting is a reversal of the removal procedure, noting the following points.

a) *Fit new seals to all disturbed injector unions **(see illustration)**.*

b) *Apply a smear of engine oil to the seals to aid installation, then ease the injectors and fuel rail into position ensuring that none of the seals are displaced.*

c) *On completion, pressurise the fuel system as described in Section 7. Start the engine and check for fuel leaks.*

2.0 litre models

14 Unbolt and remove the engine top cover, then disconnect the air duct from between the air cleaner and throttle body.

15 Disconnect the wiring from the inlet air temperature sensor.

16 Unbolt the wiring tray from the top of the inlet manifold, and position to one side.

17 Depress the release button and disconnect the fuel supply hose from the fuel rail **(see illustration)**

18 Depress the retaining clip(s), and disconnect the wiring connector(s) from the injector(s) **(see illustration)**.

19 Unscrew the mounting bolts and carefully ease the fuel rail, complete with injectors, from

13.11 Undo the two bolts (arrowed) and remove the injectors and fuel rail from the manifold

13.12 Slide off the retaining clip and remove the injector from the fuel rail

13.13 Renew all injector seals (arrowed) disturbed on removal

13.17 Depress the button (arrowed) and disconnect the fuel supply hose from the fuel rail

13.18 Release the clips and disconnect the injector wiring plugs (centre plug arrowed)

13.19 Undo the fuel rail mounting bolts

13.23 Disconnect the throttle potentiometer wiring plug . . .

13.24 . . . then undo the retaining screws (arrowed) and remove it from the throttle housing (1.4 litre SOHC)

the inlet manifold **(see illustration)**. Remove the O-rings from the end of each injector, and discard them; these must be renewed whenever they are disturbed.

20 Slide out the retaining clip(s) and remove the relevant injector(s) from the fuel rail. Remove the upper O-ring from each disturbed injector and discard; all disturbed O-rings must be renewed.

21 Refitting is a reversal of the removal procedure, noting the following points.

a) *Fit new O-rings to all disturbed injector unions.*

b) *Apply a smear of engine oil to the O-rings to aid installation then ease the injectors and fuel rail into position ensuring that none of the O-rings are displaced.*

c) *On completion start the engine and check for fuel leaks.*

Fuel pressure regulator

22 The fuel pressure regulator is an integral part of the fuel pump assembly and is not available separately. Refer to Section 8 for removal and refitting details.

Throttle potentiometer

23 Depress the retaining clip and disconnect the wiring connector from the throttle potentiometer **(see illustration)**.

24 Slacken and remove the two retaining screws, then disengage the potentiometer from the throttle valve spindle and remove it from the vehicle **(see illustration)**.

25 Refit in the reverse order of removal.

26 Ensure that the potentiometer is correctly engaged with the throttle valve spindle.

Electronic Control Unit (ECU)

Note: *If a new ECU is being fitted, the vehicle will not start until the immobiliser ECU has been matched to the engine management ECU. This can only be performed using dedicated test equipment. Consequently, entrust the procedure to a Peugeot dealer or suitably-equipped specialist.*

27 The ECU is located on the right-hand side of the engine compartment.

28 To remove the ECU, first disconnect the battery.

29 Unclip the wiring harness then slacken and remove the ECU mounting plate nut.

30 The plate is secured in position with an anti-tamper nut, unscrew the nut using a pair of grips then lift off the wiring bracket **(see illustration)**.

31 Free the mounting plate from the body then lift the retaining clip and disconnect the ECU wiring connector **(see illustration)**.

32 Unscrew the ECU mounting nuts (these are also anti-tamper nuts) then remove the ECU from the mounting plate.

33 Refitting is a reverse of the removal procedure ensuring the wiring connector is securely reconnected.

34 Secure the ECU and mounting plate in position with new anti-tamper nuts or standard nuts.

Idle speed stepper motor

35 The idle speed stepper motor is fitted to the rear of the throttle housing.

36 Disconnect the wiring connector from the motor **(see illustration)**.

37 Slacken and remove the retaining screws then remove the motor from the throttle housing **(see illustration)**. If necessary, remove the throttle potentiometer to improve access to the motor lower screw.

38 Refitting is a reversal of the removal procedure ensuring the seal is in good condition.

Manifold pressure sensor

39 The MAP sensor is mounted on the inlet manifold.

13.30 Using a pair of grips to unscrew the ECU mounting plate nut

13.31 Lift the retaining clip and carefully disconnect the wiring connector from the ECU

13.36 Disconnect the idle speed stepper motor wiring plug (arrowed) – 1.4 litre SOHC

13.37 Undo the retaining screws (arrowed) and remove the motor from the throttle housing

13.40a Disconnect the wiring connector (1) then undo the retaining screw (2) and remove the MAP sensor – 1.4 litre engine

13.40b ... 1.6 litre engine ...

13.40c ... and 2.0 litre engine

13.44 Disconnect the wiring connector ...

40 Disconnect the wiring connector then undo the screw and remove the sensor from the manifold **(see illustrations)**.
41 Refitting is a reversal of the removal procedure ensuring the sensor seal is in good condition.

Coolant temperature sensor

42 The coolant temperature sensor is screwed into the coolant outlet housing on the left-hand end of the cylinder head. Refer to Chapter 3, Section 7, for removal and refitting information.

Intake air temperature sensor

Note: *On later models, the intake air temperature sensor is integral with the throttle housing and is not available separately.*
43 The intake air temperature sensor is fitted to the base of the throttle housing.
44 Disconnect the wiring connector from the sensor **(see illustration)**.
45 Where applicable, release the retaining

clips **(see Tool Tip)** and ease the sensor out from the throttle housing **(see illustration)**.
46 Refitting is the reverse of removal ensuring the sensor seal is in good condition.

HAYNES HINT

The intake air temperature sensor clips can be released by passing a close-fitting ring spanner over the end of the sensor.

Crankshaft position sensor

47 The crankshaft sensor is situated on the front face of the transmission housing.
48 Disconnect the sensor wiring connector and unclip the wiring. Undo the retaining bolt and remove the sensor and

13.45 ... then unclip the intake air temperature sensor from the throttle housing – 1.4 litre SOHC engine shown

13.48a Disconnect the wiring connector then undo the retaining screw (arrowed) . . .

13.48b . . . then remove the crankshaft sensor from the front of the transmission housing

13.51a Disconnect the wiring connector then undo the retaining screw (arrowed) . . .

bracket assembly from the transmission unit **(see illustrations)**.

49 Refitting is reverse of the removal procedure.

Throttle housing heating element

Note: *The heating element is only fitted to aluminium throttle housings. Plastic housings do not need a heater.*

50 The heating element is fitted to the top of the throttle housing.

51 Disconnect the wiring connector then unscrew the retaining screw and remove the heating element from the throttle housing **(see illustrations)**.

52 Refitting is the reverse of removal.

Vehicle speed sensor

53 The vehicle speed sensor is an integral part of the speedometer drive on 1.4 litre models. Refer to Chapter 7A for removal and refitting details. On other models, the ECU receives vehicle speed data from the wheel speed sensors, via the ABS ECU.

Knock sensor

54 The knock sensor is screwed onto the rear of the cylinder block. To remove it, first disconnect the battery negative terminal.

55 To gain access to the sensor, firmly apply the handbrake then jack up the front of the vehicle and support it on axle stands *(see Jacking and vehicle support)*.

56 Disconnect the wiring connector from the sensor then unscrew the retaining bolt and remove the sensor from underneath the vehicle **(see illustration)**.

57 Refitting is the reverse of removal. Ensure the sensor and cylinder block mating surfaces are clean and dry and tighten the sensor mounting bolt to the specified torque.

Fuel cut-off inertia switch

Note: *The fuel cut-off inertia switch is only fitted to earlier models.*

58 Where fitted the fuel cut-off inertia switch is located in the left-hand rear corner of the engine compartment **(see illustration)**. To remove it, first disconnect the battery negative terminal.

59 Cut the retaining clip (where fitted) then unscrew the retaining nuts and remove the switch from the vehicle, disconnecting it from the wiring connector.

60 Refitting is the reverse of removal. On completion, reset the switch by firmly depressing its button.

Power steering pressure switch

Caution: Ensure no dirt is allowed to enter into the hydraulic system during the following procedure.

61 The power steering pressure switch is fitted to the power steering pipe located on the left-hand end of the cylinder head. To remove it, first disconnect the battery negative terminal.

13.51b . . . and remove the heating element from the throttle housing – 1.4 litre SOHC engine shown

62 Disconnect the wiring connector from the switch then wipe the area around the switch clean **(see illustration)**. Unscrew the switch and remove it from the pipe, along with its sealing washer. Plug the pipe whilst the switch is removed to minimise fluid loss and prevent the entry of dirt into the hydraulic system.

63 Refitting is the reverse of removal, using a new sealing washer. On completion, check the power steering fluid level and, if necessary, bleed the hydraulic system (see Chapter 10).

Air conditioning pressure switch

64 The air conditioning pressure switch is fitted to the refrigerant pipe located on the right-hand side of the engine compartment. Switch renewal requires the air conditioning system to be discharged and drained (see Chapter 3).

13.56 Disconnect the wiring connector (1) then undo the bolt (2) and remove the knock sensor from the cylinder block

13.58 Fuel cut-off inertia switch (where fitted) is located in the rear, left-hand corner of the engine compartment

13.62 Disconnecting the wiring connector from the power steering pressure switch

13.67a Disconnecting camshaft sensor wiring connector – 1.4 litre DOHC

13.67b Camshaft position sensor – 2.0 litre engine

Camshaft position sensor

65 On 2.0 litre DOHC engines the camshaft position sensor is located on the left-hand end of the exhaust camshaft cylinder head cover. On 1.4 litre DOHC engines the camshaft position sensor is located on the left-hand end of the inlet camshaft side at the rear of the cylinder head. On 1.4 litre models with pulse air injection, the camshaft position sensor is fitted to the rear of the coolant outlet housing on the left-hand end of the cylinder head.

66 Disconnect the battery negative terminal.

67 Disconnect the wiring connector then unscrew the retaining bolt and remove the sensor from the cylinder head/cover (see illustrations).

68 Refitting is the reverse of removal ensuring the sensor seal is in good condition.

Throttle valve positioner motor

69 The throttle valve positioner motor (where fitted) is integral with the throttle body, and is not available separately.

Accelerator pedal position sensor

70 The sensor is integral with the accelerator pedal assembly – see Section 4.

---

14 Inlet manifold – removal and refitting

Removal

Note: *Refer to the warning note in Section 1 before proceeding.*

1 Disconnect the battery negative terminal.

1.1 and 1.4 litre SOHC models

2 Remove the fuel rail and injectors as described in Section 13.

3 If not already done, disconnect the wiring connectors from the throttle housing components then unclip the harness and position it clear of the manifold

1.4 DOHC, 1.6 and 2.0 litre models

4 Remove the throttle housing as described in Section 12.

All models

5 Release the retaining clips and disconnect the vacuum servo unit pipe and purge valve pipe from the inlet manifold (see illustrations).

6 Disconnect all wiring connectors from the manifold, having first noted their fitted positions. Release the wiring from any retaining clips.

14.5a Disconnect the braking system servo vacuum pipe . . .

14.5b . . . the purge valve pipe from the inlet manifold – 1.4 litre engine . . .

14.5c . . . and purge valve pipe (arrowed) from the manifold – 1.6 litre engine . . .

14.5d . . . and 2.0 litre engine vacuum pipes (arrowed)

14.9a Inlet manifold nuts (arrowed) –
1.4 litre engine

14.9b Note the centre bracket (arrowed)
fitted to the 1.6 litre engine

14.9c Withdraw the manifold – 2.0 litre
engine

14.10a Ensure the new sealing rings are
correctly fitted to the manifold prior to
refitting . . .

14.10b . . . 1.4 litre DOHC engine . . .

14.10c . . . and 2.0 litre engine

7 Depress the release button and disconnect the fuel pipe and position it clear of the manifold.

8 Where necessary, undo the retaining bolts and remove the support bracket from the underside of the manifold.

9 Undo the manifold retaining nuts and withdraw the manifold from the engine compartment. Recover the four manifold seals and discard them; new ones must be used on refitting **(see illustrations)**.

Refitting

10 Refitting is a reverse of the relevant removal procedure, noting the following points:

a) *Ensure that the manifold and cylinder head mating surfaces are clean and dry, then locate the new seals in their recesses in the manifold* **(see illustrations)**. *Refit the manifold and tighten its retaining nuts to the specified torque.*

b) *Ensure that all relevant hoses are reconnected to their original positions and are securely held (where necessary) by the retaining clips.*

c) *Ensure the wiring is correctly routed and all connectors are securely reconnected.*

d) *Adjust the accelerator cable (where fitted) as described in Section 3.*

15 Exhaust manifold –
removal and refitting

Removal

All models except 2.0 litre models

Note: *On 1.4 litre DOHC engines it will be necessary to remove the alternator and mounting bracket first, see Chapter 5A.*

1 Disconnect the battery earth/negative lead, as described in Chapter 5A.

2 Slacken and remove the retaining screws and remove the shroud from the top of the exhaust manifold. It may be necessary to remove the engine lifting eye bracket from the left-hand end of the cylinder head, and undo the bolt and remove the oil dipstick tube **(see illustrations)**.

3 Firmly apply the handbrake, and then jack up the front of the vehicle and support it on axle stands (see *Jacking and vehicle support*). Release the screws and remove the engine undershield (where fitted).

4 On some models, a second heat shield is fitted on the underside of the manifold, above the oil filter. Undo the bolts and remove the heat shield.

5 Trace the oxygen sensors wiring back to the connectors and disconnect them.

6 Undo the nuts securing the exhaust front pipe to the manifold, and then remove the bolt securing the front pipe to its mounting bracket. Disconnect the front pipe from the manifold, and recover the gasket.

Caution: Do not place any strain on the flexible section of the exhaust front pipe (where fitted) as it is easily damaged.

7 Undo the retaining nuts securing the manifold to the head. Manoeuvre the manifold out of the engine compartment, and discard the manifold gasket(s).

2.0 litre models

8 Rotate the 6 fasteners 90° anti-clockwise and remove the plastic cover from the top of the engine.

15.2a Undo the heat shield bolts
(arrowed) . . .

15.2b . . . and the dipstick guide tube
retaining bolt (arrowed)

16.5 Disconnect the oxygen sensor wiring connector and free it from its bracket

16.6 Front pipe-to-manifold nuts (arrowed)

9 Remove the right-hand driveshaft as described in Chapter 8.
10 Undo the bolts and remove the heat shield from the exhaust manifold and right-hand driveshaft.
11 Undo the bolt and remove the exhaust pipe-to-manifold clamp.
12 Trace the oxygen sensors wiring back to the connectors and unplug them.
13 Release the exhaust system from its mounting points and lower the front pipe. Support the front pipe with a block of wood – do not let it hang unsupported.
14 Working underneath the vehicle, undo the bolts and remove the engine movement limiter link (see Chapter 2C).
15 Place a sheet of thick cardboard over the rear face of the radiator, and tilt the engine forward a little. Wedge it in this position using a block of wood.
16 Undo the manifold-to-cylinder head nuts, and manoeuvre the manifold from the vehicle. Discard the gasket.

Refitting

17 Refitting is the reverse of the removal procedure, noting the following points:
  a) *Examine all the exhaust manifold studs for signs of damage and corrosion; remove all traces of corrosion, and repair or renew any damaged studs.*
  b) *Ensure that the manifold and cylinder head sealing faces are clean and flat, and fit the new manifold gasket(s). Tighten the*

manifold retaining nuts to the specified torque.
  c) *Reconnect the front pipe to the manifold using the information given in Section 16.*
  d) *Where necessary, renew the oil dipstick tube O-ring.*
  e) *On 1.4 litre DOHC models, refit the alternator with reference to Chapter 5A.*

16 Exhaust system – general information, removal and refitting

General information

1 The exhaust system consists of four sections; the front pipe, the intermediate pipe, the catalytic converter and the tailpipe. All of the exhaust sections, are joined by flanged joints. The front pipe joints are secured by nuts and bolts, the intermediate pipe joint being of the spring-loaded ball type, to allow for movement in the exhaust system, and the other joints are secured by clamping rings.
2 The system is suspended throughout its entire length by rubber mountings.

Removal

3 Each exhaust section can be removed individually or, alternatively, the complete system can be removed as a unit. Even if only one part of the system needs attention, it is often easier to remove the whole system and separate the sections on the bench.

4 To remove the system or part of the system, first jack up the front or rear of the car and support it on axle stands (see *Jacking and vehicle support*). Alternatively, position the car over an inspection pit or on car ramps.

Front pipe

5 Trace the wiring back from oxygen sensor to its wiring connector. Disconnect the connector and free the wiring from all its clips and ties so the sensor is free to be removed with the front pipe **(see illustration)**.
6 Undo the nuts securing the front pipe flange joint to the manifold, and the single bolt securing the front pipe to its mounting bracket **(see illustration)**. Separate the flange joint and collect the gasket.
7 Slacken and remove the two nuts securing the front pipe flange joint to the intermediate pipe, and recover the spring cups and springs **(see illustration)**. Remove the bolts and collars, and then withdraw the front pipe from underneath the vehicle. Recover the wire-mesh gasket.

Intermediate pipe

8 Undo the two nuts securing the front pipe flange joint to the intermediate pipe **(see illustration 16.7)**. Recover the springs and spring cups, and withdraw the bolts and collars.
9 Slacken and remove the nut, washer and bolt from the catalytic converter clamping ring and disengage the clamp from the flange joint **(see illustration)**.
10 Free the intermediate pipe and withdraw it from underneath the vehicle **(see illustration)**. Recover the wire-mesh gasket from the front pipe joint.

Catalytic converter

11 On 1.4 litre engine models with pulse air injection, trace the wiring back from the catalytic converter oxygen sensor to its wiring connector. Disconnect the connector and free the wiring from all its clips and ties so the sensor is free to be removed with the converter.
12 On all engines, slacken and remove the nut, washer and bolt from each of the clamping rings and disengage the clamps from the flange joints.

16.7 Front pipe-to-intermediate pipe spring-loaded joint

16.9 Slacken and remove the nut, washer and bolt then free the clamping ring from the flange joint

16.10 Free the intermediate pipe from the catalytic converter and remove it from the vehicle

16.13 Free the catalytic converter pipe from its rear mounting (arrowed) and remove it from the vehicle

16.14 Tailpipe clamping ring (1) and rubber mountings (2)

16.19a Undo the retaining nuts and fasteners (slacken the centre screws then pull out the complete fastener) . . .

13 Free the catalytic converter from its mounting rubber and withdraw it from underneath the vehicle **(see illustration)**.

Tailpipe

14 Slacken and remove the nut, washer and bolt from the tailpipe clamping ring and disengage the clamp from the flange joint **(see illustration)**.

15 Unhook the tailpipe from its mounting rubbers and remove it from the vehicle.

Complete system (minus front pipe)

16 On 1.4 litre engine models with pulse air injection, trace the wiring back from the catalytic converter oxygen sensor to its wiring connector. Disconnect the connector and free the wiring from all its clips and ties so the sensor is free to be removed with the converter.

17 On all engines, undo the two nuts securing the front pipe flange joint to the intermediate pipe. Recover the springs and spring cups, and withdraw the bolts and collars.

18 Free the system from all its mounting rubbers and lower it from under the vehicle. Recover the wire-mesh gasket from the front pipe joint.

Heat shield(s)

19 The heat shields are secured to the underside of the body by various nuts and fasteners. If a shield is being removed to gain access to a component located behind it, remove the retaining nuts and/or fastener (unscrew the centre screw then pull out the complete fastener), and manoeuvre the shield out of position **(see illustrations)**. On some models it may be necessary to free the exhaust system from its mountings to gain the clearance necessary to remove the larger heat shield.

Refitting

20 Each section of exhaust is refitted by reversing the removal sequence, noting the following points:

a) *Ensure that all traces of corrosion have been removed from the flanges and renew all necessary gaskets.*

b) *Inspect the rubber mountings for signs of damage or deterioration, and renew as necessary.*

c) *Where joints are secured together by a clamping ring, apply a smear of exhaust*

16.19b . . . and manoeuvre the various heat shields away from the vehicle

system jointing paste to the flange joint to ensure a gas-tight seal. Insert the bolt through the clamping ring and fit the washer. Ensure the bolt and washer cut-outs are correctly engaged with the clamping ring then securely tighten the nut.

d) *Prior to tightening the exhaust system fasteners, ensure that all rubber mountings are correctly located, and that there is adequate clearance between the exhaust system and vehicle underbody.*

Chapter 4 Part B:
Fuel and exhaust systems – diesel models

Contents

Degrees of difficulty

Easy, suitable for novice with little experience 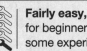	**Fairly easy,** suitable for beginner with some experience	**Fairly difficult,** suitable for competent DIY mechanic	**Difficult,** suitable for experienced DIY mechanic	**Very difficult,** suitable for expert DIY or professional

Specifications

General
System type . . . .   HDi (High-pressure Diesel injection) with full electronic control, direct injection and turbocharger

Designation:
  1.4 litre . . . .   Bosch EDC 16
  2.0 litre . . . .   Bosch EDC 15C2
Firing order . . . .   1-3-4-2 (No 1 at flywheel end)
Fuel system operating pressure . . . .   200 to 1350 bars (according to engine speed)
Idle speed . . . .   800 ± 20 rpm (controlled by ECU)
Engine cut-off speed . . . .   5000 rpm (controlled by ECU)

High-pressure fuel pump
Type:
  1.4 litre CP3.2
  2.0 litre . . . .   Bosch CP 1
Direction of rotation . . . .   Clockwise, viewed from sprocket end

Injectors
Type . . . .   Electromagnetic

Turbocharger
Type:
  1.4 litre . . . .   KKK
  2.0 litre . . . .   Garrett GT15 or KKK K03
Boost pressure (approximate) . . . .   1 bar at 3000 rpm

Torque wrench settings

	Nm	lbf ft
Accumulator rail mounting bolts	23	17
Accumulator rail-to-fuel injector fuel pipe unions*:		
1.4 litre engine:		
Stage 1	17	13
Stage 2	22	16
2.0 litre engines:		
Injector end union:		
Stage 1	25	18
Stage 2	27	20
Rail end union:		
Stage 1	24	18
Stage 2	26	19
Camshaft position sensor bolt (1.4 litre engine).	5	4
Clamping ring nuts.	20	15
Crankshaft speed/position sensor (1.4 litre engine).	5	4
Exhaust manifold nuts	20	15
Exhaust system fasteners:		
Catalytic converter-to-manifold nuts	40	30
Fuel injector clamp bolt:		
1.4 litre engine	20	15
2.0 litre engine	30	22
Fuel injector clamp stud.	7	5
Fuel pressure sensor to accumulator rail	45	33
Fuel pump-to-accumulator rail fuel pipe unions*:		
1.4 litre engine:		
Stage 1	17	13
Stage 2	22	16
2.0 litre engines:		
Rail end union:		
Stage 1	24	18
Stage 2	26	19
Pump end union:		
Stage 1	8	6
Stage 2	26	19
High-pressure fuel pump front mounting bolts/nuts	25	18
High-pressure fuel pump rear mounting bolts/nut (8 mm)	17	13
High-pressure fuel pump sprocket nut.	50	37
Turbocharger mounting bolts/nuts.	25	18
Turbocharger oil feed pipe banjo bolts.	25	18

These torque settings are using Peugeot crow's-foot adaptors – see Section 2

---

1 General information and system operation

The fuel system consists of a rear-mounted fuel tank and fuel lift pump, a fuel filter with integral water separator, on some models a fuel cooler mounted under the car, and an electronically-controlled High-pressure Diesel injection (HDi) system, together with a turbocharger.

The exhaust system is conventional, but to meet the latest emission levels an unregulated catalytic converter and an exhaust gas recirculation system are fitted to all models. On some 2.0 litre models, an exhaust emission particulate filter is fitted – refer to Chapter 4C for further details.

The HDi system (generally known as a 'common rail' system) derives its name from the fact that a common rail (referred to as an accumulator rail), or fuel reservoir, is used to supply fuel to all the fuel injectors. Instead of an in-line or distributor type injection pump, which distributes the fuel directly to

each injector, a high-pressure pump is used, which generates a very high fuel pressure (1350 bars at high engine speed) in the accumulator rail. The accumulator rail stores fuel, and maintains a constant fuel pressure, with the aid of a pressure control valve. Each injector is supplied with high-pressure fuel from the accumulator rail, and the injectors are individually controlled via signals from the system electronic control unit (ECU). The injectors are electromagnetically operated.

In addition to the various sensors used on models with a conventional fuel injection pump; common rail systems also have a fuel pressure sensor. The fuel pressure sensor allows the ECU to maintain the required fuel pressure, via the pressure control valve.

System operation

For the purposes of describing the operation of a common rail injection system, the components can be divided into three sub-systems; the low-pressure fuel system, the high-pressure fuel system and the electronic control system.

Low-pressure fuel system

The low-pressure fuel system consists of the following components:
a) Fuel tank.
b) Fuel lift pump.
c) Fuel cooler (not all models).
d) Fuel heater (not all models).
e) Fuel filter/water trap.
f) Low-pressure fuel lines.

The low-pressure system (fuel supply system) is responsible for supplying clean fuel to the high-pressure fuel system.

High-pressure fuel system

The high-pressure fuel system consists of the following components:
a) High-pressure fuel pump with pressure control valve.
b) High-pressure fuel accumulator rail.
c) Fuel injectors.
d) High-pressure fuel lines.

After passing through the fuel filter, the fuel reaches the high-pressure pump, which forces it into the accumulator rail. As diesel fuel has a certain elasticity, the pressure in the accumulator rail remains constant, even though fuel leaves the rail each time one of the injectors operates. Additionally, a pressure control valve mounted on the high-pressure pump ensures that the fuel pressure is maintained within preset limits.

The pressure control valve is operated by the ECU. When the valve is opened, fuel is returned from the high-pressure pump to the tank, via the fuel return lines, and the pressure in the accumulator rail falls. To enable the ECU to trigger the pressure control valve correctly, the pressure in the accumulator rail is measured by a fuel pressure sensor.

The electromagnetically controlled fuel injectors are operated individually, via signals from the ECU, and each injector injects fuel directly into the relevant combustion chamber. The fact that high fuel pressure is always available allows very precise and highly flexible injection in comparison to a conventional injection pump: for example combustion during the main injection process can be improved considerably by the pre-injection of a very small quantity of fuel.

Electronic control system

The electronic control system consists of the following components:

a) Electronic control unit (ECU).
b) Crankshaft speed/position sensor.
c) Camshaft position sensor.
d) Accelerator pedal position sensor.
e) Coolant temperature sensor.
f) Fuel temperature sensor.
g) Air mass meter.
h) Fuel pressure sensor.
i) Fuel injectors.
j) Fuel pressure control valve.
k) Preheating control unit.
l) EGR solenoid valve.

The information from the various sensors is passed to the ECU, which evaluates the signals. The ECU contains electronic 'maps' which enable it to calculate the optimum quantity of fuel to inject, the appropriate start of injection, and even pre- and post-injection fuel quantities, for each individual engine cylinder under any given condition of engine operation.

Additionally, the ECU carries out monitoring and self-diagnostic functions. Any faults in the system are stored in the ECU memory, which enables quick and accurate fault diagnosis using appropriate diagnostic equipment (such as a suitable fault code reader).

System Components

High-pressure pump

The high-pressure pump is mounted on the engine in the position normally occupied by the conventional distributor fuel injection pump. The pump is driven at half engine speed by the timing belt, and is lubricated by the fuel, which it pumps.

The fuel lift pump forces the fuel into the high-pressure pump chamber, via a safety valve.

The high-pressure pump consists of three radially-mounted pistons and cylinders. The pistons are operated by an eccentric cam mounted on the pump drive spindle. As a piston moves down, fuel enters the cylinder through an inlet valve. When the piston reaches bottom dead centre (BDC), the inlet valve closes, and as the piston moves back up the cylinder, the fuel is compressed. When the pressure in the cylinder reaches the pressure in the accumulator rail, an outlet valve opens, and fuel is forced into the accumulator rail. When the piston reaches top dead centre (TDC), the outlet valve closes, due to the pressure drop, and the pumping cycle is repeated. The use of multiple cylinders provides a steady flow of fuel, minimising pulses and pressure fluctuations.

As the pump needs to be able to supply sufficient fuel under full-load conditions, it will supply excess fuel during idle and part-load conditions. This excess fuel is returned from the high-pressure circuit to the low-pressure circuit (to the tank) via the pressure control valve.

The pump incorporates a facility to effectively switch off one of the cylinders to improve efficiency and reduce fuel consumption when maximum pumping capacity is not required. When this facility is operated, a solenoid-operated needle holds the inlet valve in the relevant cylinder open during the delivery stroke, preventing the fuel from being compressed.

Accumulator rail

As its name suggests, the accumulator rail acts as an accumulator, storing fuel and preventing pressure fluctuations. Fuel enters the rail from the high-pressure pump, and each injector has its own connection to the rail. The fuel pressure sensor is mounted in the rail, and the rail also has a connection to the fuel pressure control valve on the pump.

Pressure control valve

The pressure control valve is operated by the ECU, and controls the system pressure. The valve is integral with the high-pressure pump and cannot be separated.

If the fuel pressure is excessive, the valve opens, and fuel flows back to the tank. If the pressure is too low, the valve closes, enabling the high-pressure pump to increase the pressure.

The valve is an electromagnetically operated ball valve. The ball is forced against its seat, against the fuel pressure, by a powerful spring, and also by the force provided by the electromagnet. The force generated by the electromagnet is directly proportional to the current applied to it by the ECU. The desired pressure can therefore be set by varying the current applied to the electromagnet. Any pressure fluctuations are damped by the spring.

Fuel pressure sensor

The fuel pressure sensor is mounted in the accumulator rail, and provides very precise information on the fuel pressure to the ECU.

Fuel injector

The injectors are mounted on the engine in a similar manner to conventional diesel fuel injectors. The injectors are electromagnetically operated via signals from the ECU, and fuel is injected at the pressure existing in the accumulator rail. The injectors are high-precision instruments and are manufactured to very high tolerances.

Fuel flows into the injector from the accumulator rail, via an inlet valve and an inlet throttle, and an electromagnet causes the injector nozzle to lift from its seat, allowing injection. Excess fuel is returned from the injectors to the tank via a return line. The injector operates on a hydraulic servo principle: the forces resulting inside the injector due to the fuel pressure effectively amplify the effects of the electromagnet, which does not provide sufficient force to open the injector nozzle directly. The injector functions as follows. Five separate forces are essential to the operation of the injector.

a) A nozzle spring forces the nozzle needle against the nozzle seat at the bottom of the injector, preventing fuel from entering the combustion chamber.
b) In the valve at the top of the injector, the valve spring forces the valve ball against the opening to the valve control chamber. The fuel in the chamber is unable to escape through the fuel return.
c) When triggered, the electromagnet exerts a force which overcomes the valve spring force, and moves the valve ball away from its seat. This is the triggering force for the start of injection. When the valve ball moves off its seat, fuel enters the valve control chamber.
d) The pressure of the fuel in the valve control chamber exerts a force on the valve control plunger, which is added to the nozzle spring force.
e) A slight chamfer towards the lower end of the nozzle needle causes the fuel in the control chamber to exert a force on the nozzle needle.

When these forces are in equilibrium, the injector is in its rest (idle) state, but when a voltage is applied to the electromagnet, the forces work to lift the nozzle needle, injecting fuel into the combustion chamber. There are four phases of injector operation as follows:

a) Rest (idle) state – all forces are in equilibrium. The nozzle needle closes off the nozzle opening, and the valve spring forces the valve ball against its seat.
b) Opening – the electromagnet is triggered which opens the nozzle and triggers the injection process. The force from the electromagnet allows the valve ball to leave its seat. The fuel from the valve control chamber flows back to the tank

via the fuel return line. When the valve opens, the pressure in the valve control chamber drops, and the force on the valve plunger is reduced. However, due to the effect of the input throttle, the pressure on the nozzle needle remains unchanged. The resulting force in the valve control chamber is sufficient to lift the nozzle from its seat, and the injection process begins.

c) Injection – within a few milliseconds, the triggering current in the electromagnet is reduced to a lower holding current. The nozzle is now fully open, and fuel is injected into the combustion chamber at the pressure present in the accumulator rail.

d) Closing – the electromagnet is switched off, at which point the valve spring forces the valve ball firmly against its seat, and in the valve control chamber, the pressure is the same as that at the nozzle needle. The force at the valve plunger increases, and the nozzle needle closes the nozzle opening. The forces are now in equilibrium once more, and the injector is once more in the idle state, awaiting the next injection sequence.

ECU and sensors

The ECU and sensors are described earlier in this Section – see *Electronic control system*.

Air inlet sensor and turbocharger

An airflow sensor is fitted downstream of the air filter to monitor the quantity of air supplied to the turbocharger. The flow and routing of intake air is controlled by the engine management ECU. On these models, an engine coolant-heated matrix is fitted to the base of the air cleaner housing, to warm the incoming air, which decreases harmful exhaust emissions.

The turbochargers are of the fixed-geometry type on 2.0 litre models, and variable nozzle geometry type on the 1.4 litre model.

2 High-pressure diesel injection system – special information

Warnings and precautions

1 It is essential to observe strict precautions when working on the fuel system components, particularly the high-pressure side of the system. Before carrying out any operations on the fuel system, refer to the precautions given in *Safety first!* at the beginning of this manual, and to the following additional information.

• Do not carry out any repair work on the high-pressure fuel system unless you are competent to do so, have all the necessary tools and equipment required, and are aware of the safety implications involved.

• Before starting any repair work on the fuel system, wait at least 30 seconds

2.4 Typical plastic plug and cap set for sealing disconnected fuel pipes and components

after switching off the engine to allow the fuel circuit pressure to reduce.

• Never work on the high-pressure fuel system with the engine running.

• Keep well clear of any possible source of fuel leakage, particularly when starting the engine after carrying out repair work. A leak in the system could cause an extremely high-pressure jet of fuel to escape, which could result in severe personal injury.

• Never place your hands or any part of your body near to a leak in the high-pressure fuel system.

• Do not use steam cleaning equipment or compressed air to clean the engine or any of the fuel system components.

Procedures and information

2 Strict cleanliness must be observed at all times when working on any part of the fuel system. This applies to the working area in general, the person doing the work, and the components being worked on.

3 Before working on the fuel system components, they must be thoroughly cleaned with a suitable degreasing fluid. Specific cleaning products may be obtained from Peugeot dealers. Alternatively, a suitable brake cleaning fluid may be used. Cleanliness is particularly important when working on the fuel system connections at the following components:

a) Fuel filter.
b) High-pressure fuel pump.
c) Accumulator rail.
d) Fuel injectors.
e) High-pressure fuel pipes.

4 After disconnecting any fuel pipes or components, the open union or orifice must be immediately sealed to prevent the entry of dirt or foreign material. Plastic plugs and caps in various sizes are available in packs from motor factors and accessory outlets, and are particularly suitable for this application (see illustration). Fingers cut from disposable rubber gloves should be used to protect components such as fuel pipes, fuel injectors and wiring connectors, and can be secured in place using elastic bands. Suitable gloves of this type are available at no cost from most petrol station forecourts.

5 Whenever any of the high-pressure fuel

2.7 Two crow's-foot adaptors will be necessary for tightening the fuel pipe unions

pipes are disconnected or removed, new pipes must be obtained for refitting.

6 On the completion of any repair on the high-pressure fuel system, Peugeot recommend the use of a leak-detecting compound. This is a powder which is applied to the fuel pipe unions and connections and is white when dry. Any leak in the system will cause the product to darken indicating the source of the leak.

7 The torque wrench settings given in the Specifications must be strictly observed when tightening component mountings and connections. This is particularly important when tightening the high-pressure fuel pipe unions. To enable a torque wrench to be used on the fuel pipe unions, two Peugeot crow's-foot adaptors are required. Suitable alternatives are available from motor factors and accessory outlets (see illustration).

3 Fuel system – priming and bleeding

1 Should the fuel supply system be disconnected between the fuel tank and high-pressure pump, it is necessary to prime the fuel system. This is achieved by operating the hand priming pump until resistance is felt (2.0 litre models) or fuel appears in the transparent fuel supply pipe in the engine compartment (1.4 litre models) (see illustration). Remove the plastic cover from the top of the engine to access the priming

3.1 Operate the hand priming pump until fuel clear of bubbles appears in the fuel pipe (arrowed) – 1.4 litre engine

4.3a Slacken the clip and disconnect the turbo outlet hose (arrowed) . . .

4.3b . . . then undo the retaining bolts (arrowed) . . .

4.3c . . . pivot the right-hand end of the box up and disengage it from the turbo outlet stud (arrowed)

pump. **Note:** *A hand priming pump is not fitted to all 2.0 litre models.*
2 Once this is achieved, operate the starter until the engine starts.

| 4 | Air cleaner assembly and inlet ducts – removal and refitting |

Air cleaner & inlet ducts removal

1.4 litre models

1 Pull the plastic engine cover up and remove it.
2 Slacken the turbocharger inlet hose clip, and release the diesel priming bulb from its

brackets at the right-hand end of the housing.
3 Slacken the clip securing the turbo outlet hose, undo the bolt securing the resonator box, and the bolt securing the resonator box to the turbocharger, swivel the box up and remove it **(see illustrations)**.
4 Undo the two screws and remove the air cleaner housing, disconnecting any wiring plugs as necessary as the housing is withdrawn **(see illustrations)**.
5 To remove the air inlet ducting, slacken the retaining clips and remove the relevant section of ducting. Some of the air ducting in the engine compartment may be retained by plastic expansion rivets. Push down the centre pin then pull the entire rivet from place **(see illustration)**. The air deflector in the left-

hand front corner of the engine compartment simply lifts from place and, upon refitting, located over a clip on the front of the electrical box. The ducting at the rear of the engine is only accessible once the battery tray has been removed (see Chapter 5A).

2.0 litre models

6 Undo the four fasteners and lift off the engine cover **(see illustrations)**.
7 Disconnect the air mass meter wiring plug.
8 Slacken the retaining clips and disconnect the flexible air inlet duct from the air mass meter **(see illustration)**.
9 Where fitted, disconnect the wiring plug from the accelerator pedal position sensor, adjacent to the air cleaner housing.

4.4a Undo the two air cleaner housing screws (arrowed)

4.4b The rear of the air cleaner housing locates in two rubber mountings (arrowed)

4.5 Push in the centre pin, then prise the complete plastic rivet (arrowed) from place, and remove the air inlet ducting

4.6a Undo the fasteners (arrowed) . . .

4.6b . . . and remove the plastic engine style cover

4.8 Slacken the clip (arrowed) and disconnect the flexible ducting from the air mass meter

4.11 Depress the clip (arrowed) and slide the housing up from the bracket

10 Rotate the accelerator pedal position sensor quadrant, and release the inner cable from the quadrant.

11 Release the retaining clip, then lift up the housing. Where fitted, slide the heater matrix out from the housing, and disconnect the water drain hose **(see illustration)**.

12 To remove the air cleaner air inlet duct, depress the retaining lug and slide the duct from the bracket **(see illustration)**.

13 Remove the front bumper as described in Chapter 11.

14 Push in the centre pins a little, then prise out the complete plastic rivets securing the inlet ducting to the bumper bar.

15 Manoeuvre the ducting from the engine compartment.

Intake air resonator removal

1.4 litre models

16 To remove the resonator, pull up and remove the plastic cover from the top of the

4.23 Air inlet ducting – 2.0 litre engine

1 Air cleaner housing bracket
2 Inlet ducting
3 Air filter element
4 Air cleaner housing
5 Air mass meter
6 Air inlet ducting
7 Rigid plastic ducting

4.12 Depress the lug (arrowed) and slide the duct from the bracket

engine, then make a note of its fitted position, and slacken the outlet ducting clamp. It must be refitted into its original position.

17 Undo the bolt securing the resonator box, and the bolt securing the turbocharger outlet pipe to the box **(see illustrations 4.3a, 4.3b and 4.3c)**.

18 Lift up the right-hand end of the ducting, and remove the box and ducting from position.

Turbocharger ducting removal

Note: *For 1.4 litre models, see Air cleaner & inlet ducts removal.*

2.0 litre models

19 The rigid ducts at the rear of the engine, connecting the turbocharger to the air inlet duct and to the inlet manifold, are inaccessible with the engine in the car. To gain access it will be necessary to remove the front suspension subframe as described in Chapter 10.

20 Once access has been gained, undo the bolt securing the duct to the inlet manifold elbow.

21 At the lower end, undo the bolt securing the duct to the turbocharger. Lift off the duct and recover the seal from the lower end.

22 Remove the turbocharger-to-inlet manifold rigid plastic duct, slacken the clamps, and release the connecting hose from the inlet manifold elbow. Slacken the clip securing the connecting hose at the lower end of the duct to the turbocharger. Release the attachment strap from the lug on the turbocharger and

5.5 Unclip the inner cable end fitting (1) from the top of the pedal then remove the retaining clip (2) securing the outer cable to the bulkhead

withdraw the duct from the engine **(see illustration)**.

23 Slacken the clamps securing the intake ducting to the intermediate manifold, undo the bolt and manoeuvre the assembly from position.

24 The remaining ducting is secured by hose clamps. Prior to removing any ducting, note the fitted positions of any vacuum hoses or electrical wiring/connections to aid refitting.

Refitting

25 Refitting is a reverse of the removal procedure. Examine the condition of the seals and retaining clips and renew if necessary.

26 Where applicable, refit the front suspension subframe as described in Chapter 10.

27 Where necessary, reconnect and adjust the accelerator cable as described in Section 5.

---

5 Accelerator cable – removal, refitting and adjustment

Note: *Some models do not have an accelerator cable fitted.*

Removal

1 Where applicable, undo the fasteners and lift off the engine cover.

2 Rotate the accelerator pedal position sensor quadrant, and release the inner cable from the quadrant. On 2.0 litre engines, working in the engine compartment, unscrew the two bolts and free the accelerator pedal position sensor bracket from the side of the air cleaner housing. Detach the accelerator inner cable from the sensor, and then pull the outer cable out from sensor bracket, complete with the spring clip.

3 Withdraw the outer cable from the grommet in the pedal position sensor body, recover the flat washer from the end of the cable and remove the spring clip.

4 Release the cable from the remaining clips and brackets in the engine compartment, noting its routing.

5 Working in the passenger compartment, reach up under the facia, depress the ends of the cable end fitting, and detach the inner cable from the top of the accelerator pedal **(see illustration)**.

6 Release the outer cable grommet from the pedal mounting bracket, then tie a length of string to the end of the cable.

7 Return to the engine compartment, release the cable grommet from the bulkhead and withdraw the cable. When the end of the cable appears, untie the string and leave it in position – it can then be used to draw the cable back into position on refitting.

Refitting

8 Refitting is a reversal of removal, but ensure that the cable is routed as noted before removal and, on completion, adjust the cable as follows.

5.10 Remove all freeplay from the cable then fit the spring clip to the last exposed groove on the outer cable (2.0 litre engine shown)

7.1 The arrows on the pump cover indicate supply and return (arrowed)

9.2 Undo the two nuts (arrowed) securing the fuel cooler

Adjustment

9 Remove the spring clip from the accelerator outer cable. Ensuring that the pedal position sensor quadrant is against its stop, gently pull the cable out of its grommet until all free play is removed from the inner cable.

10 With the cable held in this position, refit the spring clip to the last exposed outer cable groove in front of the rubber grommet and washer **(see illustration)**. When the clip is refitted and the outer cable is released, there should be only a small amount of free play in the inner cable.

11 Have an assistant depress the accelerator pedal, and check that the pedal position sensor quadrant opens fully and returns smoothly to its stop.

12 Where applicable, refit the engine cover on completion.

6 Accelerator pedal – removal and refitting

Refer to Chapter 4A.

7 Fuel lift pump – removal and refitting

The diesel fuel lift pump is located in the same position as the conventional fuel pump on petrol models, and the removal and refitting procedures are virtually identical **(see**

illustration). Refer to Chapter 4A. **Note:** *No lift pump is fitted to the 1.4 litre engine, but the fuel gauge sender unit is located in the fuel tank – the same position as other models.*

8 Fuel gauge sender unit – removal and refitting

The fuel gauge sender unit is integral with the fuel lift pump. Refer to Section 7.

9 Fuel tank and cooler – removal and refitting

Fuel tank

Refer to Chapter 4A.

Fuel cooler

Removal

1 The fuel cooler is located under the right-hand side of the vehicle, under the driver's side footwell. Jack up the rear of the vehicle, and support it on axle stands (see *Jacking and vehicle support*).

2 Working underneath the vehicle, undo the two retaining nuts, and release the cooler from the locating holes **(see illustration)**.

3 Depress the release buttons and disconnect the fuel feed and return hoses from the cooler. Be prepared for fuel spillage, and plug the

hose and cooler openings to prevent dirt ingress **(see illustration)**.

Refitting

4 Refitting is a reversal of removal,

10 High-pressure fuel pump – removal and refitting

> ⚠️ *Warning: Refer to the information contained in Section 2 before proceeding.*

Note: *A new fuel pump-to-accumulator rail high-pressure fuel pipe will be required for refitting.*

Removal

1 Disconnect the battery (see Chapter 5A) and remove the timing belt as described in Chapter 2D. After removal of the timing belt, temporarily refit the right-hand engine mounting but do not fully tighten the bolts.

1.4 litre engine

2 Remove the cylinder head cover/air filter housing as described in Chapter 2D.

3 Depress the clip buttons and disconnect the fuel supply and return hoses from the pump **(see illustration)**. Plug the end of the hoses to prevent dirt ingress.

4 Hold the pump sprocket stationary, and loosen the centre nut securing it to the pump shaft. The manufacturers recommend using an 8 mm pin inserted through the pulley and into the pump support **(see illustration)**.

9.3 Depress the release button (arrowed) and disconnect the hose

10.3 Depress the release buttons (arrowed) and disconnect the fuel supply and return hoses from the pump

10.4 Stop the fuel pump sprocket from rotating by inserting an 8 mm drill bit or pin through the sprocket into the backplate

Tool Tip 1: Make a sprocket releasing tool from a short strip of steel. Drill two holes in the strip to correspond with the two holes in the sprocket. Drill a third hole just large enough to accept the flats of the sprocket retaining nut.

5 The fuel pump sprocket is a taper fit on the pump shaft and it will be necessary to make up a tool to release it from the taper **(see Tool Tip 1)**. Partially unscrew the sprocket retaining nut, fit the home-made tool, and secure it to the sprocket with two 7.0 mm bolts and nuts. Prevent the sprocket from rotating as before, and screw down the nuts, forcing the sprocket off the shaft taper. Once the taper is released, remove the tool, unscrew the nut fully, and remove the sprocket from the pump shaft.

6 Undo the unions and remove the pump-to-accumulator rail metal pipe. Counterhold the pump union with a second spanner – the union screwed into the pump must not be

10.8b . . . and the bolts securing the bracket to the cylinder head

10.11 Undo the bolt (arrowed) to release the plastic wiring harness guide

10.6 Counterhold the pump union with a second spanner whilst slackening the accumulator-to-pump pipe union

allowed to unscrew **(see illustration)**. Discard the pipe; a new one must be fitted.

7 Disconnect the wiring plugs from the pump, noting their fitted positions.

8 Undo the nuts/bolts and remove the pump support bracket from the rear of the pump, and the bracket on the cylinder head **(see illustrations)**.

9 Remove the EGR valve with reference to Chapter 4C.

10 Undo the three bolts, and remove the pump **(see illustration)**.

Caution: The high-pressure fuel pump is manufactured to extremely close tolerances and must not be dismantled in any way. Do not unscrew the fuel pipe male union on the rear of the pump, or attempt to remove the sensor, piston de-activator switch, or the seal on the pump shaft. No

10.10 Unscrew the three bolts (arrowed) and remove the pump

10.13 Press in the buttons (arrowed) and disconnect the fuel supply and return hose quick-release fitting at the connections

10.8a Undo the pump rear support bracket bolts/nut (arrowed) . . .

parts for the pump are available separately and if the unit is in any way suspect it must be renewed.

2.0 litre engines

11 Undo the bolts securing the plastic wiring harness guide to the front of the engine **(see illustration)**. It will be necessary to lift up the wiring harness as far as possible for access to the rear of the fuel pump. If necessary, disconnect the relevant wiring connectors to enable the harness and guide assembly to be moved further for additional access.

12 Place a suitable container beneath the fuel filter, then loosen the drain plug and drain the fuel. Retighten the plug.

13 Clean the feed and supply lines to the fuel filter, then unclip the fuel filter from its bracket and disconnect the quick-release feed and supply lines **(see illustration)**. Tape over or plug the openings in the filter and lines, to prevent entry of dust and dirt.

14 Unbolt and remove the fuel filter support bracket.

15 Hold the pump pulley/sprocket stationary, and loosen the centre nut securing it to the pump shaft. The manufacturers recommend using a pin inserted through the pulley and into the cylinder head, however, a homemade forked tool engaged with the pulley holes can be used instead **(see illustration and Tool Tip 2)**.

Tool Tip 2: A sprocket holding tool can be made from two lengths of steel strip bolted together to form a forked end. Bend the ends of the strip through 90° to form the fork 'prongs'.

10.15 Using the home-made tools to remove the fuel pump sprocket

10.17 Unscrew the unions and remove the high pressure fuel pipe

10.18 Undo the nut and bolt (arrowed) securing the fuel pump rear mounting to the mounting bracket

16 The fuel pump sprocket is a taper fit on the pump shaft and it will be necessary to make up a tool to release it from the taper (**see Tool Tip 1**). Partially unscrew the sprocket retaining nut, fit the home-made tool, and secure it to the sprocket with two 7.0 mm bolts. Prevent the sprocket from rotating as before, and unscrew the sprocket retaining nut. The nut will bear against the tool, as it is undone, forcing the sprocket off the shaft taper. Once the taper is released, remove the tool, unscrew the nut fully, and remove the sprocket from the pump shaft.

17 Thoroughly clean the high-pressure fuel pipe unions on the fuel pump and accumulator rail. Using an open-ended spanner, unscrew the union nuts securing the high-pressure fuel pipe to the fuel pump and accumulator rail. Counterhold the unions on the pump and accumulator rail with a second spanner, while unscrewing the union nuts. Withdraw the high-pressure fuel pipe and plug or cover the open unions to prevent dirt entry (**see illustration**). Note that a new high-pressure fuel pipe will be required for refitting. **Note:** *The fuel lines must be renewed every time they are removed, as it is possible for minute metal particles to enter them as a result of tightening the union nuts. If these particles enter the fuel injectors, fuel at high-pressure can enter the combustion chambers unrestricted.*

18 Unscrew the nut and bolt securing the fuel pump rear mounting to the mounting bracket (**see illustration**).

19 Disconnect the wiring connector at the pressure control valve on the rear of the fuel

pump (orange wire), and at the piston de-activator switch on the top of the pump.

20 Disconnect the low-pressure hoses from the fuel pump, then tape over the openings. Move the hoses to one side.

21 Unscrew the nut and two bolts securing the front of the fuel pump to the mounting bracket (**see illustrations**). Withdraw the pump and lift it off the engine.

Caution: The high-pressure fuel pump is manufactured to extremely close tolerances and must not be dismantled in any way. Do not unscrew the fuel pipe male union on the rear of the pump, or attempt to remove the pressure control valve, piston de-activator switch, or the seal on the pump shaft. No parts for the pump are available separately and if the unit is in any way suspect it must be renewed.

Refitting

1.4 litre engine

22 Locate the pump in the mounting bracket, and refit the three mounting screws. Tighten them to the specified torque.

23 Refit the sprocket to the pump shaft, and tighten the retaining nut to the specified torque, holding the sprocket by the same method used on removal.

24 Reconnect the pump wiring plugs.

25 Refit the pump rear support bracket, tightening the bolts/nut to the specified torque.

26 Refit the EGR valve (see Chapter 4C).

27 Fit a new metal fuel pipe between the pump and the accumulator rail. The unions at

each end of the pipe must be tightened to the specified torque in two stages. Use a second spanner to counterhold the union screwed into the pump. Do not allow the union to move.

28 The remainder of refitting is a reversal of removal.

2.0 litre engines

29 Locate the pump on the mounting bracket, and refit the front retaining nut and the two bolts. Refit the nut and bolt securing the fuel pump rear mounting to the mounting bracket, and then tighten all the mountings to the specified torque.

30 Refit the low pressure hoses and tighten the clips.

31 Reconnect the wiring to the pressure control valve and piston de-activator switch.

32 Refit the mounting bracket to the rear of the fuel pump and tighten the bolts.

33 Remove the blanking plugs from the fuel pipe unions on the pump and accumulator rail. Locate a new high-pressure fuel pipe over the unions and screw on the union nuts finger tight at this stage.

34 Refit the pump sprocket and retaining nut and tighten the nut to the specified torque. Prevent the sprocket rotating as the nut is tightened using the sprocket holding tool.

35 Using a torque wrench and crow's-foot adaptor, tighten the fuel pipe union nuts to the specified torque. Counterhold the unions on the pump and accumulator rail with an open-ended spanner, while tightening the union nuts (**see illustration**).

36 Reposition and secure the plastic wiring

10.21a Fuel pump front mounting bolts (arrowed) . . .

10.21b . . . and mounting nut (arrowed)

10.35 Tighten the fuel pipe union nuts using a torque wrench and crow's-foot adaptor

harness guide to the front of the engine, and reconnect any additional wiring disconnected for access.

37 Refit the filter mounting bracket to the engine and securely tighten the retaining bolts. Locate the fuel filter back in position in the mounting bracket.

38 Remove the blanking plugs and reconnect the supply and return hose quick-release fittings at the fuel filter, and at the connections above the fuel pump. Secure the hoses with their respective retaining clips.

All engines

39 Refit the timing belt as described in Chapter 2D.

40 With everything reassembled and reconnected, and observing the precautions listed in Section 2, start the engine and allow it to idle. Check for leaks at the high-pressure fuel pipe unions with the engine idling. If satisfactory, increase the engine speed to 4000 rpm and check again for leaks.

41 Take the car for a short road test and check for leaks once again on return. If any leaks are detected, obtain and fit another new high-pressure fuel pipe. **Do not** attempt to cure even the slightest leak by further tightening of the pipe unions. During the road test, initialise the engine management ECU as follows. Engage third gear and stabilise the engine at 1000 rpm, then accelerate fully up to 3500 rpm.

11 Accumulator rail – removal and refitting

⚠ Warning: *Refer to the information contained in Section 2 before proceeding.*
Note: *A complete new set of high-pressure fuel pipes will be required for refitting.*

Removal

1 Disconnect the battery (refer to Chapter 5A).
2 Remove the plastic cover from the top of the engine. On 1.4 litre models, the cover pulls up from place; on 2.0 litre models, undo the four fasteners and lift away the cover.

1.4 litre models

3 Remove the cylinder head cover/air filter housing as described in Chapter 2D.

4 Clean the area around the high-pressure fuel pipes to and from the accumulator rail, then unscrew the pump-to-accumulator rail pipe unions. Use a second spanner to counterhold the union screwed in to the pump body **(see illustration 10.6)**. The screwed-in union must not be allowed to move. Remove the pipe.

5 Repeat the procedure on the accumulator rail-to-injector fuel pipes. Use a second spanner to counterhold the unions screwed in to the injectors **(see illustration)**. These unions must not be allowed to move. Note their fitted locations and remove the pipes.

6 Plug the openings in the accumulator rail and fuel pump to prevent dirt ingress.

7 Disconnect the pressure sensor wiring plug from the accumulator rail **(see illustration)**.

8 Disconnect the fuel return pipe from the rail **(see illustration)**.

9 Unscrew the two rail mounting bolts and

11.5 Use a second spanner to counterhold the fuel injector unions whilst slackening the pipe unions

11.8 Depress the release button (arrowed) and disconnect the fuel return hose

11.10a Disconnect the wiring connectors at the fuel injectors . . .

manoeuvre it from place **(see illustration)**.
Note: *Peugeot insist that the fuel pressure sensor on the accumulator rail must not be removed.*

2.0 litre models

10 Disconnect the wiring connectors at the fuel injectors and at the piston de-activator switch on the top of the fuel pump **(see illustrations)**.

11 Release the retaining clip and disconnect the crankcase ventilation hose from the cylinder head cover. Position it to one side, then remove the plastic engine cover support bracket from the right-hand front end of the engine.

12 Undo the two nuts securing the plastic wiring harness guide to the cylinder head. Lift the guide off the two mounting studs and move it clear of the accumulator rail **(see illustration)**. Disconnect any additional

11.7 Disconnect the accumulator rail pressure sensor wiring plug

11.9 Remove the accumulator rail mounting bolts (arrowed)

11.10b . . . and at the piston de-activator switch on top of the fuel pump

11.12 Undo the two nuts and lift off the plastic wiring harness guide

11.16a Using two spanners, unscrew the fuel pipe unions at the accumulator rail . . .

11.16b . . . and at each injector

wiring connectors as necessary to enable the harness and guide assembly to be moved further for increased access.

13 At the connections above the fuel pump, disconnect the fuel supply and return hose quick-release fittings using a small screwdriver to release the locking clip. Suitably plug or cover the open unions to prevent dirt entry.

14 Similarly disconnect the supply and return hose quick-release fittings at the fuel filter, and plug or cover the open unions. Release the fuel hoses from the relevant retaining clips.

15 Thoroughly clean all the high-pressure fuel pipe unions on the accumulator rail, fuel pump and injectors. Using an open-ended spanner, unscrew the union nuts securing the high-pressure fuel pipe to the fuel pump and accumulator rail. Counterhold the unions on the pump and accumulator rail with a second spanner, while unscrewing the union nuts. Withdraw the high-pressure fuel pipe and plug or cover the open unions to prevent dirt entry.

16 Again using two spanners, hold the unions and unscrew the union nuts securing the high-pressure fuel pipes to the fuel injectors and accumulator rail **(see illustrations)**. Withdraw the high-pressure fuel pipes and plug or cover the open unions to prevent dirt entry.

17 Disconnect the wiring connector fuel pressure sensor on the accumulator rail.

11.18 Undo the three accumulator rail mounting bolts (arrowed)

18 Undo the three bolts securing the accumulator rail to the cylinder head and withdraw the rail from its location **(see illustration)**.

Caution: Do not attempt to remove the four high-pressure fuel pipe male unions from the accumulator rail. These parts are not available separately and if disturbed are likely to result in fuel leakage on reassembly.

Refitting

19 Locate the accumulator rail in position, refit and finger-tighten the mounting bolts.

20 Reconnect the accumulator pressure sensor wiring plug.

21 Fit the new pump-to-rail high pressure pipe, and only finger-tighten the unions at first, then tighten the unions to the Stage 1 torque setting, followed by the Stage 2 torque setting. Use a second spanner to counterhold the union screwed into the pump body.

22 Fit the new set of rail-to-injector high pressure pipes, and finger tighten the unions. If it's not possible to fit the new pipes to the injector unions, remove and refit the injectors as described in Section 12, and try again.

23 Tighten the accumulator mounting bolts to the specified torque.

24 Tighten the rail-to-injector pipe unions to the Stage 1 torque setting, followed by the Stage 2 setting. Use a second spanner to counterhold the injector unions.

25 The remainder of refitting is a reversal of removal, noting the following points:

a) *Ensure all wiring connectors and harnesses are correctly refitting and secured.*

b) *Reconnect the battery as described in Chapter 5A.*

c) *Observing the precautions listed in Section 2, start the engine and allow it to idle. Check for leaks at the high-pressure fuel pipe unions with the engine idling. If satisfactory, increase the engine speed to 4000 rpm and check again for leaks. Take the car for a short road test and check for leaks once again on return. If any leaks*

are detected, obtain and fit additional new high-pressure fuel pipes as required. Do not attempt to cure even the slightest leak by further tightening of the pipe unions. During the road test, initialise the engine management ECU as follows. Engage third gear and stabilise the engine at 1000 rpm, then accelerate fully up to 3500 rpm.

12 Fuel injectors – removal and refitting

⚠ *Warning: Refer to the information contained in Section 2 before proceeding.*

Note: *The following procedure describes the removal and refitting of the injectors as a complete set, however each injector may be removed individually if required. New copper washers, upper seals, injector clamp retaining nuts and a high-pressure fuel pipe will be required for each disturbed injector when refitting.*

Removal

1 Remove the plastic cover from the top of the engine. On 1.4 litre models, the cover pulls up from place; on 2.0 litre models, undo the four screws and lift away the cover.

1.4 litre models

2 Remove the cylinder head cover/air filter housing as described in Chapter 2D.

3 Clean the area around the high-pressure fuel pipes between the injectors and the accumulator rail, then unscrew the pipe unions. Use a second spanner to counterhold the union screwed in to the injector body **(see illustration 11.5)**. The injectors screwed-in unions must not be allowed to move. Remove the pipes. Plug the openings in the accumulator rail and injectors to prevent dirt ingress.

4 Extract the retaining circlip and disconnect

12.4 Prise out the circlip and disconnect the fuel leak-off pipe

12.5a Undo the injector clamp bolt . . .

12.5b . . . and remove the clamp

the leak-off pipe from each fuel injector **(see illustration)**.

5 Unscrew the injector retaining bolt, and remove the clamp. If loose, recover the clamp locating dowel from the cylinder head **(see illustrations)**.

6 Carefully pull or lever the injector from place. Do not lever against or pull on the solenoid housing at the top of the injector.

7 Remove the copper washer and the upper seal from each injector, or from the cylinder head if they remained in place during injector removal **(see illustration)**. New copper washers and upper seals will be required for refitting. Cover the injector hole in the cylinder head to prevent dirt ingress.

8 Examine each injector visually for any signs of obvious damage or deterioration. If any defects are apparent, renew the injector(s).
Caution: The injectors are manufactured to extremely close tolerances and must not be dismantled in any way. Do not unscrew the fuel pipe union on the side of the injector, or separate any parts of the injector body. Do not attempt to clean carbon deposits from the injector nozzle or carry out any form of ultrasonic or pressure testing.

2.0 litre models

9 Disconnect the battery (see Chapter 5A), then unscrew the four fasteners and remove

12.5c If it's loose, remove the locating dowel (arrowed)

the plastic cover from the top of the engine.

10 Disconnect the wiring connectors at the fuel injectors **(see illustration)**.

11 Release the retaining clip and disconnect the crankcase ventilation hose from the cylinder head cover. Position it to one side.

12 Undo the two nuts securing the plastic wiring harness guide to the cylinder head. Lift the guide off the two mounting studs and move it clear of the accumulator rail. Disconnect any additional wiring connectors as necessary to enable the harness and guide assembly to be moved to one side.

13 Thoroughly clean all the high-pressure

12.7 Fuel injector upper seal (A) and copper washer (B)

fuel pipe unions on the fuel injectors and accumulator rail. Using two open-ended spanners, unscrew the union nuts securing the high-pressure fuel pipes to the fuel injectors and accumulator rail **(see illustrations 11.16a and 11.16b)**. Withdraw the high-pressure fuel pipes and plug or cover the open unions on the injectors and accumulator rail to prevent dirt entry. Note that a new high-pressure fuel pipe will be required for each removed injector when refitting.

14 Extract the retaining circlip and disconnect the leak-off pipe from each fuel injector **(see illustration)**.

12.10 Disconnect the injector wiring

12.14 Extract the circlip and disconnect the injector leak-off pipes

12.15a Unscrew the injector clamp retaining nut . . .

12.15b . . . and remove the washer

12.16 Withdraw the injectors, together with their clamps, from the cylinder head

15 Unscrew the nut(s) and remove the washer(s) securing each injector clamp to its cylinder head stud(s) **(see illustrations)**. Note that new clamp nuts will be required for refitting.

16 Withdraw the injectors, together with their clamps, from the cylinder head. Slide the clamp off the injector once it is clear of the mounting stud. If the injectors are a tight fit in the cylinder head and cannot be released, two screwdrivers may be used to carefully lever them out **(see illustration)**. Alternatively, unscrew one mounting stud using a stud extractor and slide off the injector clamp. Using an open-ended spanner engaged with the clamp locating slot on the injector body, free the injector by twisting it and at the same time lifting it upwards.

17 Recover the injector clamp locating dowel from the cylinder head **(see illustration)**.

18 Remove the copper washer and the upper seal from each injector, or from the cylinder head if they remained in place during injector removal. New copper washers and upper seals will be required for refitting.

19 Examine each injector visually for any signs of obvious damage or deterioration. If any defects are apparent, renew the injector(s).

Caution: The injectors are manufactured to extremely close tolerances and must not be dismantled in any way. Do not unscrew the fuel pipe union on the side of the injector, or separate any parts of the injector body. Do not attempt to clean carbon deposits from the injector nozzle or carry out any form of ultrasonic or pressure testing.

12.17 Recover the clamp locating dowel from the cylinder head

20 If the injectors are in a satisfactory condition, plug the fuel pipe union (if not already done) and suitably cover the electrical element and the injector nozzle.

Refitting

21 Locate a new upper seal on the body of each injector, and place a new copper washer on the injector nozzle **(see illustrations)**.

22 Refit the injector clamp locating dowels to the cylinder head.

23 Place the injector clamp in the slot on each injector body and refit the injectors to the cylinder head. Guide the clamp over the mounting stud and onto the locating dowel as each injector is inserted. Ensure the upper injector seals are correctly located in the cylinder head.

24 Fit the washer and a new injector clamp retaining nut to each mounting stud. Tighten the nuts finger tight only at this stage.

25 Working on one fuel injector at a time, remove the blanking plugs from the fuel pipe unions on the accumulator rail and the relevant injector. Locate a new high-pressure fuel pipe over the unions and screw on the union nuts. Take care not to cross-thread the nuts or strain the fuel pipes as they are fitted. Once the union nut threads have started, finger-tighten the nuts only at this stage.

26 When all the fuel pipes are in place, tighten the injector clamp retaining nuts to the specified torque.

27 Using an open-ended spanner, hold each fuel pipe union in turn and tighten the union nut to the specified torque using a torque wrench and crow's-foot adaptor **(see illustration)**. Tighten all the disturbed union nuts in the same way.

28 The remainder of refitting is a reversal of removal, following the points listed in Paragraph 25 of the previous Section.

13 Engine management system components – testing, removal and refitting

Testing

1 If a fault is suspected in the electronic control side of the system, first ensure that all the wiring connectors are securely connected and free of corrosion. Ensure that the suspected problem is not of a mechanical nature, or due to poor maintenance; ie, check that the air cleaner filter element is clean, the engine breather hoses are clear and undamaged, and that the cylinder

12.21a Locate a new upper seal on the body of each injector . . .

12.21b . . . and place a new copper washer on the injector nozzle

12.27 Using a torque wrench and crow's-foot adaptor, tighten the fuel pipe union nuts

13.7 Unscrew the mounting nut (see text) and remove the mounting bracket

13.8 Disconnect the wiring connector (1) then undo the retaining nuts (2) and remove the ECU from the mounting plate

13.12 Disconnect the crankshaft position sensor wiring plug

compression pressures are correct, referring to Chapters 1B and 2D for further information.

2 If these checks fail to reveal the cause of the problem, the vehicle should be taken to a Peugeot dealer or suitably-equipped garage for testing.

3 A diagnostic socket is located behind the trim panel inside the passenger compartment, to which a fault code reader or other suitable test equipment can be connected. By using the code reader or test equipment, the engine management ECU (and the various other vehicle system ECUs) can be interrogated, and any stored fault codes can be retrieved. This will allow the fault to be quickly and simply traced, alleviating the need to test all the system components individually, which is a time-consuming operation that carries a risk of damaging the ECU.

Electronic control unit (ECU)

Note: *If a new ECU is to be fitted, this work must be entrusted to a Peugeot dealer or suitably-equipped specialist. It is necessary to initialise the new ECU after installation, which requires the use of dedicated Peugeot diagnostic equipment.*

4 Before carrying out the following procedure, disconnect the battery (see Chapter 5A). Reconnect the battery on completion of refitting.

5 The ECU is located on the right-hand side of the engine compartment.

6 Unclip the wiring harness then slacken and

remove the ECU mounting plate nut. The plate is secured in position with an anti-tamper nut; unscrew the nut using a pair of grips.

7 Remove the bracket then free the mounting plate from the body **(see illustration)**.

8 Lift the retaining clip and disconnect the ECU wiring connector then unscrew the mounting nuts (these are also anti-tamper nuts) and remove the ECU from the mounting plate **(see illustration)**.

9 Refitting is a reverse of the removal procedure, ensuring the wiring connector is securely reconnected. Secure the ECU and mounting plate in position with new anti-tamper nuts or standard nuts.

Crankshaft speed/position sensor

Note: *Before carrying out the following procedure, disconnect the battery (refer to Chapter 5A). Reconnect the battery on completion of refitting.*

1.4 litre models

10 The crankshaft position sensor is located adjacent to the crankshaft pulley on the right-hand end of the engine. Slacken the right-hand front roadwheel bolts, and then jack the front of the vehicle up and support it on axle stands (see *Jacking and vehicle support*). Remove the right-hand front roadwheel.

11 Push in the centre pins a little, then prise out the rivets and remove the wheel arch liner.

12 Disconnect the sensor wiring plug **(see illustration)**.

13 Undo the bolt and remove the sensor.

14 Refitting is a reversal of removal, tightening the sensor retaining bolt securely.

2.0 litre models

15 The crankshaft speed/position sensor is located at the top of the transmission bellhousing, directly above the engine flywheel. To gain access, remove the air cleaner assembly as described in Section 4, and then remove the battery and battery tray (see Chapter 5A).

16 Undo the retaining nuts and bolts and release the plastic wiring harness guide from its mountings **(see illustration)**.

17 Working below the thermostat housing, disconnect the wiring connector from the crankshaft speed/position sensor.

18 Slacken the bolt securing the sensor to the bellhousing **(see illustration)**. It is not necessary to remove the bolt completely as the sensor mounting flange is slotted.

19 Turn the sensor body to clear the mounting bolt, and then withdraw the sensor from the bellhousing **(see illustration)**.

20 Refitting is reverse of the removal procedure ensuring the sensor retaining bolt is securely tightened.

Camshaft position sensor

Note: *Before carrying out the following procedure, disconnect the battery (refer to Chapter 5A). Reconnect the battery on completion of refitting.*

21 The camshaft position sensor is mounted on the right-hand end of the cylinder head cover, directly behind the camshaft sprocket.

13.16 Release the plastic wiring harness guide for access to the crankshaft position sensor

13.18 Slacken the bolt securing the sensor to the bellhousing

13.19 Turn the sensor body to clear the bolt and withdraw it from the bellhousing

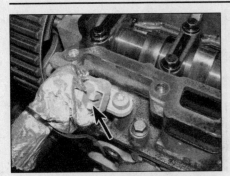

13.23 Disconnect the camshaft position sensor wiring plug (arrowed)

1.4 litre models

22 Remove the upper timing belt cover, as described in Chapter 2D.
23 Unplug the sensor wiring connector **(see illustration)**.
24 Undo the bolt and pull the sensor from position.
25 Upon refitting, position the sensor so that the air gap between the sensor end and the webs of the signal wheel is 1.2 mm, measured with feeler gauges, for a used sensor. If fitting a new sensor, the small tip of the sensor must be just touching one of the three webs of the signal wheel. Tighten the sensor retaining bolt to the specified torque **(see illustration)**.
26 The remainder of refitting is a reversal of removal.

2.0 litre models

27 Remove the timing belt upper and intermediate covers as described in Chapter 2D.
28 Disconnect the sensor wiring connector **(see illustration)**.
29 Undo the retaining bolt and lift the sensor off the cylinder head cover **(see illustration)**.
30 To refit and adjust the sensor position, locate the sensor on the cylinder head cover and loosely refit the retaining bolt.
31 The air gap between the tip of the sensor and the signal wheel at the rear of the camshaft sprocket hub must be set to 1.2 mm, using feeler blades. Clearance for the feeler blades is limited with the timing belt and camshaft sprocket in place, but it is just possible if the feeler blades are bent through 90° they can be inserted through the holes in

13.32 Insert feeler gauges bent 90° through the sprocket to measure the camshaft position sensor air gap

13.25 The gap between the end of the sensor and the webs of the signal wheel must be 1.2 mm (used sensor only)

the sprocket to rest against the inner face of the signal wheel.
32 With the feeler blades placed against the target plate, move the sensor toward the sprocket until it just contacts the feeler blades. Hold the sensor in this position and tighten the retaining bolt **(see illustration)**.
33 With the gap correctly adjusted, reconnect the sensor wiring connector, then refit the timing belt upper and intermediate covers as described in Chapter 2D.

Accelerator pedal position sensor

Note: *Before carrying out the following procedure, disconnect the battery (refer to Chapter 5A). Reconnect the battery on completion of refitting.*

Models without accelerator cable

34 On these models, the pedal sensor is integral with the accelerator pedal assembly. Refer to the relevant Section of Chapter 4A for the pedal removal procedure.

Models with accelerator cable

35 The accelerator pedal position sensor is located in the left-hand front corner of the engine compartment.
36 Remove the air cleaner assembly as described in Section 4.
37 Undo the two nuts and bolts and remove the sensor assembly from the mounting bracket on the side of the air cleaner housing.
38 Refitting is reverse of the removal procedure.

Coolant temperature sensor

39 Refer to Chapter 3, Section 7.

13.40 Fuel temperature sensor (arrowed) – 1.4 litre engine

13.28 Disconnect the wiring . . .

13.29 . . . and remove the sensor

Fuel temperature sensor

Warning: Refer to the information contained in Section 2 before proceeding.
Note: *Before carrying out the following procedure, disconnect the battery (refer to Chapter 5A). Reconnect the battery on completion of refitting.*

1.4 litre models

40 The sensor is clipped in to the plastic fuel manifold at the right-hand rear end of the cylinder head. To remove the sensor, disconnect the wiring plug, and then unclip the sensor from the manifold. Be prepared for fuel spillage **(see illustration)**.
41 Refitting is a reversal of removal.

2.0 litre models

42 The fuel temperature sensor is located to the left-hand side of the oil filler cap **(see illustration)**.
43 Undo the four plastic fasteners and lift off the engine cover.

13.42 Fuel temperature sensor (arrowed) – 2.0 litre engine

13.53a Air mass meter wiring plug (arrowed) – 1.4 litre engine

13.53b Air mass meter wiring plug – 2.0 litre engine

14.3 Inlet manifold retaining nuts (A) and bolts (B)

44 Disconnect the fuel temperature sensor wiring connector.

45 Thoroughly clean the area around the sensor and its location.

46 Suitably protect the components below the sensor and have plenty of clean rags handy. Be prepared for considerable fuel spillage.

47 Release the retaining clips and detach the sensor from the fuel pipes.

48 Refit the sensor to the fuel pipes, ensuring the clips fully engage.

49 Reconnect the sensor wiring plug.

50 Refit the engine plastic cover.

All models

51 Observing the precautions listed in Section 2, start the engine and allow it to idle. Check for leaks at the fuel temperature sensor with the engine idling. If satisfactory, increase the engine speed to 4000 rpm and check again for leaks. Take the car for a short road test and check for leaks once again on return. If any leaks are detected, obtain and fit a new sensor.

Air mass meter

Note: *Before carrying out the following procedure, disconnect the battery (refer to Chapter 5A). Reconnect the battery on completion of refitting.*

52 Air mass meter is located in the intake ducting from the air cleaner housing. On 1.4 litre models, pull the plastic cover from its mountings on top of the engine.

53 Disconnect the meter wiring plug **(see illustrations)**.

54 Slacken the retaining clips and disconnect the air inlet ducting from either side of the air mass meter. Suitably plug or cover the turbocharger rigid inlet duct, using clean rag to prevent any dirt or foreign material from entering. On 1.4 litre models, the air cleaner outlet is bolted to the air mass meter.

55 Refitting is reverse of the removal procedure.

Fuel pressure sensor

56 The fuel pressure sensor is integral with the accumulator rail, and is not available separately. Peugeot insist that the sensor is not removed from the rail.

Fuel pressure control valve

57 The fuel pressure control valve is integral with the high-pressure fuel pump and cannot be separated.

Preheating system control unit

58 Refer to Chapter 5C.

EGR solenoid valve

59 Refer to Chapter 4C, Section 2.

Vehicle speed sensor

60 The engine management ECU receives the vehicle speed signal from the wheels speed sensors via the ABS ECU. Refer to Chapter 9 for wheel speed sensor removal.

14 Inlet manifold – removal and refitting

1.4 litre engine

1 The inlet manifold is integral with the cylinder head cover. Refer to Chapter 2D.

2.0 litre engines

Note: *Renew the manifold gasket when refitting.*

Removal

2 The inlet manifold is located on the rear of the cylinder head, together with the exhaust manifold. First, remove the exhaust manifold as described in Section 15.

3 Undo the four bolts and four nuts securing

15.2a Undo the exhaust manifold nuts, recover the spacers, and remove the manifold

the inlet manifold flanges to the cylinder head **(see illustration)** and recover the washers. If preferred, the lower mounting nuts may be loosened and not removed, as the lower inlet manifold holes are slotted to allow the manifold to be lifted upwards once the upper bolts have been removed.

4 Lift the manifold off the cylinder head studs and recover the gasket.

Refitting

5 Refitting is reverse of the removal procedure, bearing in mind the following points.

a) Ensure that the manifold and cylinder head mating faces are clean, with all traces of old gasket removed.

b) Use a new gasket when refitting the manifold.

c) Ensure that all fixings and attachments are securely tightened.

d) Refit the exhaust manifold as described in Section 15.

15 Exhaust manifold – removal and refitting

Removal

1.4 litre engine

1 Remove the turbocharger as described in Section 17.

2 Undo the retaining nuts, recover the spacers, and remove the manifold. Recover the gasket **(see illustrations)**.

15.2b Recover the manifold gasket

15.7 Unscrew the turbocharger oil feed pipe union nut

15.8 Withdraw the oil feed pipe and remove the filter

15.9a Undo the oil return pipe flange securing bolts (arrowed) . . .

2.0 litre engines

3 The exhaust manifold is located on the rear of the cylinder head and access is very limited. First, apply the handbrake, and then jack up the front of the vehicle and support it on axle stands (see *Jacking and vehicle support*).

4 Disconnect the battery (see Chapter 5A).

5 Remove the exhaust front pipe with reference to Section 18.

6 Remove the turbocharger inlet and outlet ducts as described in Section 4.

7 Unscrew the union nut securing the turbocharger oil feed pipe to the cylinder block, then withdraw the pipe from its location **(see illustration)**.

8 Remove the filter from the end of the oil feed pipe, and examine it for contamination **(see illustration)**. Clean or renew if necessary.

9 Undo the two bolts securing the oil return pipe flange to the turbocharger. Separate the flange and recover the gasket **(see illustrations)**.

10 Remove the exhaust gas recirculation (EGR) valve and connecting pipe from the exhaust manifold as described in Chapter 4C.

11 Undo the exhaust manifold retaining nuts and recover the spacers from the studs **(see illustrations)**.

12 Undo the nut and bolt securing the base of the turbocharger to the support bracket on the cylinder block.

13 Withdraw the turbocharger and exhaust manifold off the mounting studs and remove the assembly from the engine. Recover the manifold gasket **(see illustrations)**.

15.9b . . . separate the flange and recover the gasket

Refitting

14 Refitting is a reverse of the removal procedure, bearing in mind the following points:

a) Ensure that the manifold and cylinder head mating faces are clean, with all traces of old gasket removed.

b) Use new gaskets when refitting the manifold to the cylinder head and, on 2.0 litre engines, the oil return pipe flange to the turbocharger.

c) Tighten the exhaust manifold retaining nuts to the specified torque.

d) On 2.0 litre engines, refit the EGR valve and connecting pipe as described in Chapter 4C, Section 2.

e) Refit the turbocharger rear inlet and outlet ducts as described in Section 4.

f) Refit the exhaust front pipe as described in Section 18.

15.11a Undo the exhaust manifold retaining nuts (arrowed) . . .

16 Turbocharger –
description and precautions

Description

1 A turbocharger is fitted to increase engine efficiency by raising the pressure in the inlet manifold above atmospheric pressure. Instead of the air simply being sucked into the cylinders, it is forced in.

2 Energy for the operation of the turbocharger comes from the exhaust gas. The gas flows through a specially shaped housing (the turbine housing) and, in so doing, spins the turbine wheel. The turbine wheel is attached to a shaft, at the end of which is another vaned wheel known as the compressor wheel. The compressor wheel spins in its own housing,

15.11b . . . and recover the spacers

15.13a Withdraw the turbocharger and manifold . . .

15.13b . . . and recover the gasket

and compresses the inlet air on the way to the inlet manifold.

3 Boost pressure (the pressure in the inlet manifold) is limited by a wastegate, which diverts the exhaust gas away from the turbine wheel in response to a pressure-sensitive actuator. On 1.4 litre models, the turbocharger incorporates a variable intake nozzle to improve boost pressure at low engine speeds.

4 The turbo shaft is pressure-lubricated by an oil feed pipe from the main oil gallery. The shaft 'floats' on a cushion of oil. A drain pipe returns the oil to the sump.

Precautions

5 The turbocharger operates at extremely high speeds and temperatures. Certain precautions must be observed, to avoid premature failure of the turbo, or injury to the operator.

6 Do not operate the turbo with any of its parts exposed, or with any of its hoses removed. Foreign objects falling onto the rotating vanes could cause excessive damage, and (if ejected) personal injury.

7 Do not race the engine immediately after start-up, especially if it is cold. Give the oil a few seconds to circulate.

8 Always allow the engine to return to idle speed before switching it off – do not blip the throttle and switch off, as this will leave the turbo spinning without lubrication.

9 Allow the engine to idle for several minutes before switching off after a high-speed run.

10 Observe the recommended intervals for oil and filter changing, and use a reputable oil of the specified quality. Neglect of oil

changing, or use of inferior oil, can cause carbon formation on the turbo shaft, leading to subsequent failure.

17 Turbocharger – removal, inspection and refitting

Removal

1 Apply the handbrake, then jack up the front of the vehicle and support it on axle stands (see *Jacking and vehicle support*). Undo the screws and remove the engine undershield.

1.4 litre models

Note: *Take precautions to protect the radiator from damage, if necessary, remove the radiator as described in Chapter 3.*

2 Undo the two clamp brackets and move the power steering pipes from across the top of the exhaust heat shield. If necessary the power steering pipe may need to be disconnected from the reservoir to move it to one side.

3 Undo the heat shield mounting bolts **(see illustration)**, and remove the heat shield from around exhaust and turbo unit. **Note:** *Protect the radiator from any damage before removing the heat shield.*

4 Release the clips and remove the turbocharger air intake pipe and resonator box **(see illustrations 4.3a, 4.3b and 4.3c)**.

5 Undo the bolts and remove the upper heat shield from the manifold.

6 Slacken the clip securing the front pipe/catalytic converter to the turbocharger.

17.3 Undo the heat shield retaining bolts (arrowed)

7 Undo the oil supply pipe banjo bolts and recover the sealing washers **(see illustrations)**.

8 Slacken the retaining clip and disconnect the oil return pipe from the turbocharger **(see illustration)**.

9 Unscrew the four nuts, and remove the turbocharger from the exhaust manifold **(see illustrations)**.

2.0 litre models

10 Firmly apply the handbrake then jack up the front of the vehicle and support it on axle sands (see *Jacking and vehicle support*).

11 Remove the right-hand driveshaft as described in Chapter 8.

12 Unscrew the nuts and bolts and remove the mounting link securing the rear engine/transmission mounting to the subframe. Undo the retaining bolts and remove the

17.7a Undo the turbocharger oil supply pipe banjo bolts from the cylinder block . . .

17.7b . . . and the turbocharger

17.7c Note the filter incorporated into the banjo bolt (arrowed)

17.8 Slacken the oil return hose clip (arrowed)

17.9a Undo the lower nuts (arrowed) . . .

17.9b . . . and upper nuts securing the turbocharger

17.17 Removing the connecting sleeve from the turbocharger

17.20 Turbocharger oil feed pipe union and return hose on the rear of the cylinder block

17.22 Undo the power steering pipe clip screw (1) then undo the bolts (2) and remove the flywheel lower cover plate from the transmission

rear mounting assembly from the rear of the cylinder block.

13 Remove the exhaust front pipe/catalytic converter as described in Section 18.

14 Unscrew the bolts and remove the exhaust outlet flange from the turbocharger.

15 Slacken the retaining clip and free the flexible duct from the top of the turbocharger intake pipe. Also unscrew the pipe upper mounting bolt. Unscrew the bolt securing the intake pipe to the side of the turbocharger then manoeuvre the pipe out of position. Recover the sealing ring fitted between the pipe and turbocharger.

16 Slacken the retaining clips securing the outlet pipe to its connecting sleeves on the turbocharger and inlet manifold then unclip and remove the pipe.

17 Slacken the retaining clip and remove the connecting sleeve from the turbocharger **(see illustration)**.

18 Remove the EGR valve (see Chapter 4C).

19 Unscrew the retaining bolts and remove the support bracket from the base of the turbocharger.

20 Wipe clean the area around the oil feed and return unions on the cylinder block **(see illustration)**. Where the feed pipe is secured by a union nut, unscrew the nut then free the pipe from the block and recover the filter (where fitted) from inside the pipe. Where the feed pipe is secured in position with a union bolt, unscrew the bolt and recover the sealing washers; discard the sealing washers, new ones should be used on refitting.

21 Release the retaining clip and detach the oil return hose from the block.

22 Undo the power steering pipe clip screws and free the pipes from the underside of the engine/transmission unit **(see illustration)**. Unscrew the retaining bolts and remove the flywheel lower cover plate from the transmission unit.

23 Unscrew the nuts securing the turbocharger to the exhaust manifold **(see illustration)** then manoeuvre the turbocharger downwards and out of position. If necessary, tilt the engine slightly forwards to gain the necessary clearance required to remove the turbocharger. Discard the nuts; new ones should be used on refitting.

24 Do not attempt to dismantle the turbocharger any further. If the unit is thought to be faulty take it to a turbo specialist for testing and examination. They will be able to inform you if the unit can be overhauled or will need renewing.

Inspection

25 With the turbocharger removed, inspect the housing for cracks or other visible damage.

26 Spin the turbine or the compressor wheel, to verify that the shaft is intact and to feel for excessive shake or roughness. Some play is normal, since in use, the shaft is 'floating' on a film of oil. Check that the wheel vanes are undamaged.

27 If oil contamination of the exhaust or induction passages is apparent, it is likely that turbo shaft oil seals have failed.

28 No DIY repair of the turbo is possible and none of the internal or external parts are available separately. If the turbocharger is suspect in any way a complete new unit must be obtained.

Refitting

29 Refitting is a reverse of the removal procedure, bearing in mind the following points:

a) *Ensure all mating surfaces are clean and dry.*

b) *Renew the turbocharger retaining nuts and gaskets.*

c) *Tighten all fixings to the specified torque (where given).*

d) *On 2.0 litre models, refit the driveshaft as described in Chapter 8 and check the transmission oil level as described in Chapter 1B.*

e) *Ensure all turbocharger ducts are correctly and securely reconnected.*

f) *If a new turbocharger is being fitted, change the engine oil and filter. Where applicable, also renew the filter in the oil feed pipe.*

g) *Prime the turbocharger by injecting clean engine oil through the oil feed pipe union before reconnecting the union.*

h) *When starting the engine for the first time, disconnect the injection pump wiring*

17.23 Turbocharger-to-exhaust manifold retaining nuts (arrowed)

connector(s) then turn the engine over on the starter motor until the oil pressure warning light goes out; this will allow oil to be circulated around the turbocharger bearings before the engine is started. Reconnect the injection pump then start the engine as normal.

18 Exhaust system – general information and component renewal

General information

1 According to model, the exhaust system consists of either two or three sections. Three section systems consist of a catalytic converter/front pipe, an intermediate pipe, and a tailpipe. On two section systems, the catalytic converter/front pipe and intermediate pipe are combined to form a single section.

2 The exhaust joints are of either the spring-loaded ball type (to allow for movement in the exhaust system) or clamp-ring type.

3 The system is suspended throughout its entire length by rubber mountings.

4 Each exhaust section can be removed individually or, alternatively, the complete system can be removed as a unit. Even if only one part of the system needs attention, it is often easier to remove the whole system and separate the sections on the bench.

5 To remove the system or part of the system, first jack up the front or rear of the car, and

18.8 Catalytic converter-to-turbocharger clamp bolt

18.9 Catalytic converter mounting bolts (arrowed)

18.14 Undo the nuts (arrowed) and remove the pipe along with the mountings

18.16 Unhook the tail pipe from the mountings, or undo the mounting nuts (arrowed)

support it on axle stands (see *Jacking and vehicle support*). Alternatively, position the car over an inspection pit, or on car ramps.

Catalytic converter/ front pipe removal

1.4 litre models

6 Undo the screws and remove the engine undershield.
7 Undo the bolts and remove the heat shield from the catalytic converter **(see illustration 17.3)**.
8 Slacken the retaining clamps joining the catalytic converter to the turbocharger and exhaust pipe. Take care not to damage the flexible section of the front exhaust pipe **(see illustration)**.
9 Undo the bolts securing the catalytic converter to the cylinder block and manoeuvre it down and out of the engine compartment **(see illustration)**.

2.0 litre models

10 The catalytic converter is integral with the front section of the exhaust pipe. Undo the screws and remove the engine undershield.
11 Slacken the retaining clamps securing the front pipe to the manifold and intermediate pipe.
12 Release the pipe from the rubber mountings and manoeuvre it from under the vehicle.

Intermediate pipe removal

13 Slacken the clamping-ring bolts, and disengage both clamps from the flange joints.
14 Release the pipe from its mounting rubber and remove it from underneath the vehicle. Alternatively, undo the nuts/bolts securing the mountings to the vehicle body **(see illustration)**.

Tailpipe removal

15 Slacken the tailpipe clamping ring bolts,

and disengage the clamp from the flange joint.
16 Unhook the tailpipe from its mounting rubbers, and remove it from the vehicle **(see illustration)**. Alternatively, undo the nuts/bolts securing the mountings to the vehicle body.

Complete system removal

17 Unscrew the front clamping-ring bolt and release the catalytic converter or front pipe from the turbocharger **(see illustration 18.8)**. Free the system from its mounting rubbers and remove it from underneath the vehicle. Alternatively, undo the nuts/bolts securing the mountings to the vehicle body.

Heat shield(s) removal

18 The heat shields are secured to the underside of the body by various nuts and bolts. Each shield can be removed once the relevant exhaust section has been removed. If a shield is being removed to gain access to a component located behind it, it may prove sufficient in some cases to remove the retaining nuts and/or bolts, and simply lower the shield, without disturbing the exhaust system.

Refitting

19 Each section is refitted by reversing the removal sequence, noting the following points:
  a) *Ensure that all traces of corrosion have been removed from the flanges, and renew all necessary gaskets.*
  b) *Inspect the rubber mountings for signs of damage or deterioration, and renew as necessary.*
  c) *On joints secured together by a clamping ring, apply a smear of exhaust system jointing paste to the flange joint, to ensure a gas-tight seal. Tighten the clamping ring nuts evenly and progressively, so that the clearance between the clamp halves remains equal on either side.*
  d) *Prior to tightening the exhaust system fasteners, ensure that all rubber mountings are correctly located, and that there is adequate clearance between the exhaust system and vehicle underbody.*
  e) *Where applicable, ensure no excess strain is being placed on the flexible section of the front pipe.*

Chapter 4 Part C:
Emission control systems

Contents

Degrees of difficulty

| Easy, suitable for novice with little experience | | Fairly easy, suitable for beginner with some experience | | Fairly difficult, suitable for competent DIY mechanic | | Difficult, suitable for experienced DIY mechanic | | Very difficult, suitable for expert DIY or professional | |

---

1 General information

All petrol engines use unleaded petrol and also have various other features built into the fuel system to help minimise harmful emissions. In addition, all engines are equipped with the crankcase emission control system described below. All engines are also equipped with a catalytic converter and an evaporative emission control system. Some petrol engines equipped to emission standard L4 also utilise a secondary air injection system to quickly bring the catalytic converter up to normal working temperature.

All diesel engines are also designed to meet the strict emission requirements and are equipped with a crankcase emission control system and a catalytic converter. To further reduce exhaust emissions, all diesel engines are also fitted with an exhaust gas recirculation (EGR) system.

The emission control systems function as follows.

Petrol engines

Crankcase emission control

To reduce the emission of unburned hydrocarbons from the crankcase into the atmosphere, the engine is sealed and the blow-by gases and oil vapour are drawn from inside the crankcase, through a wire-mesh oil separator, into the inlet tract to be burned by the engine during normal combustion.

Under all conditions the gases are forced out of the crankcase by the (relatively) higher crankcase pressure; if the engine is worn, the raised crankcase pressure (due to increased blow-by) will cause some of the flow to return under all manifold conditions.

Exhaust emission control

To minimise the amount of pollutants, which escape into the atmosphere, a catalytic converter is fitted in the exhaust system. The system is of the closed-loop type, in which lambda (oxygen) sensors in the exhaust system provides the fuel injection/ignition system ECU with constant feedback, enabling the ECU to adjust the mixture to provide the best possible conditions for the converter to operate.

The lambda sensors have a heating element built-in that is controlled by the ECU through the lambda sensor relay to quickly bring the sensor's tip to an efficient operating temperature. The sensor's tip is sensitive to oxygen and sends the ECU a varying voltage depending on the amount of oxygen in the exhaust gases; if the inlet air/fuel mixture is too rich, the exhaust gases are low in oxygen so the sensor sends a low-voltage signal, the voltage rising as the mixture weakens and the amount of oxygen rises in the exhaust gases. Peak conversion efficiency of all major pollutants occurs if the inlet air/fuel mixture is maintained at the chemically correct ratio for the complete combustion of petrol of 14.7 parts (by weight) of air to 1 part of fuel (the 'stoichiometric' ratio). The sensor output voltage alters in a large step at this point, the ECU using the signal change as a reference point and correcting the inlet air/fuel mixture accordingly by altering the fuel injector pulse width.

Evaporative emission control

To minimise the escape into the atmosphere of unburned hydrocarbons, an evaporative emission control system is fitted. The fuel tank filler cap is sealed and a charcoal canister is mounted behind the wheel arch liner under the right-hand side front wing to collect the petrol vapours generated in the tank when the car is parked. It stores them until they can be cleared from the canister (under the control of the fuel injection/ignition system ECU) via the purge valve into the inlet tract to be burned by the engine during normal combustion.

To ensure that the engine runs correctly when it is cold and/or idling and to protect the catalytic converter from the effects of an over-rich mixture, the purge control valve is not opened by the ECU until the engine has warmed-up, and the engine is under load; the valve solenoid is then modulated on and off to allow the stored vapour to pass into the inlet tract.

Secondary air injection

Some petrol engines equipped to emission standard L4 are also equipped with a secondary air injection system. This system is designed to reduce exhaust emissions in the period between first starting the engine and until the catalytic converter reaches operating (functioning) temperature. Introduction of air into the exhaust system during the initial start-up period, creates an 'afterburner' effect which quickly increases the temperature in the exhaust system front pipe, thus bringing the catalytic converter up to normal operating temperatures very quickly.

The system consists of an air pump, mounted at the front left-hand side of the car, an air injection valve, mounted on a bracket at the front of the cylinder head, a connecting pipe linking the valve to the exhaust manifold, and interconnecting air hoses.

The system operates for between 10 and 45 seconds after engine start-up, dependant on coolant temperature.

Diesel models

Crankcase emission control

Refer to the description for petrol engines.

Exhaust emission control

To minimise the level of exhaust pollutants released into the atmosphere, a catalytic converter is fitted in the exhaust system of all models.

The catalytic converter consists of a canister containing a fine mesh impregnated with a catalyst material, over which the hot exhaust gases pass. The catalyst speeds up the oxidation of harmful carbon monoxide, unburnt hydrocarbons and soot, effectively reducing the quantity of harmful products released into the atmosphere via the exhaust gases.

2.3a Undo the retaining screws . . .

2.3b . . . and the retaining clips . . .

2.3c . . . and remove the front and rear sections of the right-hand wheel arch liner

Exhaust gas recirculation system

This system is designed to recirculate small quantities of exhaust gas into the inlet tract, and therefore into the combustion process. This process reduces the level of oxides of nitrogen present in the final exhaust gas, which is released into the atmosphere.

The volume of exhaust gas recirculated is controlled by the system electronic control unit.

A vacuum-operated valve is fitted to the exhaust manifold, to regulate the quantity of exhaust gas recirculated. The valve is operated by the vacuum supplied by the solenoid valve.

2 Emission control systems – testing and component renewal

Petrol models

Crankcase emission control

1 The components of this system require no attention other than to check that the hose(s) are clear and undamaged at regular intervals.

Evaporative emission control

2 If the system is thought to be faulty, disconnect the hoses from the charcoal canister and purge control valve and check that they are clear by blowing through them. If the purge control valve or charcoal canister are thought to be faulty, they must be renewed.

Charcoal canister renewal

3 The charcoal canister is located under the wheel arch on the right-hand side. To gain access, slacken the right-hand front roadwheel bolts; jack up the front of the car and support it on axle stands (see *Jacking and vehicle support*). Remove the roadwheel, push in the centre pins then prise out the plastic expanding rivets, and remove the wheel arch liner **(see illustration)**.

4 Working in the engine compartment, slacken the nuts securing the canister to the body (the nuts do not need to be removed) **(see illustration)**.

5 Free the canister from the body and mark the hoses for identification purposes. Disconnect both hoses and remove the canister from the vehicle **(see illustration)**.

6 Refitting is a reverse of the removal procedure ensuring the hoses are correctly reconnected. Lower the vehicle to the ground and tighten the wheel bolts to the specified torque.

Purge valve renewal

Note: *On later models, the purge valve is integral with the canister, and cannot be renewed separately.*

7 On early models, the purge valve is located in the right-hand rear corner of the engine compartment.

8 To gain access to the valve, remove the coolant expansion tank as described in Chapter 3.

9 Disconnect the battery negative terminal then disconnect the wiring connector from the valve **(see illustration)**.

10 Disconnect the hoses from either end of the

2.4 Loosen the retaining nuts (arrowed) . . .

valve then release the valve from its retaining clip and remove it from the engine compartment, noting which way around it is fitted.

11 Refitting is a reversal of the removal procedure, ensuring the valve is fitted the correct way around and the hoses are securely connected. Refit the coolant expansion tank as described in Chapter 3.

Exhaust emission control

12 The performance of the catalytic converter can be checked only by measuring the exhaust gases using a good-quality, carefully calibrated exhaust gas analyser.

13 If the CO level at the tailpipe is too high, the vehicle should be taken to a Peugeot dealer or specialist so that the complete fuel injection and ignition systems, including the lambda sensor, can be thoroughly checked using the special diagnostic equipment. Once these have been checked and are known to

2.5a . . . then free the charcoal canister from the body and disconnect its hoses, noting their correct fitted locations

2.5b On later models depress the quick-release buttons (arrowed), and disconnect the hoses

2.9 Disconnect the wiring connector (1) and hoses (2) from the purge valve – early models

2.16 Lambda sensor – 1.6 litre model shown

2.20 Secondary air injection pump (where fitted)

2.27 Secondary air injection valve

be free from faults, the fault must be in the catalytic converter, which can be renewed as described in Part A of this Chapter.

Catalytic converter renewal

14 Refer to Part A of this Chapter.

Lambda sensor renewal

Note: *The lambda sensor is delicate and will not work if it is dropped or knocked, if its power supply is disrupted, or if any cleaning materials are used on it.*

15 Trace the wiring back from the lambda sensor(s), which are located before and after the catalytic converters. On 1.1, 1.4 and 1.6 litre petrol engines to emission level L4, one sensor is located in the exhaust manifold, and one after the catalytic converter. On 2.0 litre petrol engines one sensor is screwed into the top of the exhaust front pipe, and one after the catalytic converter. Disconnect both wiring connectors and free the wiring from any relevant retaining clips or ties.

16 Unscrew the sensor from the exhaust system front pipe/manifold and remove it along with its sealing washer **(see illustration).**

17 Refitting is a reverse of the removal procedure using a new sealing washer. Prior to installing the sensor apply a smear of high temperature grease to the sensor threads. Ensure that the sensor is securely tightened and that the wiring is correctly routed and in no danger of contacting either the exhaust system or engine.

Testing secondary air injection

18 The components of this system require no attention other than to check that the hose(s) are clear and undamaged at regular intervals.

19 Accurate testing of the system operation entails the use of diagnostic test equipment and should be entrusted to a Peugeot dealer or specialist.

Air injection pump renewal

20 The air pump is located at the front right-hand corner of the engine **(see illustration).**

21 Slacken and remove the three nuts and withdraw the pump from the mounting bracket.

22 Disconnect the air hoses and wiring connector and remove the pump.

23 Refitting is a reverse of the removal procedure, ensuring that the hoses are correctly reconnected.

Air injection valve renewal

24 Disconnect the battery (see Chapter 5A).

25 Slacken and remove the retaining screws, and remove the shroud from the top of the exhaust manifold.

26 Undo the two bolts securing the connecting pipe flange to the exhaust manifold.

27 Undo the two bolts securing the valve mounting bracket to the cylinder head **(see illustration).**

28 Withdraw the valve and connecting pipe, disconnect the air hose and remove the air injection valve and connecting pipe as an assembly.

29 If necessary, the air pipe can be removed from the valve and the valve removed from the mounting bracket after undoing the two retaining nuts. Collect the flange gasket after removal.

30 Refitting is a reverse of the removal procedure, but use a new gasket between the valve and mounting bracket.

Diesel models

Crankcase emission control

31 The components of this system require no attention other than to check that the hose(s) are clear and undamaged at regular intervals.

Exhaust emission control

32 The performance of the catalytic converter can only be checked by measuring the exhaust gases using a good-quality, carefully calibrated exhaust gas analyser.

33 If the catalytic converter is thought to be faulty, before assuming the catalytic converter is faulty, it is worth checking the problem is not due to a faulty injector(s). Refer to your Peugeot dealer for further information.

Catalytic converter renewal

34 Refer to Part B of this Chapter.

Exhaust gas recirculation system

35 Testing of the system should ideally be entrusted to a Peugeot dealer since a vacuum pump and vacuum gauge are required.

EGR valve renewal – 1.4 litre engine

36 Carefully pull the plastic cover upwards from the top of the engine.

37 Remove the air cleaner housing as described in Chapter 4B.

38 Note its fitted location, and then disconnect the vacuum pipe from the EGR valve.

39 Release the two retaining clamps fitted to the EGR pipe.

40 There are three bolts securing the EGR pipe, and two bolts securing the EGR valve. Undo the bolts and remove the pipe complete with valve. Discard the metal gasket from the valve, and the O-ring seal from the pipe – new ones must be fitted **(see illustrations).**

2.40a The EGR pipe is secured to the manifold by two screws (arrowed) . . .

2.40b . . . and to the cylinder block by one bolt (arrowed)

2.40c A new EGR pipe-to-manifold O-ring seal must be fitted

2.41 EGR solenoid valve retaining bolts (arrowed)

2.44 Remove the engine cover

2.55 EGR system solenoid valves (arrowed) are mounted on the bulkhead – 2.0 litre diesel engine

41 To remove the EGR solenoid valve, disconnect the two vacuum hoses and the wiring connector. Undo the mounting bracket bolts and remove the valve from the engine compartment **(see illustration)**.

42 Refitting is a reversal of removal.

EGR valve testing – 2.0 litre engine

43 If the EGR system is thought not to be operating correctly, the vehicle should be taken to a Peugeot dealer for testing using the special diagnostic equipment.

EGR valve renewal – 2.0 litre engine

44 Disconnect the battery negative terminal then release the fasteners (rotate them 90º to release them) and remove the engine cover **(see illustration)**.

45 Disconnect the vacuum hose from the EGR valve, which is fitted, to the top of the exhaust manifold.

46 Unscrew the nuts securing the valve to the exhaust manifold and the valve adaptor to the inlet manifold intake flange. Recover the valve gasket and discard it; a new one should be used on refitting.

47 Refitting is the reverse of removal, using a new gasket and tighten the valve nuts securely.

EGR regulator renewal

48 Firmly apply the handbrake then jack up the front of the vehicle and support it on axle stands (see *Jacking and vehicle support*).

49 To improve access, remove the battery and battery tray (see Chapter 5A).

50 Slacken the retaining clips and remove the flexible duct connecting the airflow meter to the turbocharger intake pipe. Unscrew the intake pipe upper mounting bolt. Unscrew the bolt securing the intake pipe to the side of the turbocharger then manoeuvre the pipe out of position. Recover the sealing ring fitted between the pipe and turbocharger.

51 Slacken the retaining clips securing the outlet pipe to its connecting sleeves on the turbocharger and EGR regulator and remove the pipe.

52 Slacken the retaining clip and remove the connecting sleeve from the EGR regulator.

53 Disconnect the vacuum hose then unscrew the retaining nuts and remove the EGR regulator from the inlet manifold elbow.

54 Refitting is the reverse of removal, ensuring all the intake ducts are correctly and securely refitted.

EGR solenoid valves renewal

55 The solenoid valves are mounted on the engine compartment bulkhead, directly behind the intake duct **(see illustration)**. One valve operates the EGR valve and the other the regulator; trace the vacuum hose back from the regulator and EGR valve to identify the valves.

56 Make a note of the correct fitted positions of each hose (mark the hoses to avoid confusion on refitting) then disconnect the vacuum hoses from each valve.

57 Unscrew the mounting bolts and remove the valve bracket assembly from the bulkhead. The valves can then be removed from the bracket.

58 Refitting is the reverse of removal, ensuring the vacuum hoses are securely reconnected to their original valve unions.

3 Catalytic converter – general information and precautions

1 The catalytic converter is a reliable and simple device which needs no maintenance in itself, but there are some facts of which an owner should be aware if the converter is to function properly for its full service life.

Petrol models

a) DO NOT use leaded petrol or LRP – the lead will coat the precious metals, and will eventually destroy the converter.

b) Always keep the ignition and fuel systems well-maintained.

c) If the engine develops a misfire, do not drive the car at all (or at least as little as possible) until the fault is cured.

d) DO NOT push- or tow-start the car – this will soak the catalytic converter in unburned fuel, causing it to overheat when the engine does start.

e) DO NOT switch off the ignition at high engine speeds.

f) DO NOT use fuel or engine oil additives – these may contain substances harmful to the catalytic converter.

g) DO NOT continue to use the car if the engine burns oil to the extent of leaving a visible trail of blue smoke.

h) Remember that the catalytic converter operates at very high temperatures. DO NOT, therefore, park the car in dry undergrowth, over long grass or piles of dead leaves after a long run.

i) Remember that the catalytic converter is FRAGILE – do not strike it with tools.

j) In some cases a sulphurous smell (like that of rotten eggs) may be noticed from the exhaust. This is common to many catalytic converter-equipped cars and once the car has covered a few thousand miles the problem should disappear. Sometimes this is also caused by the brand of fuel used.

k) If the converter is no longer effective it must be renewed.

Diesel models

2 Refer to parts f, g, h and i of the *petrol models* information given above.

Chapter 5 Part A:
Starting and charging systems

Contents

Degrees of difficulty

Easy, suitable for novice with little experience	Fairly easy, suitable for beginner with some experience	Fairly difficult, suitable for competent DIY mechanic	Difficult, suitable for experienced DIY mechanic	Very difficult, suitable for expert DIY or professional

Specifications

System type .... 12 volt, negative earth

Battery
Type .... Low maintenance or 'maintenance-free' sealed for life
Charge condition:
  Poor .... 12.5 volts
  Normal .... 12.6 volts
  Good .... 12.7 volts

Alternator
Type .... Denso, Valeo, Magneti Marelli, Bosch or Mitsubishi (depending on model)
Rating:
  1.1, 1.4 and 1.6 litre petrol models .... 70, 80, 90 or 120 amp
  2.0 litre petrol models .... 80, 90, 120 or 150 amp
  Diesel models .... 150 amp

Starter motor
Type .... Mitsubishi, Valeo, Ducellier, Iskra, or Bosch (depending on model)

Torque wrench settings

	Nm	lbf ft
Alternator mounting bolts:		
Petrol engines	37	27
Diesel engines	40	30
Oil pressure switch:		
Petrol engine	25	18
Diesel engine	30	22
Starter motor:		
1.4 litre diesel model	20	15
All other models	35	26

1 General information and precautions

General information

1 The engine electrical system consists mainly of the charging and starting systems. Because of their engine-related functions, these components are covered separately from the body electrical devices such as the lights, instruments, etc (which are covered in Chapter 12). On petrol engine models refer to Part B for information on the ignition system, and on diesel models refer to Part C for information on the preheating system.

2 The electrical system is of the 12 volt negative earth type.

3 The battery is of the low maintenance or 'maintenance-free' (sealed for life) type and is charged by the alternator, which is belt-driven from the crankshaft pulley.

4 The starter motor is of the pre-engaged type incorporating an integral solenoid. On starting, the solenoid moves the drive pinion into engagement with the flywheel ring gear before the starter motor is energised. Once the engine has started, a one-way clutch prevents the motor armature being driven by the engine while the pinion is disengaging from the flywheel.

Precautions

5 Further details of the various systems are given in the relevant Sections of this Chapter. While some repair procedures are given, the usual course of action is to renew the component concerned. The owner whose interest extends beyond mere component renewal should obtain a copy of the *Automotive Electrical & Electronic Systems Manual*, available from the publishers of this manual.

6 It is necessary to take extra care when working on the electrical system to avoid damage to semi-conductor devices (diodes and transistors), and to avoid the risk of personal injury. In addition to the precautions given in *Safety first!* at the beginning of this manual, observe the following when working on the system:

• *Always remove rings, watches, etc, before working on the electrical system.* Even with the battery disconnected, capacitive discharge could occur if a component's live terminal is earthed through a metal object. This could cause a shock or nasty burn.

• *Do not reverse the battery connections.* Components such as the alternator, electronic control units, or any other components having semi-conductor circuitry could be irreparably damaged.

• If the engine is being started using jump leads and a slave battery, connect the batteries *positive-to-positive* and *negative-to-negative* (see *Jump starting*). This also applies when connecting a battery charger.

• Never disconnect the battery terminals, the alternator, any electrical wiring or any test instruments when the ignition is switched on/the engine is running.

• Do not allow the engine to turn the alternator when the alternator is not connected.

• Never 'test' for alternator output by 'flashing' the output lead to earth.

• Never use an ohmmeter of the type incorporating a hand-cranked generator for circuit or continuity testing.

• Always ensure that the battery negative lead is disconnected when working on the electrical system.

• Before using electric-arc welding equipment on the car, disconnect the battery, alternator and components such as the engine management electronic control unit to protect them from the risk of damage.

• The radio/cassette unit fitted as standard equipment by Peugeot is equipped with a built-in security code to deter thieves. If the power source to the unit is cut, the anti-theft system will activate. Even if the power source is immediately reconnected, the radio/cassette unit will not function until the correct security code has been entered. Therefore, if you do not know the correct security code for the radio/cassette unit **do not** disconnect the battery negative terminal of the battery or remove the radio/cassette unit from the vehicle. Refer to *Audio unit anti-theft system* in the Reference Section for further information.

2 Electrical fault finding – general information

Refer to Chapter 12.

3 Battery – testing and charging

Testing

Standard and low maintenance battery

1 If the vehicle covers a small annual mileage, it is worthwhile checking the specific gravity of the electrolyte every three months to determine the state of charge of the battery. Use a hydrometer to make the check and compare the results with the following table. Note that the specific gravity readings assume an electrolyte temperature of 15°C; for every 10°C below 15°C subtract 0.007. For every 10°C above 15°C add 0.007.

	Ambient temperature	
	Above 25°C	Below 25°C
Fully-charged	1.210 to 1.230	1.270 to 1.290
70% charged	1.170 to 1.190	1.230 to 1.250
Discharged	1.050 to 1.070	1.110 to 1.130

2 If the battery condition is suspect, first check the specific gravity of electrolyte in each cell.

A variation of 0.040 or more between any cells indicates loss of electrolyte or deterioration of the internal plates.

3 If the specific gravity variation is 0.040 or more, the battery should be renewed. If the cell variation is satisfactory but the battery is discharged, it should be charged as described later in this Section.

Maintenance-free battery

4 In cases where a 'sealed for life' maintenance-free battery is fitted, topping-up and testing of the electrolyte in each cell is not possible. The condition of the battery can therefore only be tested using a battery condition indicator or a voltmeter.

5 Certain models may be fitted with a 'Delco' type maintenance-free battery, with a built-in charge condition indicator. The indicator is located in the top of the battery casing, and indicates the condition of the battery from its colour. If the indicator shows green, then the battery is in a good state of charge. If the indicator turns darker, eventually to black, then the battery requires charging, as described later in this Section. If the indicator shows clear/yellow, then the electrolyte level in the battery is too low to allow further use, and the battery should be renewed. **Do not** attempt to charge, load or jump start a battery when the indicator shows clear/yellow.

All battery types

6 If testing the battery using a voltmeter, connect the voltmeter across the battery and compare the result with those given in the Specifications under 'Charge condition'. The test is only accurate if the battery has not been subjected to any kind of charge for the previous six hours. If this is not the case, switch on the headlights for 30 seconds, then wait four to five minutes before testing the battery after switching off the headlights. All other electrical circuits must be switched off, so check that the doors and tailgate are fully shut when making the test.

7 If the voltage reading is less than 12.2 volts, then the battery is discharged, whilst a reading of 12.2 to 12.4 volts indicates a partially discharged condition.

8 If the battery is to be charged, remove it from the vehicle (Section 4) and charge it as described later in this Section.

Charging

Note: *The following is intended as a guide only. Always refer to the manufacturer's recommendations (often printed on a label attached to the battery) before charging a battery.*

Standard and low maintenance battery

9 Charge the battery at a rate of 3.5 to 4 amps and continue to charge the battery at this rate until no further rise in specific gravity is noted over a four hour period.

10 Alternatively, a trickle charger charging at the rate of 1.5 amps can safely be used overnight.

4.2 Remove the cover from the battery tray to gain access to the battery

11 Specially rapid 'boost' charges, which are claimed to restore the power of the battery in 1 to 2 hours, are not recommended, as they can cause serious damage to the battery plates through overheating.

12 While charging the battery, note that the temperature of the electrolyte should never exceed 38°C.

Maintenance-free battery

13 This battery type takes considerably longer to fully recharge than the standard type, the time taken being dependent on the extent of discharge, but it can take anything up to three days.

14 A constant voltage type charger is required, to be set, when connected, to 13.9 to 14.9 volts with a charger current below 25 amps. Using this method, the battery

4.3 Slacken the bolt and disconnect the clamp from the battery negative (–) terminal first . . .

should be usable within three hours, giving a voltage reading of 12.5 volts, but this is for a partially discharged battery and, as mentioned, full charging can take considerably longer.

15 If the battery is to be charged from a fully discharged state (condition reading less than 12.2 volts), have it recharged by your Peugeot dealer or local automotive electrician, as the charge rate is higher and constant supervision during charging is necessary.

---

4 Battery – removal and refitting

Note: *On models equipped with a Peugeot anti-theft alarm system, disable the alarm before disconnecting the battery (see Chapter 12). If a*

Peugeot audio unit is fitted, refer to 'Audio unit anti-theft system' in the Reference Section.

Removal

1 The battery is located on the left-hand side of the engine compartment.

2 Remove the cover from the battery tray to gain access to the battery terminals **(see illustration)**.

3 Slacken the clamp bolt and disconnect the clamp from the battery negative (–) terminal **(see illustration)**.

4 Release the quick-release lever and disconnect the clamp from the battery positive (+) terminal **(see illustration)**.

5 Unscrew the bolts and remove the battery retaining clamp then lift the battery out of its tray **(see illustration)**.

6 To remove the battery tray, undo the retaining bolts then unclip wiring from the tray. The battery tray can then be lifted out of position, freeing it from its cooling duct **(see illustrations)**. On diesel engine models it will be necessary to undo the nut and free the preheating unit from the rear of the tray (see Chapter 5C). On automatic transmission models it will be necessary to unclip and remove the transmission electronic control unit (ECU) mounting plate from the battery tray, disconnect the earth lead from the plate (see Chapter 7B, Section 9).

7 If necessary, with the tray removed, undo the retaining nut and bolts and remove the mounting plate from the top of the left-hand engine/transmission mounting **(see illustrations)**.

4.4 . . . then lift the quick-release lever and disconnect the clamp from the positive (+) terminal

4.5 Undo the retaining bolts (arrowed) and remove the battery retaining clamp

4.6a Unscrew the retaining bolts (arrowed) . . .

4.6b . . . and lift out the battery tray, freeing the wiring from the clips on the side of the tray

4.7a Unscrew the retaining nut and bolts (arrowed) . . .

4.7b . . . then remove the mounting plate from the top of the left-hand engine/ transmission mounting

Refitting

8 Refitting is a reversal of removal, but smear petroleum jelly on the terminals after reconnecting the leads, and always reconnect the positive lead first, negative lead last. If the battery tray has been removed ensure the cooling duct is securely connected to the front of the tray and all the wiring is clipped in position. Before starting the engine for the first time, turn on the ignition and wait for ten seconds to initialise the various electronic control units.

5 Charging system – testing

Note: *Refer to the warnings given in 'Safety first!' and in Section 1 of this Chapter before starting work.*

1 If the ignition warning light fails to illuminate when the ignition is switched on, first check the alternator wiring connections for security. If satisfactory, check that the warning light bulb has not blown, and that the bulbholder is secure in its location in the instrument panel. If the light still fails to illuminate, check the continuity of the warning light feed wire from the alternator to the bulbholder. If all is satisfactory, the alternator is at fault and should be renewed or taken to an auto-electrician for testing and repair.

2 If the ignition warning light illuminates when the engine is running, stop the engine and check that the drivebelt is correctly tensioned (see the relevant part of Chapter 1) and that the alternator connections are secure. If all is so far satisfactory, have the alternator checked by an auto-electrician for testing and repair.

3 If the alternator output is suspect even though the warning light works correctly, the regulated voltage may be checked as follows.

4 Connect a voltmeter across the battery terminals and start the engine.

5 Increase the engine speed until the voltmeter reading remains steady; the reading should be approximately 12 to 13 volts, and no more than 14 volts.

6 Switch on as many electrical accessories (eg, the headlights, heated rear window and heater blower) as possible, and check that the alternator maintains the regulated voltage at around 13 to 14 volts.

7 If the regulated voltage is not as stated, the fault may be due to worn brushes, weak brush springs, a faulty voltage regulator, a faulty diode, a severed phase winding or worn or damaged slip-rings. The alternator should be renewed or taken to an auto-electrician for testing and repair.

6 Auxiliary drivebelt – removal, refitting and tensioning

Refer to the procedure given for the auxiliary drivebelt in Chapter 1A or 1B (as applicable).

7 Alternator – removal and refitting

Removal

1 Disconnect the battery negative lead.

2 Slacken the auxiliary drivebelt tension and release the belt from the alternator pulley (refer to Chapter 1A or 1B – as applicable). Where necessary, remove the retaining bolts, screws and clips and remove the undercover from the engine/transmission unit to improve access.

3 Where applicable, remove the plastic engine style cover from the top of the engine **(see illustration)**.

4 On models with power steering, referring to Chapter 10, unbolt the power steering pump and position it clear of the engine taking care not to lose the spacer (where fitted) from the rear mounting **(see illustrations)**. Support the weight of the pump by tying it to the vehicle body/engine to prevent any excess strain being placed on the hydraulic pipes/hoses. **Note:** *There is no need to disconnect the pipe/hose from the pump. Release the pipes/hoses from any necessary clips to prevent them being strained.*

5 Remove the rubber cover(s) from the alternator terminals, then unscrew the retaining nut(s) and disconnect the wiring from the rear of the alternator **(see illustrations)**.

6 Where necessary, unscrew the mounting nut/bolt (as applicable) and remove the

7.3b ... then lift off the engine cover

7.4a Slacken and remove the power steering pump front mounting bolts ...

7.4b ... and rear mounting bolt (arrowed) ...

7.4c ... then position the power steering pump clear of the engine – petrol engine shown

7.5a Remove the rubber cap then unscrew the nut (arrowed) ...

7.5b ... and disconnect the wiring from the alternator – petrol engine shown

7.6 Remove the plastic cap and unbolt (arrowed) the auxiliary drivebelt idler pulley

7.7a Unscrew the front mounting bolts (arrowed) ...

7.7b ... and the rear mounting bolts (arrowed) ...

7.7c ... then withdraw the alternator from the mounting bracket – petrol engine shown

7.7d Tapered bolts with expanding collars (arrowed) which tighten inside the mounting bracket

auxiliary drivebelt tensioner/idler pulley to gain access to the alternator lower mounting bolt **(see illustrations)**. **Note:** *On some models, it will be necessary to remove the plastic cap from the idler pulley retaining bolt.*

7 Unscrew the mounting bolts, noting each correct fitted location, and manoeuvre the alternator out of position **(see illustrations)**. On diesel engines, recover the spacer/spacer and collar arrangement from each of the rear mountings. **Note:** *On some models, the mounting bolts on the rear of the alternator do not need to be removed completely. When the bolts are tightened they expand the metal collar in the mounting bracket to secure the alternator.*

Refitting

8 Refitting is a reversal of removal, noting the following.

a) *On diesel engines, ensure the spacer/ spacer and collar arrangement is correctly fitted to each rear mounting. Tighten the alternator front (drivebelt pulley end) mounting bolts to the specified torque first then tighten the rear mounting bolts to the specified torque.*

b) *On models with power steering, ensure the mounting spacer (where fitted) is correctly fitted to the rear mounting. Apply locking compound (Peugeot recommend the use of Loctite Frenetanch) to the pump mounting bolts; tighten the pump front (drivebelt pulley end) bolts to the specified torque first then tighten the rear bolts (see Chapter 10).*

c) *Refit the auxiliary drivebelt as described in Chapter 1A or 1B (as applicable).*

8 Alternator – testing and overhaul

If the alternator is thought to be suspect, it should be removed from the vehicle and taken to an auto-electrician for testing. Most auto-electricians will be able to supply and fit brushes at a reasonable cost. However, check on the cost of repairs before proceeding, as it may prove more economical to obtain a new or exchange alternator.

9 Starting system – testing

Note: *Refer to the precautions given in 'Safety first!' and in Section 1 of this Chapter before starting work.*

1 If the starter motor fails to operate when the ignition key is turned to the appropriate position, the following possible causes may be to blame.

a) *The battery is faulty.*

b) *The electrical connections between the switch, solenoid, battery and starter motor are somewhere failing to pass the necessary current from the battery through the starter to earth.*

c) *The solenoid is faulty.*

d) *The starter motor is mechanically or electrically defective.*

2 To check the battery, switch on the headlights.

If they dim after a few seconds, this indicates that the battery is discharged – recharge (see Section 3) or renew the battery. If the headlights glow brightly, operate the ignition switch and observe the lights. If they dim, then this indicates that current is reaching the starter motor; therefore the fault must lie in the starter motor. If the lights continue to glow brightly (and no clicking sound can be heard from the starter motor solenoid), this indicates that there is a fault in the circuit or solenoid – see following paragraphs. If the starter motor turns slowly when operated, but the battery is in good condition, then this shows that either the starter motor is faulty, or there is considerable resistance in the circuit.

3 If a fault in the circuit is suspected, disconnect the battery leads (including the earth connection to the body), the starter/solenoid wiring and the engine/ transmission earth strap – located on the to of the transmission housing **(see illustration)**.

9.3 Engine/transmission earth strap connection (arrowed)

10.4 Unscrew the nuts and disconnect the wiring from the starter motor solenoid

10.5 Starter motor mounting bolts – petrol engine

10.6 Remove the starter motor and recover the locating dowel (arrowed) – diesel engine shown

Thoroughly clean the connections, and reconnect the leads and wiring, then use a voltmeter or test lamp to check that full battery voltage is available at the battery positive lead connection to the solenoid, and that the earth is sound. Smear petroleum jelly around the battery terminals to prevent corrosion – corroded connections are amongst the most frequent causes of electrical system faults.

4 If the battery and all connections are in good condition, check the circuit by disconnecting the wire from the solenoid blade terminal. Connect a voltmeter or test lamp between the wire end and a good earth (such as the battery negative terminal), and check that the wire is live when the ignition switch is turned to the 'start' position. If it is, then the circuit is sound – if not the circuit wiring can be checked as described in Chapter 12.

5 The solenoid contacts can be checked by connecting a voltmeter or test lamp between the battery positive feed connection on the starter side of the solenoid, and earth. When the ignition switch is turned to the 'start' position, there should be a reading or lighted bulb, as applicable. If there is no reading or lighted bulb, the solenoid is faulty and should be renewed.

6 If the circuit and solenoid are proved sound, the fault must lie in the starter motor. In this event, it may be possible to have the starter motor overhauled by a specialist, but check on the cost of spares before proceeding, as it may prove more economical to obtain a new or exchange motor.

10 Starter motor – removal and refitting

Removal

1 Disconnect the battery negative lead.
2 Where applicable, remove the plastic engine style cover from the top of the engine **(see illustrations 7.3a and 7.3b)**.
3 So that access to the motor can be gained both from above and below, firmly apply the handbrake then jack up the front of the vehicle and support it on axle stands (see *Jacking and vehicle support*). Where necessary, remove the retaining bolts, screws and clips and remove

the undershield (where fitted) from the engine/transmission unit to improve access.
4 On all engines, slacken and remove the two retaining nuts and disconnect the wiring from the starter motor solenoid. Recover the washers under the nuts **(see illustration)**.
5 Undo the three mounting bolts, supporting the motor as the bolts are withdrawn **(see illustration)**. Recover the washers from under the bolt heads and note the locations of any wiring or hose brackets secured by the bolts.
6 Manoeuvre the starter motor out from underneath the engine and recover the locating dowel(s) from the motor/transmission (as applicable) **(see illustration)**.

Refitting

7 Refitting is a reversal of removal, ensuring that the locating dowel(s) are correctly positioned. Also make sure that any wiring or hose brackets are in place under the bolt heads as noted prior to removal.

11 Starter motor – testing and overhaul

If the starter motor is thought to be suspect, it should be removed from the vehicle and taken to an auto-electrician for testing. Most auto-electricians will be able to supply and fit brushes at a reasonable cost. However, check on the cost of repairs before proceeding, as it may prove more economical to obtain a new or exchange motor.

13.3a Oil pressure switch (arrowed) – 1.4 litre petrol engine shown

12 Ignition switch – removal and refitting

The ignition switch is integral with the steering column lock, and can be removed as described in Chapter 10.

13 Oil pressure warning light switch – removal and refitting

Removal

1 The switch is fitted at the front of the cylinder block, in the following locations:
Petrol engines:
    Screwed into the oil filter housing.
1.4 litre diesel engines:
    Adjacent to the oil dipstick guide tube.
2.0 litre diesel engines:
    Above the oil filter mounting.
Note: *On some models, access to the switch may be improved if the vehicle is jacked up and supported on axle stands, and the engine undershield removed (where fitted), so that the switch can be reached from underneath (see 'Jacking and vehicle support').*
2 Remove the protective sleeve from the wiring plug (where applicable), and then disconnect the wiring from the switch.
3 Unscrew the switch from the cylinder block, and recover the sealing washer **(see illustrations)**. Be prepared for oil spillage, and

13.3b Disconnect the wiring connector (arrowed) from the oil pressure switch – diesel engine shown

14.1a Oil level/temperature sensor location – diesel engine

14.1b Oil level sensor (arrowed) – 1.4 litre petrol engine

if the switch is to be left removed from the engine for any length of time, plug the hole in the cylinder block.

Refitting

4 Examine the sealing washer for signs of damage or deterioration and if necessary renew.

5 Refit the switch, complete with washer, and tighten it securely. Reconnect the wiring connector.

6 Lower the vehicle to the ground then check

and, if necessary, top-up the engine oil as described in *Weekly Checks*.

14 Oil level/temperature sensor
 – removal and refitting

1 The sensor is fitted in the following locations **(see illustrations)**:

1.1, 1.4 and 1.6 litre petrol engines:
Front side of the cylinder block adjacent to the oil filter housing.

2.0 litre petrol engines:
Rear side of the cylinder block at the sump-to-block joint.

1.4 litre diesel engines:
Rear side of the cylinder block, between cylinders 2 and 3.

2.0 litre diesel engines:
Rear side of the cylinder block, adjacent to the transmission housing.

2 The removal and refitting procedure is as described for the oil pressure switch in Section 13. Access is most easily obtained from underneath the vehicle.

Notes

Chapter 5 Part B:
Ignition system – petrol models

Contents

Degrees of difficulty

Easy, suitable for novice with little experience		Fairly easy, suitable for beginner with some experience		Fairly difficult, suitable for competent DIY mechanic		Difficult, suitable for experienced DIY mechanic		Very difficult, suitable for expert DIY or professional	

Specifications

General

System type	Static (distributorless) ignition system controlled by engine management ECU
Firing order	1-3-4-2 (No 1 cylinder at transmission end)
Spark plugs	See Chapter 1A Specifications
Ignition timing	Controlled by engine management ECU

Torque wrench setting

	Nm	lbf ft
Ignition HT coil bolts	8	6
Knock sensor securing bolt	20	15

1 Ignition system – general information

The ignition system is integrated with the fuel injection system to form a combined engine management system under the control of one ECU (see Chapter 4A for further information). The ignition side of the system is of the static (distributorless) type, consisting of the ignition coils and spark plugs. The ignition coils are housed in a single unit mounted directly above the spark plugs. The coils are integral with the spark plug caps and are pushed directly onto the spark plugs, one for each plug. This removes the need for any HT leads connecting the coils to the plugs.

Under the control of the ECU, the ignition coils operate on the 'wasted spark' principle, ie, each plug sparks twice for every cycle of the engine, once during the compression stroke and once during the exhaust stroke. The spark voltage is greatest in the cylinder which is under compression; in the cylinder on its exhaust stroke the compression is low and this produces a very weak spark which has no effect on the exhaust gases.

The ECU uses its inputs from the various sensors to calculate the required ignition advance setting and coil charging time, depending on engine temperature, load and speed. At idle speeds, the ECU varies the ignition timing to alter the torque characteristic of the engine, enabling the idle speed to be controlled. This system operates in conjunction with the idle speed control motor – see Chapter 4A for additional details.

A knock sensor is also incorporated into the ignition system. Mounted onto the cylinder block, the sensor detects the high-frequency vibrations caused when the engine starts to pre-ignite, or 'pink'. Under these conditions, the knock sensor sends an electrical signal to the ECU, which in turn retards the ignition advance setting in small steps until the 'pinking' ceases.

2 Ignition system – testing

⚠️ **Warning: Voltages produced by an electronic ignition system are considerably higher than those produced by conventional ignition systems. Extreme care must be taken when working on the system with the ignition switched on. Persons with surgically implanted cardiac pacemaker devices should keep well clear of the ignition circuits, components and test equipment.**

If a fault appears in the engine management (fuel injection/ignition) system, first ensure that the fault is not due to a poor electrical connection or poor maintenance; ie, check that the air cleaner filter element is clean, the spark plugs are in good condition and correctly gapped, that the engine breather hoses are clear and undamaged, referring to Chapter 1A for further information. Also check that the accelerator cable is correctly adjusted as described in Chapter 4A. If the engine is running very roughly, check the compression pressures and the valve clearances as described in Chapter 2A, B or C, where applicable.

If these checks fail to reveal the cause of the problem the vehicle should be taken to a suitably-equipped Peugeot dealer or specialist for testing. A wiring block diagnostic connector is incorporated in the engine management circuit into which a special electronic diagnostic tester can be plugged. The tester will locate the fault quickly and simply alleviating the need to test all the system components individually, which is a time-consuming operation that carries a high risk of damaging the ECU.

The only ignition system checks which can be carried out by the home mechanic are those described in Chapter 1A relating to the spark plugs. If necessary, the system wiring and connectors can be checked as described in Chapter 12 ensuring that the ECU wiring connector(s) have first been disconnected.

3.1 Disconnect the breather hose from the cylinder head cover

3 Ignition coil unit – removal, testing and refitting

Note: *Before disconnecting any wiring on the ignition system, it is recommended that the battery negative terminal be disconnected.*

Removal

SOHC engines

1 Disconnect the engine breather hose at the quick-release connections on the air cleaner air inlet duct, cylinder head cover and inlet manifold (see illustration). Move the hose to one side.

2 Unplug the wiring connector from the top of the ignition coil unit (see illustration).

3.3 Undo the coil retaining bolts (arrowed) . . .

3.2 Disconnect the wiring plug from the ignition HT coil

3 Undo the nut securing each end of the ignition coil unit to the mounting studs (see illustration). Note that it is quite likely that the stud will be released with the nut.

4 Lift the ignition coil unit upwards off the mounting studs and at the same time carefully ease the HT extension pillars away from the tops of the spark plugs. Lift the unit off the plugs and withdraw it from the engine (see illustration).

1.4 litre DOHC engines

5 Remove the plastic style cover from the top of the engine (see illustration).

6 Disconnect the wiring plug from the left-hand end of the ignition coil unit (see illustration).

7 Depress the clips and remove the breather pipes from the camshaft cover (see illustration).

3.4 . . . then ease the ignition HT coil assembly off the spark plugs and remove it from the engine

3.5 Remove the engine style cover

3.6 Disconnect the wiring plug

3.7 Depress the clips and disconnect the breather pipes

3.8 Undo the two coil pack retaining bolts (arrowed)

3.9 Using a metal bar as a handle to withdraw the ignition coil unit vertically

3.11 Disconnect the HT coil wiring plug (arrowed)

8 Undo the two mounting bolts securing the coil pack **(see illustration)**.

9 Lift the ignition coil unit upwards and at the same time carefully ease the HT extension pillars away from the tops of the spark plugs. Lift the unit off the plugs and withdraw it from the engine. The ignition coil unit can be a tight fit and must be lifted out straight up to prevent any damage. A flat bar, with a hole drilled in each end for the bolts, can be used as a handle to withdraw the ignition coil unit **(see illustration)**.

2.0 litre engines

10 Undo the six screws and lift off the plastic cover from the top of the engine.

11 Disconnect the wiring connector at the

5.1 Knock sensor retaining bolt (arrowed) – 1.4 litre engine shown

left-hand end of the ignition coil unit. Undo the three retaining bolts and lift the coil unit upwards off the spark plugs and from its location between the cylinder head covers **(see illustration)**.

Testing

12 The circuitry arrangement of the ignition coil unit on these engines is such that testing of an individual coil in isolation from the remainder of the engine management system is unlikely to prove effective in diagnosing a particular fault. Should there be any reason to suspect a faulty individual coil, the engine management system should be tested by a Peugeot dealer or specialist using diagnostic test equipment (see Section 2).

Refitting

13 Refitting is a reversal of the relevant removal procedure ensuring the wiring connectors are securely reconnected.

---

4 Ignition timing –
checking and adjustment

1 There are no timing marks on the flywheel or crankshaft pulley. The timing is constantly being monitored and adjusted by the engine management ECU, and nominal values cannot

be given. Therefore, it is not possible for the home mechanic to check the ignition timing.

2 The only way in which the ignition timing can be checked is using special electronic test equipment, connected to the engine management system diagnostic connector.

---

5 Knock sensor –
removal and refitting

Removal

1 On all engines (except 2.0 litre engine), the knock sensor is screwed into the rear face of the cylinder block **(see illustration)**, and, on 2.0 litre engines, into the front face.

2 Firmly apply the handbrake, and then jack up the front of the vehicle and support it securely on axle stands (see *Jacking and vehicle support*). Undo the screws and remove the engine undershield (where fitted).

3 Trace the wiring back from the sensor to its wiring connector, and disconnect it from the main loom.

4 Undo the sensor securing bolt and remove the sensor from the cylinder block.

Refitting

5 Refitting is a reversal of the removal procedure, ensuring that the sensor securing bolt is tightened to the specified torque.

Chapter 5 Part C:
Pre/post-heating system – diesel models

Contents

Degrees of difficulty

| **Easy,** suitable for novice with little experience 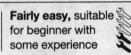 | **Fairly easy,** suitable for beginner with some experience | **Fairly difficult,** suitable for competent DIY mechanic | **Difficult,** suitable for experienced DIY mechanic | **Very difficult,** suitable for expert DIY or professional |

Specifications

Preheating system
Note: *At the time of writing no information concerning the 1.4 litre engine was available.*

2.0 litre engines
Preheating period at ambient temperature of:
–30°C	20 seconds
–10°C	5 seconds
0°C	0.5 seconds
18°C	0 seconds

Post-heating system
Note: *At the time of writing no information concerning the 1.4 litre engine was available.*

2.0 litre engines
Post-heating period at ambient temperature of:
–30°C	3 minutes
–10°C	3 minutes
0°C	1 minute
18°C	30 seconds
40°C	0 seconds

Glow plugs
Resistance (typical) . . . . 1 ohm approximately

Torque wrench settings
	Nm	lbf ft
Glow plugs:		
1.4 litre engine	8	6
2.0 litre engines	22	16

1 Pre/post-heating system
– description and testing

Description

1 To assist cold starting, diesel engines are fitted with a preheating system, which consists of four of glow plugs (one per cylinder), a glow plug relay unit, a facia-mounted warning lamp, the engine management ECU, and the associated electrical wiring.

2 The glow plugs are miniature electric heating elements, encapsulated in a metal case with a probe at one end and electrical connection at the other. Each combustion chamber has one glow plug threaded into it, with the tip of the glow plug probe positioned directly in line with incoming spray of fuel from the injectors. When the glow plug is energised, it heats up rapidly, causing the fuel passing over the glow plug probe to be heated to its optimum temperature, ready for combustion. In addition, some of the fuel passing over the glow plugs is ignited and this helps to trigger the combustion process.

3 The preheating system begins to operate as soon as the ignition key is switched to the second position, but only if the engine coolant temperature is below 20°C and the engine is turned at more than 70 rpm for 0.2 seconds. A facia-mounted warning lamp informs the driver that preheating is taking place. The lamp extinguishes when sufficient preheating has taken place to allow the engine to be started, but power will still be supplied to the glow plugs for a further period until the engine is started. If no attempt is made to start the engine, the power supply to the glow plugs is switched off after 10 seconds, to prevent battery drain and glow plug burnout.

4 With the electronically controlled diesel injection systems fitted to models in this manual, the glow plug relay unit is controlled by the engine management system ECU, which determines the necessary preheating time based on inputs from the various system sensors. The system monitors the temperature of the intake air, and then alters the preheating time (the length for which the glow plugs are supplied with current) to suit the conditions.

5 Post-heating takes place after the ignition key has been released from the 'start' position, but only if the engine coolant temperature is below 20°C, the injected fuel flow is less than a certain rate, and the engine speed is less than 2000 rpm. The glow plugs continue to operate for a maximum of 60 seconds, helping to improve fuel combustion whilst the engine is warming-up, resulting in quieter, smoother running and reduced exhaust emissions.

Testing

6 If the system malfunctions, testing is ultimately by substitution of known good units, but some preliminary checks may be made as follows.

7 Connect a voltmeter or 12 volt test lamp between the glow plug supply cable and earth (engine or vehicle metal). Make sure that the live connection is kept clear of the engine and bodywork.

8 Have an assistant switch on the ignition, and check that voltage is applied to the glow plugs. Note the time for which the warning light is lit, and the total time for which voltage is applied before the system cuts out. Switch off the ignition.

9 Compare the results with the information given in the Specifications. Warning light time will increase with lower temperatures and decrease with higher temperatures.

10 If there is no supply at all, the control unit or associated wiring is at fault.

11 To gain access to the glow plugs for further testing, remove the following components, according to model:

1.4 litre engine: Remove the cylinder head cover/manifold assembly as described in Chapter 2D.

2.0 litre engines: Undo the four plastic fasteners and remove the engine cover from the top of the engine. Disconnect the injector wiring plugs and move the wiring harness tray to one side after undoing the two retaining nuts. For access to No 4 glow plug, undo the three

bolts and move the fuel pipe support bracket to one side (see illustrations).

12 Disconnect the main supply cable and the interconnecting wire or strap from the top of the glow plugs. Be careful not to drop the nuts and washers.

13 Use a continuity tester, or a 12 volt test lamp connected to the battery positive terminal, to check for continuity between each glow plug terminal and earth. The resistance of a glow plug in good condition is very low (less than 1 ohm), so if the test lamp does not light or the continuity tester shows a high resistance, the glow plug is certainly defective.

14 If an ammeter is available, the current draw of each glow plug can be checked. After an initial surge of 15 to 20 amps, each plug should draw 12 amps. Any plug which draws much more or less than this is probably defective.

15 As a final check, the glow plugs can be removed and inspected as described in the following Section. On completion, refit any components removed for access.

2 Glow plugs – removal, inspection and refitting

Caution: If the preheating system has just been energised, or if the engine has been running, the glow plugs will be very hot.

Removal

1 Ensure the ignition is turned off. To gain access to the glow plugs, remove the components described in Section 1, according to engine.

2 Unscrew the nuts from the glow plug terminals, and recover the washers. Note that on some 2.0 litre models, an interconnecting wire/shunt is fitted between the four plugs (see illustration).

3 Where applicable, carefully move any obstructing pipes or wires to one side to enable access to the relevant glow plug(s).

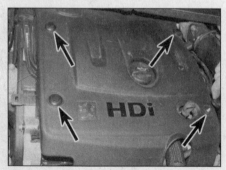

1.11a Rotate the four fasteners (arrowed) 90° anti-clockwise and pull the plastic cover from place

1.11b Undo the two nuts (arrowed) and move the wiring harness tray to one side

2.2 Undo the nuts securing the glow plug connections (arrowed)

4 Unscrew the glow plug(s) and remove from the cylinder head **(see illustration)**.

Inspection

5 Inspect each glow plug for physical damage. Burnt or eroded glow plug tips can be caused by a bad injector spray pattern. Have the injectors checked if this sort of damage is found.

6 If the glow plugs are in good physical condition, check them electrically using a 12 volt test lamp or continuity tester as described in the previous Section.

7 The glow plugs can be energised by applying 12 volts to them to verify that they heat up evenly and in the required time. Observe the following precautions.

  a) *Support the glow plug by clamping it carefully in a vice or self-locking pliers. Remember it will become red-hot.*
  b) *Make sure that the power supply or test lead incorporates a fuse or overload trip to protect against damage from a short-circuit.*
  c) *After testing, allow the glow plug to cool for several minutes before attempting to handle it.*

8 A glow plug in good condition will start to glow red at the tip after drawing current for 5 seconds or so. Any plug which takes much longer to start glowing, or which starts glowing in the middle instead of at the tip, is defective.

Refitting

9 Refit by reversing the removal operations. Apply a smear of copper-based anti-seize compound to the plug threads and tighten the glow plugs to the specified torque. Do not overtighten, as this can damage the glow plug element.

10 Refit any components removed for access.

| 3 | Pre/post-heating system relay unit – removal and refitting |

Removal

1 The unit is located on the left-hand front side of the engine compartment where it is mounted onto the rear of the battery tray.

2 Disconnect the battery negative lead (see Chapter 5A).

3 Unscrew the retaining nut securing the relay control unit to the battery tray **(see illustration)**, take care not to lose the bolt from the battery tray.

4 Unscrew the retaining nuts and free the main feed and supply wires from the base of the unit, then disconnect the wiring connector.

3.3 Undo the glow plug control unit mounting nut (arrowed) and free it from the rear of the battery tray

2.4 Unscrew the glow plugs from the cylinder head

Remove the unit from the engine compartment **(see illustration)**.

Refitting

5 Refitting is a reversal of removal, ensuring that the wiring connectors are correctly connected.

3.4 Disconnect the wiring connector (1) then unscrew the nuts (2) and disconnect the feed and supply wires from the unit

Chapter 6
Clutch

Contents

Degrees of difficulty

Easy, suitable for novice with little experience	**Fairly easy,** suitable for beginner with some experience	**Fairly difficult,** suitable for competent DIY mechanic	**Difficult,** suitable for experienced DIY mechanic	**Very difficult,** suitable for expert DIY or professional

Specifications

Type	Single dry plate with diaphragm spring. Depending on model type the release mechanism may be hydraulically operated or cable-operated.

Friction plate diameter
Petrol models:

1.1 litre models	180 mm
1.4 litre models:	
SOHC	180 mm
DOHC	200 mm
1.6 litre models	200 mm
2.0 litre models	228 mm

Diesel models:

1.4 litre models	200 mm
2.0 litre models	228 mm

Torque wrench settings

	Nm	lbf ft
Cable upper end fitting nuts	10	7
Hydraulic system components:		
Master cylinder mounting nuts	20	15
Slave cylinder mounting bolts	20	15
Slave cylinder bleed screw	7	5
Pressure plate retaining bolts:		
Petrol engine models	15	11
Diesel engine models	20	15

2.2 Clutch pedal stop bolt (shown with facia removed)

1 General information

The clutch consists of a friction plate, a pressure plate assembly, a release bearing and the release mechanism; all of these components are contained in the large cast-aluminium alloy bellhousing, sandwiched between the engine and the transmission.

The friction plate is fitted between the engine flywheel and the clutch pressure plate, and is allowed to slide on the transmission input shaft splines.

The pressure plate assembly is bolted to the engine flywheel. When the engine is running, drive is transmitted from the crankshaft, via the flywheel, to the friction plate (these components being clamped securely together by the pressure plate assembly) and from the friction plate to the transmission input shaft.

To interrupt the drive, the spring pressure must be relaxed. On the models covered in this manual, two different types of clutch release mechanism are used; right-hand drive diesel engine models have a hydraulically-operated clutch release mechanism while all other models have a cable-operated clutch release mechanism.

On the hydraulically-operated release mechanism, the clutch pedal is connected to the master cylinder pushrod. The master cylinder is mounted on the engine compartment bulkhead and is connected to the slave cylinder mounted on the front of the transmission unit. The hydraulic fluid for the system is taken from the braking system master cylinder fluid reservoir, which is linked to the clutch master cylinder via the pipe on the side of the reservoir. Depressing the clutch pedal moves the piston in the master cylinder forwards. Hydraulic pressure in the pipe/hose forces the piston in the slave cylinder forwards which in turn moves the clutch release fork.

On the cable-operated clutch, the clutch pedal is linked to the clutch release fork lever by a cable. Depressing the clutch pedal pulls the control cable inner wire, and this moves the release fork.

On all clutches, as the clutch release fork moves, it presses the release bearing against the pressure plate spring fingers. This causes the springs to deform and releases the clamping force on the pressure plate.

2 Clutch – adjustment

Cable-operated clutch

1 The clutch cable incorporates an automatic adjustment mechanism and therefore requires no regular adjustment. If the automatic adjustment mechanism is thought to be faulty it can be checked as follows.

2 Reach up behind the facia and locate the clutch pedal stop bolt. Back off the stop bolt until a small amount of freeplay is present then screw the bolt in until all freeplay is removed from the cable, without tensioning the cable at all (see illustration).

3 To gain access to the transmission end of the cable, remove the air cleaner housing as described in the relevant part of Chapter 4. To further improve access, also remove the battery and battery tray as described in Chapter 5A.

4 Pull back on the clutch release fork lever and check that the fork moves at least 5 mm. Have an assistant operate the clutch pedal a few times to operated the clutch adjustment mechanism then measure the release lever travel during a full pedal stroke (ensure there are no obstructions beneath the clutch pedal); this should be at least 24 mm (see illustrations). If the release lever will not move backwards when pulled, or the lever travel is less than specified, the automatic adjustment mechanism is faulty and the cable should be renewed.

5 On completion of the check, refit all components removed for access.

Hydraulically-operated clutch

6 The hydraulic circuit is self-adjusting and requires no regular adjustment. Should there be any problems with the clutch, bleed the hydraulic circuit. If this fails to solve the problem; renew the hydraulic system components.

3 Clutch cable – removal and refitting

Removal

1 To gain access to the transmission end of the cable remove the air cleaner housing as described in the relevant part of Chapter 4. Where necessary, also remove the battery, battery tray and mounting plate (see Chapter 5A).

2 Working in the engine compartment, free the inner cable fitting from the end of the

2.4a Pull back on the release lever fork and measure the amount of movement (1) . . .

2.4b . . . then measure the release lever travel (2) during a full pedal stroke to check the cable self-adjust mechanism – see text (petrol engine shown)

3.2a Free the inner cable fitting from the release lever . . .

3.2b . . . then unclip the outer cable from the transmission bracket (petrol engine shown)

4 Clutch pedal – removal and refitting

release fork lever then unclip the outer cable end fitting and grommet from the bracket on the transmission unit **(see illustrations)**. Work back along the cable, releasing it from any relevant clips and guides whilst noting its correct routing.

3 Working inside the vehicle, reach up and unhook the cable from the upper end of the clutch pedal **(see illustration)**. Note that access to the upper end of the pedal is very poor and can only be improved by removing the steering column (see Chapter 10).

4 On right-hand drive models, remove the coolant expansion tank as described in Chapter 3. Unscrew the cable end fitting retaining nuts then free the cable end fitting and grommet from the bulkhead and remove the cable from the vehicle **(see illustration)**.

5 On left-hand drive models, return to the engine compartment, then release the outer cable end fitting and grommet from the bulkhead. Withdraw the cable forwards and remove it from the vehicle.

6 Examine the cable, looking for worn end fittings or a damaged outer casing, and for signs of fraying of the inner wire. Check the cable's operation; the inner wire should move smoothly and easily through the outer casing. Remember that a cable that appears serviceable when tested off the car may well be much heavier in operation when in its working position. Renew the cable if it shows signs of excessive wear or any damage or the automatic adjustment mechanism is faulty.

Refitting

7 Apply a thin smear of multi-purpose grease to the inner cable end fittings and lubricate the outer cable grommets with a silicone-based lubricant spray to ease installation.

8 Route the cable correctly around the engine compartment then pass the cable through the engine compartment bulkhead.

9 On right-hand drive models, locate the outer cable end fitting on the studs and tighten its retaining nuts to the specified torque.

10 On left-hand drive models, push firmly on the outer cable end fitting to ensure its grommet is correctly seated in the bulkhead.

11 On all models, from inside the vehicle, hook the inner cable onto the clutch pedal, and check that it is correctly located.

12 Ensuring that the cable is correctly routed and retained by all the relevant retaining clips and guides, engage the inner cable with the release fork lever then locate the outer cable in the transmission bracket, ensuring its grommet is correctly seated.

13 Operate the clutch pedal several times to operate the automatic adjustment mechanism.

14 Check the operation of the adjustment mechanism as described in Section 2 then refit all components removed for access. On right-hand drive models refit the coolant expansion tank as described in Chapter 3 and top-up the cooling system.

Removal

Cable-operated clutch

1 To improve access to the transmission end of the clutch cable remove the air cleaner housing as described in the relevant part of Chapter 4. Where necessary, also remove the battery, battery tray and mounting plate (see Chapter 5A).

2 Free the inner cable fitting from the end of the release fork lever then unclip the outer cable end fitting and grommet from the bracket on the transmission unit **(see illustrations 3.2a and 3.2b)**.

3 To improve access to the clutch pedal, remove the steering column as described in Chapter 10.

4 Unhook the clutch cable from the upper end of the pedal **(see illustration 3.3)**.

5 Where necessary, carefully unhook and remove the assistance spring assembly from the side of the pedal.

6 Unhook the return spring (where fitted) from the pedal then slacken and remove the pivot bolt and nut **(see illustration)**. Manoeuvre the clutch pedal and (where fitted) return spring out of position and slide the spacer out from the pedal pivot.

7 Examine all components for signs of wear or damage and renew as necessary.

Hydraulically-operated clutch

8 To improve access to the clutch pedal, remove the steering column as described in Chapter 10.

9 Remove the pivot clip securing the master cylinder pushrod to the clutch pedal. To remove the pivot clip, unhook its lower retaining tang then pivot it upwards slightly before sliding it out of position.

10 Remove the pedal as described in paragraphs 5 to 7.

Refitting

Cable-operated clutch

11 Apply a smear of multi-purpose grease

3.3 Release the clip (1) and unhook the cable end fitting (2) from the top of the clutch pedal (shown with facia removed)

3.4 On right-hand drive models undo the nuts (arrowed) and free the cable end fitting from the bulkhead

4.6 Unscrew the nut (1) and withdraw the clutch pedal pivot bolt (2) (shown with facia removed)

5.4 Prise out the securing clip, and disconnect the hydraulic pipe

5.14 Lever out the hydraulic pipe securing clip

5.16 Undo the two clutch slave cylinder mounting bolts (arrowed)

to the spacer and insert it into the pedal pivot bore. Where necessary, refit the return spring to the pedal pivot.

12 Refit the pedal assembly and insert the pivot bolt, tightening its nut securely. Ensure the return spring (where fitted) is correctly located.

13 Refit the assistance spring assembly (where fitted), ensuring it is correctly located on both the pedal and bracket.

14 Hook the cable end fitting back onto the upper end of the pedal.

15 Working in the engine compartment, engage the inner cable with the release fork lever then locate the outer cable in the transmission bracket, ensuring its grommet is correctly seated (lubricate the grommet with a silicone-based spray to ease installation).

16 Operate the clutch pedal several times to operate the automatic adjustment mechanism.

17 Check the operation of the adjustment mechanism as described in Section 2 then refit all components removed for access (see the relevant parts of Chapters 4, 5 and 10 – as applicable).

Hydraulically-operated clutch

18 Install the pedal as described in paragraphs 11 to 13.

19 Align the pedal with the master cylinder pushrod and securely refit the pivot clip.

20 Refit the steering column (where removed) as described in Chapter 10.

5 Clutch hydraulic system components – removal and refitting

⚠ **Warning: Hydraulic fluid is poisonous; wash off immediately and thoroughly in the case of skin contact, and seek immediate medical advice if any fluid is swallowed or gets into the eyes. Certain types of hydraulic fluid are inflammable, and may ignite when allowed into contact with hot components; when servicing any hydraulic system, it is safest to assume that the fluid is inflammable, and to take precautions against the risk of fire as though it is petrol that is being handled. Hydraulic fluid is also**

an effective paint stripper, and will attack plastics; if any is spilt, it should be washed off immediately, using copious quantities of fresh water. Finally, it is hygroscopic (it absorbs moisture from the air) – old fluid may be contaminated and unfit for further use. When topping-up or renewing the fluid, always use the recommended type, and ensure that it comes from a freshly-opened sealed container.

Master cylinder

Removal

1 From inside the vehicle, remove the pivot clip securing the master cylinder pushrod to the clutch pedal. To remove the pivot clip, unhook its lower retaining tang then pivot it upwards slightly before sliding it out of position.

2 Remove the coolant expansion tank as described in Chapter 3.

3 Remove all traces of dirt from the exterior of the master cylinder.

4 Disconnect the fluid supply hose union on the side of the master cylinder then prise out the circlip from the master cylinder union and disconnect the clutch pipe **(see illustration)**. Plug the master cylinder unions and pipe ends to minimise fluid loss and prevent the entry of dirt. Refit the circlip correctly to the groove in the master cylinder.

5 Unscrew the mounting nuts securing the master cylinder to the bulkhead. Manoeuvre the master cylinder out of position and recover the seal fitted between the cylinder and bulkhead.

6 At the time of writing it was unclear whether it was possible to overhaul the master cylinder. Refer to your Peugeot dealer for the latest information on parts availability.

Refitting

7 Prior to refitting, ensure the circlip is correctly fitted to the master cylinder union.

8 Fit the seal to the rear of the master cylinder and then locate the master cylinder on its studs. Refit the mounting nuts, tightening them to the specified torque.

9 Reconnect the hydraulic pipe to the master

cylinder, making sure it is securely retained by the circlip, and then reconnect the fluid supply hose securely.

10 Align the pedal with the master cylinder pushrod and securely refit the pivot clip.

11 Bleed the hydraulic system as described in Section 6.

12 Once the clutch is functioning correctly, refit the coolant expansion tank (see Chapter 3) and top-up the cooling system.

Slave cylinder

Removal

13 To improve access to the slave cylinder, remove the air cleaner housing as described in Chapter 4A or 4B.

14 Prise out the circlip from the slave cylinder union and disconnect the clutch pipe **(see illustration)**. Plug the slave cylinder union and pipe end to minimise fluid loss and prevent the entry of dirt. Refit the circlip correctly to the groove in the cylinder.

15 Release the wiring harness from its retaining clips and position it clear of the slave cylinder.

16 Slacken and remove the bolts securing the slave cylinder to the front of the transmission housing then manoeuvre the cylinder out of position **(see illustration)**.

17 At the time of writing it was unclear whether it was possible to overhaul the slave cylinder. Refer to your Peugeot dealer for the latest information on parts availability.

Refitting

18 Prior to refitting, ensure the circlip is correctly fitted to the slave cylinder union.

19 Engage the slave cylinder with the release fork lever and seat it correctly on the transmission unit. Refit the slave cylinder retaining bolts, tightening them to the specified torque.

20 Reconnect the clutch pipe to the cylinder, ensuring it is securely retained by the circlip. Clip the wiring harness back into position.

21 Bleed the hydraulic system as described in Section 6.

22 Once the clutch is functioning correctly, refit the air cleaner housing (see Chapter 4A or 4B).

6.6 Clutch slave cylinder bleed screw (arrowed – viewed from above)

6 Clutch hydraulic system – bleeding

⚠️ *Warning: Hydraulic fluid is poisonous; wash off immediately and thoroughly in the case of skin contact, and seek immediate medical advice if any fluid is swallowed or gets into the eyes. Certain types of hydraulic fluid are inflammable, and may ignite when allowed into contact with hot components; when servicing any hydraulic system, it is safest to assume that the fluid is inflammable, and to take precautions against the risk of fire as though it is petrol that is being handled. Hydraulic fluid is also an effective paint stripper, and will attack plastics; if any is spilt, it should be washed off immediately, using copious quantities of fresh water. Finally, it is hygroscopic (it absorbs moisture from the air) – old fluid may be contaminated and unfit for further use. When topping-up or renewing the fluid, always use the recommended type, and ensure that it comes from a freshly-opened sealed container.*

1 The correct operation of any hydraulic system is only possible after removing all air from the components and circuit; this is achieved by bleeding the system. During the bleeding procedure, add only clean, unused hydraulic fluid of the recommended type; never re-use fluid that has already been bled from the system. Ensure that sufficient fluid is available before starting work.

2 If hydraulic fluid has been lost from the

6.14 Check the operation of the clutch by measuring the distance (X) between the clutch pedal and bulkhead at the point where the clutch engages/disengages – see text

system, or air has entered because of a leak, ensure that the fault is cured before proceeding further.

3 Park the vehicle on level ground.

4 Collect a clean glass jar, a suitable length of plastic or rubber tubing which is a tight fit over the bleed screw, and a ring spanner to fit the screw. The aid of an assistant will also help, although clutch bleeding can be performed by an individual since the pedal will stay depressed and will not automatically spring back to the fully raised position.

5 Unscrew the master cylinder reservoir cap (the clutch master cylinder shares the same reservoir as the braking system) and fill the reservoir right up to the base of the filler neck. Refit the cap loosely, and remember to maintain the fluid level at least above the DANGER level line throughout the procedure, or there is a risk of further air entering the system.

6 Remove the dust cap from the slave cylinder bleed screw located on the front of the transmission unit **(see illustration)**. Remove all traces of dirt then fit the spanner and tube to the screw, place the other end of the tube in the jar, and pour in sufficient fluid to cover the end of the tube.

7 Slacken the bleed screw approximately one complete turn.

8 Operate the clutch pedal by hand rapidly through twelve complete downward and upward strokes, at the rate of approximately one stroke a second; on the twelfth stroke leave the pedal fully depressed.

9 Return to the engine compartment and securely tighten the bleed screw.

10 Raise the clutch pedal fully.

11 Fill the master cylinder reservoir back up to the base of the filler neck then loosely refit the cap.

12 Repeat the operations described in paragraphs 7 to 10.

13 Top-up the master cylinder fluid level to the MAXI mark then refit the reservoir cap.

14 Operate the clutch pedal through approximately 40 strokes and check the operation of the clutch pedal. There should be a distance of at least 35 mm between the pedal and bulkhead at the point where the clutch disengages/engages **(see illustration)**. If the pedal feels at all spongy, air must still be present in the system, and further bleeding is required. Failure to bleed properly after a reasonable repetition of the bleeding procedure may be due to worn master cylinder seals.

15 When bleeding is complete, wash off any spilt fluid then tighten the bleed screw to the specified torque and refit the dust cap.

16 Check the hydraulic fluid level in the master cylinder reservoir, and top-up if necessary (see *Weekly checks*). Discard any fluid that has been bled from the system; it will not be fit for re-use.

7 Clutch assembly – removal, inspection and refitting

Note: *Although some friction materials no longer contain asbestos, it is safest to assume they do, and to take precautions accordingly.*

⚠️ *Warning: Dust created by clutch wear and deposited on the clutch components may contain asbestos, which is a health hazard. DON'T blow it out with compressed air, nor inhale any of it. DO NOT use petrol or petroleum-based solvents to clean off the dust. Brake system cleaner or methylated spirit should be used to flush the dust into a suitable receptacle. After the clutch components are wiped clean with rags, dispose of the contaminated rags and cleaner in a sealed, marked container.*

Removal

1 Unless the complete engine/transmission unit is to be removed from the car and separated for major overhaul (see Chapter 2E), the clutch can be reached by removing the transmission as described in Chapter 7A.

2 Before disturbing the clutch, use chalk or a marker pen to mark the relationship of the pressure plate assembly to the flywheel.

3 Working in a diagonal sequence, slacken the pressure plate bolts by half a turn at a time, until spring pressure is released and the bolts can be unscrewed by hand.

4 Prise the pressure plate assembly off its locating dowels, and collect the friction plate, noting which way round the plate is fitted **(see illustrations)**.

7.4a Free the pressure plate from its locating dowels . . .

7.4b . . . and remove the friction plate, noting which way around it is fitted

7.14 Ensure the friction plate is fitted the correct way around with its spring hub (B) facing away from the flywheel side (A)

7.17 Align the friction plate centrally inside the pressure plate ...

Inspection

Note: *Due to the amount of work necessary to remove and refit clutch components, it is considered good practice to renew the clutch friction plate, pressure plate assembly and release bearing as a matched set, even if only one of these is worn enough to require renewal. It is worth considering the renewal of the clutch components on a preventive basis if the engine and/or transmission have been removed for some other reason.*

5 Remove the clutch assembly.

6 When cleaning clutch components, read first the warning at the beginning of this Section; remove dust using a clean, dry cloth, and working in a well-ventilated atmosphere.

7 Check the friction plate facings for signs of wear, damage or oil contamination. If the friction material is cracked, burnt, scored or damaged, or if it is contaminated with oil or grease (shown by shiny black patches), the friction plate must be renewed.

8 If the friction material is still serviceable, check that the centre boss splines are unworn, that the torsion springs are in good condition and securely fastened, and that all the rivets are tight. If any wear or damage is found, the friction plate must be renewed.

9 If the friction material is fouled with oil, this

7.18 ... then tighten the pressure plate bolts evenly and progressively to the specified torque

must be due to an oil leak from the crankshaft left-hand oil seal, from the sump-to-cylinder block joint, or from the transmission input shaft. Renew the seal or repair the joint, as appropriate, as described in the appropriate Part of Chapter 2 or 7A, before installing the new friction plate.

10 Check the pressure plate assembly for obvious signs of wear or damage; shake it to check for loose rivets or worn or damaged fulcrum rings, and check that the drive straps securing the pressure plate to the cover do not show signs (such as a deep yellow or blue discoloration) of overheating. If the diaphragm spring is worn or damaged, or if its pressure is in any way suspect, the pressure plate assembly should be renewed.

11 Examine the machined bearing surfaces of the pressure plate and of the flywheel; they should be clean, completely flat, and free from scratches or scoring. If either is discoloured from excessive heat, or shows signs of cracks, it should be renewed – although minor damage of this nature can sometimes be polished away using emery paper.

12 Check that the release bearing contact surface rotates smoothly and easily, with no sign of noise or roughness. Also check that the surface itself is smooth and unworn, with no signs of cracks, pitting or scoring. If there is any doubt about its condition, the bearing must be renewed (see Section 8).

Refitting

13 On reassembly, ensure that the bearing surfaces of the flywheel and pressure plate are completely clean, smooth, and free from oil or grease. Use solvent to remove any protective grease from new components.

14 Fit the friction plate so that its spring hub assembly faces away from the flywheel; there may be a marking showing which way round the plate is to be refitted **(see illustration)**.

15 Refit the pressure plate assembly, aligning the marks made on dismantling (if the original pressure plate is re-used), and locating the

pressure plate on its three locating dowels. Fit the pressure plate bolts, but tighten them only finger-tight, so that the friction plate can still be moved.

16 The friction plate must now be centralised, so that when the transmission is refitted, its input shaft will pass through the splines at the centre of the friction plate.

17 Centralisation can be achieved by passing a screwdriver or other long bar through the friction plate and into the hole in the crankshaft; the friction plate can then be moved around until it is centred on the crankshaft hole. Alternatively, a clutch-aligning-tool can be used to eliminate the guesswork; these can be obtained from most accessory shops **(see illustration)**. A home-made aligning tool can be fabricated from a length of metal rod or wooden dowel which fits closely inside the crankshaft hole, and has insulating tape wound around it to match the diameter of the friction plate splined hole.

18 When the friction plate is centralised, tighten the pressure plate bolts evenly and progressively in a diagonal sequence to the specified torque setting **(see illustration)**.

19 Check the clutch release mechanism (see Section 8) then refit the transmission as described in Chapter 7A.

---

8 Clutch release mechanism – removal, inspection and refitting

Note: *Refer to the warning concerning the dangers of asbestos dust at the beginning of Section 7.*

Removal

1 Unless the complete engine/transmission unit is to be removed from the car and separated for major overhaul (see Chapter 2E), the clutch release mechanism can be reached by removing the transmission only, as described in Chapter 7A.

8.2 Free the release bearing from the fork and slide it off the guide sleeve (petrol model shown)

8.3a Tap out the roll-pin . . .

8.3b . . . then remove the release lever from the top of the fork shaft

Petrol engine models

2 Unhook the release bearing from the fork, and slide it off its guide sleeve **(see illustration)**.

3 Drive out the roll pin, and remove the release lever from the top of the release fork shaft **(see illustrations)**. Discard the roll-pin – a new one must be used on refitting.

4 Depress the retaining tabs, then free the upper bush from the housing and slide it off the release fork shaft. Disengage the shaft from its lower bush, and manoeuvre it out from the transmission **(see illustrations)**. The lower pivot bush can then be removed from the transmission housing.

Diesel engine models

5 Free the rubber gaiter from the transmission housing and remove it from the release fork.

6 Unclip the fork balljoint from its pivot stud then remove the fork and bearing assembly from the transmission unit.

Inspection

7 Check the release mechanism, renewing any component, which is worn or damaged. Carefully check all bearing surfaces and points of contact.

8 When checking the release bearing itself, note that it is often considered worthwhile to renew it as a matter of course. Check that the contact surface rotates smoothly and easily, with no sign of noise or roughness, and that the surface itself is smooth and unworn, with no signs of cracks, pitting or scoring. If there is any doubt about its condition, the bearing must be renewed.

Refitting

Petrol engine models

9 Apply a smear of molybdenum disulphide grease (Peugeot recommend the use of Molykote BR2 Plus) to the shaft pivot bushes and the contact surfaces of the release fork, bearing and guide tube. **Note:** *Ensure no grease is applied to the input shaft splines.*

10 Locate the lower pivot bush in the transmission; ensuring it is securely retained by its locating tangs, and insert the release fork **(see illustration)**. Slide the upper bush down the release fork shaft, and clip it into position in the transmission housing.

11 Refit the release lever to the shaft, aligning it with the shaft hole, and secure it in position by tapping a new roll-pin fully into position.

12 Slide the release bearing onto the guide shaft and engage its tabs correctly with the release fork.

13 Check the operation of the release mechanism then refit the transmission as described in Chapter 7A.

Diesel engine models

14 Apply a smear of molybdenum disulphide grease (Peugeot recommend the use of Molykote BR2 Plus) to the contact surfaces of the release fork, bearing and guide tube. **Note:** *Ensure no grease is applied to the input shaft splines.*

15 Ensure the pivot stud is securely fitted to the transmission housing.

16 Engage the release bearing tabs with the end of the release fork then manoeuvre the assembly into position. Locate the bearing on its guide sleeve then press the fork firmly onto its pivot stud. Check the operation of the release mechanism; ensuring the fork is a secure fit on the stud.

17 Fit the gaiter to the fork and seat it correctly in the transmission housing.

18 Refit the transmission as described in Chapter 7A.

8.4a Unclip the upper pivot bush from the transmission housing and slide it off the shaft . . .

8.4b . . . then free the shaft from its lower bush (arrowed) and manoeuvre it out of position

8.10 On refitting ensure the lower bush lug is correctly located in the transmission housing

Chapter 7 Part A:
Manual transmission

Contents

Degrees of difficulty

Easy, suitable for novice with little experience	**Fairly easy,** suitable for beginner with some experience	**Fairly difficult,** suitable for competent DIY mechanic	**Difficult,** suitable for experienced DIY mechanic	**Very difficult,** suitable for expert DIY or professional

Specifications

General

Type	Manual, five forward speeds and reverse. Synchromesh on all forward speeds

Designation:
Petrol engine models:	
1.1, 1.4 and 1.6 litre	MA5
2.0 litre	BE4/5
Diesel engine models:	
1.4 litre	MA5
2.0 litre	BE4/5

Lubrication

Capacity:	
MA5 transmissions	2.0 litres
BE4/5 transmissions	1.9 litres
Recommended oil type	See *Lubricants and fluids*
Recommended gearchange linkage grease:	
Relay lever pivot ball	Esso 3106 Grease
Relay lever pivot and link rod balljoints	Esso Norva 275 Grease

Torque wrench settings

	Nm	lbf ft
MA5 transmission		
Clutch release bearing guide sleeve bolts	12	9
Engine-to-transmission fixing bolts	40	30
Gearchange linkage fixings:		
Relay lever pivot bolt	30	22
Linkage rod-to-lever pivot bolt	8	6
Gearchange lever mounting nuts	8	6
Left-hand engine/transmission mounting:		
Mounting bracket-to-transmission nuts	25	18
Mounting bracket-to-body bolts	19	14
Mounting-to-bracket bolts	30	22
Mounting centre nut	65	48
Oil drain plug	25	18
Oil filler/level plug	25	18
Rear mounting link:		
Link-to-mounting bolt	50	37
Link-to-subframe bolt	39	29
Reversing light switch	25	18
Roadwheel bolts	90	66

Torque wrench settings (continued)

	Nm	lbf ft
BE4/5 transmission		
Clutch release bearing guide sleeve bolts	12	9
Engine-to-transmission fixing bolts	55	41
Gearchange linkage fixings:		
Relay lever pivot bolt	30	22
Linkage rod-to-lever pivot bolt	8	6
Gearchange lever mounting nuts	8	6
Left-hand engine/transmission mounting:		
Mounting bracket-to-body bolts	19	14
Mounting stud to bracket	50	37
Mounting-to-bracket bolts	30	22
Mounting centre nut	65	48
Mounting bracket to transmission	60	44
Oil drain plug	35	26
Oil filler/level plug	22	16
Rear mounting link:		
Link-to-mounting bolt	50	37
Link-to-subframe bolt	35	26
Reversing light switch	25	18
Roadwheel bolts	90	66
Speedometer drive housing bolts	15	11

1 General information

1 The transmission is contained in a cast-aluminium alloy casing bolted to the engine's left-hand end, and consists of the gearbox and final drive differential – often called a transaxle.

2 Drive is transmitted from the crankshaft via the clutch to the input shaft, which has a

2.3a Slacken and remove the retaining screws (arrowed) . . .

2.3b . . . and fasteners . . .

splined extension to accept the clutch friction plate, and rotates in sealed ball bearings. From the input shaft, drive is transmitted to the output shaft, which rotates in a roller bearing at its right-hand end, and a sealed ball-bearing at its left-hand end. From the output shaft, the drive is transmitted to the differential crownwheel, which rotates with the differential case and planetary gears, thus driving the sun gears and driveshafts. The rotation of the planetary gears on their shaft allows the inner roadwheel to rotate at a slower speed than the outer roadwheel when the car is cornering.

3 The input and output shafts are arranged side-by-side, parallel to the crankshaft and driveshafts, so that their gear pinion teeth are in constant mesh. In the neutral position, the output shaft gear pinions rotate freely, so that drive cannot be transmitted to the crownwheel.

4 Gear selection is via a floor-mounted lever and selector rod mechanism. The selector rod causes the appropriate selector fork to move its respective synchrosleeve along the shaft, to lock the gear pinion to the synchro-hub. Since the synchro-hubs are splined to the output shaft, this locks the pinion to the shaft, so that drive can be transmitted. To ensure

2.3c . . . and remove the front section of the left-hand wheel arch liner

that gearchanging can be made quickly and quietly, a synchromesh system is fitted to all forward gears, consisting of baulk rings and spring-loaded fingers, as well as the gear pinions and synchro-hubs. The synchromesh cones are formed on the mating faces of the baulk rings and gear pinions.

2 Manual transmission – draining and refilling

Note: *A suitable square section wrench may be required to undo the transmission filler/ level and drain plugs on some models. These wrenches can be obtained from most motor factors or your Peugeot dealer.*

1 This operation is much quicker and more efficient if the car is first taken on a journey of sufficient length to warm the engine/transmission up to normal operating temperature.

2 Park the car on level ground, switch off the ignition and apply the handbrake firmly. For improved access, jack up the front of the car and support it securely on axle stands (see *Jacking and vehicle support*). Note that the car must be level to ensure accuracy when refilling and checking the oil level.

3 On 2.0 litre diesel engine models, undo the bolts securing the left-hand inner cover to the wing valance and undercover, and remove the cover to gain access to the transmission filler/level plug. On all other engines, to improve access to the filler/level plug, remove the retaining screws and fasteners (pull out the centre pin then remove the complete fasteners) and remove the front section of the left-hand wheel arch liner **(see illustrations)**.

4 Wipe clean the area around the filler/level plug, which is situated on the left-hand end of the transmission, next to the end cover. Unscrew the filler/level plug from the

2.4a Unscrewing the transmission unit filler/level plug – MA5 transmission

2.4b Unscrewing the transmission filler/level plug – BE4/5 transmission

2.5a Unscrewing the transmission drain plug – MA5 transmission

transmission and recover the sealing washer **(see illustrations)**.

5 Position a suitable container under the drain plug (situated at the rear of the transmission) and unscrew the plug. On MA5 transmissions, the plug is on the left-hand side of the differential housing; on BE4/5 transmissions, it is on the base of the differential housing **(see illustrations)**. Where necessary, remove the retaining bolts, screws and clips and remove the undercover from the engine/transmission unit to gain access to the drain plug.

6 Allow the oil to drain completely into the container. If the oil is hot, take precautions against scalding. Clean both the filler/level and the drain plugs, being especially careful to wipe any metallic particles off the magnetic inserts. Discard the original sealing washers; they should be renewed whenever they are disturbed.

7 When the oil has finished draining, clean the drain plug threads and those of the transmission casing, fit a new sealing washer and refit the drain plug, tightening it to the specified torque wrench setting. Refit the undercover (where fitted) then lower the vehicle to the ground.

8 Refilling the transmission is an extremely awkward operation. Above all, allow plenty of time for the oil level to settle properly before checking it. Note that the car must be parked on flat level ground when checking the oil level.

9 Refill the transmission with the exact amount of the specified type of oil then check the oil level as described in the relevant part of Chapter 1; if the correct amount was poured into the transmission and a large amount

flows out on checking the level, refit the filler/level plug and take the car on a short journey so that the new oil is distributed fully around the transmission components, then check the level again on your return. Once the oil level is correct, securely refit the inner cover/wheel arch liner (as applicable).

3 Gearchange linkage – removal and refitting

1 Firmly apply the handbrake, and then jack up the front of the vehicle and support it on axle stands (see *Jacking and vehicle support*).
2 To improve access to the transmission end of the linkage, remove the battery and battery tray (see Chapter 5A).
3 To gain access to the gearchange lever end of the linkage, remove the exhaust system heat shields (where fitted), Remove the retaining nuts and/or fasteners (unscrew the centre screw then pull out the complete fastener), and manoeuvre the shields out of position. On some models it may be necessary to free the exhaust system from its mountings to gain the clearance necessary to remove the larger heat shield (see the relevant part of Chapter 4).
4 Slacken and remove the nut, and withdraw the pivot bolt securing the linkage rod to the base of the gearchange lever **(see illustration)**.
5 Using a flat-bladed screwdriver, carefully lever the three link rods off their balljoints on the transmission **(see illustration)**. Disengage the linkage rod from the relay lever, and remove

it from underneath the vehicle, complete with its link rods.
6 Slacken and remove the relay lever pivot bolt, then manoeuvre the relay lever and link rod out of position, noting the correct fitted locations of the spacer, pivot bushes and washers fitted to the centre of the lever.
7 Inspect all the linkage components for signs of wear or damage, paying particular attention to the pivot bushes and link rod balljoints, and renew worn components as necessary. If necessary, the gearchange lever can be removed as follows.
8 Unclip the gearchange lever gaiter from the centre console then pull off the knob from the gearchange lever and remove the gaiter. Slacken and remove the gearchange lever retaining nuts and lift off the retaining plate (where fitted) then lower the lever out from underneath the vehicle.
9 Peel back the lower gaiter from the base of the gearchange lever, then disengage the lever mounting plate, and slide the upper gaiter up the lever to gain access to the gearchange lever pivot ball. Examine the lever components for signs of wear or damage, paying particular attention to the rubber gaiters, and renew components as necessary. The lever can be separated from its baseplate after the retaining ring has been unclipped.

Refitting

10 Refitting is a reversal of the removal procedure, noting the following points:
 a) *Apply a smear of the special grease (see Specifications) to the relay lever pivot ball,*

2.5b Transmission drain plug location – BE4/5 transmission

3.4 Unscrew the nut and withdraw the pivot bolt securing the linkage rod to the gearchange lever

3.5 Carefully lever the link rods off their balljoints on the transmission unit

4.3 Unscrew the nut and remove the lower arm balljoint clamp bolt

the link rod balljoints and the relay lever pivot bushes.

b) Ensure that the gearchange lever rubber gaiters are correctly seated before refitting the lever assembly to the vehicle.

c) Apply a drop of locking compound (Peugeot recommend Loctite Frenetanch) to the threads of the relay lever pivot bolt prior to refitting.

d) Tighten all fixings to their specified torques (where given) and ensure that the link rods are securely pressed onto their balljoints.

4 Oil seals – renewal

Driveshaft oil seals

1 Chock the rear wheels, apply the handbrake, and then jack up the front of the car and support it on axle stands (see *Jacking and vehicle support*). Remove the appropriate front roadwheel.

2 Drain the transmission oil as described in Section 2.

3 Slacken and remove the suspension lower arm balljoint clamp bolt and nut **(see illustration)**. Discard the nut – a new one must be used on refitting.

4 Pull down on the lower arm to free its balljoint from the swivel hub **(see Tool Tip)**. Once the balljoint is freed from the swivel hub,

4.6b ... then rotate the bolts through 90° to disengage their offset heads (arrowed) from the bearing (shown with driveshaft removed for clarity)

To free the lower arm, attach a long bar (such as a jack handle) securely to the lower arm. Fit a block of wood to the inner end of the bar, to act as a pivot, and then use the bar to pull the lower arm out from the swivel hub.

peg the lower arm in position by inserting a suitable socket in between the top of the arm inner end and the subframe **(see illustration)**.

5 Recover the protector plate from lower arm balljoint **(see illustration)**.

Right-hand seal

6 Loosen the two intermediate bearing retaining bolt nuts, then rotate the bolts through 90° so that their offset heads are clear of the bearing outer race **(see illustrations)**.

7 Carefully pull the swivel hub assembly outwards, and pull on the inner end of the driveshaft to free the intermediate bearing from its mounting bracket.

4.5 Remove the protector plate from the lower arm balljoint

4.8 Free the right-hand driveshaft from the transmission and slide off the dust seal

4.4 Secure the lower arm clear of the swivel hub by inserting a socket in between the top of the arm and the subframe

8 Once the driveshaft end is free from the transmission, slide the dust seal/plate off the inner end of the shaft, noting which way around it is fitted, and support the inner end of the driveshaft to avoid damaging the constant velocity joints or gaiters **(see illustration)**.

9 Carefully prise the oil seal out of the transmission, using a large flat-bladed screwdriver **(see illustration)**.

10 Remove all traces of dirt from the area around the oil seal aperture, then apply a smear of grease to the outer lip of the new oil seal. Fit the new seal into its aperture, and drive it squarely into position using a suitable tubular drift (such as a socket), which bears only on the hard outer edge of the seal, until it abuts its locating shoulder. If the seal was supplied with a plastic protector sleeve, leave

4.6a On the right-hand driveshaft, slacken the two intermediate bearing retaining bolt nuts . . .

4.9 Use a large flat-bladed screwdriver to lever the right-hand oil seal out of position

4.16 On refitting ensure the dust seal is tight against the oil seal

4.20 Removing the left-hand oil seal (MA5 transmission shown)

4.27 Unscrew the retaining bolts and slide the clutch bearing guide sleeve off the input shaft

this in position until the driveshaft has been refitted.

11 Thoroughly clean the driveshaft splines, and then apply a thin film of grease to the oil seal lip.

12 Slide the dust seal/plate into position on the end of the shaft, ensuring that its flat surface is facing the transmission.

13 Carefully locate the inner driveshaft splines with those of the differential sun gear, taking care not to damage the oil seal, then align the intermediate bearing with its mounting bracket, and push the driveshaft fully into position. If necessary, use a soft-faced mallet to tap the outer race of the bearing into position in the mounting bracket.

14 Fit the protector plate to the lower arm balljoint.

15 Align the lower arm balljoint with the swivel hub. Remove the socket (used to peg the arm in position) and seat the balljoint shank correctly in the swivel hub. Insert the clamp bolt then fit the new nut and tighten to the specified torque (see Chapter 10).

16 Ensure that the intermediate bearing is correctly seated, and then rotate its retaining bolts back through 90°, so that their offset heads are resting against the bearing outer race. Evenly and progressively tighten the retaining bolt nuts to the specified torque (see Chapter 10). Ensure that the dust seal/plate is tight against the driveshaft oil seal **(see illustration)**.

17 Refit the roadwheel, then lower the vehicle

to the ground and tighten the roadwheel bolts to the specified torque.

18 Refill the transmission with the specified type and amount of oil, and check the level using the information given in the relevant part of Chapter 1.

Left-hand seal

19 Pull the swivel hub assembly outwards and withdraw the driveshaft inner constant velocity joint from the transmission, taking care not to damage the driveshaft oil seal. Support the driveshaft, to avoid damaging the constant velocity joints or gaiters.

20 Renew the oil seal as described above in paragraphs 9 to 11 **(see illustration)**.

21 Carefully locate the inner constant velocity joint splines with those of the differential sun gear, taking care not to damage the oil seal, and push the driveshaft fully into position. Where fitted, remove the plastic protector from the oil seal.

22 Fit the protector plate to the lower arm balljoint.

23 Align the lower arm balljoint with the swivel hub. Remove the socket (used to peg the arm in position) and seat the balljoint shank correctly in the swivel hub. Insert the clamp bolt then fit the new nut and tighten to the specified torque (see Chapter 10).

24 Refit the roadwheel, then lower the vehicle to the ground and tighten the roadwheel bolts to the specified torque.

25 Refill the transmission with the specified type and amount of oil, and check the level

using the information given in the relevant part of Chapter 1.

Input shaft oil seal

26 Remove the transmission as described in Section 7.

27 Undo the three bolts securing the clutch release bearing guide sleeve in position, and slide the guide off the input shaft, along with its sealing ring or gasket (as applicable) **(see illustration)**. Recover any shims or thrustwashers, which have stuck to the rear of the guide sleeve, and refit them to the input shaft.

28 Carefully lever the oil seal out of the guide using a suitable flat-bladed screwdriver **(see illustration)**.

29 Before fitting a new seal, check the input shaft's seal rubbing surface for signs of burrs, scratches or other damage, which may have caused the seal to fail in the first place. It may be possible to polish away minor faults of this sort using fine abrasive paper; however, more serious defects will require the renewal of the input shaft. Ensure that the input shaft is clean and greased, to protect the seal lips on refitting.

30 Dip the new seal in clean oil, and fit it to the guide sleeve.

31 Fit a new sealing ring or gasket (as applicable) to the rear of the guide sleeve, then carefully slide the sleeve into position over the input shaft. Refit the retaining bolts and tighten them to the specified torque setting **(see illustrations)**.

4.28 Carefully lever the seal out of the housing, noting which way around it is fitted

4.31a Fit a new sealing ring/gasket (as applicable) . . .

4.31b . . . then slide the housing assembly back onto the input shaft

5.4a Disconnecting the wiring connector from the reversing light switch – MA5 transmission

5.4b Reversing light switch – BE4/5 transmission

32 Take the opportunity to inspect the clutch components if not already done (Chapter 6). Finally, refit the transmission as described in Section 7.

Selector shaft oil seal

MA5 transmission

33 On this transmission, to renew the selector shaft seal, the transmission must be dismantled. This task should therefore be entrusted to a Peugeot dealer or transmission specialist.

BE4/5 transmission

34 Park the car on level ground, apply the handbrake, then jack up the front of the vehicle and support it on axle stands (see *Jacking and vehicle support*). Remove the left-hand front roadwheel.

35 Using a large flat-bladed screwdriver, lever the link rod balljoint off the transmission selector shaft, and disconnect the link rod.

36 Using a large flat-bladed screwdriver, carefully prise the selector shaft seal out of the housing, and slide it off the end of the shaft.

37 Before fitting a new seal, check the selector shaft's seal rubbing surface for signs of burrs, scratches or other damage, which

may have caused the seal to fail in the first place. It may be possible to polish away minor faults of this sort using fine abrasive paper; however, more serious defects will require the renewal of the selector shaft.

38 Apply a smear of grease to the new seal's outer edge and sealing lip, then carefully slide the seal along the selector rod. Press the seal fully into position in the transmission housing.

39 Refit the link rod to the selector shaft, ensuring that its balljoint is pressed firmly onto the shaft. Lower the car to the ground.

5 Reversing light switch – testing, removal and refitting

Testing

1 The reversing light circuit is controlled by a plunger-type switch, screwed into the top of the transmission casing. If a fault develops, first ensure that the circuit fuse has not blown.

2 To test the switch, disconnect the wiring connector, and use a multimeter (set to the resistance function) or a battery-and-bulb test circuit to check that there is continuity

between the switch terminals only when reverse gear is selected. If this is not the case, and there are no obvious breaks or other damage to the wires, the switch is faulty, and must be renewed.

Removal

3 Where necessary, to improve access to the switch, remove the air cleaner housing intake duct assembly/battery and battery tray (as applicable – see the relevant part of Chapter 4 and 5A).

4 Disconnect the wiring connector, and then unscrew the switch from the transmission casing along with its sealing washer **(see illustrations)**.

Refitting

5 Fit a new sealing washer to the switch, then screw it back into position in the top of the transmission housing and tighten it to the specified torque setting. Refit the wiring plug, and test the operation of the circuit. Refit any components removed for access.

6 Speedometer drive – removal and refitting

Note: *On models without a speedometer drive assembly in the transmission* **(see illustration)**, *the vehicle speed data is received from the engine management ECU. This information is supplied from the wheel speed sensors and the ABS ECU.*

Removal

1 Chock the rear wheels, firmly apply the handbrake, and then jack up the front of the car and support it on axle stands (see *Jacking and vehicle support*). The speedometer drive is on the rear of the transmission housing, next to the inner end of the right-hand driveshaft.

2 Disconnect the wiring connector from the speedometer drive **(see illustration)**.

6.1 Blanking plug (arrowed) on models which receive vehicle speed data from the engine management system

6.2 Disconnect the wiring connector (1) then undo the retaining bolt (2) and withdraw the speedometer drive assembly

6.7a On BE4/5 transmissions, unscrew the retaining bolts . . .

6.7b . . . and remove the housing, sealing ring and drive pinion from the transmission unit (shown with transmission removed)

6.8 On BE4/5 transmissions ensure the drive pinion dogs are correctly engaged with the gear slots (arrowed) on refitting

3 Slacken and remove the retaining bolt and remove the heat shield (where fitted). Withdraw the speedometer drive and driven pinion assembly from the transmission housing, along with its sealing ring.
4 If necessary, the pinion can be slid out of the housing, and the oil seal can be removed from the top of the housing. Examine the pinion for signs of damage, and renew if necessary. Renew the housing sealing ring as a matter of course.
5 If the driven pinion is worn or damaged, also examine the drive pinion in the transmission housing for similar signs.
6 On MA5 transmissions, to renew the drive pinion, the transmission must be dismantled and the differential gear removed. This task should therefore be entrusted to a Peugeot dealer or a transmission specialist.
7 On BE4/5 transmissions, to remove the drive pinion, first disengage the right-hand driveshaft from the transmission, as described in paragraphs 1 to 7 of Section 4. Undo the three retaining bolts, and remove the speedometer drive housing from the transmission, along with its sealing ring. Remove the drive pinion from the differential gear, and recover any adjustment shims from the gear **(see illustrations)**.

Refitting

8 On BE4/5 transmissions, where the drive pinion has been removed, refit the adjustment shims to the differential gear, then locate the speedometer drive on the gear, ensuring it

is correctly engaged in the gear slots **(see illustration)**. Fit a new sealing ring to the rear of the speedometer drive housing, then refit the housing to the transmission and tighten its retaining bolts to the specified torque. Inspect the driveshaft oil seal for signs of wear, and renew if necessary. Refit the driveshaft to the transmission, with reference to Section 4.
9 On all models, apply a smear of grease to the lips of the seal and to the driven pinion shaft, and slide the pinion into position in the speedometer drive.
10 Fit a new sealing ring to the speedometer drive and refit it to the transmission, ensuring that the drive and driven pinions are correctly engaged. Refit the drive retaining bolt, complete with heat shield (where fitted), and tighten securely.
11 Reconnect the wiring connector to the speedometer drive then lower the vehicle to the ground.

7 Manual transmission – removal and refitting

Removal

1 Chock the rear wheels, then firmly apply the handbrake. Jack up the front of the vehicle, and securely support it on axle stands (see *Jacking and vehicle support*). Remove both front roadwheels.
2 Drain the transmission's oil as described

in Section 2, and then refit the drain and filler plugs, and tighten to their specified torque settings.
3 Remove both driveshafts as described in Chapter 8.
4 Remove the battery, battery tray and mounting plate (see Chapter 5A).
5 Remove the air cleaner housing and intake duct and (where fitted) the crankshaft sensor as described in the relevant part of Chapter 4.
6 Remove the starter motor (Chapter 5A).
7 Where applicable, detach the clutch cable from the transmission unit as described in Chapter 6.
8 On hydraulic clutch models, unscrew the mounting bolts and free the clutch slave cylinder and hydraulic hose from transmission unit (see Chapter 6).
9 Disconnect the wiring connectors from the reversing light switch and the speedometer drive. Undo the retaining nut/bolt(s), and disconnect the earth straps from the top of the transmission housing **(see illustrations)**. Free the wiring from any relevant retaining clips, and position it clear of the transmission.
10 Using a flat-bladed screwdriver, carefully lever the three gearchange mechanism link rods off their respective balljoints on the transmission. Position the rods clear of the transmission.
11 Undo the retaining bolt(s), and remove the flywheel lower cover plate (where fitted) from the transmission.
12 On BE4/5 transmissions, remove the speedometer drive gear housing and gear assembly from the transmission as described in Section 6. On diesel engines also unscrew the bolts securing the coolant heater bracket to the top of the transmission unit.
13 Place a jack with a block of wood beneath the engine, to take the weight of the engine. Alternatively, attach a couple of lifting eyes to the engine, and fit a hoist or support bar to take the engine weight.
14 Place a jack and block of wood beneath the transmission, and raise the jack to take the weight of the transmission.
15 Slacken and remove the centre nut and washer from the left-hand engine/transmission mounting then undo the mounting bolts and remove the mounting. Unscrew the bolts

7.9a Unscrew the nut and bolt and detach the earth leads from the transmission unit – MA5 transmission

7.9b Unscrew the bolt (arrowed) and disconnect the earth lead from the transmission unit – BE4/5 transmission

7.15a Slacken and remove the centre nut and washer (1) then undo the mounting bolts (2) . . .

7.15b . . . and lift off the mounting rubber

7.15c Unscrew the mounting bolts (locations arrowed) and remove the left-hand mounting bracket from the body

securing the mounting bracket to the body and remove the bracket (see illustrations).
16 On MA5 transmissions, undo the three retaining nuts and remove the mounting plate from the top of the transmission (see illustration).

17 On BE4/5 transmissions, slide the spacer off the mounting stud, then unscrew the stud from the top of the transmission housing and remove it along with its washer. If the mounting stud is tight, a universal stud extractor can be used to unscrew it (see illustrations).

18 On all models, unscrew the nuts and bolts and remove the mounting link securing the rear engine/transmission mounting to the subframe (see illustration).
19 With the jack positioned beneath the transmission taking the weight, slacken and

7.16 On MA5 transmissions undo the nuts (arrowed) and remove the mounting bracket from the top of the transmission unit

7.17a On BE4/5 transmissions slide off the spacer . . .

7.17b . . . and unscrew the left-hand mounting stud from the top of the transmission unit

7.18 Unscrew the mounting nuts and bolts and remove the mounting link securing the rear mounting to the subframe

remove the remaining bolts securing the transmission housing to the engine. Note the correct fitted positions of each bolt, and the necessary brackets, as they are removed, to use as a reference on refitting. Make a final check that all components have been disconnected, and are positioned clear of the transmission so that they will not hinder the removal procedure.

20 With the bolts removed, move the trolley jack and transmission to the left, to free it from its locating dowels. If necessary, lower the engine slightly to enable the transmission to be freed.

Caution: Take great care not to place any excess strain on the exhaust system or damage the radiator if the engine is moved. On models equipped with air conditioning, care must also be taken to ensure the auxiliary drivebelt pulleys do not damage the air conditioning pipes on the right-hand side of the engine compartment.

21 Once the transmission is free, lower the jack and manoeuvre the unit out from under the car. Remove the locating dowels from the transmission or engine if they are loose, and keep them in a safe place.

Refitting

22 The transmission is refitted by a reversal of the removal procedure, bearing in mind the following points:

a) *Prior to refitting, check the clutch assembly and release mechanism*
components (see Chapter 6). Lubricate the release bearing guide with a little high melting-point grease (Peugeot recommend the use of Molykote BR2 plus). Do not apply too much grease, otherwise there is a possibility of the grease contaminating the clutch friction plate, and ensure no grease is applied to the input shaft/friction plate splines.

b) *Ensure that the locating dowels are correctly positioned prior to installation.*

c) *On BE4/5 transmissions, apply thread-locking fluid to the left-hand engine/transmission mounting stud threads, prior to refitting it to the transmission. Tighten the stud to the specified torque.*

d) *Tighten all nuts and bolts to the specified torque (where given).*

e) *Renew the driveshaft oil seals, then refit the driveshafts (see Chapter 8).*

f) *Reconnect the clutch cable/refit the slave cylinder (see Chapter 6).*

g) *On completion, refill the transmission with the specified type and quantity of lubricant, as described in the relevant part of Chapter 1.*

8 Manual transmission overhaul – general information

1 Overhauling a manual transmission is a difficult and involved job for the DIY home mechanic. In addition to dismantling and reassembling many small parts, clearances must be precisely measured and, if necessary, changed by selecting shims and spacers. Internal transmission components are also often difficult to obtain, and in many instances, extremely expensive. Because of this, if the transmission develops a fault or becomes noisy, the best course of action is to have the unit overhauled by a specialist repairer, or to obtain an exchange reconditioned unit.

2 Nevertheless, it is not impossible for the more experienced mechanic to overhaul the transmission, provided the special tools are available, and the job is done in a deliberate step-by-step manner, so that nothing is overlooked.

3 The tools necessary for an overhaul include internal and external circlip pliers, bearing pullers, a slide hammer, a set of pin punches, a dial test indicator, and possibly a hydraulic press. In addition, a large, sturdy workbench and a vice will be required.

4 During dismantling of the transmission, make careful notes of how each component is fitted, to make reassembly easier and more accurate.

5 Before dismantling the transmission, it will help if you have some idea what area is malfunctioning. Certain problems can be closely related to specific areas in the transmission, which can make component examination and renewal easier. Refer to the *Fault Finding* Section for more information.

Notes

Chapter 7 Part B:
Automatic transmission

Contents

Degrees of difficulty

| Easy, suitable for novice with little experience | 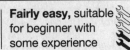 | Fairly easy, suitable for beginner with some experience | 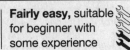 | Fairly difficult, suitable for competent DIY mechanic | 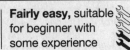 | Difficult, suitable for experienced DIY mechanic | 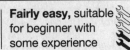 | Very difficult, suitable for expert DIY or professional | |

Specifications

General
Type	Auto-adaptive four-speed electronically controlled automatic with three driving modes (Normal, Sport and Snow)
Designation	AL4

Lubrication
Recommended fluid.	See *Lubricants and fluids*
Capacity:	
Refilling after draining.	4.5 litres*
From dry	6.0 litres

* If the torque converter is also removed and drained, add a further 2 litres

Torque wrench settings
	Nm	lbf ft
Engine-to-transmission fixing bolts	35	26
Fluid cooler centre bolt.	50	37
Fluid drain plug.	33	24
Fluid filler plug	24	18
Fluid level plug	24	18
Fluid pressure sensor bolts	9	7
Input shaft speed sensor bolt.	10	7
Left-hand engine/transmission mounting	Refer to Chapter 2A, 2B, 2C or 2D	
Multifunction switch retaining bolts	10	7
Output shaft speed sensor bolt	10	7
Rear mounting link	Refer to Chapter 2A, 2B, 2C or 2D	
Roadwheel bolts.	90	66
Torque converter-to-driveplate nuts:		
Stage 1	10	7
Stage 2	30	22

1 General information

1 Some models were offered with the option of a four-speed electronically-controlled automatic transmission, consisting of a torque converter, an epicyclic geartrain, and hydraulically-operated clutches and brakes. The unit is controlled by the electronic control unit (ECU) via the electrically-operated solenoid valves in the hydraulic block within the transmission unit. The transmission has three driving modes; Normal, Sport and Snow modes; the mode buttons are situated on the right-hand side of the selector lever and the mode indicator lights are incorporated in the instrument panel.

2 The Normal mode is the standard mode for driving in which the transmission shifts up at relatively low engine speeds to combine reasonable performance with economy. If the transmission unit is switched into Sport mode, the transmission will shift up only at high engine speeds, giving improved acceleration and overtaking performance. In Snow mode, the transmission will select 2nd gear when the vehicle pulls away from a standing start; this helps maintain traction on slippery surfaces.

3 The torque converter provides a fluid coupling between the engine and transmission, which acts as an automatic clutch, and also provides a degree of torque multiplication when accelerating.

4 The epicyclic geartrain provides either of the four forward or one reverse gear ratios, according to which of its component parts are held stationary or allowed to turn. The components of the geartrain are held or released by brakes and clutches, which are controlled by the ECU via the electrically-operated solenoid valves in the hydraulic unit. A fluid pump within the transmission provides the necessary hydraulic pressure to operate the brakes and clutches.

5 Driver control of the transmission is by a six-position selector lever. The transmission has a 'drive' position, and a 'hold' facility on the first three gear ratios. The 'drive' position D provides automatic changing throughout the range of all four gear ratios, and is the one to select for normal driving. An automatic kickdown facility shifts the transmission down a gear if the accelerator pedal is fully depressed. The 'hold' facility is very similar, but limits the number of gear ratios available – ie, when the selector lever is in the 3 position, only the first three ratios can be selected; in the 2 position, only the first two can be selected. When the lever is in the 2 position, the transmission can be locked in first gear using the button on the right-hand side of the selector lever. These lower ratio 'hold' settings are useful for providing engine braking when travelling down steep gradients, or for preventing unwanted selection of top gear on twisty roads. Note, however, that the transmission should *never* be shifted down at high engine speeds.

6 On some models, the selector lever is equipped with a shift-lock function. This prevents the selector lever being moved from the P position unless the brake pedal is depressed.

7 Due to the complexity of the automatic transmission, any repair or overhaul work must be left to a Peugeot dealer with the necessary special equipment for fault diagnosis and repair. The contents of the following Sections are therefore confined to supplying general information, and any service information and instructions that can be used by the owner.
Note: *The automatic transmission unit is of the 'auto-adaptive' type. This means that it takes into account your driving style and modifies the transmission shift points to provide optimum performance and economy to suit. When the battery is disconnected, the transmission will lose its memory and will resort to one of its many base shift programs. The transmission will then relearn the optimum shift points when the vehicle is driven a few miles. During these first few miles of driving, there maybe a noticeable difference in performance whilst the transmission adapts to your individual style.*

2 Automatic transmission fluid – draining and refilling

Note: *A suitable square section wrench may be required to undo the transmission filler plug. These wrenches can be obtained from most motor factors or your Peugeot dealer.*
Note: *The transmission unit is equipped with a fluid wear sensor to inform the driver when the fluid needs renewing (the ECU flashes the Sport and Snow mode indicator lights when fluid renewal is necessary). If the transmission unit is drained and refilled with new fluid, this sensor should be reset. This can only be done using the Peugeot diagnostic test box.*

Draining

1 This operation is much quicker and more efficient if the car is first taken on a journey of sufficient length to warm the engine/transmission up to normal operating temperature.

2 Park the car on level ground, switch off the ignition and apply the handbrake firmly. For

2.3 Unscrewing the transmission drain plug. The smaller plug (arrowed) in the centre of the drain plug is the level plug

improved access, jack up the front of the car and support it securely on axle stands (see *Jacking and vehicle support*).

3 Position a suitable container under the drain plug, situated on the base of the transmission. Unscrew the drain plug (the smaller plug in the centre of the drain plug is the level plug – see Chapter 1A or 1B) and recover the sealing washer **(see illustration)**. Allow the fluid to drain completely into the container.

⚠ *Warning: If the fluid is hot, take precautions against scalding.*

4 Clean the drain plug, being especially careful to wipe off any metallic particles. Discard the sealing washer; it should be renewed whenever it is disturbed.

5 When the fluid has finished draining, clean the drain plug threads and those of the transmission casing, fit a new sealing washer and refit the drain plug, tightening it to the specified torque wrench setting. If the car was raised for the draining operation, now lower it to the ground.

Refilling

6 To improve access to the filler plug, remove the battery and battery tray as described in Chapter 5A. If necessary, also unclip the selector cable end fitting from its balljoint on the transmission lever.

7 Wipe clean the area around the filler plug, which is situated directly behind the transmission selector lever **(see illustration)**. Unscrew the filler plug from the transmission and recover the sealing washer.
Caution: Do not unscrew the selector shaft bolt (located in front of the selector lever).

8 Carefully refill the transmission with the correct amount of the specified type of fluid. Fit the new sealing washer to the filler plug then refit the plug, tightening it to the specified torque. Reconnect the selector cable to the lever (where disconnected – support the lever when pressing the cable onto its balljoint to prevent the lever being bent) then refit the battery (see Chapter 5A).

9 Take the vehicle on a short journey to warm the transmission up to normal operating temperature.

10 On your return, check the transmission fluid level as described in Chapter 1A or 1B.

2.7 Transmission filler plug (1) location. DO NOT remove the selector shaft bolt (2)

3 Selector cable – adjustment

1 To gain access to the transmission end of the selector cable, remove the battery and battery tray as described in Chapter 5A.
2 Position the selector lever firmly against its detent in the P (park) position. There are two possible types of adjustment mechanism on the selector cable end fitting; identify which type is present and proceed as follows.
3 Where the locking plunger spring is not visible, release the plunger retaining clip and allow the plunger to extend fully from the end fitting **(see illustration)**. Ensure the transmission unit selector lever is pushed fully towards the rear then lock up the adjustment mechanism by depressing the plunger back into the end fitting.
4 If the locking plunger spring is visible, push the plunger fully into the end fitting and hold it in position **(see illustration)**. Ensure the transmission unit selector lever is pushed fully towards the rear then lock up the adjustment mechanism by releasing the plunger.
5 Check the operation of the selector lever before refitting the battery tray and battery (see Chapter 5A).

4 Selector cable – removal and refitting

Removal

1 Firmly apply the handbrake, and then jack up the front of the vehicle and support it on axle stands (see *Jacking and vehicle support*). Position the selector lever in the P position.
2 To gain access to the transmission end of the selector cable, remove the battery and battery tray as described in Chapter 5A.
3 Unclip the selector cable end fitting from the balljoint on the transmission lever. Remove the retaining clip and free the cable from the transmission bracket **(see illustrations)**.
4 To gain access to the base of the selector lever, remove the exhaust system heat shield(s). Remove the retaining nuts and/or fasteners (unscrew the centre screw then pull out the complete fastener), and manoeuvre the shields out of position. On some models it may be necessary to free the exhaust system from its mountings to gain the clearance necessary to remove the larger heat shield.
5 Unclip the cover plate from the base of the selector lever housing and recover its seal.
6 Lever the selector cable off the selector lever balljoint then free the outer cable from the front of the housing and manoeuvre it out of position. Recover the seal fitted between the outer cable and housing.

3.3 On selector cables where the locking plunger spring is not visible, release the retaining clip (1) to extend the plunger (2) and unlock the adjustment mechanism

Refitting

7 Refitting is the reverse of removal, noting the following points.
a) Renew the cable and selector cover plate seals if they show signs of damage or deterioration.
b) Support the transmission selector lever when pressing the cable onto its balljoint to prevent the lever being bent.
c) Ensure the cable end fitting and cover plate and correctly seated on the selector lever housing to ensure a watertight seal.
d) Adjust the cable as described in Section 3 before refitting all components removed for access.

5 Selector lever assembly – removal and refitting

Removal

1 Carry out the operations described in paragraphs 1 to 4 of Section 4.
2 Remove the centre console as described in Chapter 11.
3 Disconnect the wiring connector(s) from the lever assembly then remove the connector bracket from the rear of the selector lever.
4 Free the mode switch from the selector lever gate panel then unclip and remove the panel.

4.3a Unclip the selector cable end fitting (arrowed) from its balljoint . . .

3.4 On selector cables where the spring (arrowed) is visible, depress the plunger to release the adjustment mechanism

5 Slacken and remove the selector lever mounting nuts and bolts then remove the upper section of the selector lever housing.
6 Working underneath the vehicle, free the selector lever housing from the underbody then manoeuvre the lever and cable assembly out of position. If necessary, separate the cable from the lever as described in paragraphs 5 and 6 of Section 4.

Refitting

7 Refitting is the reverse of removal, noting the following points.
a) If the lever and cable have been separated, renew the cable and selector cover plate seals if they show signs of damage or deterioration.
b) Ensure the cable end fitting and cover plate and correctly seated on the selector lever housing to ensure a water-tight seal.
c) Adjust the cable as described in Section 3 before refitting all components removed for access.

6 Speedometer drive – removal and refitting

Refer to Chapter 7A, Section 6.

4.3b . . . then remove the retaining clip (arrowed) and free the cable from the transmission unit

7.2 Unscrew the nut and remove the lower arm balljoint clamp bolt

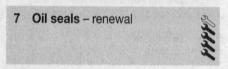

7 Oil seals – renewal

TOOL TIP

To free the lower arm, attach a long bar (such as a jack handle) securely to the lower arm. Fit a block of wood to the inner end of the bar, to act as a pivot, and then use the bar to pull the lower arm out from the swivel hub.

7.3 Secure the lower arm clear of the swivel hub by inserting a socket in between the top of the arm and the subframe

Driveshaft oil seals

1 Chock the rear wheels, apply the handbrake, and then jack up the front of the car and support it on axle stands (see *Jacking and vehicle support*). Remove the appropriate front roadwheel.

2 Slacken and remove the suspension lower arm balljoint clamp bolt and nut **(see illustration)**. Discard the nut – a new one must be used on refitting.

3 Pull down on the lower arm to free its balljoint from the swivel hub **(see Tool Tip)**. Once the balljoint is freed from the swivel hub, peg the lower arm in position by inserting a suitable socket in between the top of the arm inner end and the subframe **(see illustration)**.

4 Recover the protector plate from lower arm balljoint **(see illustration)**.

Right-hand seal

5 Loosen the two intermediate bearing retaining bolt nuts, then rotate the bolts through 90° so that their offset heads are clear of the bearing outer race **(see illustrations)**.

6 Carefully pull the swivel hub assembly outwards, and pull on the inner end of the driveshaft to free the intermediate bearing from its mounting bracket.

7 Once the driveshaft end is free from the transmission, remove the dust seal/plate (as applicable) off the inner end of the shaft, noting which way around it is fitted, and support the inner end of the driveshaft to avoid damaging the constant velocity joints or gaiters.

8 Remove the O-ring from the differential sun gear shaft then carefully remove the oil seal from of the transmission, taking care not to damage the shaft or housing. To remove the seal, carefully punch or drill two small holes opposite each other into the seal. Screw a self-tapping screw into each hole and pull on the screws to extract the seal.

9 Remove all traces of dirt from the area around the oil seal aperture, then apply a smear of grease to the outer edge and sealing lip of the new oil seal. Ease the new seal onto the shaft, taking care not to damage its lip, and into its aperture. Drive the seal squarely into position using a suitable tubular drift (such as a socket), which bears only on the hard outer edge of the seal.

10 Once the seal is correctly installed, fit a new O-ring to the sun gear shaft and slide along until it abuts the seal.

11 Fit the dust seal/plate onto the end of the driveshaft, ensuring that its flat surface is facing the transmission.

12 Carefully locate the inner driveshaft

splines with those of the differential sun gear, and then align the intermediate bearing with its mounting bracket, and push the driveshaft fully into position. If necessary, use a soft-faced mallet to tap the outer race of the bearing into position in the mounting bracket.

13 Fit the protector plate to the lower arm balljoint.

14 Align the lower arm balljoint with the swivel hub. Remove the socket (used to peg the arm in position) and seat the balljoint shank correctly in the swivel hub. Insert the clamp bolt then fit the new nut and tighten to the specified torque (see Chapter 10).

15 Ensure that the intermediate bearing is correctly seated, and then rotate its retaining bolts back through 90°, so that their offset heads are resting against the bearing outer race. Evenly and progressively tighten the retaining bolt nuts to the specified torque (see Chapter 8). Ensure that the dust seal/plate is tight against the driveshaft oil seal.

16 Refit the roadwheel, then lower the vehicle to the ground and tighten the roadwheel bolts to the specified torque.

Left-hand seal

17 Pull the swivel hub assembly outwards and withdraw the driveshaft inner constant velocity joint from the transmission, taking care not to damage the driveshaft oil seal. Support the driveshaft, to avoid damaging the constant velocity joints or gaiters.

7.4 Remove the protector plate from the lower arm balljoint

7.5a On the right-hand driveshaft, slacken the two intermediate bearing retaining bolt nuts . . .

7.5b . . . then rotate the bolts through 90° to disengage their offset heads (arrowed) from the bearing (shown with driveshaft removed for clarity)

7.27 Unscrew the nut and clamp bolt (arrowed) and free the selector lever from the transmission shaft

8.4 Release the retaining clips and disconnect the coolant hoses (arrowed) from the fluid cooler (viewed from above)

8.5 Transmission fluid cooler centre bolt (1) and seals (2)

18 Carefully prise the oil seal out of the transmission, using a large flat-bladed screwdriver.

19 Remove all traces of dirt from the area around the oil seal aperture, then apply a smear of grease to the outer lip of the new oil seal. Fit the new seal into its aperture, and drive it squarely into position using a suitable tubular drift (such as a socket), which bears only on the hard outer edge of the seal, until it abuts its locating shoulder. If the seal was supplied with a plastic protector sleeve, leave this in position until the driveshaft has been refitted.

20 Thoroughly clean the driveshaft splines, and then apply a thin film of grease to the oil seal lip.

21 Carefully locate the inner constant velocity joint splines with those of the differential sun gear, taking care not to damage the oil seal, and push the driveshaft fully into position. Where fitted, remove the plastic protector from the oil seal.

22 Fit the protector plate to the lower arm balljoint.

23 Align the lower arm balljoint with the swivel hub. Remove the socket (used to peg the arm in position) and seat the balljoint shank correctly in the swivel hub. Insert the clamp bolt then fit the new nut and tighten to the specified torque (see Chapter 10).

24 Refit the roadwheel, then lower the vehicle to the ground and tighten the roadwheel bolts to the specified torque.

Selector shaft oil seal

25 To gain access to the transmission selector shaft, remove the battery and battery tray as described in Chapter 5A.

26 Position the selector lever firmly against its detent mechanism in the P position.

27 Slacken and remove the nut and clamp bolt securing the selector lever to the transmission shaft **(see illustration)**. Make alignment marks between the shaft and lever then free the lever from the shaft.

28 Remove the retaining clip and free the selector cable from transmission bracket **(see illustration 4.3b)**. Position the cable clear of the selector shaft.

29 Make alignment marks between the

multifunction switch and transmission unit then unscrew the retaining bolts and remove the switch.

30 Carefully remove the oil seal from of the transmission, taking care not to damage the shaft or housing. To remove the seal, carefully punch or drill two small holes opposite each other into the seal. Screw a self-tapping screw into each hole and pull on the screws to extract the seal.

31 Remove all traces of dirt from the area around the oil seal aperture, then apply a smear of grease to the outer edge and sealing lip of the new oil seal. Ease the new seal onto the shaft, taking care not to damage its lip, and press it squarely into its aperture.

32 Locate the multifunction switch back on the selector shaft. Align the marks made prior to removal then refit the switch bolts, tightening them to the specified torque.

33 Seat the selector cable in the transmission bracket and engage the selector lever with the transmission shaft. Ensure the marks made on removal are correctly aligned then refit the lever clamp bolt and nut and tighten securely.

34 Secure the selector cable in position with the retaining clip then adjust the cable as described in Section 3.

35 Refit all components removed for access.

Torque converter seal

36 Remove the transmission unit as described in Section 10.

37 Carefully slide the torque converter off the transmission shaft whilst being prepared for fluid spillage.

38 Note the correct fitted position of the seal in the housing then carefully lever it out of position, taking care not to mark the housing or shaft.

39 Remove all traces of dirt from the area around the oil seal aperture. Ease the new seal into its aperture, ensuring its sealing lip is facing inwards, then press it squarely into position.

40 Engage the torque converter with the transmission shaft splines and slide it into position, taking care not to damage the oil seal.

41 Refit the transmission unit as described in Section 10.

8 Fluid cooler –
removal and refitting

Caution: Be careful not to allow dirt into the transmission unit during this procedure.

Removal

1 The fluid cooler is mounted on the rear of the transmission housing. To gain access to the cooler, remove the battery, battery tray and mounting plate as described in Chapter 5A.

2 Remove all traces of dirt from around the fluid cooler before proceeding.

3 Using a hose clamp or similar, clamp both the fluid cooler coolant hoses to minimise coolant loss during subsequent operations.

4 Release the retaining clips, and disconnect both coolant hoses from the fluid cooler – be prepared for some coolant spillage **(see illustration)**. Wash off any spilt coolant immediately with cold water, and dry the surrounding area before proceeding further.

5 Slacken and remove the fluid cooler centre bolt, and remove the cooler from the transmission. Remove the seal from the centre bolt, and the two seals fitted to the rear of the cooler, and discard them; new ones must be used on refitting **(see illustration)**.

Refitting

6 Lubricate the new seals with clean automatic transmission fluid, then fit the two new seals to the rear of the fluid cooler, and a new seal to the centre bolt.

7 Locate the fluid cooler on the rear of transmission housing then refit the centre bolt. Ensure the cooler is correctly positioned then tighten the centre bolt to the specified torque setting.

8 Reconnect the coolant hoses to the fluid cooler, and secure them in position with their retaining clips. Remove the hose clamps then refit the battery (see Chapter 5A).

9 Top-up the cooling system as described in *Weekly checks* and check the transmission unit fluid level as described in Chapter 1A or 1B.

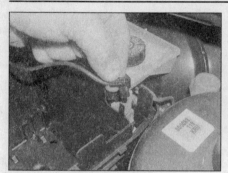

9.2a Disconnect the earth lead from the ECU mounting plate . . .

9.2b . . . then unclip the plate from the battery tray

9.3 Release the retaining clip and disconnect the wiring connector from the ECU

9 Transmission control system components – removal and refitting

Electronic control unit (ECU)

Note: *The automatic transmission electronic control system relies on accurate communication between the engine management ECU and the automatic transmission ECU. If the accelerator cable is removed and/or adjusted, or if either ECU is renewed, then both ECUs must be 'initialised'. The initialisation procedure requires access to specialised electronic test equipment and so it is recommended that this operation is entrusted to a suitably-equipped Peugeot dealer.*

Removal

1 Remove the battery (see Chapter 5A).
2 Disconnect the earth lead from the ECU mounting plate then release the plate tabs from the battery tray slots and lift the assembly out of position **(see illustrations)**.
3 Lift the retaining clip and disconnect the wiring connector from the ECU then remove the ECU and mounting plate from the vehicle

(see illustration). If necessary, undo the retaining nuts and separate the ECU and mounting plate.

Refitting

4 Refitting is the reverse of removal, ensuring the wiring connector is securely reconnected.

Output shaft speed sensor

Caution: Be careful not to allow dirt into the transmission unit during this procedure.

Removal

5 The output shaft sensor is fitted to the rear of the transmission unit.
6 To gain access to the sensor, remove the battery and battery tray as described in Chapter 5A.
7 Trace the sensor wiring back to its connector, located next to the transmission main wiring harness connector. Unclip connector from its bracket then disconnect it **(see illustration)**.
8 Wipe clean the area around the sensor then slacken and remove the sensor retaining bolt. Remove the sensor along with its sealing ring; discard the sealing ring, a new one must be used on refitting.

Refitting

9 Refitting is the reverse of removal, noting the following points.
a) Fit a new sealing ring to the sensor and tighten the sensor bolt to the specified torque.
b) On completion, check the transmission fluid level as described in Chapter 1A or 1B.

Input shaft speed sensor

Caution: Be careful not to allow dirt into the transmission unit during this procedure.

Removal

10 The input shaft speed sensor is located on the left-hand end of the transmission unit.
11 To gain access to the sensor, chock the rear wheels, firmly apply the handbrake then jack up the front of the vehicle and securely support it on axle stands (see *Jacking and vehicle support*). Remove the left-hand front roadwheel.
12 To gain access to the main wiring connector, remove the battery and battery tray (see Chapter 5A).
13 Lift the retaining clip and disconnect the main wiring connector from the top of the transmission unit **(see illustration)**.

9.7 Disconnecting the output shaft speed sensor wiring connector

9.13 Release the retaining clip (arrowed) then disconnect the main wiring connector from the transmission unit

9.14a Unscrew the two bolts (arrowed) and free the connector from the transmission unit

9.14b Cut the cable tie . . .

9.14c . . . then slide the cover off the rear of the connector

14 Unscrew the two bolts and free the main wiring connector from the transmission unit. Cut the cable tie securing the wiring to the connector cover then release the clips and slide the cover off the connector **(see illustrations)**.

15 Trace the wiring back from the sensor being removed to the main wiring connector, freeing it from all the relevant retaining clips and ties. Carefully release the retaining clips then slide the sensor connector out from the rear of the main connector, noting which way around it is fitted **(see illustration)**.

16 Wipe clean the area around the sensor. Slacken and remove the retaining bolt then remove the sensor along with its sealing ring **(see illustration)**. Discard the sealing ring; a new one must be used on refitting.

Refitting

17 Refitting is the reverse of removal, noting the following points.

a) Fit a new sealing ring to the sensor and tighten the sensor bolt to the specified torque.

b) Ensure the sensor wiring is correctly routed and retained by all the necessary clips and ties.

c) Clip the sensor wiring back into the main wiring connector, ensuring it is fitted the right way around. Slide the cover back onto the main connector, ensuring it is clipped securely in position, and secure the wiring to the cover with a new

cable tie. Secure the connector to the transmission unit with the retaining bolts.

d) On completion, check the transmission fluid level as described in Chapter 1A or 1B.

Fluid pressure sensor

Caution: Be careful not to allow dirt into the transmission unit during this procedure.

Removal

18 The fluid pressure sensor is located on the base of the transmission unit.

19 To gain access to the sensor, chock the rear wheels, firmly apply the handbrake then jack up the front of the vehicle and securely support it on axle stands (see *Jacking and vehicle support*). Remove the left-hand front roadwheel.

20 Drain the transmission fluid as described in Section 2.

21 Disconnect the sensor connector from the main wiring connector as described in paragraphs 12 to 15.

22 Wipe clean the area around the sensor then slacken and remove the sensor retaining bolts **(see illustration)**. Remove the sensor along with its sealing ring; discard the sealing ring, a new one must be used on refitting.

Refitting

23 Refitting is the reverse of removal, noting the following points.

a) Fit a new sealing ring to the sensor and tighten the sensor bolts to the specified torque.

b) Ensure the sensor wiring is correctly routed and retained by all the necessary clips and ties.

c) Clip the sensor wiring back into the main wiring connector, ensuring it is fitted the right way around. Slide the cover back onto the main connector, ensuring it is clipped securely in position, and secure the wiring to the cover with a new cable tie.

d) On completion, refill the transmission with fluid as described in Section 2.

Multifunction switch

Note: *The multifunction switch is slotted to allow for adjustment. Accurate adjustment requires the use of the special Peugeot electronic test equipment and so must be entrusted to a suitably-equipped Peugeot dealer. If the original switch is to be refitted, ensure accurate alignment marks are made prior to removal.*

Removal

24 Remove the battery and battery tray (see Chapter 5A).

25 Position the selector lever firmly against its detent mechanism in the P position.

26 Slacken and remove the nut and clamp bolt securing the selector lever to the transmission shaft **(see illustration 7.27)**. Make alignment marks between the shaft and lever then free the lever from the shaft.

27 Remove the retaining clip and free the selector cable from transmission bracket. Position the cable clear of the selector shaft.

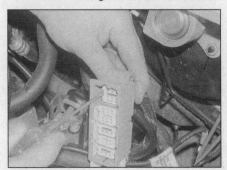

9.15 Release the retaining clips and free the relevant wiring connector from the main connector

9.16 Input shaft sensor retaining bolt (arrowed)

9.22 Fluid pressure sensor is secured to the base of the transmission unit by two bolts (arrowed)

10.2a Slacken and remove the retaining screws (arrowed) . . .

10.2b . . . and fasteners . . .

10.2c . . . and remove the front section of the left-hand wheel arch liner

28 Disconnect the switch connector from the main wiring connector as described in paragraphs 12 to 15.

29 Make accurate alignment marks between the multifunction switch and transmission unit then unscrew the retaining bolts and remove the switch.

Refitting

30 Locate the multifunction switch back on the selector shaft. Align the marks made prior to removal then refit the switch bolts, tightening them to the specified torque.

31 Clip the sensor wiring back into the main wiring connector, ensuring it is fitted the right way around. Slide the cover back onto the main connector, ensuring it is clipped securely in position, and secure the wiring to the cover with a new cable tie. Locate the connector on the transmission unit and securely tighten its retaining bolts.

32 Reconnect the main wiring connector to the transmission unit.

33 Seat the selector cable in the transmission bracket and engage the selector lever with the transmission shaft. Ensure the marks made on removal are correctly aligned then refit the lever clamp bolt and nut and tighten securely.

34 Secure the selector cable in position with the retaining clip then adjust the cable as described in Section 3.

35 Refit the battery and battery tray (see Chapter 5A).

10 Automatic transmission – removal and refitting

Removal

1 Chock the rear wheels, then firmly apply the handbrake. Jack up the front of the vehicle, and securely support it on axle stands (see *Jacking and vehicle support*). Remove both front roadwheels.

2 Undo the screws securing the front section of the left-hand wheel arch liner to the base of the bumper. Remove the fasteners (pull out the centre pin then remove the complete fastener) securing the liner section to the body then manoeuvre the front section of the liner out from underneath the wing **(see illustrations)**.

3 Remove both driveshafts as described in Chapter 8.

4 Remove the automatic transmission ECU as described in Section 9.

5 Remove the battery tray and mounting plate (see Chapter 5A).

6 Remove the air cleaner housing and intake duct as described in Chapter 4A. With the housing removed, undo the bolt and remove the housing mounting bracket from the left-hand side of the engine compartment. Also remove the crankshaft sensor.

7 Remove the starter motor (Chapter 5A).

8 Unclip the selector cable end fitting off the balljoint on the transmission lever. Remove the retaining clip then free the outer cable from its bracket and position it clear of the transmission unit **(see illustrations 4.3a and 4.3b)**.

9 Using a hose clamp or similar, clamp both the fluid cooler coolant hoses to minimise coolant loss. Release the retaining clips and disconnect both coolant hoses from the fluid cooler – be prepared for some coolant spillage **(see illustration 8.4)**. Wash off any spilt coolant immediately with cold water, and dry the surrounding area before proceeding further.

10 Lift the retaining clip and disconnect the main wiring connector from the transmission wiring block, located at the rear of the unit. Also disconnect the output shaft speed sensor wiring connector (located next to the main connector) then position the wiring harness clear of the transmission unit **(see illustrations 9.13 and 9.7)**.

11 Disconnect the wiring connector from the speedometer drive. Undo the retaining nut/bolt(s), and disconnect the earth straps from the top of the transmission housing **(see illustration)**. Free the wiring from any relevant retaining clips, and position it clear of the transmission.

12 Undo the retaining bolts and remove the lower driveplate cover plate (where fitted) from the transmission.

13 Access to the torque converter retaining nuts is gained via the starter motor aperture. Use a socket and extension bar to rotate the crankshaft pulley to align the first nut with the aperture **(see illustration)**. Unscrew the nut then rotate the crankshaft 120°. Remove the second nut then rotate the crankshaft another 120° Unscrew the third and final nut and discard all three nuts; new ones must be used on refitting.

14 To ensure that the torque converter does not fall out as the transmission is removed, secure it in position using a length of metal strip bolted to one of the starter motor bolt holes.

15 Place a jack with a block of wood beneath the engine, to take the weight of the engine. Alternatively, attach a couple of lifting eyes to the engine, and fit a hoist or support bar to take the engine weight.

16 Place a jack and block of wood beneath the transmission, and raise the jack to take the weight of the transmission.

10.11 Unscrew the bolts (arrowed) and disconnect the earth leads from the transmission unit

10.13 Access to the torque converter nuts (1) is gained via the starter motor aperture

10.17a Unscrew the centre nut (1) and mounting bolts (2) . . .

10.17b . . . then lift off the left-hand mounting

10.17c Unscrew the bolts (locations arrowed) and remove the mounting bracket from the body

17 Slacken and remove the centre nut and washer from the left-hand engine/transmission mounting then undo the mounting bolts and remove the mounting. Unscrew the bolts securing the mounting bracket to the body and remove the bracket **(see illustrations)**.

18 Slide the spacer off the mounting stud, then unscrew the stud from the top of the transmission housing and remove it along with its washer. If the mounting stud is tight, a universal stud extractor can be used to unscrew it.

19 Unscrew the nuts and bolts and remove the mounting link securing the rear engine/transmission mounting to the subframe **(see illustrations)**.

20 With the jack positioned beneath the transmission taking the weight, slacken and remove the remaining bolts securing the transmission housing to the engine. Note the correct fitted positions of each bolt and the necessary brackets as they are removed, to use as a reference on refitting. Make a final check that all components have been disconnected, and are positioned clear of the transmission so that they will not hinder the removal procedure.

21 With the bolts removed, move the trolley jack and transmission to the left, to free it from its locating dowels. If necessary, lower the

engine slightly to enable the transmission to be freed.

Caution: Take great care not to place any excess strain on the exhaust system or damage the radiator if the engine is moved. On models equipped with air conditioning, care must also be taken to ensure the auxiliary drivebelt pulleys do not damage the air conditioning pipes on the right-hand side of the engine compartment.

22 Once the transmission is free, lower the jack and manoeuvre the unit out from under the car. Remove the locating dowels from the transmission or engine if they are loose, and keep them in a safe place.

Refitting

23 Ensure that the bush fitted to the centre of the crankshaft is in good condition, and apply a little Molykote BR2 grease to the torque converter centring pin.

Caution: Do not apply too much; otherwise there is a possibility of the grease contaminating the torque converter.

24 Ensure that the engine/transmission locating dowels are correctly positioned then raise the transmission unit into position. Align the torque converter studs with the driveplate holes then engage the transmission unit with the engine.

Caution: Do not allow the weight of the

transmission unit to hang on the torque converter as the unit is installed.

25 With the transmission and engine correctly joined, refit the transmission-to-engine unit bolts and tighten them to the specified torque.

26 Screw the new nuts onto the torque converter studs, tightening them lightly only, rotating the crankshaft as necessary. Tighten all three nuts to the specified Stage 1 torque setting. Once all have been tightened to the Stage 1 torque, go around and tighten them to the specified Stage 2 torque setting.

27 The remainder of refitting is the reverse of removal, noting the following.

a) Apply thread-locking fluid to the left-hand engine/transmission mounting stud threads, prior to refitting it to the transmission. Tighten the stud to the specified torque.

b) Tighten all nuts and bolts to the specified torque (where given).

c) Renew the driveshaft oil seals, then refit the driveshafts (see Chapter 8).

d) Reconnect the selector cable and adjust as described in Section 3.

e) On completion, check the transmission fluid level as described in Chapter 1A or 1B.

11 Automatic transmission overhaul – general information

1 In the event of a fault occurring with the transmission, it is first necessary to determine whether it is of an electrical, mechanical or hydraulic nature and, to do this, special test equipment is required. It is therefore essential to have the work carried out by a Peugeot dealer if a transmission fault is suspected.

2 Do not remove the transmission from the car for possible repair before professional fault diagnosis has been carried out, since most tests require the transmission to be in the vehicle.

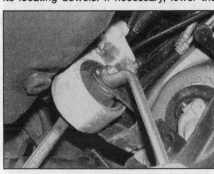

10.19a Unscrew the mounting nuts and bolts . . .

10.19b . . . and remove the rear mounting link

Chapter 8
Driveshafts

Contents

Degrees of difficulty

Easy, suitable for novice with little experience	**Fairly easy,** suitable for beginner with some experience	**Fairly difficult,** suitable for competent DIY mechanic	**Difficult,** suitable for experienced DIY mechanic	**Very difficult,** suitable for expert DIY or professional

Specifications

Lubrication (overhaul only – see text)

Lubricant type/specification	Use only special grease supplied in sachets with gaiter kits – joints are otherwise pre-packed with grease and sealed

Torque wrench settings

	Nm	lbf ft
Driveshaft retaining nut:		
Staked nut	245	181
Nut retained with locking cap and R-clip	325	240
Intermediate bearing retaining bolt nuts:		
Petrol engine models	10	7
Diesel engine models	13	10
Roadwheel bolts	90	66
Suspension lower arm balljoint clamp bolt nut	40	30

1 General information

1 Drive is transmitted from the differential to the front wheels by means of two solid-steel driveshafts of unequal length.

2 Both driveshafts are splined at their outer ends, to accept the wheel hubs, and are threaded so that each hub can be fastened by a large nut. The inner end of each driveshaft is splined, to accept the differential sun gear.

3 Constant velocity (CV) joints are fitted to each end of the driveshafts, to ensure that the smooth and efficient transmission of power at all suspension and steering angles. On petrol engine models, the outer constant velocity joints are of the spider-and-yoke type; on diesel engine models, they are of the ball-and-cage type. The inner constant velocity joints are of the tripod type on all models.

4 On the right-hand side, due to the length of the driveshaft, the inner constant velocity joint is situated approximately halfway along the shaft's length, and an intermediate support bearing is mounted in the engine/transmission rear mounting bracket. The inner end of the driveshaft passes through the bearing (which prevents any lateral movement of the driveshaft inner end) and the inner constant velocity joint outer member.

2 Driveshafts – removal and refitting

Caution: Do not allow the vehicle to rest on its wheels with one or both driveshafts removed, as damage to the wheel bearing(s) may result. If moving the vehicle is unavoidable, temporarily insert the outer end of the driveshaft(s) in the hub(s) and tighten the hub nut(s): in this case, the inner end(s) of the driveshaft(s) must be supported, for example by suspending with string from the vehicle underbody. Do not allow the driveshaft to hang down under its own weight.

Removal

1 If necessary, slacken the driveshaft nut (see paragraphs 4 to 6).

2 Chock the rear wheels of the car and firmly apply the handbrake. Jack up the front of the car and support it on axle stands (see *Jacking and vehicle support*). Remove the appropriate front roadwheel. Where necessary, remove the retaining bolts, screws and clips and remove the undershield (where fitted) from beneath the engine/transmission unit.

3 Drain the transmission oil or fluid as described in Chapter 7A or 7B (as applicable) or be prepared for some fluid loss as the shafts are removed.

4 On models where the driveshaft nut is staked, using a hammer and a chisel or similar tool, tap up the staking securing the driveshaft

2.4 Where the driveshaft nut is staked in position, relieve the staking with a suitable chisel-nosed tool

2.5a Where the driveshaft nut is secured with an R-clip, withdraw the R-clip . . .

2.5b . . . then remove the locking cap

2.6 Have an assistant firmly depress the brake pedal whilst you slacken the driveshaft nut (note wheel bolts – arrowed)

Tool Tip 1: Using a fabricated tool to hold the front hub stationary whilst the driveshaft nut is slackened.

2.7 Unscrew the nut and withdraw the lower arm balljoint clamp bolt

retaining nut in position **(see illustration)**. Note that a new retaining nut must be used on refitting.

5 On models where the driveshaft nut is secured by an R-clip, withdraw the R-clip and remove the locking cap from the driveshaft retaining nut **(see illustrations)**.

6 Refit at least two roadwheel bolts to the front hub, and tighten them securely. Have an assistant firmly depress the brake pedal to prevent the front hub from rotating then, using a socket and a long extension bar, slacken

Tool Tip 2: To free the lower arm, attach a long bar (such as a jack handle) securely to the lower arm. Fit a block of wood to the inner end of the bar, to act as a pivot, and then use the bar to pull the lower arm out from the swivel hub.

and remove the driveshaft retaining nut **(see illustration)**. Alternatively, a tool can be fabricated from two lengths of steel strip (one long, one short) and a nut and bolt; the nut and bolt forming the pivot of a forked tool. Bolt the tool to the hub using two wheel bolts, and hold the tool to prevent the hub from rotating as the driveshaft retaining nut is undone **(see Tool Tip 1)**. This nut is very tight; make sure that there is no risk of pulling the car off the axle stands (see *Jacking and vehicle support*). **Note:** *If the roadwheel trim allows access to the driveshaft nut, the initial slackening can be done with the vehicle resting on its wheels on the ground.*

7 Slacken and remove the suspension lower arm balljoint clamp bolt and nut **(see**

2.10 Free the lower arm balljoint from the swivel hub and remove the protector plate (arrowed)

illustration). Discard the nut – a new one must be used on refitting.

Left-hand driveshaft

8 Turn the steering onto full right-hand lock.

9 Pull down on the lower arm to free its balljoint from the swivel hub **(see Tool Tip 2)**. Once the balljoint is freed from the swivel hub, peg the lower arm in position by inserting a suitable socket in between the top of the arm inner end and the subframe **(see illustration 2.15)**.

10 Recover the protector plate from lower arm balljoint **(see illustration)**.

11 Carefully pull the swivel hub assembly outwards, and withdraw the driveshaft outer constant velocity joint from the hub assembly **(see illustration)**. If necessary, the shaft can

2.11 Free the driveshaft outer joint from the swivel hub . . .

2.12 . . . then free the inner joint from the transmission and remove the driveshaft from the vehicle

2.13a On the right-hand driveshaft, slacken the two intermediate bearing retaining bolt nuts . . .

2.13b . . . then rotate the bolts through 90° to disengage their offset heads (arrowed) from the bearing (shown with driveshaft removed for clarity)

be tapped out of the hub using a soft-faced mallet.

12 Support the driveshaft, and then withdraw the inner constant velocity joint from the transmission, taking care not to damage the driveshaft oil seal. Remove the driveshaft from the vehicle **(see illustration)**.

Right-hand driveshaft

13 Loosen the two intermediate bearing retaining bolt nuts, then rotate the bolts through 90°, so that their offset heads are clear of the bearing outer race **(see illustrations)**.

14 Turn the steering onto full left-hand lock.

15 Pull down on the lower arm to free its balljoint from the swivel hub **(see Tool Tip 2)** Once the balljoint is freed from the swivel hub, peg the lower arm in position by inserting a suitable socket in between the top of the arm inner end and the subframe **(see illustration)**.

16 Recover the protector plate from lower arm balljoint **(see illustration)**.

17 Carefully pull the swivel hub assembly outwards, and withdraw the driveshaft outer constant velocity joint from the hub assembly **(see illustration)**. If necessary, the shaft can be tapped out of the hub using a soft-faced mallet.

18 Support the outer end of the driveshaft, then pull on the inner end of the shaft to free the intermediate bearing from its mounting bracket.

19 Once the driveshaft end is free from the

transmission, slide the dust seal/plate off the inner end of the shaft, noting which way around it is fitted, and remove the driveshaft **(see illustration)**.

Refitting

20 Before installing the driveshaft, examine the driveshaft oil seal in the transmission for signs of damage or deterioration and, if necessary, renew it, referring to Chapter 7A or 7B for further information. (Having got this far it is worth renewing the seal as a matter of course.)

21 Thoroughly clean the driveshaft splines, and the apertures in the transmission and hub assembly. Apply a thin film of multi-purpose grease (Peugeot recommend the use of Total 3945) to the oil seal lips, and to the driveshaft outer joint splines and shoulders. Check that all gaiter clips are securely fastened.

Left-hand driveshaft

22 Offer up the driveshaft, and locate the joint splines with those of the differential sun gear, taking great care not to damage the oil seal. Push the joint fully into position.

23 Locate the outer constant velocity joint splines with those of the swivel hub, and slide the joint back into position in the hub.

24 Fit the protector plate to the lower arm balljoint.

25 Align the lower arm balljoint with the swivel hub. Remove the socket (used to peg the arm in position) and seat the balljoint

shank correctly in the swivel hub, aligning the protector plate tang with the hub slot. Insert the clamp bolt then fit the new nut and tighten to the specified torque.

26 Lubricate the inner face and threads of the driveshaft retaining nut with clean engine oil (Peugeot recommend the use of Molykote D321R) and fit it to the end of the driveshaft (a new nut must be used on models with a staked nut). Use the method employed on removal to prevent the hub from rotating, and tighten the driveshaft retaining nut to the specified torque. Check that the hub rotates freely.

27 On models where the driveshaft nut is staked, stake the new nut into the driveshaft

2.15 Secure the lower arm clear of the swivel hub by inserting a socket in between the top of the arm and the subframe

2.16 Recover the protector plate from lower arm balljoint

2.17 Free the driveshaft outer joint from the swivel hub . . .

2.19 . . . then free the intermediate bearing from its bracket and recover the dust seal from the shaft inner end

2.27 Where the driveshaft nut is staked in position, tighten the new nut then stake it firmly into the driveshaft groove

2.39 Secure the right-hand driveshaft intermediate bearing in position then slide the dust seal tight up against the oil seal

3 Driveshaft rubber gaiters – renewal

1 Remove the driveshaft from the car as described in Section 2 and proceed as described under the relevant sub-heading.

groove using a hammer and punch **(see illustration)**.

28 On models where the driveshaft nut is secured by an R-clip, engage the locking cap with the driveshaft nut so that one of its cut-outs is aligned with the driveshaft hole. Secure the cap in position with the R-clip **(see illustrations 2.5a and 2.5b)**.

29 Refit the roadwheel and undershield (where fitted), then lower the vehicle to the ground and tighten the roadwheel bolts to the specified torque.

30 Top-up/refill the transmission with the specified type and amount of fluid/oil, and check the level using the information given in Chapter 7A or 7B.

Right-hand driveshaft

31 Check that the intermediate bearing rotates smoothly, without any sign of roughness or undue free play between its inner and outer races. If necessary, renew the bearing as described in Section 5. Examine the dust seal for signs of damage or deterioration, and renew if necessary.

32 Apply a smear of grease to the outer race of the intermediate bearing, and to the inner lip of the dust seal.

33 On models with an automatic transmission unit, check the condition of the O-ring fitted to the differential sun gear shaft. Renew the O-ring if it shows signs of damage or deterioration.

34 On all models, pass the inner end of the

shaft through the bearing mounting bracket, then carefully slide the dust seal/plate into position on the driveshaft, ensuring that its flat surface is facing the transmission.

35 Carefully locate the inner driveshaft splines with those of the differential sun gear, taking care not to damage the oil seal. Align the intermediate bearing with its mounting bracket, and push the driveshaft fully into position. If necessary, use a soft-faced mallet to tap the outer race of the bearing into position in the mounting bracket.

36 Locate the outer constant velocity joint splines with those of the swivel hub, and slide the joint back into position in the hub.

37 Fit the protector plate to the lower arm balljoint.

38 Align the lower arm balljoint with the swivel hub. Remove the socket (used to peg the arm in position) and seat the balljoint shank correctly in the swivel hub, aligning the protector plate tang with the hub slot. Insert the clamp bolt then fit the new nut and tighten to the specified torque.

39 Ensure that the intermediate bearing is correctly seated, and then rotate its retaining bolts back through 90°, so that their offset heads are resting against the bearing outer race. Evenly and progressively tighten the retaining bolt nuts to the specified torque. Ensure that the dust seal/plate is tight against the driveshaft oil seal **(see illustration)**.

40 Carry out the operations described above in paragraphs 26 to 30.

Outer joint

2 Secure the driveshaft in a vice equipped with soft jaws. Mark the position of the gaiter on the driveshaft then release the two gaiter retaining clips. If necessary, the gaiter retaining clips can be cut to release them.

3 Slide the gaiter down the shaft, to expose the outer constant velocity joint. Scoop out the excess grease.

4 Using a hammer and suitable soft metal drift, sharply strike the inner member of the outer joint to drive it off the end of the shaft. The joint is retained on the driveshaft by a circlip, and striking the joint in this manner forces the circlip into its groove, so allowing the joint to slide off.

5 Once the joint assembly has been removed, remove the circlip from the groove in the driveshaft splines, and discard it. A new circlip must be fitted on reassembly.

6 Withdraw the gaiter from the driveshaft.

7 With the constant velocity joint removed from the driveshaft, thoroughly clean the joint and dry it thoroughly. Carry out a visual inspection of the joint.

8 Move the inner splined driving member from side-to-side, to expose each ball in turn at the top of its track. Examine the balls for cracks, flat spots, or signs of surface pitting.

9 Inspect the ball tracks on the inner and outer members. If the tracks have widened, the balls will no longer be a tight fit. At the same time, check the ball cage windows for wear or cracking between the windows.

10 If, on inspection, any of the constant velocity joint components are found to be worn or damaged, it will be necessary to renew the complete joint assembly (where available), or even the complete driveshaft (where no joint components are available separately). Refer to your Peugeot dealer for further information on parts availability. If the joint is in satisfactory condition, obtain a repair kit consisting of a new gaiter, circlip, retaining clips, and the correct type and quantity of grease.

11 Tape over the splines on the end of the driveshaft, to protect the new gaiter. Slide the gaiter onto the shaft and locate it correctly on the driveshaft. **Note:** *Some driveshaft kits may supply a plastic bush, which goes onto the driveshaft, and the small end of the gaiter fits onto it (see illustrations)*.

12 Remove the tape and fit the new circlip to the driveshaft, ensuring it is correctly

3.11a Slide the new plastic bush (arrowed – where fitted) and seat it in its recess in the shaft . . .

3.11b . . . then slide the gaiter along the shaft and seat it on top of the plastic bush

3.12 Fit the new circlip to the groove in the driveshaft splines . . .

3.13 . . . then locate the joint outer member on the splines and slide it over the circlip. Ensure that the joint is firmly retained by the circlip . . .

located in the driveshaft groove **(see illustration)**.

13 Locate the outer joint on the driveshaft splines and slide it on until the inner member abuts the circlip **(see illustration)**. Tap the joint outer member sharply with a hammer and soft-metal drift to force the inner member over the circlip and fully onto the driveshaft. Pull on the joint assembly to make sure it is securely retained by the circlip.

14 Work the grease well into the ball tracks of the joint and fill the gaiter with any excess **(see illustration)**.

3.19a Wrap the retaining clip around the gaiter (twice if possible) and pull it tight using a pair of pliers and a hook fabricated out of welding rod

15 Locate the outer lip of the gaiter in the groove(s) on the joint outer member and ensure the gaiter inner end is correctly seated in the driveshaft groove. Where there is no groove, align the gaiter with the marks made prior to removal.

16 Ensure the gaiter is correctly located then lift the inner lip of the gaiter to equalise the air pressure inside.

17 Ensure the gaiter is correctly located then secure it in position with the retaining clips. Note that there are two possible types of retaining clip, which are secured as follows.

18 The most frequently used type of clip simply clips around the gaiter and is secured in position by crimping its raised section. In the absence of the special tool, carefully compress the clip raised section using a pair of side-cutters, taking great care not to cut through the clip.

19 The other type of clip is in the form of a metal strap with a buckle at one end. Pass the end of the strap through the buckle slot the seat the clip on the gaiter; if sufficient clip is available wrap the clip twice around the gaiter. In the absence of the special tool, use a hook fabricated out of welding rod and a pair of pliers to pull the clip tight to remove all slack, then bend the strap back over the buckle. Cut off the excess then bend the strap end

3.14 . . . then pack the joint and gaiter with the grease supplied

behind the buckle before folding the buckle firmly down onto the strap to secure the clip in position **(see illustrations)**.

20 Check the joint moves smoothly in all directions then refit the driveshaft as described in Section 2.

Inner joint

21 Remove the outer constant velocity joint as described in paragraphs 2 to 5.

22 Tape over the splines on the driveshaft and carefully remove the outer joint gaiter. It is recommended that the outer gaiter is also renewed, regardless of its apparent condition.

23 Mark the position of the inner joint gaiter

3.19b Bend the clip back over the buckle then cut off the excess

3.19c Fold the clip end underneath the buckle . . .

3.19d . . . then fold the buckle firmly down onto the clip to secure it in position

on the driveshaft then cut/release the two gaiter retaining clips **(see illustration)**.

24 Free the gaiter from the inner joint outer member then remove the outer member and spring from the shaft **(see illustrations)**. Slide the gaiter off and remove it from the shaft.

25 Thoroughly clean the joint. Check the tripod joint bearings and joint outer member for signs of wear, pitting or scuffing on their bearing surfaces. Check that the bearing rollers rotate smoothly and easily around the tripod joint, with no traces of roughness.

26 If, on inspection, the tripod joint or outer member reveal signs of wear or damage, it will be necessary to renew the complete driveshaft assembly, since the joint is not available separately. If the joint is in satisfactory condition, obtain a repair kit consisting of a new gaiter, retaining clips, and the correct type and quantity of grease. Although not strictly necessary, it is also recommended that the outer constant velocity joint gaiter is renewed, regardless of its apparent condition.

27 On reassembly, pack the inner joint with the grease supplied in the gaiter kit. Work the grease well into the bearing tracks and rollers, while twisting the joint.

28 Clean the shaft, using emery cloth to remove any rust or sharp edges which may damage the gaiter. Slide the gaiter inner end plastic bush (where fitted) onto the shaft and locate it in the groove. Slide the gaiter onto the shaft and locate it correctly in the driveshaft groove.

29 Fit the spring to the end of the driveshaft then refit the outer member, engaging it correctly with the gaiter.

30 Ensure the gaiter is correctly located then lift the inner lip of the gaiter to equalise the air pressure inside. Fit both the inner and outer retaining clips, securing them in position using the information given in paragraphs 17 to 19 **(see illustration)**. Ensure that the gaiter retaining clips are securely tightened, then check that the joint moves freely in all directions.

31 Refit the outer constant velocity joint components using the information given in paragraph 12 to 20.

32 Check the joints move smoothly in all directions then refit the driveshaft as described in Section 2.

4 Driveshaft overhaul – general information

1 If any of the checks described in Chapter 1A or 1B reveal wear in any driveshaft joint, first remove the roadwheel trim or centre cap (as appropriate).

2 On models with a staked driveshaft nut, if the staking is still effective, the driveshaft nut should be correctly tightened; if in doubt, relieve the staking, then tighten the nut to the specified torque and restake it into the driveshaft grooves. Refit the roadwheel trim or centre cap (as applicable), and repeat the check on the remaining driveshaft nut.

3.23 Cut the inner and outer clips (arrowed) to release them

3.24b . . . and recover the spring

3 On models where the driveshaft nut is secured by an R-clip, if the R-clip is fitted, the driveshaft nut should be correctly tightened, if in doubt, remove the R-clip and locking cap, and use a torque wrench to check that the nut is securely fastened. Once tightened, refit the locking cap and R-clip, then refit the centre cap or trim. Repeat this check on the remaining driveshaft nut.

4 Road test the vehicle, and listen for a metallic clicking from the front as the vehicle is driven slowly in a circle on full-lock. If a clicking noise is heard, this indicates wear in the outer constant velocity joint. This means that the joint must be renewed; reconditioning is not possible.

5 If vibration, consistent with roadspeed, is felt through the car when accelerating, there is a possibility of wear in the inner constant velocity joints.

6 To check the joints for wear, remove the driveshafts, and then dismantle them as described in Section 3; if any wear or free play is

5.3 Using a long-reach bearing puller to remove the intermediate bearing from the right-hand driveshaft

3.24a Free the inner joint outer member from the gaiter . . .

3.30 Ensure the gaiter retaining clips are both securely fitted

found, the affected joint must be renewed. In the case of the inner joints (and, on some models, the outer joints), this means that the complete driveshaft assembly must be renewed, as the joints are not available separately. Refer to your Peugeot dealer for information on the availability of driveshaft components.

5 Right-hand driveshaft intermediate bearing – renewal

Note: *A suitable bearing puller will be required, to draw the bearing and collar off the driveshaft end.*

1 Remove the right-hand driveshaft as described in Section 2 of this Chapter.

2 Check that the bearing outer race rotates smoothly and easily, without any signs of roughness or undue free play between the inner and outer races. If necessary, renew the bearing as follows.

3 Using a long-reach universal bearing puller, carefully draw the collar and intermediate bearing off the driveshaft inner end **(see illustration)**. Apply a smear of grease to the inner race of the new bearing, and then fit the bearing over the end of the driveshaft. Using a hammer and suitable piece of tubing which bears only on the bearing inner race, tap the new bearing into position on the driveshaft, until it abuts the constant velocity joint outer member. Once the bearing is correctly positioned, tap the bearing collar onto the shaft until it contacts the bearing inner race.

4 Check that the bearing rotates freely, then refit the driveshaft.

Chapter 9
Braking system

Contents

Degrees of difficulty

Easy, suitable for novice with little experience	**Fairly easy,** suitable for beginner with some experience	**Fairly difficult,** suitable for competent DIY mechanic	**Difficult,** suitable for experienced DIY mechanic	**Very difficult,** suitable for expert DIY or professional

Specifications

Front brakes

Type	Disc, with single-piston sliding caliper
Disc diameter:	
2.0 litre engine models	266.0 mm
All other models	247.0 mm
Disc thickness:	
New:	
Solid disc	13.0 mm
Ventilated disc	20.4 mm
Minimum thickness:	
Solid disc	11.0 mm
Ventilated disc	18.4 mm
Maximum disc run-out	0.05 mm
Brake pad friction material minimum thickness	2.0 mm

Rear drum brakes

Drum internal diameter:	
Models fitted with ABS:	
New	203.0 mm
Maximum	205.0 mm
All other models*:	
New	180.0 mm
Maximum	183.0 mm
Brake shoe friction material minimum thickness	1.5 mm

Some models fitted with an automatic transmission unit maybe equipped with the larger drums

Rear disc brakes

Type	Solid disc, with single-piston sliding caliper
Disc diameter	247.0 mm
Disc thickness:	
New	8.0 mm
Minimum thickness.	6.0 mm
Maximum disc run-out	0.05 mm
Brake pad friction material minimum thickness	2.0 mm

Torque wrench settings

	Nm	lbf ft
ABS wheel sensor retaining bolt	9	7
Brake pedal pivot shaft nut	15	11
Brake pipe union nuts	15	11
Front brake caliper:		
Guide pin bolts*	30	22
Mounting bracket bolts*	105	77
Front brake disc screws	10	7
Handbrake lever mounting nuts	15	11
Load-sensitive pressure regulating valve bolt	18	13
Master cylinder-to-servo unit nuts	20	15
Rear caliper mounting bolts	110	80
Rear hub nut*	200	148
Rear wheel cylinder retaining bolts	8	6
Roadwheel bolts	90	66
Vacuum pump retaining nut and bolts – diesel engine	20	15
Vacuum servo unit/pedal bracket/crossover linkage mounting nuts	20	15

Do not re-use

1 General information

1 The braking system is of the servo-assisted, dual-circuit hydraulic type. The arrangement of the hydraulic system is such that each circuit operates one front and one rear brake from a tandem master cylinder. Under normal circumstances, both circuits operate in unison. However, in the event of hydraulic failure in one circuit, full braking force will still be available at two wheels. An Anti-lock Braking System (ABS) was available as an optional extra on all models (refer to Section 22 for further information on ABS operation).

2 The disc brakes are actuated by single-piston sliding type calipers, which ensure that equal pressure is applied to each disc pad.

3 The rear drum brakes incorporate leading and trailing shoes, which are actuated by twin-piston wheel cylinders. A self-adjust mechanism is incorporated, to automatically compensate for brake shoe wear. As the brake shoe linings wear, the footbrake operation automatically operates the adjuster mechanism, which effectively lengthens the shoe strut and repositions the brake shoes to maintain the lining-to-drum clearance. The hydraulic pressure applied to the rear brakes is regulated by the pressure control valve(s) to help prevent rear wheel lock-up during emergency braking

4 The handbrake provides an independent mechanical means of rear brake application.

5 On diesel engines, there is insufficient vacuum in the inlet manifold to operate the braking system servo effectively at all times. To overcome this problem, a vacuum pump is fitted to the engine to provide sufficient vacuum to operate the servo unit. The vacuum pump is mounted on the end of the cylinder head, and driven directly off the end of the camshaft.

Note: *When servicing any part of the system, work carefully and methodically; also observe scrupulous cleanliness when overhauling any part of the hydraulic system. Always renew components (in axle sets, where applicable) if in doubt about their condition, and use only genuine Peugeot parts, or at least those of known good quality. Note the warnings given in 'Safety first!' and at relevant points in this Chapter concerning the dangers of asbestos dust and hydraulic fluid.*

2 Hydraulic system – bleeding

⚠ **Warning: Hydraulic fluid is poisonous; wash off immediately and thoroughly in the case of skin contact, and seek immediate medical advice if any fluid is swallowed or gets into the eyes. Certain types of hydraulic fluid are inflammable, and may ignite when allowed into contact with hot components; when servicing any hydraulic system, it is safest to assume that the fluid is inflammable, and to take precautions against the risk of fire as though it is petrol that is being handled. Hydraulic fluid is also an effective paint stripper, and will attack plastics. If any is spilt, it should be washed off immediately, using copious quantities of fresh water. Finally, it is hygroscopic (it absorbs moisture from the air) – old fluid may be contaminated and unfit for further use. When topping-up or renewing the fluid, always use the recommended type, and ensure that it comes from a freshly-opened sealed container.**

Note: *If difficulty is experienced in bleeding the braking circuit on models with ABS, this maybe due to air being trapped in the ABS hydraulic unit. If this is the case then the vehicle should be taken to a Peugeot dealer so that the system can be bled using special equipment.*

General

1 The correct operation of any hydraulic system is only possible after removing all air from the components and circuit; this is achieved by bleeding the system.

2 During the bleeding procedure, add only clean, unused hydraulic fluid of the recommended type; never re-use fluid that has already been bled from the system. Ensure that sufficient fluid is available before starting work.

3 If there is any possibility of incorrect fluid being already in the system, the brake components and circuit must be flushed completely with uncontaminated, correct fluid, and new seals should be fitted to the various components.

4 If hydraulic fluid has been lost from the system, or air has entered because of a leak, ensure that the fault is cured before proceeding further.

5 Park the vehicle on level ground, then chock the wheels and release the handbrake.

6 Check that all pipes and hoses are secure, unions tight and bleed screws closed. Clean any dirt from around the bleed screws.

7 Unscrew the master cylinder reservoir cap, and top the master cylinder reservoir up to the MAX level line; refit the cap loosely, and remember to maintain the fluid level at least above the DANGER level line throughout the procedure, or there is a risk of further air entering the system.

8 There is a number of one-man, do-it-yourself brake bleeding kits currently available from motor accessory shops. It is recommended that one of these kits is used whenever possible, as they greatly simplify the bleeding operation, and also reduce the risk of expelled air and fluid being drawn back into the system. If such a kit is not available, the basic (two-man) method must be used, which is described in detail below.

9 If a kit is to be used, prepare the vehicle as described previously, and follow the kit

manufacturer's instructions, as the procedure may vary slightly according to the type being used; generally, they are as outlined below in the relevant sub-section.

10 Whichever method is used, the same sequence must be followed (paragraphs 11 and 12) to ensure the removal of all air from the system.

Bleeding sequence

11 If the system has been only partially disconnected, and suitable precautions were taken to minimise fluid loss, it should be necessary only to bleed that part of the system (ie, the primary or secondary circuit).

12 If the complete system is to be bled, then it should be done working in the following sequence:

a) *Left-hand front brake.*
b) *Right-hand front brake.*
c) *Left-hand rear brake.*
d) *Right-hand rear brake.*

Bleeding

Basic (two-man) method

13 Collect a clean glass jar, a suitable length of plastic or rubber tubing which is a tight fit over the bleed screw, and a ring spanner to fit the screw. The help of an assistant will also be required.

14 Remove the dust cap from the first screw in the sequence. Fit the spanner and tube to the screw, place the other end of the tube in the jar, and pour in sufficient fluid to cover the end of the tube.

15 Ensure that the master cylinder reservoir fluid level is maintained at least above the DANGER level line throughout the procedure.

16 Have the assistant fully depress the brake pedal several times to build-up pressure, and then maintain it on the final down stroke.

17 While pedal pressure is maintained, unscrew the bleed screw (approximately one turn) and allow the compressed fluid and air to flow into the jar. The assistant should maintain pedal pressure, following it down to the floor if necessary, and should not release it until instructed to do so. When the flow stops, tighten the bleed screw again, have the assistant release the pedal slowly, and recheck the reservoir fluid level.

18 Repeat the steps given in paragraphs 16 and

17 until the fluid emerging from the bleed screw is free from air bubbles. If the master cylinder has been drained and refilled, and air is being bled from the first screw in the sequence, allow approximately five seconds between cycles for the master cylinder passages to refill.

19 When no more air bubbles appear, tighten the bleed screw securely, remove the tube and spanner, and refit the dust cap. Do not over tighten the bleed screw.

20 Repeat the procedure on the remaining screws in the sequence, until all air is removed from the system and the brake pedal feels firm again.

Using a one-way valve kit

21 As their name implies, these kits consist of a length of tubing with a one-way valve fitted, to prevent expelled air and fluid being drawn back into the system; some kits include a translucent container, which can be positioned so that the air bubbles can be more easily seen flowing from the end of the tube.

22 The kit is connected to the bleed screw, which is then opened (**see illustration**). The user returns to the driver's seat, depresses the brake pedal with a smooth, steady stroke, and slowly releases it; this is repeated until the expelled fluid is clear of air bubbles.

23 Note that these kits simplify work so much that it is easy to forget the master cylinder reservoir fluid level; ensure that this is maintained at least above the DANGER level line at all times.

Using a pressure-bleeding kit

24 These kits are usually operated by the reservoir of pressurised air contained in the spare tyre. However, note that it will probably be necessary to reduce the pressure to a lower level than normal; refer to the instructions supplied with the kit.

25 By connecting a pressurised, fluid-filled container to the master cylinder reservoir, bleeding can be carried out simply by opening each screw in turn (in the specified sequence), and allowing the fluid to flow out until no more air bubbles can be seen in the expelled fluid.

26 This method has the advantage that the large reservoir of fluid provides an additional safeguard against air being drawn into the system during bleeding.

27 Pressure-bleeding is particularly effective when bleeding 'difficult' systems, or when bleeding the complete system at the time of routine fluid renewal.

All methods

28 When bleeding is complete, and firm pedal feel is restored, wash off any spilt fluid, tighten the bleed screws, and refit their dust caps.

29 Check the hydraulic fluid level in the master cylinder reservoir, and top-up if necessary (*Weekly checks*).

30 Discard any fluid that has been bled from the system; it will not be fit for re-use.

31 Check the feel of the brake pedal. If it feels at all spongy, air must still be present in the system, and further bleeding is required. Failure to bleed properly after a reasonable repetition of the bleeding procedure may be due to worn master cylinder seals.

3	Hydraulic pipes and hoses – renewal	

Note: *Before starting work, refer to the note at the beginning of Section 2 concerning the dangers of hydraulic fluid.*

1 If any pipe or hose is to be renewed, minimise fluid loss by first removing the master cylinder reservoir cap, then tightening it down onto a piece of polythene to obtain an airtight seal. Alternatively, flexible hoses can be sealed, if required, using a proprietary brake hose clamp; metal brake pipe unions can be plugged (if care is taken not to allow dirt into the system) or capped immediately they are disconnected. Place a wad of rag under any union that is to be disconnected, to catch any spilt fluid.

2 If a flexible hose is to be disconnected, unscrew the brake pipe union nut before removing the spring clip, which secures the hose to its mounting bracket (**see illustration**).

3 To unscrew the union nuts, it is preferable to obtain a brake pipe spanner of the correct size; these are available from most large motor accessory shops (**see illustration**). Failing this, a close-fitting open-ended spanner will

2.22 Using a one-way valve kit to bleed a front brake caliper

3.2 Unscrew the brake pipe union nut (A) then remove the retaining clip (B) and free the flexible hose (C) from its bracket

3.3 Using a brake pipe spanner to slacken a brake pipe union nut

be required, though if the nuts are tight or corroded, their flats may be rounded-off if the spanner slips. In such a case, a self-locking wrench is often the only way to unscrew a stubborn union, but it follows that the pipe and the damaged nuts must be renewed on reassembly. Always clean a union and surrounding area before disconnecting it. If disconnecting a component with more than one union, make a careful note of the connections before disturbing any of them.

4 If a brake pipe is to be renewed, it can be obtained, cut to length and with the union nuts and end flares in place, from Peugeot dealers. All that is then necessary is to bend it to shape, following the line of the original, before fitting it to the car. Alternatively, most motor accessory shops can make up brake pipes from kits, but this requires very careful measurement of the original, to ensure that the new one is of the correct length. The safest answer is usually to take the original to the shop as a pattern.

5 On refitting, do not overtighten the union nuts. It is not necessary to exercise brute force to obtain a sound joint.

6 Ensure that the pipes and hoses are correctly routed, with no kinks, and that they are secured in the clips or brackets provided. After fitting, remove the polythene from the reservoir, and bleed the hydraulic system as described in Section 2. Immediately wash off any spilt fluid, and check carefully for fluid leaks.

4 Front brake pads – renewal

⚠️ **Warning: Renew both sets of front brake pads at the same time – never renew the pads on only one wheel, as uneven braking may result. Note that the dust created by wear of the pads may contain asbestos, which is a health hazard. Never blow it out with compressed air, and don't inhale any of it. An approved filtering mask should be worn when working on the brakes. DO NOT use petrol or petroleum-based solvents to clean brake parts; use brake cleaner or methylated spirit only.**

4.3 Slacken and remove the caliper lower guide pin bolt . . .

Note: *New guide pin bolts must be used on refitting.*

1 Apply the handbrake, then jack up the front of the vehicle and support it on axle stands (see *Jacking and vehicle support*). Remove the front roadwheels.

2 Push the piston into its bore by pulling the caliper outwards.

3 Slacken and remove the caliper lower guide pin bolt; discard the bolt – a new bolt must be used on refitting **(see illustration)**.

4 Pivot the caliper upwards to gain access to the brake pads **(see illustration)**.

5 Withdraw the two brake pads from the caliper mounting bracket **(see illustration)**.

6 First measure the thickness of each brake pad's friction material. If either pad is worn at any point to the specified minimum thickness or less, all four pads must be renewed **(see illustration)**. Also, the pads should be renewed if any are fouled with oil or grease; there is no proper way of degreasing friction material, once contaminated. If any of the brake pads are worn unevenly, or are fouled with oil or grease, trace and rectify the cause before reassembly. New brake pads are available from Peugeot dealers.

7 If the brake pads are still serviceable, carefully clean them using a clean, fine wire brush or similar, paying particular attention to the sides and back of the metal backing. Clean out the grooves (where present) in the friction material, and pick out any large embedded particles of dirt or debris. Carefully clean the pad locations in the caliper body/mounting bracket.

4.4 . . . then pivot the caliper upwards . . .

8 Prior to fitting the pads, check that the guide pins are free to slide easily in the caliper mounting bracket, and check that the rubber guide pin gaiters are undamaged. Brush the dust and dirt from the caliper and piston, but **do not** inhale it, as it is injurious to health. Inspect the dust seal around the piston for damage, and the piston for evidence of fluid leaks, corrosion or damage. If attention to any of these components is necessary, refer to Section 10.

9 If new brake pads are to be fitted, the caliper piston must be pushed back into the cylinder to make room for them. Either use a G-clamp or similar tool, or use suitable pieces of wood as levers. Provided that the master cylinder reservoir has not been overfilled with hydraulic fluid, there should be no spillage, but keep a careful watch on the fluid level while retracting the piston. If the fluid level rises above the MAX level line at any time, the surplus should be syphoned off or ejected via a plastic tube connected to the bleed screw (see Section 2). **Note:** *Do not syphon the fluid by mouth, as it is poisonous; use a syringe or an old antifreeze tester.*

10 Install the pads in the caliper mounting bracket, ensuring that the friction material of each pad is against the brake disc. Ensure the pad anti-rattle springs are correctly located in the bracket then pivot the caliper down into position.

11 Align the cut-outs in the guide pin with the caliper slot then fit the new guide pin bolt **(see illustration)**. Ensure the bolt plate is correctly located in the guide pin cut-outs (the plate prevents the guide pin rotating as the bolt is

4.5 . . . and withdraw the brake pads from the caliper bracket

4.6 Measuring brake pad friction material thickness

4.11 Ensure the bolt plate (A) engages correctly with the caliper slot (B) and guide pin slots (C) when fitting the guide pin bolt

5.2a Pull out the clip ...

5.2b ... from the guide plate at the lower edge of the pads (arrowed)

5.2c Gently tap the guide plate to the outside ...

5.2d ... and remove it

5.2e Slide out the inner pad ...

5.2f ... and outer pad

tightened) then tighten the bolt to the specified torque.

12 Depress the brake pedal repeatedly until the pads are pressed into firm contact with the brake disc, and normal (non-assisted) pedal pressure is restored.

13 Repeat the above procedure on the remaining front brake caliper.

14 Refit the roadwheels, then lower the vehicle to the ground and tighten the roadwheel bolts to the specified torque.

15 Finally, check the fluid level (*Weekly checks*).

Caution: New pads will not give full braking efficiency until they have bedded-in. Be prepared for this, and avoid hard braking as far as possible for the first hundred miles or so after pad renewal.

5 Rear brake pads – renewal

⚠️ *'Warning: Renew both sets of rear brake pads at the same time – never renew the pads on only one wheel, as uneven braking may result. Note that the dust created by wear of the pads may contain asbestos, which is a health hazard. Never blow it out with compressed air, and don't inhale any of it. An approved filtering mask should be worn when working on the brakes. DO NOT use petrol or petroleum-based solvents to clean brake parts; use brake cleaner or methylated spirit only.*

1 Apply the handbrake, then slacken the rear roadwheel bolts. Jack up the rear of the

vehicle and support it on axle stands (see *"Jacking and vehicle support"*). Remove both rear roadwheels.

2 Follow the relevant accompanying photos

5.2g If any of the pads' friction material thickness is less than 2.0 mm, renew all 4 pads

5.2i The piston must be set with the slot horizontal, and the small grooves (arrowed) also horizontal

(illustrations 5.2a to 5.2p) for the actual pad replacement procedure. Be sure to stay in order and read the caption under each illustration, and note the following points:

5.2h If new pads are to be fitted, push the caliper piston back whilst rotating it clockwise at the same time. Keep an eye on the fluid level in the reservoir!

5.2j Clean the caliper using a soft brush and brake cleaner

5.2k Smear a little anti-seize grease onto the rear of the pads

5.2l Fit the springs to the upper part of each pad

5.2m Slide the outer pad into place – friction material against the disc

5.2n Fit the inner pad. The lug (arrowed) on the pad backing plate must align with the slot in the piston

5.2o Slide in the guide plate from the outside ...

5.2p ... and refit the retaining clip

a) New pads may have an adhesive foil on the backplates. Remove this foil prior to installation.

b) Clean the caliper guide surfaces with non-abrasive cleaners only, and apply a little brake assembly (Copperslip) grease.

c) When pushing the caliper piston back to accommodate new pads, keep a close eye on the fluid level in the reservoir.

3 Depress the brake pedal repeatedly, until the pads are pressed into firm contact with the brake disc, and normal (non-assisted) pedal pressure is restored.

4 Repeat the above procedure on the remaining rear brake caliper.

5 Apply a little anti-seize grease to the hub surface, then refit the roadwheels, lower the vehicle to the ground and tighten the roadwheel bolts to the specified torque.

6 Check the hydraulic fluid level as described in *Weekly checks*.

Caution: New pads will not give full braking efficiency until they have bedded-in. Be prepared for this, and avoid hard braking as far as possible for the first hundred miles or so after pad renewal.'

6 Rear brake shoes –
check and renewal

⚠️ **Warning: Brake shoes must be renewed on both rear wheels at the same time – never renew** the shoes on only one wheel, as uneven braking may result. Also, the dust created by wear of the shoes may contain asbestos, which is a health hazard. Never blow it out with compressed air, and don't inhale any of it. An approved filtering mask should be worn when working on the brakes. DO NOT use petrol or petroleum-based solvents to clean brake parts; use brake cleaner or methylated spirit only.

Check

1 Remove the brake drum (see Section 9).

2 Working carefully, and taking the necessary precautions, remove all traces of brake dust from the brake drum, backplate and shoes.

3 Measure the thickness of the friction material of each brake shoe at several points; if either shoe is worn at any point to the specified minimum thickness or less, all four shoes must be renewed as a set. The shoes should also be renewed if any are fouled with oil or grease; there is no proper way of degreasing friction material, once contaminated.

4 If any of the brake shoes are worn unevenly, or fouled with oil or grease, trace and rectify the cause before reassembly.

Renewal

5 To renew the brake shoes, proceed as described under the relevant sub-heading. Prior to removing the shoes, take careful note of the correct fitted positions of the springs and adjuster strut, to use as a guide on reassembly.

Bosch brake shoes

6 Using a pair of pliers, remove the shoe retainer spring cups by depressing and turning them through 90°. With the cups removed, lift off the springs and withdraw the retainer pins **(see illustrations)**.

6.6a Bosch rear brake shoe components

A Leading shoe
B Trailing shoe
C Lower pivot point
F Adjuster strut mechanism
1 Upper return spring
2 Lower return spring
3 Retainer pin, spring and cup
4 Adjuster strut-to-trailing shoe spring

6.6b Remove the spring cup . . .

6.6c . . . and recover the spring and retainer pin

6.7a Ease the shoes out from the lower pivot point . . .

6.7b . . . then unhook and remove the lower return spring

6.8a Free the both shoes from the wheel cylinder . . .

6.8b . . . then detach the handbrake cable and remove the shoe and strut assembly from the vehicle

6.8c Whilst the shoe assembly is removed, wrap a stout elastic band around the wheel cylinder to prevent the pistons being accidentally expelled

6.9a Note the correct fitted locations of the springs . . .

6.9b . . . and strut components before separating the shoe and strut assembly

7 Ease the shoes out one at a time from the lower pivot point, to release the tension of the return spring, then disconnect the lower return spring from both shoes (see illustrations).

8 Ease the upper end of both shoes out from their wheel cylinder locations, taking care not to damage the wheel cylinder seals, and disconnect the handbrake cable from the trailing shoe. The brake shoe and adjuster strut assembly can then be manoeuvred out of position and away from the backplate. Do not depress the brake pedal until the brakes are reassembled; wrap an elastic band around the wheel cylinder pistons to retain them (see illustrations).

9 With the shoe and adjuster strut assembly on a bench, make a note of the correct fitted positions of the springs and adjuster strut, to use

as a guide on reassembly (see illustrations).
10 Carefully unhook the adjuster strut bolt retaining spring from the leading shoe. Pivot the leading shoe out from the adjuster strut

6.10a Unhook the adjuster strut bolt spring . . .

bolt then detach the leading shoe and return spring from the trailing shoe. Unhook the adjuster strut from the trailing shoe and recover the spring (see illustrations).

6.10b . . . then pivot the leading shoe off the bolt and remove the shoe and upper return spring

6.10c Unhook the adjuster strut from the trailing shoe, noting which way around its spring is fitted

6.11 Check the adjuster strut bolt for signs of wear or damage

11 Withdraw the adjuster bolt from the strut, and carefully examine the assembly for signs of wear or damage (see illustration). Pay particular attention to the threads of the adjuster bolt and the knurled adjuster wheel, and renew if necessary. Note that left-hand and right-hand struts are not interchangeable. Also note that the strut adjuster bolts are not interchangeable; the left-hand strut bolt has a left-handed thread, and the right-hand bolt a right-handed thread.

12 All return springs should be renewed, regardless of their apparent condition; spring kits are available from Peugeot dealers.

13 Ensure that the components on the end of the strut are correctly positioned, and then apply a little high melting-point grease to the threads of the adjuster bolt (Peugeot recommend the use of Lubritherm G200). Screw the adjuster wheel onto the bolt until only a small gap exists between the wheel and the head of the bolt, and then fit the bolt in the strut.

14 Fit the adjuster strut retaining spring to the trailing shoe, ensuring that the shorter hook of the spring is engaged with the shoe. Attach the adjuster strut to the spring end, and then ease the strut into its slot in the trailing shoe (see illustration).

15 Engage the upper return spring with the trailing shoe, then hook the leading shoe onto the other end of the spring. Lever the leading

shoe down until the adjuster bolt head is correctly located in its groove. Once the bolt is correctly located, hook its retaining spring into the slot on the leading shoe (see illustration).

16 Peel back the rubber protective caps, and check the wheel cylinder for fluid leaks or other damage; check that both cylinder pistons are free to move easily. Refer to Section 12, if necessary, for information on wheel cylinder renewal.

17 Prior to installation, clean the backplate, and apply a thin smear of high-temperature brake grease or anti-seize compound (Peugeot recommend the use of Lubritherm G200) to all those surfaces of the backplate which bear on the shoes, particularly the wheel cylinder pistons and lower pivot point (see illustration). Do not allow the lubricant to foul the friction material.

18 Remove the elastic band fitted to the wheel cylinder then manoeuvre the shoe and strut assembly into position. Attach the handbrake cable to the trailing shoe then locate the upper end of both shoes correctly with the wheel cylinder pistons. Fit the lower return spring to both shoes then ease the shoes into position on the lower pivot point.

19 Tap the shoes to centralise them with the backplate, then refit the shoe retainer pins and springs, and secure them in position with the spring cups.

20 Using a screwdriver, turn the strut adjuster wheel to expand the shoes until the brake drum just slides over the shoes.

21 Refit the brake drum (see Section 9).

22 Repeat the above procedure on the remaining rear brake.

23 Once both sets of rear shoes have been renewed, adjust the lining-to-drum clearance by repeatedly depressing the brake pedal with the handbrake fully released. Whilst depressing the pedal, have an assistant listen to the rear drums, to check that the adjuster strut is functioning correctly; if so, a clicking sound will be emitted by the strut as the pedal is depressed.

24 Check and, if necessary, adjust the handbrake as described in Section 18.

25 On completion, check the hydraulic fluid level as described in Weekly checks.
Caution: New shoes will not give full braking efficiency until they have bedded-in. Be prepared for this, and avoid hard braking as far as possible for the first hundred miles or so after shoe renewal.

Lucas brake shoes

26 Make a note of the correct fitted positions of the springs and adjuster strut, to use as a guide on reassembly (see illustration).

27 As a precaution on models with ABS, unbolt the rear wheel sensor and position it clear of the backplate (see Section 23).

28 Carefully unhook the upper return spring and remove it from the brake shoes.

29 Unhook the adjusting lever spring then remove the retaining hook and strut adjusting lever from the leading shoe.

30 Using a pair of pliers, remove the leading shoe retainer spring cup by depressing it and turning through 90°. Lift off the spring, and then withdraw the retainer pin (see illustrations 6.6b and 6.6c). Free the leading shoe from the lower pivot point and adjuster strut then remove the shoe and lower return spring.

31 Remove the adjuster strut assembly from the trailing shoe.

32 Remove the trailing shoe retainer spring cup, spring and pin as described above, then detach the handbrake cable and remove the

6.14 Hook the shorter end of the spring onto the trailing shoe, then attach the adjuster strut and locate it on the shoe, ensuring it is correctly engaged with the handbrake lever

6.15 Fit the upper return spring and leading shoe. Ensure the shoe is correctly located in the bolt slot then hook the bolt spring into position

6.17 Lubricate the shoe contact surfaces of the rear backplate with a smear of high melting-point grease

1 Leading shoe
2 Trailing shoe
3 Lower pivot point
4 Upper return spring
5 Lower return spring
6 Retainer pin, spring
   and cup
7 Adjusting lever
   spring
8 Retaining hook
9 Strut adjusting lever

6.26 Lucas rear brake shoe components

shoe from the vehicle. Do not depress the brake pedal until the brakes are reassembled; wrap a strong elastic band around the wheel cylinder pistons to retain them **(see illustration 6.8c)**.

33 Withdraw the forked end from the strut, and carefully examine the assembly for signs of wear or damage. Pay particular attention to the threads and the knurled adjuster wheel, and renew if necessary. Note that left-hand and right-hand struts are not interchangeable; the left-hand fork has a right-handed thread, and **the right-hand fork a left-handed thread.**

34 All return springs should be renewed, regardless of their apparent condition; spring kits are available from Peugeot dealers.

35 Peel back the rubber protective caps, and check the wheel cylinder for fluid leaks or other damage; check that both cylinder pistons are free to move easily. Refer to Section 12, if necessary, for information on wheel cylinder renewal.

36 Prior to installation, clean the backplate, and apply a thin smear of high-temperature brake grease or anti-seize compound (Peugeot recommend the use of Lubritherm G200) to all those surfaces of the backplate which bear on the shoes, particularly the wheel cylinder pistons and lower pivot point. Do not allow the lubricant to foul the friction material. Also lubricate the adjuster strut threads.

37 Ensure that the handbrake lever stop-peg is correctly located against the edge of the

trailing shoe, and remove the elastic band fitted to the wheel cylinder.

38 Connect the handbrake cable to the trailing shoe lever then locate the upper end of the shoe in the wheel cylinder piston. Refit the retainer pin and spring, and secure it in position with the spring cup.

39 Screw in the adjuster wheel until the minimum strut length is obtained, then hook the strut into position on the trailing shoe. Position the adjuster strut forked end so that the notched side of its cut-out faces outwards **(see illustration)**.

40 Hook the lower return spring onto the trailing shoe then fit the leading shoe to the spring. Locate the leading shoe in position, ensuring that it is correctly engaged with the adjuster strut fork, and then secure it in position with the retainer pin, spring and spring cup.

41 Fit the strut adjusting lever to the leading shoe pin. Ensure the lever is correctly engaged with the adjuster strut forked end and wheel then secure it in position with the retaining hook.

42 Fit the adjusting lever spring to the leading shoe ensuring the shorter hook of the spring is engaged with the lever.

43 Install the upper return spring, then tap the shoes to centralise them with the backplate.

44 On models with ABS, clean the rear wheel sensor body and its location in the backplate. Also clean the threads of the sensor retaining bolt. Lubricate the sensor body with multi-purpose grease (Peugeot recommend Esso Norva 275). Ensure the sensor tip is clean then seat the sensor in position in the backplate. Apply a drop of thread locking compound to the threads of the sensor bolt then install the bolt, tightening it to the specified torque.

45 Using a screwdriver, turn the strut adjuster wheel to expand the shoes until the brake drum just slides over the shoes.

46 Refit the brake drum as described in Section 9.

47 Repeat the above procedure on the remaining rear brake.

48 Once both sets of rear shoes have been renewed, adjust the lining-to-drum clearance by repeatedly depressing the brake pedal with the handbrake fully released. Whilst depressing the pedal, have an assistant listen to the rear drums, to check that the adjuster strut is functioning correctly; if so, a clicking sound will be emitted by the strut as the pedal is depressed.

49 Check and, if necessary, adjust the handbrake as described in Section 18.

50 On completion, check the hydraulic fluid level as described in *Weekly checks*.

Caution: New shoes will not give full braking efficiency until they have bedded-in. Be prepared for this, and avoid hard braking as far as possible for the first hundred miles or so after shoe renewal.

6.39 Ensure the adjuster strut forked end is positioned so its notched side (1) faces outwards and its flat side (2) inwards

7 Front brake disc – inspection, removal and refitting

Note: *Before starting work, refer to the note at the beginning of Section 4 concerning the dangers of asbestos dust.*

Inspection

Note: *If either disc requires renewal, BOTH should be renewed at the same time, to ensure even and consistent braking. New brake pads should also be fitted.*

1 Apply the handbrake, then jack up the front of the car and support it on axle stands (see *Jacking and vehicle support*). Remove the appropriate front roadwheel.

2 Slowly rotate the brake disc so that the full area of both sides can be checked; remove the brake pads if better access is required to the inboard surface. Light scoring is normal in the area swept by the brake pads, but if heavy scoring or cracks are found, the disc must be renewed.

3 It is normal to find a lip of rust and brake dust around the disc's perimeter; this can be scraped off if required. If, however, a lip has formed due to excessive wear of the brake pad swept area, then the disc's thickness must be measured using a micrometer. Take measurements at several places around the disc, at the inside and outside of the pad swept area; if the disc has worn at any point to the specified minimum thickness or less, the disc must be renewed **(see illustration)**.

4 If the disc is thought to be warped, it can be checked for run-out. Either use a dial gauge mounted on any convenient fixed point, while the disc is slowly rotated, or use feeler blades to measure (at several points all around the disc) the clearance between the disc and a fixed point, such as the caliper mounting bracket **(see illustration)**. If the measurements obtained are at the specified maximum or beyond, the disc is excessively warped, and must be renewed; however, it is worth checking first that the hub bearing is in good condition (*Steering and suspension check* in the relevant part of Chapter 1 and/or Chapter 10).

5 Check the disc for cracks, especially around

7.3 Measuring front brake disc thickness using a micrometer

the wheel bolt holes, and any other wear or damage, and renew if necessary.

Removal

Note: *New caliper mounting bolts will be needed on refitting.*

6 Slacken and remove the two bolts securing the brake caliper mounting bracket to the swivel hub. Slide the caliper assembly off the disc and tie it to the front strut spring, to avoid placing any strain on the hydraulic brake hose **(see illustrations)**.

7 Use chalk or paint to mark the relationship of the disc to the hub, then remove the screws securing the brake disc to the hub, and remove the disc **(see illustration)**. If it is tight, lightly tap its rear face with a hide or plastic mallet.

Refitting

8 Refitting is the reverse of the removal procedure, noting the following points:

a) *Ensure that the mating surfaces of the disc and hub are clean and flat.*

b) *Align (if applicable) the marks made on removal, and tighten the disc retaining screws securely.*

c) *If a new disc has been fitted, use a suitable solvent to wipe any preservative coating from the disc before refitting the caliper.*

d) *Slide the caliper into position, ensuring the pads pass either side of the disc, then*

7.4 Checking front brake disc run-out using a dial gauge

fit the new mounting bolts and tighten them to the specified torque.

e) *Refit the roadwheel, then lower the vehicle to the ground and tighten the roadwheel bolts to the specified torque. On completion, repeatedly depress the brake pedal until normal (non-assisted) pedal pressure returns.*

8 Rear brake disc – inspection, removal and refitting

Note: *Before starting work, refer to the note at the beginning of Section 5 concerning the dangers of asbestos dust.*

Inspection

Note: *If either disc requires renewal, BOTH should be renewed at the same time, to ensure even and consistent braking. New brake pads should also be fitted.*

1 Firmly chock the front wheels, slacken the appropriate rear roadwheel bolts, and then jack up the rear of the car and support it on axle stands (see *Jacking and vehicle support*). Remove the relevant rear roadwheel.

2 Inspect the disc as described in Section 7.

Removal

3 Remove the brake pads as described in Section 5.

4 Undo the caliper mounting bolts, and slide

7.6a Unscrew the caliper bracket mounting bolts (arrowed) . . .

7.6b . . . then slide the caliper assembly off the brake disc

7.7 Undo the retaining screws (arrowed) and remove the brake disc from the hub

8.4 Undo the bolts (arrowed) securing the caliper

8.5 Undo the screws and remove the disc

9.2 Tap the cap out from the centre of the brake drum

it from position (see illustration). Discard the bolts – new ones must be fitted..

5 Use chalk or paint to mark the relationship of the disc to the hub, and then undo the screw(s) securing the disc to the hub. If necessary, gently tap the disc from behind and release it from the hub (see illustration).

Refitting

6 Refitting is the reverse of the removal procedure, noting the following points:
   a) Ensure that the mating surfaces of the disc and hub are clean and flat.
   b) Align (if applicable) the marks made on removal, and tighten the disc retaining screws to the specified torque.
   c) If a new disc has been fitted, use a suitable solvent to wipe any preservative coating from the disc, before refitting the caliper.
   d) Refit the roadwheel, then lower the vehicle to the ground and tighten the roadwheel bolts to the specified torque. Depress the brake pedal several times to force the pads back into contact with the disc.

9.3 Relieve the hub nut staking using a hammer and pointed-nose chisel

9.4 Remove the hub nut and thrustwasher . . .

remove the rear hub nut, and withdraw the thrustwasher (see illustration). Discard the hub nut – a new nut must be used on refitting.

5 It should now be possible to withdraw the brake drum and hub bearing assembly from the stub axle by hand (see illustration). It may be difficult to remove the drum due to the tightness of the hub bearing on the stub axle, or due to the brake shoes binding on the inner circumference of the drum. If the bearing is tight, tap the periphery of the drum using a hide or plastic mallet, or use a universal puller, secured to the drum with the wheel bolts, to pull it off. If the brake shoes are binding, first check that the handbrake is fully released. If necessary, fully slacken the handbrake cable adjuster nut, to obtain maximum freeplay in the cable to enable the drum to be removed.

6 Once the drum has been removed, slide the seal off the stub axle noting which way around it is fitted (see illustration). Discard the seal

– a new one must be used on refitting. If the stub axle spacer is loose, remove it and store it with the brake drum.

Inspection

Note: If either drum requires renewal, BOTH should be renewed at the same time, to ensure even and consistent braking. New brake shoes should also be fitted.

7 Working carefully, remove all traces of brake dust from the drum, but avoid inhaling the dust, as it is injurious to health.

8 Clean the outside of the drum, and check it for obvious signs of wear or damage, such as cracks around the roadwheel bolt holes; renew the drum if necessary.

9 Examine carefully the inside of the drum. Light scoring of the friction surface is normal, but if heavy scoring is found, the drum must be renewed. It is usual to find a lip on the drum's

---

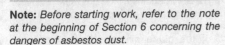

9 Rear brake drum – removal, inspection and refitting

Note: Before starting work, refer to the note at the beginning of Section 6 concerning the dangers of asbestos dust.

Removal

Note: A new rear hub nut, cap and seal must be used on refitting.

1 Chock the front wheels, then jack up the rear of the vehicle and support it on axle stands (see Jacking and vehicle support). Remove the appropriate rear wheel.

2 Using a hammer and a large flat-bladed screwdriver, carefully tap and prise the cap out of the centre of the brake drum (see illustration). Discard the cap – a new one must be used on refitting.

3 Using a hammer and chisel, tap up the staking securing the hub retaining nut to the groove in the stub axle (see illustration).

4 Using a socket and long bar, slacken and

9.5 . . . and slide off the brake drum

9.6 Remove the seal from the stub axle

9.14 Tighten the new hub nut correctly then stake it securely into the stub axle groove

inboard edge, which consists of a mixture of rust and brake dust; this should be scraped away, to leave a smooth surface which can be polished with fine (120- to 150-grade) emery paper. If, however, the lip is due to the friction surface being recessed by excessive wear, then the drum must be renewed.

10 If the drum is thought to be excessively worn, or oval, its internal diameter must be measured at several points using an internal micrometer. Take measurements in pairs, the second at right-angles to the first, and compare the two, to check for signs of ovality. Provided that it does not enlarge the drum to beyond the specified maximum diameter, it may be possible to have the drum refinished by skimming or grinding; if this is not possible, the drums on both sides must be renewed. Note that if the drum is to be skimmed, BOTH drums must be refinished, to maintain a consistent internal diameter on both sides.

Refitting

11 If a new brake drum is to be installed, install the new shoes (see Section 6) and use a suitable solvent to remove any preservative coating that may have been applied to the drum interior.

12 Lubricate the lip of the new seal with a smear of multi-purpose grease. Ensure the spacer is in position and then slide the seal onto the stub axle, ensuring its sealing lip is facing outwards (towards the hub).

13 Slide the brake drum assembly into position then refit the thrustwasher.

14 Fit the new hub nut and tighten it to the specified torque. Secure the nut in position by staking it firmly into the groove on the stub axle then tap the new hub cap into place in the centre of the brake drum **(see illustration)**.

15 Depress the footbrake several times to operate the self-adjusting mechanism.

16 Repeat the above procedure on the remaining rear brake assembly (where necessary), then check and, if necessary, adjust the handbrake cable as described in Section 18.

17 On completion, refit the roadwheel(s), then lower the vehicle to the ground and tighten the wheel bolts to the specified torque.

10 Front brake caliper – removal, overhaul and refitting

Caution: On ABS models, ensure the ignition is switched off before disconnecting any braking system hydraulic union and do not switch it back on until after the hydraulic system has been bled. Failure to do this could lead to air entering the hydraulic unit requiring the unit to be bled using special Peugeot test equipment.

Note: *Before starting work, refer to the note at the beginning of Section 2 concerning the dangers of hydraulic fluid, and to the warning at the beginning of Section 4 concerning the dangers of asbestos dust.*

Removal

Note: *New guide pin bolts must be used on refitting.*

1 Apply the handbrake, then jack up the front of the vehicle and support it on axle stands (see *Jacking and vehicle support*). Remove the appropriate roadwheel.

2 Minimise fluid loss by first removing the master cylinder reservoir cap, and then tightening it down onto a piece of polythene, to obtain an airtight seal. Alternatively, use a brake hose clamp, a G-clamp or a similar tool to clamp the flexible hose.

3 Clean the area around the brake caliper hose union, then loosen the union.

4 Slacken and remove the upper and lower caliper guide pin bolts; discard both bolts – new ones must be used on refitting.

5 Lift the caliper away from the brake disc, and then unscrew the caliper from the end of the brake hose. Note that the brake pads need not be disturbed, and can be left in position in the caliper mounting bracket.

Overhaul

6 With the caliper on the bench, wipe away all traces of dust and dirt, but *avoid inhaling the dust, as it is a health hazard.*

7 Where necessary, use a small flat-bladed screwdriver to carefully prise the dust seal retaining clip out of the caliper bore.

8 Withdraw the partially ejected piston from the caliper body, and remove the dust seal.

 If the piston cannot be withdrawn by hand, it can be pushed out by applying compressed air to the brake hose union hole. Only low pressure should be required, such as is generated by a foot pump. As the piston is expelled take great care not to trap your fingers between the piston and caliper.

9 Using a small screwdriver, extract the piston hydraulic seal, taking great care not to damage the caliper bore.

10 Thoroughly clean all components, using only methylated spirit, isopropyl alcohol or clean hydraulic fluid as a cleaning medium. Never use mineral-based solvents such as petrol or paraffin, as they will attack the hydraulic system's rubber components. Dry the components immediately, using compressed air or a clean, lint-free cloth. Use compressed air to blow clear the fluid passages.

 Warning: Wear eye protection when using compressed air.

11 Check all components, and renew any that are worn or damaged. Check particularly the cylinder bore and piston; these should be renewed (note that this means the renewal of the complete body assembly) if they are scratched, worn or corroded in any way. Similarly check the condition of the guide pins and their bores in the caliper mounting bracket; both pins should be undamaged and (when cleaned) a reasonably tight sliding fit in the mounting bracket bores. If there is any doubt about the condition of any component, renew it.

12 If the assembly is fit for further use, obtain the appropriate repair kit; the components are available from Peugeot dealers in various combinations.

13 Renew all rubber seals and gaiters disturbed on dismantling as a matter of course; these should never be re-used.

14 On reassembly, ensure that all components are absolutely clean and dry.

15 Soak the piston and the new piston (fluid) seal in clean hydraulic fluid. Smear clean fluid on the cylinder bore surface.

16 Fit the new piston (fluid) seal, using only your fingers (no tools) to manipulate it into the cylinder bore groove.

17 Fit the new dust seal to the rear of the piston and seat the outer lip of the seal in the caliper body. Carefully ease the piston squarely into the caliper bore using a twisting motion. Press the piston fully into the bore, then seat the inner lip of the dust seal in the piston groove.

18 Where fitted, install the dust seal retaining clip, ensuring that it is correctly seated in the caliper groove.

19 If the guide pins are being renewed, lubricate the pin shafts with the special grease supplied in the repair kit, or a copper-based high-temperature brake grease or anti-seize compound. Locate the new gaiters in the pin grooves then insert the pins into the caliper bracket. Seat the gaiters correctly in the mounting bracket grooves then check both guide pins slide smoothly and easily.

Refitting

20 Screw the caliper body fully onto the flexible hose union

21 Ensure the brake pads are still correctly fitted to the caliper mounting bracket then fit the caliper over the pads.

22 Align the cut-out of each guide pin with the caliper slot then fit the new guide pin bolts

10.22 Ensure the bolt plate (A) engages correctly with the caliper slot (B) and guide pin slots (C) when fitting the guide pin bolt

(see illustration). Ensure each bolt plate is correctly located in the guide pin cut-outs (the plate prevents the guide pin rotating as bolt is tightened) then tighten both bolts to the specified torque.

23 Tighten the brake hose union nut to the specified torque then remove the brake hose clamp or polythene (as applicable).

24 Bleed the hydraulic system (see Section 2). Providing the precautions described were taken to minimise brake fluid loss, it should only be necessary to bleed the relevant front brake.

25 Depress the brake pedal repeatedly, until the pads are pressed into firm contact with the brake disc, and normal (non-assisted) pedal pressure is restored.

26 Refit the roadwheel, then lower the vehicle to the ground and tighten the roadwheel bolts to the specified torque.

27 On completion check the front brake hose is in no danger of contacting the tyre when the steering is on full lock. If necessary, adjust the hose position by slackening the union nut securing the pipe to the caliper hose and remove the hose clip. Position the hose end correctly in the bracket then secure it in position with the clip. Tighten the pipe union nut to the specified torque then bleed the front brake again (see Section 2).

11 Rear brake caliper – removal, overhaul and refitting

Caution: On ABS models, ensure the ignition is switched off before disconnecting any braking system hydraulic union and do not switch it back on until after the hydraulic system has been bled. Failure to do this could lead to air entering the hydraulic unit requiring the unit to be bled using special Peugeot test equipment.
Note: *Before starting work, refer to the note at the beginning of Section 2 concerning the dangers of hydraulic fluid, and to the warning at the beginning of Section 5 concerning the dangers of asbestos dust.*
Note: *New caliper mounting bracket bolts and guide pin bolts will be required on reassembly.*

Removal

1 Chock the front wheels, slacken the relevant rear roadwheel bolts, then jack up the rear of the vehicle and support on axle stands (see *Jacking and vehicle support*). Remove the relevant rear wheel.
2 Remove the brake pads (see Section 5).
3 Minimise fluid loss by first removing the master cylinder reservoir cap, and then tightening it down onto a piece of polythene, to obtain an airtight seal. Alternatively, use a brake hose clamp, a G-clamp or a similar tool to clamp the flexible hose at the nearest convenient point to the brake caliper.
4 Wipe away all traces of dirt around the brake hose union on the caliper. Unscrew the union nut and disconnect the brake pipe from the caliper. Plug the pipe and caliper unions to minimise fluid loss and prevent dirt entry.
5 Disconnect the handbrake cable from the caliper (see Section 20), then undo the mounting bolts and remove the caliper **(see illustration 8.4)**.

Overhaul

6 At the time of writing, no parts were available to recondition the rear caliper assembly, with the exception of the guide pin bolts, guide pins and guide pin gaiters. Check the condition of the guide pins and their gaiters; both pins should be undamaged and (when cleaned) a reasonably tight sliding fit in the caliper bracket. If there is any doubt about the condition of any component, renew it.

Refitting

7 If previously removed, refit the caliper mounting bracket to the hub carrier, and tighten the new bolts to the specified torque.
8 If necessary, refit the brake pads as described in Section 5.
9 Refit the caliper and insert the new guide pin bolts, tightening them to the specified torque settings.
9 Reconnect the brake pipe to the caliper, and tighten the brake hose union nut to the specified torque. Remove the brake hose clamp or polythene (where fitted).
11 Bleed the hydraulic system as described in Section 2. Note that, providing the precautions described were taken to minimise brake fluid

12.4 Unscrew the union nut and detach the brake pipe from the rear of the wheel cylinder

loss, it should only be necessary to bleed the relevant rear brake.
12 Refit the roadwheel, then lower the vehicle to the ground and tighten the roadwheel bolts to the specified torque.

12 Rear wheel cylinder – removal and refitting

Caution: On ABS models, ensure the ignition is switched off before disconnecting any braking system hydraulic union and do not switch it back on until after the hydraulic system has been bled. Failure to do this could lead to air entering the hydraulic unit requiring the unit to be bled using special Peugeot test equipment.
Note: *Before starting work, refer to the note at the beginning of Section 2 concerning the dangers of hydraulic fluid, and to the warning at the beginning of Section 6 concerning the dangers of asbestos dust.*
Note: *New wheel cylinder retaining bolts will be needed on refitting.*

Removal

1 Remove the brake drum (see Section 9).
2 Using pliers, carefully unhook the upper brake shoe return spring, and remove it from both brake shoes. Pull the upper ends of the shoes away from the wheel cylinder to disengage them from the pistons.
3 Minimise fluid loss by first removing the master cylinder reservoir cap, and then tightening it down onto a piece of polythene, to obtain an airtight seal. Alternatively, use a brake hose clamp, a G-clamp or a similar tool to clamp the flexible hose at the nearest convenient point to the wheel cylinder.
4 Wipe away all traces of dirt around the brake pipe union at the rear of the wheel cylinder, and unscrew the union nut **(see illustration)**. Carefully ease the pipe out of the wheel cylinder, and plug or tape over its end to prevent dirt entry. Wipe off any spilt fluid immediately.
5 Unscrew the two wheel cylinder retaining bolts from the rear of the backplate, and remove the cylinder, taking great care not to allow surplus hydraulic fluid to contaminate the brake shoe linings. Discard the bolts – new ones must be used on refitting.
6 Note that it is not possible to overhaul the cylinder, since no components are available separately. If faulty, the complete wheel cylinder assembly must be renewed.

Refitting

7 Ensure that the backplate and wheel cylinder mating surfaces are clean, then spread the brake shoes and manoeuvre the wheel cylinder into position.
8 Engage the brake pipe, and screw in the union nut two or three turns to ensure that the thread has started.
9 Fit the new retaining bolts to the wheel cylinder and tighten them to the specified torque.

10 Tighten the brake pipe union nut to the specified torque then remove the clamp from the flexible brake hose, or the polythene from the master cylinder reservoir (as applicable).

11 Ensure that the brake shoes are correctly located in the cylinder pistons, and then carefully refit the brake shoe upper return spring. Use a screwdriver to stretch the spring into position.

12 Refit the brake drum (see Section 9).

13 Bleed the brake hydraulic system as described in Section 2. Providing suitable precautions were taken to minimise loss of fluid, it should only be necessary to bleed the relevant rear brake.

13 Master cylinder – removal, overhaul and refitting

Caution: On ABS models, ensure the ignition is switched off before disconnecting any braking system hydraulic union and do not switch it back on until after the hydraulic system has been bled. Failure to do this could lead to air entering the hydraulic unit requiring the unit to be bled using special Peugeot test equipment.

Note: *Before starting, refer to the warning in Section 2 on the dangers of hydraulic fluid.*

Note: *A new O-ring must be used when refitting the master cylinder.*

Removal

1 Remove the master cylinder reservoir cap and filter and syphon the hydraulic fluid from the reservoir. **Note:** *Do not syphon the fluid by mouth, as it is poisonous; use a syringe or an old anti-freeze tester.* Alternatively, open any convenient bleed screw in the system, and gently pump the brake pedal to expel the fluid through a plastic tube connected to the screw (see Section 2).

2 Disconnect the wiring connector from the brake fluid level sender unit.

3 Where applicable, disconnect the clutch master cylinder fluid supply hose from the side of the master cylinder reservoir. Plug the hose end to minimise fluid loss and prevent the entry of dirt into the system.

4 Remove the R-clip then free the fluid reservoir clip from the master cylinder pin. Carefully ease the reservoir out of from the top of the master cylinder and remove it from the vehicle.

5 Wipe clean the area around the brake pipe unions on the side of the master cylinder, and place absorbent rags beneath the pipe unions to catch any surplus fluid. Make a note of the correct fitted positions of the unions, then unscrew the union nuts and carefully withdraw the pipes. Plug or tape over the pipe ends and master cylinder orifices to minimise the loss of brake fluid, and to prevent the entry of dirt into the system. Wash off any spilt fluid immediately with cold water.

6 Slacken and remove the two nuts securing the master cylinder to the vacuum servo unit, then withdraw the unit from the engine compartment. Remove the O-ring from the rear of the master cylinder, and discard it.

Overhaul

7 At the time of writing it was unclear whether it was possible to overhaul the master cylinder. Refer to your Peugeot dealer for the latest information on parts availability.

Refitting

8 Prior to refitting, measure the distance from the tip of the vacuum servo unit pushrod to the master cylinder mating surface of the unit. This should be 22.3 mm ± 0.1 mm. If not inspect the servo unit/brake pedal for signs of a problem. If nothing obvious is found, seek the advice of a Peugeot dealer before installing the master cylinder.

9 Remove all traces of dirt from the master cylinder and servo unit mating surfaces, and fit a new O-ring to the groove on the master cylinder body. Inspect the fluid reservoir seals and renew them if they show signs of damage or deterioration.

10 Fit the master cylinder to the servo unit, ensuring that the servo unit pushrod enters the master cylinder bore centrally. Refit the master cylinder mounting nuts, and tighten them to the specified torque.

11 Wipe clean the brake pipe unions, then refit them to the master cylinder ports and tighten them to the specified torque.

12 Lubricate the seals with a smear of brake fluid then ease the fluid reservoir back into position on the reservoir. Engage the reservoir clip with the master cylinder pin and secure it in position with the R-clip.

13 Where applicable, securely reconnect the clutch fluid hose to the reservoir.

14 On all models, reconnect the wiring connector to the fluid level sender.

15 Refill the master cylinder reservoir with new fluid, and bleed the complete hydraulic system (see Section 2).

16 Bleed the clutch hydraulic system, where necessary (Chapter 6).

14 Rear brake pressure-regulating valve(s) – testing, removal and refitting

1 On models without ABS, a load-sensitive pressure regulating valve is fitted to the hydraulic circuit to the rear brakes. The valve is mounted onto the underside of the rear of the vehicle, and is attached to the rear suspension by a spring. The valve measures the load on the rear axle, via the movement of the suspension, and regulates the hydraulic pressure being applied to the rear brakes to help prevent the rear wheels locking up under heavy braking.

2 On some models the valves are incorporated into the rear wheel cylinders; on these models the valves are pressure-sensitive only and are not affected by the load being carried by the vehicle.

3 Specialist equipment is required to check the performance of the valve(s), so if the valve is thought to be faulty, the car should be taken to a suitably equipped Peugeot dealer for testing. Repairs are not possible and, if faulty, the valve must be renewed; on models with a load-sensitive valve, adjustment is possible but, again, specialist equipment is needed to carry out this procedure.

Removal

Note: *Before starting, refer to the warning in Section 2 on the dangers of hydraulic fluid.*

Load-sensitive valve

4 Firmly chock the front wheels, then jack up the rear of the vehicle and support it on axle stands (see *Jacking and vehicle support*).

5 Minimise fluid loss by first removing the master cylinder reservoir cap, and then tightening it down onto a piece of polythene, to obtain an airtight seal.

6 Wipe clean the area around the brake pipe unions on the valve, and place absorbent rags beneath the pipe unions to catch any surplus fluid **(see illustration)**. To avoid confusion on refitting, make alignment marks between the pipes and valve.

7 Slacken the union nuts and disconnect the brake pipes from the valve. Plug or tape over the pipe ends and valve orifices, to minimise the loss of brake fluid, and to prevent the entry of dirt into the system. Wash off any spilt fluid immediately with cold water.

8 Slacken and remove the valve retaining bolt then unhook the valve spring from its bolt and remove the valve assembly from underneath the vehicle.

Pressure-sensitive valve

9 The valve is an integral part of the rear wheel cylinder. Refer to Section 12 for removal details.

Refitting

Load-sensitive valve

10 Prior to refitting, clean the valve retaining bolt threads and apply a few drops of thread-locking compound (Peugeot recommend the use of Loctite Frenetanch) to the bolt.

14.6 Load-sensitive pressure regulating valve brake pipe unions (A) and retaining bolt (B)

11 Manoeuvre the valve assembly into position, and hook the spring onto its suspension bolt. Align the valve correctly with its mounting bracket and secure it in position with the retaining bolt, tightening it to the specified torque.

12 Reconnect the brake pipes to their specific unions on the valve and tighten their union nuts to the specified torque.

13 Remove the polythene from the master cylinder reservoir and bleed the complete hydraulic system as described in Section 2. If a new valve assembly has been fitted, it is recommended that the vehicle is taken to a Peugeot dealer so the valve operation can be checked and, if necessary, adjusted using their special test equipment.

Pressure-sensitive valve

14 Refit the wheel cylinder as described in Section 12.

15 Brake pedal –
removal and refitting

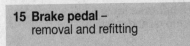

Removal

1 Access to the pedal is poor with the facia in position. The only way access can be significantly improved is to remove the facia as described in Chapter 11.

2 On left-hand drive models, remove the stop-light switch (see Section 21).

3 On all models, remove the pivot clip securing the servo unit pushrod (left-hand drive models) or crossover linkage (right-hand drive models) to the brake pedal. To remove the pivot clip, unhook its lower retaining tang then pivot it upwards slightly before sliding it out of position **(see illustrations 16.9a and 16.9b)**.

4 Slacken and remove the pivot bolt and nut then manoeuvre the brake pedal out of position **(see illustration)**. Slide the spacer out from the pedal pivot.

5 Examine all components for signs of wear or damage and renew as necessary.

Refitting

6 Apply a smear of multi-purpose grease to

15.4 Unscrew the nut (A) and withdraw the brake pedal bolt (B) pivot (shown with facia removed)

the spacer and insert it into the pedal pivot bore.

7 Manoeuvre the pedal into position, making sure it is correctly engaged with the servo unit/crossover linkage (as applicable). Insert the pivot bolt and nut, tightening it to the specified torque.

8 Align the pedal with the pushrod/linkage (as applicable) and insert the pivot clip, ensuring it is securely clipped in position.

9 On left-hand drive models, install the stop-light switch (see Section 21)

10 Where necessary, refit the facia (see Chapter 11).

16 Vacuum servo unit –
testing, removal and refitting

Testing

1 To test the operation of the servo unit, depress the footbrake several times to exhaust the vacuum, then start the engine whilst keeping the pedal firmly depressed. As the engine starts, there should be a noticeable 'give' in the brake pedal as the vacuum builds-up. Allow the engine to run for at least two minutes, and then switch it off. If the brake pedal is now depressed it should feel normal, but further applications should result in the pedal feeling firmer, with the pedal stroke decreasing with each application.

2 If the servo does not operate as described,

first inspect the servo unit check valve as described in Section 17. On diesel engine models, also check the operation of the vacuum pump as described in Section 25.

3 If the servo unit still fails to operate satisfactorily, the fault lies within the unit itself. Repairs to the unit are not possible – if faulty, the servo unit must be renewed.

Removal

Note: A new servo mounting gasket will be required on refitting.

Right-hand drive models

4 Remove the battery and battery tray as described in Chapter 5A.

5 Remove the master cylinder as described in Section 13.

6 Disconnect the vacuum hose from servo unit check valve.

7 Where applicable, detach the clutch cable from the transmission unit (see Chapter 6).

8 On all models, remove the glovebox as described in Chapter 11, Section 27.

9 Remove the pivot clip securing the crossover linkage to the servo unit pushrod. To remove the pivot clip, unhook its lower retaining tang then pivot it upwards slightly before sliding it out of position **(see illustrations)**.

10 Unscrew the nuts securing the crossover linkage plate to the servo unit studs and the bolt securing the plate to the upper mounting bracket **(see illustration)**.

11 Release the retaining clips on the servo unit bore then ease the servo unit end of the crossover linkage slightly away from the bulkhead to gain access to the servo retaining clips (where fitted). Slide the clips off the servo unit studs.

12 Return to the engine compartment and remove the servo unit. Recover the seal, which is fitted between the servo unit and bulkhead, and discard it – a new one must be used on refitting.

Left-hand drive models

13 Remove the battery and battery tray as described in Chapter 5A.

14 Remove the master cylinder as described in Section 13.

15 Disconnect the vacuum hose from servo unit check valve.

16 Where applicable, detach the clutch cable from the transmission unit (see Chapter 6).

16.9a Unhook the base of the pivot clip then pivot it upwards . . .

16.9b . . . and slide it out from the servo unit pushrod

16.10 Unscrew the mounting nuts (A) and bracket bolt (B) then release the servo unit retaining clips (C)

17 Remove the pivot clip securing the brake pedal to the servo unit pushrod. To remove the pivot clip, unhook its lower retaining tang then pivot it upwards slightly before sliding it out of position.

18 Disconnect the wiring connector from the stop-light switch.

19 Unscrew the nuts securing the pedal mounting-bracket to the servo unit studs and the bolt securing the bracket assembly to the upper mounting bracket.

20 Release the retaining clips located at the top and bottom of the servo unit bore then ease the pedal bracket assembly away from the bulkhead to gain access to the servo retaining clips (where fitted). **Note:** *If necessary, disconnect the steering column from the steering gear pinion to gain the necessary clearance required to position the pedal bracket assembly clear (see Chapter 10).*

21 Slide the retaining clips off the servo unit studs.

22 Return to the engine compartment and remove the servo unit. Recover the seal, which is fitted between the servo unit and bulkhead, and discard it – a new one must be used on refitting.

Refitting

23 Refitting is the reverse of removal, noting the following points.

  a) *Prior to refitting measure the distance from the end of the vacuum servo unit pushrod to the servo unit master cylinder mating surface. This should be 22.3 ± 0.1 mm; if not seek the advice of a Peugeot dealer.*

  b) *Ensure the servo unit and bulkhead mating surfaces are clean and dry and fit a new seal to the rear of the servo.*

  c) *Secure the servo in position with the retaining clips and tighten the servo unit/ pedal bracket nuts to the specified torque.*

  d) *Refit the master cylinder (Section 13) and bleed the complete hydraulic system (Section 2).*

17 Vacuum servo unit check valve – removal, testing and refitting

Removal

1 Slacken the retaining clip (where fitted), and disconnect the vacuum hose from the servo unit check valve.

2 Withdraw the valve from its rubber sealing grommet, using a pulling and twisting motion. Remove the grommet from the servo.

Testing

3 Examine the check valve for signs of damage, and renew if necessary. The valve may be tested by blowing through it in both directions. Air should flow through the valve in one direction only – when blown through from the servo unit end of the valve. Renew the valve if this is not the case.

4 Examine the rubber sealing grommet and flexible vacuum hose for signs of damage or deterioration, and renew as necessary.

Refitting

5 Fit the sealing grommet into the servo unit.

6 Ease the check valve into position, taking care not to displace or damage the grommet. Reconnect the vacuum hose to the valve, and tighten its retaining clip (as applicable).

7 On completion, start the engine and check the check valve-to-servo unit connection for signs of air leaks.

18 Handbrake – adjustment

1 To check the handbrake adjustment, first apply the footbrake firmly several times with the handbrake released to establish correct shoe-to-drum or pad-to-disc clearance, then apply and release the handbrake several times to ensure that the self-adjust mechanism is fully adjusted. Applying normal moderate pressure, pull the handbrake lever to the fully applied position, counting the number of clicks emitted from the handbrake ratchet mechanism. If adjustment is correct, there should be 4 to 7 clicks before the handbrake is fully applied. If this is not the case, adjust as follows.

2 Chock the front wheels, then jack up the rear of the vehicle and support it on axle stands (see *Jacking and vehicle support*).

3 For access to the handbrake adjuster nut, remove the rear section of the centre console (Chapter 11).

4 Apply and release the handbrake a few times whilst observing the handbrake lever equaliser plate. The plate must remain square to the handbrake lever as the lever is applied and released. If not, there is a fault with the cables, which must be rectified before adjustment can be carried out.

5 If the cables are operating freely, fully release the handbrake lever and then slacken the adjuster nut **(see illustration)**.

6 Start the engine and apply the footbrake approximately forty times; this will ensure the self-adjusting mechanism is correctly adjusted.

7 Switch the engine off and then tighten the adjuster nut until all the freeplay is removed from both handbrake cables. Fully apply and release the handbrake at least ten times to settle the cables in position.

8 With the handbrake lever set on the second notch of the ratchet mechanism, rotate the adjuster nut so that only a slight drag can be felt when the rear wheels/hubs are turned. Once this is so, fully release the handbrake lever, and check that the wheels/hubs rotate freely. Check the adjustment by applying the handbrake fully, counting the clicks (no more than eight) from the handbrake ratchet and, if necessary, re-adjust.

9 Check the operation of the handbrake

18.5 Remove the rear section of the centre console to gain access to the handbrake cable adjuster nut (arrowed)

warning light (the light should illuminate when the lever is set on the first notch of the ratchet mechanism) then refit the centre console, and lower the vehicle to the ground.

19 Handbrake lever – removal and refitting

Removal

1 Remove the rear section of the centre console (Chapter 11).

2 Slacken the handbrake adjuster nut to obtain maximum freeplay in the cables, and disengage the inner cables from the handbrake lever equaliser plate.

3 Slacken and remove the three handbrake lever retaining nuts, and remove the lever from the vehicle **(see illustration)**.

Refitting

4 Refitting is a reversal of removal, tightening the handbrake lever nuts to the specified torque. Prior to refitting the centre console, adjust the handbrake (see Section 18).

20 Handbrake cables – removal and refitting

Removal

1 Remove the rear section of the centre console (Chapter 11). The handbrake cable

19.3 Handbrake lever is secured to the floor by three nuts (arrowed)

20.5 Prise off the retaining clip and free the handbrake cable from the underside of the fuel tank

HAYNES
HiNT

Release the handbrake cable end fitting clips by passing a close-fitting ring spanner over the end fitting.

20.7 Free the outer cable end fitting from the backplate and remove the cable from the vehicle

20.8 Disconnect the handbrake cable from the caliper lever and bracket (arrowed)

consists of two sections, a right and a left-hand section, which are linked to the lever by an equaliser plate. Each section can be removed as follows.

2 Slacken the handbrake lever adjuster nut **(see illustration 18.5)** to obtain maximum free play in the cable(s), and disengage the inner cables from the handbrake lever plate.

3 Firmly chock the front wheels, then jack up the rear of the vehicle and support it on axle stands (see *Jacking and vehicle support*).

4 Referring to the relevant part of Chapter 4, remove the exhaust system heat shield(s) to gain access to the front end of the handbrake cables.

5 Prise off the retaining clip and free the cable from its guide on the underside of the fuel tank **(see illustration)**.

6 Free the front end of the outer cable from the body, then work back along the length of the cable, freeing it from all its retaining clips and guides.

7 On models with drum brakes, remove the rear brake shoes from the relevant side as described in Section 6. Release the retaining clips **(see Tool Tip)** then free the handbrake outer cable out from the brake backplate, and remove it from underneath the vehicle **(see illustration)**.

8 On models with disc brakes, Release the cable end fitting from the lever on the brake caliper, and remove the cable from the support bracket **(see illustration)**.

Refitting

9 Refitting is a reversal of the removal procedure, adjusting the handbrake as described in Section 18.

21 Stop-light switch – removal, refitting and adjustment

Removal

1 On left-hand drive models, the stop-light switch is located on the pedal bracket behind the facia. On right-hand drive models the switch is fitted to the left-hand end of the pedal crossover linkage.

2 Reach up behind the facia and disconnect the wiring connector then pull the switch out from the pedal bracket **(see illustrations)**.

Refitting and adjustment

3 Hold the brake pedal down then press the switch fully into the mounting bracket (this will require the aid of an assistant on right-hand drive models).

4 Slowly release the brake pedal and pull it back up to its stop; the pedal will automatically adjust the position of the switch in the mounting bracket.

5 Reconnect the wiring connector, and check the operation of the stop-lights.

22 Anti-lock Braking System (ABS) – general information

1 ABS is available on all models covered by this manual. The system comprises of a hydraulic unit **(see illustration)** and the four roadwheel sensors. The hydraulic unit contains the electronic control unit (ECU), the eight solenoid valves (two for each brake – one inlet and one outlet) and the electrically-driven return pump. The purpose of the system is to prevent the wheel(s) locking during heavy braking. This is achieved by automatic release of the brake on the relevant wheel, followed by re-application of the brake.

21.2a Disconnect the wiring connector . . .

21.2b . . . then pull the stop-light switch out of its mounting bracket (shown with facia removed for clarity)

22.1 ABS hydraulic unit (arrowed) location

2 The solenoid valves are controlled by the ECU, which receives signals from the four wheel sensors (front sensors are fitted to the swivel hubs, and the rear wheel sensors are fitted to the rear of the backplates), which monitor the speed of rotation of each wheel. By comparing these signals, the ECU can determine the speed at which the vehicle is travelling. It can then use this speed to determine when a wheel is decelerating at an abnormal rate, compared to the speed of the vehicle, and therefore predicts when a wheel is about to lock. During normal operation, the ABS system has no effect on braking and the hydraulic system functions in the same way as a non-ABS system.

3 If the ECU senses that a wheel is about to lock, it closes the relevant outlet solenoid valve in the hydraulic unit, which then isolates the brake on the relevant wheel, effectively sealing-in hydraulic pressure.

4 If the speed of rotation of the wheel continues to decrease at an abnormal rate, the ECU opens the relevant inlet solenoid valve and operates the return pump, which returns the hydraulic fluid back to the master cylinder, releasing the brake. Once the speed of rotation of the wheel returns to an acceptable rate, the pump stops and the solenoid valves switch again. This allows hydraulic master cylinder pressure to return to the caliper/ wheel cylinder (as applicable), which reapplies the brake. This cycle can be carried out many times a second.

5 The action of the solenoid valves and return pump creates pulses in the hydraulic circuit. When the ABS system is functioning, these pulses can be felt through the brake pedal.

6 The operation of the ABS is dependent on electrical signals. To prevent the system responding to any inaccurate signals, a built-in safety circuit monitors all signals received by the ECU. If an inaccurate signal or low battery voltage is detected, the system is automatically shut down and the warning light in the instrument panel is illuminated to inform the driver that the ABS system is not operational. Normal braking should still be available, however.

7 If a fault does develop in the ABS system, the vehicle must be taken to a Peugeot dealer for fault diagnosis and repair.

23 Anti-lock Braking System (ABS) components – removal and refitting

Hydraulic unit

Caution: Disconnect the battery before disconnecting the hydraulic unions from the hydraulic unit and do not reconnect the battery until after the hydraulic system has been bled. Plug the hydraulic unions of the unit and ensure it is stored upright (in the same position as it is fitted to the vehicle) and is not tipped onto its side, or upside down. Failure to do this could lead to air entering the unit, requiring the unit to be bled using special Peugeot test equipment on refitting.

Note: *Before starting work, refer to the note at the beginning of Section 2 concerning the dangers of hydraulic fluid.*

Removal

1 Disconnect the battery negative lead.

2 Apply the handbrake, then jack up the front of the vehicle and support it on axle stands (see *Jacking and vehicle support*). Remove the front roadwheels.

3 Remove all traces if dirt from the exterior of the hydraulic unit and then disconnect the wiring connector **(see illustrations)**.

4 Mark the locations of the hydraulic fluid pipes to ensure correct refitting, then unscrew the union nuts, and disconnect the pipes from the hydraulic unit. Be prepared for fluid spillage, and plug the open ends of the pipes and the hydraulic unit, to prevent dirt ingress and further fluid loss.

5 Slacken and remove the three mounting bracket nuts and remove the hydraulic unit from the vehicle, keeping the unit upright **(see illustration)**.

Refitting

6 Manoeuvre the unit into position and securely tighten its mounting bolts.

7 Reconnect the hydraulic pipes to the correct unions on the unit and tighten the union nuts to the specified torque.

8 Securely reconnect the hydraulic unit wiring connector.

9 Bleed the complete hydraulic system as described in Section 2. Once the system is correctly bled, reconnect the battery.

Front wheel sensor

Removal

10 Disconnect the battery negative lead.

11 Apply the handbrake, then jack up the front of the vehicle and support securely on axle stands (see *Jacking and vehicle support*). To improve access, remove the front roadwheel.

12 Slacken and remove the retaining nut and remove the protective shield (where fitted) from the sensor **(see illustrations)**.

13 Trace the wiring back from the sensor and separate the two halves of the wiring connector. Release the wiring from the all the relevant clips and ties, noting its routing.

14 Slacken and remove the retaining bolt and

23.3a Release the locking lever (arrowed) . . .

23.3b . . . and disconnect the wiring connector (arrowed)

23.5 Hydraulic unit mounting bracket retaining nuts (arrowed)

23.12a Undo the retaining nut (arrowed) . . .

23.12b . . . and remove the sensor protective cover

23.14 Front wheel sensor retaining bolt (arrowed)

withdraw the sensor from the swivel hub **(see illustration)**.

Refitting

15 Ensure the mating surfaces of the sensor and swivel hub are clean and apply a little grease to the sensor body (Peugeot recommend Esso Norva 275) before refitting.
16 Make sure the sensor tip is clean then ease it into position in the swivel hub.
17 Clean the threads of the sensor bolt and apply a few drops of thread-locking compound. Refit the bolt and tighten it to the specified torque.
18 Work along the sensor wiring, making sure it is correctly routed, and securing it in position with all the relevant clips and ties. Reconnect the wiring connector.
19 Refit the protective shield (where fitted) and securely tighten its bolts. Lower the vehicle and (where necessary) tighten the wheel bolts to the specified torque.

Rear wheel sensor

Removal

20 Chock the front wheels, then jack up the rear of the vehicle and support it on axle stands (see *Jacking and vehicle support*).
21 Trace the wiring back from the sensor and separate the two halves of the wiring connector. Release the wiring from the all the relevant clips and ties, noting its routing.

24.3 Vacuum pump mounting bolts (arrowed) – 1.4 litre model shown

23.22 Rear wheel sensor retaining bolt (arrowed)

22 Slacken and remove the retaining bolt and withdraw the sensor from the rear hub assembly **(see illustration)**.

Refitting

23 Ensure the mating surfaces of the sensor and swivel hub are clean and apply a little grease (Peugeot recommend Esso Norva 275) to the sensor body before refitting.
24 Make sure the sensor tip is clean then ease it into position in the backplate.
25 Clean the threads of the sensor bolt and apply a few drops of thread-locking compound. Refit the bolt and tighten it to the specified torque.
26 Work along the sensor wiring, making sure it is correctly routed, and securing it in position with all the relevant clips and ties. Reconnect the wiring connector then lower the vehicle.

24 Vacuum pump (diesel engine models) – removal and refitting

Removal

1 The pump is located at the left-hand end of the cylinder head. If necessary, to improve access to the vacuum pump, remove the plastic engine style cover, the air cleaner duct (see Chapter 4B), battery and battery box/tray (see Chapter 5A)

24.4a Vacuum pump O-ring seals location (A) and gauze filter (B) – 2.0 litre model shown

2 Depress the retaining clip button and disconnect the vacuum hose from the pump.
3 Slacken and remove the retaining bolts/nut (as applicable) securing the pump to the left-hand end of the cylinder head, then remove the pump **(see illustration)**. Discard the sealing rings – new ones must be used on refitting.

Refitting

4 Fit new sealing ring(s) to the pump recess(es), then align the drive dog with the slot in the end of the camshaft, and refit the pump to the cylinder head, ensuring that the sealing ring(s) remain correctly seated **(see illustrations)**.
5 Refit the pump mounting bolts/nut (as applicable) and tighten them securely.
6 Reconnect the vacuum hose to the pump, ensuring its retaining clip engages correctly, and (where necessary) refit the air cleaner duct.

25 Vacuum pump (diesel engine models) – testing and overhaul

1 The operation of the braking system vacuum pump can be checked using a vacuum gauge.
2 Disconnect the vacuum pipe from the pump, and connect the gauge to the pump union using a suitable length of hose.
3 Start the engine and allow it to idle, and then measure the vacuum created by the pump. As a guide, after one minute, a minimum of approximately 500 mm Hg should be recorded. If the vacuum registered is significantly less than this, it is likely that the pump is faulty. However, seek the advice of a Peugeot dealer before condemning the pump.
4 Overhaul of the vacuum pump is not possible, since no components are available separately for it. If faulty, the complete pump assembly must be renewed.

24.4b Ensure the pump drive dog engages with the slot in the end of the camshaft (arrowed)

Chapter 10
Suspension and steering

Contents

Degrees of difficulty

Easy, suitable for novice with little experience	**Fairly easy,** suitable for beginner with some experience	**Fairly difficult,** suitable for competent DIY mechanic	**Difficult,** suitable for experienced DIY mechanic	**Very difficult,** suitable for expert DIY or professional

Specifications

Steering

Power steering fluid type . . . .   See *Lubricants and fluids*

Wheel alignment and steering angles

Front:
  Camber . . . .   0° ± 30'
  Castor:
    Manual steering . . . .   2° ± 30'
    Power steering . . . .   3° ± 30'
  Wheel toe setting . . . .   0° 7' ± 4' (0.75 ± 0.5 mm) toe-in
Rear:
  Camber:
    All models (except 2.0 litre Estate) . . . .   -1° ± 30'
    2.0 litre Estate models . . . .   -1° 30' ± 30'
  Wheel toe setting:
    Cabriolet Coupe . . . .   0° 15' ± 4'
    All other models . . . .   0° 28' ± 4'

Roadwheels

Type . . . .   Pressed-steel or aluminium alloy (depending on model)
Tyre pressures . . . .   See end of *Weekly checks*

Torque wrench settings

	Nm	lbf ft
Front suspension		
Anti-roll bar:		
Mounting clamp bolts.....................................	104	77
Connecting link nuts......................................	36	27
Lower arm balljoint clamp bolt...............................	40	30
Lower arm mounting bolts..................................	141	104
Strut upper mounting bolts	20	15
Strut upper mounting retaining nut	45	33
Strut-to-swivel hub bolt	54	40
Subframe mounting bolts...................................	110	81
Rear suspension		
Rear axle mounting bolts	110	81
Shock absorber lower mounting bolt..........................	150	111
Shock absorber upper mounting bolt	70	52
Tie rod to centre yoke (2.0 litre models)......................	105	77
Tie rod to hub mounting (2.0 litre models)	105	77
Torsion bar end bolts	20	15
Centre yoke to crossmember (2.0 litre models)	30	22
Steering		
Power steering pump:		
Mounting bolts	25	18
Feed pipe union nut	20	15
Feed pipe clip bolt	20	15
Steering column mounting nuts and bolts.....................	40	30
Steering column universal joint clamp bolt nut	25	18
Steering gear:		
Mounting studs..	10	7
Mounting nuts..	80	59
Power steering feed and return pipe clamp bolt	20	15
Power steering pipe union nuts	8	6
Steering wheel bolt.......................................	35	26
Track rod balljoint (to swivel hub) nut........................	35	26
Track rod balljoint locknut	45	33
Track rod inner balljoint to steering rack	70	52
Roadwheels		
Wheel bolts..	90	66

1 General information

1 The independent front suspension is of the MacPherson strut type, incorporating coil springs and integral telescopic shock absorbers. The MacPherson struts are located by transverse lower suspension arms, which utilise rubber inner mounting bushes, and incorporate a balljoint at the outer ends. The front swivel hubs, which carry the wheel bearings, brake calipers and the hub/disc assemblies, are bolted to the MacPherson struts and connected to the lower arms via the balljoints. A front anti-roll bar is fitted to most models. The anti-roll bar is rubber-mounted onto the subframe, and is connected directly to the front suspension struts.
2 The rear suspension is of the independent trailing arm type, which consists of two trailing arms, linked by a tubular crossmember. Torsion

bars linking the trailing arms are situated in front of and behind the crossmember. On most models an anti-roll bar linking the arms passes through the centre of the crossmember. On 2.0 litre models, there are extra tie-rods fitted to the rear axle.
3 The complete rear axle assembly is mounted onto the vehicle underbody by four 'Pay Free' rubber mountings. These mountings are designed to move slightly under extreme cornering forces. This movement of the rear axle assembly has the effect of actually turning the rear wheels slightly, to help steer the vehicle in the required direction. This improves the handling of the vehicle when cornering at high speeds.
4 The steering column has a universal joint fitted in the centre of its length, which is connected to an intermediate shaft having a second universal joint at its lower end. The lower universal joint is clamped to the steering gear pinion by means of a clamp bolt.
5 The steering gear is mounted onto the front

subframe, and is connected by two track rods, with balljoints at their outer ends, to the steering arms projecting rearwards from the swivel hubs. The track rod ends are threaded, to facilitate adjustment.
6 Power-assisted steering is fitted as standard on some models, and is available as an option on most others. The hydraulic steering system is powered by a belt-driven pump, which is driven off the crankshaft pulley.

2 Front swivel hub assembly
– removal and refitting

Note: *All self-locking nuts disturbed on removal must be renewed as a matter of course. These include the track rod balljoint nut, lower suspension arm balljoint clamp bolt nut, and the swivel hub clamp bolt nut. New brake caliper mounting bolts must also be used on refitting.*

2.3 Where the driveshaft nut is staked in position, relieve the staking with a suitable chisel-nosed tool

2.4a Where the driveshaft nut is secured with an R-clip, withdraw the R-clip . . .

2.4b . . . then remove the locking cap

Removal

1 If necessary, slacken the driveshaft nut (see paragraphs 3 to 5).

2 Chock the rear wheels of the car and firmly apply the handbrake. Jack up the front of the car and support it on axle stands (see *Jacking and vehicle support*). Remove the appropriate front roadwheel.

3 On models where the driveshaft nut is staked, using a hammer and a chisel or similar tool, tap up the staking securing the driveshaft retaining nut in position **(see illustration)**. Note that a new retaining nut must be used on refitting.

4 On models where the driveshaft nut is secured by an R-clip, withdraw the R-clip and remove the locking cap from the driveshaft retaining nut **(see illustrations)**.

5 Refit at least two roadwheel bolts to the front hub, and tighten them securely. Have an assistant firmly depress the brake pedal to prevent the front hub from rotating then, using a socket and a long extension bar, slacken and remove the driveshaft retaining nut **(see illustration)**. Alternatively, a tool can be fabricated from two lengths of steel strip (one long, one short) and a nut and bolt; the nut and bolt forming the pivot of a forked tool. Bolt the tool to the hub using two wheel bolts, and hold the tool to prevent the hub from rotating as the driveshaft retaining nut is undone (see Chapter 8, Section 2). **Note:** *If the roadwheel trim allows access to the driveshaft nut, the*

2.5 Have an assistant firmly depress the brake pedal whilst you slacken the driveshaft nut (note wheel bolts – arrowed)

initial slackening can be done with the vehicle resting on its wheels on the ground.

6 If the hub bearings are to be disturbed, remove the brake disc as described in Chapter 9. If not, unscrew the two bolts securing the brake caliper mounting bracket assembly to the swivel hub, and slide the caliper assembly off the disc **(see illustration)**. Using a piece of wire or string, tie the caliper to the front suspension coil spring, to avoid placing any strain on the hydraulic brake hose. Discard the caliper mounting bolts – they must be renewed whenever they are disturbed.

7 Slacken and remove the bolt securing the support bracket (where fitted) to the top of the swivel hub.

2.6 Tie the brake caliper to the coil spring to prevent the brake hose being strained

8 On models with ABS, remove the wheel sensor from the swivel hub as described in Chapter 9.

9 On all models, slacken and remove the nut securing the steering gear track rod balljoint to the swivel hub, and release the balljoint tapered shank using a balljoint separator **(see illustration)**.

10 Slacken and remove the suspension lower arm balljoint clamp bolt and nut **(see illustration)**. Discard the nut – a new one must be used on refitting.

11 Undo the nut and withdraw the swivel hub-to-suspension strut clamp bolt **(see illustration)**. Discard the nut – a new one must be used on refitting.

12 Pull down on the lower arm to free its

2.9 Releasing a track rod balljoint using a balljoint separator

2.10 Unscrew the nut and remove the balljoint clamp bolt from the swivel hub

2.11 Undo the nut and withdraw the strut clamp bolt from the swivel hub

TOOL TIP

To free the lower arm, attach a long bar (such as a jack handle) securely to the lower arm. Attach a block of wood to the inner end of the bar, to act as a pivot, then use the bar to pull the lower arm out from the swivel hub.

2.12 Pull the lower arm down and hold it in position by inserting a socket (arrowed) in between the arm and subframe

2.13 Remove the protector plate from the lower arm balljoint

balljoint from the swivel hub **(see Tool Tip)**. Once the balljoint is freed from the swivel hub, peg the lower arm in position by inserting a suitable socket in between the top of the arm inner end and the subframe **(see illustration)**.

13 Recover the protector plate from lower arm balljoint **(see illustration)**.

14 Free the swivel hub assembly from the end of the strut, then release it from the outer constant velocity joint splines, and remove it from the vehicle. If the swivel hub is a tight fit on the strut, use a large flat-bladed screwdriver to carefully open up the clamp a little.

Refitting

15 Ensure that the driveshaft outer constant velocity joint and hub splines are clean and dry. Apply a thin film of multi-purpose grease (Peugeot recommend the use of Total 3945) to the driveshaft outer joint splines then slide the hub fully onto the driveshaft splines.

16 Slide the hub assembly fully onto the suspension strut, aligning the split in the hub clamp with the lug on the base of the strut. Also ensure that the stop bosses on the strut are in contact with the top surface of the swivel hub. Insert the swivel hub-to-suspension strut

clamp bolt then fit a new nut and tighten it to the specified torque.

17 Fit the protector plate to the lower arm balljoint.

18 Align the lower arm balljoint with the swivel hub. Remove the socket (used to peg the arm in position) and seat the balljoint shank correctly in the swivel hub, aligning the protector plate tang with the hub slot. Insert the clamp bolt then fit the new nut and tighten to the specified torque.

19 Locate the track rod balljoint in the swivel hub, then fit a new retaining nut and tighten it to the specified torque **(see illustration)**.

20 Referring to Chapter 9, refit the brake disc (where removed) to the hub and tighten its retaining screws to the specified torque. Slide the brake caliper assembly into position, ensuring the pads pass either side of the disc, then fit the new mounting bolts and tighten them to the specified torque (see Chapter 9).

21 Where necessary, refit the ABS wheel sensor as described in Chapter 9.

22 Refit the wiring support bracket (where fitted) to the top of the swivel hub, and tighten its retaining bolt securely.

23 Lubricate the inner face and threads of the driveshaft retaining nut with a smear of oil (Peugeot recommend the use of Molykote D321R) and fit it to the end of the driveshaft (a new nut must be used on models with a staked nut). Use the method employed

on removal to prevent the hub from rotating, and tighten the driveshaft retaining nut to the specified torque (see Chapter 8). Check that the hub rotates freely.

24 On models where the driveshaft nut is staked, stake the new nut into the driveshaft groove using a hammer and punch **(see illustration)**.

25 On models where the driveshaft nut is secured by an R-clip, engage the locking cap with the driveshaft nut so that one of its cut-outs is aligned with the driveshaft hole. Secure the cap in position with the R-clip.

26 Refit the roadwheel, then lower the vehicle to the ground and tighten the roadwheel bolts to the specified torque.

---

3 Front hub bearings – renewal

Note: *The bearing is a sealed, pre-adjusted and pre-lubricated, double-row roller type, and is intended to last the car's entire service life without maintenance or attention. Never overtighten the driveshaft nut beyond the specified torque wrench setting in an attempt to 'adjust' the bearing.*

Note: *A press will be required to dismantle and rebuild the assembly; if such a tool is not available, a large bench vice and spacers (such*

2.19 Tighten the track rod balljoint nut to the specified torque

2.24 Where the driveshaft nut needs to be staked, stake it firmly into the driveshaft with a hammer and punch

3.3 Front hub bearing retaining circlip (arrowed)

4.3 Retain the balljoint shank and unscrew the nut securing the anti-roll bar connecting link to the strut

4.5 Unscrew the nut and withdraw the lower arm balljoint clamp bolt

as large sockets) will serve as an adequate substitute. The bearing's inner races are an interference fit on the hub; if the inner race remains on the hub when it is pressed out of the hub carrier, a knife-edged bearing puller will be required to remove it. A new bearing retaining circlip must be used on refitting.

1 Remove the swivel hub assembly as described in Section 2.

2 Support the swivel hub securely on blocks or in a vice. Using a tubular spacer, which bears only on the inner end of the hub flange, press the hub flange out of the bearing. If the bearing's outboard inner race remains on the hub, remove it using a bearing puller (see note above).

3 Extract the bearing retaining circlip from the inner end of the swivel hub assembly **(see illustration)**.

4 Where necessary, refit the inner race back in position over the ball cage, and securely support the inner face of the swivel hub. Using a tubular spacer that bears only on the inner race, press the complete bearing assembly out of the swivel hub.

5 Thoroughly clean the hub and swivel hub, removing all traces of dirt and grease, and polish away any burrs or raised edges which might hinder reassembly. Check both for cracks or any other signs of wear or damage, and renew them if necessary. Renew the circlip, regardless of its apparent condition.

6 On reassembly, apply a light film of oil to the bearing outer race and hub flange shaft, to aid installation of the bearing.

7 Securely support the swivel hub, and locate

the bearing in the hub. Press the bearing fully into position, ensuring that it enters the hub squarely, using a tubular spacer that bears only on the bearing outer race.

8 Once the bearing is correctly seated, secure the bearing in position with the new circlip, ensuring that it is correctly located in the groove in the swivel hub.

9 Securely support the outer face of the hub flange, and locate the swivel hub bearing inner race over the end of the hub flange. Press the bearing onto the hub, using a tubular spacer that bears only on the inner race of the hub bearing, until it seats against the hub shoulder. Check that the hub flange rotates freely, and wipe off any excess oil or grease.

10 Refit the swivel hub assembly as described in Section 2.

4 Front suspension strut – removal and refitting

Note: *All self-locking nuts disturbed on removal must be renewed as a matter of course. These include the track rod balljoint nut, lower suspension arm balljoint clamp bolt nut, anti-roll bar connecting link nut and the swivel hub clamp bolt nut.*

Removal

1 Chock the rear wheels of the car and firmly apply the handbrake. Jack up the front of the car and support it on axle stands (see *Jacking and vehicle support*). Remove the appropriate front roadwheel.

2 Slacken and remove the bolt securing the support bracket (where fitted) to the top of the swivel hub.

3 Unscrew the nut and free the anti-roll bar connecting link (where fitted) from the strut **(see illustration)**. Discard the nut – a new one must be used on refitting.

4 Slacken and remove the nut securing the steering gear track rod balljoint to the swivel hub, and release the balljoint tapered shank using a balljoint separator.

5 Slacken and remove the suspension lower arm balljoint clamp bolt and nut **(see illustration)**. Discard the nut – a new one must be used on refitting.

6 Undo the nut and withdraw the swivel hub-to-suspension strut clamp bolt **(see illustration)**. Discard the nut – a new one must be used on refitting.

7 Pull down on the lower arm to free its balljoint from the swivel hub **(see Tool Tip in Section 2)**. Once the balljoint is freed from the swivel hub, peg the lower arm in position by inserting a suitable socket in between the top of the arm inner end and the subframe **(see illustration)**.

8 Recover the protector plate from lower arm balljoint.

9 Free the swivel hub assembly from the end of the strut. If the swivel hub is a tight fit on the strut, use a large flat-bladed screwdriver to carefully open up the clamp a little. Position the swivel hub assembly clear of the strut and seat it on the lower arm balljoint **(see illustration)**. Tie the upper end of the hub

4.6 Unscrew the nut and withdraw the strut clamp bolt from the swivel hub

4.7 Pull down on the lower arm and peg it in position by inserting a socket (arrowed) between the top of the arm and subframe

4.9 Free the swivel hub assembly from the base of the strut and locate it back on the lower arm balljoint

4.10a Unscrew the upper mounting bolts (arrowed) . . .

4.10b . . . then manoeuvre the strut out from underneath the wheel arch

4.12 Ensure the strut is correctly located in the swivel hub then tighten its clamp bolt nut to the specified torque

assembly securely to the body to ensure no excess strain is placed on the brake hose or driveshaft joints.

10 Unscrew the strut upper mounting bolts then manoeuvre the strut out from underneath the wheel arch and remove it from the vehicle **(see illustrations)**.

Refitting

11 Manoeuvre the strut assembly into position. Locate its upper mounting plate correctly on the body and refit the upper mounting bolts.

12 Slide the hub assembly fully onto the suspension strut, aligning the split in the hub clamp with the lug on the base of the strut. Also ensure that the stop bosses on the strut are in contact with the top surface of the swivel hub. Insert the swivel hub-to-suspension strut

clamp bolt then fit a new nut and tighten it to the specified torque **(see illustration)**.

13 Fit the protector plate to the lower arm balljoint **(see illustration)**.

14 Align the lower arm balljoint with the swivel hub. Remove the socket (used to peg the arm in position) and seat the balljoint shank correctly in the swivel hub, aligning the protector plate tang with the hub slot. Insert the clamp bolt then fit the new nut and tighten to the specified torque.

15 Engage the track rod balljoint in the swivel hub, then fit a new retaining nut and tighten it to the specified torque.

16 Locate the anti-roll bar connecting link (where fitted) in the strut bracket. Fit the new nut to the link and tighten it to the specified torque.

17 Refit the bracket (where fitted) to the top of the swivel hub, and tighten its retaining bolt securely.

18 Refit the roadwheel, then lower the vehicle to the ground and tighten the roadwheel bolts to the specified torque.

5 Front suspension strut – overhaul

⚠️ *Warning: Before attempting to dismantle the front suspension strut, a suitable tool to hold the coil spring in compression must be obtained. Adjustable coil spring compressors are readily available, and are recommended for this operation. Any attempt to dismantle the strut without such a tool is likely to result in damage or personal injury.*

Note: *A new mounting plate nut must be used on reassembly.*

1 Remove the strut as described in Section 4.

2 Clean away all external dirt, then mount the strut upright in a vice.

3 Fit the spring compressors, and compress the coil spring until all tension is relieved from the upper spring seat **(see illustration)**.

4 Remove the cap then slacken the upper mounting plate nut whilst retaining the shock absorber piston with an Allen key **(see illustrations)**. Remove the mounting plate nut and washer. Discard the nut – a new one must be fitted on reassembly.

5 Lift off the mounting plate, bearing, upper spring seat and flat washer **(see illustrations)**.

4.13 Refit the protector plate to the lower arm balljoint

5.3 Compress the coil spring using spring compressors until all spring pressure is relieved from the seats

5.4a Remove the cap . . .

5.4b . . . then slacken the upper mounting plate nut whilst retaining the strut piston

5.5a Lift off the upper mounting plate . . .

5.5b . . . followed by the bearing (1), upper spring seat (2) and flat washer (3)

5.6 Slide the dust cover and rubber bump stop off the piston

5.12 Fit the coil spring, ensuring its end is correctly located against the stop (arrowed) on the lower seat

6 Remove the coil spring then slide off the piston dust cover and rubber damper stop (see illustration).

7 With the strut now dismantled, examine all the components for wear, damage or deformation, and check the upper bearing for smoothness of operation. Renew any of the components as necessary.

8 Examine the strut for signs of fluid leakage. Check the strut piston for signs of pitting along its entire length, and check the strut body for signs of damage. While holding it in an upright position, test the operation of the strut by moving the piston through a full stroke, and then through short strokes of 50 to 100 mm. In both cases, the resistance felt should be smooth and continuous. If the resistance is jerky, or uneven, or if there is any visible sign

of wear or damage to the strut, renewal is necessary.

9 If any doubt exists about the condition of the coil spring, carefully remove the spring compressors, and check the spring for distortion and signs of cracking. Renew the spring if it is damaged or distorted, or if there is any doubt as to its condition.

10 Inspect all other components for signs of damage or deterioration, and renew any that are suspect.

11 Ensure all components are clean and dry then slide the rubber damper stop and dust cover onto the strut.

12 Fit the coil spring, ensuring its end is correctly located against the stop on the lower seat (see illustration).

13 Fit the flat washer to the piston then install

the upper spring seat. Position the upper spring seat stop against the spring end (see illustrations).

14 Fit the bearing to the upper seat then fit the upper mounting plate. Fit the washer and new nut and tighten it to the specified torque (see illustrations).

15 Ensure the spring ends are still correctly positioned against their stops then carefully release the spring compressor and remove it from the strut.

16 Seat the damper stop and dust cover correctly in the upper spring seat.

17 Refit the strut as described in Section 4.

6 Front suspension lower arm – removal, overhaul and refitting

Note: *A new lower arm balljoint clamp bolt nut and lower arm mounting bolt nuts will be required on refitting.*

Removal

1 Chock the rear wheels of the car and firmly apply the handbrake. Jack up the front of the car and support it on axle stands (see *Jacking and vehicle support*). Remove the appropriate front roadwheel.

2 Slacken and remove the suspension lower arm balljoint clamp bolt and nut (see illustration). Discard the nut – a new one must be used on refitting.

5.13a Fit the flat washer . . .

5.13b . . . then fit the upper spring seat, positioning its stop (arrowed) against the spring end

5.14a Fit the washer . . .

5.14b . . . and the new upper mounting plate nut, tightening it to the specified torque

6.2 Unscrew the nut and withdraw the balljoint clamp bolt from the swivel hub

6.3 Unscrew the nuts and remove the lower arm mounting bolts (rear bolt shown) from the top of the subframe

3 Slacken and remove the front and rear mounting nuts and bolts securing the lower arm to the subframe **(see illustration)**. Discard the nuts – new ones must be used on refitting.

4 Free the lower arm balljoint from the swivel hub and remove the arm from the vehicle, taking care not to lose the protector plate from balljoint **(see Tool Tip in Section 2)**.

Overhaul

5 Thoroughly clean the lower arm and the area around the arm mountings, removing all traces of dirt and underseal if necessary, then check carefully for cracks, distortion or any other signs of wear or damage, paying particular attention to the pivot bushes. The pivot bushes are a press-fit in the arm and can be renewed separately. However, bush renewal requires the use of a hydraulic press and suitable mandrels and should therefore be entrusted to a Peugeot dealer.

6 Check that the lower arm balljoint moves freely, without any sign of roughness; check also that the balljoint gaiter shows no sign of deterioration, and is free from cracks and splits. The gaiter is available separately but if the balljoint is damaged, the lower arm will have to be renewed.

Refitting

7 Refit the protector plate to the balljoint then manoeuvre the lower arm assembly into position. Engage the balljoint shank with the

swivel hub, aligning the protector plate tang with the hub slot, and then insert the front and rear mounting bolts from above.

8 Fit the new nuts to the lower arm mounting bolts and tighten them to the specified torque.

9 Ensure the balljoint is correctly seated in the swivel hub then insert the clamp bolt. Fit a new nut to the clamp bolt and tighten it to the specified torque.

10 Refit the roadwheel, then lower the vehicle to the ground and tighten the roadwheel bolts to the specified torque.

---

7 Front suspension lower arm balljoint – removal and refitting

1 The balljoint is integral with the lower arm. The gaiter is available separately but if the balljoint is worn or damaged the lower arm will have to be renewed (see Section 6).

---

8 Front suspension anti-roll bar – removal and refitting

Note: *New anti-roll bar mounting bolt and connecting link nuts will be needed on refitting.*

Removal

1 Chock the rear wheels, firmly apply the handbrake, and then jack up the front of the vehicle and support it on axle stands (see *Jacking and vehicle support*).

2 On petrol engine models, remove the exhaust system intermediate pipe (see Chapter 4A).

3 On all models, undo the nuts securing the left- and right-hand connecting links to the anti-roll bar **(see illustration)**. Retain the connecting link balljoint with a Torx key to prevent rotation as the nut is slackened. Discard the nuts, new ones should be used on refitting, and position both connecting links clear of the anti-roll bar.

4 Slacken and remove the two anti-roll bar mounting clamp retaining bolts and nuts **(see illustration)**. Discard the nuts – new ones must be used on refitting.

5 Free both mounting both clamps from the subframe then manoeuvre the anti-roll bar out from underneath the vehicle. Remove the mounting bushes from the bar.

6 Carefully examine the anti-roll bar components for signs of wear, damage or deterioration, paying particular attention to the mounting bushes. Renew worn components as necessary.

Refitting

7 Fit the rubber mounting bushes to the anti-roll bar, ensuring that the flats on the inside of each bush engage with the corresponding flats on the anti-roll bar and the bush split is facing towards the rear.

8 Offer up the anti-roll bar, and manoeuvre it into position on the subframe.

9 Ensure the mounting bushes are still correctly engaged with the bar flats then refit the mounting clamps. Hook the end of each clamp into on the subframe and engage the clamps with the bushes. Install the mounting clamp bolts and fit the new nuts, tightening them lightly only.

10 Refit the connecting links to the anti-roll bar ends and fit the new nuts, tightening them to the specified torque.

11 Tighten the anti-roll bar mounting clamp bolts to the specified torque.

12 On petrol engine models refit the exhaust system intermediate pipe (see Chapter 4A).

13 On completion, lower the vehicle to the ground.

---

9 Front suspension anti-roll bar connecting link – removal and refitting

Note: *New connecting link securing nuts must be used on refitting.*

Removal

1 Firmly apply the handbrake, and then jack up the front of the car and support it on axle stands (see *Jacking and vehicle support*). Remove the roadwheel to improve access to the link.

2 Slacken and remove the nuts securing the connecting link to the strut and anti-roll bar, and remove the link from the vehicle **(see illustration)**. Retain the link balljoint shank

8.3 Unscrew the nuts and free the connecting link from each end of the anti-roll bar

8.4 Unscrew the nuts and bolts securing the anti-roll bar mounting clamps to the subframe

9.2 Retain the balljoint shanks with a Torx wrench whilst slackening the connecting link nuts

with a Torx key to prevent rotation as the nut is slackened.

3 Examine the connecting link for signs of damage, paying particular attention to the mounting bushes or balljoints (as applicable). If any sign of damage is found, renew if necessary. It is not possible to renew the bushes or balljoints separately. Note that the connecting link retaining nuts must be renewed as a matter of course.

Refitting

4 Manoeuvre the connecting link into position and engage it with the anti-roll bar and strut. Fit the new nuts to the connecting link and tighten to the specified torque.

5 Refit the roadwheel then lower the vehicle to the ground and tighten the wheel bolts to the specified torque.

10 Rear hub assembly – removal and refitting

1 The rear hub is an integral part of the brake drum. Refer to Chapter 9 for details on brake drum removal and refitting.

11 Rear hub bearings – renewal

Note: *The bearing is intended to last the car's entire service life without maintenance or attention. Never overtighten the hub nut beyond the specified torque wrench setting, in an attempt to 'adjust' the bearings.*

1 Remove the rear brake drum (Chapter 9).

2 Extract the bearing retaining circlip from the centre of the brake drum **(see illustration)**.

3 Prise out the hub seal seating ring from the rear of the drum **(see illustration)**.

4 Securely support the outer face of the drum hub, then press or drive the bearing out of position, using a tubular drift which bears on the bearing inner race. Alternatively, the bearing can be removed using an improvised tool made up from a suitable socket or tube, washers, nut and a suitable long bolt or threaded rod **(see illustration)**.

5 Thoroughly clean the hub, removing all

11.2 Extract the rear hub bearing circlip

traces of dirt and grease, and polish away any burrs or raised edges which might hinder reassembly. Check the hub for cracks or any other signs of wear or damage, and renew them if necessary. The bearing, circlip and seal seating ring must be renewed whenever they are disturbed. Note that a bearing kit is available from Peugeot dealers.

6 Examine the stub axle shaft for signs of wear or damage, and if necessary renew it. The stub axle is an interference fit in the trailing arm, and can either be tapped out of position, using a hammer and a soft-metal drift, or pushed out using a heavy-duty bearing puller. When installing the new stub axle, align its splines with those of the trailing arm, and drive or press it fully into position in the arm.

7 On reassembly, apply a light film of clean engine oil to the bearing outer race, to aid installation of the bearing.

11.4 Using a socket and drawbolt arrangement to draw the bearing out from the drum

11.3 Prise out the hub seal seating ring from the rear of the drum

8 Securely support the inner face of the drum hub, and locate the bearing in the hub bore. Press the bearing fully into position; ensuring it enters the hub squarely, using a tubular spacer that bears only on the bearing outer race. Alternatively, the bearing can be drawn into position with the improvised tool used previously, but note that a different socket or tube will be required to bear on the bearing outer race **(see illustrations)**.

9 Ensure that the bearing is correctly seated against the hub shoulder, and secure it in position with the new circlip. Ensure that the circlip is correctly seated in its hub groove.

10 Tap the new hub seal seating ring into position in the rear of the hub, taking care not to damage the seal seating surface **(see illustrations)**.

11 Refit the brake drum (see Chapter 9) using the new seal.

11.8a Locate the new bearing in the drum . . .

11.8b . . . and draw it squarely into position

11.10a Fit the new hub seal seating ring to the rear of the drum . . .

11.10b . . . and tap it squarely into position

12 Rear suspension components – general

1 Although it is possible to remove the rear suspension torsion bars, trailing arms and anti-roll bar independently of the complete rear axle assembly, it is essential to have certain special tools available to complete the work successfully.

2 Due to the complexity of the tasks, and the requirement for special tools to accurately set the suspension geometry on refitting, the removal and refitting of individual rear suspension components is considered to be beyond the scope of DIY work, and should be entrusted to a Peugeot dealer.

3 On 2.0 litre models, there are additional tie-rods and centre mounting yoke attached to the rear axle. Although these are relevantly easy to remove and refit, special tools are required to set-up the rear suspension geometry **(see illustrations)**.

4 Procedures for removal and refitting of the rear shock absorbers, and the complete rear axle assembly are given in Sections 13 and 14 respectively.

13 Rear shock absorber – removal, testing and refitting

Note: *New shock absorber mounting nuts must be used on refitting.*

Removal

1 Chock the front wheels, then jack up the rear of the vehicle and support it on axle stands (see *Jacking and vehicle support*). Remove the relevant rear roadwheel.

2 Using a trolley jack, raise the trailing arm until the shock absorber is slightly compressed.

3 Slacken and remove the nuts and washers from both the upper and lower shock absorber mounting bolts **(see illustrations)**.

4 Withdraw the mounting bolts, noting which way round they are fitted, and manoeuvre the shock absorber out from underneath the vehicle.

12.3a Centre yoke and tie-rods (arrowed) on rear axle

Testing

5 Examine the shock absorber for signs of fluid leakage or damage. Test the operation of the shock absorber, while holding it in an upright position, by moving the piston through a full stroke and then through short strokes of 50 to 100 mm. In both cases, the resistance felt should be smooth and continuous. If the resistance is jerky, or uneven, or if there is any visible sign of wear or damage, renewal is necessary. Also check the rubber mounting bushes for damage and deterioration. Renew the complete unit if any damage or excessive wear is evident; the mounting bushes are not available separately. Inspect the shanks of the mounting bolts for signs of wear or damage, and renew as necessary.

Refitting

6 Prior to refitting the shock absorber, mount it upright in the vice, and operate it fully through several strokes in order to prime it. Apply a smear of multi-purpose grease to both the shock absorber mounting bolts.

7 Manoeuvre the shock absorber into position, and insert its mounting bolts. Fit the new nuts to the mounting bolts, but do not tighten them yet.

8 Measure the distance between the shock absorber bolt head centres, and adjust the position of the jack under the trailing arm until a distance of 317.5 mm is obtained between the bolt centres. Once the trailing arm is correctly positioned, tighten the upper and lower mounting bolt nuts to the specified torque.

12.3b Tie-rod outer mounting bolt (arrowed)

9 Refit the roadwheel, then lower the car to ground and tighten the roadwheel bolts to the specified torque.

14 Rear axle assembly – removal, overhaul and refitting

Removal

1 Firmly chock the front wheels, then jack up the rear of the vehicle and support it on axle stands (see *Jacking and vehicle support*). Remove both rear roadwheels, then lower the spare wheel out from underneath the rear of the vehicle, and unhook the wheel carrier.

2 Remove the relevant exhaust system components and heat shield(s) (see the relevant part of Chapter 4).

3 Referring to Chapter 9, fully slacken the handbrake cable adjuster nut and detach both handbrake cables from the lever plate. From underneath the vehicle, work along the length of each cable, and free them from any retaining clips, which secure them to the vehicle underbody. Note the routing of the cables to ensure correct refitting.

4 Where necessary, disconnect the ABS wheel sensors at the wiring connectors, and free the sensor wiring from any retaining clips securing them to the vehicle underbody.

5 Trace the brake pipes back from the backplates to their unions on/in front of the axle **(see illustration)**. Wipe clean the area around the unions then slacken the union nuts and disconnect the pipes. Plug the hose/

13.3a Slacken and remove the upper . . .

13.3b . . . and lower mounting nuts and bolts and remove the rear shock absorber

14.5 Rear brake pipe union (arrowed) on the right-hand side of the axle

14.7a Rear axle front mounting bolt (arrowed)

14.7b Rear axle rear mounting bolt (arrowed)

pipe ends and valve unions (as applicable), to minimise fluid loss and prevent the entry of dirt into the hydraulic system.

6 Make a final check that all necessary components have been disconnected and positioned so that they will not hinder the removal procedure, then position a trolley jack beneath the centre of the rear axle assembly. Raise the jack until it is supporting the weight of the axle.

7 Slacken and remove the four bolts and washers securing the axle mounting bushes to the vehicle underbody **(see illustrations)**.

8 Lower the jack and axle assembly out of position, and remove it from underneath the car.

Overhaul

9 Examine the rear axle mountings for signs of damage or deterioration of the mounting rubber. If any mounting shows signs of damage or deterioration, all four mountings should be renewed as a set, do not renew the mountings individually. The mountings are a press-fit in the crossmember; renewal requires the use of a hydraulic press and suitable mandrels and should therefore be entrusted to a Peugeot dealer.

Refitting

10 Position the rear axle assembly onto the jack and carefully raise it up into position, taking care not to crush the brake pipes or trap the cables/wiring.

11 Align the axle mountings with the vehicle underbody and refit the mounting bolts, tightening them to the specified torque.

12 Referring to Chapter 9, carry out the following.

a) *Reconnect the brake pipes, tightening the union nuts to the specified torque. Ensure the pipes/hoses are correctly routed and retained by all the relevant clips.*

b) *Reconnect the handbrake cables to the lever, ensuring they are correctly routed and retained by all the relevant clips.*

c) *On models with ABS, reconnect the rear wheel sensor wiring connectors, ensuring the wiring is correctly routed and retained by all the relevant clips.*

13 Refit the rear section of the exhaust system (see the relevant part of Chapter 4).

14 Refit the spare wheel and carrier.

15 Refit the roadwheels then lower the vehicle to the ground and tighten the wheel bolts to the specified torque.

16 Bleed the complete braking system hydraulic circuit as described in Chapter 9 then adjust the handbrake cable.

17 If the axle assembly has been overhauled/renewed, have the vehicle ride height checked at the earliest opportunity.

---

15 Vehicle ride height – checking

1 Checking of the vehicle ride height requires the use of Peugeot special tools to accurately compress the suspension in a suspension checking bay.

2 The operation should be entrusted to a Peugeot dealer, as it not possible to carry out checking accurately without the use of the appropriate tools.

---

16 Steering wheel – removal and refitting

Note: *Models equipped with an airbag have the word AIRBAG stamped on the steering wheel pad.*

16.9a On models with a driver's airbag, unclip the horn wiring connector from the wheel . . .

Models without an airbag

Removal

1 Set the front wheels in the straight-ahead position, and release the steering lock by inserting the ignition key.

2 Carefully ease off the steering wheel centre pad, then slacken and remove the steering wheel retaining bolt.

3 Mark the steering wheel and steering column shaft in relation to each other, then lift the steering wheel off the column splines.

> **HAYNES HiNT**
> *If the wheel is tight, tap it up near the centre, using the palm of your hand, or twist it from side-to-side, whilst pulling to release it from the shaft splines.*

Refitting

4 Ensure that the indicator switch stem is in its central position (failure to do this could lead to the steering wheel lug breaking the switch tab) then engage the wheel with the column splines, aligning the mark made on removal.

5 Clean the threads of the steering wheel bolt then apply a drop of locking compound (Peugeot recommend Loctite Frenetanch) to its threads. Fit the retaining bolt and tighten it to the specified torque.

6 Refit the centre pad to the wheel.

Models with an airbag

> ⚠ *Warning: Refer to the precautions given in Chapter 12 about the airbag system before proceeding.*

Removal

7 Remove the airbag unit from the steering wheel (see Chapter 12).

8 Set the front wheels in the straight-ahead position, and release the steering lock by inserting the ignition key.

9 Unclip the horn wiring connector from the wheel then disconnect the connector and remove the horn wiring **(see illustrations)**.

16.9b . . . then disconnect the connector and remove the wiring

16.10 Slacken and remove the steering wheel retaining bolt

10 Slacken and remove the steering wheel retaining bolt **(see illustration)**.
11 Mark the steering wheel and steering column shaft in relation to each other then carefully lift wheel off the column splines. As the wheel is removed, pass the horn and airbag wiring connectors down through the wheel, taking care not to strain the wiring **(see illustration)**.

HAYNES HiNT *If the wheel is tight, tap it up near the centre, using the palm of your hand, or twist it from side-to-side, whilst pulling to release it from the shaft splines.*

Refitting

12 Prior to refitting, ensure the airbag contact unit is correctly centralised (see Chapter 12, Section 23).
13 Ensure that the indicator switch stem is in its central position (failure to do this could lead to the steering wheel lug breaking the switch tab) then pass the airbag unit and horn wiring up through the wheel. Engage the wheel the column splines, aligning the mark made on removal.
14 Clean the threads of the steering wheel retaining bolt and apply a drop of locking compound (Peugeot recommend Loctite Frenetanch) to its threads. Fit the bolt and tighten it to the specified torque **(see illustration)**.
15 Reconnect the horn wiring then clip the connector back onto the steering wheel.
16 Refit the airbag unit as described in Chapter 12.

16.11 Free the steering wheel from the column and remove it, taking care not to strain the horn/airbag wiring

17 Steering column – removal, inspection and refitting

Removal

1 Disconnect the battery negative terminal.
2 Remove the steering wheel (see Section 16).
3 Rotate the fastener a quarter-of-a-turn (90°) and remove the lower cover from the driver's side of the facia.
4 Undo the retaining screws and free the lower shroud from the column. Trace the audio unit control stalk back to its wiring connector then disconnect the connector and remove the shroud and switch as an assembly **(see illustration)**.

17.4 Disconnect the audio unit control stalk wiring connector and remove the lower shroud

16.14 Treat the threads of the steering wheel bolt with locking compound prior to refitting

5 Unclip and remove the upper shroud from the steering column.
6 On models equipped with an airbag, remove the contact unit from the column as described in Chapter 12.
7 On all models, carefully unclip the immobiliser ring and free it from the ignition switch/steering column lock **(see illustration)**.
8 Slacken and remove the three screws securing the combination switch bracket to the top of the column. Disconnect the wiring connectors from the base of the switches and remove the bracket assembly **(see illustrations)**.
9 Release the retaining clips and disconnect the ignition switch wiring connectors from the fusebox and wiring harness **(see illustration)**.
10 Free the wiring harness from the steering column cover then unclip the cover and

17.7 Unclip the immobiliser ring from the ignition switch/steering lock

17.8a Undo the retaining screws (arrowed) . . .

17.8b . . . and remove the combination switch bracket assembly, disconnecting the switch wiring connectors

17.9 Trace the ignition switch back to its wiring connectors (lift the retaining clip to disconnect the connector – arrowed)

17.10 Unclip and remove the cover from the steering column

17.11a Unclip the ends (arrowed) of the safety clip . . .

17.11b . . . then slide the clip (arrowed) off the base of the steering column

17.12a Slacken and remove the upper mounting nuts . . .

17.12b . . . and lower mounting bolts . . .

17.12c . . . and remove the steering column from the vehicle

remove it from the steering column **(see illustration)**.

11 Expand the ends of the safety clip and remove it from the base of the steering column **(see illustrations)**. Using paint or a suitable marker pen, make alignment marks between the column and steering gear pinion. Slacken and remove the nut and clamp bolt and detach the column from the steering gear pinion.

12 Slacken and remove the column upper mounting nuts and lower mounting bolts then manoeuvre the column out of position **(see illustrations)**.

Inspection

Note: *New steering columns are supplied with a safety clip fitted to the upper universal joint to protect the joint during handling. Remove this clip once the column is correctly installed.*

13 The steering column incorporates a telescopic safety feature. In the event of a front-end crash, the shaft collapses and prevents the steering wheel injuring the driver. Before refitting the steering column, examine the column and mountings for signs of damage and deformation, and renew as necessary.

14 Check the steering shaft for signs of free play in the column bushes, and check the universal joints for signs of damage or roughness in the joint bearings. If any damage or wear is found on the steering column universal joints or shaft bushes, the column must be renewed as an assembly.

Refitting

15 Manoeuvre the column into position and engage it with its upper mounting studs. Fit the upper mounting nuts and lower bolts tighten them lightly only.

16 Release the column height adjustment lever then tighten the column upper mounting nuts to the specified torque. Lock the height adjustment mechanism again then tighten the lower mounting bolts to the specified torque.

17 Engage the column universal joint with the steering gear pinion, aligning the marks made on removal, and secure it in position with the safety clip. Refit the clamp bolt and nut and tighten it to the specified torque.

18 Securely reconnect the ignition switch wiring connectors then clip the cover back onto the column. Ensure the cover is correctly fitted and clip the wiring harness back into position.

19 Reconnect the wiring to the combination switches then seat the bracket assembly back on the column. Securely tighten the bracket screws.

20 Clip the immobiliser sensor ring back onto the ignition switch/steering lock.

21 On models with an airbag, refit the contact unit as described in Chapter 12.

22 On all models, reconnect the audio unit control switch wiring connector then refit the upper and lower shrouds to the column and securely tighten the retaining screws.

23 Refit the steering wheel (Section 16) then reconnect the battery.

18 Ignition switch/steering column lock – removal and refitting

Removal

1 Disconnect the battery negative terminal.

2 Rotate the fastener a quarter-of-a-turn (90°) and remove the lower cover from the driver's side of the facia **(see illustration)**.

3 Undo the retaining screws and free the lower shroud from the column. Trace the audio unit control stalk back to its wiring connector then disconnect the connector and remove the shroud and switch as an assembly.

18.2 Rotate then fastener 90° and remove the lower cover from the facia

18.4 Unclip and remove the upper shroud from the steering column

18.5 Free the immobiliser ring from the lock

18.6a Disconnect the ignition switch wiring connectors from the fusebox (arrowed) . . .

18.6b . . . and wiring harness (arrowed)

18.7 Slacken and remove the retaining screw from the front of the lock housing

18.9 With the key correctly positioned, depress the detent clip (arrowed) and withdraw the lock from the steering column

4 Unclip and remove the upper shroud from the steering column **(see illustration)**.

5 Carefully unclip the immobiliser ring and free it from the ignition switch/steering column lock **(see illustration)**.

6 Release the retaining clips and disconnect the ignition switch wiring connectors from the fusebox and wiring harness **(see illustrations)**.

7 Slacken and remove the retaining screw from the front of the ignition switch/steering column lock housing **(see illustration)**.

8 Insert the ignition key and rotate it so that it is aligned with the mark positioned halfway between the A and M marks on the barrel.

9 With the key correctly positioned, depress the lock detent clip then withdraw the lock from the steering column **(see illustration)**.

Refitting

10 Align the key with the mark positioned halfway between the A and M marks then feed the wiring through the steering column lock housing and seat the lock barrel in position. Refit the retaining screw and tighten it securely.

11 Securely reconnect the ignition switch wiring connectors then check the operation of the switch and steering lock.

12 Clip the immobiliser sensor ring back onto the ignition switch/steering lock.

13 Reconnect the audio unit control switch wiring connector then refit the upper and lower shrouds to the column and securely tighten the retaining screws.

14 Refit the lower cover to the facia then reconnect the battery.

19 Steering gear assembly – removal, overhaul and refitting

Note: *New steering gear mounting studs and nuts and track rod balljoint nuts will be required on refitting. A balljoint separator tool will be required for this operation. On models with power steering, new O-rings will also be required for the pipe-to-steering gear unions.*

Removal

1 Working inside the vehicle, expand the ends of the safety clip and remove it from the base of the steering column **(see illustrations 17.11a and 17.11b)**. Using paint or a suitable marker pen, make alignment marks between the column and steering gear pinion. Slacken and remove the nut and clamp bolt and detach the column from the steering gear pinion. Free the inner rubber seal from the bulkhead and remove it from the steering gear.

2 Chock the rear wheels, firmly apply the handbrake, then jack up the front of the vehicle and support on axle stands (see *Jacking and vehicle support*). Remove both front roadwheels. Where necessary, remove the retaining bolts, screws and clips and remove the undercover (where fitted) from beneath the engine/transmission unit.

3 Slacken and remove the nuts securing the

steering gear track rod balljoints to the swivel hubs, and release the balljoint tapered shanks using a universal balljoint separator. Discard the nuts; new ones must be used on refitting.

4 On petrol engine models, remove the exhaust system intermediate pipe as described in Chapter 4A. On diesel engine models unscrew the nuts securing the exhaust mounting bracket to the rear of the subframe.

5 On models equipped with power steering, using brake hose clamps, clamp both the supply and return flexible hoses to minimise fluid loss. Slacken and remove the bolt securing the fluid feed and return pipe clamp to the steering gear **(see illustration)**. Free the pipes from the steering gear assembly; be prepared for fluid spillage, and position a suitable container beneath the pipes whilst

19.5 Feed and return pipe clamp bolt (arrowed) – models with power steering

19.7a Unscrew the steering gear nuts and washers from the base of the subframe . . .

19.7b . . . then unscrew the mounting studs . . .

19.7c . . . and recover the washers fitted between the steering gear and top of the subframe

unscrewing the union nuts. Plug the pipe ends and steering gear orifices, to prevent fluid leakage and to keep dirt out of the hydraulic system. Note that new sealing rings for the pipes must be used on refitting.

6 On all models, slacken and remove the nut and bolt securing the engine/transmission unit rear mounting link to the mounting.

7 Slacken and remove the nuts and washers securing the steering gear to the subframe. Once the nuts are removed, unscrew the mounting studs from the underside of the steering gear and recover the washers fitted between the steering gear and subframe **(see illustrations)**. Discard the studs and nuts; new ones should be used on refitting.

8 Support the subframe assembly with a jack then slacken and remove the four bolts securing the subframe to the vehicle body **(see illustrations)**. Lower the subframe slightly to enable access to be gained to the steering gear.

9 Free the steering gear outer rubber seal from the bulkhead then manoeuvre the steering gear from underneath the driver's side wheel arch, positioning the subframe clear as necessary.

Overhaul

10 Examine the steering gear assembly for signs of wear or damage, and check that the rack moves freely throughout the full length of its travel, with no signs of roughness or

19.8a Front subframe front mounting bolt (arrowed)

19.8b Front subframe rear mounting bolt (arrowed)

excessive free play between the steering gear pinion and rack. It is possible to overhaul the steering gear assembly housing components, but this task should be entrusted to a Peugeot dealer. The only components which can be renewed easily by the home mechanic are the steering gear gaiters, the track rod balljoints and the track rods. Track rod, track rod balljoint and steering gear gaiter renewal procedures are covered in Sections 24, 23 and 20 respectively.

11 On models with power steering, inspect all the steering gear fluid unions for signs of leakage, and check that all union nuts are securely tightened. Also examine the steering gear hydraulic ram for signs of fluid leakage or damage, and if necessary renew it.

12 Inspect the inner and outer rubber seals for signs of damage or deterioration and renew as necessary.

Refitting

13 Engage the outer rubber seal with the steering gear. On right-hand drive models fit the seal so the DD slot in the seal is engaged with the tab on the steering gear; on left-hand drive models fit the seal so the DG slot is engaged with the steering gear tab **(see illustration)**.

14 Ensure the outer rubber seal is correctly installed then manoeuvre the steering gear into position. Position the washers in between the steering gear and subframe then align the steering gear with the subframe. Fit the new mounting studs, ensuring they pass through the washers, and tighten them to the specified torque **(see illustration)**.

19.13 On right-hand drive models fit the outer seal (1) so that its DD slot is engaged with the tab (A) on the steering gear housing (on left-hand drive models align the DG slot with the tab)

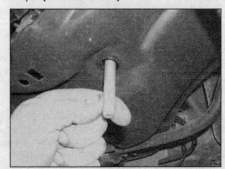

19.14 Fit the new studs to the steering gear, ensuring they pass through the washers

15 Seat the outer seal correctly on the bulkhead then align the subframe with its mountings. Refit the subframe mounting bolts and tighten them to the specified torque.

16 Fit the washers and new mounting nuts to the steering gear studs and tighten to the specified torque.

17 Refit the engine/transmission rear mounting link bolt and nut and tighten to the specified torque (see the relevant part of Chapter 2).

18 On models with power steering, remove the O-rings from the ends of the feed and return pipe unions. Fit the new O-rings, lubricating them with a smear of power steering fluid, and then ease them back into position in the steering gear. Ensure both pipes are correctly located then refit the clamp bolt and tighten to the specified torque.

19 On petrol engine models, refit the exhaust intermediate pipe (see Chapter 4A). On diesel engine models, locate the exhaust mounting bracket in the subframe and securely tighten its retaining nuts.

20 On all models, locate the track rod balljoints back in the swivel hubs. Fit the new nuts to the balljoints and tighten them to the specified torque.

21 Refit the roadwheels then lower the vehicle to the ground and tighten the wheel bolts to the specified torque.

22 Refit the inner rubber seal ensuring it is correctly engaged with the bulkhead and steering gear pinion. Engage the column universal joint with the steering gear pinion, aligning the marks made on removal, and secure it in position with the safety clip. Refit the clamp bolt and nut, tightening it to the specified torque.

23 On models with power steering, remove the hose clamps (where fitted) from the power steering hoses, then top-up the fluid reservoir and bleed the hydraulic system as described in Section 21.

24 On all models, on completion check and, if necessary, adjust the front wheel alignment as described in Section 25.

20 Steering gear rubber gaiters – renewal

1 Remove the track rod balljoint as described in Section 23.

2 To improve access to the left-hand gaiter, remove the battery and battery tray (see Chapter 5A).

3 Mark the correct fitted position of the gaiter on the track rod. Free the breather pipe from the inner edge of the gaiter, then release the retaining clips and slide the gaiter off the steering gear housing and track rod end.

4 Thoroughly clean the track rod and the steering gear housing, using fine abrasive paper to polish off any corrosion, burrs or sharp edges which might damage the new gaiter's sealing lips on installation. Scrape off all the grease from the old gaiter, and apply it to the track rod inner balljoint. (This assumes that grease has not been lost or contaminated as a result of damage to the old gaiter. Use fresh grease if in doubt – Peugeot recommend Total N3924 or N3945.)

5 Carefully slide the new gaiter onto the track rod end, and locate it on the steering gear housing, ensuring the breather pipe union is uppermost. Align the outer edge of the gaiter with the mark made on the track rod prior to removal, and then secure it the gaiter in position with new retaining clips. Ensure the gaiter is securely fitted then reconnect the breather pipe.

6 Refit the track rod balljoint as described in Section 23. Where necessary, install the battery (see Chapter 5A).

21 Power steering system – bleeding

1 This procedure will only be necessary when any part of the hydraulic system has been disconnected.

2 Referring to *Weekly checks*, remove the fluid reservoir filler cap, and top-up with the specified fluid to the C level mark.

3 With the engine stopped, slowly move the steering from lock-to-lock several times to purge out the trapped air, then top-up the level in the fluid reservoir. Repeat this procedure until the fluid level in the reservoir does not drop any further.

4 Start the engine and allow it to idle for a few minutes without turning the steering wheel. Keep fluid level topped-up whilst the engine idles. Once the fluid level stabilises, slowly move the steering from lock-to-lock several times to purge out any remaining air in the system. Repeat this procedure until bubbles cease to appear in the fluid reservoir.

5 If, when turning the steering, an abnormal noise is heard from the fluid lines, it indicates that there is still air in the system. Check this by turning the wheels to the straight-ahead position and switching off the engine. If the fluid level in the reservoir rises, then air is present in the system, and further bleeding is necessary.

6 Once all traces of air have been removed from the power steering hydraulic system, turn the engine off and allow the system to cool. Once cool, check that the fluid level is correct (see *Weekly checks*), topping-up if necessary.

22 Power steering pump – removal and refitting

Removal

1 Release the drivebelt tension as described in the relevant part of Chapter 1, and unhook the drivebelt from the pump pulley. The power steering pump is mounted directly above the alternator, on the front of the engine. Unclip and remove the screenwash reservoir neck to improve access to the pump.

2 On diesel engine models, remove the engine cover.

3 Slacken and remove the bolt securing the feed pipe clip to the side of the pump.

4 Wipe clean the area around the feed pipe union on the top of the pump. Unscrew the union nut and detach the pipe from the pump; be prepared for some fluid spillage as the pipe is disconnected, and plug the pipe end and pump unions to minimise fluid loss and prevent the entry of dirt into the system **(see illustration)**. **Note:** *Access to the union nut is awkward; Peugeot produce a special socket (0720E) to enable the nut to the slackened/ tightened.*

5 Slacken and remove the front and rear bolts securing the pump to its mounting bracket **(see illustration)**.

6 Free the pump from the bracket and (where necessary) recover the spacer from the rear mounting. Release the retaining clip, and disconnect the return hose from the base of the pump, being prepared for fluid spillage

22.4 Unscrew the nut and disconnect the feed pipe from the power steering pump

22.5 The pump front mounting bolts are accessed through the holes in the drivebelt pulley

22.6 Lift the pump away from its mounting bracket and disconnect the fluid return hose (arrowed) from the base of the pump

(see illustration). Plug the hose end then remove the pump from the vehicle and drain the fluid reservoir contents.

Refitting

7 Manoeuvre the pump into position and securely reconnect the return hose.

8 Ensure the spacer (where fitted) is correctly fitted to the rear mounting then seat the pump on its bracket.

9 Apply a drop of locking compound (Peugeot recommend the use of Loctite Frenetanch) to the threads of the pump lower front mounting bolt then refit all the bolts. Tighten the front (drivebelt pulley end) mounting bolts to the specified torque first, and then tighten the rear mounting bolts to the specified torque.

10 Reconnect the feed pipe to the pump and screw the union nut in a few turns. Refit the bolt securing the pipe clip to the pump then tighten the union nut to the specified torque followed by the clip bolt.

11 Refit the drivebelt to the pump pulley as described in the relevant part of Chapter 1.

12 Refill the fluid reservoir with fresh fluid then bleed the hydraulic system as described in Section 21.

23 Track rod balljoint – removal and refitting

Note: *A new track rod balljoint nut must be used on refitting.*

Removal

1 Apply the handbrake, then jack up the front of the vehicle and support it on axle stands (see *Jacking and vehicle support*). Remove the appropriate front roadwheel.

2 If the balljoint is to be re-used, use a straight-edge and a scriber, or similar, to mark its relationship to the track rod.

3 Hold the track rod, and unscrew the balljoint locknut by a quarter of a turn. Do not move the locknut from this position, as it will serve as a handy reference mark on refitting.

4 Slacken and remove the nut securing the track rod balljoint to the swivel hub, and release the balljoint tapered shank using a

23.4 Releasing a track rod balljoint using a balljoint separator

universal balljoint separator **(see illustration).** Discard the nut – a new one must be used when refitting.

5 Counting the **exact** number of turns necessary to do so, unscrew the balljoint from the track rod end.

6 Count the number of exposed threads between the end of the balljoint and the locknut, and record this figure. If a new balljoint is to be fitted, unscrew the locknut from the old balljoint.

7 Carefully clean the balljoint and the threads. Renew the balljoint if its movement is sloppy or too stiff, if excessively worn, or if damaged in any way; carefully check the stud taper and threads. If the balljoint gaiter is damaged, the complete balljoint assembly must be renewed; it is not possible to obtain the gaiter separately.

Refitting

8 If a new balljoint is to be fitted, screw the locknut onto its threads, and position it so that the same number of exposed threads are visible as was noted prior to removal **(see illustration). Note:** *Peugeot give an initial setting for the locknut if both balljoints are to be renewed; the locknut should be positioned so the specified length of thread is visible between the balljoint and locknut.*

9 Screw the balljoint into the track rod by the number of turns noted on removal. This should bring the balljoint locknut to within a

23.8 The initial setting for a track rod balljoint is made by measuring the amount of exposed thread (X) visible

Models with manual steering – X = 18 mm
Models with power steering – X = 13 mm

quarter of a turn from the locknut, with the alignment marks that were made on removal (if applicable) lined up.

10 Refit the balljoint shank to the swivel hub, and then fit a new retaining nut and tighten it to the specified torque.

11 Refit the roadwheel, then lower the vehicle to the ground and tighten the roadwheel bolts to the specified torque.

12 Check and, if necessary, adjust the front wheel toe setting as described in Section 25, then tighten the balljoint locknut to the specified torque.

24 Track rod – removal and refitting

Note: *Access to the track rod inner balljoints with the steering gear installed is poor. To improve access remove the steering gear as described in Section 19.*
Note: *Peugeot manufacture a special wrench (0707), which fits the track rod balljoint enabling it to be easily unscrewed from the steering rack.*

Removal

1 Remove the track rod balljoints as described in Section 23.

2 Disconnect the breather pipe then release the retaining clips and slide the steering gear gaiter off the end of the track rod – refer to Section 20 for further information. It is recommended that the gaiter is renewed, regardless of its apparent condition.

3 Unscrew the track rod inner balljoint from the steering rack end, preventing the steering rack from turning by holding the steering rack with a pair of grips using a stout cloth to protect the rack surface. Take great care not to mark the surfaces of the rack and balljoint.

4 Remove the track rod assembly and examine its inner balljoint for signs of slackness or tight spots, and check that the track rod itself is straight and free from damage. If necessary, renew the track rod.

Refitting

5 Screw the track rod inner balljoint into the steering rack, and tighten it to the specified torque whilst retaining the steering rack with a pair of grips, using a stout cloth to protect against damage. Again, take great care not to damage or mark the track rod balljoint or steering rack.

6 Carefully slide the new gaiter onto the track rod end, and locate it on the steering gear housing, ensuring the breather pipe union is uppermost. Align the outer edge of the gaiter with the mark made on the track rod prior to removal, and then secure it the gaiter in position with new retaining clips. Ensure the gaiter is securely fitted then reconnect the breather pipe.

7 Refit the track rod balljoint as described in Section 23.

25 Wheel alignment and steering angles – general information

General

1 A car's steering and suspension geometry is defined in four basic settings – all angles are expressed in degrees (toe settings are also expressed as a measurement); the relevant settings are camber, castor, steering axis inclination, and toe-setting. With the exception of front wheel toe-setting, none of these settings are adjustable.

Front wheel toe setting – checking and adjustment

2 Due to the special measuring equipment necessary to accurately check the wheel alignment, and the skill required to use it properly, checking and adjustment is best left to a Peugeot dealer or similar expert. Note that most tyre-fitting shops now possess sophisticated checking equipment. The following is provided as a guide, should the owner decide to carry out a DIY check.

3 The front wheel toe setting is checked by measuring the distance between the front and rear inside edges of the roadwheel rims. Proprietary toe measurement gauges are available from motor accessory shops. Adjustment is made by screwing the balljoints in or out of their track rods, to alter the effective length of the track rod assemblies.

4 For **accurate** checking, the vehicle **must** be at the kerb weight, ie, unladen and with a full tank of fuel, and the ride height must be correct (see Section 15).

5 Before starting work, check first that the tyre sizes and types are as specified, then check the tyre pressures and tread wear, the roadwheel run-out, the condition of the hub bearings, the steering wheel free play, and the condition of the front suspension components (see the relevant part of Chapter 1). Correct any faults found.

6 Park the vehicle on level ground, check that the front roadwheels are in the straight-ahead position, then rock the rear and front ends to settle the suspension. Release the handbrake, and roll the vehicle backwards 1 metre, then forwards again, to relieve any stresses in the steering and suspension components.

7 Measure the distance between the front edges of the wheel rims and the rear edges of the rims. Subtract the front measurement from the rear measurement, and check that the result is within the specified range.

8 If adjustment is necessary, apply the handbrake, then jack up the front of the vehicle and support it securely on axle stands (see *Jacking and vehicle support*). Turn the steering wheel onto full-left lock, and record the amount of exposed thread on the right-hand track rod balljoint. Now turn the steering onto full-right lock, and record the number of threads on the left-hand balljoint. If there is the same amount of thread visible on both sides, then subsequent adjustment should be made equally on both sides. If more thread is visible on one side than the other, it will be necessary to compensate for this during adjustment. **Note:** *Peugeot give an initial setting for the length of visible thread on each balljoint* **(see illustration 23.8)**. *It is most important that after adjustment, the same amount of thread is visible on each track rod end.*

9 First clean the track rod balljoint threads; if they are corroded, apply penetrating fluid before starting adjustment. Release the rubber gaiter outer clips (where necessary), and peel back the gaiters; apply a smear of grease to the inside of the gaiters, so that both are free, and will not be twisted or strained as their respective track rods are rotated.

10 Use a straight-edge and a scriber or similar to mark the relationship of each track rod to its balljoint then, holding each track

25.10 Adjusting the front wheel toe setting

rod in turn, unscrew its locknut fully **(see illustration)**.

11 Alter the length of the track rods, bearing in mind the note made in paragraph 8. Screw them onto or off of the balljoints, rotating the track rod using an open-ended spanner fitted to the flats provided on the track rod. Shortening the track rods (screwing them onto their balljoints) will reduce toe-in/increase toe-out.

12 When the setting is correct, hold the track rods and tighten the balljoint locknuts to the specified torque. Check the length of each track rod is equal by measuring the amount of exposed thread is equal on both balljoints. If they are not the same, then the adjustment has not been made equally, and problems will be encountered with tyre scrubbing in turns; also, the steering wheel spokes will no longer be horizontal when the wheels are in the straight-ahead position.

13 If the track rod lengths are the same, lower the vehicle to the ground and recheck the toe setting; re-adjust if necessary. When the setting is correct, tighten the track rod balljoint locknuts to the specified torque. Ensure that the rubber gaiters are seated correctly, and are not twisted or strained, and secure them in position with new retaining clips (where necessary).

Chapter 11
Bodywork and fittings

Contents

Degrees of difficulty

Easy, suitable for novice with little experience	Fairly easy, suitable for beginner with some experience	Fairly difficult, suitable for competent DIY mechanic	Difficult, suitable for experienced DIY mechanic	Very difficult, suitable for expert DIY or professional

Specifications

Torque wrench settings	Nm	lbf ft
Bonnet release lever bolt	6	4
Facia mounting bolts	19	14
Front seat mounting bolts	25	18
Rear seat back mounting bolts	23	17
Seat belt/inertia reel mounting bolts	30	22

1 General information

1 The bodyshell is made of pressed-steel sections, and is available in both three- or five-door Hatchback, Estate and Cabriolet Coupe versions. Most components are welded together, but some use is made of structural adhesives. The front wings are bolted on.
2 The bonnet, doors and some other vulnerable panels are made of zinc-coated metal, and are further protected by being coated with an anti-chip primer prior to being sprayed.
3 Extensive use is made of plastic materials, mainly in the interior, but also in exterior components. The front and rear bumpers and the front grille are injection-moulded from a synthetic material, which is very strong, and yet light. Plastic components such as wheel arch liners are fitted to the underside of the vehicle, to improve the body's resistance to corrosion.

2 Maintenance – bodywork and underframe

1 The general condition of a vehicle's bodywork is the one thing that significantly affects its value. Maintenance is easy, but needs to be regular. Neglect, particularly after minor damage, can lead quickly to further deterioration and costly repair bills. It is important also to keep watch on those parts of the vehicle not immediately visible, for instance the underside, inside all the wheel arches, and the lower part of the engine compartment.
2 The basic maintenance routine for the bodywork is washing – preferably with a lot of water, from a hose. This will remove all the loose solids, which may have stuck to the vehicle. It is important to flush these off in such a way as to prevent grit from scratching the finish. The wheel arches and underframe need washing in the same way, to remove any accumulated mud, which will retain moisture and tend to encourage rust. Paradoxically enough, the best time to clean the underframe and wheel arches is in wet weather, when the mud is thoroughly wet and soft. In very wet weather, the underframe is usually cleaned of large accumulations automatically, and this is a good time for inspection.
3 Annually, preferably just prior to winter, the underbody should be washed down and any damage to the wax coating repaired using underseal.
4 After washing paintwork, wipe off with a chamois leather to give an unspotted clear finish. A coat of clear protective wax polish will give added protection against chemical pollutants in the air. If the paintwork sheen has dulled or oxidised, use a cleaner/polisher combination to restore the brilliance of the shine. This requires a little effort, but such

dulling is usually caused because regular washing has been neglected. Care needs to be taken with metallic paintwork, as a special non-abrasive cleaner/polisher is required to avoid damage to the finish. Always check that the door and ventilator opening drain holes and pipes are completely clear, so that water can be drained out. Brightwork should be treated in the same way as paintwork. Windscreens and windows can be kept clear of the smeary film, which often appears, by the use of proprietary glass cleaner. Never use any form of wax or other body or chromium polish on glass.

3 Maintenance – upholstery and carpets

1 Mats and carpets should be brushed or vacuum-cleaned regularly, to keep them free of grit. If they are badly stained, remove them from the vehicle for scrubbing or sponging, and make quite sure they are dry before refitting. Seats and interior trim panels can be kept clean by wiping with a damp cloth and a proprietary upholstery cleaner. If they do become stained (which can be more apparent on light-coloured upholstery), use a little liquid detergent and a soft nail brush to scour the grime out of the grain of the material. Do not forget to keep the headlining clean in the same way as the upholstery. When using liquid cleaners inside the vehicle, do not over-wet the surfaces being cleaned. Excessive damp could get into the seams and padded interior, causing stains, offensive odours or even rot. If the inside of the vehicle gets wet accidentally, it is worthwhile taking some trouble to dry it out properly, particularly where carpets are involved. *Do not leave oil or electric heaters inside the vehicle for this purpose.*

4 Minor body damage – repair

Minor scratches

1 If the scratch is very superficial, and does not penetrate to the metal of the bodywork, repair is very simple. Lightly rub the area of the scratch with a paintwork renovator, or a very fine cutting paste, to remove loose paint from the scratch, and to clear the surrounding bodywork of wax polish. Rinse the area with clean water.
2 Apply touch-up paint to the scratch using a fine paint brush; continue to apply fine layers of paint until the surface of the paint in the scratch is level with the surrounding paintwork. Allow the new paint at least two weeks to harden, and then blend it into the surrounding paintwork by rubbing the scratch area with a paintwork renovator or a very fine cutting paste. Finally apply wax polish.
3 Where the scratch has penetrated right through to the metal of the bodywork, causing

the metal to rust, a different repair technique is required. Remove any loose rust from the bottom of the scratch with a penknife, and then apply rust-inhibiting paint, to prevent the formation of rust in the future. Using a rubber or nylon applicator, fill the scratch with bodystopper paste. If required, this paste can be mixed with cellulose thinners, to provide a very thin paste, which is ideal for filling narrow scratches. Before the stopper-paste in the scratch hardens, wrap a piece of smooth cotton rag around the top of a finger. Dip the finger in cellulose thinners, and quickly sweep it across the surface of the stopper-paste in the scratch; this will ensure that the surface of the stopper-paste is slightly hollowed. The scratch can now be painted over as described earlier in this Section.

Dents

4 When deep denting of the vehicle's bodywork has taken place, the first task is to pull the dent out, until the affected bodywork almost attains its original shape. There is little point in trying to restore the original shape completely, as the metal in the damaged area will have stretched on impact, and cannot be reshaped fully to its original contour. It is better to bring the level of the dent up to a point, which is about 3 mm below the level of the surrounding bodywork. In cases where the dent is very shallow anyway, it is not worth trying to pull it out at all. If the underside of the dent is accessible, it can be hammered out gently from behind, using a mallet with a wooden or plastic head. Whilst doing this, hold a suitable block of wood firmly against the outside of the panel, to absorb the impact from the hammer blows and thus prevent a large area of the bodywork from being 'belled-out'.
5 Should the dent be in a section of the bodywork, which has a double skin, or some other factor making it inaccessible from behind, a different technique is called for. Drill several small holes through the metal inside the area – particularly in the deeper section. Then screw long self-tapping screws into the holes, just sufficiently for them to gain a good purchase in the metal. Now the dent can be pulled out by pulling on the protruding heads of the screws with a pair of pliers.
6 The next stage of the repair is the removal of the paint from the damaged area, and from an inch or so of the surrounding 'sound' bodywork. This is accomplished most easily by using a wire brush or abrasive pad on a power drill, although it can be done just as effectively by hand, using sheets of abrasive paper. To complete the preparation for filling, score the surface of the bare metal with a screwdriver or the tang of a file, or alternatively, drill small holes in the affected area. This will provide a really good 'key' for the filler paste.
7 To complete the repair, see the Section on filling and respraying.

Rust holes or gashes

8 Remove all paint from the affected area, and from an inch or so of the surrounding 'sound' bodywork, using an abrasive pad or a wire brush on a power drill. If these are not available, a few sheets of abrasive paper will do the job most effectively. With the paint removed, you will be able to judge the severity of the corrosion, and therefore decide whether to renew the whole panel (if this is possible) or to repair the affected area. New body panels are not as expensive as most people think, and it is often quicker and more satisfactory to fit a new panel than to attempt to repair large areas of corrosion.

9 Remove all fittings from the affected area, except those, which will act as a guide to the original shape of the damaged bodywork (eg headlight shells etc). Then, using tin snips or a hacksaw blade, remove all loose metal and any other metal badly affected by corrosion. Hammer the edges of the hole inwards, in order to create a slight depression for the filler paste.

10 Wire-brush the affected area to remove the powdery rust from the surface of the remaining metal. Paint the affected area with rust-inhibiting paint; if the back of the rusted area is accessible, treat this also.

11 Before filling can take place, it will be necessary to block the hole in some way. This can be achieved by the use of aluminium or plastic mesh, or aluminium tape.

12 Aluminium or plastic mesh, or glass-fibre matting, is probably the best material to use for a large hole. Cut a piece to the approximate size and shape of the hole to be filled, then position it in the hole so that its edges are below the level of the surrounding bodywork. It can be retained in position by several blobs of filler paste around its periphery.

13 Aluminium tape should be used for small or very narrow holes. Pull a piece off the roll, trim it to the approximate size and shape required, then pull off the backing paper (if used) and stick the tape over the hole; it can be overlapped if the thickness of one piece is insufficient. Burnish down the edges of the tape with the handle of a screwdriver or similar, to ensure that the tape is securely attached to the metal underneath.

Filling and respraying

14 Before using this Section, see the Sections on dent, minor scratch, rust holes and gash repairs.

15 Many types of bodyfiller are available, but generally speaking, those proprietary kits which contain a tin of filler paste and a tube of resin hardener are best for this type of repair; some can be used directly from the tube. A wide, flexible plastic or nylon applicator will be found invaluable for imparting a smooth and well-contoured finish to the surface of the filler.

16 Mix up a little filler on a clean piece of card or board – measure the hardener carefully (follow the maker's instructions on the pack), otherwise the filler will set too rapidly or too slowly. Using the applicator, apply the filler paste to the prepared area; draw the applicator across the surface of the filler to achieve the correct contour and to level the surface. As

soon as a contour that approximates to the correct one is achieved, stop working the paste – if you carry on too long, the paste will become sticky and begin to 'pick-up' on the applicator. Continue to add thin layers of filler paste at 20-minute intervals, until the level of the filler is just proud of the surrounding bodywork.

17 Once the filler has hardened, the excess can be removed using a metal plane or file. From then on, progressively finer grades of abrasive paper should be used, starting with a 40-grade production paper, and finishing with a 400-grade wet-and-dry paper. Always wrap the abrasive paper around a flat rubber, cork, or wooden block – otherwise the surface of the filler will not be completely flat. During the smoothing of the filler surface, the wet-and-dry paper should be periodically rinsed in water. This will ensure that a very smooth finish is imparted to the filler at the final stage.

18 At this stage, the 'dent' should be surrounded by a ring of bare metal, which in turn should be encircled by the finely 'feathered' edge of the good paintwork. Rinse the repair area with clean water, until all of the dust produced by the rubbing-down operation has gone.

19 Spray the whole area with a light coat of primer – this will show up any imperfections in the surface of the filler. Repair these imperfections with fresh filler paste or bodystopper, and once more smooth the surface with abrasive paper. If bodystopper is used, it can be mixed with cellulose thinners, to form a really thin paste, which is ideal for filling small holes. Repeat this spray-and-repair procedure until you are satisfied that the surface of the filler, and the feathered edge of the paintwork, are perfect. Clean the repair area with clean water, and allow to dry fully.

20 The repair area is now ready for final spraying. Paint spraying must be carried out in a warm, dry, windless and dust-free atmosphere. This condition can be created artificially if you have access to a large indoor working area, but if you are forced to work in the open, you will have to pick your day very carefully. If you are working indoors, dousing the floor in the work area with water will help to settle the dust, which would otherwise be in the atmosphere. If the repair area is confined to one body panel, mask off the surrounding panels; this will help to minimise the effects of a slight mismatch in paint colours. Bodywork fittings (e.g. chrome strips, door handles etc) will also need to be masked off. Use genuine masking tape, and several thicknesses of newspaper, for the masking operations.

21 Before commencing to spray, agitate the aerosol can thoroughly, and then spray a test area (an old tin, or similar) until the technique is mastered. Cover the repair area with a thick coat of primer; the thickness should be built up using several thin layers of paint, rather than one thick one. Using 400-grade wet-and-dry paper, rub down the surface of the primer until it is really smooth. While doing this, the work area should be thoroughly doused with

water, and the wet-and-dry paper periodically rinsed in water. Allow to dry before spraying on more paint.

22 Spray on the top coat, again building up the thickness by using several thin layers of paint. Start spraying at the top of the repair area, and then, using a side-to-side motion, work downwards until the whole repair area and about 2 inches of the surrounding original paintwork is covered. Remove all masking material 10 to 15 minutes after spraying on the final coat of paint.

23 Allow the new paint at least two weeks to harden, then, using a paintwork renovator or a very fine cutting paste, blend the edges of the paint into the existing paintwork. Finally, apply wax polish.

Plastic components

24 With the use of more and more plastic body components by the vehicle manufacturers (e.g. bumpers. spoilers, and in some cases major body panels), rectification of more serious damage to such items has become a matter of either entrusting repair work to a specialist in this field, or renewing complete components. Repair of such damage by the DIY owner is not really feasible, owing to the cost of the equipment and materials required for effecting such repairs. The basic technique involves making a groove along the line of the crack in the plastic, using a rotary burr in a power drill. The damaged part is then welded back together, using a hot air gun to heat up and fuse a plastic filler rod into the groove. Any excess plastic is then removed, and the area rubbed down to a smooth finish. It is important that a filler rod of the correct plastic is used, as body components can be made of a variety of different types (eg polycarbonate, ABS, polypropylene).

25 Damage of a less serious nature (abrasions, minor cracks etc) can be repaired by the DIY owner using a two-part epoxy filler repair material. Once mixed in equal proportions, this is used in similar fashion to the bodywork filler used on metal panels. The filler is usually cured in twenty to thirty minutes, ready for sanding and painting.

26 If the owner is renewing a complete component himself, or if he has repaired it with epoxy filler, he will be left with the problem of finding a suitable paint for finishing which is compatible with the type of plastic used. At one time, the use of a universal paint was not possible, owing to the complex range of plastics encountered in body component applications. Standard paints, generally speaking, will not bond to plastic or rubber satisfactorily. However, it is now possible to obtain a plastic body parts finishing kit, which consists of a pre-primer treatment, a primer and coloured top coat. Full instructions are normally supplied with a kit, but basically, the method of use is to first apply the pre-primer to the component concerned, and allow it to dry for up to 30 minutes. Then the primer is applied, and left to dry for about an hour before finally applying the special-coloured

6.2a Pull out the centre pins and remove the fasteners securing the grille panel in position . . .

6.2b . . . then release the lower retaining clips (arrowed) and unclip the grille panel from the bumper in an upwards direction

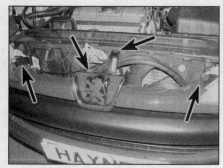

6.3a Undo the retaining screws (arrowed) . . .

top coat. The result is a correctly coloured component, where the paint will flex with the plastic or rubber, a property that standard paint does not normally possess.

5 Major body damage – repair

1 Where serious damage has occurred, or large areas need renewal due to neglect, it means that complete new panels will need welding-in, and this is best left to professionals. If the damage is due to impact, it will also be necessary to check completely the alignment of the bodyshell, and this can only be carried out accurately by a Peugeot dealer using special jigs. If the body is left misaligned, it is

primarily dangerous, as the car will not handle properly, and secondly, uneven stresses will be imposed on the steering, suspension and possibly transmission, causing abnormal wear, or complete failure, particularly to such items as the tyres.

6 Front bumper – removal and refitting

Removal

1 Open the bonnet. For improved access, apply the handbrake, and then jack up the front of the vehicle and support securely on axle stands (see *Jacking and vehicle support*).
2 Remove the four fasteners (pull out the

centre pin then remove the complete fastener) securing the grille panel to the top of the front panel. Release the lower retaining clips and unclip the grille panel from the front trim panel in an upward direction **(see illustrations)**.
3 Slacken and remove the retaining screws securing the front trim panel in position. Carefully unclip the trim panel from the inner edge of each headlight then unclip the ends of the panel from each wing and remove the panel from the vehicle **(see illustrations)**.
4 Slacken and remove the three bumper upper retaining bolts **(see illustration)**.
5 Undo the screws securing the front section of the left-hand wheel arch liner to the base of the bumper. Remove the fasteners securing the liner section to the body then manoeuvre the front section of the liner out from underneath the wing **(see illustrations)**.

6.3b . . . then unclip each end of the panel from the wing . . .

6.3c . . . and remove the front trim panel from the vehicle

6.4 Slacken and remove the three bumper retaining bolts

6.5a Undo the screws (arrowed) . . .

6.5b . . . then pull out the centre pins and remove the retaining fasteners . . .

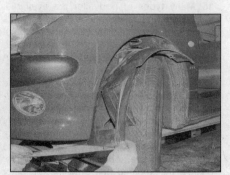

6.5c . . . and remove the front section of each wheel arch liner

6.7a Unscrew the nut (arrowed) securing the bumper ends to each wing . . .

6.7b . . . and the bolts securing the base of the bumper to the body

6.8 On models with front foglights, disconnect the wiring connector from each foglight

6.9 Free each end of the bumper from the wings and remove the bumper from the vehicle

7.2a Undo the retaining screws (one side arrowed) . . .

7.2b . . . and the retaining screws (arrowed) – Estate model shown

6 Remove the front section of the right-hand wheel arch liner in the same way.

7 Unscrew the nut securing each end of the bumper to the wings, and the two bolts securing the base of the bumper to the body **(see illustrations)**.

8 On models with foglights, disconnect the battery negative lead, and then disconnect the foglight wiring connectors **(see illustration)**.

9 Carefully free the bumper ends from the wings and withdraw the bumper from the front of the vehicle **(see illustration)**. On models equipped with headlight washers, disconnect the washer hose as the bumper is removed.

Refitting

10 Refitting is a reversal of removal, ensuring the bumper is correctly engaged with the wings.

7 Rear bumper – removal and refitting

Removal

1 For improved access, chock the front wheels, then jack up the rear of the vehicle and support securely on axle stands (see *Jacking and vehicle support*).

2 Open the tailgate/boot lid, and remove the bumper upper retaining screws **(see illustrations)**.

3 Undo the screw securing the right-hand wheel arch inner shield to the base of the bumper then remove the retaining fastener fasteners (pull out the centre pin then remove the complete fastener) and manoeuvre the shield out of position **(see illustrations)**. Remove the left-hand shield in the same way.

4 Working under the bumper, unscrew the two nuts securing the base of the bumper to

7.3a Undo the retaining screw . . .

7.3b . . . then remove the fastener (arrowed) . . .

7.3c . . . and remove the wheel arch inner shield from the rear bumper

7.4a Unscrew the nuts securing the base of the bumper to the vehicle . . .

7.4b . . . and the nut securing each end of the bumper to the body

7.5 Remove the rear bumper from the vehicle, disconnecting the wiring connector from the foglight

the body and the nut securing each end of the bumper in position **(see illustrations)**.

5 Free the ends of the bumper and remove the bumper from the vehicle, disconnecting the wiring connector from the rear foglight **(see illustration)**.

Refitting

6 Refitting is a reversal of removal.

8 Bonnet – removal, refitting and adjustment

Removal

1 Open the bonnet and have an assistant support it, then, using a pencil or felt tip pen, mark the outline of each bonnet hinge relative to the bonnet, to use as a guide on refitting.

2 Disconnect the windscreen washer fluid hose from its connector then unclip the hose from the bonnet **(see illustrations)**.

3 Unscrew the bonnet retaining nuts and, with the help of the assistant, carefully lift the bonnet from the vehicle **(see illustration)**. Store the bonnet out of the way in a safe place.

4 Inspect the bonnet hinges for signs of wear and free play at the pivots, and if necessary renew. Each hinge is secured to the body by two bolts. On refitting, apply a smear of multi-purpose grease to the hinges.

Refitting and adjustment

5 With the aid of an assistant, offer up the bonnet and loosely fit the retaining bolts. Align the hinges with the marks made on removal,

and then tighten the retaining nuts securely. Reconnect the windscreen washer hose and clip it securely to the bonnet.

6 Close the bonnet, and check for alignment with the adjacent panels. If necessary, slacken the hinge bolts and re-align the bonnet to suit. Once the bonnet is correctly aligned, tighten the hinge bolts securely.

7 Once the bonnet is correctly aligned, check that the bonnet fastens and releases in a satisfactory manner.

9 Bonnet release cable – removal and refitting

Removal

1 Remove the bonnet lock as described in Section 10.

2 Remove the retaining clips and free the outer cable from the front panel **(see illustration)**. Tie a length of string to the end of the cable then work back along the cable, freeing it from any retaining clips whilst noting its correct routing. Free the cable grommet from the bulkhead.

3 On left-hand drive models, to improve access to the release lever, remove the built-in systems interface (BSI) unit from the base of the fusebox (see Chapter 12).

4 On all models, reach up under the facia and unscrew the bolt securing the bonnet release lever to the body **(see illustration)**.

8.2a Disconnect the washer fluid hose from its connector . . .

8.2b . . . and unclip the hose from the bonnet

8.3 Unscrew the nuts (arrowed) securing the bonnet to the hinges and remove the bonnet from the vehicle

9.2 Release the retaining clips (arrowed) and free the bonnet release cable from the front panel

9.4 Bonnet release lever bolt (arrowed)

10.3 Disconnecting the bonnet lock switch wiring connector

10.4a Unscrew the bolts (arrowed) . . .

10.4b . . . then free the bonnet lock from the front panel and disconnect the release cable

5 Withdraw the release lever and cable assembly from the vehicle. When the end of the cable appears, untie the string and leave it in position; it can then be used to draw the cable back into position on refitting.

Refitting

6 Prior to refitting, lubricate the cable grommet with a silicone-based spray lubricant.
7 Tie the string to the end of the cable then use the string to draw the cable through the bulkhead and into the engine compartment.
8 Ensure the cable is correctly routed and retained by all the necessary clips then untie the string. Pull the cable grommet through and seat it correctly in the bulkhead.
9 Ensure the grommet is correctly located then seat the release cable lever correctly on

11.2 Unscrew the bolt securing the check strap to the door pillar

the body, tightening its retaining bolt to the specified torque. On left-hand drive models, refit the built-in system interface (BSI) unit (see Chapter 12).
10 Seat the outer cable correctly in the front panel. Ensure the cable is correctly routed then secure it in position with all the retaining clips.
11 Refit the bonnet lock as described in Section 10.

10 Bonnet lock – removal and refitting

Removal

1 Open the bonnet.
2 Remove the four fasteners (pull out the centre pin then remove the complete fastener) securing the grille panel to the top of the front panel. Release the lower retaining clips and unclip the grille panel from the front trim panel in an upward direction **(see illustrations 6.2a and 6.2b)**.
3 Trace the wiring back from the lock switch (where fitted) to its wiring connector. Free the connector from its retaining clip and separate the two halves of the connector **(see illustration)**.
4 Unscrew the retaining bolts and free the lock from the front panel then unclip the release cable and remove the lock from the vehicle **(see illustrations)**.

Refitting

5 Attach the lock to the release cable then seat the lock on the front panel and securely tighten its retaining bolts.
6 Reconnect the lock switch wiring connector and clip the connector onto the front panel.
7 Check the operation of the bonnet lock then refit the grille panel and secure it in position with the fasteners.

11 Door – removal, refitting and adjustment

Front door

Removal

1 Disconnect the battery negative lead.
2 Open the door then unscrew the bolt securing the door check strap to the pillar **(see illustration)**.
3 Rotate the door wiring harness connector locking ring anti-clockwise and disconnect the connector from the socket in the door pillar **(see illustration)**.
4 Have an assistant support the door, and then unscrew the pivot pins from the upper and lower hinges **(see illustration)**. The door can then be removed from the vehicle.
Caution: The door is heavy.

11.3 Rotate the locking ring anti-clockwise and disconnect the door connector from the pillar

11.4 Unscrew the hinge pins and remove the door from the vehicle

11.5a The hinges are secured to the door by a single bolt . . .

11.5b . . . and to the pillar by two bolts (arrowed)

5 If necessary, with the door removed, undo the retaining bolts and remove the hinges from the body and door **(see illustrations)**. Take care not to lose the hinge locating dowels.

Refitting

6 If the hinges were removed, ensure the locating dowels are in position, and then refit the hinges to the body and door. Tighten the hinge retaining bolts securely. If the paintwork around the hinges has been damaged, paint the affected area with a suitable touch-up brush to prevent corrosion.

7 Lubricate the hinge pivot pins with multi-purpose grease. With the aid of an assistant, offer up the door to the vehicle taking care not to damage the paintwork. Refit the pivot pins to the upper and lower hinges and tighten them securely.

8 Reconnect the door wiring connector and secure it in position by rotating the locking ring until the index marks align.

9 Seat the check link on the pillar and securely tighten its retaining bolt.

10 Reconnect the battery then close the door and check the door alignment.

Adjustment

11 Close the door and check its alignment with the surrounding panels. The hinges are located on dowels (unless they have been removed) so it is not possible to slacken the hinge bolts and reposition the hinges on the door/body. If the door is not correctly aligned,

check the hinges are not worn or damaged. If necessary, remove the door and renew the hinges.

12 If adjustment is necessary, remove the door and unbolt the hinge from the body. Refit the hinge to the body without the locating dowels, tightening the hinge bolts lightly, and install the door. Align the door correctly with its surrounding panels then tighten the hinge bolts securely; the bolts can be accessed from behind the wheel arch once the liner has been freed.

Rear door

Removal

13 Disconnect the battery negative lead.

14 Open the front door to gain access to the rear door wiring harness connector. Rotate the connector locking ring anti-clockwise and disconnect the connector from the socket in the door pillar **(see illustration)**.

15 Unscrew the bolt securing the door check strap to the pillar.

16 Have an assistant support the door, and then unscrew the pivot pins from the upper and lower hinges **(see illustration)**. The door can then be removed from the vehicle.

Caution: The door is heavy.

17 If necessary, with the door removed, undo the retaining bolts and remove the hinges from the body and door. Take care not to lose the locating dowel fitted to the door side of the hinge.

Refitting

18 If the hinges were removed, ensure the locating dowel is in position, and then refit the hinges to the body and door. Ensure the hinges are correctly located then tighten their retaining bolts securely. If the paintwork around the hinges has been damaged, paint the affected area with a suitable touch-up brush to prevent corrosion.

19 Lubricate the hinge pivot pins with multi-purpose grease. With the aid of an assistant, offer up the door to the vehicle taking care not to damage the paintwork. Refit the pivot pins to the upper and lower hinges and tighten them securely.

20 Reconnect the door wiring connector and secure it in position by rotating the locking ring until the index marks align.

21 Seat the check link on the pillar and securely tighten its retaining bolt.

22 Reconnect the battery then close the door and check the door alignment.

Adjustment

23 Close the door and check its alignment with the surrounding panels. The door side of the hinge is located on a dowel (unless it has been removed) and the body side of the hinges has built-in locating pin, so it is not possible to slacken the hinge bolts and reposition the hinges on the door/body. If the door is not correctly aligned, check the hinges are not worn or damaged. If necessary, remove the door and renew the hinges.

24 If adjustment is necessary, remove the door and door hinges. Enlarge the hinge locating pin holes in the pillar slightly using a drill. Refit the hinges to the door without the locating dowels and refit the hinges to the pillar. Lightly tighten the hinge bolts and install the door. Align the door correctly with its surrounding panels then tighten the hinge bolts securely.

12 Door inner trim panel
– removal and refitting

Note: *Door trim panel design varies according to the specification level of the vehicle and therefore some of the trim panel fasteners locations on your vehicle may be different to those shown in the accompanying illustrations.*

Removal

1 Fully lower the window glass then disconnect the battery negative terminal. Proceed as described under the relevant sub-heading.

Front door

2 Carefully unclip the exterior mirror inner trim panel from the front of the door. On models with manually-adjusted mirrors, remove the rubber gaiter from the adjustment handle prior to unclipping the trim panel. Rotate the

11.14 Rotate the locking ring anti-clockwise and disconnect the door wiring connector

11.16 Unscrew the hinge pins and remove the rear door

12.2a Unclip the exterior mirror inner trim panel from the door

12.2b Rotate the tweeter speaker (where fitted) to free it from the mirror panel

12.4 Carefully prise out the handle surround from the trim panel

12.5 Remove the retaining screw (arrowed) at the edge of the panel – Cabriolet Coupe shown

12.6 Undo the screw securing the trim panel pocket in position

12.7 Unclip the base of the trim panel from the door then remove the panel in an upwards direction

tweeter speaker (where fitted) to free it from the panel then remove the panel from the vehicle **(see illustrations)**.

3 On models with manually-operated windows, pull the window winder regulator handle off its spindle and remove it, along with the spacer.

4 Carefully prise out the door lock inner handle surround from the panel **(see illustration)**.

5 Slacken and remove the retaining screw(s) from the front and rear edge of the trim panel **(see illustration)**.

6 Slacken and remove the screw securing the trim panel pocket to the door **(see illustration)**.

7 Make a final check that all the retaining screws have been removed then carefully

unclip the base of the trim panel from the door and manoeuvre it upwards and away from the door **(see illustration)**.

Rear door

8 On models with manually-operated windows, pull the window winder regulator handle off its spindle **(see illustration)**.

9 Carefully prise out the door lock inner handle surround from the panel **(see illustration)**.

10 Slacken and remove the retaining screw securing the trim panel pocket to the door.

11 Carefully unclip the base of the trim panel from the door and manoeuvre it upwards and away from the door **(see illustration)**.

Refitting

12 Refitting is a reversal of removal. Prior to

refitting, check the trim panel retaining studs for signs of damage and renew any that were broken on removal.

13 Door handles and lock components – removal and refitting

Door lock inner handle

Removal

1 Remove the inner trim panel as described in Section 12.

2 Remove the alignment peg(s) from the top of the foam insulation panel then carefully peel/cut the panel away from the door sufficiently

12.8 On models with manual windows, pull off the regulator handle and remove the spacer (arrowed)

12.9 Unclip the inner handle surround from the trim panel

12.11 Unclip the base of the trim panel from the door then remove the panel in an upwards direction

13.2a Remove the alignment peg(s) . . .

13.2b . . . then carefully cut the insulation panel away from the door to gain access to the handle/lock (front door shown)

13.3 Free the inner handle from the door and unhook it from the end of the link rod

to gain access to the handle and lock **(see illustrations)**. **Note:** *This is likely to result in the insulation panel being torn or damaged. If this is the case, remove the panel completely and discard it and obtain a new panel for use on refitting. On the rear door the loudspeaker and housing will need to be removed from the door (see Chapter 12) before the insulation panel can be removed.*

3 Slide the handle forwards to unclip it from the door, and then detach it from the end of the link rod **(see illustration)**.

Refitting

4 Engage the handle with the link rod then clip the handle securely into the door.

5 Check the operation of the handle and lock assembly then securely stick the insulation panel back to the door **(see illustrations)**. **Note:** *If a new insulation panel is being fitted, remove all traces of the original adhesive from the door with a suitable solvent. Align the new panel with the door then install the alignment peg(s) before carefully sticking the panel to the door, ensuring its is not creased or torn. On the rear door, refit the loudspeaker (see Chapter 12).*

6 Refit the inner trim panel as described in Section 12.

Front door lock

Removal

7 Remove the inner handle and lock cylinder from the door as described elsewhere in this section.

8 Fully raise the window glass.

9 Free the inner handle link rod from its guide **(see illustration)**.

10 Unclip and detach the exterior handle link rod from the lock.

11 Peel the lock button foam guide away from the door so it is free to be removed with the lock assembly **(see illustration)**.

12 Slacken and remove the three screws securing the lock to the door **(see illustration)**.

13 Manoeuvre the lock out of position then release the retaining clip and disconnect the wiring connector **(see illustration)**.

Refitting

14 Refitting is the reverse of removal. Prior to sticking the insulation panel to the door, reconnect the battery and check the operation

13.5a Install the alignment peg(s) . . .

13.5b . . . then stick the insulation panel securely to the door, taking care not to crease or tear it (rear door shown)

13.9 Unclip the handle link rod from its guide

13.11 Free the lock button foam guide from the door

13.12 Undo the screws (arrowed) securing the lock to the door

13.13 Manoeuvre the lock assembly out of position then lift the retaining clip and disconnect its wiring connector

13.19 Door handle is secured in position with pop rivets (arrowed)

13.21 Remove the plug from the rear of the front door . . .

13.22 . . . then insert the removal tool in through the hole and screw it into the lock cylinder retaining clip

of the lock and handles. If all is well stick the panel securely in position (see paragraph 5) then refit the trim panel (Section 12).

Front door exterior handle

Note: *A pop rivet gun and suitable rivets will be required on refitting.*

Removal

15 Remove the inner trim panel as described in Section 12.
16 Remove the alignment peg(s) from the top of the foam insulation panel then carefully peel/cut the panel away from the door sufficiently to gain access to the handle and lock. **Note:** *This is likely to result in the insulation panel being torn or damaged. If this is the case, remove the panel completely, discard it and obtain a new panel for use on refitting.*
17 Fully raise the window glass.
18 Unclip and detach the exterior handle link rod from the lock.
19 Lift the handle then carefully drill the heads off the pop rivets securing the handle to the door **(see illustration)**.
Caution: Take care not to damage the handle/door when drilling out the rivets.

Refitting

20 Refitting is the reverse of removal, securing the handle in position with new pop rivets. Prior to sticking the insulation panel to the door, reconnect the battery and check the operation of the lock and handles. If all is well stick the panel securely in position (see paragraph 5) then refit the trim panel (Section 12).

Front door lock cylinder

Note: *This procedure requires the use of Peugeot special lock removal tool. A suitable alternative can be made by brazing a medium-size self-tapping screw to the end of a piece of rod.*

Removal/refitting with special tool

21 Open the door. Prise out the plug from the rear of the door to gain access to the lock cylinder retaining clip **(see illustration)**.
22 Carefully insert the removal tool in through the door aperture and screw it securely into the retaining clip **(see illustration)**.
23 Pull on the tool to release the retaining clip from the lock cylinder then manoeuvre the lock cylinder out of position **(see illustration)**. Whilst the lock cylinder is removed, leave the removal tool in position.
24 Ensure the lock cylinder seal is in good condition then manoeuvre the cylinder into position. Engage the lock cylinder pin with the lock then seat the cylinder in the door. Hold the lock cylinder firmly against the door then secure it in position by sliding the retaining clip onto the lock. Ensure the lock cylinder is securely retained by the clip then check the operation of the lock assembly **(see illustration)**. Unscrew the removal tool from the retaining clip then refit the access plug to the door. **Note:** *Do not remove the tool from the retaining clip until you are certain the lock cylinder and retaining clip are correctly fitted.*

Removal/refitting without special tool

25 Remove the inner trim panel as described in Section 12.
26 Remove the alignment peg(s) from the top of the foam insulation panel then carefully peel/cut the panel away from the door sufficiently to gain access to the handle and lock. **Note:** *This is likely to result in the insulation panel being torn or damaged. If this is the case, remove the panel completely, discard it and obtain a new panel for use on refitting.*
27 Fully raise the window glass.
28 Slide the retaining clip off the lock cylinder then manoeuvre the cylinder out from the door.
29 Refitting is the reverse of removal. Prior to sticking the insulation panel to the door, reconnect the battery and check the operation of the lock and handles. If all is well stick the panel securely in position (see paragraph 5) then refit the trim panel (Section 12).

Rear door lock

Removal

30 Remove the inner handle as described in paragraphs 1 to 3.
31 Fully raise the window glass.
32 Free the inner handle link rod from its guide.
33 Unclip the inner locking button pivot from the door **(see illustration)**. Free the button link rod from its guide and ease the button out of its foam guide so it is free to be removed with the lock.

13.23 Pull the tool to the rear to release the retaining clip then manoeuvre the lock cylinder out of position

13.24 Ensure the lock cylinder pin (1) engages correctly with the lock then secure the lock cylinder in position by sliding the retaining clip (2) back into position (shown with panel removed)

13.33 Unclip the inner locking button pivot from the door and free the button from its foam guide

34 Slacken and remove the three screws securing the lock to the door **(see illustration)**.

35 Release the retaining clip and disconnect the wiring connector from the lock then manoeuvre the lock assembly out of position **(see illustration)**.

Refitting

36 Refitting is the reverse of removal. Prior to sticking the insulation panel to the door, reconnect the battery and check the operation of the lock and handles. If all is well stick the panel securely in position (see paragraph 5) then refit the trim panel (Section 12).

Rear door exterior handle – except Estate models

Note: *A pop rivet gun and suitable rivets will be required on refitting.*

Removal

37 Lift the handle then carefully drill the heads off the pop rivets securing the handle to the door. The handle can then be removed from the door.

Caution: Take care not to damage the handle/door when drilling out the rivets.

Refitting

40 Refitting is the reverse of removal.

Rear door exterior handle – Estate models

Removal

39 Open the rear door, unclip the blanking plugs from inside he door pillar, and then undo the retaining nuts **(see illustrations)**.

40 Carefully unclip the door handle from the outside of the door and disconnect the linkage rod from the rear of the handle **(see illustrations)**.

Refitting

41 Refitting is the reverse of removal, making sure the linkage rod is securely located.

13.34 Remove the retaining screws (arrowed) . . .

13.35 . . . then disconnect the wiring connector and manoeuvre the lock out from the rear door

13.39a Remove the blanking plugs . . .

13.39b . . . and undo the retaining nuts (arrowed)

---

14 Door window glass and regulator – removal and refitting

Removal

1 Remove the inner trim panel as described in Section 12.

2 Remove the alignment peg(s) from the top of the foam insulation panel then carefully peel/cut the panel away from the door sufficiently to gain access to the regulator and window glass **(see illustrations 13.2a and 13.2b)**. Note: *This is likely to result in the insulation panel being torn or damaged. If this is the case, remove the panel completely and discard it and obtain a new panel for use on*

refitting. On the rear door the loudspeaker and housing will need to be removed from the door (see Chapter 12) before the insulation panel can be removed.

Window glass

3 Remove the inner sealing strip from the top of the door, noting which way around it is fitted **(see illustration)**.

4 Position the window approximately two-thirds of the way down so access can be gained to the glass retaining clips/bolts on the regulator guide(s) (the front window has two clips/bolts and guides, the rear window has one).

5 On all models (except Cabriolet Coupe), depress the retaining clip(s) with a screwdriver then release the window glass from the

13.40a Carefully unclip the door handle . . .

13.40b . . . and unclip the linkage rod (arrowed)

14.3 Remove the inner sealing strip from the top of the door

14.5a Depress the retaining clip (arrowed) and slide the window glass out from the regulator guide . . .

14.5b . . . then lift it out from the door

14.6a On Cabriolet Coupe models undo the front retaining bolt (arrowed) . . .

regulator guide(s) and carefully manoeuvre it upwards and out from the top of the door **(see illustrations)**.

6 On Cabriolet Coupe models, remove the two retaining bolts from the window regulator guides and carefully manoeuvre it upwards and out from the top of the door **(see illustrations)**.

Window regulator

Note: *On some models, the window regulator is held in position using pop rivets. A pop rivet gun and suitable rivets will be required on refitting this type.*

7 Remove the window glass as described in paragraphs 3 to 6

8 On models with electric windows, release the retaining clip and disconnect the wiring

connector from the regulator motor **(see illustration)**.

9 On all models (except Cabriolet Coupe), carefully drill the heads off the pop rivets securing the regulator mechanism to the door **(see illustrations)**.

Caution: Take care not to damage the regulator/door when drilling out the rivets.

10 On Cabriolet Coupe models, remove the rubber grommets and undo the retaining nuts from the window regulator guides **(see illustrations)**.

11 Before the front door regulator is removed, it will be necessary to unclip the regulator cable clip from the door. Free the regulator mechanism from the door and manoeuvre it out of position **(see illustration)**.

14.6b . . . and the rear retaining bolt (arrowed)

14.8 On models with electric windows disconnect the wiring connector from the regulator motor

14.9a Carefully drill the heads off all the pop rivets securing the regulator to the door

14.9b If the front door regulator is being removed free the cable clip from the door

14.10a Remove the lower retaining nuts (one arrowed) . . .

14.10b . . . and upper retaining nuts (one arrowed)

14.11 Manoeuvre the regulator out through the door aperture

14.15a Carefully cut around the foam insulation panel . . .

14.15b . . . and remove from the rear quarter panel

14.16 Unclip the weather strip from the top of the rear quarter panel

Rear side window glass – Cabriolet Coupe models

12 Remove the rear seat cushion as described in Section 24.

13 Release the retaining clips and withdraw the upper trim panel from the rear quarter panel **(see illustrations 26.20a and 26.20b)**.

14 Release the retaining clips and withdraw the inner rear trim panel **(see illustrations 26.21a and 26.21b)**.

15 Carefully peel/cut the foam insulation panel away from the rear panel aperture **(see illustration)**, to gain access to the regulator and window glass. **Note:** *There are two insulation panels, an inner and outer panel. It is likely to result in the insulation panel being torn or damaged. If this is the case, remove the panel completely and discard it and obtain a new panel for use on refitting.*

16 Unclip the weather strip from the top of the rear quarter panel **(see illustration)**.

17 Slacken the two upper mounting bolts and push the assembly towards the inside of the vehicle and retighten the bolts **(see illustration)**.

18 Slacken the lower regulator mounting bolt **(see illustration)**.

19 Raise the rear window until the window regulator mounting bolts are in view, and then remove the three bolts **(see illustration)**.

20 Support the window glass and lower the window regulator slightly, and then carefully manoeuvre the glass out from the rear panel.

Rear window regulator – Cabriolet Coupe models

21 Remove the rear window glass as described in paragraphs 12 to 20.

22 Release the retaining clip and disconnect the wiring connector from the regulator motor **(see illustration)**.

23 Remove the lower regulator mounting bolt **(see illustration 14.18)**.

24 Slacken and remove the two upper mounting bolts **(see illustration 14.17)**.

25 Free the regulator mechanism from the aperture and manoeuvre it out of the rear panel.

Refitting

Window glass

26 Manoeuvre the glass back into position in the door/quarter panel and engage it with the regulator guide(s). Ensure the glass is securely retained by the guide clip(s) or retaining nuts.

27 On Cabriolet Coupe models, tighten the lower regulator mounting bolt. Also slacken the upper retaining bolts, push the assembly towards the outside of the vehicle and retighten the bolts.

28 Refit the sealing strip to the top of the door/quarter panel, ensuring it is the correct way around.

29 Check the operation of the window then securely stick the insulation panel back to the door. **Note:** *If a new insulation panel is being fitted, remove all traces of the original adhesive from the door with a suitable solvent. Align the new panel with the door then install the alignment pegs before carefully sticking the panel to the door, ensuring its is not creased or torn* **(see illustrations 13.5a and 13.5b)**. *On the rear door, refit the loudspeaker (see Chapter 12).*

30 Refit the inner trim panel as described in the relevant Section of this Chapter.

Window regulator

31 Where applicable, remove the remnants of the original rivets from the regulator/door. Then manoeuvre the regulator into position in the door and align it with its mountings. **Note:** *If the front door mechanism is being installed, take great care not to twist the regulator cables on installation.*

32 Ensure the regulator is correctly positioned then secure it in position with retaining nuts or new pop rivets.

33 Refit the window glass as described in paragraphs 26 to 30.

34 Reconnect the wiring connector (where

14.17 Slacken the two retaining bolts (arrowed)

14.18 Slacken the lower mounting bolt (arrowed)

14.19 Undo the three retaining nuts (arrowed)

14.22 Disconnect the wiring connector (arrowed)

15.3 Pull out the centre pin and remove the fastener securing the luggage compartment side trim panel to the body

15.4 Remove the courtesy light from the left-hand upper trim panel and disconnect it from the wiring connector

15.5a Undo the retaining screws (arrowed) . . .

necessary) then check the operation of the window before securely sticking the insulation panel back to the door. **Note:** *If a new insulation panel is being fitted, remove all traces of the original adhesive from the door with a suitable solvent. Align the new panel with the door then install the alignment peg(s) before carefully sticking the panel to the door, ensuring its is not creased or torn (see illustrations 13.5a and 13.5b). On the rear door, refit the loudspeaker (see Chapter 12).*

35 Refit the inner trim panel as described in the relevant Section of this Chapter.

---

15 Tailgate/boot lid and support struts – removal and refitting

Hatchback tailgate

Note: *Obtain a connector to enable the tailgate washer hose to be joined on refitting.*

Removal

1 Open the tailgate and then disconnect the battery negative lead.
2 Fold down the rear seats then remove the parcel shelf.
3 Remove the fastener(s) (pull out the centre

pin then remove the complete fastener) and free the luggage compartment left-hand side trim panel from the body to gain access to the tailgate wiring connector **(see illustration)**.
4 Remove the luggage compartment courtesy light from the upper trim panel and disconnect it from the wiring connector **(see illustration)**.
5 Slacken and remove the retaining screws securing the left-hand upper trim panel to the rear pillar then unclip the panel and free it from the body **(see illustrations)**.
6 Unscrew the bolt securing the tailgate earth lead to the rear pillar then lift the retaining clip and disconnect the tailgate wiring harness connector. Release the wiring from its retaining

clips then free the wiring harness grommet from the body and withdraw the wiring **(see illustrations)**.
7 Free the tailgate washer hose grommet from the right-hand side of the body and cut the tailgate washer hose; a connector will be required to rejoin the hose on refitting **(see illustration)**. **Note:** *If it is not wished to cut the washer hose, remove the high-level stop-light (see Chapter 12, Section 7) then withdraw the hose from the tailgate.*
8 Have an assistant support the tailgate then carefully lift the retaining clips and detach both support struts from the tailgate **(see illustration)**.
9 Unscrew the nuts securing the hinges to the

15.5b . . . then unclip the left-hand upper trim panel from the body

15.6a Disconnect the tailgate wiring harness connector (1) and unbolt the earth lead (2) . . .

15.6b . . . then free the wiring harness grommet from the body and withdraw the wiring

15.7 Free the washer hose grommet from the right-hand side of the body and cut the tailgate washer hose

15.8 Lift the retaining clip and detach each support strut from the tailgate

15.9 Unscrew the nuts securing the tailgate to the hinges and remove the tailgate

15.14a Undo the grab handle securing screws . . .

15.14b . . . and release the retaining clips

tailgate, and then carefully remove the tailgate from the vehicle (see illustration).

10 Inspect the hinges for signs of wear or damage. If renewal is necessary, free the tailgate sealing strip from the top of its aperture then carefully unclip the upper trim panel from the rear of the roof. Carefully peel back the headlining to gain access to the hinge nuts. Draw around the outline of each hinge then undo the retaining nuts and remove the hinges from the vehicle. Fit the new hinges, aligning them with the marks made prior to removal, and securely tighten the hinge retaining nuts. Clip the headlining back into position and refit the upper trim panel. Ensure the panel is correctly refitted then seat the sealing strip back on the body.

15.15 Tailgate wiring loom grommet (arrowed)

Refitting

11 Refitting is a reversal of removal. Prior to refitting the trim panels, reconnect the battery and check the operation of all the tailgate electrical components. On completion, ensure the tailgate is correctly aligned with its surrounding panels; adjustments can be made by slackening the hinge bolts and reposition the tailgate and by adjusting the tailgate rubber buffers.

Estate tailgate

Removal

12 Remove the tailgate glass as described in Section 21.

13 Open the tailgate, and then disconnect the battery negative lead.

14 Undo the retaining screws and remove the handle from the inner trim panel, and then release the securing clips and remove the inner trim panel from the tailgate (see illustrations).

15 Disconnect the wiring connectors from the electrical components inside the tailgate and withdraw the loom from the top of the tailgate (see illustration).

16 With the aid of an assistant, support the tailgate, mark the position of the upper hinge mounting brackets on each side of the vehicle, and then slacken and remove the retaining nuts (see illustration). Carefully remove the tailgate from the vehicle.

Refitting

17 Refitting is a reversal of removal. Prior to refitting the trim panels, reconnect the battery and check the operation of all the tailgate electrical components. On completion, ensure the tailgate is correctly aligned with its surrounding panels; adjustments can be made by slackening the hinge bolts and reposition the tailgate and by adjusting the tailgate rubber buffers.

Cabriolet Coupe boot assembly

Note: *This is a complex procedure and will need an assistant to carry out some of the procedures. The vehicle will need to be with the roof in the up position.*

Removal

18 Make sure the both rear quarter glass windows are in the lowered position and then disconnect the battery negative lead.

19 Open the boot lid and release the luggage cover screen from its clips (see illustration) and fold it away.

20 Using the Allen key (4 mm) supplied with the vehicle breakdown kit, turn the hydraulic unit load reduction screw on the hydraulic pump a quarter of a turn in the anti-clockwise direction (see illustration).
Caution: Always make sure the hydraulic pump load reduction screw has been set in the safe position before working on any components.

15.16 Tailgate hinge retaining nuts (arrowed)

15.19 Release the luggage cover from its retaining clips (arrowed)

15.20 Allen key (arrowed) to adjust hydraulic unit load reduction screw

15.21 Removing the inner trim cover from the luggage compartment

15.22 Removing the side trim cover from the luggage compartment

15.23 Move the retaining hook (arrowed) to release the catch

21 Remove the retaining clips and remove the upper cover from the rear of the luggage compartment (see illustration).

22 Remove the retaining clips and remove the both side trim panels from the luggage compartment (see illustration).

23 Move the retaining hook to release the lower striker plate on the upper part of the boot lid (see illustration).

24 Close the complete boot lid and open the upper part of the boot lid from the rear screen backwards.

25 Lock the upper part of the boot lid by inserting the Allen key (4 mm) supplied with the vehicle breakdown kit, into the hinge bracket on the right-hand rear of the vehicle (see illustrations).

 Warning: Always make sure the upper part of the boot lid is locked in position and cannot move before working on any components.

26 Release the upper and lower retaining clips and remove the hydraulic struts complete with pipes, do not disconnect the hydraulic lines. Unclip any cable-ties from the hydraulic pipes and move the struts to one side (see illustration).

27 Disconnect the wiring connector and release the wiring harness from the left-hand side of the luggage compartment (see illustration). Work your way along the wiring harness and release it from any cable-ties.

28 With the aid of an assistant, release the roof catches and carefully fold the roof assembly into the luggage compartment. Take care not to damage the roof assembly as it is lowered.

29 Remove the rear seat cushion as described in Section 24.

30 Release the retaining clips and withdraw the upper trim panel from the rear quarter panel (see illustrations 26.20a and 26.20b).

31 Release the retaining clips and withdraw the inner rear trim panel (see illustrations 26.21a and 26.21b).

32 Undo the retaining nuts and remove the rear headrests (see illustrations 26.59a and 26.59b).

33 Remove the retaining clips and unclip the rear trim panel from the vehicle (see illustrations 26.60a and 26.60b).

34 Withdraw the Allen key from the hinge bracket on the right-hand rear of the vehicle (see illustrations 15.25a and 15.25b).

35 Close the upper part of the boot lid, securing it in the locking catch and open the complete boot lid assembly.

36 With the aid of an assistant, support the boot lid and release the securing clips and disconnect the struts from the boot lid (see illustration).

37 With the aid of an assistant, lower the boot lid until it rests on the lock, without locking it.

38 Mark the position of the upper hinge mounting brackets on each side of the vehicle,

15.25a Locking the upper boot lid in the open position . . .

15.25b . . . using an Allen key (arrowed) – supplied in the breakdown kit

15.26 Strut upper retaining clip (arrowed)

15.27 Disconnect the wiring loom connectors (arrowed)

15.36 Release the securing clip (arrowed) from the strut

15.38 Hinge mounting bracket retaining nuts (arrowed)

15.42a Unclip the plastic cover . . .

15.42b . . . undo the securing screws (arrowed) . . .

and then slacken and remove the retaining nuts **(see illustration)**.

39 Check that there is nothing still attached to the boot lid and, with the aid of an assistant, lift the boot lid assembly from the vehicle and place it somewhere safe.

Refitting

40 Refitting is a reversal of removal, noting the following points:

a) *An assistant will be required to help refit the boot assembly.*

b) *Ensure the boot lid is correctly aligned with its surrounding panels.*

c) *Tighten the upper hinge mounting nuts in the position noted on removal.*

d) *Prior to refitting the trim panels, reconnect the battery and check the operation of all the boot lid assembly electrical components.*

e) *Make sure all the hydraulic pipes and*

wiring loom are securely refitted using cable-ties, to prevent any damage to them.

f) *Using the Allen key (4 mm) supplied with the vehicle breakdown kit, turn the hydraulic unit load reduction screw on the hydraulic pump a quarter of a turn in the clockwise direction (see illustration 15.20).*

Cabriolet Coupe boot upper cover

Note: *The vehicle will need to be with the roof in the up position.*

Removal

41 Open the boot lid and release the luggage cover screen from its clips **(see illustration 15.19)** and fold it away.

42 Unclip the plastic cover, and then undo

the retaining screws and remove the handle from the inner trim panel. Release the securing clips and remove the inner trim panel from the boot lid **(see illustrations)**.

43 Close the complete boot lid and open the upper part of the boot lid from the rear screen backwards.

44 Lock the upper part of the boot lid by inserting the Allen key (4 mm) supplied with the vehicle breakdown kit into the hinge bracket on the right-hand rear of the vehicle (see illustrations 15.25a and 15.25b).

⚠ **Warning: Always make sure the upper part of the boot lid is locked in position and cannot move before working on any components.**

45 Slacken and remove the three securing screws and remove the plastic trim cover from the underside of the boot upper cover **(see illustration)**.

46 Undo the retaining nuts and remove the catch from the underside of the boot lid **(see illustration)**.

47 Working your way around the outside edge of the upper boot lid cover, unclip the wiring loom and cables from any retaining clips **(see illustration)**.

48 With the aid of an assistant, support the upper boot lid, mark the position of the hinge mounting brackets on each side of the vehicle, and then slacken and remove the retaining bolts **(see illustration)**. Carefully remove the upper boot lid from the vehicle.

Refitting

49 Refitting is a reversal of removal. On

15.42c . . . and release the retaining clips

15.45 Undo the three retaining screws (arrowed)

15.46 Undo the two catch retaining nuts (arrowed)

15.47 Release the wiring and cables from the retaining clips

15.48 Slacken and remove the bolts (arrowed)

15.51 Lift the retaining clips and free the support strut from its balljoints

16.3a Release the retaining clips . . .

16.3b . . . and remove the lock cover

completion, ensure the upper boot lid is correctly aligned with its surrounding panels.

Support struts

Removal

50 Support the tailgate/boot lid in the open position, with the help of an assistant, or using a stout piece of wood.
51 Using a small flat-bladed screwdriver, carefully lift the retaining clips and unhook the support strut from its balljoints **(see illustration)**.

Refitting

52 Refitting is a reversal of removal ensuring the strut is fitted the correct way around and is securely held by its retaining clips.

16 Tailgate/boot lid lock components – removal and refitting

Removal

1 Open the tailgate/boot lid, and then disconnect the battery negative terminal.
2 Undo the retaining screws and remove the grab handle from the inside of the tailgate/ boot lid. Release the retaining clips and carefully unclip the inner trim panel from the tailgate/boot lid.
3 On Estate models, open the tailgate glass and remove the plastic cover from the tailgate glass locking catch **(see illustrations)**.

Lock catch – Hatchback

4 Unclip the lock link rod from the handle assembly **(see illustration)**.
5 Unscrew the two retaining screws and remove the lock catch from the tailgate **(see illustrations)**.

Lock handle – Hatchback

6 Unclip the lock link rod from the handle assembly.
7 Disconnect the wiring connector from the central locking motor.
8 Unscrew the two retaining nuts then manoeuvre the handle assembly out of position. If necessary the outer trim strip can then be unclipped and removed from the tailgate **(see illustrations)**.

16.4 Unclip the link rod from the handle . . .

16.5a . . . then undo the retaining screws (arrowed) . . .

16.5b . . . and remove the lock assembly from the tailgate

16.8a Undo the retaining nuts (arrowed) . . .

16.8b . . . and remove the lock handle from the tailgate

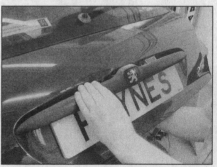

16.8c With the lock handle removed, the outer trim strip can be unclipped

16.9 Disconnect the wiring connector (arrowed)

16.10 Undo the two lock retaining screws (arrowed)

16.11 Undo the four retaining nuts (arrowed)

16.12 Disconnect the wiring connectors

16.13 Unclip the handle from the trim panel

16.14 Lock assembly linkage rods (arrowed)

Lock catch – Estate

9 Disconnect the wiring connector from the lock assembly **(see illustration)**.
10 Unscrew the two retaining screws and remove the lock from the tailgate **(see illustration)**.

Lock handle – Estate

11 Undo the retaining nuts and release the lock handle trim from above the rear number plate **(see illustration)**.
12 Disconnect the wiring connectors from the door handles and the number plate lights **(see illustration)**.
13 Release the securing clip and withdraw

the tailgate handle from the outer trim panel **(see illustration)**.

Lock assembly – Cabriolet Coupe

14 Unclip the lock link rods from the lock assembly **(see illustration)**.
15 Unscrew the two retaining screws and remove the lock catch from the boot lid **(see illustration)**.
16 Unscrew the three retaining screws and remove the lock from the boot lid **(see illustration)**.

Refitting

17 Refitting is the reverse of removal ensuring

the link rods are securely reconnected. Check the operation of the lock and handle before refitting the trim panel.

17 Central locking components – removal and refitting

Door lock motor

1 Each door lock motor is integral with the lock assembly and cannot be renewed separately. If the motor is faulty, the complete lock assembly must be renewed (see Section 13).

16.15 Lock catch retaining bolts (arrowed)

16.16 Boot lock retaining screws (arrowed)

17.3a Disconnect the wiring connector then undo the retaining screw (arrowed) and remove the tailgate lock motor

17.3b Undo the two retaining screws (arrowed) – Cabriolet Coupe model

19.5 Disconnect the mirror wiring connector . . .

Tailgate/boot lock motor

2 Carefully unclip the inner trim panel from the tailgate/boot lid.

3 Disconnect the wiring connector then undo the retaining screw and remove the motor from the lock linkage **(see illustrations)**.

4 Refitting is the reverse of removal. Check the operation of the motor before refitting the trim panel.

Electronic control unit (ECU)

5 The central locking system control unit (ECU) and the remote signal receiver are an integral part of the built-in systems interface (BSI) unit. Refer to Chapter 12 for removal and refitting details.

Remote control batteries

6 Using a small screwdriver, carefully prise the two halves of the transmitter apart, and remove the battery, noting which way round it is fitted.

7 Fit the new battery, ensuring that it is fitted the correct way round; the battery and transmitter terminals are marked + and – to avoid confusion. Clip the transmitter back together and check the operation of the transmitter. If the transmitter does not function correctly, reprogram the unit as follows.

a) Press and hold the transmitter locking button until the indicator light on the transmitter stops flashing then release the button. The indicator light should remain on.

b) With the indicator light lit, press the locking button twice then insert the key and turn on the ignition. Wait at least three seconds then switch the ignition off. The transmitter should now be reprogrammed and function as normal.

18 Electric window components renewal – general information

Window switches

1 Refer to Chapter 12.

Window winder motors

2 At the time of writing it was unclear whether the window winder motors were available separately or whether the complete regulator assembly would have to be renewed. Refer to your Peugeot dealer for the latest information. Regulator removal and refitting is described in Section 14.

19 Exterior mirrors and associated components – removal and refitting

Manually-adjusted mirror

1 Remove the rubber gaiter from the mirror adjustment handle, then carefully unclip the mirror inner trim panel from the door. Where necessary, rotate the tweeter speaker (where

fitted) to free it from the panel then remove the panel from the vehicle.

2 Slacken and remove the three retaining screws and remove the mirror from the door. Recover the rubber seal, which is fitted between the door and mirror; if the seal is damaged, it must be renewed.

3 Refitting is the reverse of removal, ensuring the seal is correctly positioned.

Electrically-adjusted mirror

4 Carefully unclip the mirror inner trim panel from the door. Where necessary, rotate the tweeter speaker to free it from the panel then remove the panel from the vehicle **(see illustrations 12.2a and 12.2b)**.

5 Disconnect the mirror wiring connector **(see illustration)**.

6 Slacken and remove the three retaining screws and remove the mirror from the door. Recover the rubber seal which is fitted between the door and mirror. If the seal is damaged, it must be renewed **(see illustrations)**.

7 Refitting is the reverse of removal, ensuring the seal is correctly positioned **(see illustration)**.

Mirror glass

Note: *The mirror glass is clipped in position. Removal of the glass is likely to result in breakage if carried out carelessly. It is advisable to wear gloves when carrying out this procedure.*

8 Tilt the mirror glass fully inwards. Insert a small flat-bladed screwdriver inbetween the

19.6a . . . then undo the retaining screws (arrowed) . . .

19.6b . . . and remove the mirror assembly from the door

19.7 On refitting, ensure the mirror seal is correctly fitted

19.8 Unhook the mirror glass retaining clip (arrowed) . . .

19.9 . . . then unclip the glass and disconnect the wiring connectors (arrowed) from the heating element

19.10 Ensure the retaining clip is correctly fitted before refitting the glass to the housing

outer edge of the mirror glass and housing, and unhook the retaining clip from the rear of the mirror **(see illustration)**.

9 Once the clip has been released, carefully unclip the glass from the motor/adjuster. Take great care when removing the glass; do not use excessive force as the glass is easily broken. Remove the glass from the mirror, where necessary, disconnecting the wiring connectors from the mirror heating element **(see illustration)**.

10 On refitting, ensure the retaining clips is correctly fitted to the rear of the glass then reconnect the wiring (where necessary) and clip the glass onto the mirror/adjuster, taking care not to break it **(see illustration)**. Ensure the glass is clipped securely into position and adjust as necessary.

Mirror switch

11 Refer to Chapter 12.

Mirror motor

12 Remove the mirror glass as described above.
13 Undo the retaining screws and free the motor from the housing. Disconnect the wiring and remove the motor.
14 Refitting is the reverse of removal.

Outside temperature sensor

Note: *This is fitted to the passenger side mirror.*

15 Remove the mirror glass as described above.

16 Undo the retaining screws and free the motor from the mirror housing.
17 Slacken and remove the two screws from the base of the mirror housing **(see illustration)**.
18 Carefully, taking great care not to damage the plastic, ease the temperature sensor out from the base of the mirror housing.
19 Mark the sensor wires for identification then cut the wires and remove the sensor.
20 Refitting is the reverse of removal, ensuring the sensor wires are correctly reconnected (Peugeot recommend that the wires are soldered) and insulated.

20 Rear quarter window (three-door models) – removal and refitting

Window glass

Removal

1 From inside the vehicle, slacken and remove the screw securing the window to the opening catch and recover the nut and rubber washer from the outside of the window **(see illustrations)**.
2 Support the glass, then remove the screws, nuts and rubber washers securing the glass panel to the hinges. Remove the window from the vehicle.

Refitting

3 Refitting is the reverse of removal, ensuring

the rubber washers are correctly positioned between the window and nuts.

Window hinges

Removal

4 Remove the button from the seat belt upper mounting height adjuster then undo the retaining screw and remove the trim cover from the mounting.
5 Unscrew the mounting bolt and free the belt from the height adjuster.
6 Unclip the top of the pillar upper trim panel and free it from the pillar.
7 Undo the screw securing the window to the hinge and recover the nut and rubber washer from the outside of the window. Slacken and remove the screw securing the hinge to the body and remove the hinge.

Refitting

8 Refitting is the reverse of removal, ensuring the rubber washers are correctly positioned between the window and nuts. Prior to refitting the trim panel, ensure the window is correctly aligned with its surrounding panels.

Window opening catch

Note: *A pop rivet gun and suitable rivets will be required on refitting.*

Removal

9 Peel back the luggage compartment side trim panel then slacken and remove the rear pillar upper trim panel retaining screws. Unclip

19.17 Mirror housing screws (1) and temperature sensor (2)

20.1a On three-door models, undo the screw securing the rear quarter window to the catch . . .

20.1b . . . and recover the nut and rubber washer from the outside of the glass

20.11 Rear quarter window catch is secured to the body by three pop rivets (arrowed)

21.3 Pull back the rubber cover and remove the retaining screw

21.4 Removing the trim panel from the top of the glass

the panel and free it from the body to gain access to the catch.

10 Slacken and remove the screw securing the catch to the window and recover the nut and rubber washer from the outside of the window (see illustrations 20.1a and 20.1b).

11 Carefully drill the heads off the pop rivets securing the catch to the body and remove the catch from the vehicle (see illustration).

Caution: Take care not to damage the catch/body when drilling out the rivets.

Refitting

12 Refitting is the reverse of removal, securing the catch to the body with new pop rivets. Ensure the rubber washer is correctly positioned between the nut and window.

---

one has plenty of practice, to obtain a secure, waterproof fit. Furthermore, the task carries a high risk of breakage; this applies especially to the laminated glass windscreen. In view of this, owners are strongly advised to have this sort of work carried out by one of the many specialist windscreen fitters.

2 On Estate models, the rear tailgate glass is hinged and can be opened; this type of glass can be removed as described in the following paragraphs.

Estate tailgate glass

Removal

3 Open the tailgate and remove the two screws from the hinges. Note that on the left-hand hinge the rubber cover will need to be

pulled back to access the retaining screw (see illustration).

4 Shut the tailgate and open the tailgate glass, undo the retaining screw and remove the trim panel from the top of the glass (see illustration).

5 Disconnect the wiring connector and the washer pipe from the upper rear spoiler (see illustrations).

6 Undo the retaining screws and withdraw the spoiler from the top of the tailgate glass (see illustration).

7 Support the glass and release the securing clip, then disconnect the strut from the rear glass (see illustration).

8 Disconnect the heated rear window wiring connector from by the left-hand hinge bracket (see illustration).

---

21 Windscreen and tailgate glass – general information, removal and refitting

General information

1 These areas of glass are secured by the tight fit of the weatherstrip in the body aperture, and are bonded in position with a special adhesive. Renewal of such fixed glass is a difficult, messy and time-consuming task, which is considered beyond the scope of the home mechanic. It is difficult, unless

21.5a Disconnect the wiring connector . . .

21.5b . . . and the washer pipe

21.6 Undo the outer spoiler retaining screws

21.7 Release the clip (arrowed) from the strut

21.8 Disconnect the wiring connector (arrowed)

21.9 With the glass supported, undo the retaining nuts – one side arrowed

9 Support the glass and undo the retaining nuts from the hinges **(see illustration)**. With the nuts removed, carefully manoeuvre the glass from the tailgate.

Refitting

10 Refitting is the reverse of removal.

22 Sunroof – general information

1 Due to the complexity of the sunroof mechanism, considerable expertise is needed to repair, renew or adjust the sunroof components successfully. Removal of the roof first requires the headlining to be removed which is a complex and tedious operation in itself. Therefore, any problems with the sunroof should be referred to a Peugeot dealer.
2 On Cabriolet Coupe models, the roof operation is hydraulic and therefore should only be entrusted to a specialist for any work done on the hydraulic system **(see illustration)**. See Section 26 in Chapter 12 for electrical components.

23 Body exterior fittings – removal and refitting

Wheel arch liners and body underpanels

1 The various plastic covers fitted to the underside of the vehicle are secured in position

22.2 Hydraulic pump and relays located behind inner trim panel

by a mixture of screws, nuts and retaining clips, and removal will be fairly obvious on inspection. Work methodically around the panel, removing its retaining screws and clips until the panel is free and can be removed from the underside of the vehicle. Most clips used on the vehicle are simply prised out of position. Other clips can be released by unscrewing/prising out the centre pins then removing the clip **(see illustration)**.
2 On refitting, renew any retaining clips that may have been broken on removal and ensure the panel is securely retained by all the necessary fasteners.

Body trim strips and badges

3 The various body trim strips and badges are held in position with a special adhesive tape. Removal requires the trim/badge to be heated, to soften the adhesive, and then cut away from the surface. Due to the high risk of damage to the vehicle paintwork during this operation, it is recommended that this task should be entrusted to a Peugeot dealer.

24 Seats – removal and refitting

⚠ *Warning: On models with side airbags (a side airbag label will be attached to the trim on the side of the seat base if side airbags are fitted), refer to the precautions given in Chapter 12 before proceeding.*

23.1 The most commonly used fastener is removed by pulling out its centre pin then removing the complete fastener

Front seat

1 On models with side airbags, disconnect the battery negative terminal and wait at least two minutes before proceeding. Reach in under the seat and disconnect the wiring connector from the side airbag unit.
2 Slide the seat fully forwards then slacken and remove the bolts securing the rear of the seat rails in position **(see illustration)**.
3 Slide the seat fully backwards then slacken and remove the seat rail front mounting bolts **(see illustration)**.
4 Carefully manoeuvre the seat out of position.
5 Manoeuvre the seat into position and securely reconnect its wiring connector(s) (where necessary).
6 Fit the seat rail front mounting bolts, tightening them lightly only, then slide the seat forwards and install the rear mounting bolts. Tighten the rear mounting bolts to the specified torque then slide the seat backwards again and tighten the front mounting bolts to the specified torque.
7 On models with side airbags, on completion, reconnect the battery. With the driver's door open, switch on the ignition from outside the vehicle whilst standing clear of the airbag/seat belt. Check the operation of the airbag warning light.

Rear seat cushions

Hatchback and Estate

8 Tilt the rear seat cushion forwards. Unhook the pivot clip ends from the body and remove the seat cushion from the vehicle **(see illustration)**.

24.2 Slide the front seat fully forwards and unscrew the rear mounting bolts . . .

24.3 . . . then slide the seat fully backwards and remove its front mounting bolts

24.8 Fold the rear seat cushion forwards and unhook its pivot clip ends (arrowed) from the floor

24.10 Undo the retaining nut (arrowed)

24.11 Unclip the rear of the seat cushion and remove

24.14 Unscrew the bolts securing the rear seat back centre brackets . . .

9 Refitting is the reverse of removal.

Cabriolet Coupe

10 Undo the retaining nuts from under the front edge of the rear seat cushions (see illustration).
11 Unhook the rear of the seat cushion and remove it from the vehicle (see illustration).
12 Refitting is the reverse of removal.

Rear seat back

Hatchback and Estate

13 Tilt the rear seat cushions forwards.
14 Unscrew the bolts securing the seat back centre mounting brackets to the floor (see illustration).
15 Working in the luggage compartment, unscrew the bolt securing the smaller section seat back outer mounting bracket to the floor then release the seat catch and remove the

seat back from the vehicle (see illustration).
16 If the rear seat centre belt is fitted to the seat and the larger seat back is being removed, unbolt the belt lower mounting from the floor.
17 Unscrew the bolt securing the larger section seat back outer mounting bracket to the floor then release the seat catch and remove the larger seat back from the vehicle.
18 Refit the larger seat back and lightly tighten its outer mounting bracket bolt.
19 Install the smaller seat back and fit its outer bracket bolt. Clip both seat backs in position then refit the centre mounting bracket bolts. With all bolts correctly fitted, go around and tighten them to the specified torque.
20 Where necessary, refit the centre belt lower mounting bolt and tighten to the specified torque.
21 Lower the seat cushions into position.

Cabriolet Coupe

22 Remove the rear seat cushion as described in paragraphs 10 and 11 of this Section.
23 Unscrew the nuts securing the lower part of the seat back to the floor panel (see illustration).
24 Lift the seat back upwards to release it from the two upper retaining clips and remove it from the vehicle (see illustrations).
25 Refitting is the reverse of removal.

25 Front seat belt tensioning mechanism – general information and precautions

1 Most models covered in this manual are fitted with a front seat belt tensioner system. The system is designed to instantaneously take up any slack in the seat belt in the case of a sudden frontal impact, therefore reducing the possibility of injury to the front seat occupants. Each front seat belt is fitted with the system, the tensioner being an integral part of the seat belt inertia reel.
2 The seat belt tensioners are operated by an electronic control unit (ECU), which is located behind the centre console. On models with a driver/passenger airbag, the ECU also operates the driver/passenger airbag (as applicable – see Chapter 12 for information on the airbag systems). The ECU contains a sensor, which is triggered by a frontal impact above a predetermined force. Lesser impacts, including impacts from behind, will not trigger the system.
3 When the mechanism is triggered, the fuel inside the tensioner cylinder ignites. This force retracts the inertia reel mechanism slightly, removing all slack from the seat belt, before locking it in position. The strength of the explosion is calibrated to retract the seat belt sufficiently to securely retain the occupant of the seat without forcing them into the seat. Once the tensioner has been triggered, the seat belt will be permanently locked and the assembly will have to be renewed.
4 Note the following warnings before contemplating any work on the front seat belts.

24.15 . . . and the outer bracket to the floor

24.23 Undo the seat back lower retaining nut (arrowed)

24.24a Lift the seat back upward . . .

24.24b . . . to release it from the two retaining clips (arrowed)

26.2a On three-door models, remove the trim cap and unscrew the mounting bolt (arrowed) . . .

26.2b . . . then free the anchorage bar from the body and recover the washer (arrowed)

26.2c Recover the spacer (1) and trim cap (2) fitted between the anchorage bar and body

⚠ *Warning: Before carrying out any operations on the front seat belt tensioning mechanism, disconnect the battery negative terminal and wait at least two minutes. Remove the centre console (see Section 28) then release the retaining clip and disconnect the wiring connector(s) from the seat belt tensioning/airbag system electronic control unit (ECU) (see Chapter 12). On completion of work, securely reconnect the ECU wiring connector(s) then refit the centre console. Ensure no one is inside the vehicle when the battery is reconnected then, with the driver's door open, switch on the ignition from outside the vehicle whilst standing clear of the airbag/seat belt. Check the operation of the airbag warning light.*

26.3a Remove the height adjuster button then undo the retaining screw (arrowed) and remove the trim cover from the seat belt upper mounting

⚠ *Warning: If the seat belt inertia reel is dropped, it must be renewed, even if it has suffered no apparent damage.*

⚠ *Warning: Do not allow any solvents to come into contact with the tensioner mechanism.*

⚠ *Warning: Do not subject the bodywork around the electronic control unit (ECU) to any form of shock as this could accidentally trigger the seat belt tensioner/airbag system.*

⚠ *Warning: Do not subject the inertia reel assembly to temperatures in excess of 100°C.*

⚠ *Warning: Peugeot recommend that the front seat belts must be renewed every ten years.*

26 Seat belt components
– removal and refitting

⚠ *Warning: Refer to the precautions given in Section 25 before proceeding.*

Front belt

Three-door Hatchback

1 Disconnect the battery negative terminal and wait at least two minutes. Remove the

centre console (see Section 28) then release the retaining clip and disconnect the wiring connector from the seat belt tensioning/airbag system electronic control unit (ECU) (see Chapter 12).

2 Prise off the trim cap from the lower belt anchorage bolt then slacken and remove the bolt and washer. Free the anchorage bar from the body then slide off the washer and free the bar from the seat belt. Recover the spacer and trim cap fitted between the anchorage bar mounting and body (see illustrations).

3 Remove the button from the seat belt upper mounting height adjuster then undo the retaining screw and remove the trim cover from the mounting. Unscrew the mounting bolt and free the belt from the height adjuster (see illustrations).

4 Unclip the top of the pillar upper trim panel then free the panel from the seat belt and remove it from the vehicle (see illustration). If necessary, the height adjuster mechanism can then be unbolted from the pillar.

5 Lift out the parcel shelf then remove the seat cushion and back as described in Section 24.

6 Prise off the trim cap from the rear seat belt lower mounting bolt then slacken and remove the bolt and washer. Free the belt and recover the spacer fitted between the belt and body (see illustrations).

7 Peel back the luggage compartment side trim panel then slacken and remove the upper trim panel retaining screws. Unclip the panel and free it from the rear seat belt (see

26.3b Unscrew the mounting bolt and free the seat belt from the height adjuster

26.4 Unclip the upper trim panel from the pillar and free it from the seat belt

26.6a Remove the trim cap then unscrew the rear seat belt lower mounting bolt . . .

26.6b . . . and recover the spacer (arrowed) fitted between the belt and body

26.7a Undo the retaining screws (arrowed) . . .

26.7b . . . then unclip the upper trim panel from the rear pillar

illustrations). If the left-hand panel is being removed, it will also be necessary to remove the courtesy light from the panel.

8 Open the rear quarter window and free the window sealing strip from the top of the rear seat side trim panel. Unclip the side trim panel from the body then free the seat belt guide and seat belt from the panel and remove the panel from the vehicle (see illustrations).

9 Disconnect the wiring connector from the seat belt tensioner mechanism (see illustration).

10 Slacken and remove the inertia reel mounting bolt and remove the seat belt assembly from the vehicle.

11 Refitting is a reversal of removal, ensuring the mounting bolts are tightened to the specified torque and the tensioner wiring connector is securely reconnected. Ensure the trim panels are clipped securely in position and are correctly located behind the edges of the sealing strips

Five-door Hatchback and Estate

12 To improve access, remove the relevant front seat as described in Section 24.

13 Remove the trim cap from the seat belt lower mounting bolt then slacken and remove the mounting bolt and washer (see illustration).

26.8a Free the window sealing strip from the top of the panel . . .

14 Remove the button from the seat belt upper mounting height adjuster then undo the retaining screw and remove the trim cover from the mounting. Unscrew the mounting bolt and free the belt from the height adjuster (see illustrations).

26.8b . . . and unclip the rear seat side trim panel from the body

26.8c Unclip the seat belt guide then free the trim panel from the seat belt

26.9 Front seat belt inertia reel tensioner wiring connector (1) and mounting bolt (2)

26.13 On five-door models, prise off the trim cap then slacken and remove the seat belt lower mounting bolt

26.14a Unclip the button from the height adjuster lever . . .

26.14b . . . then undo the retaining screw and remove the trim cover (arrowed)

26.14c Unscrew the upper mounting bolt and free the seat belt from the height adjuster

26.15a Unclip the upper trim panel from the pillar . . .

26.15b . . . then free the lower trim panel from the pillar and belt

26.16 Disconnect the wiring connector from the seat belt tensioner mechanism . . .

26.17 . . . then unscrew the inertia reel mounting bolt and remove the seat belt

26.20a Release the securing clip . . .

26.20b . . . and unclip the trim panel

15 Unclip the upper trim panel from the pillar and free it from the seat belt then unclip the lower trim panel from the pillar **(see illustrations)**. If necessary, the height adjuster mechanism can also be unbolted from the pillar.

16 Disconnect the wiring connector from the seat belt tensioner mechanism **(see illustration)**.

17 Slacken and remove the inertia reel mounting bolt and remove the seat belt assembly from the vehicle **(see illustration)**.

18 Refitting is a reversal of removal, ensuring the mounting bolts are tightened to the specified torque and the tensioner wiring connector is securely reconnected. Ensure the trim panels are clipped securely in position and are correctly located behind the edges of the sealing strips.

Cabriolet Coupe

19 Remove the rear seat cushion as described in Section 24.

20 Release the retaining clips and withdraw the upper trim panel from the rear quarter panel **(see illustrations)**.

21 Release the retaining clips undo the retaining screw and withdraw the inner rear trim panel **(see illustrations)**.

22 Remove the plastic cover from the seat belt lower mounting point, and then unscrew the mounting bolt and free the belt from the guide bracket **(see illustration)**.

23 Disconnect the wiring connector from the seat belt tensioner mechanism **(see illustration)**.

26.21a Remove the lower retaining clip (arrowed) . . .

26.21b . . . release the upper retaining clip . . .

26.21c . . . and remove the inner trim panel

26.22 Unclip the cover and remove the lower mounting bolt (arrowed)

26.23 Disconnect the wiring connector (arrowed)

26.24 Inertia reel seat belt mounting bolt (arrowed)

26.31 Unscrew the bolt and free the rear seat belt upper mounting from the body

26.32 Rear seat belt inertia reel mounting bolt (arrowed)

24 Slacken and remove the inertia reel mounting bolt and remove the seat belt assembly from the vehicle **(see illustration)**.

25 Refitting is a reversal of removal, ensuring the mounting bolts are tightened to the specified torque and the tensioner wiring connector is securely reconnected. Ensure the trim panels are clipped securely in position and are correctly located behind the edges of the sealing strips.

Rear side belt

Three-door Hatchback

26 Remove the parcel shelf.

27 Remove the rear seat back as described in Section 24.

28 Prise off the trim cap from the rear seat belt lower mounting bolt then slacken and remove the bolt and washer. Free the belt and recover the spacer fitted between the belt and body **(see illustrations 26.6a and 26.6b)**.

29 Remove the fastener (pull out the centre pin then remove the complete fastener) and free the luggage compartment side trim panel from the body to gain access to the inertia reel.

30 Slacken and remove the retaining screws securing the rear pillar upper trim panel in position. Unclip the panel from the body and free it from the seat belt; if the left-hand panel is being removed, it will also be necessary to remove the courtesy light from the panel **(see illustrations 26.7a and 26.7b)**.

31 Unscrew the seat belt upper mounting bolt and recover the spacer fitted between the belt and body **(see illustration)**.

32 Slacken and remove the inertia reel mounting bolt and remove the seat belt assembly from the vehicle **(see illustration)**.

33 Refitting is a reversal of removal. Ensure that all washers and/or spacers are positioned as noted before removal, and tighten all mounting bolts to the specified torque. Ensure the trim panels are clipped securely in position and are correctly located behind the edges of the sealing strips.

Five-door Hatchback

34 Remove the parcel shelf.

35 Remove the rear seat back as described in Section 24.

36 Remove the trim cap then unscrew the seat belt lower mounting bolt and washer. Recover the spacer fitted between the belt and body **(see illustrations)**.

26.36a On five-door models, prise off the trim cap . . .

37 Remove the fastener(s) (pull out the centre pin then remove the complete fastener) and free the luggage compartment side trim panel from the body to gain access to the inertia reel.

38 Slacken and remove the retaining screws securing the rear pillar upper trim panel in position **(see illustrations)**. Unclip the panel from the body and free it from the seat belt; if the left-hand panel is being removed, it will also be necessary to remove the courtesy light from the panel.

39 Unscrew the seat belt upper mounting bolt and recover the spacer fitted between the belt and body **(see illustration)**.

40 Slacken and remove the inertia reel mounting bolt and remove the seat belt assembly from the vehicle.

41 Refitting is a reversal of removal, ensuring

26.36b . . . then unscrew the lower mounting bolt and recover the spacer (arrowed) fitted between the belt and body

26.38a Undo the retaining screws (arrowed) . . .

26.38b . . . then unclip the upper trim panel from the rear pillar

26.39 Unscrew the upper mounting bolt and recover the spacer (arrowed) fitted between the belt and body

26.44 Unclip the plastic cap (arrowed) from the upper seat belt mounting

26.45 Unclip the trim panel from the rear pillar

26.46a Undo the front retaining screw (arrowed) . . .

the mounting bolts are tightened to the specified torque. Ensure the trim panels are clipped securely in position and are correctly located behind the edges of the sealing strips.

Estate

42 Where applicable, remove the parcel shelf.
43 Remove the rear seat back as described in Section 24.
44 Remove the trim caps then unscrew the seat belt lower and upper mounting bolt and washer. Recover the spacer fitted between the belt and body (see illustration).
45 Unclip the trim panel from the rear pillar (see illustration).
46 Remove the fastener(s) and free the

luggage compartment side trim panel from the body to gain access to the inertia reel (see illustrations).
47 Slacken and remove the inertia reel mounting bolt and remove the seat belt assembly from the vehicle (see illustration).
48 Refitting is a reversal of removal, ensuring the mounting bolts are tightened to the specified torque. Ensure the trim panels are clipped securely in position and are correctly located behind the edges of the sealing strips.

Cabriolet Coupe

49 Remove the rear seat cushion as described in Section 24.
50 Release the retaining clips and withdraw the upper trim panel from the rear quarter

panel (see illustrations 26.51a and 26.51b).
51 Release the retaining clips and withdraw the inner rear trim panel (see illustrations 26.21a, 26.21b and 26.21c).
52 Slacken and remove the mounting bolts from the seat belt lower anchorage point and the inertia reel mounting bolt and remove the seat belt assembly from the vehicle (see illustration).
53 Refitting is a reversal of removal. Ensure that all washers and/or spacers are positioned as noted before removal, and tighten all mounting bolts to the specified torque. Ensure the trim panels are clipped securely in position and are correctly located behind the edges of the sealing strips.

Rear belt buckles and lap belt

Hatchback and Estate

54 The assemblies can simply be unbolted from the floor panel, after folding the rear seat cushion forwards (see illustration). Note the locations of any washers and spacers, to ensure correct refitting.
55 Refitting is a reversal of removal. Ensure that all washers and/or spacers are positioned as noted before removal, and tighten all mounting bolts to the specified torque.

Cabriolet Coupe

56 Remove the rear seat cushion and backs as described in Section 24.
57 Release the retaining clips and withdraw

26.46b . . . and the rear retaining screw (arrowed) . . .

26.46c . . . and carefully unclip the side trim panel

26.47 Inertia reel seat belt mounting bolt (arrowed)

26.52 Undo the two seat belt mounting bolts (arrowed)

26.54 The rear seat belt buckles and lap belt are bolted to the floor

26.59a Undo the retaining nuts (arrowed) . . .

26.59b . . . and remove the headrest

26.60a Release the retaining clips . . .

the upper trim panel from both of the rear quarter panels **(see illustrations 26.20a and 26.02b)**.

58 Release the retaining clips and withdraw the inner rear trim panel from each side of the rear seat **(see illustrations 26.21a, 26.21b and 26.21c)**.

59 Undo the retaining nuts and remove the rear headrests **(see illustrations)**.

60 Remove the retaining clips and unclip the rear trim panel from the vehicle **(see illustrations)**.

61 Unbolt the belt buckles from the floor panel **(see illustration)**. Note the locations of any washers and spacers, to ensure correct refitting.

62 Refitting is a reversal of removal. Ensure that all washers and/or spacers are positioned as noted before removal, and tighten all mounting bolts to the specified torque.

Rear inertia reel centre belt

Note: *New headrest guides will be required on refitting.*

63 Remove the seat back as described in Section 24.

64 Depress the locking buttons and slide out the rear headrests from the seat back.

65 Remove the headrest guides from the seat. To do this, grab each guide firmly and rotate it to break its retaining tabs then pull it out of the seat assembly. If this fails to remove the guides, saw off the guide head whilst taking great care not to damage the

seat upholstery (as a precaution, make up a protective template out of cardboard and fit this between the saw and upholstery).

66 Undo the retaining screws and remove the seat belt trim cover from the top of the seat.

67 Unclip the upholstery from the sides and top of the seat back and peel back the foam to gain access to the inertia reel. Unbolt the inertia reel and remove the belt from the seat.

68 Refitting is the reverse of removal, ensuring the upholstery and headrest guides are securely clipped in position. Refit the seat back as described in Section 24.

27 Interior trim – removal and refitting

Interior trim panels

1 The interior trim panels are retained using either or various types of trim fastener, usually studs or clips.

2 Check that there are no other panels overlapping the one to be removed; usually there is a sequence that has to be followed that will become obvious on close inspection. Where the panel is next to a door/window sealing strip, if necessary, free the sealing strip from the body to ensure it does not hinder panel removal.

3 Remove all obvious fasteners, such as screws. If the panel will not come free, it is held by hidden clips or fasteners. These are usually situated around the edge of the panel and are released by prising the panel away from the body. The best way of releasing such clips without the correct tool, is to use a large flat-bladed screwdriver to carefully release the panel, taking care not to damage the panel or paintwork.

4 When removing a panel **never** use excessive force or the panel may be damaged; always check carefully that all fasteners have been removed or release before attempting to remove the panel.

5 Refitting is the reverse of removal. Prior to refitting check the condition of all retaining clips and renew any which show signs of damage or deterioration. Ensure the panel is securely clipped in position and retained by all the necessary fasteners and screws to prevent annoying rattles and squeaks. Where the panel is next to a door/window sealing strip, ensure that it is correctly located behind the edge of the strip.

Glovebox

6 Open up the glovebox lid then carefully unclip the base of the lid from its retaining clips. Free the lid stays from the glovebox compartment and remove the lid from the facia **(see illustration)**.

7 Slacken and remove the glovebox

26.60b . . . and remove the plastic trim panel

26.61 Belt buckle retaining bolt (arrowed)

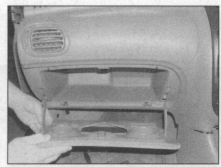

27.6 Unclip the glovebox lid from its retaining clips and remove it from the facia

27.7a Slacken and remove the retaining screws (arrowed) . . .

27.7b . . . noting the correct fitted direction of the retaining clips fitted to the lower screws . . .

27.8 . . . then manoeuvre the glovebox compartment out of position

compartment retaining screws, noting the correct fitted locations of the lid retaining clips **(see illustrations)**.

8 Free the glovebox compartment from the facia then manoeuvre it downwards and out from under the facia **(see illustration)**. Where necessary, disconnect the wiring connectors from the glovebox light and switch as the compartment is removed.

9 Refitting is the reverse of removal.

Carpets

10 The passenger compartment floor carpet is in one piece, and is secured at its edges by screws or various types of clips.

11 Carpet removal and refitting is reasonably straightforward, but time-consuming, due to the fact that all adjoining trim panels must be

removed first, as must components such as the seats and centre console.

Headlining

12 The headlining is bonded to the roof, and can be withdrawn only once all fittings such as the grab handles, sun visors, overhead console, windscreen, centre and rear pillar trim panels, and associated panels have been removed. The door, tailgate and sunroof aperture weatherstrips will also have to be prised clear.

13 Note that headlining removal requires considerable skill and experience if it is to be carried out without damage, and is therefore best entrusted to an expert (the headlining must also be heated with a hot air gun to soften the adhesive and carefully prised away from the roof).

28 Centre console – removal and refitting

Removal

1 Carefully, taking care not to mark the switch or console, prise the switch(es) out from the rear section of the centre console. Disconnect the wiring connector(s) and remove the switch(es) **(see illustrations)**.

2 Unclip the access cover from the rear of the centre console rear section to gain access to the retaining screw. Undo the retaining screw and remove the console rear section from the vehicle **(see illustrations)**.

3 Unscrew the handbrake lever mounting nuts and free the handbrake lever from the

28.1a Unclip the switches from the console rear section . . .

28.1b . . . and disconnect the wiring

28.2a Unclip the access cover . . .

28.2b . . . then slacken and remove the retaining screw . . .

28.2c . . . and lift off the console rear section

28.3 Unscrew the nuts (arrowed) and free the handbrake lever from the floor

28.4 On manual transmission models unclip the gearchange lever gaiter from the console

28.5 On automatic transmission models unclip the selector lever surround from the console

28.6a Carefully prise out the window/ mirror switch assembly . . .

28.6b . . . and disconnect its wiring connectors

28.8 Unclip the cover (1) to gain access to the console front retaining screws (2)

28.9a Remove the ashtray assembly . . .

floor, taking care not to strain the cables **(see illustration)**. If necessary, referring to Chapter 9, slacken the cable adjuster nut to obtain maximum freeplay in the cables to enable the lever to be moved.

4 On manual transmission models, unclip the gearchange lever gaiter from the console **(see illustration)**.

5 On automatic transmission models, carefully unclip the selector lever surround from the console **(see illustration)**.

6 On models with electric front windows/ electrically-operated exterior mirrors, carefully prise out the window/mirror switch out from the centre console front section. Disconnect

the wiring connector and remove the switch **(see illustrations)**.

7 On models without electric front windows/ mirrors, unclip and remove the storage compartment from the console.

8 On all models, unclip the trim cover from the front of the console to gain access to the front retaining screws **(see illustration)**.

9 Remove the ashtray and unclip the ashtray illumination bulbholder from the console **(see illustrations)**.

10 Slacken and remove the console front section front retaining screws and the rear retaining nut. Lift the rear of the console front section and disconnect the wiring connectors

from the cigarette lighter. Free the front of the console from the facia and manoeuvre it out of position **(see illustrations)**.

Refitting

11 Refitting is the reverse of removal, noting the following.
   a) *Ensure the wiring is correctly routed and securely reconnected.*
   b) *Tighten the handbrake lever mounting nuts to the specified torque (see Chapter 9). Check and, if necessary, adjust the handbrake adjustment before refitting the console rear section.*
   c) *On completion check the operation of all the switches.*

28.9b . . . and free the illumination bulbholder from the console

28.10a Unscrew the front screws and rear nut . . .

28.10b . . . then manoeuvre the console front section out of position

29.5a Undo the retaining screws (arrowed) . . .

29.5b . . . then unclip the centre vent panel from the facia

29.6a Undo the retaining screws (arrowed) . . .

29 Facia panel assembly
– removal and refitting

 HAYNES HiNT *Attach an identification label to each wiring connector as it is disconnected. The labels can then be used on refitting to ensure that all wiring is correctly routed through the relevant facia apertures.*

Removal

1 Disconnect the battery negative terminal.

2 Remove the centre console (see Section 28).
3 Remove the steering column as described in Chapter 10.
4 Remove the following components as described in Chapter 12.
a) Instrument panel.
b) Clock/multifunction unit.
c) Facia switch panel.
d) Audio unit.
5 Slacken and remove the retaining screws securing the top of the centre vent panel to the facia. Carefully unclip the panel and remove it from the facia (see illustrations).
6 Slacken and remove the four screws then release the upper retaining clip(s) and free the

heating/ventilation control unit from the facia (see illustrations).
7 Unscrew the two bolts securing the centre of the facia to the heating/ventilation housing and upper bolt securing the facia to the body (see illustrations).
8 Unscrew the bolt securing the facia centre mounting bracket to the floor and the two bolts securing the bracket to the facia frame.
9 Unscrew the bolt and detach the facia panel earth lead from the floor (see illustration).
10 Release the retaining clips and disconnect the facia harness wiring connectors located next to the fusebox. Unclip the brown-coloured connector and the black-coloured connector from the bracket (see illustrations).

29.6b . . . then unclip the heating/ventilation control unit from the facia

29.7a Unscrew the two bolts (arrowed) securing the facia to the heating/ventilation housing . . .

29.7b . . . and the single bolt securing it to the body

29.9 Unscrew the bolt (arrowed) and detach the facia earth lead from the floor

29.10a Disconnect the facia harness wiring connectors located next to the fusebox . . .

29.10b . . . then unclip the brown and black wiring connectors (arrowed) and from the facia bracket

11 Unscrew the facia mounting bolt located in the instrument panel aperture **(see illustration)**.

12 Carefully prise out the end covers from the left- and right-hand end of the facia. Disconnect the aerial lead from its connector located behind the passenger side cover **(see illustrations)**.

13 Unscrew the bolts securing the left- and right-hand ends of the facia to the bulkhead.

14 With the aid of an assistant, lift the facia up slightly then manoeuvre it away from the bulkhead, freeing it from the heating/ventilation housing and control panel **(see illustration)**.

Refitting

15 Manoeuvre the facia into position, ensuring the wiring connectors are correctly routed through the necessary facia apertures. Locate the facia correctly on the bulkhead, ensuring that the facia vents engage correctly with the heating/ventilation housing. Also ensure the control panel is correctly engaged with the facia.

16 Refit the bolts securing the facia ends to the bulkhead, the facia bolt located in the instrument panel aperture and the bolt securing the centre mounting bracket to the floor. Tighten all bolts by hand then tighten them to the specified torque in the following order:
   a) *Centre mounting bracket bolt-to-body bolt.*
   b) *Left-and right-hand end bolts.*
   c) *Instrument panel aperture bolt.*
   d) *Centre mounting bracket-to-facia bracket bolts*

17 Reconnect the aerial lead to the connector located at the passenger end of the facia then refit the end covers to the facia.

18 Clip the brown and black connectors back onto the facia bracket then securely reconnect all the facia wiring connectors.

19 Reconnect the facia and wiring harness earth leads to the floor, tightening the retaining bolt securely.

20 Refit the bolts and screws securing the facia to the heating/ventilation housing and control panel, tightening them securely.

21 Clip the centre vent panel into position and secure it in position with the retaining screws.

22 Refit the audio unit, facia switch panel,

29.11 Unscrew the facia mounting bolt located in the instrument panel aperture

29.12b Aerial lead connector (1) and facia left-hand end mounting bolts (2)

clock/multifunction unit and instrument panel, as described in Chapter 12.

23 Refit the steering column as described in Chapter 10.

24 Refit the centre console as described in Section 28.

25 Reconnect the battery. With the driver's door open, switch on the ignition from outside the vehicle whilst standing clear of the airbag/seat belt. Check the operation of the airbag warning light then check that all electrical components and switches function correctly.

30 Roof assembly (Cabriolet Coupe models) – removal and refitting

Note: *An assistant will be needed to carry out some of the procedures. The vehicle will need to be with the roof in the up position to start.*

29.12a Unclip the left- and right-hand end covers from the facia

29.14 Removing the facia assembly

Roof

Removal

1 Make sure the both rear quarter glass windows are in the lowered position and then disconnect the battery negative lead.

2 Open the boot lid and release the luggage cover screen from its clips **(see illustration)** and fold it away.

3 Using the Allen key (4 mm) supplied with the vehicle breakdown kit, turn the hydraulic unit load reduction screw on the hydraulic pump a quarter of a turn in the anti-clockwise direction **(see illustration)**.

Caution: Always make sure the hydraulic pump load reduction screw has been set in the safe position before working on any components.

4 Remove the retaining clips and remove the upper cover from the rear of the luggage compartment **(see illustration)**.

30.2 Unclip the luggage cover

30.3 Turning the hydraulic unit load reduction screw

30.4 Removing the inner trim from the luggage compartment

30.5 Disconnect the wiring harness connectors (arrowed)

30.7a Locking the upper boot lid in the open position . . .

30.7b . . . using an Allen key (arrowed) – supplied in the breakdown kit

5 Disconnect the wiring connector and release the wiring harness from the left-hand side of the luggage compartment **(see illustration)**.

Work your way along the wiring harness and release it from any cable-ties.

6 Close the complete boot lid and open the upper part of the boot lid from the rear screen backwards.

7 Lock the upper part of the boot lid by inserting the Allen key (4 mm) supplied with the vehicle breakdown kit, into the hinge bracket on the right-hand rear of the vehicle **(see illustrations)**.

⚠ *Warning: Always make sure the upper part of the boot lid is locked in position and cannot move before working on any components.*

30.8a Inserting a bar (deep socket) . . .

30.8b . . . into the hinge to lock it in position

8 With the aid of an assistant, release the roof catches and carefully fold the roof assembly back into the intermediate position (rear screen vertical). Lock the hinges in place by inserting a round metal bar (long deep socket) into the hinge bracket **(see illustrations)**.

⚠ *Warning: Always make sure the roof assembly is locked in position and cannot move before working on any components.*

9 Remove the retaining clip from the lower edge of the trim panel and unclip the outer trim panel from the rear screen panel **(see illustrations)**.

10 Remove the two retaining clips from the lower edge of the trim panel and unclip the inner trim panel from the rear screen panel **(see illustrations)**.

11 Unclip the inner trim panel from the roof panel, releasing it from the roof locking catch **(see illustration)**.

12 To remove the roof panel, mark the position of the mounting brackets on each

30.9a Release the retaining clip . . .

30.9b . . . and carefully unclip the trim panel

30.10a Release the two retaining clips (arrowed) . . .

30.10b . . . and carefully unclip the trim panel

30.11 Unclip the upper roof trim panel

30.12 Roof panel bracket mounting nuts (arrowed)

30.13a Remove the upper mounting bolts (arrowed) . . .

30.13b . . . and the lower mounting bolts (arrowed)

side, and then, with the aid of an assistant, slacken and remove the retaining nuts **(see illustration)**. Check that there is nothing still attached, and then lift the roof panel from the vehicle and place it somewhere safe.

13 To remove the rear screen panel, mark the position of the mounting brackets on each side, and then, with the aid of an assistant, slacken and remove the retaining bolts **(see illustrations)**. Check that there is nothing still attached, and then lift the rear screen panel from the vehicle and place it somewhere safe.

Refitting

14 Refitting is a reversal of removal, noting the following points:
a) *An assistant will be required to help refit the roof and rear screen panels.*
b) *Tighten the hinge mounting nuts/bolts in*

the position noted on removal.
c) *Using the Allen key (4 mm) supplied with the vehicle breakdown kit, turn the hydraulic unit load reduction screw on the hydraulic pump a quarter of a turn in the clockwise direction* **(see illustration 30.3)**.

Roof catch

Removal

15 Unclip the inner trim panel from the roof panel, releasing it from the roof locking catch **(see illustration 30.11)**.

16 Undo the retaining screws and remove the catch from the roof panel **(see illustration)**.

Refitting

17 Refitting is a reversal of removal.

30.16 Roof catch retaining screws (arrowed)

Chapter 12
Body electrical systems

Contents

Degrees of difficulty

Easy, suitable for novice with little experience	Fairly easy, suitable for beginner with some experience	Fairly difficult, suitable for competent DIY mechanic	Difficult, suitable for experienced DIY mechanic	Very difficult, suitable for expert DIY or professional

Specifications

General

System type . . . . 12 volt negative earth

Bulbs

	Type	Wattage
Direction indicator light	Bayonet	21
Direction indicator side repeater	Push-fit	5
Front foglight	H1	55
Front sidelights.	Push-fit	5
Headlights:		
Models with combined dip/main beam bulb	H4	60/55
Models with separate main and dipped beam bulbs	H7	55
Number plate light	Push-fit	5
Rear foglight.	Bayonet	21
Reversing light	Bayonet	21
Stop/tail light	Bayonet	21/5

Torque wrench settings	Nm	lbf ft
Airbag system:		
Control unit retaining nuts	8	6
Driver's airbag retaining screws	10	7
Passenger airbag retaining nuts.	4	3
Tailgate wiper motor:		
Spindle nut	25	18
Wiper arm nut	20	15
Windscreen wiper arm nut	25	18

1 General information

⚠ **Warning: Before carrying out any work on the electrical system, read through the precautions given in 'Safety first!' at the beginning of this manual, and in Chapter 5A.**

1 The electrical system is of 12 volt negative earth type. Power for the lights and all electrical accessories is supplied by a lead-acid type battery, which is charged by the alternator.

2 Many of the body electrical systems are controlled by individual electronic control units (ECUs) and these are in turn controlled by a main ECU known as a Built-in Systems Interface (BSI). The various ECUs and the BSI exchange data with each other via a multiplex network. The multiplex network is a two-wire system linking the BSI with the system ECUs and is termed by Peugeot as CAN (controlled area network) and VAN (vehicle area network). Essentially this means that the BSI and the ECUs controlling the 'comfort' systems, safety systems, security systems and entertainment systems in the vehicle are all interconnected via Vehicle Area Networks **(see illustration)**.

3 An ECU connected to the multiplex network only receives some of the data needed for it to operate directly, with the remaining data being supplied by the other ECUs on the network. Because the ECUs share information via the network, several ECUs can control the operation of the same system. Also, one ECU can control several systems in an autonomous manner. The BSI is the manager of this information interchange as well as also being responsible for the control of certain vehicle systems itself. The BSI has a full diagnostic capability whereby any fault in any of the ECUs on the multiplex network can be traced using diagnostic equipment connected to the vehicle diagnostic connector. Should any fault develop with a system on the network, have the self-diagnosis facility interrogated by a Peugeot dealer or suitably-equipped specialist.

4 This Chapter covers repair and service procedures for the various electrical components not associated with the engine. Information on the battery, alternator and starter motor can be found in Chapter 5A.

5 It should be noted that, prior to working on any component in the electrical system, the battery should first be disconnected; to prevent the possibility of electrical short-circuits (see Chapter 5A).

2 Electrical fault finding – general information

Note: *Refer to the precautions given in 'Safety first!' and in Section 1 of this Chapter before starting work. The following tests relate to testing of the main electrical circuits, and should not be used to test delicate electronic circuits (such as anti-lock braking systems), particularly where an electronic control unit (ECU) is used.*

General

1 A typical electrical circuit consists of an electrical component; any switches, relays, motors, fuses, fusible links or circuit breakers related to that component, and the wiring and connectors which link the component to both the battery and the chassis. To help to pinpoint a problem in an electrical circuit, wiring diagrams are included at the end of this Chapter.

2 Before attempting to diagnose an electrical fault, first study the appropriate wiring diagram, to obtain a more complete understanding of the components included in the particular circuit concerned. The possible sources of a fault can be narrowed down by noting whether other components related to the circuit are operating properly. If several components or circuits fail at one time, the problem is likely to be related to a shared fuse or earth connection.

3 Electrical problems usually stem from simple causes, such as loose or corroded connections, a faulty earth connection, a blown fuse, a melted fusible link, or a faulty relay (refer to Section 3 for details of testing relays). Visually inspect the condition of all fuses, wires and connections in a problem circuit before testing the components. Use the wiring diagrams to determine which terminal connections will need to be checked, in order to pinpoint the trouble spot.

4 The basic tools required for electrical fault finding include a circuit tester or voltmeter (a 12 volt bulb with a set of test leads can also be used for certain tests); a self-powered test light (sometimes known as a continuity tester); an ohmmeter (to measure resistance); a battery and set of test leads; and a jumper wire, preferably with a circuit breaker or fuse incorporated, which can be used to bypass suspect wires or electrical components. Before attempting to locate a problem with test instruments, use the wiring diagram to determine where to make the connections.

5 To find the source of an intermittent wiring fault (usually due to a poor or dirty connection, or damaged wiring insulation), a 'wiggle' test can be performed on the wiring. This involves wiggling the wiring by hand, to see if the fault occurs as the wiring is moved. It should be possible to narrow down the source of the fault to a particular section of wiring. This method of testing can be used in conjunction with any of the tests described in the following sub-Sections.

6 Apart from problems due to poor connections, two basic types of fault can occur in an electrical circuit – open-circuit, or short-circuit.

7 Open-circuit faults are caused by a break somewhere in the circuit, which prevents current from flowing. An open-circuit fault will prevent a component from working, but will not cause the relevant circuit fuse to blow.

8 Short-circuit faults are caused by a 'short' somewhere in the circuit, which allows the current flowing in the circuit to 'escape' along an alternative route, usually to earth. Short-circuit faults are normally caused by a breakdown in wiring insulation, which allows a feed wire to touch either another wire, or an earthed component such as the bodyshell. A short-circuit fault will normally cause the relevant circuit fuse to blow.

Note: *As an aid to economy and to prevent battery discharge, certain functions of the electrical system can only be used for 30 minutes after the engine has been stopped. Bear this in mind when tracing power supply faults on these systems.*

Functions affected

Windscreen wipers.
Electric windows.
Sunroof.
Courtesy lights.
Audio equipment.

1.2 Multiplexing – Vehicle Area Network (VAN)

1 Built-in Systems Interface (BSI)
2 Electric windows
3 Fuel additive ECU (2.0 litre diesel with particulate filter)
4 Anti-theft alarm
5 Central locking transmitter
6 Sunroof motor
7 Power steering pump
8 Engine management ECU
9 Steering column combination switches
10 ABS control unit
11 ESP control unit
12 Automatic transmission ECU
13 Airbag ECU
14 Fusebox
15 Air conditioning ECU
16 Instrument cluster
17 CD player
18 Multifunction display
19 Parking aid ECU
20 Radio
21 Radio/telephone ECU

After this period the BSI (Built-in Systems Interface) cuts the power to these circuits. To restore power, start the engine. It is also possible for the BSI to turn off certain functions (heater blower, heated rear window) depending on the state of charge of the battery. When tracing a fault, ensure the battery is in a good state of charge.

Finding an open-circuit

9 To check for an open-circuit, connect one lead of a circuit tester or voltmeter to either the negative battery terminal or a known good earth.

10 Connect the other lead to a connector in the circuit being tested, preferably nearest to the battery or fuse.

11 Switch on the circuit, bearing in mind that some circuits are live only when the ignition switch is moved to a particular position.

12 If voltage is present (indicated either by the tester bulb lighting or a voltmeter reading, as applicable), this means that the section of the circuit between the relevant connector and the battery is problem-free.

13 Continue to check the remainder of the circuit in the same fashion.

14 When a point is reached at which no voltage is present, the problem must lie between that point and the previous test point with voltage. Most problems can be traced to a broken, corroded or loose connection.

Finding a short-circuit

15 To check for a short-circuit, first disconnect the load(s) from the circuit (loads are the components which draw current from a circuit, such as bulbs, motors, heating elements, etc).

16 Remove the relevant fuse from the circuit, and connect a circuit tester or voltmeter to the fuse connections.

17 Switch on the circuit, bearing in mind that some circuits are live only when the ignition switch is moved to a particular position.

18 If voltage is present (indicated either by the tester bulb lighting or a voltmeter reading, as applicable), this means that there is a short-circuit.

19 If no voltage is present, but the fuse still blows with the load(s) connected, this indicates an internal fault in the load(s).

Finding an earth fault

20 The battery negative terminal is connected to 'earth' – the metal of the engine/transmission and the car body – and most systems are wired so that they only receive a positive feed, the current returning via the metal of the car body. This means that the component mounting and the body form part of that circuit. Loose or corroded mountings can therefore cause a range of electrical faults, ranging from total failure of a circuit, to a puzzling partial fault. In particular, lights may shine dimly (especially when another

circuit sharing the same earth point is in operation), motors (eg, wiper motors or the radiator cooling fan motor) may run slowly, and the operation of one circuit may have an apparently unrelated effect on another. Note that on many vehicles, earth straps are used between certain components, such as the engine/transmission and the body, usually where there is no metal-to-metal contact between components, due to flexible rubber mountings, etc.

21 To check whether a component is properly earthed, disconnect the battery, and connect one lead of an ohmmeter to a known good earth point. Connect the other lead to the wire or earth connection being tested. The resistance reading should be zero; if not, check the connection as follows.

22 If an earth connection is thought to be faulty, dismantle the connection, and clean back to bare metal both the bodyshell and the wire terminal or the component earth connection mating surface. Be careful to remove all traces of dirt and corrosion, and then use a knife to trim away any paint, so that a clean metal-to-metal joint is made. On reassembly, tighten the joint fasteners securely; if a wire terminal is being refitted, use serrated washers between the terminal and the bodyshell, to ensure a clean and secure connection. When the connection is remade, prevent the onset of corrosion in the future by applying a coat of petroleum jelly or silicone-based grease, or by spraying on (at regular intervals) a proprietary ignition sealer or water-dispersant lubricant.

3.3a Rotate the fastener 90° . . .

3.5a Using the removal tool supplied to remove a fuse

3 Fuses and relays – general information

Fuses

1 Fuses are designed to break a circuit when a predetermined current is reached, in order to protect the components and wiring, which could be damaged by excessive current flow. Any excessive current flow will be due to a fault in the circuit, usually a short-circuit (see Section 2).

2 The majority of fuses are located behind the lower cover on the driver's side of the facia. Additional fuses (including the larger, higher-rated fuses) are located in the fuse/relay box on the left-hand side of the engine compartment.

3 To gain access to the facia fuses, rotate the cover fastener through 90° then remove the cover from the facia (see illustrations). To gain access to the fuses in the engine compartment, simply unclip the cover from the fuse/relay box.

4 A list of circuits each fuse protects is given on the fusebox cover.

5 To remove a fuse, first switch off the circuit concerned (or the ignition), and then pull the fuse out of its terminals (see illustrations). The wire within the fuse should be visible; if the fuse has blown it will be broken or melted.

6 Always renew a fuse with one of the correct rating, never use a fuse with a different rating from that specified. The fuse rating is stamped

3.3b . . . then remove the lower cover to gain access to the fusebox

3.5b Additional fuses are located in the fuse/relay box in the engine compartment

3.8a Remove the fasteners (arrowed) and remove the relay plate . . .

3.8b . . . from the front panel to gain access to the cooling fan relays (arrowed)

3.11 Relays inside the hydraulic pump insulated cover

on the top of the fuse, the fuses are also colour-coded as follows. Refer to the wiring diagrams for details of the fuse ratings and the circuits protected.

Colour	Rating
Orange	5A
Red	10A
Blue	15A
Yellow	20A
Clear or white	25A
Green	30A

7 Never renew a fuse more than once without tracing the source of the trouble. If the new fuse blows immediately, find the cause before renewing it again; a short to earth as a result of faulty insulation is most likely. Where a fuse

protects more than one circuit, try to isolate the fault by switching on each circuit in turn (where possible) until the fuse blows again. Always carry a supply of spare fuses of each relevant rating on the vehicle; a spare of each rating should be clipped into the fusebox.

Relays

8 The majority of relay functions are incorporated into the built-in system interface (BSI) unit (see Section 24). Other relays are located in the fuse/relay box in the engine compartment and the cooling fan relay(s) is/are located in front panel (see illustrations).
9 If a circuit or system controlled by a relay develops a fault and the relay is suspect, operate the system. If the relay is functioning, it should be possible to hear it 'click' as it is energised. If this is the case, the fault lies with the components or wiring of the system. If the relay is not being energised, then either the relay is not receiving a main supply or a switching voltage, or the relay itself is faulty. Testing is by the substitution of a known good unit, but be careful – while some relays are identical in appearance and in operation, others look similar but perform different functions.
10 To remove a relay, first ensure that the relevant circuit is switched off. The relay can then simply be pulled out from the socket, and pushed back into position.

11 On Cabriolet Coupe models, there are two relays for the roof and boot lid hydraulic system located in the luggage compartment next to the hydraulic pump (see illustration).

4 Switches – removal and refitting

Note: *Disconnect the battery negative lead before removing any switch, and reconnect the lead after refitting the switch.*

Ignition switch/ steering column lock

1 Refer to Chapter 10.

Steering column combination switches

2 Rotate the fastener a quarter-of-a-turn (90°) and remove the lower cover from the driver's side of the facia.
3 Undo the retaining screws and free the lower shroud from the column. Trace the audio unit control stalk wiring back to its connector then disconnect the connector and remove the shroud and switch as an assembly. Unclip and remove the upper shroud from the steering column (see illustrations).
4 To remove an individual switch assembly, remove the retaining screws then slide the

4.3a Undo the retaining screws (arrowed) then free the lower shroud from the steering column . . .

4.3b . . . disconnect the audio unit control stalk wiring connector and remove the shroud

4.3c Unclip the upper shroud and remove it from the column

4.4a To remove an individual switch, undo the screws (arrowed) . . .

4.4b . . . then slide the switch out of the holder and disconnect its wiring connector

4.5a To remove the complete assembly, undo the retaining screws (arrowed) . . .

4.5b . . . then lift off the switch and bracket assembly, disconnecting its wiring connectors

4.9 Undo the screws (arrowed) and remove the audio unit switch from the lower shroud

4.12a Unclip the switch panel from the facia . . .

switch out of its holder, disconnecting the wiring connector as it becomes accessible **(see illustrations)**.

5 To remove the complete switch and mounting bracket assembly it will first be necessary to remove the steering wheel (see Chapter 10). On models with a driver's airbag also remove the contact unit as described in Section 23. On all models, undo the retaining screws then remove the assembly from the top of the steering column, disconnecting the wiring connectors from the switches **(see illustrations)**.

6 Refitting is the reverse of removal, ensuring the wiring connectors are securely reconnected.

Audio unit control stalk switch

7 Rotate the fastener a quarter-of-a-turn (90°)

and remove the lower cover from the driver's side of the facia.

8 Undo the retaining screws and free the lower shroud from the column. Trace the audio unit control stalk wiring back to its connector then disconnect the connector and remove the shroud and switch as an assembly **(see illustrations 4.3a and 4.3b)**.

9 Undo the retaining screws and separate the audio control switch and lower shroud **(see illustration)**.

10 Refitting is a reversal of removal, ensuring that the switch wiring is routed as noted before removal.

Facia-mounted switches

11 Rotate the fastener a quarter-of-a-turn (90°)

and remove the lower cover from the driver's side of the facia.

12 Unclip the switch panel from the facia and disconnect the wiring connectors from the switches. Each individual switch can then be unclipped and remove from the panel **(see illustrations)**.

13 Refitting is the reverse of removal.

Hazard warning light switch

14 Carefully unclip the clock/multifunction unit surround from the top of the facia and remove it, disconnecting the wiring connector from the hazard warning light switch **(see illustration)**.

4.12b . . . and disconnect the switch wiring connectors

4.12c Each individual switch can then be pushed out of the panel

4.14 Unclip clock/multifunction unit surround from the facia and disconnect the hazard warning light switch wiring connector (arrowed) . . .

4.15 . . . the switch can then be unclipped from the surround

15 Unclip the switch and remove it from the surround **(see illustration)**.
16 Refitting is the reverse of removal.

Centre console switches

17 Carefully, taking care not to mark the switch or console, prise the relevant switch assembly out from the centre console **(see illustration)**.
18 Disconnect the switch from the wiring connector(s) and remove it from the vehicle **(see illustration)**.
19 Refitting is the reverse of removal.

Heating/ventilation control panel switches

20 The switches are an integral part of the heater/ventilation control panel, and cannot be renewed separately. If any switch is faulty, the complete control panel must be renewed – refer to Chapter 3 for details.

4.17 Carefully prise the switch out from the console . . .

Overhead console switches

21 The overhead console switches are an integral part of the courtesy light unit(s). If a switch is faulty the light unit will have to be renewed (see Section 6).

Stop-light switch

22 Refer to Chapter 9.

Handbrake warning light switch

23 Remove the rear section of the centre console as described in Chapter 11.
24 Carefully unclip the warning light switch from the floor and disconnect it from the wiring connector **(see illustrations)**. **Note: *If there is insufficient slack in the wiring to enable this to be done, it will be necessary to free the handbrake lever from the floor (see Chapter 9). Access to the wiring connector***

4.18 . . . and disconnect its wiring connectors

can then be gained by reaching in through the lever aperture.
25 Refitting is the reverse of removal.

Courtesy light switch

26 The courtesy light switches are an integral part of the door lock assemblies. Refer to Chapter 11 for door lock removal and refitting details.

Luggage area light switch

27 Open the tailgate/boot lid, and then undo the retaining screws and remove the grab handle from the inner trim panel. Working your way around the panel remove the retaining clips and unclip the panel from the tailgate/boot lid **(see illustrations)**.
28 Disconnect the wiring connector from the switch then undo the retaining bolt and remove the switch from the tailgate **(see illustration)**.
29 Refitting is the reverse of removal, ensuring the trim panel is correctly fitted to the tailgate.

4.24a Carefully prise the handbrake warning light switch out from the floor . . .

4.24b . . . and disconnect it from the wiring connector

4.27a Unclip the plastic cover (Cabriolet Coupe)

4.27b Undo the retaining screws (Estate model) . . .

4.27c . . . and release the retaining clips

4.28 Disconnect the wiring connector then undo the bolt (arrowed) and remove the switch from the tailgate

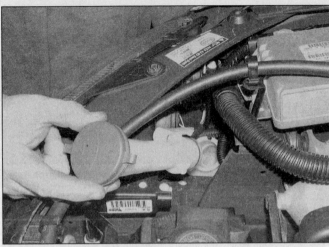

5.2 Unclip the washer reservoir filler neck to improve access to the right-hand headlight unit

5.3a On models with a combined dip/main beam bulb, disconnect the wiring connector . . .

Wiper rain sensor switch

30 Carefully unclip the rear view mirror housing from its mounting on the inside of the windscreen by pushing it gently upwards.
31 Disconnect the wiring connector then carefully release the side retaining clips and remove the rain sensor from the windscreen.
Caution: Do not touch the rain sensor lens or the windscreen glass in the area of the sensor. These areas must be kept spotlessly clean if the sensor is to function correctly.
32 Refitting is the reverse of removal, ensuring the sensor is securely retained by its clips. If a new sensor is being fitted, it will be necessary to remove the protective film from the sensor prior to installation. On completion, check the sensor operation by spraying the screen with water (wiper stalk in the auto position).

Glovebox illumination switch

33 Open the glovebox lid.
34 Carefully prise the switch out of position then disconnect it from the wiring connector.
35 Refitting is the reverse of removal.

5 Bulbs (exterior lights) – renewal

General

1 Whenever a bulb is renewed, note the following points:
 a) *Disconnect the battery negative lead before starting work.*
 b) *Remember that, if the light has just been in use, the bulb may be extremely hot.*
 c) *Always check the bulb contacts and holder, ensuring that there is clean metal-to-metal contact between the bulb and its live(s) and earth. Clean off any corrosion or dirt before fitting a new bulb.*
 d) *Wherever bayonet-type bulbs are fitted*

(see Specifications), ensure that the live contact(s) bear firmly against the bulb contact.
 e) *Always ensure that the new bulb is of the correct rating, and that it is completely clean before fitting it; this applies particularly to headlight/foglight bulbs (see below).*

Headlight

Note: On models with ABS, it may be necessary to remove the LH headlamp completely (as described is Section 7) to gain access to the bulb.
2 To improve access to the right-hand headlight, unclip the filler neck from the washer reservoir **(see illustration)**.
3 On models with a combined dipped/main beam bulb, disconnect the wiring connector from the rear of the headlight bulb then remove the rubber dust cover from the headlight unit, noting its correct fitted location **(see illustrations)**.
4 On models with separate dipped and main beam bulbs, release the retaining clip then remove the access cover from the rear of the headlight unit. Disconnect the wiring connector from the relevant bulb.
5 On all models, unhook the ends of the bulb retaining clip and release it from the rear of

5.3b . . . then remove the rubber dust cover from the headlight

the headlight unit. Withdraw the bulb **(see illustrations)**.
6 When handling the new bulb, use a tissue or clean cloth to avoid touching the glass with the fingers; moisture and grease from the skin can cause blackening and rapid failure of this type of bulb. If the glass is accidentally touched, wipe it clean using methylated spirit.
7 Install the new bulb, ensuring that its locating tabs are correctly seated in the light cut-outs, and secure it in position with the retaining clip.
8 On models with a combined dipped/main beam bulb, refit the rubber dust cover,

5.5a Unhook the retaining clip (arrowed) . . .

5.5b . . . then remove the bulb

5.11a Free the sidelight bulbholder from the rear of the headlight . . .

5.11b . . . then pull the bulb out from the holder

5.13 Open the flap in the wheel arch liner

ensuring it is correctly seated on the headlight unit and bulb, then reconnect the bulb wiring connector.

9 On models with separate dipped and main beam bulbs, reconnect the wiring connector. Ensure the seal is in good condition then securely refit the access cover to the headlight unit.

10 Where necessary, clip the filler neck securely back onto the washer reservoir.

Front sidelight

11 Rotate the bulbholder and free it from the rear of the headlight unit. The bulb is of the capless (push-fit) type, and can be removed by simply pulling it out of the holder **(see illustrations)**.

12 Refitting is the reverse of the removal procedure, ensuring that the bulbholder seal is in good condition.

Front foglight

13 Rotate the wheel onto full lock then open the flap in the wheel arch liner to gain access to the rear of the foglight unit **(see illustration)**.

14 Rotate the cover anti-clockwise and remove it from the foglight **(see illustration)**.

15 Disconnect the wiring connector from the foglight bulb **(see illustration)**.

16 Unhook the end of the bulb retaining clip and release it from the rear of the foglight unit **(see illustration)**. Withdraw the bulb.

17 When handling the new bulb, use a tissue

or clean cloth to avoid touching the glass with the fingers; moisture and grease from the skin can cause blackening and rapid failure of this type of bulb. If the glass is accidentally touched, wipe it clean using methylated spirit.

18 Install the new bulb, ensuring that its locating tabs are correctly seated in the light cut-outs. Secure the bulb in position with the retaining clip then reconnect the wiring connector.

19 Ensure the seal is in good condition then securely refit the cover to the rear of the foglight unit. Securely close the wheel arch liner flap.

Front direction indicator

20 Rotate the bulbholder and free it from the top of the headlight unit **(see illustration)**. The bulb is a bayonet-fit in the holder, and can be removed by pressing it in and rotating it anti-clockwise.

21 Refitting is the reverse of the removal procedure, ensuring that the bulbholder seal is in good condition.

Direction indicator side repeater

22 Push the light unit to one side, to free its retaining clips, and then ease it out from the front wing **(see illustration)**.

23 Rotate the bulbholder anti-clockwise and free it from the rear of the light. The bulb is of the capless (push-fit) type, and can be

5.14 Rotate the cover anti-clockwise and remove it from the foglight (shown with bumper removed for clarity)

5.15 Disconnect the wiring connector from the bulb . . .

5.16 . . . then unhook the retaining clip and withdraw the foglight bulb

5.20 Rotate the direction indicator bulbholder to free it from the headlight

5.22 Ease the side repeater light unit out from the wing . . .

5.23a . . . then free the bulbholder from the light . . .

5.23b . . . and pull out the bulb

5.26a Unscrew the bulbholder nut (1) using the tool (2) supplied . . .

removed by simply pulling it out of the holder **(see illustrations)**.

24 Refitting is a reversal of the removal procedure.

Rear light

Hatchback

25 Remove the rear light unit as described in Section 7.

26 Unscrew the bulbholder retaining nut and

remove the bulbholder from the light unit. The nut can be unscrewed using the tool supplied which is clipped to the rear of the light unit; if the tool has never been used it will still be moulded to the rear light shell; break the tab to release it **(see illustrations)**.

Estate

27 Remove the rear light unit as described in Section 7.

28 The bulbholder can be removed from

the light unit by releasing the retaining clips and withdrawing the bulbholder **(see illustrations)**.

Cabriolet Coupe

29 Remove the rear light unit as described in Section 7.

30 Unscrew the bulbholder retaining nut and remove the bulbholder from the light unit. The nut can be unscrewed using the tool supplied which is clipped to the rear of the light unit;

5.26b . . . if the tool has not been used before it will still be moulded onto the light unit

5.26c Remove the bulbholder from the light unit

5.28a Release the retaining clips . . .

5.28b . . . and withdraw the bulbholder

5.30a Undo the bulb holder retaining nut . . .

5.30b . . . and withdraw the bulbholder

5.30c If tool still in place, break the tool of the side of the bulbholder . . .

5.30d . . . fit the tool over the nut and unscrew it

if the tool has never been used it will still be moulded to the rear light shell; break the tab to release it **(see illustrations)**.

All models

31 All the bulbs have bayonet fittings. The relevant bulb can be removed by pressing it in slightly and rotating it anti-clockwise **(see illustration)**. Note that the stop/tail light bulb has offset pins to ensure it is fitted the correct way around.

32 Refitting is the reverse of removal, ensuring the light unit and bulbholder seals are in good condition. Where applicable, make sure the locating pegs on the rear of the light unit are located correctly in the body panel **(see illustration 7.25a and 7.25b)**.

Rear foglight

33 Reach up behind the bumper then release

5.30e Store the tool on the peg provided on the rear of the bulb holder

the retaining clip and push the light unit out from the rear bumper.

34 Rotate the bulbholder anti-clockwise and free it from the rear of the light unit. The bulb is a bayonet-fit in the holder, and can be

5.31 Remove the relevant bulb by pressing it in and rotating it anti-clockwise

removed by pressing it in and rotating it anti-clockwise **(see illustrations)**.

35 Refitting is the reverse of the removal procedure, ensuring the bulbholder seal is in good condition.

High-level stop-light

Note: *On some models, the high-level brake light unit is a complete sealed unit. The bulbs on this type cannot be renewed; a complete light unit will be required.*

36 Remove the light unit as described in Section 7.

37 Where applicable, release the retaining clips and detach the bulbholder from the light unit. Each bulb is of the capless (push-fit) type, and can be removed by simply pulling it out of the bulbholder **(see illustrations)**.

38 Refitting is the reverse of removal. Do not overtighten the light unit retaining nuts, as the plastic is easily broken.

5.34a Rotate the bulbholder anti-clockwise to free it from the light unit . . .

5.34b . . . then remove the bulb by pressing it in and rotating it anti-clockwise

5.37a Unclip the bulbholder from the rear of the high-level stop-light . . .

5.37b . . . and pull out the relevant bulb

5.40a Carefully unclip the lens from the number plate light . . .

5.40b . . . and pull out the bulb

Number plate light

39 Remove the light unit as described in Section 7.

40 Carefully unclip and remove the lens from the number plate light unit. The bulb is of the capless (push-fit) type, and can be removed by simply pulling it out of the light unit **(see illustrations)**.

41 Refitting is the reverse of the removal procedure, ensuring that the lens is securely clipped in position.

6 Bulbs (interior lights) – renewal

General

1 Refer to Section 5, paragraph 1.

Courtesy light and map reading light

2 Using a flat bladed-screwdriver, carefully ease the light unit out of position and disconnect it from the wiring connector **(see illustration)**.

3 Release the bulbholder from the light unit. The bulb is of the capless (push-fit) type, and can be removed by simply pulling it out of the bulbholder **(see illustrations)**.

4 Refitting is the reverse of the removal procedure

Instrument panel illumination/warning lights

5 Remove the instrument panel as described in Section 9.

6 Twist the relevant bulbholder anti-clockwise and remove it from the rear of the instrument panel **(see illustration)**. All bulbs are integral with their holders.

7 Ensure the new bulb is off the correct rating

then securely fit the holder to the rear of the instrument panel.

8 Refit the instrument panel as described in Section 9.

Heating/ventilation control panel illumination bulb

Manual heater

9 Remove the control panel as described in Chapter 3.

10 Pull off the knob from the air recirculation flap lever **(see illustration)**.

11 Carefully release the retaining clips and

6.2 Carefully prise the courtesy light unit out of position

6.3a Free the bulbholder from the rear of the light . . .

6.3b . . . then pull the bulb out from its holder

6.6 Rotate the bulbholder anti-clockwise and remove it from the rear of the instrument panel

6.10 Pull off the knob from the air recirculation lever . . .

6.11a ... then carefully release the retaining clips (arrowed) ...

6.11b ... and separate the two halves of the heating/ventilation manual control panel

6.11c The illumination bulbs (arrowed) can then be pulled out

separate the two halves of the control panel. The illumination bulbs can then be pulled out of position **(see illustrations)**.
Caution: Do not use excessive force when separating the control panel, as the panel is easily broken. Do not attempt to remove the LEDs from the control panel; these are an integral part of the panel and cannot be renewed separately.
12 Fit the new bulb(s) then reassemble the control panel, engaging the control knobs with their shafts. Check the operation of the panel controls and switches then refit the knob to the recirculation lever.
13 Refit the control panel as described in Chapter 3.

Automatic climate control system
14 At the time of writing no information it

was unclear whether the illumination bulbs were an integral part of the control panel or whether they could be renewed separately. Refer to your Peugeot dealer for the latest available information. Control panel removal and refitting is described in Chapter 3.

Clock/multifunction unit illumination bulb
15 Carefully unclip the clock/multifunction unit surround from the top of the facia and remove it, disconnecting the wiring connector from the hazard warning light switch **(see illustration)**.
16 Rotate the relevant bulbholder anti-clockwise and remove it from the top of the clock/multifunction unit **(see illustration)**. The bulb is integral with the holder.

17 Securely fit the new bulbholder then reconnect the switch wiring connector and clip the surround back into position.

Centre console ashtray illumination bulb
18 Unclip the ashtray and remove it from the centre console.
19 Free the bulbholder from the console and pull the bulb out from its holder.
20 Securely fit the new bulb to its holder then clip the holder back into position on the console. Refit the ashtray.

Cigarette lighter illumination bulb
21 Remove the centre console as described in Chapter 11.
22 Carefully release retaining clips and slide the illumination light assembly off the base of the lighter, taking care not to break its electrical contacts **(see illustration)**.
23 Unclip the bulbholder from the base of the assembly then pull the bulb out from the holder **(see illustration)**.
24 Fit the new bulb then clip the bulbholder back into the assembly.
25 Slide the light assembly onto the metal insert and clip it securely onto the plastic outer.
26 Ensure the cigarette lighter is correctly assembled then refit the centre console.

Switch illumination bulbs
27 All of the switches are fitted with illumination bulbs. On most switches, these bulbs are an integral part of the switch and cannot be renewed separately. Bulb renewal will therefore require renewal of the complete switch assembly (see Section 4).

6.16 Rotate the relevant bulbholder anti-clockwise and remove it from the unit

6.15 Unclip the clock/multifunction unit surround from the facia and disconnect the switch wiring connector (arrowed)

6.22 Unclip the illumination light assembly from the cigarette lighter ...

6.23 ... and free the bulbholder

7   Exterior light units –
removal and refitting

Note: *Disconnect the battery negative lead before removing any light unit, and reconnect the battery after refitting light unit.*

7.1 If the left-hand headlight is being removed, pull up the retaining clip pin and remove the air intake deflector

7.2a Pull out the centre pin and remove each fastener securing the grille panel in position . . .

7.2b . . . then release the retaining clips (arrowed) and remove the panel in an upwards direction

Headlight

1 Open the bonnet. If the left-hand headlight is being removed, pull out the retaining clip pin and remove the air intake water deflector from the top of the headlight unit **(see illustration)**.

2 Remove the four fasteners (pull out the centre pin then remove the complete fastener) securing the grille panel to the top of the front panel. Release the lower retaining clips and unclip the grille panel from the front trim panel in an upward direction **(see illustrations)**.

3 Slacken and remove the retaining screws securing the front trim panel in position. Carefully unclip the trim panel from the inner edge of each headlight then unclip the ends of the panel from each wing and remove the panel from the vehicle **(see illustrations)**.

4 Slacken and remove the three mounting bolts and free the headlight unit from its mounting pin. Disconnect the wiring connectors from the headlight unit then manoeuvre the unit out of position **(see illustrations)**.

5 On models equipped with a headlight-levelling system, if necessary, remove the motor from the rear of the light unit by rotating it anti-clockwise and carefully unclipping its balljoint from the rear of the reflector unit **(see illustration)**.

6 Prior to refitting ensure the levelling system motor (where fitted) is correctly installed.

7 Offer up the headlight unit and securely reconnect its wiring connectors.

7.3a Undo the retaining screws (arrowed) . . .

7.3b . . . then unclip the panel ends from the wings . . .

7.3c . . . and remove the front trim panel from the vehicle

7.4a Slacken and remove upper mounting bolts (arrowed) . . .

7.4b . . . and lower mounting bolt (arrowed) . . .

7.4c . . . then disconnect the wiring connectors and remove the headlight unit

7.5 Rotate the levelling motor and unclip it from the rear of the unit

7.8 Ensure the headlight bracket (1) engages correctly with the pin (2) when refitting the headlight unit

8 Align the headlight bracket with the mounting pin on the outer edge of the body then seat the headlight in position, ensuring its locating tab is correctly located in the cut-out in the wing **(see illustration)**.

9 Refit the headlight mounting bolts. Tighten all the bolts lightly then securely tighten the bolts in the following order.
  a) *Upper, outermost bolt.*
  b) *Lower bolt.*
  c) *Upper, innermost bolt*

10 Check the operation of the headlight then clip the front trim panel into position and securely tighten its retaining screws. Clip the grille panel onto the trim panel and secure it in position with the fasteners.

11 Check the headlight beam alignment using the information given in Section 8.

7.12a Remove the retaining screws (arrowed) . . .

Front foglight

12 Undo the screws securing the front section of the relevant wheel arch liner to the base of the bumper. Remove the fasteners securing the liner section to the body then manoeuvre the front section of the liner out from underneath the wing **(see illustrations)**.

13 Disconnect the wiring connector from the foglight **(see illustration)**.

14 Undo the lower retaining screw then free the foglight unit and remove it from the bumper **(see illustration)**. **Note:** *If the left-hand foglight is being removed, remove the air cleaner housing intake duct to improve access to the light unit (see Chapter 4A or 4B).*

15 Refitting is the reverse of removal. If necessary adjust the foglight aim using the adjuster on the rear of the light unit.

7.12b . . . and fasteners . . .

Direction indicator side repeater

16 Push the light unit to one side, to free its retaining clips, and then ease it out from the wing panel **(see illustration)**.

17 Disconnect the wiring connector and remove the light unit from the vehicle **(see illustration)**.

18 Refitting is a reversal of the removal procedure.

Rear light unit

Hatchback

19 Remove the fastener(s) (pull out the centre pin then remove the complete fastener) and free the luggage compartment side trim panel from the body to gain access to the rear of the light unit **(see illustration)**.

7.12c . . . and manoeuvre the front section of the wheel arch liner out from under the wing

7.13 Disconnect the wiring connector from the foglight . . .

7.14 . . . then undo the retaining screw (1) and remove the foglight from the front bumper (note the adjuster – 2)

7.16 Ease the side repeater light out from the wing . . .

7.17 . . . and disconnect it from the wiring connector

7.19 Pull out the centre pin then remove the fastener securing the luggage compartment side trim panel in position

7.20a Disconnect the wiring connector (1) then unscrew the wing nut (2) . . .

7.20b . . . and remove the rear light unit

7.21a Carefully unclip the trim panel . . .

7.21b . . . and remove it from the rear pillar

7.22a Undo the plastic retaining nuts (arrowed) . . .

7.22b . . . withdraw the light unit . . .

20 Disconnect the wiring connector from the light unit then unscrew the wing nut and remove the light unit from the vehicle (see illustrations).

Estate

21 Open the tailgate and unclip the inner trim panel from the inside of the rear pillar (see illustrations).
22 Unscrew the plastic retaining nuts and withdraw the light unit, disconnecting the wiring connector on removal (see illustrations).

Cabriolet Coupe

23 Open the boot lid, and then open the flap

7.22c . . . and disconnect the wiring connector

in the luggage side trim panel to gain access to the rear of the light unit (see illustration).
24 Disconnect the wiring connector from

7.23 Open the access panel in the inner trim panel

the light unit then unscrew the wing nut and remove the light unit from the vehicle (see illustrations).

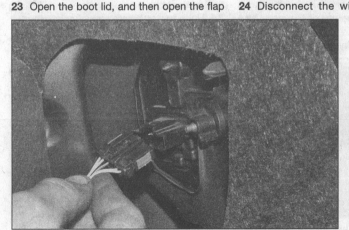

7.24a Disconnect the wiring connector . . .

7.24b . . . and undo the plastic wing nut (arrowed)

7.25a Locating peg (arrowed) – Estate

7.25b Locating peg (arrowed) – Cabriolet Coupe

7.27 Push the rear foglight unit out from the bumper and disconnect its wiring connector

All models

25 Refitting is the reverse of removal, ensuring the light unit seal is in good condition. Where applicable, make sure the locating pegs on the rear of the light unit are located correctly in the body panel **(see illustrations)**.

Rear foglight

26 Reach up behind the bumper then release the retaining clip and push the light unit out from the rear bumper.
27 Disconnect the wiring connector and remove the light unit from the vehicle **(see illustration)**.
28 Refitting is the reverse of the removal procedure.

High-level stop-light

Hatchback

29 Open the tailgate the unscrew the nuts securing the light unit to the tailgate **(see illustration)**. Carefully push on the light unit studs to ease the unit out from the tailgate spoiler.
30 Disconnect the washer hose and wiring connector and remove the light unit from the tailgate **(see illustration)**.
31 Refitting is the reverse of removal. Do not overtighten the light unit retaining nuts, as the plastic is easily broken.

Estate

32 Open the tailgate and remove the two screws from the hinges. Note on the left-hand hinge the rubber cover will need to be pulled back to access the retaining screw **(see illustration)**.

7.29 Unscrew the retaining nuts (arrowed) then push the high-level stop-light out of position

7.32 Pull back the rubber cover and remove the retaining screw

33 Shut the tailgate and open the tailgate glass, undo the retaining screw and remove the trim panel from the top of the glass **(see illustration)**.
34 Disconnect the wiring connector and the

7.30 Disconnect the washer hose and wiring connector (arrowed) then remove the light unit from the tailgate

7.33 Removing the trim panel from the top of the glass

washer pipe from the upper rear spoiler **(see illustrations)**.
35 Undo the retaining screws and withdraw the spoiler from the top of the tailgate glass **(see illustration)**.

7.34a Disconnect the wiring connector . . .

7.34b . . . and the washer pipe

7.35 Undo the outer spoiler retaining screws

7.36 Undo the two retaining screws (arrowed

7.39a Locking the upper boot lid in the open position . . .

7.39b . . . using an Allen key (arrowed) – supplied in the breakdown kit

7.40 Undo the two nuts (arrowed)

7.43a Release the retaining clips and push the number plate light unit out of the tailgate . . .

7.43b . . . then disconnect its wiring connector

36 Undo the two retaining screws and remove the high-level stop-light (**see illustration**).
37 Refitting is the reverse of removal.

Cabriolet Coupe

38 With the boot lid in the closed position, open the upper part of the boot lid from the rear screen backwards.
39 Lock the upper part of the boot lid by inserting the Allen key (4 mm) supplied with the vehicle breakdown kit into the hinge bracket on the right-hand rear of the vehicle (**see illustrations**).

 Warning: Always make sure the upper part of the boot lid is locked in position and cannot move before working on any components.

40 Disconnect the wiring connector, undo the two retaining nuts and remove the high-level

stop-light unit from the upper boot lid panel (**see illustration**).
41 Refitting is the reverse of removal.

Number plate light

Hatchback

42 Open the tailgate and then carefully unclip the inner trim panel from the tailgate.
43 Release the retaining clips then push the relevant light unit out from the tailgate. Disconnect the wiring connector and remove the light unit (**see illustrations**).
44 Refitting is the reverse of removal.

Estate

45 Open the tailgate and unclip the light unit from the trim panel above the number plate (**see illustration**).
46 Disconnect the wiring connector as the light unit is removed (**see illustration**).

Cabriolet Coupe

47 Open the boot lid and unclip the lens cover from the light unit (**see illustration**).

7.45 Unclip the light unit . . .

7.46 . . . and disconnect the wiring connector

7.47 Unclip the lens from the light unit

7.48a Unclip the light unit . . .

7.48b . . . and disconnect the wiring connector

8.2 Headlight beam adjustment screw locations (arrowed). The outer screw is accessed through the hole in the panel

9.3 Unclip the instrument panel shroud from the facia (shown with steering wheel removed for clarity)

9.4 Undo the retaining screw . . .

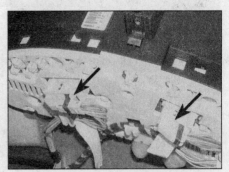

9.5 . . . then unclip and remove the instrument panel, disconnecting its wiring connectors (arrowed)

48 Using a small screwdriver unclip the light unit from the boot lid panel, and then disconnect the wiring connector as the light unit is removed **(see illustrations).**

8 Headlight beam alignment – general information

1 Accurate adjustment of the headlight beam is only possible using optical beam-setting equipment, and this work should therefore be carried out by a Peugeot dealer or suitably-equipped workshop.
2 For reference, the headlights can be adjusted using a suitable-sized Allen key to

11.2 Unclip the clock/multifunction unit surround from the facia and disconnect the wiring connector (arrowed)

rotate the adjuster assemblies fitted to the rear of each light unit. The outer adjuster alters the vertical height of the beam, whilst the inner adjuster alters the horizontal position of the beam **(see illustration).**
3 On models equipped with headlight-levelling, ensure the adjuster switch is set to position 0 before the headlights are adjusted. On models not equipped with headlight-levelling, ensure the manual adjuster on the rear of each headlight unit is set to position 0 before adjustment (where fitted).

9 Instrument panel – removal and refitting

Removal

1 Disconnect the battery negative terminal.
2 To improve access, release the height adjuster lever and fully lower the steering column.
3 Starting at the bottom of the shroud, carefully unclip the shroud and remove it from the facia **(see illustration).**
4 Slacken and remove the instrument panel retaining screw **(see illustration).**
5 Remove the instrument panel assembly from the facia, disconnecting the wiring connectors as they become accessible **(see illustration).**

Refitting

6 Securely reconnect the wiring connectors to the instrument panel and clip the panel back into position in the facia. Refit the panel retaining screw, tightening it securely.
7 Clip the instrument panel shroud back onto the facia.
8 Reconnect the battery and check the operation of the panel warning lights to ensure they are functioning correctly.

10 Instrument panel components – removal and refitting

At the time of writing, it was unclear if any of the instrument panel components were available separately. Refer to your Peugeot dealer for the latest parts information; they will advise you on the best course of action should the instrument(s) develop a fault.

11 Clock/multifunction unit – removal and refitting

Removal

1 Disconnect the battery negative terminal.
2 Carefully unclip the clock/multifunction unit surround from the top of the facia and remove it, disconnecting the wiring connector from the hazard warning light switch **(see illustration).**

11.3a Undo the retaining screws (arrowed) . . .

11.3b . . . and remove the clock/ multifunction unit, disconnecting its wiring connectors

12.2 Unclip the illumination light assembly from the cigarette lighter

3 Undo the retaining screws then remove the clock/multifunction unit, disconnecting its wiring connector as it becomes accessible (**see illustrations**).

Refitting

4 Reconnect the wiring connector then seat the clock/multifunction unit back in position. Refit the unit retaining screws, tightening them securely.

5 Reconnect the wiring connector to the hazard warning light switch then clip the surround back onto the facia.

12 Cigarette lighter – removal and refitting

Removal

1 Remove the centre console as described in Chapter 11.

2 Carefully release retaining clips and slide the illumination light assembly off the base of the lighter, taking great care not to break its electrical contacts (**see illustration**).

3 Pull out the lighter element then release the tangs and push out the metal insert. The plastic outer section can then be removed from the console (**see illustrations**).

Refitting

4 Align the plastic outer section tab with the cut-out then insert it into the console.

5 Align the bulbholder contact on the metal insert with the holder tangs on the plastic outer then clip the insert into position.

6 Slide the illumination light assembly onto the metal insert and clip it securely onto the plastic outer.

7 Ensure the cigarette lighter is correctly assembled then refit the centre console as described in Chapter 11.

13 Horn – removal and refitting

Removal

1 The horn is located behind the front bumper, on the right-hand side. To gain access, firmly apply the handbrake then jack up the front of the vehicle, and support it securely on axle stands (see *Jacking and vehicle support*).

2 Disconnect the wiring connector(s) then slacken the mounting nut and remove the horn from the vehicle (**see illustration**).

Refitting

3 Refitting is a reversal of removal.

14 Wiper arm – removal and refitting

Note: *The wiper arms are a very tight fit on their spindles and it is likely that a puller will be needed to remove them safely, without damage.*

12.3a Unclip and remove the metal insert . . .

12.3b . . . then slide out the plastic outer section

13.2 Horn mounting nut (1) and wiring connector (2) (viewed from front with bumper removed)

14.2a Unclip the securing peg . . .

14.2b . . . and withdraw the plastic cover

14.3 On right-hand drive models the driver's side wiper arm has a dual pivot arrangement (arrowed)

Removal

1 Operate the wiper motor, then switch it off so that the wiper arm returns to the

14.4 Using a puller to free a wiper arm from its spindle

at-rest position. Stick tape to the screen alongside the wiper blade to ensure correct refitment.

2 Lift up the wiper arm spindle nut cover (where fitted) then slacken and remove the spindle nut. On the rear wiper arm (Estate models), using a small screwdriver unclip the securing peg and withdraw the plastic cover from the wiper arm retaining nut (see illustrations).

3 On right-hand drive models the driver's side front wiper arm incorporates a linkage at its lower end and is also fixed to a pivot by a second nut; remove this nut as well (see illustration).

4 Lift the blade off the glass, and pull the wiper arm off its spindle. If the arm is very tight, free it from the spindle using a suitable puller (see illustration).

Refitting

5 Ensure that the wiper arm and spindle splines are clean and dry, and then refit the arm to the spindle, aligning the wiper blade with the tape fitted on removal.

6 Refit the spindle nut, tightening it securely, and clip the nut plastic cover (where fitted) back into position.

15 Windscreen wiper motor and linkage – removal and refitting

Removal

1 Disconnect the battery negative lead.

2 Remove the wiper arms (see Section 14).

3 On petrol engine models, remove the air cleaner housing-to-inlet manifold intake duct to improve access (see Chapter 4A).

4 Free the sealing strip from the top of the bulkhead then, starting at the inner end and working outwards, carefully unclip the left-hand section of the water deflector panel. Free the panel from the right-hand section and remove it from base of the windscreen (see illustrations).

5 Unscrew the mounting bolt, located directly beneath the wiper motor (see illustration).

6 Unscrew the retaining nut and washer from each wiper arm spindle then free the wiper motor assembly from the body. Disconnect the wiring connector then manoeuvre the assembly out of position (see illustrations).

15.4a Free the sealing strip from the top of the bulkhead . . .

15.4b . . . then unclip and remove the left-hand section of the water deflector panel (retaining clips arrowed)

15.5 Slacken and remove the mounting bolt from beneath the wiper motor

15.6a Unscrew the nut and remove the washer from each wiper spindle

15.6b Disconnect the wiring connector . . .

15.6c . . . then manoeuvre the wiper motor assembly out of position

15.7 Wiper motor shaft nut (1) and retaining bolts (2)

16.4 Carefully drill the heads of the rivets (arrowed) securing the wiper motor bracket to the tailgate

7 If necessary, mark the relative positions of the motor shaft and crank, then unscrew the retaining nut and washer and free the wiper linkage from the motor spindle **(see illustration)**. Unscrew the motor retaining bolts and separate the motor and linkage.

Refitting

8 Refitting is a reversal of removal, ensuring all fasteners are securely tightened. Ensure the water deflector panel is securely clipped in position prior to refitting the wiper arms.

16 Tailgate window wiper motor – removal and refitting

Removal

Hatchback

Note: *A pop rivet gun and suitable rivets will be required on refitting.*

1 Disconnect the battery negative lead.
2 Remove the wiper arm (see Section 14), and then unscrew the wiper motor spindle nut.
3 Open the tailgate and then unclip the inner trim panel from the tailgate.
4 Using a 7.5 mm drill, carefully drill the heads off the pop rivets securing the wiper motor bracket to the tailgate **(see illustration)**. To prevent the rivets falling into the tailgate, position a cloth on either side of the motor.

Caution: Take care not to damage the motor and tailgate when drilling out the rivets.

5 With the three rivets removed, disconnect the wiring connector and remove the wiper motor from the tailgate **(see illustration)**. Take care not to lose the collars from the motor mounting rubbers.
6 Remove the wiper motor sealing grommet from the tailgate glass.
7 Remove the cloths and recover the remnants of each rivet from the motor bracket/tailgate. Ensure all traces of rivet are removed.
8 If necessary, undo the three bolts and separate the wiper motor and bracket **(see illustration)**.

Estate

9 Disconnect the battery negative lead.

16.5 Disconnect the wiring connector and remove the wiper motor assembly from the tailgate

10 Remove the wiper arm (see Section 14), and then unscrew the wiper motor spindle nut.
11 Open the tailgate glass and then undo the retaining screw and unclip the inner trim panel from the wiper motor **(see illustration)**.
12 Disconnect the wiring connector from the wiper motor, and then undo the three mounting nuts **(see illustrations)**.
13 Remove the wiper motor from the tailgate glass, and then remove the wiper motor sealing grommet from the tailgate glass. Where applicable, retrieve any spacers from the motor mounting bracket.

Refitting

14 Prior to refitting check the sealing grommet and rubber mountings for signs of damage or deterioration and renew as necessary.

16.8 Unscrew the bolts (arrowed) and separate the wiper motor and bracket

16.11 Remove the inner trim panel

16.12a Disconnect the wiring connector (arrowed)

16.12b Wiper motor mounting nuts (arrowed)

16.15a Ensure the rubber grommet is correctly fitted to the tailgate glass ...

16.15b ... and the mounting rubbers and collars are correctly fitted to the motor mounting bracket

17.2 Unclip the filler neck and remove it from the washer fluid reservoir

15 Ensure the rubber grommet is correctly fitted to the tailgate glass, and the rubber mountings and collars/spacers are correctly fitted to the motor mounting bracket **(see illustrations)**.

16 Manoeuvre the wiper motor into position and secure it in position with new pop rivets/ mounting nuts. Tighten the wiper motor spindle nut to the specified torque wrench setting.

17 Reconnect the wiring connector to the motor then refit the trim panel to the tailgate/ wiper motor.

18 Refit the wiper arm as described in Section 14 then reconnect the battery.

17.6 Disconnect the washer hoses ...

17.7 ... and wiring connector from the washer pump

17 Washer system components – removal and refitting

1 The washer reservoir is located behind the right-hand front wing and supplies both the windscreen and tailgate washers via the same pump. On models equipped with headlight washers, the reservoir also supplies the headlight washer jets via an additional pump.

Washer fluid reservoir

2 Working in the engine compartment, unclip the filler neck from the reservoir **(see illustration)**.

3 Jack up the front of the vehicle, and support it securely on axle stands (see *Jacking and*

vehicle support). To improve access, remove the right-hand roadwheel.

4 Undo the screws securing the front section of the right-hand wheel arch liner to the base of the bumper. Remove the fasteners securing the liner section to the body then manoeuvre the front section of the liner out from underneath the wing.

5 On models with front foglights, remove the right-hand foglight unit (see Section 7).

6 Note the correct fitted location of the washer hoses (if necessary, mark them for identification purposes) then disconnect the hoses from the washer pump(s) **(see illustration)**.

7 Disconnect the wiring connector(s) from the washer pump(s) **(see illustration)**.

8 Slacken and remove the retaining bolt then free the reservoir from the body and

manoeuvre it out from underneath the wing **(see illustration)**.

9 Refitting is the reverse of removal, ensuring that the hoses are securely reconnected. Refill the reservoir and check for leaks.

Washer pump

10 Proceed as described in paragraphs 3 to 7 and disconnect the hose(s) and wiring connector from the pump (there is no need to remove the foglight).

11 Position a container beneath the reservoir to catch the washer fluid as the pump is removed.

12 Carefully ease the pump out from the reservoir, and recover its sealing grommet **(see illustrations)**. Wash off any spilt fluid with cold water.

13 Refitting is the reverse of removal, using

17.8 Unscrew the mounting bolt (arrowed – shown with bumper removed) and remove the washer fluid reservoir

17.12a Ease the washer pump out of position ...

17.12b ... and remove the sealing grommet from the reservoir

17.17 Unclip the bulbholder from the rear of the high-level stop-light

17.18a Disconnect the washer hose . . .

17.18b . . . then rotate the washer jet 90° and remove it from the light

a new sealing grommet if the original shows signs of damage or deterioration. Refill the reservoir and check the pump grommet for leaks on completion.

Windscreen washer jet

14 Open the bonnet to gain access to the base of the windscreen washer jets. Disconnect the washer hose(s) from the relevant jet, then depress the retaining clips and ease the jet out of position.
15 On refitting, securely connect the jet to the hose then clip it into the bonnet. Check the operation of the jet. If necessary, adjust the nozzles using a pin aiming one nozzle to a point slightly above the centre of the

swept area of the screen and the other to a point slightly below the centre point to ensure complete coverage.

Tailgate washer jet

16 Remove the high-level stop-light unit as described in Section 7.
17 Release the retaining clips and detach the light unit from the bulbholder **(see illustration)**.
18 Disconnect the washer hose from the jet then free the jet from the light unit, by rotating it a quarter-of-a-turn **(see illustrations)**.
19 Refitting is the reverse of removal. Do not overtighten the light unit retaining nuts, as the plastic is easily broken. The washer jet is not adjustable.

Headlight washer jet

20 Remove the bumper as described in Chapter 11.
21 Disconnect the washer hose from the washer jet then unscrew the retaining nuts and remove the jet from the bumper.
22 Refitting is the reverse of removal.

---

18 Audio unit/CD autochanger – removal and refitting

Note: *The following procedure is for the range of equipment fitted by Peugeot.*

Audio unit

Removal

1 Ensure the audio unit is switched off.
2 Insert a small screwdriver/punch into the hole on each side of the unit and pushing it in until the clip releases **(see illustration)**.
3 Once both retaining clips have been released, slide the audio unit out of position. Disconnect the wiring connections and aerial lead and remove the unit from the vehicle **(see illustration)**.

Refitting

4 Prior to refitting, reset the audio unit retaining clips.
5 Securely reconnect the aerial lead and wiring connectors then slide the unit back into position, taking care not to trap the wiring.
6 Switch on the unit and enter the security code (see *Audio unit anti-theft system* section in the Reference section at the end of this manual).

CD autochanger

Removal

7 Remove the screws and/or fastener(s) (pull out the centre pin then remove the complete fastener) and free the luggage compartment side trim panel from the body to gain access to the CD autochanger **(see illustrations)**.

18.2 Release the retaining clips by inserting a screwdriver/punch into each of the holes . . .

18.3 . . . then withdraw the audio unit from facia and disconnect its wiring connectors and aerial lead (arrowed)

18.7a Remove the screw and hook . . .

18.7b . . . and the fasteners and peel back the luggage compartment side trim panel to gain access to the CD autochanger

18.8a Slide the CD autochanger out of its bracket . . .

18.8b . . . then disconnect its wiring connector

8 Slide the CD autochanger unit out of its mounting bracket then release the retaining clip and disconnect its wiring connector (**see illustrations**).

9 If necessary, the mounting bracket can then be unbolted from the body.

Refitting

10 Refitting is the reverse of removal.

---

19 Loudspeakers –
  removal and refitting

Removal

Front door speaker

1 Remove the door inner trim panel as described in Chapter 11.

2 Slacken and remove the retaining screws then remove the speaker from the door, disconnecting the wiring connector as it becomes accessible (**see illustrations**).

3 If necessary, carefully drill the heads off the pop rivets securing the speaker housing to the door then remove the housing.

Caution: Take care not to damage the

housing and door when drilling out the rivets.

Front door tweeter

4 Carefully unclip the exterior mirror inner trim panel from the front of the door (**see illustration**). On models with manually-adjusted mirrors, remove the rubber gaiter from the adjustment handle prior to unclipping the trim panel.

5 Rotate the tweeter speaker to free it from the trim panel and disconnect it from the wiring connector (**see illustration**).

Rear speaker – five-door models

Note: *A pop rivet gun and suitable rivets will be required on refitting.*

6 Remove the door inner trim panel as described in Chapter 11.

7 Carefully drill the heads off the pop rivets securing the speaker assembly to the door.

8 Release the retaining clips then free the speaker from its housing, disconnecting the wiring connector as it becomes accessible (**see illustration**).

9 If necessary, the speaker housing can then

19.2a Undo the retaining screws
(arrowed) . . .

19.2b . . . then remove the front door speaker from its housing, disconnecting its wiring connector

19.4 Unclip the mirror inner trim panel from the door . . .

19.5 . . . and rotate the tweeter speaker to free it from the panel

19.8 Drill out the pop rivets then unclip the speaker from the rear door and disconnect its wiring connector

19.9 The speaker housing can then be unclipped and removed from the door

19.11a On three-door models, undo the retaining screws (arrowed) . . .

19.11b . . . then unclip the upper trim panel from the rear pillar

19.12a Remove the trim cap and unscrew the mounting bolt (arrowed) . . .

19.12b . . . then free the anchorage bar from the body and recover the washer (arrowed)

19.12c Recover the spacer (1) and trim cap (2) fitted between the anchorage bar and body

be unclipped and removed from the door **(see illustration)**.

Rear speaker – three-door models

10 Lift out the parcel shelf then remove the seat cushion and back as described in Chapter 11.

11 Peel back the luggage compartment side trim panel then slacken and remove the upper trim panel retaining screws. Unclip the panel

and free it from the rear seat belt. If the left-hand panel is being removed, it will also be necessary to remove the courtesy light from the panel **(see illustrations)**.

12 Prise off the trim cap from the front seat belt lower anchorage bolt then slacken and remove the bolt and washer. Free the anchorage bar from the body then slide off the washer and free the bar from the seat belt. Recover the spacer and trim cap fitted

between the anchorage bar mounting and body **(see illustrations)**.

13 Remove the button from the seat belt upper mounting height adjuster then undo the retaining screw and remove the trim cover from the mounting. Unscrew the mounting bolt and free the belt from the height adjuster **(see illustrations)**.

14 Unclip the top of the pillar upper trim panel then free the panel from the seat

19.13a Remove the height adjuster button then undo the retaining screw (arrowed) and remove the trim cover from the seat belt upper mounting

19.13b Unscrew the mounting bolt and free the seat belt from the height adjuster

19.14 Unclip the upper trim panel from the pillar and free it from the seat belt

19.15a Remove the trim cap then unscrew the rear seat belt lower mounting bolt . . .

19.15b . . . and recover the spacer (arrowed) fitted between the belt and body

belt and remove it from the vehicle **(see illustration)**.

15 Prise off the trim cap from the rear seat belt lower mounting bolt then slacken and remove the bolt and washer. Free the belt and recover the spacer fitted between the belt and body **(see illustrations)**.

16 Open the rear quarter window and free the window sealing strip from the top of the rear seat side trim panel. Unclip the side trim panel from the body then free the seat belt guide and seat belt from the panel and remove the panel from the vehicle **(see illustrations)**.

17 If necessary, remove the foam insulation ring from around the speaker to gain access to the speaker screws **(see illustration)**.

18 Slacken and remove the retaining screws then remove the speaker from the body, disconnecting the wiring connector as it becomes accessible.

Rear speaker – Cabriolet Coupe

19 Remove the rear seat cushion as described in Chapter 11.

20 Release the retaining clips and withdraw the upper trim panel from the rear quarter panel – see Chapter 11, Section 26.

21 Release the retaining clips and withdraw the inner rear trim panel – see Chapter 11, Section 26.

22 Slacken and remove the retaining screws **(see illustration),** and then remove the speaker from the body,

disconnecting the wiring connector as it becomes accessible.

Refitting

23 Refitting is a reversal of removal, ensuring the seat belt mounting bolts are tightened to the specified torque (see Chapter 11). Ensure the trim panels are clipped securely in position and are correctly located behind the edges of the sealing strips.

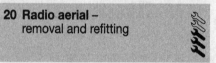

20 Radio aerial – removal and refitting

Removal

1 The aerial is a screw-fit in its base and is easily removed.

2 To remove the complete aerial on models where the aerial is mounted on the rear of the roof, open the tailgate then free the tailgate sealing strip from the top of its aperture. Carefully unclip the upper trim panel from the rear of the roof and peel back the headlining to gain access to the aerial nut.

3 To remove the complete aerial on models where the aerial is at the front of the roof, carefully prise the courtesy light out of position, disconnecting it from the wiring

19.16a Free the window sealing strip from the top of the panel . . .

19.16b . . . and unclip the rear seat side trim panel from the body

19.16c Unclip the seat belt guide then free the trim panel from the seat belt

19.17 Peel back the foam insulation ring to gain access to the speaker screws

19.22 Speaker retaining screws (arrowed)

20.3a Where the aerial is mounted at the front of the roof, prise out the courtesy light . . .

20.3b . . . and disconnect it from the wiring connector . . .

20.3c . . . then unclip the light surround

connector, then unclip the light surround from the headlining **(see illustrations)**.

4 Remove the insulating cap then slacken and remove the nut **(see illustrations)**. Detach the aerial lead and lift the aerial off from the roof, complete with its rubber seal.

Refitting

5 Refitting is the reverse of removal.

---

21 Engine immobiliser and anti-theft alarm system – general information

20.4a Remove the insulating cap . . .

20.4b . . . then unscrew the aerial retaining nut (arrowed)

Note: *This information is applicable only to the systems fitted by Peugeot as standard equipment.*

Engine immobiliser

1 An engine immobiliser system is fitted as standard to all models and the system is operated automatically every time the ignition key is inserted/removed.

2 The immobiliser system ensures the vehicle can only be started using the original Peugeot ignition key. The key contains an electronic chip (transponder), which is programmed with a code. When the key is inserted into the ignition switch it uses the current present in the sensor ring (which is fitted to the ignition switch housing) to send a signal to the immobiliser electronic control unit (ECU). The ECU is incorporated into the built-in systems interface (BSI) unit (see Section 24). The ECU checks this code every time the ignition is switched on. If the key code does not match the ECU code, the ECU will disable the starter, fuel and ignition (as applicable) to prevent the engine being started.

3 When the vehicle is new, a confidential security card is supplied along with the other vehicle documentation. This card contains the security code, which your Peugeot dealer requires when carrying out any work on the immobiliser system. Keep this card in a safe place at home; never store it in the vehicle. If the ignition key is lost, a new one can be obtained from a Peugeot dealer. Take the confidential security card and all the existing keys along to your Peugeot dealer who will

supply a new key and reprogram all the keys with a new security code; this will render the lost key useless.

Caution: Without the confidential security card, it will not be possible to have the keys and immobiliser system reprogrammed. If you have purchased the vehicle second-hand, as a precaution have all the keys and the immobiliser system reprogrammed with a new security code. This will ensure the keys in your possession are the only ones able to start the vehicle and render all other keys useless.

4 Any problems with the engine immobiliser system should be referred to a Peugeot dealer.

Anti-theft alarm system

5 Most models covered in this were also equipped with an anti-theft alarm system as standard equipment. The system was available as a option on all other models. The alarm is automatically armed when the deadlocking is set using the remote central locking transmitter and is disarmed when the doors are unlocked using the remote transmitter. The alarm system has switches on the bonnet, tailgate and each of the doors and also has ultrasonic sensing, which detects movement inside the vehicle via sensors mounted on either side of the vehicle interior.

6 When the system is activated, the direction indicators will flash continuously for two seconds and the indicator light on the alarm switch, fitted to the rear section of the centre

console, will flash continuously. **Note:** *If the bonnet, tailgate or one of the doors are not properly closed when the alarm is set, the siren will sound briefly. If the bonnet/tailgate/door (as applicable) is properly closed within 45 seconds the alarm will activate. If not the alarm will remain disarmed.*

7 If for some reason the remote central locking transmitter fails whilst the alarm is armed, the alarm can be disarmed using the key. To do this, open the door with the key, and then enter the vehicle, noting that the alarm will sound as the door is opened. Insert the key and switch on the ignition, the immobiliser will recognise the key and will switch off the alarm.

8 If required, the ultrasonic sensing facility of the alarm can be switched off, whilst retaining the switched side of the system. To switch off the ultrasonic sensing, with the ignition switched off, depress the alarm switch (mounted on the rear section of the centre console) until the alarm indicator light on the switch is continuously lit. Get out of the vehicle and operate the deadlocking function using the remote transmitter to arm the alarm. The direction indicators will flash as normal but only the switched (door, tailgate and bonnet) side of the alarm system will be operational. This facility is useful, as it allows you to leave the windows/sunroof open, and still arm the alarm. If the windows/sunroof are left open with the ultrasonic sensing not switched off, the alarm may be falsely triggered by a gust of wind.

9 Prior to disconnecting the battery, the alarm system should be disabled; this will prevent the alarm sounding when the battery is disconnected/reconnected. To do this, switch on the ignition then immediately depress and hold the alarm switch for two seconds; the indicator light on the switch should then flash rapidly for approximately three seconds indicating the alarm has been disabled. Switch off the ignition and disconnect the battery negative terminal. Once the battery has been reconnected, operate the deadlocking with the remote transmitter then unlock the vehicle. The alarm will be set as normal; the next time the deadlocking is set.

10 Should the alarm system become faulty, the vehicle should be taken to a Peugeot dealer for examination.

22 Airbag system – general information and precautions

Driver and passenger airbags

1 Both a driver's and passenger airbag are fitted as standard to some models in the range; on other models they were available as an optional extra. Models fitted with a driver's airbag have the word AIRBAG stamped on the airbag unit (fitted to the centre of the steering wheel). Models also equipped with a passenger airbag also have the word AIRBAG stamped on the passenger airbag unit (fitted to the facia unit). The airbag system comprises of the airbag unit(s) (complete with gas generators), the control unit (with an integral impact sensor) and a warning light in the instrument panel.

2 The airbag system is triggered in the event of a heavy frontal impact above a predetermined force, depending on the point of impact. The airbag is then inflated within milliseconds, and forms a safety cushion between the driver and steering wheel and (where fitted) the passenger and facia. This prevents contact between the upper body and wheel/facia, and therefore greatly reduces the risk of injury. The airbag then deflates almost immediately. The control unit also operates the front seat belt tensioner mechanisms at the same time (see Chapter 11).

3 Every time the ignition is switched on, the airbag control unit performs a self-test. The self-test takes approximately six seconds and during this time the warning light in the instrument panel will be illuminated. After the self-test is complete, the warning light will go out (unless the passenger airbag unit has been deactivated – see paragraph 4). If the warning light fails to come on, remains illuminated after the self-test period, or comes on at any time when the vehicle is being driven, there is a fault in the airbag system. The vehicle should be taken to a Peugeot dealer for examination at the earliest possible opportunity.

4 Most vehicles with a passenger airbag are equipped with a disabling switch on the facia. The switch is operated using the ignition key and switches off the passenger airbag (it is not possible to disable the driver's airbag) to

enable a rear-facing child seat to be installed in the passenger seat. Whilst the passenger airbag is disabled, the airbag warning light on the instrument panel will remain illuminated all the time.

⚠ **Warning: Before carrying out any operations on the airbag system, disconnect the battery negative terminal and wait at least two minutes. Remove the centre console (see Chapter 11) then release the retaining clip and disconnect the wiring connector(s) from the airbag control unit; if necessary remove the facia panel bracket mounting bolt to gain the clearance necessary to disconnect the connector. When the operations are complete, securely reconnect the control unit and tighten the facia bracket bolt to the specified torque (where removed) then refit the centre console (see Chapter 11). Make sure no one is inside the vehicle when the battery is reconnected then, with the driver's door open, switch the ignition on from outside vehicle and check the operation of the airbag warning light.**

⚠ **Warning: Do not subject the area of the body around the control unit to any form of shock, which could trigger the system.**

⚠ **Warning: Note that the airbags must not be subjected to temperatures in excess of 100°C. When the airbag is removed, ensure that it is stored the correct way up (pad upwards) to prevent possible inflation.**

⚠ **Warning: Do not allow any solvents or cleaning agents to contact the airbag assemblies. They must be cleaned using only a damp cloth.**

⚠ **Warning: The airbags and control unit are both sensitive to impact. If either is dropped or damaged they should be renewed.**

⚠ **Warning: Disconnect the airbag control unit wiring connector prior to using arc welding equipment on the vehicle.**

⚠ **Warning: On models with a passenger airbag, never fit a rear-facing child seat to the front passenger seat unless the passenger airbag has been disabled (see paragraph 4).**

⚠ **Warning: Peugeot recommend that the airbag units be renewed every ten years.**

Side airbags

5 On some models, in addition to the driver and passenger airbag units, side airbags are also fitted to the seat back of each front seat (a side airbag label will be attached to the trim on the side of the seat base if side airbags are fitted). Each airbag unit has its own control unit, which is mounted onto the vehicle body on the outside of each front seat. The side airbags are not linked in anyway and operate individually.

6 The relevant side airbag is triggered in the event of a heavy side impact above a

predetermined force. The airbag is then inflated within milliseconds, and forms a safety cushion between the driver/passenger (as applicable) and the door. This prevents contact between the upper body and door, and therefore greatly reduces the risk of injury. The airbag then deflates almost immediately.

7 Every time the ignition is switched on, the control unit performs a self-test. The self-test takes approximately six seconds and during this time the side airbag warning light in the instrument panel will be illuminated. After the self-test is complete, the warning light will go out. If the warning light fails to come on, remains illuminated after the self-test period, or comes on at any time when the vehicle is being driven, there is a fault in the airbag system. The vehicle should be taken to a Peugeot dealer for examination at the earliest possible opportunity.

⚠ **Warning: Before carrying out any operations on the front seats, disconnect the battery negative terminal and wait at least two minutes. Reach in under the seats and disconnect the wiring connector from the side airbag unit of each seat. When the operations are complete, reconnect the wiring connectors to the airbags. Make sure no one is inside the vehicle when the battery is reconnected then, with the driver's door open, switch the ignition on from outside vehicle and check the operation of the airbag warning light.**

⚠ **Warning: Do not subject the area of the body around the control units to any form of shock which could trigger the system.**

⚠ **Warning: Note that the airbags must not be subjected to temperatures in excess of 100°C.**

⚠ **Warning: The side airbags and control units are sensitive to impact. If either is dropped or damaged they should be renewed.**

⚠ **Warning: Disconnect the side airbag control unit wiring connectors prior to using arc welding equipment on the vehicle.**

⚠ **Warning: Peugeot recommend that the airbag units be renewed every ten years.**

23 Airbag system components – removal and refitting

⚠ **Warning: Refer to the precautions given in Section 23 before carrying out the following operations.**

Note: Two different air bags may be fitted. The airbag may be retained by bolts or a retaining clip.

Driver's airbag – bolted type

Removal

1 Disconnect the battery negative terminal

23.3a Undo the retaining screws then lift the airbag unit away from the steering wheel . . .

23.3b . . . and disconnect its wiring connectors (arrowed)

23.8a Insert a screwdriver into the hole in the front face of the steering wheel boss ...

23.8b ... pull the screwdriver handle rearwards ...

23.8c ... to release the retaining clips (arrowed)

23.9 Disconnect the wiring plugs as the airbag is withdrawn

and wait at least two minutes. Remove the centre console (see Chapter 11) then release the retaining clip and disconnect the wiring connector(s) from the airbag control unit **(see illustration 23.22)**. If necessary, remove the facia bracket lower mounting bolt to gain the clearance necessary to disconnect the connector.

2 Slacken and remove the two airbag unit retaining screws from the rear of the steering wheel, rotating the wheel as necessary to gain access to the screws.

3 Return the steering wheel to the straight-ahead position, and then carefully lift the airbag unit away from the wheel, disconnecting the wiring connectors as they become accessible **(see illustrations)**.

⚠️ *Warning: Do not knock or drop the airbag unit and store it the correct way up with its padded surface uppermost.*

Refitting

4 Securely reconnect the wiring connectors then seat the airbag unit in the steering wheel, ensuring the wiring does not become trapped.

5 Fit the airbag unit retaining screws and tighten them evenly and progressively to the specified torque.

6 Securely reconnect the airbag control unit wiring connector(s). Refit the facia mounting bracket bolt (where removed), tightening it to the specified torque, then refit the centre console (see Chapter 11). Make sure no one is inside the vehicle then reconnect the

battery. With the driver's door open, switch the ignition on from outside vehicle and check the operation of the warning light.

Drivers airbag – clipped type

Removal

7 Disconnect the battery negative terminal and wait at least 2 minutes.

8 With the wheels and steering wheel in the 'straight-ahead' position, insert a screwdriver into the hole in the front face of the steering wheel boss. Pull the screwdriver handle rearwards to release the spring clips **(see illustrations)**.

9 Carefully lift the airbag from place, disconnecting the wiring plugs as they become accessible **(see illustration)**.

23.14 Unclip the glovebox lid from its retaining clips and remove it from the facia

⚠️ *Warning! Do not drop or knock the airbag unit and store it the correct way up with its padded surface uppermost.*

Refitting

10 Reconnect the wiring plugs, and press the airbag into place. Ensure the retaining clips engage fully.

11 With no-one inside the cabin, then reconnect the battery negative terminal. With the drivers door open, switch on the ignition from outside the vehicle and check the operation of the warning light.

Passenger airbag

Removal

12 Disconnect the battery negative terminal and wait at least two minutes. Remove the centre console (see Chapter 11) then release the retaining clip and disconnect the wiring connector(s) from the airbag control unit **(see illustration 23.27)**. If necessary, remove the facia bracket lower mounting bolt to gain the clearance necessary to disconnect the connector.

13 Remove the audio unit as described in Section 18.

14 Open up the glovebox lid then carefully unclip the base of the lid from its retaining clips. Free the lid stays from the glovebox compartment and remove the lid from the facia **(see illustration)**.

15 Slacken and remove the glovebox compartment retaining screws, noting the

23.15a Slacken and remove the retaining screws (arrowed) . . .

23.15b . . . noting the correct fitted direction of the retaining clips fitted to the lower screws . . .

23.16 . . . then manoeuvre the glovebox compartment out of position

correct fitted locations of the lid retaining clips **(see illustrations)**.

16 Free the glovebox compartment from the facia then manoeuvre it downwards and out from under the facia **(see illustration)**. Where necessary, disconnect the wiring connectors from the glovebox light and switch as the compartment is removed.

17 Carefully unclip the clock/multifunction unit surround from the top of the facia and remove it, disconnecting the wiring connector from the hazard warning light switch **(see illustration)**.

18 Slacken and remove the retaining screws securing the top of the centre vent panel to the facia. Carefully unclip the panel and remove it from the facia.

19 Prise out the end cover from the passenger end of the facia **(see illustration)**.

20 Carefully prise the vent out from the passenger end of the facia, taking great care not to mark the vent or facia **(see illustration)**.

21 Rotate the fastener through 90° and remove the lower cover from the driver's side of the facia.

22 Trace the passenger airbag unit wiring back across the facia, freeing it from the retaining clips, and disconnect it from the wiring connector located next to the fusebox.

23 Working through the glovebox aperture, slacken and remove the seven retaining screws securing the airbag panel to the rear of the facia and the four nuts securing the passenger airbag in position **(see illustration)**. The airbag panel and unit can then be removed from the facia, taking care not to strain the airbag wiring.

Refitting

24 Fit the airbag unit and panel to the facia, ensuring the wiring is correctly routed. Fit all the retaining screws and tighten the airbag unit nuts to the specified torque.

25 Secure the airbag wiring in position with the retaining clips and securely reconnect its wiring connector.

26 The remainder of refitting is the reverse of removal. On completion, securely reconnect the airbag control unit wiring connector(s). Refit the facia mounting bracket bolt (where removed), tightening it to the specified torque, then refit the centre console (see Chapter 11). Make sure no one is inside the vehicle then reconnect the battery. With the driver's door open, switch the ignition on from outside vehicle and check the operation of the warning light.

Airbag control unit

Removal

27 Disconnect the battery negative terminal and wait at least two minutes. Remove the centre console (see Chapter 11) then release the retaining clip and disconnect the wiring connector(s) from the airbag control unit **(see illustration)**. If necessary, remove the facia bracket lower mounting bolt to gain the clearance necessary to disconnect the connector.

28 Unscrew the retaining nuts then remove the control unit from the vehicle.

23.17 Unclip the clock/multifunction unit surround from the facia and disconnect the switch wiring connector (arrowed)

23.19 Unclip the end cover from the passenger end of the facia . . .

23.20 . . . then prise out the passenger end vent

23.23 Airbag panel retaining screw (1) and passenger airbag unit nut (2) locations

23.27 Release the retaining clip and disconnect the wiring connector from the airbag control unit

23.35a Undo the retaining screws securing the lower shroud to the steering column . . .

23.35b . . . then disconnect the audio unit control stalk wiring connector and remove the shroud

23.37 Free the contact unit wiring connectors (arrowed) from the steering column and disconnect them

Refitting

29 Refit the control unit, making sure the arrow on the top of the unit is pointing towards the front of the vehicle. Refit the control unit retaining nuts and tighten them to the specified torque.

30 Securely reconnect the airbag control unit wiring connector(s).

31 Refit the facia mounting bracket bolt (where removed), tightening it to the specified torque, then refit the centre console (see Chapter 11). Make sure no one is inside the vehicle then reconnect the battery. With the driver's door open, switch the ignition on from outside vehicle and check the operation of the warning light.

Driver's airbag wiring contact unit

Removal

32 Remove the driver's airbag as described in paragraphs 1 to 3.

33 Remove the steering wheel as described in Chapter 10. Ensure the front wheels are pointing in the straight-ahead position.

34 Rotate the fastener a quarter-of-a-turn (90°) and remove the lower cover from the driver's side of the facia.

35 Undo the retaining screws and free the lower shroud from the column. Trace the audio unit control stalk back to its wiring connector then disconnect the connector, and remove the shroud and switch as an assembly **(see illustrations)**.

36 Unclip and remove the upper shroud from the steering column.

37 Unclip the contact unit wiring connectors from the column then release the retaining clips and separate the two halves of each connector **(see illustration)**.

38 Release the retaining clip and carefully free the immobiliser ring from the ignition switch/steering column lock.

39 Slacken and remove the retaining screws and remove the contact unit from the top of the steering column, taking care not to strain the wiring **(see illustrations)**.

Refitting

40 Prior to refitting it is necessary to ensure the contact unit is correctly centralised, with the arrow markings on the top of the unit correctly aligned, and that the front wheels are pointing in the straight-ahead position. If there is any doubt about the unit position, rotate the contact insert in a clockwise direction until resistance is felt. From this point, rotate the insert back through two to two and a half rotations until the arrow markings on the top surface of the unit are correctly aligned; the wiring harness will now be at the bottom. Do not rotate the unit from now onwards.

41 Slide the contact unit into position, making sure its wiring is correctly routed, and engage it with the switch housing on the column. Ensure that the contact ring is correctly seated then refit its retaining screws, tightening them securely.

42 Reconnect the contact unit wiring connectors then clip the connectors back onto the bracket.

43 Reconnect the audio unit control stalk wiring connector then refit the shrouds to the steering column. Ensure the wiring is not trapped by the shrouds then refit and securely tighten the lower shroud screws.

44 Refit the steering wheel as described in Chapter 10, then refit the airbag unit as described in paragraphs 4 to 6.

Side airbag unit

45 Removal and refitting of the side airbag units should be entrusted to a Peugeot dealer. The seat must be dismantled to enable the airbag unit to removed/refitted.

Side airbag control unit

Removal

46 Remove the relevant front seat as described in Chapter 11.

47 Referring to Section 26 of Chapter 11, on three-door models remove the rear seat side trim panel as described in paragraphs 2 to 8, and on five-door models remove the pillar upper and lower trim panels as described in paragraphs 12 to 15.

48 On all models, peel back the carpet to gain access to the side airbag control unit.

49 Disconnect the wiring connector then undo the retaining nuts and remove the control unit from the vehicle.

Refitting

50 Refitting is the reverse of removal, tightening the control unit retaining nuts to the specified torque.

23.39a Undo the retaining screws (arrowed) . . .

23.39b . . . then remove the contact unit, taking care not to strain the wiring

24 Built-in Systems Interface (BSI) unit – general information, removal and refitting

General information

1 The built-in systems interface (BSI) unit is an electronic control unit, which controls a variety of functions, normal controlled by individual control units and relays. The BSI unit is located behind the lower cover on the driver's side of facia where it is situated directly beneath the fusebox; the unit has six fuses plugged into it.

24.5 Unclip the cover from the base of the fusebox to gain access to the BSI unit (shown with facia removed for clarity)

The BSI unit controls the following functions (not all functions are fitted to all models).
• *Direction indicator/hazard warning lights.*
• *Windscreen/tailgate wiper motors.*
• *Rear screen heating element.*
• *Immobiliser system.*
• *Anti-theft alarm system.*
• *Lights-on/ignition key warning buzzer.*
• *Central locking/deadlocking, including the remote central locking receiver.*
• *Door open indicator.*
• *Courtesy light delay timer.*
• *Automatic transmission audible warning system.*

2 Should any of the above functions become faulty, first check the condition of the fuses. If this fails to locate the problem, take the vehicle to a Peugeot dealer for testing. The only satisfactory way to test the BSI unit is by substitution with another unit which is know to be functioning correctly.

Removal

3 Disconnect the battery negative terminal.
4 Rotate the fastener a quarter-of-a-turn (90º) and remove the lower cover from the driver's side of the facia.
5 Carefully unclip the protective cover from the underside of the fusebox to gain access to the BSI unit **(see illustration)**.
6 Undo the retaining screw then release the retaining clip and pivot the BSI unit downwards to free it from the base of the fusebox **(see illustrations)**.
7 Release the retaining clips then disconnect all the wiring connectors and remove the BSI unit from the vehicle **(see illustration)**.

24.6a Undo the retaining screw then release the retaining clip (arrowed) . . .

Refitting

8 Refitting is the reverse of removal, ensuring the wiring connectors are all securely reconnected.

25 Satellite navigation system – general information

1 A satellite navigation system was offered as an optional extra on some models. The navigation unit and remote control are located in the glovebox. Refer to the manufacturer's handbook supplied with the vehicle for operating instructions. Any problems with the system must be referred to a Peugeot dealer.

26 Roof and boot (Cabriolet Coupe models) – general information, removal and refitting

General information

1 An electro-hydraulic system is used to move the roof, boot lid and rear shelf. The hydraulic system is made up of a pump, hydraulic struts and hydraulic pipes. Due to the complexity of this system, it should be entrusted to a specialist for any work done on the hydraulic system. The hydraulic pump is located inside the luggage compartment, at the right-hand side, behind the trim panel at the rear of the back seats **(see illustration)**.
2 Before any work is carried out on the roof and boot lid assembly, the hydraulic

24.6b . . . and free the BSI unit from the base of the fusebox

24.7 Release the retaining clips then disconnect the wiring connectors and remove the BSI unit

system will need to be put in the safe mode. This is done by using the Allen key (4 mm) supplied with the vehicle breakdown kit, turn the hydraulic unit load reduction screw on the hydraulic pump a quarter of a turn in the anti-clockwise direction. After the work has been done, the load reduction screw will need to be turned back a quarter of a turn in the clockwise direction **(see illustration)**.
Caution: Always make sure the hydraulic pump load reduction screw has been set in the safe position before working on any components.
3 The system is controlled by an electronic control unit (ECU), which receives information from various switches. The switches determine the position of the roof and then transmit a signal to the ECU, which then operates the hydraulic pump via relays. The ECU is located inside the luggage compartment, at the left-hand side, behind the trim panel at the rear of the back seats **(see illustration)**.

26.1 Location of hydraulic pump

26.2 Allen key inserted in the hydraulic unit load reduction screw

26.3 Location of ECU – inner trim panel removed

26.5a Wiring (arrowed) for roof catch switch

26.5b Wiring (arrowed) for boot catch switch

26.5c Switch (arrowed) for luggage cover

4 The ECU controls the following functions:
- *The opening and closing of the retractable roof.*
- *The opening and closing of the upper boot lid cover.*
- *Moving the rear shelf panel to allow the roof to be lowered.*
- *Lowering or raising the side windows.*

5 There are 11 switches in total that are installed in the roof and boot lid assembly.
- *Roof locking catch switch – left-hand side* **(see illustration)**.
- *Boot catch in closed position switch* **(see illustration)**.
- *Luggage cover extended in the open position switch* **(see illustration)**.
- *Upper boot cover catch in locked position switch – left-hand side* **(see illustration)**.
- *Upper boot cover catch in locked position switch – right-hand side.*
- *Roof locking catch switch – right-hand side.*
- *Rear shelf in place switch.*
- *Rear shelf in stored position switch.*
- *Upper boot cover catch in open position switch.*
- *Retractable roof in the open position switch.*
- *Retractable roof in the closed position switch.*

ECU

Removal

6 Disconnect the battery negative lead.
7 Open the boot lid and remove the retaining clips from the trim panel at the rear of the luggage compartment, remove the trim panel **(see illustrations)**.

26.5d Wiring (arrowed) for boot lid upper cover catch switch

26.7b . . . and remove the inner trim panel

8 Release the securing clip and slide the ECU from the body panel, disconnect the wiring connectors and remove the ECU from the vehicle **(see illustration)**.

26.7a Release the retaining clips (one arrowed) . . .

26.8 Slide the ECU to the rear of the vehicle to remove

Refitting

9 Refitting is the reverse of removal, ensuring the wiring connectors are all securely reconnected.

PEUGEOT 206 wiring diagrams

Diagram 1

Key to symbols

Bulb	
Flashing bulb	
Switch	
Multiple contact switch (ganged)	
Fuse/fusible link and current rating	F5 30A
Resistor	
Variable resistor	
Variable resistor	
Wire splice, soldered joint or unspecified connector	

Item no.	2
Pump/motor	M
Gauge/meter	
Earth point & location	E4
Diode	
Light emitting diode (LED)	
Solenoid actuator	
Heating element	
Connecting wires	

Dashed outline denotes part of a larger item, containing in this case an electronic or solid state device.

C2   - connector pin identification.

2Ve   - 2 pin green connector.

The prime method of wire identification is by using the terminal pin numbers (moulded into each component or connector and shown in the diagrams) together with the number code printed on each wire. To relate each diagram to the vehicle wiring, locate the relevant component or connector illustrated and find the wire(s) connected to the terminal pin(s) as shown in the diagram.

Caution: Whilst a number (indicating the function of that wire) may be printed on each wire, this is not always the case, and in such instances, this is reflected by the absence of such wire numbering on our diagrams. Similarly, numbering of the connector/component terminal pins is not always available from the manufacturers' source information and may also be missing from our diagrams. In these cases, it may be necessary to refer to your local dealer for further information.

Note that the conventional method of using colour coding does not apply – whilst the wires on the vehicle will be coloured, the wire colour has no relevance. Accordingly, the wires on our diagrams all appear in black.

Earth locations

E1	On front of engine
E2	On bulkhead behind battery
E3	Behind RH headlight
E4	On sill at base of LH 'A' pillar
E5	Behind LH headlight
E6	LH front sill
E7	Below LH rear tail light
E8	Under centre console

Engine fusebox 5

Fuse	Rating	Circuit protected
MF01	20A	Engine cooling fan
MF02	60A	ABS & ESP control units
MF03	30A	ABS & ESP control units
MF04	70A	Passenger fusebox (BSI)
MF05	70A	Passenger fusebox (BSI)
MF06	30A	Not used
MF07	30A	Ignition switch
MF08	30A	Radio amplifier
F1	10A	Reversing light switch, high speed fan relay, vehicle speed sensor, preheat control unit, air flow sensor, water in fuel sensor, electric power steering pump
F2	15A	Fuel gauge, canister purge valve
F3	10A	ABS & ESP control units
F4	10A	Auto. trans. & engine management control units
F5	10A	Engine management control unit
F6	15A	LH & RH front foglights
F7	20A	Headlight washer pump
F8	20A	EGR valve, cooling fan relay, low speed cooling fan relay, engine mangement control unit, Diesel high pressure regulator
F9	15A	LH headlight dip beam
F10	15A	RH headlight dip beam
F11	10A	LH headlight main beam
F12	15A	RH headlight main beam
F13	15A	Horn
F14	10A	Front/rear screen washer pump
F15	30A	Ignition coil, Diesel heater, engine management, air flow sensor, Diesel injection pump, throttle body, inlet air solenoid valve, EGR valve, fuel injectors, oxygen sensors
F16	30A	Pulse air pump, horn
F17	30A	Windscreen wiper motor
F18	40A	Heater blower motor, air conditioning

Passenger fusebox (BSI) 6

Fuse	Rating	Circuit protected
F1	15A	Steering column switch unit, heated seat relay, alarm
F4	20A	Multifunction screen, navigation control unit, radio, sunroof control unit, LH & RH rear light unit, radio/telephone transmitter/receiver
F5	15A	Auto. trans. control unit, diagnostic connector
F6	10A	Auto. trans., ESP steering angle sensor, radio
F7	15A	Driving school control unit, diagnostic connector, alarm, auto.trans. hydraulic block, radio/telephone transmitter/receiver, cruise control safety switch
F9	30A	Rear electric windows, alarm
F10	40A	Heated rear screen, LH & RH heated mirror assembly
F11	15A	Rear wiper motor
F12	30A	Sunroof, driver's door mirror/window control switch, sunroof/window control switch
F14	10A	Steering column switch unit, rain/brightness sensor, engine fusebox, airbag control unit, alarm
F15	15A	Multifunction screen, navigation control unit, radio, A/C control unit, instrument cluster
F16	30A	Central locking
F20	10A	RH stop light
F21	15A	LH stop light, high level stop light
F22	20A	Interior lighting & accessory sockets

Engine fusebox 5

Passenger fusebox 6

H33507

Connector colours

Ba	White	**Or**	Orange
Be	Blue	**Rg**	Red
Bg	Beige	**Rs**	Pink
Gr	Grey	**Ve**	Green
Jn	Yellow	**Vi**	Mauve
Mr	Brown	**VJ**	Green/
Nr	Black		Yellow

Key to items

1 Battery
2 Starter motor
3 Alternator
4 Ignition switch
5 Engine fusebox
6 Passenger fusebox (BSI)
7 Preheat control unit (Diesel)
8 Instrument cluster
   a = alternator warning light
   b = glow plug warning light

9 Glow plugs
10 Engine management contol unit
11 Steering column switch unit
12 Horn
13 Front accessory socket
14 Ashtray illumination light
15 Cigar lighter

Diagram 2

H33508

Typical starting & charging system

Typical preheating system (Diesel)

Typical cigar lighter & front accessory socket

Typical horn

Connector colours

Ba	White	**Or**	Orange
Be	Blue	**Rg**	Red
Bg	Beige	**Rs**	Pink
Gr	Grey	**Ve**	Green
Jn	Yellow	**Vi**	Mauve
Mr	Brown	**VJ**	Green/
Nr	Black		Yellow

Key to items

1 Battery
4 Ignition switch
5 Engine fusebox
6 Passenger fusebox (BSI)
8 Instrument cluster
   c = front foglight warning light
   d = rear foglight warning light
10 Engine management control unit
11 Steering column switch unit
17 Coolant temperature sensor

18 A/C pressostat
19 Diagnostic connector
20 Two speed resistor
21 Engine cooling fan
22 LH rear light unit
   a = stop light
   b = reversing light
24 RH rear light unit
   a = stop light
   b = reversing light

25 High level stop light
26 LH front foglight
27 RH front foglight
28 Rear foglight
29 Stop light switch
30 Reversing light switch
31 High speed fan relay
32 Low speed fan relay

Diagram 3

H33509

Typical engine cooling fan

Typical stop & reversing lights

Typical front/rear foglights

Connector colours

Ba	White	**Or**	Orange
Be	Blue	**Rg**	Red
Bg	Beige	**Rs**	Pink
Gr	Grey	**Ve**	Green
Jn	Yellow	**Vi**	Mauve
Mr	Brown	**VJ**	Green/
Nr	Black		Yellow

Key to items

1 Battery
4 Ignition switch
5 Engine fusebox
6 Passenger fusebox (BSI)
8 Instrument cluster
  e = LH indicator warning light
  f = RH indicator warning light
  g = dip beam warning light
  h = main beam warning light
11 Steering column switch unit
22 LH rear light unit
  c = tail light
  d = direction indicator

23 RH rear light unit
  (as above)
33 LH side light
34 RH side light
35 LH number plate light
36 RH number plate light
37 Rain/brightness sensor
38 Hazard warning switch
39 LH front direction indicator
40 RH front direction indicator
41 LH indicator side repeater
42 RH indicator side repeater

43 LH headlight
  a = dip beam
  b = main beam
44 RH headlight
  (as above)
45 LH headlight levelling adjuster
46 RH headlight levelling adjuster
47 Headlight levelling switch

Diagram 4

H33510

Typical side, tail & number plate lights

Typical direction indicators & hazard warning lights

Typical headlights & headlight levelling

Connector colours

Ba White	**Or** Orange		
Be Blue	**Rg** Red		
Bg Beige	**Rs** Pink		
Gr Grey	**Ve** Green		
Jn Yellow	**Vi** Mauve		
Mr Brown	**VJ** Green/		
Nr Black	Yellow		

Key to items

1 Battery
4 Ignition switch
5 Engine fusebox
6 Passenger fusebox (BSI)
11 Steering column switch unit
22 LH rear light unit
37 Rain/brightness sensor
50 Glove box light
51 Glovebox light switch
52 Luggage compartment light
53 Luggage compartment light switch
54 Front interior light
55 Rear interior light
56 Map reading light
57 LH front door lock assembly
58 RH front door lock assembly
59 LH rear door lock assembly
60 RH rear door lock assembly
61 Front/rear washer pump
62 Windscreen wiper motor
63 Headlight washer pump
64 Rear screen wiper motor

Diagram 5

H33511

Typical interior lighting

Typical wash/wipe & headlight washer

Connector colours

Ba	White	**Or**	Orange
Be	Blue	**Rg**	Red
Bg	Beige	**Rs**	Pink
Gr	Grey	**Ve**	Green
Jn	Yellow	**Vi**	Mauve
Mr	Brown	**VJ**	Green/
Nr	Black		Yellow

Key to items

1   Battery
4   Ignition switch
5   Engine fusebox
6   Passenger fusebox (BSI)
8   Instrument cluster
10 Engine management control unit
68 Air conditioning control panel
69 LH mirror assembly
  a = heating element
  b = mirror control motors
  c = mirror retraction motor
  d = outside air temperature sensor
70 RH mirror assembly
  (as above)
71 Heated rear window
72 Door mirror/electric window
  control switch
73 Heater blower motor
74 Heater blower control module
75 Sunroof assembly

Diagram 6

H33512

Typical heated rear window & mirrors

Typical electric mirrors

Typical heater blower (models without A/C)

Typical electric sunroof

Connector colours

Ba White
Be Blue
Bg Beige
Gr Grey
Jn Yellow
Mr Brown
Nr Black

Or Orange
Rg Red
Rs Pink
Ve Green
Vi Mauve
VJ Green/
    Yellow

Key to items

1 Battery
4 Ignition switch
5 Engine fusebox
6 Passenger fusebox (BSI)
11 Steering column switch unit
57 LH front door lock assembly
58 RH front door lock assembly
59 LH rear door lock assembly

60 RH rear door lock assembly
69 LH mirror assembly
70 RH mirror assembly
72 Door mirror/electric window
    control switch
80 Tailgate lock motor
81 High frequency transmitter
82 Heated seat relay (part of)

83 Rear window isolator switch
84 LH front electric window motor
85 RH front electric window motor
86 LH rear electric window motor
87 RH rear electric window motor
88 LH rear window switch
89 RH rear window switch

Diagram 7

H33513

Typical central locking

Typical electric windows

Connector colours

Ba	White	**Or**	Orange
Be	Blue	**Rg**	Red
Bg	Beige	**Rs**	Pink
Gr	Grey	**Ve**	Green
Jn	Yellow	**Vi**	Mauve
Mr	Brown	**VJ**	Green/
Nr	Black		Yellow

Key to items

1 = Battery
4 = Ignition switch
5 = Engine fusebox
6 = Passenger fusebox (BSI)
8 = Instrument cluster
i = water in fuel warning light
j = stop warning light
k = seatbelt warning light
l = speedometer
m = tachometer
n = coolant temp. gauge
o = oil temp. gauge
p = fuel gauge
q = oil pressure/temp. warning light

r = brake system warning light
s = low fuel warning light
10 Engine management control unit
11 Steering column switch unit
17 Coolant temperature sensor
92 Multifunction display
93 Audio unit
94 Amplifier
95 LH rear bass speaker
96 LH rear speaker
97 LH front door speaker
98 LH front tweeter
99 RH rear bass speaker
100 RH rear speaker

101 RH front door speaker
102 RH front tweeter
103 Oil pressure switch
104 Navigation control unit
105 Oil temp./level sensor
106 Seatbelt switch
107 Handbrake switch
108 Water in fuel sensor
109 Vehicle speed sensor
110 Engine speed sensor
111 Fuel gauge/fuel pump
112 Low brake fluid switch

Diagram 8

H33514

Typical audio system

Typical instrument cluster (part of)

Notes

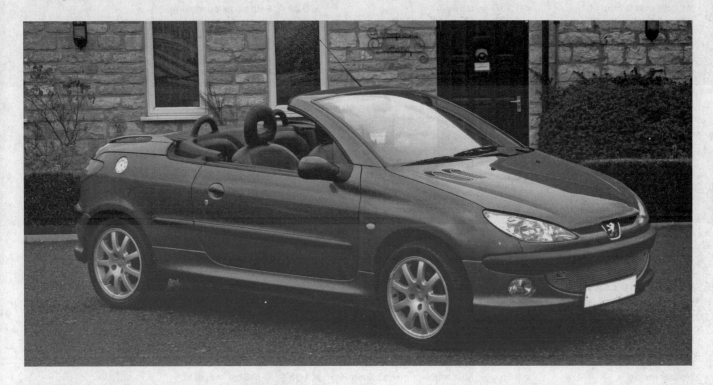

Dimensions and weights

Note: *All figures are approximate, and may vary according to model. Refer to manufacturer's data for exact figures.*

Dimensions

Saloon:

Overall length	3835 mm
Overall width (excluding mirrors)	1673 mm
Overall height (unladen)	1425 mm
Wheelbase	2442 mm

SW (Estate):

Overall length	4028 mm
Overall width (excluding mirrors)	1664 mm
Overall height (unladen)	1460 mm
Wheelbase	2442 mm

Cabriolet Coupe:

Overall length	3835 mm
Overall width (excluding mirrors)	1673 mm
Overall height (unladen)	1373 mm
Wheelbase	2442 mm

Weights*

Kerb weight	985 to 1215 kg
Maximum gross vehicle weight	1405 to 1614 kg
Maximum gross train (vehicle and trailer) weight	1920 to 2504 kg

Maximum towing weight†:

Unbraked trailer	485 to 570 kg
Braked trailer	700 to 1100 kg

* Refer to the Vehicle Identification Plate for the exact figures for your vehicle – see 'Vehicle identification'
† Ensure the combined weight of the trailer and vehicle never exceeds the gross train weight when towing.

Conversion factors

Length (distance)

Inches (in)	x 25.4	= Millimetres (mm)	x 0.0394	= Inches (in)	
Feet (ft)	x 0.305	= Metres (m)	x 3.281	= Feet (ft)	
Miles	x 1.609	= Kilometres (km)	x 0.621	= Miles	

Volume (capacity)

Cubic inches (cu in; in³)	x 16.387	= Cubic centimetres (cc; cm³)	x 0.061	= Cubic inches (cu in; in³)
Imperial pints (Imp pt)	x 0.568	= Litres (l)	x 1.76	= Imperial pints (Imp pt)
Imperial quarts (Imp qt)	x 1.137	= Litres (l)	x 0.88	= Imperial quarts (Imp qt)
Imperial quarts (Imp qt)	x 1.201	= US quarts (US qt)	x 0.833	= Imperial quarts (Imp qt)
US quarts (US qt)	x 0.946	= Litres (l)	x 1.057	= US quarts (US qt)
Imperial gallons (Imp gal)	x 4.546	= Litres (l)	x 0.22	= Imperial gallons (Imp gal)
Imperial gallons (Imp gal)	x 1.201	= US gallons (US gal)	x 0.833	= Imperial gallons (Imp gal)
US gallons (US gal)	x 3.785	= Litres (l)	x 0.264	= US gallons (US gal)

Mass (weight)

Ounces (oz)	x 28.35	= Grams (g)	x 0.035	= Ounces (oz)
Pounds (lb)	x 0.454	= Kilograms (kg)	x 2.205	= Pounds (lb)

Force

Ounces-force (ozf; oz)	x 0.278	= Newtons (N)	x 3.6	= Ounces-force (ozf; oz)
Pounds-force (lbf; lb)	x 4.448	= Newtons (N)	x 0.225	= Pounds-force (lbf; lb)
Newtons (N)	x 0.1	= Kilograms-force (kgf; kg)	x 9.81	= Newtons (N)

Pressure

Pounds-force per square inch (psi; lbf/in²; lb/in²)	x 0.070	= Kilograms-force per square centimetre (kgf/cm²; kg/cm²)	x 14.223	= Pounds-force per square inch (psi; lbf/in²; lb/in²)
Pounds-force per square inch (psi; lbf/in²; lb/in²)	x 0.068	= Atmospheres (atm)	x 14.696	= Pounds-force per square inch (psi; lbf/in²; lb/in²)
Pounds-force per square inch (psi; lbf/in²; lb/in²)	x 0.069	= Bars	x 14.5	= Pounds-force per square inch (psi; lbf/in²; lb/in²)
Pounds-force per square inch (psi; lbf/in²; lb/in²)	x 6.895	= Kilopascals (kPa)	x 0.145	= Pounds-force per square inch (psi; lbf/in²; lb/in²)
Kilopascals (kPa)	x 0.01	= Kilograms-force per square centimetre (kgf/cm²; kg/cm²)	x 98.1	= Kilopascals (kPa)
Millibar (mbar)	x 100	= Pascals (Pa)	x 0.01	= Millibar (mbar)
Millibar (mbar)	x 0.0145	= Pounds-force per square inch (psi; lbf/in²; lb/in²)	x 68.947	= Millibar (mbar)
Millibar (mbar)	x 0.75	= Millimetres of mercury (mmHg)	x 1.333	= Millibar (mbar)
Millibar (mbar)	x 0.401	= Inches of water (inH₂O)	x 2.491	= Millibar (mbar)
Millimetres of mercury (mmHg)	x 0.535	= Inches of water (inH₂O)	x 1.868	= Millimetres of mercury (mmHg)
Inches of water (inH₂O)	x 0.036	= Pounds-force per square inch (psi; lbf/in²; lb/in²)	x 27.68	= Inches of water (inH₂O)

Torque (moment of force)

Pounds-force inches (lbf in; lb in)	x 1.152	= Kilograms-force centimetre (kgf cm; kg cm)	x 0.868	= Pounds-force inches (lbf in; lb in)
Pounds-force inches (lbf in; lb in)	x 0.113	= Newton metres (Nm)	x 8.85	= Pounds-force inches (lbf in; lb in)
Pounds-force inches (lbf in; lb in)	x 0.083	= Pounds-force feet (lbf ft; lb ft)	x 12	= Pounds-force inches (lbf in; lb in)
Pounds-force feet (lbf ft; lb ft)	x 0.138	= Kilograms-force metres (kgf m; kg m)	x 7.233	= Pounds-force feet (lbf ft; lb ft)
Pounds-force feet (lbf ft; lb ft)	x 1.356	= Newton metres (Nm)	x 0.738	= Pounds-force feet (lbf ft; lb ft)
Newton metres (Nm)	x 0.102	= Kilograms-force metres (kgf m; kg m)	x 9.804	= Newton metres (Nm)

Power

Horsepower (hp)	x 745.7	= Watts (W)	x 0.0013	= Horsepower (hp)

Velocity (speed)

Miles per hour (miles/hr; mph)	x 1.609	= Kilometres per hour (km/hr; kph)	x 0.621	= Miles per hour (miles/hr; mph)

Fuel consumption*

Miles per gallon, Imperial (mpg)	x 0.354	= Kilometres per litre (km/l)	x 2.825	= Miles per gallon, Imperial (mpg)
Miles per gallon, US (mpg)	x 0.425	= Kilometres per litre (km/l)	x 2.352	= Miles per gallon, US (mpg)

Temperature

Degrees Fahrenheit = (°C x 1.8) + 32   Degrees Celsius (Degrees Centigrade; °C) = (°F - 32) x 0.56

It is common practice to convert from miles per gallon (mpg) to litres/100 kilometres (l/100km), where mpg x l/100 km = 282

Spare parts are available from many sources, including maker's appointed garages, accessory shops, and motor factors. To be sure of obtaining the correct parts, it may sometimes be necessary to quote the vehicle identification number. If possible, it can also be useful to take the old parts along for positive identification. Items such as starter motors and alternators maybe available under a service exchange scheme – any parts returned should be clean.

Our advice regarding spare part sources is:

Officially appointed garages

This is the best source of parts, which are peculiar to your car, and are not otherwise generally available (eg, badges, interior trim, certain body panels, etc). It is also the only place at which you should buy parts if the vehicle is still under warranty.

Accessory shops

These are very good places to buy materials and components needed for the maintenance of your car (oil, air and fuel filters, spark plugs, light bulbs, drivebelts, oils and greases, brake pads, touch-up paint, etc). Components of this nature sold by a reputable shop are of the same standard as those used by the car manufacturer.

Besides components, these shops will also sell tools and general accessories, usually have convenient opening hours, charge lower prices, and can often be found close to home. Some accessory shops also have parts counters where components needed for almost any repair job can be purchased or ordered.

Motor factors

Good factors will stock all the more important components, which wear out comparatively quickly and can sometimes supply individual components needed for the overhaul of a larger assembly. They may also handle work such as cylinder block re-boring, crankshaft regrinding and balancing, etc.

Tyre and exhaust specialists

These outlets may be independent or members of a local or national chain. They frequently offer competitive prices when compared with a main dealer or local garage, but it will pay to obtain several quotes before making a decision. Also ask what 'extras' may be added to the quote – for instance, fitting a new valve and balancing the wheel are both often charged on top of the price of a new tyre.

Other sources

Beware of parts or materials obtained from market stalls, car boot sales or similar outlets. Such items are not invariably sub-standard, but there is little chance of compensation if they do prove unsatisfactory. In the case of safety-critical components such as brake pads there is the risk not only of financial loss but also of an accident causing injury or death.

Vehicle identification

Modifications are a continuing and unpublicised process in vehicle manufacture, quite apart from major model changes. Spare parts manuals and lists are compiled upon a numerical basis, the individual vehicle identification numbers being essential for correct identification of the part concerned.

When ordering spare parts, always give as much information as possible. Quote the car model; year of manufacture, body and engine numbers as appropriate.

The *vehicle identification number (VIN) plate* is inside the luggage compartment, riveted onto the rear of the body (just beneath the tailgate lock). The plate carries the vehicle identification number (VIN) and vehicle weight information **(see illustration)**.

The *vehicle identification number (VIN)* is also stamped onto the rear of the body, on the right-hand side of the VIN plate and onto the left-hand side of the engine compartment bulkhead where it is visible through the base of the windscreen **(see illustrations)**.

The engine number is situated on the front face of the cylinder block, and can be found in the following locations:

a) *On petrol engines the engine number is located on the left-hand side of the cylinder block. The number is either stamped directly onto the block or is stamped onto a plate, which is riveted to the block.*
b) *On diesel engines the engine number is stamped on the base of the cylinder block on the flat surface located on the left-hand side of the oil filter/cooler.*

Note: *The first part of the engine number gives the engine code – eg, KFX.*

The paint code is on the label stuck to the top of the left-hand suspension turret.

Vehicle identification number (VIN) plate is fixed to the rear of the luggage compartment

The vehicle identification number is also stamped onto the rear of the body, on the right-hand side of the VIN plate . . .

. . . and on the left-hand side of the bulkhead where it is visible through the windscreen

Whenever servicing, repair or overhaul work is carried out on the car or its components, observe the following procedures and instructions. This will assist in carrying out the operation efficiently and to a professional standard of workmanship.

Joint mating faces and gaskets

When separating components at their mating faces, never insert screwdrivers or similar implements into the joint between the faces in order to prise them apart. This can cause severe damage which results in oil leaks, coolant leaks, etc upon reassembly. Separation is usually achieved by tapping along the joint with a soft-faced hammer in order to break the seal. However, note that this method may not be suitable where dowels are used for component location.

Where a gasket is used between the mating faces of two components, a new one must be fitted on reassembly; fit it dry unless otherwise stated in the repair procedure. Make sure that the mating faces are clean and dry, with all traces of old gasket removed. When cleaning a joint face, use a tool which is unlikely to score or damage the face, and remove any burrs or nicks with an oilstone or fine file.

Make sure that tapped holes are cleaned with a pipe cleaner, and keep them free of jointing compound, if this is being used, unless specifically instructed otherwise.

Ensure that all orifices, channels or pipes are clear, and blow through them, preferably using compressed air.

Oil seals

Oil seals can be removed by levering them out with a wide flat-bladed screwdriver or similar implement. Alternatively, a number of self-tapping screws may be screwed into the seal, and these used as a purchase for pliers or some similar device in order to pull the seal free.

Whenever an oil seal is removed from its working location, either individually or as part of an assembly, it should be renewed.

The very fine sealing lip of the seal is easily damaged, and will not seal if the surface it contacts is not completely clean and free from scratches, nicks or grooves. If the original sealing surface of the component cannot be restored, and the manufacturer has not made provision for slight relocation of the seal relative to the sealing surface, the component should be renewed.

Protect the lips of the seal from any surface which may damage them in the course of fitting. Use tape or a conical sleeve where possible. Where indicated, lubricate the seal lips with oil before fitting and, on dual-lipped seals, fill the space between the lips with grease.

Unless otherwise stated, oil seals must be fitted with their sealing lips toward the lubricant to be sealed.

Use a tubular drift or block of wood of the appropriate size to install the seal and, if the seal housing is shouldered, drive the seal down to the shoulder. If the seal housing is unshouldered, the seal should be fitted with its face flush with the housing top face (unless otherwise instructed).

Screw threads and fastenings

Seized nuts, bolts and screws are quite a common occurrence where corrosion has set in, and the use of penetrating oil or releasing fluid will often overcome this problem if the offending item is soaked for a while before attempting to release it. The use of an impact driver may also provide a means of releasing such stubborn fastening devices, when used in conjunction with the appropriate screwdriver bit or socket. If none of these methods works, it may be necessary to resort to the careful application of heat, or the use of a hacksaw or nut splitter device. Before resorting to extreme methods, check that you are not dealing with a left-hand thread!

Studs are usually removed by locking two nuts together on the threaded part, and then using a spanner on the lower nut to unscrew the stud. Studs or bolts which have broken off below the surface of the component in which they are mounted can sometimes be removed using a stud extractor.

Always ensure that a blind tapped hole is completely free from oil, grease, water or other fluid before installing the bolt or stud. Failure to do this could cause the housing to crack due to the hydraulic action of the bolt or stud as it is screwed in.

For some screw fastenings, notably cylinder head bolts or nuts, torque wrench settings are no longer specified for the latter stages of tightening, "angle-tightening" being called up instead. Typically, a fairly low torque wrench setting will be applied to the bolts/nuts in the correct sequence, followed by one or more stages of tightening through specified angles.

When checking or retightening a nut or bolt to a specified torque setting, slacken the nut or bolt by a quarter of a turn, and then retighten to the specified setting. However, this should not be attempted where angular tightening has been used.

Locknuts, locktabs and washers

Any fastening which will rotate against a component or housing during tightening should always have a washer between it and the relevant component or housing.

Spring or split washers should always be renewed when they are used to lock a critical component such as a big-end bearing retaining bolt or nut. Locktabs which are folded over to retain a nut or bolt should always be renewed.

Self-locking nuts can be re-used in non-critical areas, providing resistance can be felt when the locking portion passes over the bolt or stud thread. However, it should be noted that self-locking stiffnuts tend to lose their effectiveness after long periods of use, and should then be renewed as a matter of course.

Split pins must always be replaced with new ones of the correct size for the hole.

When thread-locking compound is found on the threads of a fastener which is to be re-used, it should be cleaned off with a wire brush and solvent, and fresh compound applied on reassembly.

Special tools

Some repair procedures in this manual entail the use of special tools such as a press, two or three-legged pullers, spring compressors, etc. Wherever possible, suitable readily-available alternatives to the manufacturer's special tools are described, and are shown in use. In some instances, where no alternative is possible, it has been necessary to resort to the use of a manufacturer's tool, and this has been done for reasons of safety as well as the efficient completion of the repair operation. Unless you are highly-skilled and have a thorough understanding of the procedures described, never attempt to bypass the use of any special tool when the procedure described specifies its use. Not only is there a very great risk of personal injury, but expensive damage could be caused to the components involved.

Environmental considerations

When disposing of used engine oil, brake fluid, antifreeze, etc, give due consideration to any detrimental environmental effects. Do not, for instance, pour any of the above liquids down drains into the general sewage system, or onto the ground to soak away. Many local council refuse tips provide a facility for waste oil disposal, as do some garages. You can find your nearest disposal point by calling the Environment Agency on 08708 506 506 or by visiting www.oilbankline.org.uk.

Note: It is illegal and anti-social to dump oil down the drain. To find the location of your local oil recycling bank, call 08708 506 506 or visit www.oilbankline.org.uk.

The jack supplied with the vehicle should only be used for changing the road wheels – see *Wheel changing* at the front of this manual. When carrying out any other kind of work, raise the vehicle using a hydraulic (or 'trolley') jack, and always supplement the jack with axle stands at the vehicle jacking points.

When using a hydraulic jack or axle stands, always position the jack head or axle stand head under one of the relevant jacking points; the jacking point is the area in between the cut-outs on the sill **(see illustration)**. Use a block of wood between the jack or axle stand and the sill – the block of wood should have a groove cut into it, into which the welded flange of the sill will locate.

Do not attempt to jack the vehicle under the front crossmember, the sump, or any of the suspension components.

The jack supplied with the vehicle locates in the jacking points on the underside of the sills – see *Wheel changing*. Ensure that the jack head is correctly engaged before attempting to raise the vehicle.

Never work under, around, or near a raised vehicle, unless it is adequately supported in at least two places.

Jacking points are between the cut-outs (arrowed) on the base of the sill (shown with the vehicle jack in position)

Audio unit anti-theft system

The audio unit fitted as standard equipment by Peugeot is equipped with a built-in security code, to deter thieves. If the power source to the unit is cut, the anti-theft system will activate. Even if the power source is reconnected, the audio unit will not function until the correct security code has been entered. Therefore, if you do not know the correct security code for the audio unit, **do not** disconnect the battery negative terminal, or remove the audio unit from the vehicle.

To enter the security code, first switch the unit on; the display will show 'Code'. The security code can then be entered using the station buttons 1 to 6 on the unit. For example if the code is 5345; press button 5, followed by button 3, button 4 and finally button 5. Once the correct code is displayed, the audio unit will automatically come on. If you make a mistake when entering one of the first three digits of the security code; switch the audio unit off and start again.

If an incorrect code is entered, the display will show four dashes, after which the radio will be locked for between 5 minutes and an hour, depending on how many attempts have been made. If an incorrect code is entered, the audio unit must be switched on and left untouched until the display shows the 'Code' prompt again, and allows you to re-enter the security code

If the security code is lost or forgotten, seek the advice of your Peugeot dealer. On presentation of proof of ownership, a Peugeot dealer will be able to provide you with a new code.

Introduction

A selection of good tools is a fundamental requirement for anyone contemplating the maintenance and repair of a motor vehicle. For the owner who does not possess any, their purchase will prove a considerable expense, offsetting some of the savings made by doing-it-yourself. However, provided that the tools purchased meet the relevant national safety standards and are of good quality, they will last for many years and prove an extremely worthwhile investment.

To help the average owner to decide which tools are needed to carry out the various tasks detailed in this manual, we have compiled three lists of tools under the following headings: *Maintenance and minor repair, Repair and overhaul,* and *Special.* Newcomers to practical mechanics should start off with the *Maintenance and minor repair* tool kit, and confine themselves to the simpler jobs around the vehicle. Then, as confidence and experience grow, more difficult tasks can be undertaken, with extra tools being purchased as, and when, they are needed. In this way, a *Maintenance and minor repair* tool kit can be built up into a *Repair and overhaul* tool kit over a considerable period of time, without any major cash outlays. The experienced do-it-yourselfer will have a tool kit good enough for most repair and overhaul procedures, and will add tools from the *Special* category when it is felt that the expense is justified by the amount of use to which these tools will be put.

Maintenance and minor repair tool kit

The tools given in this list should be considered as a minimum requirement if routine maintenance, servicing and minor repair operations are to be undertaken. We recommend the purchase of combination spanners (ring one end, open-ended the other); although more expensive than open-ended ones, they do give the advantages of both types of spanner.

☐ *Combination spanners:*
  Metric - 8 to 19 mm inclusive
☐ *Adjustable spanner - 35 mm jaw (approx.)*
☐ *Spark plug spanner (with rubber insert) - petrol models*
☐ *Spark plug gap adjustment tool - petrol models*
☐ *Set of feeler gauges*
☐ *Brake bleed nipple spanner*
☐ *Screwdrivers:*
  Flat blade - 100 mm long x 6 mm dia
  Cross blade - 100 mm long x 6 mm dia
  Torx - various sizes (not all vehicles)
☐ *Combination pliers*
☐ *Hacksaw (junior)*
☐ *Tyre pump*
☐ *Tyre pressure gauge*
☐ *Oil can*
☐ *Oil filter removal tool (if applicable)*
☐ *Fine emery cloth*
☐ *Wire brush (small)*
☐ *Funnel (medium size)*
☐ *Sump drain plug key (not all vehicles)*

Repair and overhaul tool kit

These tools are virtually essential for anyone undertaking any major repairs to a motor vehicle, and are additional to those given in the *Maintenance and minor repair* list. Included in this list is a comprehensive set of sockets. Although these are expensive, they will be found invaluable as they are so versatile - particularly if various drives are included in the set. We recommend the half-inch square-drive type, as this can be used with most proprietary torque wrenches.

The tools in this list will sometimes need to be supplemented by tools from the *Special* list:

☐ *Sockets to cover range in previous list (including Torx sockets)*
☐ *Reversible ratchet drive (for use with sockets)*
☐ *Extension piece, 250 mm (for use with sockets)*
☐ *Universal joint (for use with sockets)*
☐ *Flexible handle or sliding T "breaker bar" (for use with sockets)*
☐ *Torque wrench (for use with sockets)*
☐ *Self-locking grips*
☐ *Ball pein hammer*
☐ *Soft-faced mallet (plastic or rubber)*
☐ *Screwdrivers:*
  Flat blade - long & sturdy, short (chubby), and narrow (electrician's) types
  Cross blade – long & sturdy, and short (chubby) types
☐ *Pliers:*
  Long-nosed
  Side cutters (electrician's)
  Circlip (internal and external)
☐ *Cold chisel - 25 mm*
☐ *Scriber*
☐ *Scraper*
☐ *Centre-punch*
☐ *Pin punch*
☐ *Hacksaw*
☐ *Brake hose clamp*
☐ *Brake/clutch bleeding kit*
☐ *Selection of twist drills*
☐ *Steel rule/straight-edge*
☐ *Allen keys (inc. splined/Torx type)*
☐ *Selection of files*
☐ *Wire brush*
☐ *Axle stands*
☐ *Jack (strong trolley or hydraulic type)*
☐ *Light with extension lead*
☐ *Universal electrical multi-meter*

Sockets and reversible ratchet drive

Brake bleeding kit

Torx key, socket and bit

Hose clamp

Angular-tightening gauge

Special tools

The tools in this list are those which are not used regularly, are expensive to buy, or which need to be used in accordance with their manufacturers' instructions. Unless relatively difficult mechanical jobs are undertaken frequently, it will not be economic to buy many of these tools. Where this is the case, you could consider clubbing together with friends (or joining a motorists' club) to make a joint purchase, or borrowing the tools against a deposit from a local garage or tool hire specialist.

The following list contains only those tools and instruments freely available to the public, and not those special tools produced by the vehicle manufacturer specifically for its dealer network. You will find occasional references to these manufacturers' special tools in the text of this manual. Generally, an alternative method of doing the job without the vehicle manufacturers' special tool is given. However, sometimes there is no alternative to using them. Where this is the case and the relevant tool cannot be bought or borrowed, you will have to entrust the work to a dealer.

- [ ] *Angular-tightening gauge*
- [ ] *Valve spring compressor*
- [ ] *Valve grinding tool*
- [ ] *Piston ring compressor*
- [ ] *Piston ring removal/installation tool*
- [ ] *Cylinder bore hone*
- [ ] *Balljoint separator*
- [ ] *Coil spring compressors (where applicable)*
- [ ] *Two/three-legged hub and bearing puller*
- [ ] *Impact screwdriver*
- [ ] *Micrometer and/or vernier calipers*
- [ ] *Dial gauge*
- [ ] *Tachometer*
- [ ] *Fault code reader*
- [ ] *Cylinder compression gauge*
- [ ] *Hand-operated vacuum pump and gauge*
- [ ] *Clutch plate alignment set*
- [ ] *Brake shoe steady spring cup removal tool*
- [ ] *Bush and bearing removal/installation set*
- [ ] *Stud extractors*
- [ ] *Tap and die set*
- [ ] *Lifting tackle*

Buying tools

Reputable motor accessory shops and superstores often offer excellent quality tools at discount prices, so it pays to shop around.

Remember, you don't have to buy the most expensive items on the shelf, but it is always advisable to steer clear of the very cheap tools. Beware of 'bargains' offered on market stalls, on-line or at car boot sales. There are plenty of good tools around at reasonable prices, but always aim to purchase items which meet the relevant national safety standards. If in doubt, ask the proprietor or manager of the shop for advice before making a purchase.

Care and maintenance of tools

Having purchased a reasonable tool kit, it is necessary to keep the tools in a clean and serviceable condition. After use, always wipe off any dirt, grease and metal particles using a clean, dry cloth, before putting the tools away. Never leave them lying around after they have been used. A simple tool rack on the garage or workshop wall for items such as screwdrivers and pliers is a good idea. Store all normal spanners and sockets in a metal box. Any measuring instruments, gauges, meters, etc, must be carefully stored where they cannot be damaged or become rusty.

Take a little care when tools are used. Hammer heads inevitably become marked, and screwdrivers lose the keen edge on their blades from time to time. A little timely attention with emery cloth or a file will soon restore items like this to a good finish.

Working facilities

Not to be forgotten when discussing tools is the workshop itself. If anything more than routine maintenance is to be carried out, a suitable working area becomes essential.

It is appreciated that many an owner-mechanic is forced by circumstances to remove an engine or similar item without the benefit of a garage or workshop. Having done this, any repairs should always be done under the cover of a roof.

Wherever possible, any dismantling should be done on a clean, flat workbench or table at a suitable working height.

Any workbench needs a vice; one with a jaw opening of 100 mm is suitable for most jobs. As mentioned previously, some clean dry storage space is also required for tools, as well as for any lubricants, cleaning fluids, touch-up paints etc, which become necessary.

Another item which may be required, and which has a much more general usage, is an electric drill with a chuck capacity of at least 8 mm. This, together with a good range of twist drills, is virtually essential for fitting accessories.

Last, but not least, always keep a supply of old newspapers and clean, lint-free rags available, and try to keep any working area as clean as possible.

Micrometers

Dial test indicator ("dial gauge")

Oil filter removal tool (strap wrench type)

Compression tester

Bearing puller

This is a guide to getting your vehicle through the MOT test. Obviously it will not be possible to examine the vehicle to the same standard as the professional MOT tester. However, working through the following checks will enable you to identify any problem areas before submitting the vehicle for the test.

It has only been possible to summarise the test requirements here, based on the regulations in force at the time of printing. Test standards are becoming increasingly stringent, although there are some exemptions for older vehicles.

An assistant will be needed to help carry out some of these checks.

The checks have been sub-divided into four categories, as follows:

1 Checks carried out **FROM THE DRIVER'S SEAT**

2 Checks carried out **WITH THE VEHICLE ON THE GROUND**

3 Checks carried out **WITH THE VEHICLE RAISED AND THE WHEELS FREE TO TURN**

4 Checks carried out on **YOUR VEHICLE'S EXHAUST EMISSION SYSTEM**

---

1 Checks carried out **FROM THE DRIVER'S SEAT**

Handbrake (parking brake)

☐ Test the operation of the handbrake. Excessive travel (too many clicks) indicates incorrect brake or cable adjustment.

☐ Check that the handbrake cannot be released by tapping the lever sideways. Check the security of the lever mountings.

☐ If the parking brake is foot-operated, check that the pedal is secure and without excessive travel, and that the release mechanism operates correctly.

☐ Where applicable, test the operation of the electronic handbrake. The brake should engage and disengage without excessive delay. If the warning light does not extinguish when the brake is disengaged, this could indicate a fault which will need further investigation.

Footbrake

☐ Depress the brake pedal and check that it does not creep down to the floor, indicating a master cylinder fault. Release the pedal, wait a few seconds, then depress it again. If the pedal travels nearly to the floor before firm resistance is felt, brake adjustment or repair is necessary. If the pedal feels spongy, there is air in the hydraulic system which must be removed by bleeding.

☐ Check that the brake pedal is secure and in good condition. Check also for signs of fluid leaks on the pedal, floor or carpets, which would indicate failed seals in the brake master cylinder.

☐ Check the servo unit (when applicable) by operating the brake pedal several times, then keeping the pedal depressed and starting the engine. As the engine starts, the pedal will move down slightly. If not, the vacuum hose or the servo itself may be faulty.

Steering wheel and column

☐ Examine the steering wheel for fractures or looseness of the hub, spokes or rim.

☐ Move the steering wheel from side to side and then up and down. Check that the steering wheel is not loose on the column, indicating wear or a loose retaining nut. Continue moving the steering wheel as before, but also turn it slightly from left to right.

☐ Check that the steering wheel is not loose on the column, and that there is no abnormal movement of the steering wheel, indicating wear in the column support bearings or couplings.

☐ Check that the ignition lock (where fitted) engages and disengages correctly.

☐ Steering column adjustment mechanisms (where fitted) must be able to lock the column securely in place with no play evident.

Windscreen, mirrors and sunvisor

☐ The windscreen must be free of cracks or other significant damage within the driver's field of view. (Small stone chips are acceptable.) Rear view mirrors must be secure, intact, and capable of being adjusted.

☐ The driver's sunvisor must be capable of being stored in the "up" position.

Seat belts and seats

Note: *The following checks are applicable to all seat belts, front and rear.*

☐ Examine the webbing of all the belts (including rear belts if fitted) for cuts, serious fraying or deterioration. Fasten and unfasten each belt to check the buckles. If applicable, check the retracting mechanism. Check the security of all seat belt mountings accessible from inside the vehicle, ensuring any height adjustable mountings lock securely in place.

☐ Seat belts with pre-tensioners, once activated, have a "flag" or similar showing on the seat belt stalk. This, in itself, is not a reason for test failure.

☐ The front seats themselves must be securely attached and the backrests must lock in the upright position.

Doors

☐ Both front doors must be able to be opened and closed from outside and inside, and must latch securely when closed.

Bonnet and boot/tailgate

☐ The bonnet and boot/tailgate must latch securely when closed.

2 Checks carried out WITH THE VEHICLE ON THE GROUND

Vehicle identification

☐ Number plates must be in good condition, secure and legible, with letters and numbers correctly spaced – spacing at (A) should be 33 mm and at (B) 11 mm. At the front, digits must be black on a white background and at the rear black on a yellow background. Other background designs (such as honeycomb) are not permitted.

☐ The VIN plate and/or homologation plate must be permanently displayed and legible.

Electrical equipment

☐ Switch on the ignition and check the operation of the horn.

☐ Check the windscreen washers and wipers, examining the wiper blades; renew damaged or perished blades. Also check the operation of the stop-lights.

☐ Check the operation of the sidelights and number plate lights. The lenses and reflectors must be secure, clean and undamaged.

☐ Check the operation and alignment of the headlights. The headlight reflectors must not be tarnished and the lenses must be undamaged.

☐ Switch on the ignition and check the operation of the direction indicators (including the instrument panel tell-tale) and the hazard warning lights. Operation of the sidelights and stop-lights must not affect the indicators - if it does, the cause is usually a bad earth at the rear light cluster. Indicators should flash at a rate of between 60 and 120 times per minute – faster or slower than this could indicate a fault with the flasher unit or a bad earth at one of the light units.

☐ Check the operation of the rear foglight(s), including the warning light on the instrument panel or in the switch.

☐ The warning lights must illuminate in accordance with the manufacturer's design. For most vehicles, the ABS and other warning lights should illuminate when the ignition is switched on, and (if the system is operating properly) extinguish after a few seconds. Refer to the owner's handbook.

Footbrake

☐ Examine the master cylinder, brake pipes and servo unit for leaks, loose mountings, corrosion or other damage. If ABS is fitted, this unit should also be examined for signs of leaks or corrosion.

☐ The fluid reservoir must be secure and the fluid level must be between the upper (**A**) and lower (**B**) markings.

☐ Inspect both front brake flexible hoses for cracks or deterioration of the rubber. Turn the steering from lock to lock, and ensure that the hoses do not contact the wheel, tyre, or any part of the steering or suspension mechanism. With the brake pedal firmly depressed, check the hoses for bulges or leaks under pressure.

Steering and suspension

☐ Have your assistant turn the steering wheel from side to side slightly, up to the point where the steering gear just begins to transmit this movement to the roadwheels. Check for excessive free play between the steering wheel and the steering gear, indicating wear or insecurity of the steering column joints, the column-to-steering gear coupling, or the steering gear itself.

☐ Have your assistant turn the steering wheel more vigorously in each direction, so that the roadwheels just begin to turn. As this is done, examine all the steering joints, linkages, fittings and attachments. Renew any component that shows signs of wear or damage. On vehicles with power steering, check the security and condition of the steering pump, drivebelt and hoses.

☐ Check that the vehicle is standing level, and at approximately the correct ride height.

Shock absorbers

☐ Depress each corner of the vehicle in turn, then release it. The vehicle should rise and then settle in its normal position. If the vehicle continues to rise and fall, the shock absorber is defective. A shock absorber which has seized will also cause the vehicle to fail.

Exhaust system

☐ Start the engine. With your assistant holding a rag over the tailpipe, check the entire system for leaks. Repair or renew leaking sections.

3 Checks carried out **WITH THE VEHICLE RAISED AND THE WHEELS FREE TO TURN**

Jack up the front and rear of the vehicle, and securely support it on axle stands. Position the stands clear of the suspension assemblies. Ensure that the wheels are clear of the ground and that the steering can be turned from lock to lock.

Steering mechanism

☐ Have your assistant turn the steering from lock to lock. Check that the steering turns smoothly, and that no part of the steering mechanism, including a wheel or tyre, fouls any brake hose or pipe or any part of the body structure.

☐ Examine the steering rack rubber gaiters for damage or insecurity of the retaining clips. If power steering is fitted, check for signs of damage or leakage of the fluid hoses, pipes or connections. Also check for excessive stiffness or binding of the steering, a missing split pin or locking device, or severe corrosion of the body structure within 30 cm of any steering component attachment point.

Front and rear suspension and wheel bearings

☐ Starting at the front right-hand side, grasp the roadwheel at the 3 o'clock and 9 o'clock positions and rock gently but firmly. Check for free play or insecurity at the wheel bearings, suspension balljoints, or suspension mount-ings, pivots and attachments.

☐ Now grasp the wheel at the 12 o'clock and 6 o'clock positions and repeat the previous inspection. Spin the wheel, and check for roughness or tightness of the front wheel bearing.

☐ If excess free play is suspected at a component pivot point, this can be confirmed by using a large screwdriver or similar tool and levering between the mounting and the component attachment. This will confirm whether the wear is in the pivot bush, its retaining bolt, or in the mounting itself (the bolt holes can often become elongated).

☐ Carry out all the above checks at the other front wheel, and then at both rear wheels.

Springs and shock absorbers

☐ Examine the suspension struts (when applicable) for serious fluid leakage, corrosion, or damage to the casing. Also check the security of the mounting points.

☐ If coil springs are fitted, check that the spring ends locate in their seats, and that the spring is not corroded, cracked or broken.

☐ If leaf springs are fitted, check that all leaves are intact, that the axle is securely attached to each spring, and that there is no deterioration of the spring eye mountings, bushes, and shackles.

☐ The same general checks apply to vehicles fitted with other suspension types, such as torsion bars, hydraulic displacer units, etc. Ensure that all mountings and attachments are secure, that there are no signs of excessive wear, corrosion or damage, and (on hydraulic types) that there are no fluid leaks or damaged pipes.

☐ Inspect the shock absorbers for signs of serious fluid leakage. Check for wear of the mounting bushes or attachments, or damage to the body of the unit.

Driveshafts (fwd vehicles only)

☐ Rotate each front wheel in turn and inspect the constant velocity joint gaiters for splits or damage. Also check that each driveshaft is straight and undamaged.

Braking system

☐ If possible without dismantling, check brake pad wear and disc condition. Ensure that the friction lining material has not worn excessively, (A) and that the discs are not fractured, pitted, scored or badly worn (B).

☐ Examine all the rigid brake pipes underneath the vehicle, and the flexible hose(s) at the rear. Look for corrosion, chafing or insecurity of the pipes, and for signs of bulging under pressure, chafing, splits or deterioration of the flexible hoses.

☐ Look for signs of fluid leaks at the brake calipers or on the brake backplates. Repair or renew leaking components.

☐ Slowly spin each wheel, while your assistant depresses and releases the footbrake. Ensure that each brake is operating and does not bind when the pedal is released.

black smoke means unburnt fuel (dirty air cleaner element, or other fuel system fault).

□ An exhaust gas analyser for measuring carbon monoxide (CO) and hydrocarbons (HC) is now needed. If one cannot be hired or borrowed, have a local garage perform the check.

CO emissions (mixture)

□ The MOT tester has access to the CO limits for all vehicles. The CO level is measured at idle speed, and at 'fast idle' (2500 to 3000 rpm). The following limits are given as a general guide:

At idle speed – Less than 0.5% CO
At 'fast idle' – Less than 0.3% CO
Lambda reading – 0.97 to 1.03

□ If the CO level is too high, this may point to poor maintenance, a fuel injection system problem, faulty lambda (oxygen) sensor or catalytic converter. Try an injector cleaning treatment, and check the vehicle's ECU for fault codes.

HC emissions

□ The MOT tester has access to HC limits for all vehicles. The HC level is measured at 'fast idle' (2500 to 3000 rpm). The following limits are given as a general guide:

At 'fast idle' – Less then 200 ppm

□ Excessive HC emissions are typically caused by oil being burnt (worn engine), or by a blocked crankcase ventilation system ('breather'). If the engine oil is old and thin, an oil change may help. If the engine is running badly, check the vehicle's ECU for fault codes.

Diesel models

□ The only emission test for diesel engines is measuring exhaust smoke density, using a calibrated smoke meter. The test involves accelerating the engine at least 3 times to its maximum unloaded speed.

Note: *On engines with a timing belt, it is VITAL that the belt is in good condition before the test is carried out.*

□ With the engine warmed up, it is first purged by running at around 2500 rpm for 20 seconds. A governor check is then carried out, by slowly accelerating the engine to its maximum speed. After this, the smoke meter is connected, and the engine is accelerated quickly to maximum speed three times. If the smoke density is less than the limits given below, the vehicle will pass:

Non-turbo vehicles: 2.5m-1
Turbocharged vehicles: 3.0m-1

□ If excess smoke is produced, try fitting a new air cleaner element, or using an injector cleaning treatment. If the engine is running badly, where applicable, check the vehicle's ECU for fault codes. Also check the vehicle's EGR system, where applicable. At high mileages, the injectors may require professional attention.

□ Examine the handbrake mechanism, checking for frayed or broken cables, excessive corrosion, or wear or insecurity of the linkage. Check that the mechanism works on each relevant wheel, and releases fully, without binding.

□ It is not possible to test brake efficiency without special equipment, but a road test can be carried out later to check that the vehicle pulls up in a straight line.

Fuel and exhaust systems

□ Inspect the fuel tank (including the filler cap), fuel pipes, hoses and unions. All components must be secure and free from leaks. Locking fuel caps must lock securely and the key must be provided for the MOT test.

□ Examine the exhaust system over its entire length, checking for any damaged, broken or missing mountings, security of the retaining clamps and rust or corrosion.

Wheels and tyres

□ Examine the sidewalls and tread area of each tyre in turn. Check for cuts, tears, lumps, bulges, separation of the tread, and exposure of the ply or cord due to wear or damage. Check that the tyre bead is correctly seated on the wheel rim, that the valve is sound and properly seated, and that the wheel is not distorted or damaged.

□ Check that the tyres are of the correct size for the vehicle, that they are of the same size and type on each axle, and that the pressures are correct.

□ Check the tyre tread depth. The legal minimum at the time of writing is 1.6 mm over the central three-quarters of the tread width. Abnormal tread wear may indicate incorrect front wheel alignment or wear in steering or suspension components.

□ If the spare wheel is fitted externally or in a separate carrier beneath the vehicle, check that mountings are secure and free of excessive corrosion.

Body corrosion

□ Check the condition of the entire vehicle structure for signs of corrosion in load-bearing areas. (These include chassis box sections, side sills, cross-members, pillars, and all suspension, steering, braking system and seat belt mountings and anchorages.) Any corrosion which has seriously reduced the thickness of a load-bearing area (or is within 30 cm of safety-related components such as steering or suspension) is likely to cause the vehicle to fail. In this case professional repairs are likely to be needed.

□ Damage or corrosion which causes sharp or otherwise dangerous edges to be exposed will also cause the vehicle to fail.

Towbars

□ Check the condition of mounting points (both beneath the vehicle and within boot/hatchback areas) for signs of corrosion, ensuring that all fixings are secure and not worn or damaged. There must be no excessive play in detachable tow ball arms or quick-release mechanisms.

4 Checks carried out on **YOUR VEHICLE'S EXHAUST EMISSION SYSTEM**

Petrol models

□ The engine should be warmed up, and running well (ignition system in good order, air filter element clean, etc).

□ Before testing, run the engine at around 2500 rpm for 20 seconds. Let the engine drop to idle, and watch for smoke from the exhaust. If the idle speed is too high, or if dense blue or black smoke emerges for more than 5 seconds, the vehicle will fail. Typically, blue smoke signifies oil burning (engine wear);

Engine

- [ ] Engine fails to rotate when attempting to start
- [ ] Engine rotates, but will not start
- [ ] Engine difficult to start when cold
- [ ] Engine difficult to start when hot
- [ ] Starter motor noisy or excessively-rough in engagement
- [ ] Engine starts, but stops immediately
- [ ] Engine idles erratically
- [ ] Engine misfires at idle speed
- [ ] Engine misfires throughout the driving speed range
- [ ] Engine hesitates on acceleration
- [ ] Engine stalls
- [ ] Engine lacks power
- [ ] Engine backfires
- [ ] Oil pressure warning light on with engine running
- [ ] Engine runs-on after switching off
- [ ] Engine noises

Cooling system

- [ ] Overheating
- [ ] Overcooling
- [ ] External coolant leakage
- [ ] Internal coolant leakage
- [ ] Corrosion

Fuel and exhaust systems

- [ ] Excessive fuel consumption
- [ ] Fuel leakage and/or fuel odour
- [ ] Excessive noise or fumes from exhaust system

Clutch

- [ ] Pedal travels to floor – no pressure or very little resistance
- [ ] Clutch fails to disengage (unable to select gears)
- [ ] Clutch slips (engine speed rises, with no increase in vehicle speed)
- [ ] Judder as clutch is engaged
- [ ] Noise when depressing or releasing clutch pedal

Manual transmission

- [ ] Noisy in neutral with engine running
- [ ] Noisy in one particular gear
- [ ] Difficulty engaging gears
- [ ] Jumps out of gear
- [ ] Vibration
- [ ] Lubricant leaks

Automatic transmission

- [ ] Fluid leakage
- [ ] Transmission fluid brown, or has burned smell
- [ ] General gear selection problems
- [ ] Transmission will not downshift (kick down) on full throttle
- [ ] Engine won't start in any gear, or starts in gears other than P or N
- [ ] Transmission slips, shifts roughly, is noisy, or has no drive in forward or reverse gears

Driveshafts

- [ ] Clicking or knocking noise on turns (at slow speed on full-lock)
- [ ] Vibration when accelerating or decelerating

Braking system

- [ ] Vehicle pulls to one side under braking
- [ ] Noise (grinding or high-pitched squeal) when brakes applied
- [ ] Excessive brake pedal travel
- [ ] Brake pedal feels spongy when depressed
- [ ] Excessive brake pedal effort required to stop vehicle
- [ ] Judder felt through brake pedal or steering wheel when braking
- [ ] Brakes binding
- [ ] Rear wheels locking under normal braking

Suspension and steering systems

- [ ] Vehicle pulls to one side
- [ ] Wheel wobble and vibration
- [ ] Excessive pitching and/or rolling around corners, or during braking
- [ ] Wandering or general instability
- [ ] Excessively-stiff steering
- [ ] Excessive play in steering
- [ ] Lack of power assistance
- [ ] Tyre wear excessive

Electrical system

- [ ] Battery will not hold a charge for more than a few days
- [ ] Ignition/no-charge warning light stays on with engine running
- [ ] Ignition/no-charge warning light fails to come on
- [ ] Lights inoperative
- [ ] Instrument readings inaccurate or erratic
- [ ] Horn inoperative, or unsatisfactory in operation
- [ ] Windscreen/tailgate wipers failed, or unsatisfactory in operation
- [ ] Windscreen/tailgate washers failed, or unsatisfactory in operation
- [ ] Electric windows inoperative, or unsatisfactory in operation
- [ ] Central locking system inoperative, or unsatisfactory in operation

Introduction

The vehicle owner who does his or her own maintenance according to the recommended service schedules should not have to use this section of the manual very often. Modern component reliability is such that provided those items subject to wear or deterioration are inspected or renewed at the specified intervals, sudden failure is comparatively rare. Faults do not usually just happen as a result of sudden failure, but develop over a period of time. Major mechanical failures in particular are usually preceded by characteristic symptoms over hundreds or even thousands of miles. Those components, which do occasionally fail without warning, are often small and easily carried in the vehicle.

With any fault-finding, the first step is to decide where to begin investigations. Sometimes this is obvious, but on other occasions, a little detective work will be necessary. The owner who makes half a dozen haphazard adjustments or replacements may be successful in curing a fault (or its symptoms), but will be none the wiser if the fault recurs, and ultimately may have spent more time and money than was necessary. A calm and logical approach will be found to be more satisfactory in the long run. Always take into account any warning signs or abnormalities that may have been noticed in the period preceding the fault – power loss, high or low gauge readings, unusual smells, etc – and remember that failure of components such as fuses or spark plugs may only be pointers to some underlying fault.

The pages which follow provide an easy-reference guide to the more common problems which may occur during the operation of the vehicle. These problems and their possible causes are grouped under headings denoting various components or systems, such as Engine, Cooling system, etc. The general Chapter which deals with the problem is also shown in brackets; refer to the relevant part of that Chapter for system-specific information. Whatever the fault, certain basic principles apply. These are as follows:

Verify the fault. This is simply a matter of being sure that you know what the symptoms are before starting work. This is particularly important if you are investigating a fault for someone else, who may not have described it very accurately.

Don't overlook the obvious. For example, if the vehicle won't start, is there fuel in the tank? (Don't take anyone else's word on this particular point, and don't trust the fuel gauge either!) If an electrical fault is indicated, look for loose or broken wires before digging out the test gear.

Cure the disease, not the symptom. Substituting a flat battery with a fully charged one will get you off the hard shoulder, but if the underlying cause is not attended to, the new battery will go the same way. Similarly, changing oil-fouled spark plugs (petrol models) for a new set will get you moving again, but remember that the reason for the fouling (if it wasn't simply an incorrect grade of plug) will have to be found and corrected.

Don't take anything for granted. Particularly, don't forget that a 'new' component may itself be defective (especially if it's been rattling around in the boot for months), and don't leave components out of a fault diagnosis sequence just because they are new or recently fitted. When you do finally diagnose a difficult fault, you'll probably realise that all the evidence was there from the start.

Diesel fault diagnosis

The majority of starting problems on small diesel engines are electrical in origin. The mechanic who is familiar with petrol engines but less so with diesel may be inclined to view the diesel's injectors and pump in the same light as the spark plugs and distributor, but this is generally a mistake.

When investigating complaints of difficult starting for someone else, make sure that the correct starting procedure is understood and is being followed. Some drivers are unaware of the significance of the preheating warning light – many modern engines are sufficiently forgiving for this not to matter in mild weather, but with the onset of winter, problems begin.

As a rule of thumb, if the engine is difficult to start but runs well when it has finally got going, the problem is electrical (battery, starter motor or preheating system). If poor performance is combined with difficult starting, the problem is likely to be in the fuel system. The low-pressure (supply) side of the fuel system should be checked before suspecting the injectors and high-pressure pump. The most common fuel supply problem is air getting into the system, and any pipe from the fuel tank forwards must be scrutinised if air leakage is suspected. Normally the pump is the last item to suspect, since unless it has been tampered with, there is no reason for it to be at fault.

Engine

Engine fails to rotate when attempting to start

- ☐ Battery terminal connections loose or corroded (*Weekly checks*).
- ☐ Battery discharged or faulty (Chapter 5A).
- ☐ Broken, loose or disconnected wiring in the starting circuit (Chapter 5A).
- ☐ Defective starter motor (Chapter 5A).
- ☐ Starter pinion or flywheel/driveplate ring gear teeth loose or broken (Chapter 2A or 2B and 5A).
- ☐ Engine earth strap broken or disconnected (Chapter 5A).

Engine rotates, but will not start

- ☐ Fuel tank empty.
- ☐ Battery discharged (engine rotates slowly) (Chapter 5A).
- ☐ Battery terminal connections loose or corroded (*Weekly checks*).
- ☐ Worn, faulty or incorrectly-gapped spark plugs – petrol models (Chapter 1A).
- ☐ Preheating system faulty – diesel models (Chapter 5C).
- ☐ Engine management system fault – petrol models (Chapter 4A).
- ☐ Air in fuel system – diesel models (Chapter 4B).
- ☐ Fuel injector/injection pump fault – diesel models (Chapter 4B).
- ☐ Low cylinder compressions (Chapter 2A or 2B).
- ☐ Major mechanical failure (e.g. camshaft drive) (Chapter 2A or 2B).

Engine difficult to start when cold

- ☐ Battery discharged (Chapter 5A).
- ☐ Battery terminal connections loose or corroded (*Weekly checks*).
- ☐ Worn, faulty or incorrectly-gapped spark plugs – petrol models (Chapter 1A).
- ☐ Preheating system faulty – diesel models (Chapter 5C).
- ☐ Engine management system fault – petrol models (Chapter 4A).
- ☐ Fast idle valve incorrectly adjusted – 1.9 litre diesel model (Chapter 4B).
- ☐ Fuel injector/injection pump fault – diesel models (Chapter 4B).

Engine difficult to start when hot

- ☐ Engine management system fault – petrol models (Chapter 4A).
- ☐ Fuel injector/injection pump fault – diesel models (Chapter 4B).
- ☐ Low cylinder compressions (Chapter 2A or 2B).

Starter motor noisy or excessively rough in engagement

- ☐ Starter pinion or flywheel/driveplate ring gear teeth loose or broken (Chapters 2A or 2B and 5A).
- ☐ Starter motor mounting bolts loose or missing (Chapter 5A).
- ☐ Defective starter motor (Chapter 5A).

Engine starts, but stops immediately

- ☐ Vacuum leak at the throttle housing/inlet manifold – petrol models (Chapter 4A).
- ☐ Engine management system fault – petrol models (Chapter 4A).
- ☐ Air in fuel system – diesel models (Chapter 4B).
- ☐ Fuel injector/injection pump fault – diesel models (Chapter 4B).

Engine idles erratically

- ☐ Vacuum leak at the throttle housing/inlet manifold – petrol models (Chapter 4A).
- ☐ Worn, faulty or incorrectly-gapped spark plugs – petrol models (Chapter 1A).
- ☐ Engine management system fault – petrol models (Chapter 4A).
- ☐ Air in fuel system – diesel models (Chapter 4B).
- ☐ Fuel injector/injection pump fault – diesel models (Chapter 4B).
- ☐ Uneven or low cylinder compressions (Chapter 2A or 2B).
- ☐ Camshaft lobes worn (Chapter 2A or 2B).
- ☐ Timing belt incorrectly fitted (Chapter 2A or 2B).

Engine misfires at idle speed

- ☐ Worn, faulty or incorrectly-gapped spark plugs – petrol models (Chapter 1A).
- ☐ Vacuum leak at the throttle housing/inlet manifold – petrol models (Chapter 4A).
- ☐ Engine management system fault – petrol models (Chapter 4A).
- ☐ Faulty injector(s) – diesel models (Chapter 4B).
- ☐ Uneven or low cylinder compressions (Chapter 2A or 2B).
- ☐ Disconnected, leaking, or perished crankcase ventilation hoses (Chapter 4C).

Engine misfires throughout the driving speed range

- ☐ Fuel filter blocked (Chapter 1A or 1B).
- ☐ Fuel pump faulty (Chapter 4A or 4B).
- ☐ Fuel tank vent blocked, or fuel pipes restricted (Chapter 4A or 4B).
- ☐ Worn, faulty or incorrectly-gapped spark plugs – petrol models (Chapter 1A).
- ☐ Vacuum leak at the throttle housing/inlet manifold – petrol models (Chapter 4A).
- ☐ Engine management system fault – petrol models (Chapter 4A).
- ☐ Fuel injector/injection pump fault – diesel models (Chapter 4B).
- ☐ Faulty ignition HT coil – petrol models (Chapter 5B).
- ☐ Uneven or low cylinder compressions (Chapter 2A or 2B).

Engine hesitates on acceleration

- ☐ Worn, faulty or incorrectly-gapped spark plugs – petrol models (Chapter 1A).
- ☐ Vacuum leak at the throttle housing/inlet manifold – petrol models (Chapter 4A).
- ☐ Engine management system fault – petrol models (Chapter 4A).
- ☐ Fuel injector/injection pump fault – diesel models (Chapter 4B).

Engine stalls

- ☐ Fuel filter blocked (Chapter 1A or 1B).
- ☐ Fuel pump faulty (Chapter 4A or 4B).
- ☐ Fuel tank vent blocked, or fuel pipes restricted (Chapter 4A or 4B).
- ☐ Worn, faulty or incorrectly-gapped spark plugs – petrol models (Chapter 1A).
- ☐ Vacuum leak at the throttle housing/inlet manifold – petrol models (Chapter 4A).
- ☐ Engine management system fault – petrol models (Chapter 4A).
- ☐ Fuel injector/injection pump fault – diesel models (Chapter 4B).

Engine lacks power

- ☐ Timing belt incorrectly fitted (Chapter 2A or 2B).
- ☐ Fuel filter blocked (Chapter 1A or 1B).
- ☐ Fuel pump faulty (Chapter 4A or 4B).
- ☐ Uneven or low cylinder compressions (Chapter 2A or 2B).
- ☐ Worn, faulty or incorrectly-gapped spark plugs – petrol models (Chapter 1A).
- ☐ Vacuum leak at the throttle housing/inlet manifold – petrol models (Chapter 4A).
- ☐ Engine management system fault – petrol models (Chapter 4A).
- ☐ Fuel injector/injection pump fault – diesel models (Chapter 4B).
- ☐ Brakes binding (Chapters 1A or 1B and 9).
- ☐ Clutch slipping (Chapter 6).

Engine backfires

- ☐ Timing belt incorrectly fitted (Chapter 2A or 2B).
- ☐ Vacuum leak at the throttle housing/inlet manifold – petrol models (Chapter 4A).
- ☐ Engine management system fault – petrol models (Chapter 4A).

Engine (continued)

Oil pressure warning light on with engine running

- [ ] Low oil level, or incorrect oil grade (*Weekly checks*).
- [ ] Faulty oil pressure warning light switch (Chapter 5A).
- [ ] Worn engine bearings and/or oil pump (Chapter 2C).
- [ ] High engine operating temperature (Chapter 3).
- [ ] Oil pressure relief valve defective (Chapter 2A or 2B).
- [ ] Oil pick-up strainer clogged (Chapter 2A or 2B).

Engine runs-on after switching off

- [ ] Excessive carbon build-up in engine (Chapter 2C).
- [ ] High engine operating temperature (Chapter 3).
- [ ] Engine management system fault – petrol models (Chapter 4A).
- [ ] Fuel injection pump fault – diesel models (Chapter 4B).

Engine noises

Pre-ignition (pinking) or knocking during acceleration or under load

- [ ] Engine management system fault – petrol models (Chapter 4A).
- [ ] Incorrect grade of spark plug – petrol models (Chapter 1A).
- [ ] Incorrect grade of fuel – petrol models (Chapter 4A).

- [ ] Vacuum leak at the throttle housing/inlet manifold – petrol models (Chapter 4A).
- [ ] Excessive carbon build-up in engine (Chapter 2C).

Whistling or wheezing noises

- [ ] Leaking inlet manifold or throttle housing gasket – petrol models (Chapter 4A).
- [ ] Leaking vacuum hose (Chapters 4A or 4B and 9).
- [ ] Blowing cylinder head gasket (Chapter 2A or 2B).

Tapping or rattling noises

- [ ] Worn valve gear or camshaft (Chapter 2A or 2B).
- [ ] Ancillary component fault (coolant pump, alternator, etc) (Chapters 3, 5A, etc).

Knocking or thumping noises

- [ ] Worn big-end bearings (regular heavy knocking, perhaps less under load) (Chapter 2C).
- [ ] Worn main bearings (rumbling and knocking, perhaps worsening under load) (Chapter 2C).
- [ ] Piston slap (most noticeable when cold) (Chapter 2C).
- [ ] Ancillary component fault (coolant pump, alternator, etc) (Chapters 3, 5A, etc).

Cooling system

Overheating

- [ ] Insufficient coolant in system (*Weekly checks*).
- [ ] Thermostat faulty (stuck closed) (Chapter 3).
- [ ] Radiator core blocked, or grille restricted (Chapter 3).
- [ ] Electric cooling fan or sensor faulty (Chapter 3).
- [ ] Pressure cap faulty (Chapter 3).
- [ ] Inaccurate temperature gauge/sensor (Chapter 3).
- [ ] Airlock in cooling system (Chapter 1A or 1B).
- [ ] Engine management system fault – petrol models (Chapter 4A).

Overcooling

- [ ] Thermostat faulty (stuck open) (Chapter 3).
- [ ] Inaccurate temperature gauge/sensor (Chapter 3).

External coolant leakage

- [ ] Deteriorated or damaged hoses or hose clips (Chapter 1A or 1B).
- [ ] Radiator core or heater matrix leaking (Chapter 3).
- [ ] Pressure cap faulty (Chapter 3).
- [ ] Coolant pump leaking (Chapter 3).
- [ ] Boiling due to overheating (Chapter 3).
- [ ] Core plug leaking (Chapter 2C).

Internal coolant leakage

- [ ] Leaking cylinder head gasket (Chapter 2A or 2B).
- [ ] Cracked cylinder head or cylinder bore (Chapter 2A, 2B or 2C).

Corrosion

- [ ] Infrequent draining and flushing (Chapter 1A or 1B).
- [ ] Incorrect coolant mixture or inappropriate coolant type (Chapter 1A or 1B).

Fuel and exhaust systems

Excessive fuel consumption

☐ Air filter element dirty or clogged (Chapter 1A or 1B).
☐ Engine management system fault – petrol models (Chapter 4A).
☐ Faulty injector(s) – diesel models (Chapter 4B).
☐ Tyres under-inflated (*Weekly checks*).
☐ Brakes binding (Chapters 1A or 1B and 9).

Fuel leakage and/or fuel odour

☐ Damaged or corroded fuel tank, pipes or connections (Chapter 4A or 4B).

Excessive noise or fumes from exhaust system

☐ Leaking exhaust system or manifold joints (Chapters 1A or 1B and 4A or 4B).
☐ Leaking, corroded or damaged silencers or pipe (Chapters 1A or 1B and 4A or 4B).
☐ Broken mountings causing body or suspension contact (Chapters 1A or 1B and 4A or 4B).

Clutch

Pedal travels to floor – no pressure or very little resistance

☐ Broken clutch cable/faulty self-adjusting mechanism – cable-operated clutch (Chapter 6).
☐ Air in hydraulic system/faulty master or slave cylinder – hydraulically operated clutch (Chapter 6).
☐ Broken clutch release bearing or fork (Chapter 6).
☐ Broken diaphragm spring in clutch pressure plate (Chapter 6).

Clutch fails to disengage (unable to select gears)

☐ Faulty self-adjusting mechanism – cable-operated clutch (Chapter 6).
☐ Air in hydraulic system/faulty master or slave cylinder – hydraulically operated clutch (Chapter 6).
☐ Clutch disc sticking on gearbox input shaft splines (Chapter 6).
☐ Clutch disc sticking to flywheel or pressure plate (Chapter 6).
☐ Faulty pressure plate assembly (Chapter 6).
☐ Clutch release mechanism worn or incorrectly assembled (Chapter 6).

Clutch slips (engine speed rises, with no increase in vehicle speed)

☐ Faulty self-adjusting mechanism – cable-operated clutch (Chapter 6).

☐ Faulty hydraulic release system – hydraulically operated clutch (Chapter 6).
☐ Clutch disc linings excessively worn (Chapter 6).
☐ Clutch disc linings contaminated with oil or grease (Chapter 6).
☐ Faulty pressure plate or weak diaphragm spring (Chapter 6).

Judder as clutch is engaged

☐ Clutch disc linings contaminated with oil or grease (Chapter 6).
☐ Clutch disc linings excessively worn (Chapter 6).
☐ Clutch cable sticking or frayed – cable-operated clutch (Chapter 6).
☐ Faulty or distorted pressure plate or diaphragm spring (Chapter 6).
☐ Worn or loose engine or gearbox mountings (Chapter 2A or 2B).
☐ Clutch disc hub or gearbox input shaft splines worn (Chapter 6).

Noise when depressing or releasing clutch pedal

☐ Worn clutch release bearing (Chapter 6).
☐ Worn or dry clutch pedal bushes (Chapter 6).
☐ Faulty pressure plate assembly (Chapter 6).
☐ Pressure plate diaphragm spring broken (Chapter 6).
☐ Broken clutch disc cushioning springs (Chapter 6).

Manual transmission

Noisy in neutral with engine running

☐ Input shaft bearings worn (noise apparent with clutch pedal released, but not when depressed) (Chapter 7A).*
☐ Clutch release bearing worn (noise apparent with clutch pedal depressed, possibly less when released) (Chapter 6).

Noisy in one particular gear

☐ Worn, damaged or chipped gear teeth (Chapter 7A).*

Difficulty engaging gears

☐ Clutch fault (Chapter 6).
☐ Worn or damaged gear linkage (Chapter 7A).
☐ Worn synchroniser units (Chapter 7A).*

Jumps out of gear

☐ Worn or damaged gear linkage (Chapter 7A).
☐ Worn synchroniser units (Chapter 7A).*
☐ Worn selector forks (Chapter 7A).*

Vibration

☐ Lack of oil (Chapters 1 and 7A).
☐ Worn bearings (Chapter 7A).*

Lubricant leaks

☐ Leaking differential output oil seal (Chapter 7A).
☐ Leaking housing joint (Chapter 7A).*
☐ Leaking input shaft oil seal (Chapter 7A).

Although the corrective action necessary to remedy the symptoms described is beyond the scope of the home mechanic, the above information should be helpful in isolating the cause of the condition, so that the owner can communicate clearly with a professional mechanic.

Automatic transmission

Note: *Due to the complexity of the automatic transmission, it is difficult for the home mechanic to properly diagnose and service this unit. For problems other than the following, the vehicle should be taken to a Peugeot dealer service department.*

Fluid leakage

☐ Automatic transmission fluid is usually dark in colour. Fluid leaks should not be confused with engine oil, which can easily be blown onto the transmission by airflow.
☐ To determine the source of a leak, first remove all built-up dirt and grime from the transmission housing and surrounding areas using a degreasing agent, or by steam-cleaning. Drive the vehicle at low speed, so airflow will not blow the leak far from its source. Raise and support the vehicle, and determine where the leak is coming from.

Transmission fluid brown, or has burned smell

☐ Transmission fluid level low, or fluid in need of renewal (Chapter 1A and 7B).

General gear selection problems

☐ Chapter 7B deals with checking and adjusting the selector cable on automatic transmissions. The following are common problems which may be caused by a poorly-adjusted cable:

a) Engine starting in gears other than Park or Neutral.
b) Indicator panel showing a gear other than that being used.
c) Vehicle moves when in Park or Neutral.
d) Poor gear shift quality or erratic gear changes.
☐ Refer to Chapter 7B for the selector cable adjustment procedure.

Transmission will not downshift (kickdown) at full throttle

☐ Low transmission fluid level (Chapter 1A).
☐ Incorrect selector cable adjustment (Chapter 7B).

Engine won't start in any gear, or starts in gears other than Park or Neutral

☐ Incorrect multi-function switch adjustment (Chapter 7B).
☐ Incorrect selector cable adjustment (Chapter 7B).

Transmission slips, shifts roughly, is noisy, or has no drive in forward or reverse gears

☐ There are many probable causes for the above problems, but the home mechanic should be concerned with only one possibility – fluid level. Before taking the vehicle to a dealer or transmission specialist, check the fluid level as described in Chapter 1A. Correct the fluid level as necessary, or change the fluid. If the problem persists, professional help will be necessary.

Driveshafts

Clicking or knocking noise on turns (at slow speed on full-lock)

- [ ] Lack of constant velocity joint lubricant, possibly due to damaged gaiter (Chapter 8).
- [ ] Worn outer constant velocity joint (Chapter 8).

Vibration when accelerating or decelerating

- [ ] Worn inner constant velocity joint (Chapter 8).
- [ ] Bent or distorted driveshaft (Chapter 8).
- [ ] Worn intermediate bearing (Chapter 8).

Braking system

Note: *Before assuming that a brake problem exists, make sure that the tyres are in good condition and correctly inflated, that the front wheel alignment is correct, and that the vehicle is not loaded with weight in an unequal manner. Apart from checking the condition of all pipe and hose connections, any faults occurring on the anti-lock braking system should be referred to a Peugeot dealer for diagnosis.*

Vehicle pulls to one side under braking

- [ ] Worn, defective, damaged or contaminated brake pads/shoes on one side (Chapter 9).
- [ ] Seized or partially-seized front brake caliper/wheel cylinder piston (Chapter 9).
- [ ] A mixture of brake pad/shoe lining materials fitted between sides (Chapter 9).
- [ ] Brake caliper or backplate mounting bolts loose (Chapter 9).
- [ ] Worn or damaged steering or suspension components (Chapters 1A or 1B and 10).

Noise (grinding or high-pitched squeal) when brakes applied

- [ ] Brake pad or shoe friction lining material worn down to metal backing (Chapters 1A or 1B and 9).
- [ ] Excessive corrosion of brake disc or drum. May be apparent after the vehicle has been standing for some time (Chapter 9).
- [ ] Foreign object (stone chipping, etc) trapped between brake disc and shield (Chapter 9).

Excessive brake pedal travel

- [ ] Inoperative rear brake self-adjust mechanism (Chapter 9).
- [ ] Faulty master cylinder (Chapter 9).
- [ ] Air in hydraulic system (Chapter 9).
- [ ] Faulty vacuum servo unit (Chapter 9).

Brake pedal feels spongy when depressed

- [ ] Air in hydraulic system (Chapter 9).
- [ ] Deteriorated flexible rubber brake hoses (Chapters 1A or 1B and 9).
- [ ] Master cylinder mounting nuts loose (Chapter 9).
- [ ] Faulty master cylinder (Chapter 9).

Excessive brake pedal effort required to stop vehicle

- [ ] Faulty vacuum servo unit (Chapter 9).
- [ ] Disconnected, damaged or insecure brake servo vacuum hose (Chapter 9).
- [ ] Primary or secondary hydraulic circuit failure (Chapter 9).
- [ ] Seized brake caliper or wheel cylinder piston(s) (Chapter 9).
- [ ] Brake pads or brake shoes incorrectly fitted (Chapter 9).
- [ ] Incorrect grade of brake pads or brake shoes fitted (Chapter 9).
- [ ] Brake pads or brake shoe linings contaminated (Chapter 9).

Judder felt through brake pedal or steering wheel when braking

- [ ] Excessive run-out or distortion of discs/drums (Chapters 9).
- [ ] Brake pad or brake shoe linings worn (Chapters 1A or 1B and 9).
- [ ] Brake caliper or brake backplate mounting bolts loose (Chapter 9).
- [ ] Wear in suspension or steering components or mountings (Chapters 1A or 1B and 10).

Brakes binding

- [ ] Seized brake caliper or wheel cylinder piston(s) (Chapter 9).
- [ ] Incorrectly-adjusted handbrake mechanism (Chapter 9).
- [ ] Faulty master cylinder (Chapter 9).

Rear wheels locking under normal braking

- [ ] Rear brake shoe linings contaminated (Chapters 1A or 1B and 9).
- [ ] Faulty brake pressure regulator (Chapter 9).

Suspension and steering

Note: *Before diagnosing suspension or steering faults, be sure that the trouble is not due to incorrect tyre pressures, mixtures of tyre types, or binding brakes.*

Vehicle pulls to one side

- [ ] Defective tyre (*Weekly checks*).
- [ ] Excessive wear in suspension or steering components (Chapters 1A or 1B and 10).
- [ ] Incorrect front wheel alignment (Chapter 10).
- [ ] Damage to steering or suspension components (Chapter 1A or 1B).

Wheel wobble and vibration

- [ ] Front roadwheels out of balance (vibration felt mainly through the steering wheel) (Chapters 1A or 1B and 10).
- [ ] Rear roadwheels out of balance (vibration felt throughout the vehicle) (Chapters 1A or 1B and 10).
- [ ] Roadwheels damaged or distorted (Chapters 1A or 1B and 10).
- [ ] Faulty or damaged tyre (*Weekly checks*).
- [ ] Worn steering or suspension joints, bushes or components (Chapters 11A or 1B and 10).
- [ ] Wheel bolts loose (Chapters 1A or 1B and 10).

Excessive pitching and/or rolling around corners, or during braking

- [ ] Defective shock absorbers (Chapters 1A or 1B and 10).
- [ ] Broken or weak spring and/or suspension part (Chapters 1A or 1B and 10).
- [ ] Worn or damaged anti-roll bar or mountings (Chapter 10).

Wandering or general instability

- [ ] Incorrect front wheel alignment (Chapter 10).
- [ ] Worn steering or suspension joints, bushes or components (Chapters 1A or 1B and 10).
- [ ] Roadwheels out of balance (Chapters 1A or 1B and 10).
- [ ] Faulty or damaged tyre (*Weekly checks*).
- [ ] Wheel bolts loose (Chapters 1A or 1B and 10).
- [ ] Defective shock absorbers (Chapters 1A or 1B and 10).

Excessively-stiff steering

- [ ] Lack of steering gear lubricant (Chapter 10).
- [ ] Seized track rod end balljoint or suspension balljoint (Chapters 1A or 1B and 10).

- [ ] Broken or incorrectly-adjusted auxiliary drivebelt – power steering (Chapter 1A or 1B).
- [ ] Incorrect front wheel alignment (Chapter 10).
- [ ] Steering gear or column bent or damaged (Chapter 10).

Excessive play in steering

- [ ] Worn steering column intermediate shaft universal joint (Chapter 10).
- [ ] Worn steering track rod end balljoints (Chapters 1A or 1B and 10).
- [ ] Worn steering gear (Chapter 10).
- [ ] Worn steering or suspension joints, bushes or components (Chapters 1A or 1B and 10).

Lack of power assistance

- [ ] Broken or incorrectly-adjusted auxiliary drivebelt (Chapter 1A or 1B).
- [ ] Incorrect power steering fluid level (*Weekly checks*).
- [ ] Restriction in power steering fluid hoses (Chapter 1A or 1B).
- [ ] Faulty power steering pump (Chapter 10).
- [ ] Faulty steering gear (Chapter 10).

Tyre wear excessive

Tyre treads exhibit feathered edges

- [ ] Incorrect toe setting (Chapter 10).

Tyres worn in centre of tread

- [ ] Tyres over-inflated (*Weekly checks*).

Tyres worn on inside and outside edges

- [ ] Tyres under-inflated (*Weekly checks*).

Tyres worn on inside or outside edges

- [ ] Incorrect camber/castor angles (wear on one edge only) (Chapter 10).
- [ ] Worn steering or suspension joints, bushes or components (Chapters 1A or 1B and 10).
- [ ] Excessively-hard cornering.
- [ ] Accident damage.

Tyres worn unevenly

- [ ] Tyres/wheels out of balance (*Weekly checks*).
- [ ] Excessive wheel or tyre run-out (Chapter 1A or 1B).
- [ ] Worn shock absorbers (Chapters 1A or 1B and 10).
- [ ] Faulty tyre (*Weekly checks*).

Electrical system

Note: *For problems associated with the starting system, refer to the faults listed under 'Engine' earlier in this Section.*

Battery won't hold a charge for more than a few days

- ☐ Battery defective internally (Chapter 5A).
- ☐ Battery terminal connections loose or corroded (*Weekly checks*).
- ☐ Auxiliary drivebelt broken, worn or incorrectly adjusted (Chapter 1A or 1B).
- ☐ Alternator not charging at correct output (Chapter 5A).
- ☐ Alternator or voltage regulator faulty (Chapter 5A).
- ☐ Short-circuit causing continual battery drain (Chapters 5A and 12).

Ignition/no-charge warning light stays on with engine running

- ☐ Auxiliary drivebelt broken, worn, or incorrectly adjusted (Chapter 1A or 1B).
- ☐ Internal fault in alternator or voltage regulator (Chapter 5A).
- ☐ Broken, disconnected, or loose wiring in charging circuit (Chapter 5A).

Ignition/no-charge warning light fails to come on

- ☐ Warning light bulb blown (Chapter 12).
- ☐ Broken, disconnected, or loose wiring in warning light circuit (Chapter 12).
- ☐ Alternator faulty (Chapter 5A).

Lights inoperative

- ☐ Bulb blown (Chapter 12).
- ☐ Corrosion of bulb or bulb holder contacts (Chapter 12).
- ☐ Blown fuse (Chapter 12).
- ☐ Faulty relay (Chapter 12).
- ☐ Broken, loose, or disconnected wiring (Chapter 12).
- ☐ Faulty switch (Chapter 12).

Instrument readings inaccurate or erratic

Instrument readings increase with engine speed

- ☐ Faulty voltage regulator (Chapter 12).

Fuel or temperature gauges give no reading

- ☐ Faulty gauge sensor unit (Chapter 3).
- ☐ Wiring open-circuit (Chapter 12).
- ☐ Faulty gauge (Chapter 12).

Fuel or temperature gauges give continuous maximum reading

- ☐ Faulty gauge sensor unit (Chapter 3).
- ☐ Wiring short-circuit (Chapter 12).
- ☐ Faulty gauge (Chapter 12).

Horn inoperative, or unsatisfactory in operation

Horn operates all the time

- ☐ Horn push either earthed or stuck down (Chapter 12).
- ☐ Horn cable-to-horn push earthed (Chapter 12).

Horn fails to operate

- ☐ Blown fuse (Chapter 12).
- ☐ Cable or cable connections loose, broken or disconnected (Chapter 12).
- ☐ Faulty horn (Chapter 12).

Horn emits intermittent or unsatisfactory sound

- ☐ Cable connections loose (Chapter 12).
- ☐ Horn mountings loose (Chapter 12).
- ☐ Faulty horn (Chapter 12).

Electrical system (continued)

Windscreen/tailgate wipers failed, or unsatisfactory in operation

Wipers fail to operate, or operate very slowly

- ☐ Wiper blades stuck to screen, or linkage seized or binding (Chapters 1A or 1B and 12).
- ☐ Blown fuse (Chapter 12).
- ☐ Cable or cable connections loose, broken or disconnected (Chapter 12).
- ☐ Faulty built-in system interface (BSI) unit (Chapter 12).
- ☐ Faulty wiper motor (Chapter 12).

Wiper blades sweep over too large or too small an area of the glass

- ☐ Wiper arms incorrectly positioned on spindles (Chapter 12).
- ☐ Excessive wear of wiper linkage (Chapter 12).
- ☐ Wiper motor or linkage mountings loose or insecure (Chapter 12).

Wiper blades fail to clean the glass effectively

- ☐ Wiper blade rubbers worn or perished (*Weekly checks*).
- ☐ Wiper arm tension springs broken, or arm pivots seized (Chapter 12).
- ☐ Insufficient windscreen washer additive to adequately remove road film (Weekly checks).

Windscreen/tailgate washers failed, or unsatisfactory in operation

One or more washer jets inoperative

- ☐ Blocked washer jet (*Weekly checks*).
- ☐ Disconnected, kinked or restricted fluid hose (Chapter 12).
- ☐ Insufficient fluid in washer reservoir (*Weekly checks*).

Washer pump fails to operate

- ☐ Broken or disconnected wiring or connections (Chapter 12).
- ☐ Blown fuse (Chapter 12).
- ☐ Faulty washer switch (Chapter 12).
- ☐ Faulty washer pump (Chapter 12).

Washer pump runs for some time before fluid is emitted from jets

- ☐ Faulty one-way valve in fluid supply hose (Chapter 12).

Electric windows inoperative, or unsatisfactory in operation

Window glass will only move in one direction

- ☐ Faulty switch (Chapter 12).

Window glass slow to move

- ☐ Regulator seized or damaged, or in need of lubricant (Chapter 11).
- ☐ Door internal components or trim fouling regulator (Chapter 11).
- ☐ Faulty motor (Chapter 11).

Window glass fails to move

- ☐ Blown fuse (Chapter 12).
- ☐ Broken or disconnected wiring or connections (Chapter 12).
- ☐ Faulty motor (Chapter 11).

Central locking system inoperative, or unsatisfactory in operation

Complete system failure

- ☐ Blown fuse (Chapter 12).
- ☐ Broken or disconnected wiring or connections (Chapter 12).
- ☐ Faulty built-in system interface (BSI) unit (Chapter 12).

Door/tailgate locks but will not unlock, or unlocks but will not lock

- ☐ Broken or disconnected link rod(s) (Chapter 11).
- ☐ Faulty lock motor (Chapter 11).

One lock fails to operate

- ☐ Broken or disconnected wiring or connections (Chapter 12).
- ☐ Faulty lock motor (Chapter 11).
- ☐ Broken, binding or disconnected link rod(s) (Chapter 11).

A

ABS (Anti-lock brake system) A system, usually electronically controlled, that senses incipient wheel lockup during braking and relieves hydraulic pressure at wheels that are about to skid.

Air bag An inflatable bag hidden in the steering wheel (driver's side) or the dash or glovebox (passenger side). In a head-on collision, the bags inflate, preventing the driver and front passenger from being thrown forward into the steering wheel or windscreen.

Air cleaner A metal or plastic housing, containing a filter element, which removes dust and dirt from the air being drawn into the engine.

Air filter element The actual filter in an air cleaner system, usually manufactured from pleated paper and requiring renewal at regular intervals.

Air filter

Allen key A hexagonal wrench which fits into a recessed hexagonal hole.

Alligator clip A long-nosed spring-loaded metal clip with meshing teeth. Used to make temporary electrical connections.

Alternator A component in the electrical system which converts mechanical energy from a drivebelt into electrical energy to charge the battery and to operate the starting system, ignition system and electrical accessories.

Alternator (exploded view)

Ampere (amp) A unit of measurement for the flow of electric current. One amp is the amount of current produced by one volt acting through a resistance of one ohm.

Anaerobic sealer A substance used to prevent bolts and screws from loosening. Anaerobic means that it does not require oxygen for activation. The Loctite brand is widely used.

Antifreeze A substance (usually ethylene glycol) mixed with water, and added to a vehicle's cooling system, to prevent freezing of the coolant in winter. Antifreeze also contains chemicals to inhibit corrosion and the formation of rust and other deposits that would tend to clog the radiator and coolant passages and reduce cooling efficiency.

Anti-seize compound A coating that reduces the risk of seizing on fasteners that are subjected to high temperatures, such as exhaust manifold bolts and nuts.

Anti-seize compound

Asbestos A natural fibrous mineral with great heat resistance, commonly used in the composition of brake friction materials. Asbestos is a health hazard and the dust created by brake systems should never be inhaled or ingested.

Axle A shaft on which a wheel revolves, or which revolves with a wheel. Also, a solid beam that connects the two wheels at one end of the vehicle. An axle which also transmits power to the wheels is known as a live axle.

Axle assembly

Axleshaft A single rotating shaft, on either side of the differential, which delivers power from the final drive assembly to the drive wheels. Also called a driveshaft or a halfshaft.

B

Ball bearing An anti-friction bearing consisting of a hardened inner and outer race with hardened steel balls between two races.

Bearing

Bearing The curved surface on a shaft or in a bore, or the part assembled into either, that permits relative motion between them with minimum wear and friction.

Big-end bearing The bearing in the end of the connecting rod that's attached to the crankshaft.

Bleed nipple A valve on a brake wheel cylinder, caliper or other hydraulic component that is opened to purge the hydraulic system of air. Also called a bleed screw.

Brake bleeding

Brake bleeding Procedure for removing air from lines of a hydraulic brake system.

Brake disc The component of a disc brake that rotates with the wheels.

Brake drum The component of a drum brake that rotates with the wheels.

Brake linings The friction material which contacts the brake disc or drum to retard the vehicle's speed. The linings are bonded or riveted to the brake pads or shoes.

Brake pads The replaceable friction pads that pinch the brake disc when the brakes are applied. Brake pads consist of a friction material bonded or riveted to a rigid backing plate.

Brake shoe The crescent-shaped carrier to which the brake linings are mounted and which forces the lining against the rotating drum during braking.

Braking systems For more information on braking systems, consult the *Haynes Automotive Brake Manual*.

Breaker bar A long socket wrench handle providing greater leverage.

Bulkhead The insulated partition between the engine and the passenger compartment.

C

Caliper The non-rotating part of a disc-brake assembly that straddles the disc and carries the brake pads. The caliper also contains the hydraulic components that cause the pads to pinch the disc when the brakes are applied. A caliper is also a measuring tool that can be set to measure inside or outside dimensions of an object.

Camshaft A rotating shaft on which a series of cam lobes operate the valve mechanisms. The camshaft may be driven by gears, by sprockets and chain or by sprockets and a belt.

Canister A container in an evaporative emission control system; contains activated charcoal granules to trap vapours from the fuel system.

Canister

Carburettor A device which mixes fuel with air in the proper proportions to provide a desired power output from a spark ignition internal combustion engine.

Carburettor

Castellated Resembling the parapets along the top of a castle wall. For example, a castellated balljoint stud nut.

Castellated nut

Castor In wheel alignment, the backward or forward tilt of the steering axis. Castor is positive when the steering axis is inclined rearward at the top.

Catalytic converter A silencer-like device in the exhaust system which converts certain pollutants in the exhaust gases into less harmful substances.

Catalytic converter

Circlip A ring-shaped clip used to prevent endwise movement of cylindrical parts and shafts. An internal circlip is installed in a groove in a housing; an external circlip fits into a groove on the outside of a cylindrical piece such as a shaft.

Clearance The amount of space between two parts. For example, between a piston and a cylinder, between a bearing and a journal, etc.

Coil spring A spiral of elastic steel found in various sizes throughout a vehicle, for example as a springing medium in the suspension and in the valve train.

Compression Reduction in volume, and increase in pressure and temperature, of a gas, caused by squeezing it into a smaller space.

Compression ratio The relationship between cylinder volume when the piston is at top dead centre and cylinder volume when the piston is at bottom dead centre.

Constant velocity (CV) joint A type of universal joint that cancels out vibrations caused by driving power being transmitted through an angle.

Core plug A disc or cup-shaped metal device inserted in a hole in a casting through which core was removed when the casting was formed. Also known as a freeze plug or expansion plug.

Crankcase The lower part of the engine block in which the crankshaft rotates.

Crankshaft The main rotating member, or shaft, running the length of the crankcase, with offset "throws" to which the connecting rods are attached.

Crankshaft assembly

Crocodile clip See Alligator clip

D

Diagnostic code Code numbers obtained by accessing the diagnostic mode of an engine management computer. This code can be used to determine the area in the system where a malfunction may be located.

Disc brake A brake design incorporating a rotating disc onto which brake pads are squeezed. The resulting friction converts the energy of a moving vehicle into heat.

Double-overhead cam (DOHC) An engine that uses two overhead camshafts, usually one for the intake valves and one for the exhaust valves.

Drivebelt(s) The belt(s) used to drive accessories such as the alternator, water pump, power steering pump, air conditioning compressor, etc. off the crankshaft pulley.

Accessory drivebelts

Driveshaft Any shaft used to transmit motion. Commonly used when referring to the axleshafts on a front wheel drive vehicle.

Driveshaft

Drum brake A type of brake using a drum-shaped metal cylinder attached to the inner surface of the wheel. When the brake pedal is pressed, curved brake shoes with friction linings press against the inside of the drum to slow or stop the vehicle.

Drum brake assembly

E

EGR valve A valve used to introduce exhaust gases into the intake air stream.

EGR valve

Electronic control unit (ECU) A computer which controls (for instance) ignition and fuel injection systems, or an anti-lock braking system. For more information refer to the *Haynes Automotive Electrical and Electronic Systems Manual.*

Electronic Fuel Injection (EFI) A computer controlled fuel system that distributes fuel through an injector located in each intake port of the engine.

Emergency brake A braking system, independent of the main hydraulic system, that can be used to slow or stop the vehicle if the primary brakes fail, or to hold the vehicle stationary even though the brake pedal isn't depressed. It usually consists of a hand lever that actuates either front or rear brakes mechanically through a series of cables and linkages. Also known as a handbrake or parking brake.

Endfloat The amount of lengthwise movement between two parts. As applied to a crankshaft, the distance that the crankshaft can move forward and back in the cylinder block.

Engine management system (EMS) A computer controlled system which manages the fuel injection and the ignition systems in an integrated fashion.

Exhaust manifold A part with several passages through which exhaust gases leave the engine combustion chambers and enter the exhaust pipe.

Exhaust manifold

F

Fan clutch A viscous (fluid) drive coupling device which permits variable engine fan speeds in relation to engine speeds.

Feeler blade A thin strip or blade of hardened steel, ground to an exact thickness, used to check or measure clearances between parts.

Feeler blade

Firing order The order in which the engine cylinders fire, or deliver their power strokes, beginning with the number one cylinder.

Flywheel A heavy spinning wheel in which energy is absorbed and stored by means of momentum. On cars, the flywheel is attached to the crankshaft to smooth out firing impulses.

Free play The amount of travel before any action takes place. The "looseness" in a linkage, or an assembly of parts, between the initial application of force and actual movement. For example, the distance the brake pedal moves before the pistons in the master cylinder are actuated.

Fuse An electrical device which protects a circuit against accidental overload. The typical fuse contains a soft piece of metal which is calibrated to melt at a predetermined current flow (expressed as amps) and break the circuit.

Fusible link A circuit protection device consisting of a conductor surrounded by heat-resistant insulation. The conductor is smaller than the wire it protects, so it acts as the weakest link in the circuit. Unlike a blown fuse, a failed fusible link must frequently be cut from the wire for replacement.

G

Gap The distance the spark must travel in jumping from the centre electrode to the side

Adjusting spark plug gap

electrode in a spark plug. Also refers to the spacing between the points in a contact breaker assembly in a conventional points-type ignition, or to the distance between the reluctor or rotor and the pickup coil in an electronic ignition.

Gasket Any thin, soft material - usually cork, cardboard, asbestos or soft metal - installed between two metal surfaces to ensure a good seal. For instance, the cylinder head gasket seals the joint between the block and the cylinder head.

Gasket

Gauge An instrument panel display used to monitor engine conditions. A gauge with a movable pointer on a dial or a fixed scale is an analogue gauge. A gauge with a numerical readout is called a digital gauge.

H

Halfshaft A rotating shaft that transmits power from the final drive unit to a drive wheel, usually when referring to a live rear axle.

Harmonic balancer A device designed to reduce torsion or twisting vibration in the crankshaft. May be incorporated in the crankshaft pulley. Also known as a vibration damper.

Hone An abrasive tool for correcting small irregularities or differences in diameter in an engine cylinder, brake cylinder, etc.

Hydraulic tappet A tappet that utilises hydraulic pressure from the engine's lubrication system to maintain zero clearance (constant contact with both camshaft and valve stem). Automatically adjusts to variation in valve stem length. Hydraulic tappets also reduce valve noise.

I

Ignition timing The moment at which the spark plug fires, usually expressed in the number of crankshaft degrees before the piston reaches the top of its stroke.

Inlet manifold A tube or housing with passages through which flows the air-fuel mixture (carburettor vehicles and vehicles with throttle body injection) or air only (port fuel-injected vehicles) to the port openings in the cylinder head.

J

Jump start Starting the engine of a vehicle with a discharged or weak battery by attaching jump leads from the weak battery to a charged or helper battery.

L

Load Sensing Proportioning Valve (LSPV) A brake hydraulic system control valve that works like a proportioning valve, but also takes into consideration the amount of weight carried by the rear axle.

Locknut A nut used to lock an adjustment nut, or other threaded component, in place. For example, a locknut is employed to keep the adjusting nut on the rocker arm in position.

Lockwasher A form of washer designed to prevent an attaching nut from working loose.

M

MacPherson strut A type of front suspension system devised by Earle MacPherson at Ford of England. In its original form, a simple lateral link with the anti-roll bar creates the lower control arm. A long strut - an integral coil spring and shock absorber - is mounted between the body and the steering knuckle. Many modern so-called MacPherson strut systems use a conventional lower A-arm and don't rely on the anti-roll bar for location.

Multimeter An electrical test instrument with the capability to measure voltage, current and resistance.

N

NOx Oxides of Nitrogen. A common toxic pollutant emitted by petrol and diesel engines at higher temperatures.

O

Ohm The unit of electrical resistance. One volt applied to a resistance of one ohm will produce a current of one amp.

Ohmmeter An instrument for measuring electrical resistance.

O-ring A type of sealing ring made of a special rubber-like material; in use, the O-ring is compressed into a groove to provide the sealing action.

O-ring

Overhead cam (ohc) engine An engine with the camshaft(s) located on top of the cylinder head(s).

Overhead valve (ohv) engine An engine with the valves located in the cylinder head, but with the camshaft located in the engine block.

Oxygen sensor A device installed in the engine exhaust manifold, which senses the oxygen content in the exhaust and converts this information into an electric current. Also called a Lambda sensor.

P

Phillips screw A type of screw head having a cross instead of a slot for a corresponding type of screwdriver.

Plastigage A thin strip of plastic thread, available in different sizes, used for measuring clearances. For example, a strip of Plastigage is laid across a bearing journal. The parts are assembled and dismantled; the width of the crushed strip indicates the clearance between journal and bearing.

Plastigage

Propeller shaft The long hollow tube with universal joints at both ends that carries power from the transmission to the differential on front-engined rear wheel drive vehicles.

Proportioning valve A hydraulic control valve which limits the amount of pressure to the rear brakes during panic stops to prevent wheel lock-up.

R

Rack-and-pinion steering A steering system with a pinion gear on the end of the steering shaft that mates with a rack (think of a geared wheel opened up and laid flat). When the steering wheel is turned, the pinion turns, moving the rack to the left or right. This movement is transmitted through the track rods to the steering arms at the wheels.

Radiator A liquid-to-air heat transfer device designed to reduce the temperature of the coolant in an internal combustion engine cooling system.

Refrigerant Any substance used as a heat transfer agent in an air-conditioning system. R-12 has been the principle refrigerant for many years; recently, however, manufacturers have begun using R-134a, a non-CFC substance that is considered less harmful to the ozone in the upper atmosphere.

Rocker arm A lever arm that rocks on a shaft or pivots on a stud. In an overhead valve engine, the rocker arm converts the upward movement of the pushrod into a downward movement to open a valve.

Rotor In a distributor, the rotating device inside the cap that connects the centre electrode and the outer terminals as it turns, distributing the high voltage from the coil secondary winding to the proper spark plug. Also, that part of an alternator which rotates inside the stator. Also, the rotating assembly of a turbocharger, including the compressor wheel, shaft and turbine wheel.

Runout The amount of wobble (in-and-out movement) of a gear or wheel as it's rotated. The amount a shaft rotates "out-of-true." The out-of-round condition of a rotating part.

S

Sealant A liquid or paste used to prevent leakage at a joint. Sometimes used in conjunction with a gasket.

Sealed beam lamp An older headlight design which integrates the reflector, lens and filaments into a hermetically-sealed one-piece unit. When a filament burns out or the lens cracks, the entire unit is simply replaced.

Serpentine drivebelt A single, long, wide accessory drivebelt that's used on some newer vehicles to drive all the accessories, instead of a series of smaller, shorter belts. Serpentine drivebelts are usually tensioned by an automatic tensioner.

Serpentine drivebelt

Shim Thin spacer, commonly used to adjust the clearance or relative positions between two parts. For example, shims inserted into or under bucket tappets control valve clearances. Clearance is adjusted by changing the thickness of the shim.

Slide hammer A special puller that screws into or hooks onto a component such as a shaft or bearing; a heavy sliding handle on the shaft bottoms against the end of the shaft to knock the component free.

Sprocket A tooth or projection on the periphery of a wheel, shaped to engage with a chain or drivebelt. Commonly used to refer to the sprocket wheel itself.

Starter inhibitor switch On vehicles with an automatic transmission, a switch that prevents starting if the vehicle is not in Neutral or Park.

Strut See MacPherson strut.

T

Tappet A cylindrical component which transmits motion from the cam to the valve stem, either directly or via a pushrod and rocker arm. Also called a cam follower.

Thermostat A heat-controlled valve that regulates the flow of coolant between the cylinder block and the radiator, so maintaining optimum engine operating temperature. A thermostat is also used in some air cleaners in which the temperature is regulated.

Thrust bearing The bearing in the clutch assembly that is moved in to the release levers by clutch pedal action to disengage the clutch. Also referred to as a release bearing.

Timing belt A toothed belt which drives the camshaft. Serious engine damage may result if it breaks in service.

Timing chain A chain which drives the camshaft.

Toe-in The amount the front wheels are closer together at the front than at the rear. On rear wheel drive vehicles, a slight amount of toe-in is usually specified to keep the front wheels running parallel on the road by offsetting other forces that tend to spread the wheels apart.

Toe-out The amount the front wheels are closer together at the rear than at the front. On front wheel drive vehicles, a slight amount of toe-out is usually specified.

Tools For full information on choosing and using tools, refer to the *Haynes Automotive Tools Manual*.

Tracer A stripe of a second colour applied to a wire insulator to distinguish that wire from another one with the same colour insulator.

Tune-up A process of accurate and careful adjustments and parts replacement to obtain the best possible engine performance.

Turbocharger A centrifugal device, driven by exhaust gases, that pressurises the intake air. Normally used to increase the power output from a given engine displacement, but can also be used primarily to reduce exhaust emissions (as on VW's "Umwelt" Diesel engine).

U

Universal joint or U-joint A double-pivoted connection for transmitting power from a driving to a driven shaft through an angle. A U-joint consists of two Y-shaped yokes and a cross-shaped member called the spider.

V

Valve A device through which the flow of liquid, gas, vacuum, or loose material in bulk may be started, stopped, or regulated by a movable part that opens, shuts, or partially obstructs one or more ports or passageways. A valve is also the movable part of such a device.

Valve clearance The clearance between the valve tip (the end of the valve stem) and the rocker arm or tappet. The valve clearance is measured when the valve is closed.

Vernier caliper A precision measuring instrument that measures inside and outside dimensions. Not quite as accurate as a micrometer, but more convenient.

Viscosity The thickness of a liquid or its resistance to flow.

Volt A unit for expressing electrical "pressure" in a circuit. One volt that will produce a current of one ampere through a resistance of one ohm.

W

Welding Various processes used to join metal items by heating the areas to be joined to a molten state and fusing them together. For more information refer to the *Haynes Automotive Welding Manual*.

Wiring diagram A drawing portraying the components and wires in a vehicle's electrical system, using standardised symbols. For more information refer to the *Haynes Automotive Electrical and Electronic Systems Manual*.

Note: *References throughout this index are in the form* **"Chapter number"** • **"Page number"**. *So, for example, 2A•15 refers to page 15 of Chapter 2A.*

Note: *References throughout this index are in the form* **"Chapter number"** • **"Page number"**. *So, for example, 2A•15 refers to page 15 of Chapter 2A.*

Note: *References throughout this index are in the form "Chapter number" • "Page number". So, for example, 2A•15 refers to page 15 of Chapter 2A.*

Haynes Manuals – The Complete UK Car List

Title	Book No.
ALFA ROMEO Alfasud/Sprint (74 - 88) up to F *	0292
Alfa Romeo Alfetta (73 – 87) up to E *	0531
AUDI 80, 90 & Coupe Petrol (79 – Nov 88) up to F	0605
Audi 80, 90 & Coupe Petrol (Oct 86 – 90) D to H	1491
Audi 100 & A6 Petrol & Diesel (May 91 – May 97) H to P	3504
Audi A3 Petrol & Diesel (96 – May 03) P to 03	4253
Audi A3 Petrol & Diesel (June 03 – Mar 08) 03 to 08	4884
Audi A4 Petrol & Diesel (95 – 00) M to X	3575
Audi A4 Petrol & Diesel (01 – 04) X to 54	4609
Audi A4 Petrol & Diesel (Jan 05 – Feb 08) 54 to 57	4885
AUSTIN A35 & A40 (56 – 67) up to F *	0118
Mini (59 – 69) up to H *	0527
Mini (69 – 01) up to X	0646
Austin Healey 100/6 & 3000 (56 – 68) up to G *	0049
BEDFORD/Vauxhall Rascal & Suzuki Supercarry (86 – Oct 94) C to M	3015
BMW 1-Series 4-cyl Petrol & Diesel (04 – Aug 11) 54 to 11	4918
BMW 316, 320 & 320i (4-cyl)(75 – Feb 83) up to Y *	0276
BMW 3- & 5- Series Petrol (81 – 91) up to J	1948
BMW 3-Series Petrol (Apr 91 – 99) H to V	3210
BMW 3-Series Petrol (Sept 98 – 06) S to 56	4067
BMW 3-Series Petrol & Diesel (05 – Sept 08) 54 to 58	4782
BMW 5-Series 6-cyl Petrol (April 96 – Aug 03) N to 03	4151
BMW 5-Series Diesel (Sept 03 – 10) 53 to 10	4901
BMW 1500, 1502, 1600, 1602, 2000 & 2002 (59 – 77) up to S *	0240
CHRYSLER PT Cruiser Petrol (00-09) W to 09	4058
CITROEN 2CV, Ami & Dyane (67 – 90) up to H	0196
Citroen AX Petrol & Diesel (87- 97) D to P	3014
Citroen Berlingo & Peugeot Partner Petrol & Diesel (96 – 10) P to 60	4281
Citroen C1 Petrol (05 – 11) 05 to 11	4922
Citroen C3 Petrol & Diesel (02 – 09) 51 to 59	4890
Citroen C4 Petrol & Diesel (04 – 10) 54 to 60	5576
Citroen C5 Petrol & Diesel (01 – 08) Y to 08	4745
Citroen C15 Van Petrol & Diesel (89 – Oct 98) F to S	3509
Citroen CX Petrol (75 – 88) up to F	0528
Citroen Saxo Petrol & Diesel (96 – 04) N to 54	3506
Citroen Visa Petrol (79 – 88) up to F	0620
Citroen Xantia Petrol & Diesel (93 – 01) K to Y	3082
Citroen XM Petrol & Diesel (89 – 00) G to X	3451
Citroen Xsara Petrol & Diesel (97 – Sept 00) R to W	3751
Citroen Xsara Picasso Petrol & Diesel (00 – 02) W to 52	3944
Citroen Xsara Picasso (Mar 04 – 08) 04 to 58	4784
Citroen ZX Diesel (91 – 98) J to S	1922
Citroen ZX Petrol (91 – 98) H to S	1881
FIAT 126 (73 – 87) up to E *	0305
Fiat 500 (57 – 73) up to M *	0090
Fiat 500 & Panda (04 – 12) 53 to 61	5558
Fiat Bravo & Brava Petrol (95 – 00) N to W	3572
Fiat Cinquecento (93 – 98) K to R	3501
Fiat Panda (81 – 95) up to M	0793
Fiat Punto Petrol & Diesel (94 – Oct 99) L to V	3251
Fiat Punto Petrol (Oct 99 – July 03) V to 03	4066
Fiat Punto Petrol (03 – 07) 03 to 07	4746

Title	Book No.
Fiat Punto Petrol (Oct 99 – 07) V to 07	5634
Fiat X1/9 (74 – 89) up to G *	0273
FORD Anglia (59 – 68) up to G *	0001
Ford Capri II (& III) 1.6 & 2.0 (74 – 87) up to E *	0283
Ford Capri II (& III) 2.8 & 3.0 V6 (74 – 87) up to E	1309
Ford C-Max Petrol & Diesel (03 – 10) 53 to 60	4900
Ford Escort Mk I 1100 & 1300 (68 – 74) up to N *	0171
Ford Escort Mk I Mexico, RS 1600 & RS 2000 (70 – 74) up to N *	0139
Ford Escort Mk II Mexico, RS 1800 & RS 2000 (75 – 80) up to W *	0735
Ford Escort (75 – Aug 80) up to V *	0280
Ford Escort Petrol (Sept 80 – Sept 90) up to H	0686
Ford Escort & Orion Petrol (Sept 90 – 00) H to X	1737
Ford Escort & Orion Diesel (Sept 90 – 00) H to X	4081
Ford Fiesta Petrol (Feb 89 – Oct 95) F to N	1595
Ford Fiesta Petrol & Diesel (Oct 95 – Mar 02) N to 02	3397
Ford Fiesta Petrol & Diesel (Apr 02 – 08) 02 to 58	4170
Ford Fiesta Petrol & Diesel (08 – 11) 58 to 11	4907
Ford Focus Petrol & Diesel (98 – 01) S to Y	3759
Ford Focus Petrol & Diesel (Oct 01 – 05) 51 to 05	4167
Ford Focus Petrol (05 – 09) 54 to 09	4785
Ford Focus Diesel (05 – 09) 54 to 09	4807
Ford Fusion Petrol & Diesel (02 – 11) 02 to 61	5566
Ford Galaxy Petrol & Diesel (95 – Aug 00) M to W	3984
Ford Galaxy Petrol & Diesel (00 – 06) X to 06	5556
Ford Granada Petrol (Sept 77 – Feb 85) up to B *	0481
Ford Ka (96 – 08) P to 58	5567
Ford Mondeo Petrol (93 – Sept 00) K to X	1923
Ford Mondeo Petrol & Diesel (Oct 00 – Jul 03) X to 03	3990
Ford Mondeo Petrol & Diesel (July 03 – 07) 03 to 56	4619
Ford Mondeo Petrol & Diesel (Apr 07 – 12) 07 to 61	5548
Ford Mondeo Diesel (93 – Sept 00) L to X	3465
Ford Sierra V6 Petrol (82 – 91) up to J	0904
Ford Transit Connect Diesel (02 – 11) 02 to 11	4903
Ford Transit Diesel (Feb 86 – 99) C to T	3019
Ford Transit Diesel (00 – Oct 06) X to 56	4775
Ford 1.6 & 1.8 litre Diesel Engine (84 – 96) A to N	1172
HILLMAN Imp (63 – 76) up to R *	0022
HONDA Civic (Feb 84 – Oct 87) A to E	1226
Honda Civic (Nov 91 – 96) J to N	3199
Honda Civic Petrol (Mar 95 – 00) M to X	4050
Honda Civic Petrol & Diesel (01 – 05) X to 55	4611
Honda CR-V Petrol & Diesel (02 – 06) 51 to 56	4747
Honda Jazz (02 to 08) 51 to 58	4735
JAGUAR E-Type (61 – 72) up to L *	0140
Jaguar Mk I & II, 240 & 340 (55 – 69) up to H *	0098
Jaguar XJ6, XJ & Sovereign, Daimler Sovereign (68 – Oct 86) up to D	0242
Jaguar XJ6 & Sovereign (Oct 86 – Sept 94) D to M	3261
Jaguar XJ12, XJS & Sovereign, Daimler Double Six (72 – 88) up to F	0478
JEEP Cherokee Petrol (93 – 96) K to N	1943
LAND ROVER 90, 110 & Defender Diesel (83 – 07) up to 56	3017
Land Rover Discovery Petrol & Diesel (89 – 98) G to S	3016

Title	Book No.
Land Rover Discovery Diesel (Nov 98 – Jul 04) S to 04	4606
Land Rover Discovery Diesel (Aug 04 – Apr 09) 04 to 09	5562
Land Rover Freelander Petrol & Diesel (97 – Sept 03) R to 53	3929
Land Rover Freelander (97 – Oct 06) R to 56	5571
Land Rover Series II, IIA & III 4-cyl Petrol (58 – 85) up to C	0314
Land Rover Series II, IIA & III Petrol & Diesel (58 – 85) up to C	5568
MAZDA 323 (Mar 81 – Oct 89) up to G	1608
Mazda 323 (Oct 89 – 98) G to R	3455
Mazda B1600, B1800 & B2000 Pick-up Petrol (72 – 88) up to F	0267
Mazda MX-5 (89 – 05) G to 05	5565
Mazda RX-7 (79 – 85) up to C *	0460
MERCEDES-BENZ 190, 190E & 190D Petrol & Diesel (83 – 93) A to L	3450
Mercedes-Benz 200D, 240D, 240TD, 300D & 300TD 123 Series Diesel (Oct 76 – 85) up to C	1114
Mercedes-Benz 250 & 280 (68 – 72) up to L *	0346
Mercedes-Benz 250 & 280 123 Series Petrol (Oct 76 – 84) up to B *	0677
Mercedes-Benz 124 Series Petrol & Diesel (85 – Aug 93) C to K	3253
Mercedes-Benz A-Class Petrol & Diesel (98 – 04) S to 54	4748
Mercedes-Benz C-Class Petrol & Diesel (93 – Aug 00) L to W	3511
Mercedes-Benz C-Class (00 – 07) X to 07	4780
Mercedes-Benz Sprinter Diesel (95 – Apr 06) M to 06	4902
MGA (55 – 62)	0475
MGB (62 – 80) up to W	0111
MGB 1962 to 1980 (special edition) *	4894
MG Midget & Austin-Healey Sprite (58 – 80) up to W *	0265
MINI Petrol (July 01 – 06) Y to 56	4273
MINI Petrol & Diesel (Nov 06 – 13) 56 to 13	4904
MITSUBISHI Shogun & L200 Pick-ups Petrol (83 – 94) up to M	1944
MORRIS Minor 1000 (56 – 71) up to K	0024
NISSAN Almera Petrol (95 – Feb 00) N to V	4053
Nissan Almera & Tino Petrol (Feb 00 – 07) V to 56	4612
Nissan Micra (83 – Jan 93) up to K	0931
Nissan Micra (93 – 02) K to 52	3254
Nissan Micra Petrol (03 – Oct 10) 52 to 60	4734
Nissan Primera Petrol (90 – Aug 99) H to T	1851
Nissan Qashqai Petrol & Diesel (07 – 12) 56 to 62	5610
OPEL Ascona & Manta (B-Series) (Sept 75 – 88) up to F *	0316
Opel Ascona Petrol (81 – 88)	3215
Opel Ascona Petrol (Oct 91 – Feb 98)	3156
Opel Corsa Petrol (83 – Mar 93)	3160
Opel Corsa Petrol (Mar 93 – 97)	3159
Opel Kadett Petrol (Oct 84 – Oct 91)	3196
Opel Omega & Senator Petrol (Nov 86 – 94)	3157
Opel Vectra Petrol (Oct 88 – Oct 95)	3158
PEUGEOT 106 Petrol & Diesel (91 – 04) J to 53)	1882
Peugeot 107 Petrol (05 – 11) 05 to 11	4923
Peugeot 205 Petrol (83 – 97) A to P	0932
Peugeot 206 Petrol & Diesel (98 – 01) S to X	3757

* Classic reprint

Title	Book No.
Peugeot 206 Petrol & Diesel (02 – 06) 51 to 06	4613
Peugeot 207 Petrol & Diesel (06 – July 09) 06 to 09	4787
Peugeot 306 Petrol & Diesel (93 – 02) K to 02	3073
Peugeot 307 Petrol & Diesel (01 – 08) Y to 58	4147
Peugeot 308 Petrol & Diesel (07 – 12) 07 to 12	5561
Peugeot 405 Diesel (88 – 97) E to P	3198
Peugeot 406 Petrol & Diesel (96 – Mar 99) N to T	3394
Peugeot 406 Petrol & Diesel (Mar 99 – 02) T to 52	3982
Peugeot 407 Diesel (04 -11) 53 to 11	5550
PORSCHE 911 (65 – 85) up to C	0264
Porsche 924 & 924 Turbo (76 – 85) up to C	0397
RANGE ROVER V8 Petrol (70 – Oct 92) up to K	0606
RELIANT Robin & Kitten (73 – 83) up to A *	0436
RENAULT 4 (61 – 86) up to D *	0072
Renault 5 Petrol (Feb 85 – 96) B to N	1219
Renault 19 Petrol (89 – 96) F to N	1646
Renault Clio Petrol (91 – May 98) H to R	1853
Renault Clio Petrol & Diesel (May 98 – May 01) R to Y	3906
Renault Clio Petrol & Diesel (June 01 – 05) Y to 55	4168
Renault Clio Petrol & Diesel (Oct 05 – May 09) 55 to 09	4788
Renault Espace Petrol & Diesel (85 – 96) C to N	3197
Renault Laguna Petrol & Diesel (94 – 00) L to W	3252
Renault Laguna Petrol & Diesel (Feb 01 – May 07) X to 07	4283
Renault Megane & Scenic Petrol & Diesel (96 – 99) N to T	3395
Renault Megane & Scenic Petrol & Diesel (Apr 99 – 02) T to 52	3916
Renault Megane Petrol & Diesel (Oct 02 – 08) 52 to 58	4284
Renault Scenic Petrol & Diesel (Sept 03 – 06) 53 to 06	4297
Renault Trafic Diesel (01 – 11) Y to 11	5551
ROVER 216 & 416 Petrol (89 – 96) G to N	1830
Rover 211, 214, 216, 218 & 220 Petrol & Diesel (Dec 95 – 99) N to V	3399
Rover 25 & MG ZR Petrol & Diesel (Oct 99 – 06) V to 06	4145
Rover 414, 416 & 420 Petrol & Diesel (May 95 – 99) M to V	3453
Rover 45 / MG ZS Petrol & Diesel (99 – 05) V to 55	4384
Rover 618, 620 & 623 Petrol (93 – 97) K to P	3257
Rover 75 / MG ZT Petrol & Diesel (99 – 06) S to 06	4292
Rover 820, 825 & 827 Petrol (86 – 95) D to N	1380
Rover 3500 (76 – 87) up to E *	0365
Rover Metro, 111 & 114 Petrol (May 90 – 98) G to S	1711
SAAB 95 & 96 (66 – 76) up to R *	0198
Saab 90, 99 & 900 (79 – Oct 93) up to L	0765
Saab 900 (Oct 93 – 98) L to R	3512
Saab 9000 4-cyl (85 – 98) C to S	1686
Saab 9-3 Petrol & Diesel (98 – Aug 02) R to 02	4614
Saab 9-3 Petrol & Diesel (92 – 07) 52 to 57	4749
Saab 9-3 Petrol & Diesel (07-on) 57 on	5569
Saab 9-5 4-cyl Petrol (97 – 05) R to 55	4156
Saab 9-5 (Sep 05 – Jun 10) 55 to 10	4891
SEAT Ibiza & Cordoba Petrol & Diesel (Oct 93 – Oct 99) L to V	3571
Seat Ibiza & Malaga Petrol (85 – 92) B to K	1609
Seat Ibiza Petrol & Diesel (May 02 – Apr 08) 02 to 08	4889

Title	Book No.
SKODA Fabia Petrol & Diesel (00 – 06) W to 06	4376
Skoda Felicia Petrol & Diesel (95 – 01) M to X	3505
Skoda Octavia Petrol (98 – April 04) R to 04	4285
Skoda Octavia Diesel (May 04 – 12) 04 to 61	5549
SUBARU 1600 & 1800 (Nov 79 – 90) up to H *	0995
SUNBEAM Alpine, Rapier & H120 (68 – 74) up to N *	0051
SUZUKI SJ Series, Samurai & Vitara 4-cyl Petrol (82 – 97) up to P	1942
Suzuki Supercarry & Bedford/Vauxhall Rascal (86 – Oct 94) C to M	3015
TOYOTA Avensis Petrol (98 – Jan 03) R to 52	4264
Toyota Aygo Petrol (05 – 11) 05 to 11	4921
Toyota Carina E Petrol (May 92 – 97) J to P	3256
Toyota Corolla (80 – 85) up to C	0683
Toyota Corolla (Sept 83 – Sept 87) A to E	1024
Toyota Corolla (Sept 87 – Aug 92) E to K	1683
Toyota Corolla Petrol (Aug 92 – 97) K to P	3259
Toyota Corolla Petrol (July 97 0 Feb 02) P to 51	4286
Toyota Corolla Petrol & Diesel (02 – Jan 07) 51 to 56	4791
Toyota Hi-Ace & Hi-Lux Petrol (69 – Oct 83) up to A	0304
Toyota RAV4 Petrol & Diesel (94 – 06) L to 55	4750
Toyota Yaris Petrol (99 – 05) T to 05	4265
TRIUMPH GT6 & Vitesse (62 0 74) up to N *	0112
Triumph Herald (59 – 71) up to K *	0010
Triumph Spitfire (62 – 81) up to X	0113
Triumph Stag (70 – 78) up to T *	0441
Triumph TR2, TR3, TR3A, TR4 & TR4A (52 – 67) up to F *	0028
Triumph TR5 & TR6 (67 – 75) up to P *	0031
Triumph TR7 (75 – 82) up to Y *	0322
VAUXHALL Astra Petrol (Oct 91 – Feb 98) J to R	1832
Vauxhall/Opel Astra & Zafira Petrol (Feb 98 – Apr 04) R to 04	3758
Vauxhall/Opel Astra & Zafira Diesel (Feb 98 – Apr 04) R to 04	3797
Vauxhall/Opel Astra Petrol (04 – 08)	4732
Vauxhall/Opel Astra Diesel (04 – 08)	4733
Vauxhall/Opel Astra Petrol & Diesel (Dec 09 – 13) 59 to 13	5578
Vauxhall/Opel Calibra (90 – 98) G to S	3502
Vauxhall Cavalier Petrol (Oct 88 0 95) F to N	1570
Vauxhall/Opel Corsa Diesel (Mar 93 – Oct 00) K to X	4087
Vauxhall Corsa Petrol (Mar 93 – 97) K to R	1985
Vauxhall/Opel Corsa Petrol (Apr 97 – Oct 00) P to X	3921
Vauxhall/Opel Corsa Petrol & Diesel (Oct 03 – Aug 06) 53 to 06	4617
Vauxhall/Opel Corsa Petrol & Diesel (Sept 06 – 10) 56 to 10	4886
Vauxhall/Opel Corsa Petrol & Diesel (00 – Aug 06) X to 06	5577
Vauxhall/Opel Frontera Petrol & Diesel (91 – Sept 98) J to S	3454
Vauxhall/Opel Insignia Petrol & Diesel (08 – 12) 08 to 61	5563
Vauxhall/Opel Meriva Petrol & Diesel (03 – May 10) 03 to 10	4893
Vauxhall/Opel Omega Petrol (94 – 99) L to T	3510
Vauxhall/Opel Vectra Petrol & Diesel (95 – Feb 99) N to S	3396

Title	Book No.
Vauxhall/Opel Vectra Petrol & Diesel (Mar 99 – May 02) T to 02	3930
Vauxhall/Opel Vectra Petrol & Diesel (June 02 – Sept 05) 02 to 55	4618
Vauxhall/Opel Vectra Petrol & Diesel (Oct 05 – Oct 08) 55 to 58	4887
Vauxhall/Opel Vivaro Diesel (01 – 11) Y to 11	5552
Vauxhall/Opel Zafira Petrol & Diesel (05 -09) 05 to 09	4792
Vauxhall/Opel 1.5, 1.6 & 1.7 litre Diesel Engine (82 – 96) up to N	1222
VW Beetle 1200 (54 – 77) up to S	0036
VW Beetle 1300 & 1500 (65 – 75) up to P	0039
VW 1302 & 1302S (70 – 72) up to L *	0110
VW Beetle 1303, 1303S & GT (72 – 75) up to P	0159
VW Beetle Petrol & Diesel (Apr 99 – 07) T to 57	3798
VW Golf & Jetta Mk 1 Petrol 1.1 & 1.3 (74 – 84) up to A	0716
VW Golf, Jetta & Scirocco Mk 1 Petrol 1.5, 1.6 & 1.8 (74 – 84) up to A	0726
VW Golf & Jetta Mk 1 Diesel (78 – 84) up to A	0451
VW Golf & Jetta Mk 2 Petrol (Mar 84 – Feb 92) A to J	1081
VW Golf & Vento Petrol & Diesel (Feb 92 – Mar 98) J to R	3097
VW Golf & Bora Petrol & Diesel (Apr 98 – 00) R to X	3727
VW Golf & Bora 4-cyl Petrol & Diesel (01 – 03) X to 53	4169
VW Golf & Jetta Petrol & Diesel (04 – 09) 53 to 09	4610
VW LT Petrol Vans & Light Trucks (76 – 87) up to E	0637
VW Passat 4-cyl Petrol & Diesel (May 88 – 96) E to P	3498
VW Passat 4-cyl Petrol & Diesel (Dec 96 – Nov 00) P to X	3917
VW Passat Petrol & Diesel (Dec 00 – May 05) X to 05	4279
VW Passat Diesel (June 05 – 10) 05 to 60	4888
VW Polo Petrol (Nov 90 – Aug 94) H to L	3245
VW Polo Hatchback Petrol & Diesel (94 – 99) M to S	3500
VW Polo Hatchback Petrol (00 – Jan 02) V to 51	4150
VW Polo Petrol & Diesel (02 – May 05) 51 to 05	4608
VW Transporter 1600 (68 – 79) up to V	0082
VW Transporter 1700, 1800 & 2000 (72 – 79) up to V *	0226
VW Transporter (air cooled) Petrol (79 – 82) up to Y *	0638
VW Transporter (water cooled) Petrol (82 – 90) up to H	3452
VW Type 3 (63 – 73) up to M *	0084
VOLVO 120 & 130 Series (& P1800) (61 – 70) up to M *	0203
Volvo 142, 144 & 145 (66 – 74) up to N *	0129
Volvo 240 Series Petrol (74 – 93) up to K	0270
Volvo 440, 460 & 480 Petrol (87 – 97) D to P	1691
Volvo 740 & 760 Petrol (82 – 91) up to J	1258
Volvo 850 Petrol (92 – 96) J to P	3260
Volvo 940 Petrol (90 – 98) H to R	3249
Volvo S40 & V40 Petrol (96 – Mar 04) N to 04	3569
Volvo S40 & V50 Petrol & Diesel (Mar 04 – Jun 07) 04 to 07	4731
Volvo S60 Petrol & Diesel (01 – 08) X to 09	4793
Volvo S70, V70 & C70 Petrol (96 – 99) P to V	3573
Volvo V70 / S80 Petrol & Diesel (98 – 07) S to 07	4263
Volvo V70 Diesel (June 07 – 12) 07 to 61	5557
Volvo XV60 / 90 Diesel (03 – 12) 52 to 62	5630

* Classic reprint

All the products featured on this page are available through most motor accessory shops, cycle shops and book stores. Our policy of continuous updating and development means that titles are being constantly added to the range. For up-to-date information on our complete list of titles, please telephone: (UK) +44 1963 442030 • (USA) +1 805 498 6703 • (Sweden) +46 18 124016 • (Australia) +61 9763 8100

Preserving Our Motoring Heritage

<
The Model J Duesenberg Derham Tourster. Only eight of these magnificent cars were ever built – this is the only example to be found outside the United States of America

Almost every car you've ever loved, loathed or desired is gathered under one roof at the Haynes Motor Museum. Over 300 immaculately presented cars and motorbikes represent every aspect of our motoring heritage, from elegant reminders of bygone days, such as the superb Model J Duesenberg to curiosities like the bug-eyed BMW Isetta. There are also many old friends and flames. Perhaps you remember the 1959 Ford Popular that you did your courting in? The magnificent 'Red Collection' is a spectacle of classic sports cars including AC, Alfa Romeo, Austin Healey, Ferrari, Lamborghini, Maserati, MG, Riley, Porsche and Triumph.

A Perfect Day Out

Each and every vehicle at the Haynes Motor Museum has played its part in the history and culture of Motoring. Today, they make a wonderful spectacle and a great day out for all the family. Bring the kids, bring Mum and Dad, but above all bring your camera to capture those golden memories for ever. You will also find an impressive array of motoring memorabilia, a comfortable 70 seat video cinema and one of the most extensive transport book shops in Britain. The Pit Stop Cafe serves everything from a cup of tea to wholesome, home-made meals or, if you prefer, you can enjoy the large picnic area nestled in the beautiful rural surroundings of Somerset.

> John Haynes O.B.E., Founder and Chairman of the museum at the wheel of a Haynes Light 12.

< Graham Hill's Lola Cosworth Formula 1 car next to a 1934 Riley Sports.

The Museum is situated on the A359 Yeovil to Frome road at Sparkford, just off the A303 in Somerset. It is about 40 miles south of Bristol, and 25 minutes drive from the M5 intersection at Taunton.

Open 9.30am - 5.30pm (10.00am - 4.00pm Winter) 7 days a week, *except Christmas Day, Boxing Day and New Years Day*

Special rates available for schools, coach parties and outings Charitable Trust No. 292048